BIBLICAL CRITICISM

BEYOND THE BASICS

HOLY BIBLE

EDWARD D. ANDREWS, F. DAVID FARNELL, THOMAS
HOWE, THOMAS MARSHALL, DIANNA NEWMAN

BIBLICAL CRITICISM
Beyond the Basics

Edward D. Andrews • F. David Farnell • Thomas Howe •
Thomas Marshall • Dianna Newman

Christian Publishing House

Cambridge, Ohio

CHRISTIAN PUBLISHING HOUSE

BIBLICAL CRITICISM: Beyond the Basics

ISBN-13: 978-1-945757-71-6
ISBN-10: 1-945757-71-X

Table of Contents

INTRODUCTION The History of the High Criticism 1

    Canon Dyson Hague...1

CHAPTER 1 History of Modern Criticism................................22

    F. David Farnell 22

CHAPTER 2 Grammatical-Historical Versus Historical-Critical 30

    F. David Farnell 30

CHAPTER 3 Form and Tradition Criticism 34

    F. David Farnell 34

CHAPTER 4 Historical Criticism 108

    F. David Farnell 108

CHAPTER 5 Rhetorical Criticism 144

    Thomas Marshall 144

CHAPTER 6 Reader-Response and Narrative Criticism 156

    Thomas Howe...156

CHAPTER 7 Feminist Criticism of the Bible.............................193

    Dianna Newman..193

CHAPTER 8 The Synoptic Gospels in the Ancient Church: The Testimony to the Priority of the Gospel of Matthew 215

    F. David Farnell 215

CHAPTER 9 Contemporary 21st Century Evangelical NT Criticism: Those Who Do Not Learn From the Lessons of History............................244

    F. David Farnell 244

CHAPTER 10 The Documentary Hypothesis................................304

    Edward D. Andrews..304

CHAPTER 11 The Authorship and Unity of Isaiah 347

    Edward D. Andrews..347

CHAPTER 12 Daniel Misjudged...360

    Edward D. Andrews..360

CHAPTER 13 Bible Difficulties Explained..................................378

    Edward D. Andrews..378

Bibliography 404

INTRODUCTION The History of the High Criticism

Canon Dyson Hague[1]

What is the meaning of the Higher Criticism? Why is it called higher? Higher than what?

At the outset, it must be explained that the word "Higher" is an academic term, used in this connection in a purely special or technical sense. It is not used in the popular sense of the word at all and may convey a wrong impression to the ordinary man. Nor is it meant to convey the idea of superiority. It is simply a term of contrast. It is used in contrast to the phrase, "Lower Criticism."

One of the most important branches of theology is called the science of Biblical criticism, which has for its object the study of the history and contents, and origins and purposes, of the various books of the Bible. In the early stages of the science, Biblical criticism was devoted to two great branches, the Lower, and the Higher. The Lower Criticism was employed to designate the study of the text of the Scripture and included the investigation of the manuscripts and the different readings in the various versions and codices and manuscripts in order that we may be sure we have the original words as the divinely inspired writers wrote them. The term generally used today is Textual Criticism. If the phrase were used in the twentieth-century sense, Beza, Erasmus, Bengel, Griesbach, Lachmann, Tregelles, Tischendorf, Scrivener, Westcott, and Hort would be called Lower Critics. However, the term lower criticism is not used as a rule. The Higher Criticism, on the contrary, was employed to designate the study of the historical origins, the dates, and authorship of the various books of the Bible, and that great branch of study, which in the technical language of modern theology is known as Introduction. It is a very valuable branch of Biblical science and is of the highest importance as an auxiliary in the interpretation of the Word of God. By its researches, floods of light may be thrown on the Scriptures.

The term Higher Criticism, then, means nothing more than the study of the literary structure of the various books of the Bible, and more especially of the Old Testament.[2] Now, this in itself is most laudable. It is indispensable. It is just such work as every minister, or Sunday school teacher does. He takes up his Bible Handbook, or his Introduction to the Old and New Testament, or his Survey of the Old and New Testament, or even his commentary volume of the book, to find out

---

[1] This chapter was published from 1910 to 1915. However, it is as vital and relevant as any chapter in this book, It is truly a stepping stone to Dr. Farnell's chapter 1 History of Modern Criticism. In other words, to pass it over because you the reader believe it to be out of date would be a mistake. Edward D. Andrews has edited this chapter updating term, grammar and syntax, and removing a few portions that were not relevant.

[2] The Old Testament was the focus at the time of Hague's writing, but modern day criticism focuses its attention on both equally.

1

all he can with regard to the portion of the Bible he is studying. In other words, he is looking for the author, the date, the circumstances, and purpose of its writing.

Higher Criticism Identified with Unbelief and Subjective Conclusions

In the first place, the critics who were the leaders, the men who have given name and force to the whole movement, have been men who have based their theories largely upon their own subjective conclusions. They have based their conclusions largely upon the very dubious basis of the author's style and supposed literary qualifications. Everybody knows that style is a very unsafe basis for the determination of a literary product. The greater the writer, the more versatile his power of expression and anybody can understand that the Bible is the last book in the world to be studied as a mere classic by mere human scholarship without any regard to the spirit of sympathy and reverence on the part of the student. The Bible, as has been said, has no revelation to make to unbiblical minds, which are not receptive to biblical truth, and knowing the basics of biblical interpretation.

The qualification for the perception of Biblical truth is neither philosophic nor philological (i.e., study of language) knowledge, but rather having at least a basic understanding of grammatical-historical principles of biblical interpretation. No interpreter is infallible. The only infallibility or inerrancy belonged to the original manuscripts. Each Christian has the right to interpret God's Word, to discover what it means, but this does not guarantee that they will come away with the correct meaning. The Holy Spirit will guide us into and through the truth, by way of our working in behalf of our prayers to have the correct understanding. Our working in harmony with the Holy Spirit means that we buy out the time for a personal study program, not to mention the time to prepare properly and carefully for our Christian meetings. In these studies, do not expect that the Holy Spirit is going to give us some flash of understanding miraculously, but rather understanding will come to us as we set aside our personal biases, worldviews, human imperfections, presuppositions, preunderstanding, opening our mental disposition to the Spirit's leading as we study.

German Desires

In the second place, some of the most powerful advocates of the modern Higher Critical theories have been Germans, and it is notorious to what length some German Desires can go in the direction of the subjective and of the conjectural. For hypothesis weaving and speculation, some German theological professors are unsurpassed. One of the foremost thinkers used to lay it down as a fundamental truth in philosophical and scientific enquiries that no one should give any regard to the conjectures or hypotheses of thinkers, and quoted as an axiom the great: Newton himself and his famous words, *Non fingo* hypotheses, "I do not frame hypotheses." It is notorious that some of the most learned German thinkers are men who lack in a singular degree the faculty of common sense and knowledge of human nature. Like many physical scientists, they are so preoccupied with a theory that their conclusions seem to the average mind curiously warped.

In fact, a learned man in a letter to Descartes once made an observation, which, with slight verbal alteration, might be applied to some of the German critics. He wrote, "When men sitting in their closet and consulting only their books attempt disquisitions (essays) into the Bible, they may indeed tell how they would have made the Book if God had given them that commission. That is, they may describe fantasies which correspond to the fatuity (self-satisfied unintelligence) of their own minds, but without an understanding truly Divine they can never form such an idea to themselves as the Deity had in creating it." "If," says Matthew Arnold, "you shut a number of men up to make study and learning the business of their lives, how many of them, from want of some discipline or other, seem to lose all balance of judgment, all common sense."

The learned professor of Assyriology at Oxford said that the investigation of the literary source of history has been a peculiarly German pastime. It deals with the writers and readers of the ancient Orient as if they were modern German professors, and the attempt to transform the ancient Israelites into somewhat inferior German compilers proves a strange want of familiarity with Oriental modes of thought. (Sayce 1897, 108-112)

Anti-Supernaturalists

In the third place, the dominant men of the movement were men with a strong bias against the supernatural. This is not an ex-parte (one-sided) statement at all. It is simply a matter of fact, as we shall presently show. Some of the men who have been most distinguished as the leaders of the Higher Critical movement in Germany and Holland have been men who have no faith in the God of the Bible, and no faith in either the necessity or the possibility of a personal supernatural revelation. The men who have been the voices of the movement, of whom the great majority, less widely known and less influential, have been mere echoes; the men who manufactured the articles the others distributed, have been notoriously opposed to the miraculous.

We must not be misunderstood. We distinctly repudiate the idea that all the Higher Critics were or are anti-supernaturalists. This just is not the case. The British-American School embraces within its ranks many earnest believers.[3] What we do say, as we will presently show, is that the dominant minds which have led and swayed the movement, who made the theories that the others circulated, were unbelieving in the extreme.

Then the higher critical movement has not followed its true and original purposes in investigating the Scriptures for the purposes of confirming faith and of helping believers to understand the beauties, and appreciate the circumstances of the origin of the various books, and so understand more completely the Bible?

---

[3] That certainly was the case back in 1910, but today, in 2015, the United Kingdom is filled with seminary professors, who use higher criticism, and cast doubt on the trustworthiness of God. This is also true of Canada and Australia. The seminaries in the United States are almost at the same point. For example, in the United states 62-70 percent of Bible scholar are liberal.

No. It has not; unquestionably, it has not. It has been deflected from that, largely owing to the character of the men whose ability and forcefulness have given predominance to their views. It has become identified with a system of criticism, which is based on hypotheses and suppositions, which have for their object the repudiation of the traditional theory, and has investigated the origins and forms and styles and contents. Apparently, this is not to confirm the authenticity, credibility, and reliability of the Scriptures, but to discredit in most cases their genuineness, to discover discrepancies, and throw doubt upon their authority.

The Origin of the Movement

Who, then, were the men whose views have molded the views of the leading teachers and writers of the Higher Critical school of today?

We will answer this as briefly as possible.

It is not easy to say whom the first so-called Higher Critic is, or when the movement began. However, it is not modern by any means. Broadly speaking, it has passed through three great stages:

1. The French-Dutch.

2. The German.

3. The British-American.

In its origin, it was Franco-Dutch, and speculative, if not skeptical. The views which in 1910 were accepted as axiomatic by the Continental and British-American schools of Higher Criticism seem to have been first hinted at by Carlstadt in 1521 in his work on the Canon of Scripture, and by Andreas Masius, a Belgian scholar, who published a commentary on Joshua in 1574, and a Roman Catholic priest, called Peyrere or Pererius, in his *Systematic Theology*, 1660. (LIV. Cap. i.)

However, it may really be said to have originated with Spinoza, the rationalist Dutch philosopher. In his *Tractatus Theologico-Politicus* (Cap. vii-viii), 1670, Spinoza came out boldly and impugned the traditional date and Mosaic authorship of the Pentateuch and ascribed the origin of the Pentateuch to Ezra or to some other late compiler.

Spinoza was really the fountain-head of the movement, and his line was taken in England by the British philosopher Hobbes. He went deeper than Spinoza, as an outspoken antagonist of the necessity and possibility of a personal revelation, and denied the Mosaic authorship of the Pentateuch. A few years later a French priest, called Richard Simon of Dieppe, pointed out the supposed varieties of style as indications of various authors in his *Historical Criticism of the Old Testament*, "an epoch-making work." Then another Dutchman, named Clericus (or Le Clerk), in 1685, advocated still more radical views, suggesting an Exilian and priestly authorship for the Pentateuch, and that the Pentateuch was composed by the priest sent from Babylon (2 Kings, 17), about 678, B.C., and also a kind of later editor or redactor theory. Clericus is said to have been the first critic who set forth the theory that Christ and his Apostles did not come into the world to teach the Jews criticism,

4

and that it is only to be expected that their language would be in accordance with the views of the day.

In 1753, a Frenchman named Astruc, a medical man, and reputedly, a freethinker of profligate life propounded for the first time the Jehovistic and Elohistic divisive hypothesis and opened a new era. (Briggs' *Higher Criticism of the Pentateuch*, page 46.) Astrue said that the use of the two names, Jehovah and Elohim, showed the book was composed of different documents. (The idea of the · Holy Spirit employing two words, or one here and another there, or both together as He wills, never seems to enter the thought of the Higher Critical) His work was called "*Conjectures Regarding the Original Memoirs in the Book of Genesis*," and was published in Brussels.

Astrue may be called the father of the documentary theories. He asserted there are traces of no less than ten or twelve different memoirs in the book of Genesis. He denied its Divine authority and considered the book to be disfigured by useless repetitions, disorder, and contradiction. (Hirschfelder, page 66.) For fifty years, Astruc's theory was unnoticed. The rationalism of Germany was as yet undeveloped so that the body was not yet prepared to receive the germ, or the soil the weed.

The German Critics

The next stage was largely German. Eichhorn is the greatest name in this period, the eminent Oriental professor at Goftingen who published his work on the Old Testament introduction in 1780. He put into different shape the documentary hypothesis of the Frenchman and did his work so ably that the most distinguished scholars generally adopted his views. Eichhorn's formative influence has been incalculably great. Few scholars refused to do honor to the new sun. It is through him that the name Higher Criticism has become identified with the movement. He was followed by Vater and later by Hartmann with their fragment theory, which practically undermined the Mosaic authorship, made the Pentateuch a heap of fragments, carelessly joined by one editor, and paved the way for the most radical of all divisive hypotheses.

In 1806 De Wette, Professor of Philosophy and Theology at Heidelberg published a work, which ran through six editions in four decades. His contribution to the introduction of the Old Testament instilled the same general principles as Eichhorn, and in the supplemental hypotheses assumed that Deuteronomy was composed in the age of Josiah (2 Kings 22:8). Not long after, Vatke and Leopold George (both Hegelians) unreservedly declared the post-Mosaic and post-prophetic origin of the first four books of the Bible. Then came Bleek, who advocated the idea of the Grundshift or original document and the redactor theory, and then Ewald, the father of the Crystallization theory, and then Hupfield (1853), who held that the original document was an independent compilation. Then, there was Graf, who wrote a book on the historical books of the Old Testament in 1866 and advocated the theory that the Jehovistic and Elohistic documents were written hundreds of years after Moses' time. Graf was a pupil of Reuss, the redactor of the Ezra hypothesis of Spinoza.

Then came a most influential writer, Professor Kuenen of Leyden in Holland, whose work on the Hexateuch was edited by Colenso in 1865, and his "*Religion of Israel and Prophecy in Israel*," published in England in 1874–1877. Kuenen was one of the most advanced exponents of the rationalistic school. Last, but not least, of the continental Higher Critics is Julius Wellhausen, who at one time was a theological professor in Germany, who published in 1878 the first volume of his history of Israel, and won by his scholarship the attention if not the allegiance of a number of leading theologians. (See *Higher Criticism of the Pentateuch*, Green, pages 59–88.)

It will be observed that nearly all these authors were Germans, and most of them professors of philosophy or theology.

The British-American Critics

The third stage of the movement is the British-American. The best-known names are those of Dr. Samuel Davidson, whose "*Introduction to the Old Testament*," published in 1862, was largely based on the fallacies of the German rationalists. The supplementary hypothesis passed over into England through him and with strange incongruity, he frequently borrowed from Baur. Dr. Robertson Smith, the Scotchman, recast the German theories in an English form in his works on the Pentateuch, the Prophets of Israel, and the Old Testament in the Jewish Church, first published in 1881, and followed the German school, according to Briggs, with great boldness and thoroughness. A man of deep piety and high spirituality, he combined with a sincere regard for the Word of God a critical radicalism that was strangely inconsistent. This is also true of his namesake, George Adam Smith, the most influential of the leaders in those days, a man of great insight and scriptural acumen, who in his works on Isaiah, and the twelve prophets, adopted some of the most radical and least demonstrable of the German theories, and in his later work, "*Modern Criticism and the Teaching of the Old Testament*," has gone still farther in the rationalistic direction.

Another well-known Higher Critic is Dr. S. R. Driver, the Regius professor of Hebrew at Oxford, who, in his "*Introduction to the Literature of the Old Testament*," published ten years later, and his work on the Book of Genesis, has elaborated with remarkable skill and great detail of analysis the theories and views of the continental school. Driver's work is able, very able, but it lacks originality and English independence. The hand is the hand of Driver, but the voice is the voice of Kuenen or Wellhausen.

The third well-known name is that of Dr. C. A. Briggs, for some time Professor of Biblical Theology in the Union Theological Seminary of New York. An equally earnest advocate of the German theories, he published in 1883 his "*Biblical Study*"; in 1886, his "*Messianic Prophecy*," and a little later his "*Higher Criticism of the Hexateuch*." Briggs studied the Pentateuch, as he confesses, under the guidance chiefly of Ewald. (*Hexateuch*, page 63.)

Of course, this list is a very partial one, but it gives most of the names that have become famous in connection with the movement up unto the beginning of the 20th-century, and the reader who desires more will find a complete summary of the literature of the Higher Criticism in Professor Bissell's work on the Pentateuch (Scribner's, 1892). Briggs, in his "*Higher Criticism of the Hexateuch*" (Scribner's, 1897), gives a historical summary also.

We must now investigate another question, and that is the religious views of the men most influential in this movement. In making the statement that we are about to make, we desire to deprecate the idea of there being anything uncharitable, unfair, or unkind entirely, in stating what is simply a matter of fact.

The View of the Continental Critics

Regarding the views of the Continental Critics, three things can be confidently asserted of nearly all, if not all, of the real leaders.

1. They were men who denied the validity of miracle and the validity of any miraculous narrative. What Christians consider to be miraculous they considered legendary or mythical; "legendary exaggeration of events that are entirely explicable from natural causes."

2. They were men who denied the reality of prophecy and the validity of any prophetical statement. What Christians have been accustomed to consider prophetical, they called dexterous conjectures, coincidences, fiction, or imposture.

3. They were men who denied the reality of revelation, in the sense in which the universal Christian Church has ever held it. They were avowed unbelievers of the supernatural. Their theories were excogitated on pure grounds of human reasoning. Their hypotheses were constructed on the assumption of the falsity of Scripture. As to the inspiration of the Bible, as to the Holy Scriptures from Genesis to Revelation being the Word of God, they had no such belief. We may take them one by one. Spinoza repudiated absolutely a supernatural revelation. In addition, Spinoza was one of their greatest. Eichhorn discarded the miraculous, and considered that the so-called supernatural element was an Oriental exaggeration, and Eichhorn has been called the father of Higher Criticism, and was the first man to use the term. De Wette's views as to inspiration were entirely infidel. Vatke and Leopold George were Hegelian rationalists and regarded the first four books of the Old Testament as entirely mythical. Kuenen, says Professor Sanday, wrote in the interests of an almost avowed Naturalism. That is, he was a free-thinker, an agnostic; a man who did not believe in the Revelation of the one true and living God. (*Brampton Lectures*, 1493, page 117.) He wrote from an avowedly naturalistic standpoint, says Driver (page 205). According to Wellhausen, the religion of Israel was a naturalistic evolution from heathendom, an emanation from an imperfectly monotheistic kind of semi-pagan idolatry. It was simply a human religion.

The leaders were Rationalists

In one word, the formative forces of the Higher Critical movement were rationalistic forces, and the men who were its chief authors and expositors, who "on account of purely philological criticism have acquired an appalling authority," were men who had discarded belief in God and Jesus Christ Whom He had sent. The Bible, in their view, was a mere human product. It was a stage in the literary evolution of a religious people. If it was not the resultant of a fortuitous concourse of Oriental myths and legendary accretions, and its Jahveh or Jahweh, the excogitation of a Sinaitic clan, it certainly was not given by the inspiration of God and is not the Word of the living God. "Men spoke from God as they were carried along by the Holy Spirit," said Peter. "Long ago, at many times and in many ways, God spoke to our fathers by the prophets," said Paul. Not so, said Kuenen; the prophets were not moved to speak by God. Their utterances were all their own. (Sanday, page 117.)

These then were their views, and these were the views that have so dominated modern Christianity and permeated modern ministerial thought in the two great languages of the modern world. We cannot say that they were men whose rationalism was the result of their conclusions in the study of the Bible. Nor can we say their conclusions with regard to the Bible were wholly the result of their rationalism. However, we can say, on the one hand, that inasmuch as they refused to recognize the Bible as a direct revelation from God, they were free to form hypotheses *ad libitum*. In addition, on the other hand, as they denied the supernatural, the animus that animated them in the construction of the hypotheses was the desire to construct a theory that would explain away the supernatural. Unbelief was the antecedent (precursor), not the consequent (result), of their criticism.

Now there is nothing unkind in this. There is nothing that is uncharitable, or unfair. It is simply a statement of fact, which modern authorities most freely admit.

School of Compromise

When we come to the English writing Higher Critics, we approach a much more difficult subject. The *British-American Higher Critics* represent a school of compromise. On the one hand, they practically accept the premises of the Continental school with regard to the antiquity, authorship, authenticity, and origins of the. Old Testament books. On the other hand, they refuse to go with the German rationalists in altogether denying their inspiration. They still claim to accept the Scriptures as containing a Revelation from God. But may they not hold their own peculiar views with regard to the origin and date and literary structure of the Bible without endangering either their own faith or the faith of Christians? This is the very heart of the question, and, in order that the reader may see the seriousness of the adoption of the conclusions of the critics, as brief, a resume as possible of the matter will be given.

The Point in a Nutshell

According to the faith of the universal church, the Pentateuch, that is, the first five books of the Bible is one consistent, coherent, authentic and genuine composition, inspired by God. In addition, according to the testimony of the Jews, the statements of the books themselves, the reiterated corroborations of the rest of the Old Testament, and the explicit statement of the Lord Jesus (Luke 24:44, John 5:46–47) was written by Moses (with the exception, of course, of Deut. 34, possibly written by Joshua, as the Talmud states, or probably by Ezra). These were penned about fourteen centuries before the advent of Christ, and 800 years or so before Jeremiah. Moreover, it is a portion of the Bible, which is of paramount importance, for it is the basic substratum of the whole revelation of God. Further, it is of paramount value, not because it is merely the literature of an ancient nation, but because it is the introductory section of the Word of God, bearing His authority and given by inspiration through His servant Moses. That is the faith of the Church.

The Critics' Theory

But according to the Higher Critics:

1. The Pentateuch consists of four completely diverse documents. These completely different documents were the primary sources of the composition which they call the Hexateuch: (a) The Yahwist or Jahwist, (b) the Elohist, (c) the Deuteronomist, and (d) the Priestly Code, the Grundschift, the work of the first Elohist (Sayce *Hist. Heb.*, 103), now generally known as J. E. D. P., and for convenience designated by these symbols.

2. [These critics say] these different works were composed at various periods of time, not in the fifteenth century, B. C., but in the ninth, seventh, sixth and fifth centuries; J. and E. being referred approximately to about 800 to 700 B. C.; D to about 650 to 625 B. C., and P. to about 525 to 425 B. C. According to the Graf theory, accepted by Kuenen, the Elohist documents were post-exilian, that is, they were written only five centuries or so before Christ. Genesis and Exodus as well as the Priestly Code that is, Leviticus and part of Exodus and Numbers were also post-exilic.[4]

3. These different works, moreover, represent different traditions of the national life of the Hebrews and are at variance in most important particulars.

4. And, further. They conjecture that these four suppositive documents were not compiled and written by Moses, but were probably constructed somewhat after this fashion: For some reason, and at some time, and in some way, someone, no one knows who, or why, or when, or where, wrote J. Then someone else, no one knows who, or why, or when, or where, wrote another document, which is now called E. And then at a later time, the critics only know who, or why, or when, or where, an anonymous personage, whom we may call Redactor I, took in hand the reconstruction of these documents, introduced new material, harmonized the real and apparent discrepancies, and divided the inconsistent accounts of one event into two separate transactions. Then sometime after this, perhaps one hundred years or more, no one knows who, or why, or when, or where, some anonymous personage wrote another document, which they style D. And after a while another anonymous author, no one knows who, or why, or when, or where, whom we will call Redactor II, took this in hand, compared it with J. E., revised J. E., with considerable freedom, and in addition introduced quite a body of new material. Then someone

---

[4] In truth, Genesis was written in the late 16th century (c. 1510 B.C.), while Exodus and Leviticus was written one year later, while Deuteronomy was written forty years after the exodus from Egypt, i.e., about 1410 B.C. This is 600 to more than 1,000 years before the above dates. Please see The Documentary Hypothesis chapter.

else, no one knows who, or why, or when, or where, probably, however, about 525, or perhaps 425, wrote P.; and then another anonymous Hebrew, whom we may call Redactor III, undertook to incorporate this with the triplicated composite J. E. D., with what they call redactional additions and insertions. (Green, page 88, cf. Sayce, *Early History of the Hebrews*, pages 100–105.)

It may be well to state at this point that this is not an exaggerated statement of the Higher Critical position. On the contrary, we have given here what has been described as a position "established by proofs, valid and cumulative" and "representing the most sober scholarship." The more advanced continental Higher Critics, Green says, distinguish the writers of the primary sources according to the supposed elements as J1 and J2, E1 and E2, P1, P2 and P3, and D1 and D2, nine different originals in all. The different Redactors, technically described by the symbol R., are Rj., who combined J. and E.; Rd., who added D. to J. E., and Rh., who completed the Hexateuch by combining P. with J. E. D. (*H. C. of the Pentateuch*, page 88.)

A Discredited Pentateuch

5. These four suppositive documents are, moreover, alleged to be internally inconsistent and undoubtedly incomplete. How far they are incomplete, they do not agree. How much is missing and when, where, how and by whom it was removed; whether it was some thief who stole, or copyist who tampered or editor who falsified, they do not declare.

6. In this redactory process, no limit apparently is assigned by the critic to the work of the redactors. With an utter irresponsibility of freedom, it is declared that they inserted misleading statements with the purpose of reconciling incompatible traditions; that they amalgamated what should have been distinguished, and sundered that which should have amalgamated. In one word, it is an axiomatic principle of the divisive hypothesizers that the redactors "have not only misapprehended but misrepresented the originals." (Green, page 170) They were animated by "egotistical motives." They confused varying accounts, and erroneously ascribed them to different occasions. They not only gave false and colored impressions; they destroyed valuable elements of the suppositive documents and tampered with the dismantled remnant.

7. And worst of all. The Higher Critics are unanimous in the conclusion that these documents contain three species of material:

(a) The probably true.

(b) The certainly doubtful.

(c) The positively spurious.

"The narratives of the Pentateuch are usually trustworthy, though partly mythical and legendary. The miracles recorded were the exaggerations of a later age." (Davidson, *Introduction*, page 131.) The framework of the first eleven chapters of Genesis, says George Adam Smith in his "*Modern Criticism and the Preaching of the Old Testament*," is woven from the raw material of myth and legend. He denies their historical character and says that he can find no proof in archaeology for the personal existence of characters of the Patriarchs themselves. Later on, however, in a fit of apologetic repentance, he makes the condescending admission that it is extremely probable that the stories of the Patriarchs have at the heart of them historical elements. (Pages 90–106.)

Such is the view of the Pentateuch that is accepted as conclusive by "the sober scholarship" of a number of the leading theological writers and professors of the day. It is to this the Higher Criticism reduces what the Lord Jesus called the writings of Moses.

A Discredited Old Testament

As to the rest of the Old Testament, it may be briefly said that they have dealt with it with an equally confusing hand. The time-honored traditions of the Catholic Church are set at naught, and its thesis of the relation of inspiration and genuineness and authenticity derided. As to the Psalms, the harp that was once believed to be the harp of David was not handled by the sweet Psalmist of Israel, but generally by some anonymous post-exilist;[5] and Psalms that are ascribed to David by the omniscient Lord Himself are daringly attributed to some anonymous Maccabean. Ecclesiastes, written, nobody knows when, where, and by whom, possesses just a possible grade of inspiration, though one of the critics "of cautious and well-balanced judgment" denies that it contains any at all. "Of course," says another, "it is not really the work of Solomon." (Driver, Introduction, page 470.) The Song of Songs is an idyll of human love, and nothing more. There is no inspiration in it; it contributes nothing to the sum of revelation. (Sanday, page 211.) Esther, too, adds nothing to the sum of revelation and is not historical (page 213). Isaiah was, of course, written by a number of authors. The first part, chapters 1 to 40, by Isaiah; the second by a Deutero-Isaiah and a number of anonymous authors. As to Daniel, it was a purely pseudonymous work, written probably in the second century B. C.

With regard to the New Testament: The English writing school have hitherto confined themselves mainly to the Old Testament, but if Professor Sanday, who passes as a most conservative and moderate representative of the critical school, can be taken as a sample, the historical books are "yet in the first instance strictly histories, put together by ordinary historical methods, or, in so far as the methods on which they are composed, are not ordinary, due rather to the peculiar circumstances of the case, and not to influences, which need be specially described as supernatural" (page 399). *The Second Epistle of Peter* is pseudonymous, its name counterfeit, and, therefore, a forgery, just as large parts of Isaiah, Zachariah, and Jonah, and Proverbs were supposititious and quasi-fraudulent documents. This is a straightforward statement of the position taken by what is called the moderate school of Higher Criticism. It is their own admitted position, according to their own writings.

---

[5] By post-exilist, the author means that the critics are saying this was penned after the Israelites came back from the their seventy year exile in Babylon, i.e., after 537 B.C.

The difficulty, therefore, that presents itself to the average man of today is this: How can these critics still claim to believe in the Bible as the Christian Church has ever believed it?

A Discredited Bible

There can be no doubt that Christ and His Apostles accepted the whole of the Old Testament as inspired in every portion of every part. From the first chapter of Genesis to the last chapter of Malachi, all was implicitly believed to be the very Word of God. And ever since their day the view of the Universal Christian Church has been that the Bible is the Word of God. As the twentieth article of the Anglican Church terms it, it is God's Word written. The Bible as a whole is inspired. "All that is written is God-inspired." That is; the Bible does not merely *contain* the Word of God; it *is* the Word of God. It contains a revelation. "All is not revealed, but all is inspired." This is the conservative and, up to the beginning of the 20th century, the almost universal view of the question. There are, it is well known, many theories of inspiration. But whatever view or theory of inspiration men may hold, plenary, verbal, dynamical, mechanical, superintendent, or governmental, they refer either to the inspiration of the men who wrote or to the inspiration of what is written. In one word, they imply throughout the work of God the Holy Spirit and are bound up with the concomitant ideas of authority, veracity, reliability, and truth divine. (The two strongest works on the subject from this standpoint are by Gaussen and Lee. Gaussen on the *Theopneustia* is published in an American edition by Hitchcock & Walden, of Cincinnati, and Lee on the *Inspiration of Holy Scripture* is published by Rivingtons. Bishop Wordsworth, on the "Inspiration of the Bible," is also very scholarly and strong. Rivingtons, 1875.)

The Bible can no longer, according to the critics, be viewed in this light. It *is* not the Word in the old sense of that term. It is not the Word of God in the sense that all of it is given by the inspiration of God. It merely *contains* the Word of God. In many of its parts, it is just as uncertain as any other human book. It is not even reliable history. It's records of what it does narrate as ordinary history are full of falsifications and blunders. The origin of Deuteronomy, e.g., was "a consciously refined falsification." (See Möller, page 207.)

The Real Difficulty

But do they still claim to believe that the Bible is inspired? Yes. That is, in a measure. As Dr. Driver says in his preface, "Criticism in the hands of Christian scholars does not banish or destroy the inspiration of the Old Testament; it presupposes it." That is entirely true. Criticism in the hands of Christian scholars is safe.

Excursion From Article: This may have been true in 1918, but it is no longer true. In fact, it is now liberal, moderate and even conservative "Christian" scholars, whose use of higher criticism: source, form, redaction, and the like, bear a heavy responsibility for undermining the influence of the Bible in the lives of tens of millions of people.

But the preponderating scholarship in Old Testament criticism has admittedly *not* been in the hands of men who could be described as Christian scholars. It has been in the hands of men who disavow belief in God and Jesus Christ Whom He sent. Criticism in the hands of Horne and Hengstenberg does not banish or destroy the inspiration of the Old Testament. But, in the hands of Spinoza, and Graf and Wellhausen and Kuenen, inspiration is neither pre-supposed nor possible. Dr. Briggs and Dr. Smith may avow earnest avowals of belief in the Divine character of the Bible, and Dr. Driver may assert that critical conclusions do not touch either the authority or the inspiration of the Scriptures of the Old Testament, but from first to last, they treat God's Word with an indifference almost equal to that of the Germans. They certainly handle the Old Testament as if it were ordinary literature. And in all their theories they seem like plastic wax in the hands of the rationalistic moulders. But they still claim to believe in Biblical inspiration.

A Revolutionary Theory

Their theory of inspiration must be, then, a very different one from that held by the average Christian.

In the Bampton Lectures for 1903, Professor Sanday of Oxford, as the exponent of the later and more conservative school of Higher Criticism, came out with a theory that he termed the inductive theory. It is not easy to describe what is fully meant by this, but it appears to mean the presence of what they call "a divine element" in certain parts of the Bible. What that really is he does not accurately declare. The language always vapors off into the vague and indefinite, whenever he speaks of it. In what books it is he does not say. "It is present in different books and parts of books in different degrees." "In some, the Divine element is at the maximum; in others at the minimum." He is not always sure. He is sure it is not in Esther, in Ecclesiastes, in Daniel. If it is in the historical books, it is there as conveying a religious lesson rather than as a guarantee of historic veracity, rather as interpreting than as narrating. At the same time, if the histories as far as textual construction was concerned were "natural processes carried out naturally," it is difficult to see where the Divine or supernatural element comes in. It is an inspiration that seems to have been devised as a hypothesis of compromise. In fact, it is a tenuous, equivocal, and indeterminate something, the amount of which is as indefinite as its quality. (Sanday, pages 100–398; cf. Driver, Preface, ix.)

But its most serious feature is this: It is a theory of inspiration that completely overturns the old-fashioned ideas of the Bible and its unquestioned standard of authority and truth. For whatever this so-called Divine element is, it appears to be quite consistent with defective argument, incorrect interpretation, if not what the average man would call forgery or falsification.

It is, in fact, revolutionary. To accept it, the Christian will have completely to readjust his ideas of honor and honesty, of falsehood and misrepresentation. Men used to think that forgery was a crime, and falsification a sin. Pusey, in his great work on Daniel, said that "to write a book under the name of another and to give it out to be his is, in any case, a forgery, dishonest in itself and destructive of all trustworthiness." (Pusey, *Lectures on Daniel*, page 1.) But according to the Higher Critical position, all sorts of pseudonymous material, and not a little of it believed to be true by the Lord Jesus Christ Himself, is to be found in the Bible, and no antecedent objection ought to be taken to it.

Men used to think that inaccuracy would affect reliability and that proven inconsistency would imperil credibility. But now it appears that there may not only be mistakes and errors on the part of copyists, but forgeries, intentional omissions, and misinterpretations on the part of authors, and yet, marvelous to say, faith is not to be destroyed, but to be placed on a firmer foundation. (Sanday, page 122.) They have, according to Briggs, enthroned the Bible in a higher position than ever before. (Briggs, "*The Bible, Church and Reason*," page 149.) Sanday admits that there is an element in the Pentateuch derived from Moses himself. An element! But he adds, "However much we may believe that there is a genuine Mosaic foundation in the Pentateuch, it is difficult to lay the finger upon it, and to say with confidence, here Moses himself is speaking." "The strictly Mosaic element in the Pentateuch must be indeterminate." "We ought not, perhaps, to use them (the visions of Ex. 3 and 33) without reserve for Moses himself" (pages 172–174–176). The ordinary Christian, however, will say: Surely if we deny the Mosaic authorship and the unity of the Pentateuch we must undermine its credibility. The Pentateuch claims to be Mosaic. It was the universal tradition of the Jews. It is expressly stated in nearly all the subsequent books of the Old Testament. The Lord Jesus said so most explicitly.– John 5:46–47.

If Not Moses, Who?

For this thought must surely follow to the thoughtful man: If Moses did not write the Books of Moses, who did?

If there were three or four, or six, or nine authorized original writers, why not fourteen, or sixteen, or nineteen? And then another and more serious thought must follow that. Who were these original writers, and who originated them? If there were manifest evidence of alterations, manipulations, inconsistencies, and omissions by an indeterminate number of unknown and unknowable and undateable redactors, then the question arises: who were these redactors, and how far had they authority to redact, and who gave them this authority? If the redactor was the writer, was he an inspired writer, and if he was inspired, what was the degree of his inspiration; was it partial, plenary, inductive or indeterminate? This is a question of questions: What is the guarantee of the inspiration of the redactor, and who is its guarantor? Moses we know, and Samuel we know, and Daniel we know, but you anonymous and pseudonymous, who are you? The Pentateuch, with Mosaic authorship, as Scriptural, divinely accredited, is upheld by Catholic tradition and scholarship,[6] and appeals to reason. But a mutilated cento or scrap-book of anonymous compilations, with its pre- and post-exilic redactors and redactions is confusion worse confounded.

---

[6] This is no longer true of the Catholic Church. The Protestant denominations are plagued with seminaries, scholars and church leaders who do not hold to the conservative position of the Historical-grammatical method of interpretation, but rather delve into the historical-critical method, i.e., high criticism.

At least that is the way it appears to the average Christian. He may not be an expert in philosophy or theology, but his common sense must surely be allowed its rights. And that is the way it appears, too, to such an illustrious scholar and critic as Dr. Emil Reich. (*Contemporary Review*, April 1905, page 515.)

It is not possible then to accept the Kuenen-Wellhausen theory of the structure of the Old Testament and the Sanday-Driver theory of its inspiration without undermining faith in the Bible as the Word of God. For the Bible is either the Word of God or it is not. The children of Israel were the children of the Only Living and True God, or they were not. If their Jehovah was a mere tribal deity, and their religion a human evolution; if their sacred literature was natural with mythical and pseudonymous admixtures; then the Bible is dethroned from its throne as the exclusive, authoritative, Divinely inspired Word of God. It simply ranks as one of the sacred books of the ancients with similar claims of inspiration and revelation. Its inspiration is an indeterminate quantity, and any man has a right to subject it to the judgment of his own critical insight, and to receive just as much of it as inspired as he or some other person believes to be inspired. When the contents have passed through the sieve of his judgment, the inspired residue[7] may be large, or the inspired residue may be small. If he is a conservative critic it may be relatively large, a maximum; if he is a more advanced critic it may be fairly small, a minimum. It is simply the ancient literature of a religious people containing somewhere the Word of God; "a revelation of no one knows what, made no one knows how, and lying no one knows where, except that it is to be somewhere between Genesis and Revelation, but probably to the exclusion of both." (Pusey, *Daniel*, xxviii.)

No Final Authority

Another serious consequence of the Higher Critical movement is that it threatens the Christian system of doctrine and the whole fabric of systematic theology. For up to the present time any text from any part of the Bible was accepted as a proof-text[8] for the establishment of any truth of Christian teaching. In addition, a statement from the Bible was considered an end of controversy. The doctrinal systems of the Anglican,[9] the Presbyterian, the Methodist[10] and other

---

[7] The original word here was "residuum," which means, "remainder: something left after other parts have been taken away."

[8] The term proof-text is frowned upon these days, because a text is not an island, and the context (surrounding verses), must be considered in order to get at what the author meant. Let us be frank, we all proof-text, but are the texts that one is using what the author meant by the words that he used, in the context of the surrounding verses. If one is simply pulling verses out of the context, to support a doctrine, this is bad proof-texting.

[9] Things have changed, the Anglican Church accepts historical criticism or higher criticism method of interpretation. More recent changes in the North American churches of the Anglican Communion, such as the introduction of same-sex marriage rites and the ordination of gay and lesbian people to the priesthood and episcopate, have created further separations

[10] Things have changed, the Methodist Church accepts historical criticism or higher criticism method of interpretation. The United Methodist Church "implore[s] families and churches not to reject or condemn lesbian and gay members and friends" and commits itself

Churches are all based upon the view that the Bible contains the truth, the whole truth, and nothing but the truth. (See 39 *Articles Church of England*, vi, ix, xx, etc.) They accept as an axiom that the Old and New Testaments in part, and as a whole, have been given and sealed by God the Father, God the Son, and God the Holy Spirit. All the doctrines of the Church of Christ, from the greatest to the least, are based on this. All the proofs of the doctrines are also based on this. No text was questioned; no book was doubted; all Scripture was received by the great builders of our theological systems with that unassailable belief in the inspiration of its texts, which was the position of Christ and His apostles.[11]

But now the Higher Critics think they have changed all that.

They claim that the science of criticism has dispossessed the science of systematic theology. Canon Henson tells us that the day has gone by for proof-texts and harmonies. It is not enough now for a theologian to turn to a book in the Bible, and bring out a text in order to establish a doctrine. It might be in a book, or in a portion of the Book that the German critics have proved to be a forgery or an anachronism. It might be in Deuteronomy, or in Jonah, or in Daniel, and, in that case, of course, it would be out of the question to accept it. The Christian system, therefore, will have to be re-adjusted if not revolutionized, every text and chapter and book will have to be inspected and analyzed in the light of its date, and origin, and circumstances, and authorship, and so on, and only after it has passed the examining board of the modern Franco-Dutch-German criticism will it be allowed to stand as a proof-text for the establishment of any Christian doctrine.

But the most serious consequence of this theory of the structure and inspiration of the Old Testament is that it overturns the juridical authority of our Lord Jesus Christ.

What of Christ's Authority

The attitude of Christ to the Old Testament Scriptures must determine ours. He is the Son of God. He is the truth. His is the final voice. He is the Supreme Judge. There is no appeal from that court. Christ Jesus the Lord believed and affirmed the historical veracity of the whole of the Old Testament writings implicitly (Luke 24:44). And the Canon, or collection of Books of the Old Testament, was precisely the same in Christ's time as it is today. And further. Christ Jesus, our Lord, believed and emphatically affirmed the Mosaic authority of the Pentateuch. (Matt. 5:17–18; Mark 12:26–36; Luke 16:31; John 5:46–47.) That is true, the critics say. But, then, neither Christ nor His Apostles were critical scholars! Perhaps not in the twentieth-century sense of the term. But, as a German scholar said, if they were not *critici doctores*, they were *doctores veritatis* who did not come into the world to fortify popular errors by their authority. But then they say, Christ's knowledge as man was limited. He grew in knowledge (Luke 2:52). Surely that implies His ignorance. And

---

to be in ministry with all persons, affirming that God's grace, love, and forgiveness is available to all. "Human Sexuality". The United Methodist Church. Retrieved May 09, 2015.

[11] It should be noted that absolute or full inerrancy is based on the original texts, not on translations. An English translation is considered God's Word in as much as it is a reflection of the original in English.

if His ignorance, why not His ignorance with regard to the science of historical criticism? (Gore, *Lux Mundi*, page 360; Briggs, H. C. of *Hexateuch*, page 28.) Or even if He did know more than His age, He probably spoke as He did in accommodation with the ideas of His contemporaries! (Briggs, page 29.)

In fact, what they mean is practically that Jesus did know perfectly well that Moses did not write the Pentateuch, but allowed His disciples to believe that Moses did, and taught His disciples that Moses did, simply because He did not want to upset their simple faith in the whole of the Old Testament as the actual and authoritative and Divinely revealed Word of God. (See Driver, page 12.) Or else, that Jesus imagined, like any other Jew of His day, that Moses wrote the books that bear his name and believed, with the childlike Jewish belief of His day, the literal inspiration, Divine authority and historic veracity of the Old Testament, and yet was completely mistaken, ignorant of the simplest facts, and wholly in error. In other words, He could not tell a forgery from an original, or a pious fiction from a genuine document. (The analogy of Jesus speaking of the sun rising as an instance of the theory of accommodation is a very different thing.)

This, then, is their position: Christ knew the views He taught were false, and yet taught them as truth. Or else, Christ didn't know they were false and believed them to be true when they were not true. In either case, the Blessed One is dethroned as being fully divine and a perfect man. If He did not know the books to be spurious when they were spurious and the fables and myths to be mythical and fabulous; if He accepted legendary tales as trustworthy facts, then He was not and is not omniscient. He was not only intellectually fallible, but He was also morally fallible; for He was not true enough "to miss the ring of truth" in Deuteronomy and Daniel.

And further. If Jesus did know certain of the books to be lacking in genuineness, if not spurious and pseudonymous; if He did know the stories of the Fall and Lot and Abraham and Jonah and Daniel to be allegorical and imaginary, if not unverifiable and mythical, then He was neither trustworthy nor good. "If it were not so, I would have told you." We feel, those of us who love and trust Him, that if these stories were not true, if these books were a mass of historical lies (want of veracity; lack of untruthfulness), if Abraham was an eponymous[12] hero, if Joseph was a myth of the stars, that He would have told us so. It is a matter that concerned His honor as a Teacher, as well as His knowledge as our God. As Canon Liddon has conclusively pointed out if our Lord was unreliable in these historical and documentary matters of inferior value, how can He be followed as the teacher of doctrinal truth and the revealer of God? (John 3:12.) (Liddon, *Divinity of Our Lord*, pages 475–480.)

After the Kenosis

Men say in this connection that part of the humiliation of Christ was His being touched with the infirmities of our human ignorance and fallibilities. They dwell upon the so-called doctrine of the *Kenosis*, or the emptying, as explaining His

---

[12] Eponymous means having the name that is used as the title or name of something else, especially the title of a book.

limitations satisfactorily. But Christ spoke of the Old Testament Scriptures after His resurrection. He affirmed after His glorious resurrection that "all things must be fulfilled which were written in the law of Moses, and in the prophets, and in the Psalms concerning Me." (Luke 24:44) This was not a statement made during the time of the *Kenosis* when Christ was a mere boy, or youth, or a mere Jew after the flesh (1 Cor. 13:11). It is the statement of Him Who has been declared the Son of God with power. It is the Voice that is final and overwhelming. The limitations of the *Kenosis* are all abandoned now, and yet the Risen Lord not only does not give a shadow of a hint that any statement in the Old Testament is inaccurate or that any portion thereof needed revision or correction, not only most solemnly declared that those books that we receive as the product of Moses were indeed the books of Moses, but authorized with His Divine imprimatur the whole of the Old Testament Scriptures from beginning to end.

There are, however, two or three questions that must be raised, as they will have to be faced by every student of present-day problems. The first is this: Is not refusal of the higher critical conclusions mere opposition to light and progress and the position of ignorant alarmists and obscurantists?

Not Obscurantists

It is very necessary to have our minds made perfectly clear on this point, and to remove not a little dust of misunderstanding.

The desire to receive all the light that the most fearless search for truth by the highest scholarship can yield is the desire of every true believer in the Bible. No really healthy Christian mind can advocate obscurantism. The obscurant who opposes the investigation of scholarship, and would throttle the investigators, has not the spirit of Christ. In heart and attitude, he is a Mediævalist. To use Bushnell's famous apologue, he would try to stop the dawning of the day by wringing the neck of the crowing cock. No one wants to put the Bible in a glass case. But it is the duty of every Christian who belongs to the noble army of truth lovers to test all things and to hold fast that which is good. He also has rights even though he is, technically speaking, unlearned, and to accept any view that contradicts his spiritual judgment simply because it is that of a so-called scholar, is to abdicate his franchise as a Christian and his birthright as a man. (See that excellent little work by Professor Kennedy, "Old Testament Criticism and the Rights of the Unlearned," F. H. Revell.) And in his right of private judgment he is aware that while the privilege of investigation is conceded to all, the conclusions of an avowedly prejudiced scholarship must be subjected to a peculiarly searching analysis. The most ordinary Bible reader is learned enough to know that the investigation of the Book that claims to be supernatural by those who are avowed enemies of all that is supernatural, and the study of subjects that can be understood only by men of humble and contrite heart by men who are admittedly irreverent in spirit, must certainly be received with caution. (See Parker's striking work, "*None Like It*," F. H. Revell, and his last address.)

The Scholarship Argument

The second question is also serious: Are we not bound to receive these views when they are advanced, not by rationalists, but by Christians, and not by ordinary Christians, but by men of superior and unchallengeable scholarship?

There is a widespread idea among younger men that the so-called Higher Critics must be followed because their scholarship settles the questions. This is a great mistake. No expert scholarship can settle questions that require a humble heart, a believing mind, and a reverent spirit, as well as a knowledge of Hebrew and philology; and no scholarship can be relied upon as expert which is manifestly characterized by a biased judgment, a curious lack of knowledge of human nature, and a still more curious deference to the views of men with a prejudice against the supernatural. No one can read such a suggestive and sometimes even such an inspiring writer as George Adam Smith without a feeling of sorrow that he has allowed this German bias of mind to lead him into such an assumption of infallibility in many of his positions and statements. It is the same with Driver. With a kind of *sicvolo* sic *jubeo airy ease,* he introduces assertions and propositions that would really require chapter after chapter if not even volume after volume, to substantiate. On page after page his "must be," and "could not possibly be," and "could certainly not," extort from the average reader the natural exclamation: "But why?" "Why not?" "Wherefore?" "On what grounds?" "For what reason?" "Where are the proofs?" But of proofs or reason, there is not a trace. The reader must be content with the writer's assertions. It reminds one, in fact, of the "we may well suppose," and "perhaps" of the Darwinian who offers as the sole proof of the origination of a different species his random supposition! ("Modern Ideas of Evolution," Dawson, pages 53–55.)

A Great Mistake

There is a widespread idea also among the younger students that because Graf and Wellhausen and Driver and Cheyne are experts in Hebrew that, therefore, their deductions as experts in language must be received. This, too, is a mistake. There is no such difference in the Hebrew of the so-called original sources of the Hexateuch as some suppose. The argument from language, says Professor Bissell ("*Introduction to Genesis in Colors,*" page vii), requires extreme care for obvious reasons. There is no visible cleavage line among the supposed sources. Any man of ordinary intelligence can see at once the vast difference between the English of Tennyson and Shakespeare, and Chaucer and Sir John de Mandeville. But no scholar in the world ever has or ever will be able to tell the dates of each and every book in the Bible by the style of the Hebrew. (See Sayce, "*Early History of the Hebrews,*" page 109.) The unchanging Orient knows nothing of the swift lingual variations of the Occident. Pusey, with his masterly scholarship, has shown how even the Book of Daniel, from the standpoint of philology, cannot possibly be a product of the time of the Maccabees. ("*On Daniel,*" pages 23–59.) The late Professor of Hebrew in the University of Toronto, Professor Hirschfelder, in his very learned work on Genesis, says: "We would search in vain for any peculiarity either in the language or the sense that would indicate a two-fold authorship." As far as the language of the original goes, "the most fastidious critic could not possibly detect the slightest peculiarity that would indicate it to be derived from two sources" (page 72). Dr. Emil Reich also, in his *"Bankruptcy of the Higher Criticism,"* in the Contemporary Review, April 1905, says the same thing.

Not All On One Side

A third objection remains a most serious one. It is that all the scholarship is on one side. The old-fashioned conservative views are no longer maintained by men with pretension to scholarship. The only people who oppose the Higher Critical views are the ignorant, the prejudiced, and the illiterate. (Briggs, *"Bible, Church and Reason,"* pages 240–247.)

This, too, is a matter that needs a little clearing up. In the first place, it is not fair to assert that the upholders of what are called the old-fashioned or traditional views of the Bible are opposed to the pursuit of a scientific Biblical investigation. It is equally unfair to imagine that their opposition to the views of the Continental school is based upon ignorance and prejudice.

What the Conservative school opposes is not Biblical criticism, but Biblical criticism by rationalists. They do not oppose the conclusions of Wellhausen and Kuenen because they are experts and scholars; they oppose them because the Biblical criticism of rationalists and unbelievers can be neither expert nor scientific. A criticism that is characterized by the most arbitrary conclusions from the most spurious assumptions has no right to the word scientific. And further. Their adhesion to the traditional views is not only conscientious but intelligent. They believe that the old-fashioned views are as scholarly as they are Scriptural. It is the fashion in some quarters to cite the imposing list of scholars on the side of the German school and to sneeringly assert that there is not a scholar to stand up for the old views of the Bible.

This is not the case. Hengstenberg of Basle and Berlin was as profound a scholar as Eichhorn, Vater or De Wette; and Keil or Kurtz, and Zahn and Rupprecht were competent to compete with Reuss and Kuenen. Wilhelm Möller, who confesses that he was once "immovably convinced of the irrefutable correctness of the Graf-Wellhausen hypothesis," has revised his former radical conclusions on the ground of reason and deeper research as a Higher Critic; and Professor Winckler, who has of late overturned the assured and settled results of the Higher Critics from the foundations, is, according to Orr, the leading Orientalist in Germany, and a man of enormous learning.

Sayce, the Professor of Assyriology at Oxford, has a right to rank as an expert and scholar with Cheyne, the Oriel Professor of Scripture Interpretation. Margoliouth, the Laudian Professor of Arabic at Oxford, as far as learning is concerned, is in the same rank with Driver, the Regius Professor of Hebrew, and the conclusion of this great scholar with regard to one of the widely vaunted theories of the radical school is almost amusing in its terseness.

"Is there then nothing in the splitting theories," he says in summarizing a long line of defense of the unity of the book of Isaiah; "is there then nothing in the splitting theories? To my mind, *nothing at all!"* (*"Lines of Defense,"* page 136.)

Green and Bissell are as able, if not abler, scholars than Robertson Smith and Professor Briggs, and both of these men, as a result of the widest and deepest research, have come to the conclusion that the theories of the Germans are unscientific, unhistorical, and unscholarly. The last words of Professor Green in his very able work on the "*Higher Criticism of the Pentateuch*" are most suggestive. "Would it not be wiser for them to revise their own ill-judged alliance with the enemies of evangelical truth, and inquire whether Christ's view of the Old Testament may not, after all, be the true view?"

Yes. That, after all, is the great and final question. We trust we are not ignorant. We feel sure we are not malignant. We desire to treat no man unfairly or set down aught in malice.

But we desire to stand with Christ and His Church. If we have any prejudice, we would rather be prejudiced against rationalism. If we have any bias, it must be against a teaching, which unsteadies heart and unsettles faith. Even at the expense of being thought behind the times, we prefer to stand with our Lord and Saviour Jesus Christ in receiving the Scriptures as the Word of God, without objection and without a doubt. A little learning and a little listening to rationalistic theorizers and sympathizers may incline us to uncertainty; but deeper study and deeper research will incline us as it inclined Hengstenberg and Möller, to the most profound conviction of the authority and authenticity of the Holy Scriptures, and to cry, "Thy word is very pure; therefore. Thy servant loveth it."[13]

---

[13] Canon Dyson Hague, *Chapter I: The History of the Higher Criticism*, vol. 1 **The Fundamentals: A Testimony To The Truth**, Bible Institute of Los Angeles. (Los Angeles, CA: 1910 to 1915), 9–42.

CHAPTER 1 History of Modern Criticism

F. David Farnell

Isaiah 40:8 Updated American Standard Version (UASV)	Matthew 24:35 Updated American Standard Version (UASV)
[8] The grass withers, the flower fades, but the word of our God will stand forever.	[35] Heaven and earth will pass away, but my words will not pass away.

My ancestors hail from England. My great grandparents came from Staffordshire County, England and emigrated to America at the end of the 19th century. My name "David" reflects my great grandfather "David Farnell." My great grandmother was "Rhoda Griffiths Farnell" whose life exhibited a strong commitment to the Word of God. She regularly prayed for the safety of my father, her grandson, who fought, in the American Army, alongside with the British 8th Army in World War 2 in North Africa and Italy. According to my father, his grandmother always had her afternoon tea with biscuits, as well as her mince-meat pies at Christmas that reflected her ancestry. My father always was thankful for his British grandmother's constant prayers. Her prayers brought him back safe from that horrific global conflict. Once he was home safe, she soon passed into glory speaking of seeing "God's shining light." He became a Christian because his grandmother never ceased praying. I believe that I am in ministry due also to her prayers.

When my great-grandparents left England, England had experienced many centuries of a global influence for Christianity, for it was responsible for evangelizing most of the known world. Wherever the British Empire went, British missionaries followed. Indeed, the Great Awakening in America was stirred by such a great British preacher as George Whitfield in 1730-1740. No other country in the 19th century, not even America, could claim such a heritage when my ancestors came to the United States.

Today, Christian churches, cathedrals in England stand boarded or now serve as museums or bars. British newspapers declare Christianity dead in England.[14] Indeed, even the Archbishop of England declared that she is a "post-Christian nation."[15] The British and Scottish Universities are spiritually dead, yet the irony is that American evangelicals send their students to be trained at these prestigious institutions. Ian Murray, in his excellent book, *A Scottish Christian Heritage*,[16] catalogued "The Tragedy of the Free Church of Scotland," wherein the University of Aberdeen, once a lighthouse for the inerrancy of God's Word, fell by the wayside

---

[14] http://www.telegraph.co.uk/news/religion/8633540/Ageing-Church-of-England-will-be-dead-in-20-years.html accessed on October 9, 2014.

[15] http://www.telegraph.co.uk/news/religion/10790495/Former-archbishop-of-Canterbury-We-are-a-post-Christian-nation.html accessed on October 9, 2014.

[16] Ian Murray, *A Scottish Christian Heritage* (Banner of Truth Trust, 2006).

and now is a centering of virulently anti-biblical thinking that influences many young scholars who now attend its hallowed halls and whose heart so rapidly turns away from child-like faith in the glorious gospel of Jesus Christ.

What caused Christianity in England and Scotland to fail so decisively? What turned Aberdeen and other such once great Christian center universities away from a vital belief in God's Word and trust in the Savior, the Lord Jesus Christ? Neither threat from 20th century Communism nor the might of the Nazis was able to defeat the Christian heritage: of England and Scotland. Christianity fell from within, from the carelessness of her clergy and her people who did not recognize the danger (Acts 20:28-31) inside her own gates; from self-professing academics who claimed "discipleship" of Jesus but were not genuinely or firmly committed to His Word (Matt. 10:37-38; 16:24-27) but instead with evangelistic zeal championed radical theories of German critics who assaulted God's Word and who long ago had lost their way spiritually; that destroyed the faith of the preachers that they were training in these schools, that, in turn, weakened or destroyed the faith of those who attended the sermons of these lukewarm clergy ("I wish that you were either hot or cold but you are lukewarm"–Rev. 3:15-17). The British, the Scottish Christian heritage was destroyed internally by its own membership.

America now is facing the same crisis that destroyed Christianity *from within* in the United Kingdom. Soon "Ichabod" or "the glory has departed" will be written about America's Christian heritage as was with England and Scotland. American evangelicals now send their best and brightest to radical schools in Germany, but especially England and Scotland, where long ago God's Word was weakened, rejected, and now mocked. These continental and British-trained evangelical American scholars hold vast influential sway in seminaries founded in the United States at the turn of the 20th century; schools and seminaries that once fought firmly for God's Word in the modernist-fundamentalist struggle that destroyed mainline denominations' in the United States in the first decades of that century. America evangelicalism is being threatened, not from without, but from within its own ranks. Scholarship now reigns over Lordship; radicalism over spiritual renewal and revival. The light of God's Word becomes enveloped in a growing darkness and skepticism rather than a vibrancy of trust.

John MacArthur, President of The Master's Seminary, has warned that the gravest danger to God's Word is always *from within.* He told how Christians in America and throughout the world must brace for a new onslaught of skepticism from within its own membership. As a professor of New Testament, I train seminary students in New Testament language and literature coming to The Master's Seminary from literally around the world (e.g. former Soviet Union countries, Russia, China, North Korea). These students are a monumental testimony that communism and atheistic dictatorships are not able to weaken God's people or their trust in His Word. These students, their families, indeed, their ancestors faced the onslaught from without. The faithful in Russia, China and Korea withstood the danger from without. But today, *the influx of radical scholarship from within now threatens God's people in these nations as the outward evil could not.* Indeed, Russian, Chinese, Korean Christians were safer when facing the KGB, Chinese secret police, and Korean tyranny than they are with evangelicals now trained in Continental and British Universities. Basics of Biblical Criticism will demonstrate the foundational truth of this latter assessment of the grave danger from within. These countries are now being weakened by the influx of cults, heretics, as well as radicalized, doubting Christian academics within evangelicalism.

Every Christian generation must be willing to take a stand for the Word against those whose goal is to destroy God's people from within, whether these do so deliberately, carelessly or unwittingly. Always must the faithful be vigilant. A book I have written, along with apologist Norman Geisler, entitled *The Jesus Quest The Danger From Within*, has traced this danger being faced now by Christian evangelicals. The book details the shocking degeneration of the spiritual vitality of evangelical seminaries and churches that have been infected by scholarship that reigns over the Lordship of Jesus and His Word. American at the turn of the 20th century fought off the last conflict from within, but now is rapidly losing the spiritual battle once again from within. As England and Scotland had suffered in the loss of its Christian heritage, so also American evangelicalism travels quickly down the same path toward an irreversible destruction of trust in the inerrancy of God's Word.

At the beginning of the 20th Century, World War 1 the fires of destruction engulfed Europe. In the United Kingdom, the privilege of being a torch light for the gospel had been extinguished, the embers growing cold and dark. The shameful irony of that period was that while Charles Darwin, the man who single-handedly did more damage to the church than any other in recent times with his preposterous hypothesis of evolution that had no true scientific foundation, found honor being enshrined in Westminster Abbey, while John Knox, the great Presbyterian reformer who was one of the biggest champions of the Gospel in modern times, lies buried under a parking lot with a small plate marking the spot. Oddly, a cryptic remark by German physician, Albert Schweitzer in his book written at that time, spoke of the infiltration of the German Universities long ago by a group doing great damage to the church in Germany known by the name of the "illuminati."[17]

In America during this period, a similar shadow of darkness was attempting to extinguish the glorious light of the Gospel. The Great Awakening of the 18th Century had long lost its influence. America's churches grew spiritually cold, dead, yet a small remnant remained within them. Bible colleges, originally founded for the proclamation of the Gospel in the "Colonies" had grown intellectually but decayed spiritually. Harvard, Yale, Princeton, all originally designed to train preachers, were fountain-heads of virulent atheism or rampant unbelief. This period in America was marked by several characteristics:

As in the United Kingdom who had tread a similar path previously …

(1) Evolution had gained hold in Christian institutions with Genesis 1-11 being regarded as symbolic, fiction or worse, a fairy-tale, instead of genuine history of the Divine creation of man in God's image. Adam and Eve were regarded as symbolic

---

[17] Schweizer wrote an enigmatic statement in this work, that many theologians in German "wrote under the impression of the immense influence exercised by the order of the Illuminati at the end of the eighteenth century." Albert Schweitzer, *The Quest of the Historical Jesus*. Introduction by James M. Robinson. Trans. By W. Montgomery from the first German Edition, 1906 (New York: Macmillan, 1968), 4.

rather than mankind's first parents. The catastrophism of a world-wide flood, so evidenced in the geologic columns, was dismissed as either a mere local flood or so much literary fiction.

(2) Higher criticism, what is known today as "historical criticism," assaulted not only the Old Testament but also the New Testament. Virulent doubt, unbelief pervaded the interpretation of every book of the Bible.

(3) The Gospel records, Matthew, Mark, Luke and John were dismissed as untrue, fictional or at best, symbolic rather than historical documents of Jesus' life.

(4) American denominations were training its clergy and scholarship for its religious schools and churches from German and British institutions that long ago had turned hostile to the Word of God. Future American preachers sat under prestigious professors from Oxford, Cambridge, Aberdeen, Tubingen, Gottingen, Harvard, Yale, etc. etc. etc. whose ears were filled with anti-biblical theories that denied the foundational historicity and factuality of the biblical text. The "fire in the bellies" for preaching God's Word was diminished by influencing the next generation of preachers. One could characterize the period with Jesus' words in Matthew 23:15, "Woe to you, scribes and Pharisees, hypocrites, because you travel around on sea and land to make one proselyte; and when he becomes one, you make him twice as much a son of hell as yourselves."

(5) The American Christian atmosphere filled with a desire for new thinking, i.e. "novelty" in its colleges and schools. Faithfulness to God's Word, echoing Paul's command in 2 Timothy 2:2 "The things which you have heard from me in the presence of many witnesses, entrust these to faithful men who will be able to teach others also," was dismissed as old fashioned, not in keeping with the modern world.

(6) Churches dismissed inerrancy. Errancy pervaded every part of Christian churches and schools.

(7) As a result, Jesus was lost. The first search for the "historical Jesus" was being conducted because the Gospels had lost credibility in mainline denominations. The Jesus of the Gospels was considered a fiction, so scholars searched for him in unbelieving ways.

In this dark time for America, a faithful remnant began praying. The precious Spirit of God sovereignly demonstrated his mercy to those who were praying for revival. In 1909, God moved two Christian laymen, wealthy California oil magnates who were brothers named Lyman and Milton Stewart, to set aside a large sum of money for issuing twelve volumes that would set forth the fundamentals of the Christian faith and which were to be sent free of charge to ministers of the gospel, missionaries, Sunday School superintendents, and others engaged in aggressive Christian work through the English-speaking world. A committee of twelve men who were known to be sound in the faith was chosen to have the oversight of the publication of these volumes. Entitled, *The Fundamentals*, they were a twelve-volume set published between 1910 and 1917 that set presented the fundamentals of the Christian faith. Three million individual volumes were distributed. R. A. Torrey related his own personal knowledge and experience with these volumes in the following terms, "Rev. Dr. A. C. Dixon was the first Executive Secretary of the Committee, and upon his departure for England Rev. Dr. Louis

Meyer was appointed to take his place. Upon the death of Dr. Meyer the work of the Executive Secretary developed upon me. We were able to bring out these twelve volumes according to the original plan. Some of the volumes were sent to 300,000 ministers and missionaries and other workers in different parts of the world. On the completion of the twelve volumes as originally planned the work was continued through The King's Business, published at 536 South Hope St., Los Angeles, California. Although a large number of volumes were issues than there were names on our mailing list, at last the stock became exhausted, but appeals for them kept coming in from different parts of the world."[18]

An immediate impact of *The Fundamentals* was the alerting of God's people regarding the worsening spiritual condition that the church was experiencing. God's people issued a call to assemble throughout America, rallying in defense of God's inerrant Word. Warren Wiersbe related, "[a]t that time in history, Fundamentalism was become a force to reckon with, thanks to effective preachers, popular Bible conferences and the publications that taught 'the fundamentals' and also exposed the growing apostasy of that day . . . It was a time of growth and challenge."[19] On May 25–June 1, 1919, six thousand Christians met in Philadelphia at "The World Conference on Christian Fundamentals." W. H. Griffith Thomas chaired the Resolutions Committee, while popular well-known fundamentalist preachers spoke for those days, such as W. B. Riley, R. A. Torrey, Lewis Sperry Chafer, James M. Gray and William L. Pettingill. Delegates came from 42 states in America, most of the Canadian provinces as well as seven foreign countries to rally against the infiltration of destructive higher criticism and liberalism of the day in the church. The Conference issued *God Hath Spoken* (Philadelphia: Bible Conference Committee, 1919) that consisted of 25 addresses that were delivered at the conference and stenographically recorded for posterity.[20]

Today, at the turn of the 21st Century, American churches once again are facing the *very same challenges* that they already had experienced at the beginning of the 20th century. The hour grows dark again for the glorious light of the Gospel in the United States. Basics of Biblical Criticism will detail the horrific onslaught that the church in America is now facing in the very same way that was faced at the turn of the 20th century.

The early twentieth-century church in America faced a sobering assessment of the spiritual decay of Bible understanding and interpretation, especially in terms of the inspiration and inerrancy of Scripture. At best, a partial inspiration of Scripture was promulgated among churches, with scholars arbitrarily picking and choosing portions of the OT and NT to either spiritualize or allegorize away any form of literal, plain interpretation or out rightly reject the text of Scripture altogether. In

---

[18] "Preface," in *The Fundamentals: A Testimony to the Truth*, R. A. Torrey, A. C. Dixon and others, eds. (Grand Rapids Baker Reprint, 1972), vol. 1. Reprinted without alteration or abridgment from the original, four-volume edition issues by the Bible Institute of Los Angeles in 1917.

[19] Warren Wiersbe, "Foreword," in *The Fundamentals for Today*.

[20] *God Hath Spoken (Hebrews 1:1-2) Twenty-five Addresses Delivered at the World Conference on Christian Fundamentals.* Stenographically reported under the direction of a Biblically trained expert (Philadelphia: Bible Conference Committee, 1919).

light of this very serious decay of sound Bible teaching, the early twentieth century Bible-believing community began to rally support for the Scriptures in a determined effort to counter the spiraling downward effects that mainstream denominations in America were experiencing. Because of the efforts of the faithful within the church, publications like *The Fundamentals* (1917) and Bible conferences such as "The World Conference on Christian Fundamentals" (1919) served as a rallying cry to focus attention to the dangerous drift away from the inspiration and inerrancy of God's Word. A call to interpret Scripture according to the plain, normal sense of Scripture (known also as "grammatico-historical interpretation" in contrast to "historical criticism" of the liberal denominations that caused such havoc) also became a central focus of Bible-believing Christians.

Since mainline denominations were so sorely infected, large numbers withdrew from denominations deemed now spiritually beyond repair. The faithful formed a host of Bible colleges, Christian colleges and Seminaries were founded in the first 50 or so years of the twentieth century that would promote the inspiration, inerrancy and plain, normal interpretation. Moody Bible Institute was founded in 1886 by evangelist Dwight L. Moody. In 1907 Lyman Stewart funded the production of *The Fundamentals* (mentioned above) which heralded the founding of the Bible Institute of Los Angeles. By 1912, Torrey, coming from Moody Bible Institute, became Dean of the Bible Institute of Los Angeles and assumed editorial leadership in publishing *The Fundamentals* as a four-volume work in 1917. The warning of J. Gresham Machen that "as go the theological seminaries, so goes the church" struck deep at the heart of Bible-believing scholars everywhere: "many seminaries today *are* nurseries of unbelief; and because they are nurseries of unbelief the churches that they serve have become unbelieving churches too. As go the theological seminaries, so goes the church."[21] In 1929, Machen was influential in founding Westminster Theological Seminary as a result of Princeton's direction.[22] Dallas Theological Seminary was founded in 1924,[23] and Fuller Theological Seminary was founded in 1947 by Biola graduate, Charles E. Fuller along with Harold Ockenga. These are just a select few of the many schools founded by faithful men in this period. The hope was that these new schools would preserve a faithful, orthodox view of Scripture.

After this strategic withdrawal by fundamentalists of the first generation who fought the battle to preserve Scripture from the onslaught of historical criticism as well as its subsequent searching for the historical Jesus, subsequent generations from fundamentalist groups became discontent with their isolation from liberal-dominated mainstream biblical scholarship. The lessons of history were forgotten by subsequent American generations of the battle fought at the turn of the 20th

---

[21] J. Gresham Machen, *The Christian Faith in the Modern World*. Grand Rapids: Eerdmans, 1965 [1936], 65.

[22] For a revealing look at Machen's struggle, see J. Gresham Machen, *Christianity and Liberalism* (Grand Rapids: Eerdmans, 1946 [1923]); idem. *The Virgin Birth of Christ*. Second Edition (New York and London: Harper & Brothers, 1932 [1930]; idem. *What is Faith?* (Grand Rapids: Eerdmans, 1946 [1925].

[23] For a recent recounting of the history of Dallas Theological Seminary, see John D. Hannah, *An Uncommon Union: Dallas Theological Seminary and American Evangelicalism* (Grand Rapids: Zondervan, 2009).

century. By the mid-1960s, prominent voices were scolding fundamentalists for continued isolation and dialogue and interaction once again became the rallying cry. Carl F. H. Henry's criticisms struck deep, "The preoccupation of fundamentalists with the errors of modernism, and neglect of schematic presentations of the evangelical alternative, probably gave neo-orthodoxy its great opportunity in the Anglo-Saxon world...If Evangelicals do not overcome their preoccupation with negative criticism of contemporary theological deviations at the expense of the construction of preferable alternatives to these, they will not be much of a doctrinal force in the decade ahead."[24]

Echoing similar statements, George Eldon Ladd (1911-1982) of Fuller Theological Seminary became a zealous champion of modern critical methods, arguing that the two-source hypothesis should be accepted "as a literary fact" and that form criticism "has thrown considerable light on the nature of the Gospels and the traditions they employ" adding, "Evangelical scholars should be willing to accept this light."[25] Indeed, for Ladd, critical methods have derived great benefit for evangelicals, "it has shed great light on the historical side of the Bible; and these historical discoveries are valid for all Bible students even though the presuppositions of the historical-critical method have been often hostile to an evangelical view of the Bible. Contemporary evangelicals often overlook this important fact when they condemn the critical method as such; for even while they condemn historical criticism, they are constantly reaping the benefits of its discoveries and employing critical tools."[26] Ladd asserts, "One must not forget that...everyday tools of good Bible study are the product of the historical-critical method."[27] George Ladd catalogued the trend of a "substantial group of scholars" whose background was in the camp of "fundamentalism" who had now been trained "in Europe as well as in our best universities" and were "deeply concerned with serious scholarship."[28] He also chided fundamentalists for their "major preoccupation" with defending "inerrancy of the Bible in its most extreme form," but contributing "little of creative thinking to the current debate."[29] Although Ladd acknowledged that historical-critical ideology was deeply indebted for its operation in the Enlightenment, and the German scholarship that created it openly admitted its intention of "dissolving

---

[24] Carl F. H. Henry, *Jesus of Nazareth, Savior and Lord* (London: Tyndale, 1970 (1966), 9.

[25] George Eldon Ladd, *NT and Criticism* (Grand Rapids: Eerdmans, 1967) 141, 168-169.

[26] Ladd, *NT and Criticism*, 10.

[27] Ladd offers two examples: Kittel and Friedrich, *Theological Dictionary of the New Testament* and Arndt, Gingrich, Baur and Danker, *A Greek-English Lexicon of the New Testament*; Ladd, *NT and Criticism*, 11.

[28] George E. Ladd, "The Search for Perspective," *Interpretation* XXV (1971), 47.

[29] Ladd, "The Search for Perspective," 47. In a hotly debated book, Harold Lindsell in the mid-1970s detailed the problems facing Fuller, the Southern Baptist Convention and other Christian institutions due to the encroachment of historical criticism from European influence. See Harold Lindsell, "The Strange Case of Fuller Theological Seminary," *The Battle for the Bible* (Grand Rapids: Zondervan, 1976), 106-121. Marsden's book also covers this period in *Reforming Fundamentalism* (Grand Rapids: Eerdmans, 1987).

orthodoxy's identification of the Gospel with Scripture,"[30] Ladd sent many of his students for subsequent study in Britain and Europe in order to enlarge the influence of conservatives, the latter of which influence was greatly responsible for the fundamentalist split at the turn of the twentieth century.[31]

Today, Ladd serves as the recognized paradigm for current attitudes and approaches among evangelical historical-critical scholarship in encouraging evangelical education in British and Continental institutions as well as the adoption and participation in historical criticism to some form or degree, actions which previously were greatly responsible for the fundamentalist-modernist split.[32] Lessons from what caused the last theological meltdown had long been forgotten or carelessly disregarded.[33] These schools now train the American evangelical churches producing a host of dangerous thinking regarding inspiration and inerrancy as well as plain, normal interpretation ("when the plain sense makes common sense, seek no other sense").

Bible Colleges, Christian Universities, and Seminaries, once founded to guard faithfulness to Scripture in the early and mid-20th century, are now once again becoming the hotbed of the latest teachings of the theological left of the United Kingdom and European schools. The very same errors that crept in at the beginning of the 20th Century. History now repeats. The next article will detail the destruction occurring among evangelical institutions in the 21st century.

---

[30] Ladd, "The Search for Perspective, 49 cf. Ladd's citing of this admission by Ernst Käsemann may be found in the latter's, *Essays on New Testament Themes* (London: SCM, 1964), 54-62.

[31] An example of one of Ladd's students is the late Robert Guelich who wrote *The Sermon on the Mount, A Foundation for Understanding* (Waco, TX: Word, 1982). Guelich promoted an exegesis "that . . . makes use of the literary critical tools including text, source, form, tradition, redaction, and structural criticism" and goes on to assert "for many to whom the Scriptures are vital the use of these critical tools has historically been more 'destructive' than 'constructive.' But one need not discard the tool because of its abuse."

[32] Mark Noll conducted a personal poll/survey among evangelicals and has, as a result, described Ladd as "the most widely influential figure on the current generation of evangelical Bible scholars." Ladd was "most influential" among scholars in the Institute for Biblical Research and was placed just behind John Calvin as "most influential" among scholars in the Evangelical Theological Society. See Noll, 97, 101, 112-114 [note especially p. 112 for this quote], 116, 121, 159-163, 211-226. Moreover, Marsden described Noll's book, *Between Faith and Criticism*, as making "a major contribution toward understanding twentieth-century evangelical scholarship." See George M. Marsden, *Reforming Fundamentalism* , 250 fn. 9. Since Noll marked out Ladd as the outstanding figure influencing the recent paradigm shift in twentieth-century evangelical scholarship toward favoring historical-critical methods and since Marsden promotes Noll's book as making "a major contribution toward understanding twentieth-century evangelical scholarship," this paper uses Ladd as the outstanding paradigmic example, as well as typical representative, of this drift among evangelicals toward historical-critical ideologies that favor literary dependency hypotheses.

[33] For further historical details, see F. David Farnell, "The Philosophical and Theological Bent of Historical Criticism, in *The Jesus Crisis*, 85-131.

CHAPTER 2 Grammatical-Historical Versus Historical-Critical

F. David Farnell

Great Confusion over Terminology and Practice

Overview

Much confusion exists in evangelical circles regarding grammatico-historical and historical-critical approaches to exegesis.[34] These two hermeneutical disciplines are distinct and must not be confused by evangelicals. Several factors may be cited in contrast.

1. The independence approach associates itself with the grammatico-historical hermeneutic that has its roots in the Reformation of 1517. In contrast, the historical-critical hermeneutic has its roots in deism, rationalism, and the Enlightenment. Krentz, favorable to the practice, readily admits in his The *Historical-Critical Method* relates that "Historical method is the child of the Enlightenment."[35] Maier, against historical criticism, argued, "historical criticism over against a possible divine revelation presents an inconclusive and false counterpart which basically maintains human arbitrariness and its standards in opposition to the demands of revelation."[36]

2. Because of their distinct philosophical differences and developments, the grammatico-historical method is open to the supernatural and miraculous. It assumes the Scriptures are true regarding their assertions and posits the idea that God can and does intervene in human history. In contrast, the historical-critical method assumes Troeltsch's ideological principles of (a) the principle of criticism or methodological doubt—history achieves only probability, nothing can be known with any certainty; (b) the principle of analogy (somewhat like the modern idea of uniformitarianism) that present experience becomes the criteria of probability in the past (hence, if no supernatural events occur today; then, they do not occur in the past either); and (c) correlation or mutual interdependence that postulates a closed-continuum of cause and effect with no outside divine intervention.[37] Therefore, any time evangelicals dehistoricize the gospels or the Scriptures as a whole; they practice historical-critical, not grammatico-historical hermeneutics. Grammatico-historical

---

[34] See Robert L. Thomas, "Current Hermeneutical Trends: Toward Explanation or Obfuscation?, JETS 39 (June 1996): 241-256.

[35] Edgar Krentz, *The Historical-Critical Method* (Philadelphia: Fortress, 1975), 55.

[36] Gerhard Maier, *The End of the Historical-Critical Method* (St. Louis, MO: Concordia Publishing House, 1974), 25.

[37] See Krentz, *The Historical-Critical Method*, 55; Ernest Troeltsch, "Historical and Dogmatic Method in Theology (1898)," in *Religion in History*. Essays translated by James Luther Adams and Walter F. Bense (Minneapolis: Fortress, 1991), 11-32.

exegesis does not shift the burden of proof upon the Scriptures to demonstrate their truth, reliability or historicity as does historical critical ideology like source criticism.

3. The grammatico-historical approach emphasizes an inductive approach to understanding the meaning of Scripture based on plain, normal interpretation. Its goal is to understand the Scripture as was intended by the original author.[38] It seeks single, not multiple, layers of meaning while emphasizing the perspicuity of Scripture. In contrast, the historical-critical approach does not attempt to understand the Scripture as was necessarily intended. It pursues and deductive approach that *a priori* assumes an interpretation and forces Scripture into that mold. It often practices an allegorizing hermeneutic that sees multiple layers of meaning. [39]

4. The history of dependency hypotheses associates them with historical-critical ideologies, not grammatico-historical exegesis as has been evident throughout this discussion. Dependency hypotheses arose in the modern period that has its roots in skepticism of the biblical record, especially the Gospels. Therefore, those who practice dependency hypotheses are automatically, if not unwittingly, aligned with the errancy position of historical-criticism. At root, philosophy controls the exegetical approach of historical-critical approaches like source, form/tradition, and redaction criticism.

In direct contrast, the independence approach allies itself with the grammatico-historical hermeneutic. Its critical approach to examining Scripture starts from a qualitatively different bases than historical-critical ideology.[40] Moreover, the grammatico-historical method of interpretation has been the safeguard in hermeneutics, for it downplays subjectivity and emphasizes the need for Spirit-guided objectivity in exegeting Scripture.

Historical Criticism

Historical Criticism is a product of philosophical ideologies that are inherently hostile to the Biblical text.

---

[38] Milton Terry, *Biblical Hermeneutics* (Grand Rapids: Zondervan, n.d.), 173.

[39] Evangelical drift from the single-meaning principle is alarming. Wallace, reflecting the evangelical drift into multiple-layers of meaning, argues: "One of the reasons that most NT grammarians have been reticent to accept this category [plenary genitive] is simply that most NT grammarians are Protestants. And the Protestant tradition of a singular meaning for the text (which, historically, was a reaction to the fourfold meaning employed in the Middle Ages) has been fundamental in their thinking. However, current biblical research recognizes that a given author may, at times, be *intentionally* ambiguous. The instances of double entendre, *sensus plenior* (conservative defined), puns, and word-plays in the NT all contribute to this view . . . . Tradition has to some degree prevented Protestants from seeing this." See Dan B. Wallace, *Greek Grammar Beyond the Basics* (Grand Rapids: Zondervan, 1996), 120 fn 134.

[40] For more important weaknesses of the historical-critical method, consult Maier, *The End of the Historical-Critical Method*, 11-92.

1. Please note the CHART on the Philosophical Antecedents/Developments of Historical Criticism. The Chart is simplified for easier understanding. Much more was involved, but it covers the major highlights.

2. Geisler notes,

> [W]ithin a little over one hundred years after the Reformation the philosophical seeds of modern errancy were sown. When these seeds had produced their fruit in the church a century or so later, it was because theologians had capitulated to alien philosophical presuppositions. Hence, the rise of an errant view of Scripture did not result from a discovery of factual evidence that made belief in an inerrant Scripture untenable. Rather, it resulted from the unnecessary acceptance of philosophical premises that undermined the historic belief in an infallible and inerrant Bible.[41]

Stephen Davis, far from espousing fundamentalist views, confirms this,

> What leads them to liberalism, apart from cultural and personal issues, is their acceptance of certain philosophical or scientific assumptions that are inimical to evangelical theology—e.g., assumptions about what is "believable to modern people," "consistent with modern science," acceptable by twentieth-century canons of scholarship," and the like.[42]

3. Because of its philosophical underpinnings, Historical Criticism should be seen as an ideology.

The Grammatical-Historical Method

A. The Definition–

1. It seeks to find the meaning which the authors of Scripture intended to convey and the meaning comprehended by the recipients

Special allowance/provision made for (1) inspiration, (2) Holy Spirit, and (3) inerrancy

2. **Specific Definition:** *A Study of inspired Scripture designed to discover under the guidance of the Holy Spirit the meaning of a text dictated by the principles of grammar and the facts of history*

---

[41]Norman L. Geisler, "Inductivism, Materialism, and Rationalism: Bacon, Hobbes, and Spinoza," in *The Biblical Errancy: An Analysis of Its Philosophical Roots.* Edited by Norman Geisler (Grand Rapids: Zondervan, 1981), 11. This excellent work presents a variety of articles that trace the underpinnings of historical-critical methodologies to baneful philosophical methodologies. Unfortunately, Geisler's warning has not been heeded by evangelicals who continue their connections with Historical Criticism.

[42] Stephen Davis, *The Debate about the Bible* (Philadelphia: Westminster, 1977), 139. What is refreshing about Davis's statement is the outright candor of the remark compared to some evangelicals who refuse to admit the philosophical basis of such crucial issues.

3. WARNING: EVANGELICALS HAVE WRONGLY USED GRAMMATICO-HISTORICAL AND HISTORICAL CRITICISM AS SYNONYMOUS.

4. PLEASE FOREVER REMEMBER

FORMULA:

GRAMMATICO HISTORICAL

≠ (does not equal)

HISTORICAL CRITICISM

B. The Presuppositions of Grammatico-Historical Criticism

A. Grammatico-historical has a required spiritual dimension: <u>Must</u> be indwelled by Holy Spirit to interpret Scripture properly (acceptance and understanding)–Romans 8:3; 1 Cor. 2: 6-16). Certain areas of meaning will be hidden to the natural man because he will lack the necessary spiritual guidance to use the exegetical data properly.

B. Open/Continuum. GH allows for possibility of miracles. Open to it.

C. Inspiration—inspiration possible

D. Scripture documents must be allowed to speak for themselves. Not *a priori* doubted—until documents disprove their accuracy/factuality.

E. God of the Bible is God

C. Grammatico-Historical Method is a part of the REFORMATION (HC part of Spinoza, rationalism, deism, the Enlightenment) HERITAGE! MUST DISTINGUISH PHILOSOPHIES BEHIND HC. THEY ARE NOT BEHIND REFORMATION HERITAGE.

CHAPTER 3 Form and Tradition Criticism

F. David Farnell

2 Peter 1:16 Updated American Standard Version (UASV)

[16] For we did not follow cleverly devised myths when we made known to you the power and coming of our Lord Jesus Christ, but we were eyewitnesses of his majesty.

Introduction

The historical-critical methods of form[43] and tradition[44] criticism are the natural end-products of the radical historical skepticism produced from the period of the Enlightenment and beyond. Their derivation and development radiated

---

[43] The Encarta Dictionary defines Form criticism as "a method of analyzing the Bible to determine the presumed original oral form of the written text by removing known historical conventions that emerged at a later period." Hayes and Holladay, proponents of the so-called historical-critical methodologies offer the following on Form Criticism,

"Form criticism seeks to identify various literary genres and then to classify a passage within one of these genres. Form critics also recognize that literary classification is not enough. They also try to ascertain the "situation in life" (German: *Sitz im Leben*) in which genres originated and developed. The phrase "in life" reminds us that what we experience as literary forms—something we read—originally had a "life setting." Imagining different situations in life, such as worship, teaching, preaching, and argument, enables us to appreciate the original oral form of literary genres. What we experience as formalized, written genres typically acquired their literary shape through oral repetition."–John H. Hayes; Carl R. Holladay (2010-11-05). *Biblical Exegesis*, 3rd ed. (pp. 104-105). Westminster John Knox Press. Kindle Edition.

It should be noted that these definitions make form criticism seem innocent, which could not be further from the truth. I define these approaches by historical/ideological background. The definitions **do not** reveal their true intentions, i.e. to dehistoricize and control the text as to meaning, i.e. make it suitable to the critics ideologies rather than to the plain normal sense of Scripture.

[44] The Encyclopaedia Britannica defines tradition criticism as a "study of biblical literature, method of criticism of the Hebrew Bible (Old Testament) and the New Testament that attempts to trace the developmental stages of the oral tradition, from its historical emergence to its literary presentation in scripture. Scholars of the Hebrew Bible might, for example, study the development of a narrative tradition about the patriarchs (Abraham, Isaac, and Jacob) or the judges (such as Deborah and Samuel) as it unfolded over several generations. New Testament scholars often pay special attention to the oral stage of Gospel transmission, investigating both the record of the ministry of Jesus and the development of Christian theology in the short preliterary. stage."

http://www.britannica.com/topic/tradition-criticism

It should be noted that these definitions make tradition criticism seem innocent, which could not be further from the truth. I define these approaches by historical/ideological background. The definitions **do not** reveal their true intentions, i.e. to dehistoricize and control the text as to meaning, i.e. make it suitable to the critics ideologies rather than to the plain normal sense of Scripture.

historically from an underlying foundation that was innately hostile to the biblical text, especially in terms of its origin, historicity, and validity.

More strategically, however, is the fact that the hostility of these methodologies to the biblical text strategically centers in the essential philosophical nature of these disciplines. Form and tradition criticism are inherently philosophically driven disciplines. Philosophical traditions that were inherently hostile to the biblical text were the motivating force behind the developments of these disciplines and are responsible for the history, characteristics, and methodological expressions and practices of both form and tradition criticism. This hostility to the biblical text that is displayed in form and tradition criticism is the natural consequence of their philosophical underpinnings. These philosophical movements that comprise the Presuppositional foundations and underpinnings of form and tradition criticism are also responsible for the ascendance of these methodologies to widespread predominance in biblical interpretation.

Moreover, philosophy forms the basis for all historical-critical methodologies (source, form, redaction, tradition, literary criticism) practiced in recent times. As inherently philosophical methodologies, form and tradition criticism have already prescribed agendas that reach foregone conclusions. These disciplines cannot ever hope to perform an objective analysis because their design and superstructure are predicated upon a host of assumptions that are, by their very nature, philosophical in origin and expression. One should overlook this philosophical basis of form and tradition criticism. It is, therefore, more accurate to describe such historical-critical methodologies as "ideologies" rather than methodologies.[45] As a result, form and tradition criticism as historical-critical methodologies are not capable of being "neutral" tools and have no real hopes of being so, no matter how far evangelicals try to "modify" this hermeneutical methodology. Their philosophical underpinnings preclude the possibility of neutrality or any form of objectivity or honesty in handling the biblical text.

Not only is an understanding of their philosophical bases important, but critical also to a proper understanding of form and tradition criticism is their nature as hermeneutical methodologies. These disciplines seek to make interpretive conclusions that are driven ultimately by philosophical underpinnings. Any such interpretive practices and decisions, therefore, are highly suspect due to the philosophically-driven basis of these disciplines. Indeed, much of what is considered exegesis in historical-critical methodologies is actually better described as eisegesis, i.e. the reading into the text of interpretive elements and conclusions that are extraneous and/or foreign to the text (not actually expressed through the text). Other possibilities are a priori proscribed or prohibited. Just like a child's Lego® set is capable of building only certain structures in a certain way, so is the situation with the interpretive methodologies of form and tradition criticism. As eisegetical methods, they also are acutely subjective in nature, mirroring the capricious manipulation and bias of the interpreter. In contrast to the goal of the grammatico-historical method that correctly has been to eschew subjectivity in interpretation as

---

[45]For further information on the ideological, as well as philosophical, basis of historical-critical methodologies, consult the excellent work of the post-Bultmannian turned evangelical Eta Linnemann, Historical Criticism of the Bible, Methodology or Ideology? Translated by Robert W. Yarbrough (Grand Rapids: Baker, 1990).

much as possible, form and tradition criticism, by their very nature, actively promote the imposition of subjectivity upon the text.

At first, the liberal camp of theology developed and practiced form and tradition criticism since they were most profoundly influenced by prevailing philosophical developments that arose from the Enlightenment and beyond. Liberals lauded the utilization of these disciplines since they promoted the a priori agenda of the left-wing in their interpretation of the biblical text. The post-Bultmannian Norman Perrin is typical, calling form criticism "the single most important development" in the history of gospel criticism "for it provides what must be regarded as the only satisfactory understanding of the nature of the synoptic gospel material."[46] Others have been more modest in praise. Redlich, realizing the vastly assumptive nature of form criticism, reflects a more moderate tone, "exponents of the Form-Critical school quite understandably overrate the value of their method."[47]

Sadly, the practice of form and tradition criticism has now gained a stronghold in the evangelical camp. While evangelicals, especially conservative evangelicals, at first generally adopted an apologetic stance against such hermeneutical methodologies, many are now evidencing much greater willingness to accept such methodologies in their approach to interpreting the text. Robert Guelich, in his The Sermon on the Mount (1982) following George Ladd's lead (see editor's "Introduction" that details Ladd's views), his mentor, promotes an exegesis "that . . . makes use of the literary critical tools including text, source, form, tradition, redaction, and structural criticism" and goes on to assert "for many to whom the Scriptures are vital the use of these critical tools has historically been more 'destructive' than 'constructive.' But one need not discard the tool because of its abuse."[48] Darrell Bock also follows this logic, arguing, "In the hands of a skilled exegete who uses the tools of interpretation in a way that fits what they are capable of, Form Criticism can be a fruitful aid to understanding and to exposition."[49]

Alister McGrath, in a recent article, declared that evangelicalism is the "Future of Protestantism," representing "a modern standard bearer of historic, orthodox Christianity," the "mainstream of American Protestant Christianity," and "The Christian vision of the future."[50] However, this future for orthodox Christianity will be bleak indeed if conservative evangelicals continue to increase their association with historical-critical methodologies like form criticism. This latter thought receives reinforcement in the fact that through the employment of historical-critical methods now increasingly promoted by conservative evangelicals; liberals had long ago

---

[46] Norman Perrin, *Rediscovering the Teaching of Jesus* (New York: Harper and Row, 1976), 218.

[47] See "Preface" in E. Basil Redlich, *Form Criticism, Its Value and Limitations* (London: Duckworth, 1939), n.p.

[48] Robert A. Guelich, *The Sermon on the Mount, A Foundation for Understanding* (Waco, TX.: Word, 1982), 23.

[49] Darrell L. Bock, "Form Criticism," in *New Testament Criticism and Interpretation.* Edited by David A. Black and David S. Dockery (Grand Rapids: Zondervan, 1991), 192.

[50] Alister McGrath, "Why Evangelicalism is the Future of Protestantism," Christianity Today, June 19, 1995, 18-23.

come to intellectual bankruptcy in their analysis of the Gospel material (e.g. deconstructionism).

In light of this growing acceptance of form and tradition criticism among conservative evangelicals, this chapter will analyze these hermeneutical disciplines, trace their Presuppositional and historical developments, and highlight their practice among liberals and conservative evangelicals alike in order to demonstrate the hermeneutical dangers posed by the adoption of these historical-critical methods.

The Definition and Description of Form Criticism

The renown German theologian Rudolf Bultmann (1893-1976), in essential agreement with Martin Dibelius, defines form criticism as follows:

> I am entirely in agreement with M. Dibelius when he maintains that form-criticism is not simply an exercise in aesthetics nor yet simply a process of description or classification; that is to say, it does not consist of identifying the individual units of the tradition according to their aesthetics or other characteristics and placing them in their various categories. It is much rather "to discover the origin and the history of the particular units and thereby to throw some light on the history of the tradition before it took literary form." The proper understanding of form-criticism rests upon the judgment that the literature in which the life of a given community, even the primitive Christian community, has taken shape, springs out of the quite definite conditions and wants of life from which grows up a quite definite style and quite specific forms and categories. Thus every literary category has its "life situation" (*Sitz im Leben*: Gunkel), whether it be worship in its different forms, or work, or hunting, or war. The *Sitz im Leben* is not, however, an individual historical event, but a typical situation or occupation in the life of the community.[51]

The British theologian F. F. Bruce prefers a more simple, watered-down definition: "Form criticism (Ger. Formgeschichte, 'form history') represents an endeavor to determine the oral prehistory of written documents or sources, and to classify the material according to the various "forms" or categories of narrative, discourse, and so forth."[52]

Pre-eminently an Ideology Rather Than Methodology

Yet, one must not treat these definitions in isolation, for taken out of context, they mistakenly might be interpreted to portray form criticism as a somewhat benign process. However, as will be demonstrated, form criticism involves far more than determining so-called form categories or an alleged "life situation" from which the gospel tradition arose. Both presuppositionally and historically, form criticism

---

[51] Rudolf Bultmann, *The History of the Synoptic Tradition*. Translated by John Marsh. Revised Edition (Basil Blackwell, 1963; Peabody, MA.: Hendrickson, n.d.), 3-4

[52] S. v. "Criticism," by F. F. Bruce, in ISBE, 1:822.

inherently makes strategic, a priori judgments on the historicity and factuality of the gospel records. It is an ideology as well as a methodology. Eta Linnemann, herself a former Bultmannian who turned evangelical, remarks that historical criticism, in general, is more an ideology than a methodology,

A more intensive investigation would show that underlying the historical-critical approach is a series of prejudgments which are not themselves the result of scientific investigation. They are rather dogmatic premises, statements of faith, whose foundation is the absolutizing of human reason as a controlling apparatus."[53]

Presuppositionally, certain ideologies are inherent in the methodology that contributed to the development of form criticism. Indeed, as will be seen, form criticism (and tradition criticism) would not have been conceptually possible without certain presuppositional and historical developments. The method is replete with a priori assumptions that are buttressed by little or no proof. As a result, one must investigate the presuppositional and historical development of the methodology to determine the legitimacy of the method as a hermeneutical discipline, especially in relationship to its utilization by conservative evangelicals.

The term "form criticism" comes from the German formgeschichte (English, "form history"). In German, its full title is formgeschichtliche Methode. As with such terms as redactionsgischichte (English, "redaction history or criticism" and traditionsgeschichte (English, "form history or criticism"), the original German name of the discipline subtly reveals its negative philosophical underpinnings by the usage of term geschichte instead of the term historie. While the word historie refers to objective historical facts of history (external and verifiable), the usage of geschichte dichotomizes the concept of history further into interpretations of history, i.e., history as significance, internal and non-verifiable. According to this distinction, that Jesus was a man who lived in the first century is an objective statement of historical fact, or historie, that may be verified by canons of "historical reason," while the assertion that he was the Son of God is an interpretive statement and belongs to the realm of geschichte in that it is affirmed only by an assumption of faith. In addition, such a distinction permits assertions that something may be interpretively "true" (history as significance) that may not be "true" in the sense of objectively verifiable (history as fact). For such form critics as Bultmann, no continuity exists between the Jesus of history (historie) and the Christ of Faith, i.e., geschichte the–Christ of the kerygma.[54]

According to form critics like Bultmann, the Jesus of history was a Jewish apocalyptist who died a tragic death and remains dead, while the "Risen Christ" is a mythological concept of the early church that reinterpreted the dead Jesus as the risen "Son of Man" under the influence of Jewish apocalyptic and Gnostic redemption mythology. Bultmann sought to demythologize stories of Jesus's resurrection, and, in doing so, the resurrection signifies His rising into the kerygma

---

[53] Eta Linnemann, *Historical Criticism of the Bible, Methodology or Ideology?* Translated by Robert W. Yarbrough (Grand Rapids: Baker, 1990), 111.

[54] S. v. "*Historie; Geschichte/geschichtlich; historisch*," in Handbook of Biblical Criticism. Edited by Richard N. Soulen (Atlanta: John Knox, 1981), 88-89.

to become the kerygmatic Christ. The basis of such assertions centers in a virulent anti-supernaturalism.[55]

The Prime Impetuses: Evolutionary Conceptions and Unbelief

From its conception, form criticism, as well as its background presupposition of the priority of Mark, was heavily influenced by an underlying assumption of evolution conceptions of simple to complex (for further information, see also discussion of history and presuppositions below). Kelber insightfully describes Bultmann's form-critical analysis in the following terms, "it [Bultmann's concept of the development of the synoptic tradition] was a process as natural as that of biological evolution: simplicity grew into complexity" and his [Bultmann's] form-critical model as "an effortlessly evolutionary transition from the pre-gospel stream of tradition to the written gospel."[56]

The fundamental assumption (presupposition) "which makes form criticism both necessary and possible" reveals an evolutionary-driven philosophy encrusted in the following terms: "the tradition consists basically of individual sayings and narratives joined together in the Gospels by the work of the authors."[57] These individual sayings and narratives circulated as isolated, independent units before being fixed in written form.[58] This assumed oral period usually is identified as existing somewhere between 30/33 and 60/70 C.E. or between the death of Christ and the composition of the earliest written Christian documents, hence a period of about thirty years.[59]

Guthrie, however, notes the peril of any such dogmatic speculation regarding an oral period: "The very fact that our historical data for the first thirty years of Christian history are so limited means that form critics inevitably had to draw a

---

[55] Bultmann, *Jesus Christ and Mythology*, 11-21; For an overview of Bultmann's method of demythologization, s. v. "Myth" by M. J. A. Horsnell, ISBE, vol. 3, 461-463.

[56] Werner H. Kelber, *The Oral and Written Gospel* (Philadelphia: Fortress, 1983), 5-6.

[57] McKnight, *What is Form Criticism?*, 18.

[58] An exception to this principle would be the passion narrative. Early form critics asserted that this very early existed as a connected narrative. Taylor remarks, "[T]he Gospel tradition came to be mainly a collection of isolated stories, sayings, and sayings-groups. The most important exception to the dissolving process continued to be the Passion Story which existed in the form of short accounts of the Arrest, Trial, and Crucifixion of Jesus current at different centres of primitive Christianity." See Vincent Taylor, The Formation of the Gospel Tradition (London: Macmillan, 1953), 169-170.

[59] This period varies among form critics. The period starts between C.E. 30-33 and goes anywhere between C.E. 50 and 70. For example, Dibelius saw this period as between C.E. 30 and C.E. 70. See Martin Dibelius, From Tradition to Gospel (Charles Scribner's Sons, n.d.), 9-10. Taylor sees the period from about 30 to around C.E. 50 when the alleged "Q" document was composed with the oral period ending from C. E. 65 to 100 when the Gospels and other books of the Bible were allegedly composed. Vincent Taylor, The Formation of the Gospel Tradition, 168. Most of the radical form critics place the Synoptics and John well outside the eyewitness period, dating them from late in the first century.

good deal on imagination, although none of them were conscious of doing so."[60] Thus, at its very heart, form criticism is acutely subjective. Since form critics contend that the passion narrative circulated as a continuous narrative, why could not other narratives also (e.g. Mark 1:21-39:2:1-3:6)?[61] The highly credible works of Birger Gerhardsson and Harald Riesenfeld reveals that the Jews were capable of tremendous feats of memorization that would indicate the stability of the tradition rather than instability as posited by form criticism.[62] Furthermore, a very credible case can be made that short narratives written by the eyewitness apostles may have existed.[63] These latter two points have been too readily dismissed by New Testament scholars as a whole, most likely because they would inherently refute the acutely dogmatic positions that currently predominate in both the source and form criticism.

Furthermore, the hypothesis of evolution has continued to dominate the second generation of form critics. For example, although Caird rejected the more "radical" conclusions of earlier or radical form critics like Bultmann, especially in terms of the historicity of the tradition, he supported the validity of much of form-critical principles. He boldly asserts, "Nobody is likely to dispute that some process of *natural selection* [italics mine] has been at work in the formulation of the gospel tradition."[64]

---

[60] Donald Guthrie, *New Testament Introduction*. Revised Edition (Downers Grove, IL.: InterVarsity, 1990), 210.

[61] Guthrie, New Testament Introduction, 231.

[62] For further information, see Birger Gerhardsson, *Memory and Manuscript* (Lund: C. W. K. Gleerup); *The Origins of the Gospel Traditions* (Philadelphia: Fortress, 1977); Harald Riesenfeld, The Gospel Tradition (Philadelphia: Fortress, 1970).

[63] Gundry argues, "The Apostle Matthew was a note-taker during the earthly ministry of Jesus and . . . his notes provided the basis for the bulk of the apostolic gospel tradition. The use of notebooks which were carried on one's person was very common in the Graeco-Roman world. In ancient schools outline notes (gravmmata uJpomnhmatikav) were often taken by pupils as the teacher lectured. . . . Shorthand was used possibly as early as the fourth century B. C. and certainly by Jesus time . . . . Rabbinic tradition was transmitted by the employment of catchwords and phrases which were written down in shorthand notes. Thus, from both the Hellenistic side and the Judaistic side it is wholly plausible to suppose that one from the apostolic band was a note-taker—especially since the relationship of Jesus to his disciples was that of a teacher, or rabbi, to his pupils.

As an ex-publican, whose employment and post near Capernaum on the Great West Road would have required and given a good command of Greek and instilled the habit of jotting down information, and perhaps as a Levite, whose background would have given him acquaintance with the OT in its Semitic as well as Greek forms, Mt the Apostle was admirably fitted for such a function among the unlettered disciples." See Robert H. Gundry, *The Use of the Old Testament in St. Matthew's School: With Special Reference to the Messianic Hope* (Leiden: E. J. Brill, 1967), 182-183. Goodspeed revived this hypothesis, but it has largely been ignored. Unfortunately, both Gundry and Goodspeed also held that Mark, instead of Matthew, was the first gospel written. See Edgar J. Goodspeed, *Matthew, Apostle and Evangelist* (Philadelphia: John C. Winston, 1959), 115, 159-160.

[64] George B. Caird, "The Study of the Gospels: II. Form Criticism," Expository Times LXXXVII (February 1976): 139.

Due to philosophically-motivated prejudices, rather than accepting the gospels coming from disciples whose names the Gospels bore (e.g. Matthew, John) and who were eyewitnesses of the deeds and sayings of Jesus during his earthly life or contemporaries of eyewitnesses (Mark, Luke), form critics allege that the gospels reflect the Post-Easter faith of the early church that functioned as the repository for these stories. The gospel tradition reflects the teaching of the early church not Jesus and resulted long after any eyewitness period. Similar to biological evolution that must postulate long periods of time for the origin of species, form critics sees a gradual development of the gospel tradition, long after any eyewitness period. For example, Bultmann argues that although the "date of the gospels cannot be accurately determined," Mark "was not the work of a disciple of Jesus or a member of the primitive community; and the same is true of Matthew and Luke." He asserts that Mark was the oldest gospel being composed around C.E. 70 and goes on to argue that "The composition of the Gospels of Matthew and Luke may be placed in the period from 70-100 A.D., probably nearer 100 than 70."[65] Thus, direct attestation to Jesus' words are not available, and indeed, the Gospels do not reflect Jesus' words but the thinking of the Christian community. Lightfoot, whose work served as the bridge between form and redaction criticism,[66] asserted, "It seems, then, that the form of the earthly no less than of the heavenly Christ is for the most part hidden from us. For all the inestimable value of the gospels, they yield us little more than a whisper of his voice; we trace in them but the outskirts of his ways."[67]

Fundamental Contradictions to Form Criticism: Eyewitnesses to and Biographical Interest in the Tradition

Form critics must postulate that the gospels were written well beyond the apostolic period because the acceptance of the concept of eyewitnesses to and a biographical interest in the Gospel tradition stands in direct contradiction to form criticism as well as affirms the stability of the tradition. Significantly, in Bultmann's History of the Synoptic Tradition, the term "eyewitness" does not even occur. The lack of eyewitness involvement is a basic presupposition of early form critics. Nineham comments, "According to form-critics, eyewitnesses played little direct part in the *development* of the Gospel tradition, however much they may have had to do with its original formulation . . . this opinion is no accidental or peripheral feature of the form-critical position" especially since "characteristics" and "key features" [of form-critical analysis] "are incompatible with any theory of much direct eye-witness influence after the initial stage."[68] However, the form critic, Dibelius, was forced to admit the strategic significance of the presence of eyewitnesses for the

---

[65] Bultmann, Form Criticism, Two Essays on New Testament Research, 15, 21.

[66] Richard H. Lightfoot, History and Interpretation in the Gospels (New York and London: Harper and Brothers, 1934), 225.

[67] Lightfoot, History and Interpretation in the Gospels, 225.

[68] D. E. Nineham, "Eyewitness Testimony and the Gospel Tradition—I," Journal of Theological Studies 9 (April 1958): 13.

tradition: "At the period when eyewitnesses of Jesus were still alive, it was not possible to mar the picture of Jesus in the tradition."[69]

Form critics postulate that through time and the changing conditions of the various Christian communities, these stories of Jesus gradually acquired accretions (i.e. fabrications and embellishments) that were not original, especially miraculous elements. Varied individual circumstances of the Christian communities determined what accretions were added and how such accretions took shape. The early church was interested not in the tradition for historical and literary purposes but for proclamation concerns of the church (e.g. preaching). Dibelius notes,

> The first understanding afforded by the standpoint of Formgeschichte is that there never was a "purely" historical witness to Jesus. Whatever was told of Jesus' words and deeds was always a testimony of faith as formulated for preaching and exhortation in order to convert unbelievers and confirm the faithful. What founded Christianity was not knowledge about a historical process, but the confidence that the content of the story was salvation: the decisive beginning of the End . . . .
>
> [Form Criticism] . . . undertakes to portray that the understanding of the story of Jesus, by which the various formulations of the material are dominated."[70]

However, Dibelius was not quite as radical as Bultmann regarding historical judgments, for he asserts at times, "That the words of Jesus were preserved, that they were put together to form 'speeches' with a single theme, and . . . that the sayings and parables were edited in the interest of exhortation, shows the Church's concern for shaping the life according to the commands of the Master."[71] The form critic, Ernst Käsemann, remarks, "[T]he work of the Form Critics was designed to show that the message of Jesus as given to us by the synoptists is, for the most part, not authentic but was minted by the faith of the primitive Christian community in its various stages."[72]

Guthrie strikes at the heart of the matter:

> [T]his type of form criticism is based on a definite presupposition regarding the earliest Christian period. It first is assumed that all the synoptic gospel records are community products and it then follows automatically that they become witnesses to the actual life and teaching of the church rather than to the life and teaching of Jesus.[73]

Thus, according to the developers of form criticism, the words of Jesus effectively have been lost due conversion motivations of the early church. No

---

[69] Dibelius, *From Tradition to Gospel*, 293.

[70] Dibelius, *From Tradition to Gospel*, 295.

[71] Dibelius, *From Tradition to Gospel*, 289.

[72] Ernst Käsemann, "The Problem of the Historical Jesus," *in Essays on New Testament Themes*. Translated by W. J. Montague (Philadelphia: Fortress Press, 1982), 15.

[73] Guthrie, *New Testament Introduction*, 222.

biographical interest existed in the Christian community to preserve the words of Jesus. Thus, basic to form criticism is the assumption that through time a change (evolution) in the transmission of material occurred.

A strong case, however, for the dating of the gospels and the New Testament as whole during the eyewitnesses period can be made. Interestingly, the liberal John A. T. Robinson, who formerly dated the New Testament as late reconstructions similar to the position of form critics, i.e. from C.E. 70 to early in the second century, now concludes after a rigorous re-analysis that all 27 New Testament were produced in approximately the two decades before C.E. 70 and that they are the work of the Apostles themselves or their contemporaries. He insightfully concludes, "[I]f the chronology of the documents and the pattern of development should turn out to be anything like what I have suggested, then there will be scope for numerous new trajectories to be drawn and for the rewriting of many introductions to–and ultimately theologies of–the New Testament. For dates remain disturbingly fundamental data."[74]

Not only may the early dating of the New Testament and the subsequent role of eyewitness be affirmed, but the New Testament indicates a fundamental biographical interests of the Christian community in the words and deeds of Jesus Christ, e.g., 1 Corinthians 7:10 where Paul distinguishes his words from those of Jesus; Luke 1:1-4 where Luke indicates that many had drawn up accounts based on reports handed down ("handed down"–*parevdosan*) to them from those who were "eyewitnesses and servants" (*aujtovptai* kai; *uJphrevtai*) from the very beginning (*ap j ajrch'*) of Jesus ministry and that his research was based on careful investigation (*ajkribw'*) of those eyewitness accounts; Acts and other New Testament books contain constant appeal by first century Christians that they were eyewitnesses of the events about which they spoke (e.g. Acts 2:32; 3:15; 10:41; 1 Cor. 15:1-8).

If the fact of eyewitnesses be accepted, then the concept of an unstable oral tradition is untenable for those eyewitnesses provide a guard against any substantial variation. If the apostles and their eyewitness contemporaries wrote the 27 books of the New Testament, then the New Testament offers no actual support to the form-critical evolutionary hypothesis of the tradition as brief, rounded units circulating for long periods of time that eventually were placed into a gospel record by the "Christian community." Instead, the Gospels reflect the personal reminiscences of eyewitnesses. As a result, the primary circulation of the tradition evidenced in the 27 documents of the New Testament is that which occurred in the minds of the apostles and their eyewitness contemporaries as they composed their works based on either their own personal reminiscences or those of other eyewitnesses (cf. Luke 1:1-4)! They are the true repository of the tradition reflected in New Testament rather than some later, hypothetical and nebulous entity known as the "Christian community."

---

[74] John A. T. Robinson, *Redating the New Testament* (Philadelphia: Fortress, 1976), 358. See also, John A. T. Robinson, *Can We Trust the New Testament?* (Grand Rapids: Eerdmans, 1977); "The New Testament Dating Game," Time (March 21, 1977), 95.

The Goals of Form Criticism

Because form criticism assumes a basic change in the gospel material, form critics apply certain form criteria or laws of tradition (e.g., length of episode, addition of details, presence of Semitisms) that are considered valid for determining the relative age (antiquity), original form, and historical veracity of the tradition reflected in the written sources (i.e., the gospels). Although more will be said regarding these criteria and others ("criteria of authenticity"), such criteria are also heavily based on evolutionary assumptions of gradually increasing complexity, a presuppositional antisupernatural bias against miraculous elements and the assumption that proposed "laws" of folk tradition can be applied to the gospel tradition in order to determine what aspects are late accretions and modifications (i.e., inauthentic). Bultmann contended,

> The laws governing the formulation of popular narrative and tradition may be studied in detail in the material which the Synoptists handed down. The first thing we observe is that the narrators do not give us long unified accounts but rather small single pictures, individual scenes narrated with the utmost simplicity. These always occupy but a brief space of time; apart from the Passion narrative no event or proceeding is narrated which covers more than two days. As a rule, only two speaking characters appear in these scenes, or at most three; involved proceedings are beyond the powers of the simple story teller. Where groups or crowds are present, they are treated as a unity. As such narratives pass from mouth to mouth, or when one writer takes them over from another, their fundamental character remains the same, but the details are subject to the control of fancy and are usually made more explicit or definite.[75]

Bultmann continues,

> This last task, viz., the study of the laws which govern literary transmission, can be approached by observing the manner in which the Marcan material was altered by Matthew and Luke; and also how Matthew and Luke worked over what they took from the *Logia*. Here we observe a certain regular procedure which becomes still more evident when we carry the investigation to a later tradition, particularly to the apocryphal gospels, and see how in these the gospel material received further literary development. . . . The ability to make the necessary distinctions can be developed by studying the general laws which govern popular transmission of stories and traditions in other instances, for example, in the case of folk-tales, anecdotes, and folk-songs.[76]

---

[75] See Rudolf Bultmann, "The Study of the Synoptic Gospels," in *Form Criticism, Two Essays on New Testament Research*. Translated by Frederick C. Grant (New York: Harper & Brothers, 1934), 32.

[76] Rudolf Bultmann, "The New Approach to the Synoptic Problem," *Journal of Religion* (July 1926): 345.

During this oral period, form critics postulate that these individual units of tradition were shaped by the early church as they were continually recounted by preachers, teachers and story-tellers as the occasion warranted. Davies summarizes the form-critical posture well,

> It is the first assumption of Form Critics that the Gospels are from the Church, by the Church, for the Church. The tradition about the works and words of Jesus was transmitted by the churches scattered around the Mediterranean; their evangelists, preachers, teachers, and exorcists used it and molded it, and even created parts of it. It was the needs of the churches in worship, in catechism, in apologetic, in exhortation, and in other ways that determined what tradition was transmitted and how it was used.[77]

Over time and as these fabricated accretions were gradually added, Gospel literature, assumed by form critics to be parallel to other forms of folk literature, took on definite or fixed forms through constant repetition. These forms varied according to the function that they served in the Christian community, e.g., preaching, teaching, worship, instruction, or apologetics. The technical term in form criticism that refers to that sociological setting within the life of the early Church that gave rise to the particular rhetorical forms (e.g. legends, sayings, miracle stories) is called <u>Sitz im Leben</u> (lit. "setting in life" or "life situation").[78] Hermann Gunkel first employed this term in his form-critical analysis of the Old Testament. Dibelius and Bultmann, influenced by Gunkel, applied the concept to the New Testament, especially the Gospel materials under the assumption that they had existed in oral form prior to being written down in the Gospels.[79]

Yet, both Dibelius and Bultmann conceptualized different <u>Sitz im Lebens</u> that gave rise to the tradition. While Dibelius asserted that the Sitz im Leben of the material centered in the preaching of the early church,[80] Bultmann hypothesized that the Sitz im Leben centered in apologetic concerns.[81] Furthermore, Bultmann asserted that while most of the formative process took place in the Palestinian communities, miracle stories and legends took place in the Hellenistic community

---

[77] William D. Davies, *Invitation to the New Testament, A Guide to Its Main Witnesses* (Garden City, N.Y.: Doubleday, 1966), 98.

[78] For further information, consult Martin J. Buss, "The Idea of Sitz-im Leben—History and Critique, <u>Zeitschrift für die Alttestamentliche Wissenschaft</u> 90 (1978): 157-170; See "*Sitz-im-Leben*" in Richard N. Soulen, <u>Handbook of Biblical Criticism</u> (Atlanta: John Knox, 1981), 178-179. Soulen notes that while <u>Sitz-im-Leben</u> is a technical term in form criticism to refer to a sociological setting within the life of Israel or the Church, in NT redaction criticism the term is modified to refer "to a literary setting, viz., 'the setting with in the Gospel' . . . which the various traditions (parables, miracle stories, sayings, etc.) have been given by the writers."

[79] See Dibelius, *From Tradition to Gospel*, 9; Bultmann, *History of the Synoptic Tradition*, 1-7; E. Basil Redlich, *Form Criticism, Its Value and Limitations* (London: Duckworth1939), 17-19; Robert H. Lightfoot, *History and Interpretation in the Gospels* (New York and London: Harper and Brothers, 1934), 7-15; Taylor, *The Formation of the Gospel Tradition*, 5-9.

[80] Dibelius, *From Tradition to Gospel*, 70.

[81] For example, see Bultmann, *The History of the Synoptic Tradition*, 48-49, 281-282.

which, according to Bultmann were more gullibly prone to add miraculous embellishments.[82]

Eventually, according to form criticism, the anonymous gospel writers collected and arranged these numerous individual stories into a written narrative (i.e., gospel) that reflected the needs and interests of their particular community. Presuppositionally (see below under history and presuppositions), form critics also assume the evolutionary-driven two- (German—Holtzmann) or four-source (British—Streeter) hypothesis (a.k.a. The Two-Document Hypothesis) that contends that an evangelist identified as Mark wrote his gospel first. Utilizing both Mark and a hypothetical (i.e., postulated, non-extant) document known as "Q" (German, Quelle or "source"),[83] the unknown evangelists identified as "Matthew" and "Luke" (generally assumed by form critics not to be written by the individuals whose names the Gospels bear) composed their respective gospels. However, to form critics, the gospel writers were mere collectors of tradition rather than unique contributors. Dibelius argues, "The authors of the Gospels, at least of the synoptics are not 'authors' in the literary sense but collectors. We are not, therefore, concerned first of all with their knowledge of the subject matters, but with the knowledge of those who gave the tradition its form, and this taking form was not mediated by authors but by preachers."[84] Bultmann remarks, "Mark is not sufficiently master of his material to be able to venture on a systematic construction himself."[85]

In light of these foundational constructions of form criticism, Dibelius delineated the purpose of form criticism in the following terms:

> The method of Formgeschichte has a twofold objective. In the first place, by reconstruction and analysis, it seeks to explain the origin of the tradition about Jesus, and thus to penetrate into a period previous to that in which our Gospels and their written sources were recorded. But it has a further purpose. It seeks to make clear the intention and real interest of the earliest tradition. We must show with what objective the first churches recounted stories about Jesus, passed them from mouth to mouth as independent narratives, or copied them from papyrus to papyrus. In the same manner we must examine the sayings of Jesus and

---

[82] Bultmann's strong belief in the Religionsgeschichtliche Schule (History-of-Religions School) led him to assert that a syncretistic tendency toward assimilation of mystery religion concepts led to church to Hellenize the story of Jesus: "For if the kuvrio" was essentially a cultic deity for the Hellenistic church as well, then, in order to retain the peculiar character of Christian faith—the union of the cultic deity with the historical person of Jesus—a tradition about the story of Jesus was necessary; and the analogy of Hellenistic saviors about whom stories were related could not but help to further the demand for and consequently the taking over the tradition." Bultmann, The History of the Synoptic Tradition, 369 (see also 368-374).

[83] Friedrich Daniel Ernst Schleiermacher, "Ueber die Zeugnisse des Papias von unsern beiden ersten Evangelien," Theologische Studien und Kritiken (1832), 735-768. For an excellent overview of Schleiermacher's contribution to synoptic studies, See William R. Farmer, The Synoptic Problem (Macon, GA.: Mercer, 1976), 15.

[84] Dibelius, From Tradition to Gospel, 59.

[85] Bultmann, The History of the Synoptic Tradition, 350.

ask with what intention these churches collected them, learnt them by heart and wrote them down. The present-day reader should learn to read the individual passages of the early tradition in the way they were meant, before the time when, more or less edited, they were included in the Gospels.[86]

However, Dibelius immediately admits a further purpose and design of form criticism:

The method of Formgeschichte seeks to help in answering the historical questions as to the nature and trustworthiness of our knowledge of Jesus, and also in solving a theological problem properly so-called. It shows in what way the earliest testimony about Jesus was interwoven with the earliest testimony about salvation which appeared in Jesus Christ. Thereby it attempts to emphasize and illuminate the chief elements of the message upon which Christianity was founded.[87]

Similarly, Bultmann writes that the purpose of form criticism is: "discovering what the original units of the Synoptics were, both sayings and stories, to try to establish what their historical setting was, whether they belong to a primary or secondary tradition or whether they were the product of editorial activity."[88] To Bultmann, "the aim of form-criticism is to determine the original form of a piece of narrative, a dominical saying or a parable. In the process, we learn to distinguish secondary additions and forms, and these, in turn, lead to important results for the history of the tradition."[89]

In light of these postulates, the methodological practice (i.e., objectives) of form criticism centers generally in three overall activities: 1) classification of the individual pericopes (self-contained units of teaching or narrative) of the gospel materials according to form; 2) assigning each form to a Sitz im Leben or life-situation in the early church from which the material arose and was preserved; and 3) recovery of the original form of the material during the oral period through laws of tradition (see the section on "tradition criticism").[90]

The Historical and Presuppositional Background of Form Criticism

A presuppositional and historical review of the development of form criticism is absolutely vital in determining the legitimacy or illegitimacy of form criticism as a hermeneutical discipline. Importantly, a hermeneutical methodology can only be as legitimate as the presuppositional and historical foundation upon which it is

---

[86] See "Author's Preface," in Dibelius, *From Tradition to Gospel*, n.p.

[87] See "Author's Preface," in Dibelius, *From Tradition to Gospel*, n.p.

[88] Bultmann, *The History of the Synoptic Tradition*, 2-3.

[89] Bultmann, *The History of the Synoptic Tradition*, 6.

[90]S. v. "Form Criticism" by C. Blomberg, in Dictionary of the Gospels and Jesus. Edited by Joel B. Green, Scot McKnight, and I. Howard Marshall (Downers Grove, IL.: InterVarsity, 1992), 243.

based especially since that foundation provides the raison d' être for its existence. If the foundations are hermeneutically tenuous or illegitimate, then the methodology must also be.

Conservative evangelicals who practice form-critical methodologies in isolation from its presuppositional and historical developments place themselves in a precarious position. Any attempts by conservative evangelicals at modifying form-critical principles or practicing the discipline in isolation from its antecedents are tenuous since such a practice largely ignore the justification for the discipline's existence and merely serve to underscore the dubious validity of form criticism as a legitimate hermeneutical methodology. The following is a brief sketch of the major historical developments in Gospel criticism that gave rise to form criticism.[91]

Although form criticism is a development of twentieth-century scholarship, its roots center in the period of the Enlightenment in the seventeenth and eighteenth centuries. A "prologue" to the development of form criticism was the deist and rationalist Hermann Samuel Reimarus (1694-1768), a professor of Oriental Languages in Hamburg.[92] During his life, he published a number of works advocating deism, but he is perhaps best remembered for writing a four-thousand-page manuscript entitled Apologie oder Schutzschrift für die vernünftigen Verehrer Gottes (English, "An Apologetic for the Rational Worshipers of God"). This work remained unpublished during his lifetime.

After Reimarus's death, Gotthold Ephraim Lessing (1729-1781), motivated by a profound belief in rationalism and historical skepticism from the Enlightenment, published parts of the work between 1774 and 1778 under the title of Fragmente eines Ungenannten.[93] Two fragments (the sixth and seventh published) received special attention since their purpose was to discredit Christianity. The sixth fragment, Ueber die Auferstehungsgeschichte (English, "Concerning the Resurrection Story"—1777) attempted to trump up inconsistencies in the Gospel accounts of the resurrection and asserted that the evangelists were mistaken as to the fact of the resurrection. The seventh fragment, Von dem Zwecke Jesu und seiner Jünger (English, "On the Purpose of Jesus and His Disciples"–1778), contended that Jesus was an unsuccessful political messianic pretender and that the disciples were

---

[91] For more detailed information on the presuppositional and philosophical background to historical criticism, see Chapter 2: "The Philosophical and Theological Bent of Historical Criticism."

[92] McKnight relates, "The work of Reimarus must be considered a 'prologue' rather than a beginning of the critical study of the earthly Jesus, for the ideas of Reimarus did not directly influence the works which followed. Yet the forces at work in the life of Reimarus were at work in the life and thought of others in the eighteenth century who pioneered in the historical study of Jesus and who did influence the later developments in the study." Edgar V. McKnight, What is Form Criticism? (Philadelphia: Fortress, 1969), 3-4.

[93] A recent English translation is Ralph S. Fraser, Reimarus: Fragments. Edited by Charles H. Talbert (Philadelphia: Fortress, 1970).

disappointed charlatans who stole the body of Jesus and invented the Christian faith rather than go back to work for a living after the crucifixion.[94]

The significance of Reimarus's work centers in the fact that in the age of deism, rationalism, and skepticism of the Enlightenment, the Gospels were increasingly dismissed as historical documents and instead were interpreted as dogmatic and theological documents designed to promote belief rather than convey factual accounts. Schweitzer summarizes the significance of Reimarus's work for developing gospel criticism: Reimarus shows the necessity of assuming "a creative element in the tradition" to which are ascribed "the miracles, the stories which turn on the fulfillment of Messianic prophecy, the universalistic traits and the predictions of the passion and the resurrection."[95] Perrin states of Reimarus's significance that he is the father of "Life of Jesus research altogether."[96]

The next significant development toward form criticism was the work of David Friedrich Strauss (1808-1874)[97] who popularized the "mythical" view of Scripture. Strauss characterized Reimarus as one of Christianity's "most courageous and worthy representatives" of biblical criticism in the eighteenth century.[98] While Strauss praised Reimarus, he also admired the skeptic and anti-supernaturalist, David Hume. Strauss remarked that "Hume's Essay on Miracles in particular carries with it such general conviction, that the question [of the impossibility of miracles] may be regarded as having been virtually settled."[99]

Yet, the views of Strauss were close to that of Reimarus. In 1862, Strauss published a tribute to Reimarus who maintained a rationalistic interpretation of Jesus's life.[100] In 1835-36, Strauss wrote Das Leben Jesu, kritisch bearbeitet ("The Life of Jesus Critically Examined") that set forth the concept of "myth" in the Gospel accounts. Strauss removed any element of the supernatural from history, especially biblical history. He saw a closed continuum of cause and effect that admitted no divine intervention. To Strauss, whenever the biblical data presents the supernatural or abnormal, the mythopoeic faculty has been at work. Although Strauss allowed a minimal historical framework for the life of Jesus, he considered the vast majority

---

[94] For the English text of the sixth and seventh articles respectively, see Fraser, Reimarus: Fragments, 61-269 ("Concerning the Resurrection" fragment is sandwiched by Fraser into pp. 153-200 [û10-32] in accordance with Lessing's directions—see pp. 24, 153 fn. 55 for specifics).

[95] Albert Schweitzer, The Quest of the Historical Jesus. Translated by W. Montgomery. Introduction by James M. Robinson (New York: Macmillan, 1968), 24.

[96] Norman Perrin, What is Redaction Criticism? (Philadelphia: Fortress, 1969), 4.

[97] Strauss himself espoused the philosophy of Hegel. For further information on Hegel's influence upon Strauss and others, consult such works as Cornelio Fabro, God in Exile. Translated and Edited by Arthur Gibson (Westminster, Md.: Newman, 1968); Bruno Bauer, The Trumpet of the Last Judgement Against Hegel the Atheist and Antichrist. Translated by Lawrence Stepelevich (Lewiston, N.Y.: Edwin Mellen, 1989).

[98] See David Friedrich Strauss, "Hermann Samuel Reimarus and His Apology," in Reimarus: Fragments, 44.

[99] See David Friedrich Strauss, A New Life of Jesus. Authorized Translation. Second Edition (Williams and Norgate, 1879), 199.

[100] See Strauss, "Hermann Samuel Reimarus and His Apology, in Reimarus: Fragments, 44-57.

of material in the Gospels to be myth.[101] Neill remarks regarding this work that "if Strauss's interpretation of the Gospels came to be accepted, Christianity, as it has been understood through the centuries, would come to an end in a generation."[102] The renowned form critic Rudolf Bultmann would also follow Strauss's tactic of myth in the pursuit of his form-critical analysis of the Gospels.[103]

While the virulent antisupernaturalism of the Enlightenment caused the Gospels to be viewed as dogmatic and theological documents rather than historical, another significant presuppositional development occurred that would stimulate the development of both source and form criticism: the hypothesis of evolution. Although popularized by Charles Darwin (1809-82) in his Origin of Species (1859) and The Descent of Man (1871), evolutionary concepts are ancient, and Darwin was by no means original with the hypothesis.[104] Hutchison relates, "Few factors have influenced Western thinking during the past two centuries more than the writings of Charles Darwin."[105] Evolutionary ideas had a strong, quick, and saturating impact in Britain (Darwin's homeland) and in Germany where many of the new theories regarding the origin and development of the New Testament were being germinated during the late nineteenth and early twentieth centuries.[106] However, currently, a trend exists toward more sober assessment of the true nature of evolution, not as a science but as a faith postulate based on philosophical

---

[101] For further information, see David Friedrich Strauss, The Life of Jesus Critically Examined. Edited by Peter C. Hodgson. Translated by George Eliot (Philadelphia: Fortress, 1972), 52-91 (û8-16).

[102] See Stephen Neill and Tom Wright, The Interpretation of the New Testament, 1861-1986. Second Edition (Oxford: Oxford University, 1988), 14.

[103] For an example of Bultmann's mythological approach to the Gospels, see Rudolf Bultmann, "New Testament and Mythology," in Kerygma and Myth. Edited by Hans Werner Bartsch. Translated by Reginald H. Fuller (New York: Harper & Row, 1961), 1-44; "The Case for Demythologizing," in Kerygma and Myth II. Edited by Hans-Werner Bartsch. Translated by Reginald H. Fuller (London: SPCK, 1962), 181-194; Jesus Christ and Mythology (New York: Charles Scribner's Sons, 1958).

[104] For further information, consult Henry M. Morris, The Long War Against God (Grand Rapids: Baker, 1989), 151-260; The Troubled Waters of Evolution (San Diego, CA.: Creation Life, 1982), 51-76.

[105] John C. Hutchison, "Darwin's Evolutionary Theory and 19th-Century Natural Theology," Bibliotheca Sacra 152 (July-September 1995), 334.

[106] This pervasive influence of evolution in the United Kingdom is demonstrated by an interesting side note. In the United Kingdom, the Church's celebration of Darwin is seen in his burial place at Westminster Abbey. Today, many of the world's leading evolutionists live in Britain. See "Astounding Response to Creation in Darwin's Homeland," in Acts and Facts, vol. 22, August 1993), 1. However, the great churchman and creationist, John Knox, who led the great Protestant Reformation in Scotland in the sixteenth century, has a possible burial cite (unmarked) in a automobile parking lot. Ham notes, "A man who popularized an idea that attacks the foundations of the Church, is honored by a church and buried in a prominent place for all to see. Yet, a man who stood for the authority of the Word of God is all but forgotten, and his grave is housed in a parking lot." See Ken Ham, "A Tale of Two Graves," in Creation Ex Nihilo 16 (June-August, 1994), 16-18.

naturalism. This assessment is not coming exclusively from those who may be pejoratively labeled as "fighting fundies" but also from secular sources.[107]

In terms of Old Testament, the Documentary Hypothesis or the Graf-Wellhausen hypothesis originated during the height of the popularity of evolution in philosophical circles.[108]   Rejecting Mosaic authorship, it posits a gradual development (long after Moses) of the Old Testament from simple documents (JEDP) into the complexity of the Pentateuch.[109] The hypothesis developed in the backdrop of philosophical speculations of the rationalist and pantheist Spinoza (who suggested Ezra composed the Torah), the deists, Hegelianism, and the increasing popularity of evolutionary philosophy. Twentieth century scholarship has tended to discount the Graf-Wellhausen hypothesis.[110]

Evolutionary thought thoroughly permeates the Two- (popularized and synthesized by Heinrich J. Holtzmann [1832-1910] in Die Synoptischen Evangelien [1863] in Germany) and Four-Document Hypotheses (popularized by Burnett Hillman Streeter [1874-1937] in The Four Gospels-[1924] in Britain) that assume the priority of Mark as the earliest. These Two- and Four-Document hypotheses also stand as important presuppositions since form criticism assumes these hypotheses as working bases for form-critical analysis.[111] Here again, the idea of simple to complex is seen in that Mark (, the alleged "Q" source (Quelle), material peculiar to Matthew (M), and material peculiar to Luke (L) were combined into the complex documents of Matthew and Luke.[112]   The Two- and Four-Document hypotheses developed at a time in which evolutionary philosophy was rocketing to prominence in Britain and on the continent of Europe (e.g., Germany) in the latter half of the nineteenth century.

Farmer, in his work, The Synoptic Problem (1964), insightfully identifies the evolutionary "intellectual climate" of the time as fostering the dominance of the Documentary Hypothesis in source criticism at the end of the nineteenth century.[113] Thomas Huxley (1825-1895), one of the greatest of evolutionary propagandists, championed the Marcan hypothesis. He wrote: "our canonical second Gospel, the

---

[107] For an excellent critique of evolution, consult Phillip E. Johnson, Darwin on Trial. Second Edition (Downers Grove, IL.: InterVarsity, 1993).

[108]See the interesting discussion of Gleason L. Archer, A Survey of Old Testament Introduction. Revised and Expanded (Chicago: Moody, 1994), 149-50.

[109]Thoroughgoing refutations of the Wellhausen Hypothesis appeared soon after the rise in its popularity, but they were largely ignored, e.g. William Henry Green, Unity of the Book of Genesis (New York: Scribner, 1895) and by the same author Higher Criticism of the Pentateuch (New York: Scribner, 1896). Green's works still constitute an effective refutation of the Documentary Hypothesis.

[110]For a thorough discussion of the specifics of this hypothesis, see the excellent analysis of Archer, A Survey of Old Testament Introduction, 89-171.

[111] For further information, see Pierre Benoit, "Reflections on 'Formgeschichtliche Methode,'" in Jesus and the Gospel. Translated by Benet Weatherhead (New York: Herder and Herder), 1:11-45.

[112]For further information on the details of the four source hypothesis, consult Burnett H. Streeter, The Four Gospels, A Study of Origins (London: Macmillan, 1953), 223-272.

[113] See Farmer, The Synoptic Problem, 178-190.

so-called 'Mark's' Gospel) is that which most closely represents the primitive groundwork of the three. That I take to be one of the most valuable results of New Testament criticism, of immeasurably greater importance than the discussion about dates and authorship."[114]

In Oxford Studies, Streeter wrote an essay entitled "The Literary Evolution of the Gospels."[115] William Sanday (1843-1920), the editor of Oxford Studies was an outstanding propagandists for the British Four Source Theory. He praised Streeter's essay with the following:

> I do not remember to have seen, within anything like the same compass, a picture at once so complete, so sound, and (to my mind) so thoroughly scientific, of the whole course of development in the Apostolic and sub-Apostolic age in its bearing upon literary composition in general and the composition of the Gospels in particular. It is a real evolution, and an evolution conceived as growth, in which each stage springs naturally, spontaneously, and inevitably out of the last.[116]

Farmer remarks, 'Darwin's epoch-making *Origin of Species* had been published during Sanday's student days at Oxford, and there is no doubt that in the years following, like many of the best minds of his generation, he [Sanday] drank deeply from the cup of salvation offered by the cult of 'scientism,' that is, faith in science."[117]

In addition, Edwin Abbott (1838-1926) provides another important clue in the acceptance of Mark as the first and most "primitive" gospel: antisupernaturalism. In a major article on the gospels in a 1879 Encyclopedia article, Abbott based his acceptance of the "antiquity" of Mark on the "striking proof" that it does not mention "supernatural events" like Matthew and Luke, i.e. reference to the details of Jesus' birth (e.g., virgin birth, visit of angels, star in Bethlehem) and "only the barest prediction of His resurrection."[118] Because Mark was perceived as relatively "simple," without any reference to the miraculous birth narratives and post-Resurrection appearances, the antisupernatural climate of the time naturally gravitated to the Marcan hypothesis.[119] Farmer notes, "This article exercised a profound influence upon the Synoptic Problem in England. Reliable chroniclers of biblical criticism give it a prominent place."[120]

---

[114]See Thomas H. Huxley, Science and Christian Tradition (New York: D. Appleton, 1899), 273.

[115]See Burnett H. Streeter, "The Literary Evolution of the Gospels," in Oxford Studies in the Synoptic Problem. Edited by W. Sanday (Oxford: At the Clarendon, 1911), 210-227. Streeter also used the term "evolution" in reference to the "evolution of the Gospel canon" and "evolution of Pauline canon." See Streeter, The Four Gospels, 609 (cf. 526 and 499 note 1).

[116]Sanday, Oxford Studies, xvi.

[117]Farmer, Synoptic Problem, 181.

[118]The article was originally published in 1879. For the full text, see Edwin A. Abbott, "Gospels" in Encyclopedia Britannica. R. S. Peale Reprint (Chicago: R. S. Peale, 1892), vol. X, 801-802.

[119]See Farmer's excellent discussion, The Synoptic Problem, 25-26, 178-79.

[120] Farmer, The Synoptic Problem, 70.

Yet, the perceived weakness of source criticism was that it could not push behind these alleged sources into a hypothesized oral period before the gospels took written form. Source criticism left an alleged gap of some twenty to thirty years between the time of Jesus and the first written documents. The desire to explore this period would help give rise to form-critical speculation and conjecture.[121] Furthermore, the multiplying of hypothetical sources in source criticism due to the Two- and Four-Document Hypotheses inability to explain the synoptic evidence "increasingly weakened the whole structure of the hypothesis."[122]

The scholar who was directly responsible for the development of form criticism was Johannes Heinrich Hermann Gunkel (1862-1932), an Old Testament scholar. Gunkel applied form-critical analysis to Genesis in his work <u>Sagen der Genesis</u> (English, "The Stories of Genesis").[123] In this work, Gunkel acknowledged the work of Old Testament source criticism that negated Mosaic authorship of the Pentateuch. Instead, under evolutionary influences, he viewed Genesis, as well as the rest of the Pentateuch, as developing gradually over a long period of time (well after the time of Moses), growing out of documents known as JEDP reflected in the Graf-Wellhausen hypothesis.[124] Before the documents were written, individual stories existed in oral form and modified (increased in complexity) over a long period of time.[125]

Gunkel also classified the stories of Genesis in light of the purpose (e.g., historical, ethnographical, etiological, ethnological, etymological, and cultic).[126] Although Gunkel allowed for a bare minimal kernel of historical truth in some stories of Genesis, he held that the stories of Genesis were largely mythological in character, especially the accounts of creation and the flood.[127] Kümmel notes,

> K. L. Schmidt and his like-minded colleagues, M. Dibelius and R. Bultmann, owe the most potent stimuli to the writings of the man who, after having cooperated in founding the history-of-religions school, transferred his interests to Old Testament Research—Herman Gunkel. Gunkel's method of recovering the original traditions and of discovering the spiritual presuppositions of the formation of these traditions (<u>Sitz im Leben</u> or "life situation")—a method applied especially to the Old Testament legends of the patriarchs and to the Old Testament songs—

---

[121] See the excellent discussion of Donald Guthrie, <u>New Testament Introduction</u>. Revised Edition (Downers Grove, IL.: InterVarsity, 1990), 210.

[122] Guthrie, <u>New Testament Introduction</u>, 210.

[123] See Hermann Gunkel, <u>The Stories of Genesis</u>. Translated by John J. Scullion. Edited by William R. Scott (Berkeley, CA.: BIBAL, 1994). This work was also published as <u>The Legends of Genesis: The Biblical Saga and History</u>. Translated by W. H. Carruth (New York: Schocken, 1964).

[124] Gunkel, <u>The Legends of Genesis</u>, 93-119.

[125] Gunkel, <u>The Legends of Genesis</u>, 29-31.

[126] Gunkel, <u>The Legends of Genesis</u>, 18-24.

[127] Gunkel, <u>The Legends of Genesis</u>, 11-12, 71-72, 78.

prepared the way in decisive fashion for the investigation of the gospel traditions by K. L. Schmidt and the other form critics."[128]

The Old Testament scholar and form critic, Julius Wellhausen (1844-1918) also helped take took form-critical methodologies into New Testament studies. He helped form a bridge between Old and New Testament studies.[129] Wellhausen, in his Einleitung in die drei ersten Evangelien, makes three points about Mark that developed eventually into major form-critical axioms: 1) the original source for material in the Gospel is oral tradition that circulated independently in small units; 2) the material was brought together and redacted in various ways and at various stages, only one of which was the evangelist; and 3) the material gives us information about the beliefs and circumstances of the early church as well as Jesus's ministry.[130] In his Das Evangelium Marci (1903), Wellhausen contended that the primitive tradition reflected in Mark was overlaid with editorial additions (i.e. accretions) influenced by early church theology rather than reflecting the historical situation of Jesus. Wellhausen's hypothesis helped give impetus to the form-critical speculation that the origin shaping of the material was not due to apostolic eyewitnesses but to the Christian community.[131]

For a time, source criticism had postulated that Mark was the earliest gospel, and although it reflected mythological elements like the other Gospels (Matthew, Luke, John), Mark reflected somewhat more primitive historicity than the other gospels, i.e., Mark was closest to the point of time of the original eyewitnesses so that it could be used with relative confidence as a historical source. However, Wilhelm Wrede (1859-1906), in Das Messiasgeheimnis in den Evangelien ("The Messianic Secret"–1901) would undertake a similar tactic to Reimarus in rejecting the historicity of Mark and asserting that Mark's gospel represents creative, dogmatic ideas which the evangelist imposed on the tradition, i.e., Jesus never claimed to be Messiah during his lifetime; the church superimposed this post-Resurrection idea upon the lips of Jesus.[132] Perrin remarks that "Wilhelm Wrede (1859-1906) . . . sounded the death knell" regarding the historicity of Mark "by demonstrating that a major aspect of the Marcan narratives was precisely the 'mythic.'"[133]

---

[128] Werner Georg Kümmel, The New Testament: The History of the Investigation of Its Problems (Nashville: Abingdon, 1972), 330.

[129] For further information, consult Kümmel, The New Testament, 281-284; Perrin, What is Redaction Criticism?, 13-14.

[130] Julius Wellhausen, Einleitung in die drei ersten Evangelien (Berlin: Georg Reimer, 1905), 43-57. See also Robert H. Lightfoot, History and Interpretation of the Gospels (New York and London: Harper and Brothers, 1934), 23; Perrin, What is Redaction Criticism?, 14.

[131] Guthrie, New Testament Introduction, 211.

[132] For a refutation of Wrede's assertions, consult James D. G. Dunn, "The Messianic Secret in Mark," in The Messianic Secret. Edited by Christopher Tuckett (Philadelphia: Fortress, 1983), 116-131.

[133] Perrin, What is Redaction Criticism?, 7.

Although Wrede's view was at first strongly criticized,[134] it exerted a powerful influence on early form critics who assumed as a presupposition that the framework of the gospel narratives was suspect and the contextual framework of the stories of little importance.[135] Bultmann, for example, concurred with Wrede's conclusions, arguing that Mark is not history because it "is really dominated by the theology of the Church and by a dogmatic conception of Christ."[136] Benoit relates, "This [Wrede's view] is exactly the same attitude adopted by the Form Critics. All they add to Wrede's position is a more methdological research into the way in which Christian dogma was created and elaborated by the primitive Community."[137]

With a very large portion of New Testament scholars viewing Mark as "mythical" and dogmatic (theological) rather than historical, the road now opened for the work of Karl Ludwig Schmidt (1891-1956). In his work, _Der Rahmen der Geschichte Jesu_ (1919) Schmidt concentrated on the chronological and geographical framework imposed on Mark by the evangelist. Schmidt asserted that the episodes of the Gospel accounts were isolated units of tradition linked together by the author (like pearls on a string). References to time, place, and geography did not form part of the episodes and had little value. The evangelist strung the episodes together unhistorically and artificially. Schmidt concluded his work with the following, "On the whole there is [in the Gospels] no life of Jesus in the sense of a developing story, as a chronological outline of the history of Jesus, but only isolated stories, pericopes, which have been provided with a framework."[138]

With the elimination of the belief in the integrity of the chronological and geographical framework on the Synoptics, the units of material tied together by that framework were left in isolation. These episodes came from the Christian community among whom they circulated in independent form. Schmidt speculated that these independent pericopes arose due to the development of Christian tradition of worship. However, Schmidt did not utilize the tools of form criticism to pry into an alleged oral period of the Gospels.[139]

Martin Dibelius (1883-1947) and Rudolf Bultmann (1884-1976) fully developed and refined form criticism in the New Testament. Dibelius was the first to apply form criticism to the synoptic tradition in his _Die Formgeschichte des Evangeliums_ (1919; English title, _From Tradition to Gospel_—1934). The term

---

[134] For an example of an older work that criticized Wrede, see A. E. J. Rawlinson, _St. Mark_ (London: Methuen, 1947), 258-262. For a more recent critique, see C. M. Tuckett, Editor, _The Messianic Secret_ (Philadelphia: Fortress, 1983).

[135] Guthrie, _New Testament Introduction_, 211.

[136] Bultmann, _Form Criticism, Two Essays on New Testament Research_, 23.

[137] Benoit, "Reflections on 'Formgeschichtliche Methode,'" 1:41.

[138] The quote is translated. The German text reads: "Aber im ganzen gibt es kein Leben Jesu im Sinne einer sich entwickelnden Lebensgeschichte, keinen chronologischen Aufriß der Geschichte Jesu, sondern nur Einzelgeschichten, Perikopen, die in ein Rahmenwerk gestellt sind." Karl L. Schmidt, _Der Rahmen der Geschichte Jesu_ (Darmstadt: Wissenschaftliche Buchgesellschaft, 1969), 317. The work was originally published in 1919 (Berlin: Trowitzsch & Sohn) and has never been translated into English.

[139]McKnight, _What is Form Criticism?_, 15.

formgeschichte (English, "form criticism" or "history") originated from Dibelius's use of it in his title.[140] Dibelius worked out a system for identifying the isolated gospel episodes and worked out a method for classifying their form.

Rudolf Bultmann is associated more closely with form than Dibelius or Schmidt and is most responsible for the thoroughness and maturation of the method. Bultmann's epoch-making work was Die Geschichte der synoptischen Tradition (1921) [English title, The History of the Synoptic Tradition, 1963].[141] Evolutionary dogma heavily influenced Bultmann in the formulation of his system. Because many of his professors came from the history-of-religions school, he was an advocate of that evolutionary system of thought and made significant contributions to the work of this group.[142] Bultmann's professor for his dissertation (Der Stil der paulinischen Predigt und kynisch-stoische Diatribe, ["The Style of Pauline Sermon and Cynic-Stoic Diatribe"]—1910) was the history-of-religions proponent Heitmüller. He also dedicated his primary work, History of the Synoptic Tradition, to Heitmüller. Hermann Gunkel, the renown Old Testament form critic and history-of-religions advocate, was also one of Bultmann's professors during his years as a student at Berlin University.[143] In 1921, Bultmann became Bousset's successor at Giessen, and in 1921 succeeded Heitmüller at Marburg.

Philosophically, Bultmann was also heavily influenced by Kant. Morgan writes, "His theology was shaped above all by the pious neo-Kantianism of his teacher Herrmann (1846-1922), a devout follower of Ritschl (1822-89)."[144] The existentialist thinking of Kierkegaard and especially Heidegger also deeply influenced Bultmann.[145] Becoming disillusioned with the historical Jesus of the

---

[140] Some think that Dibelius actually took over the expression from a subtitle of another book, Eduard Norden's Agnostos Theos: Untersuchungen zur Formgeschichte religiöser Rede {"The Unknown God: Inquiries into the History of the Forms of Religious Utterance"— 1913). Neill257

[141] The work has recently been reissued. Rudolf Bultmann, The History of the Synoptic Tradition. Translated by John Marsh. Revised Edition (Basil Blackwell, 1963; Peabody, MA.: Hendrickson, n.d.).

[142] Johnson notes, "In 1908, Wilhelm Heitmüller joined the Marburg faculty, and through him Bultman became immersed in the work of the history-of-religions school. Heitmüller, along with the writings of Richard Reitzenstein and Wilhelm Bousset, taught Bultmann to understand the literature of the New Testament by comparing early Christianity with other religious movements of the same era: e.g., Jewish apocalyptic or Hellenistic Gnosticism. Bultmann himself made significant contributions to the work of this group, and not surprisingly, he was invited to succeed Heitmüller at Marburg University in 1921." See Roger A. Johnson, Editor, Rudolf Bultmann, Interpreting Faith for the Modern Era (Minneapolis: Fortress, 1991), 9-10.

[143] For further information, see Bultmann, "Autobiographical Reflections," in Existence and Faith, 284.

[144] Robert Morgan, "Rudolf Bultmann," in The Modern Theologians, vol. 1 in An Introduction to Christian Theology in the Twentieth Century. Edited by David F. Ford (New York: Basil Blackwell, 1989), 109.

[145] Martin Heidegger taught at Marburg University with Bultmann from 1922-1928. For further information on Heidegger's influence, see Bultmann's personally written history, "Autobiographical Reflections," in Existence and Faith, 283-288.

liberal school, Bultmann sought to emancipate the need for historical demonstration of the Christian faith. For Bultmann, the most important element in Christian faith was an existential encounter ("a leap of faith") that demanded decision apart from historical proof.[146]

An important motivation of Bultmann in the development of his form-critical speculations also was the desire to "modernize" the gospels.[147] His approach was one of demythologization of gospel record. Strauss's concept of "myth" heavily influenced Bultmann.[148] To Bultmann, the canonical gospels contain pre-scientific conceptions of the world of nature and men that were quite outdated by modern scientific knowledge.[149] In his work, Kerygma and Myth I, Bultmann defines myth in the following terms, "Myth is used here in the sense popularized by the 'History of Religions' school. Mythology is the use of imagery to express the other worldly in terms of this world and the divine in terms of human life, the other side in terms of this side."[150] To Bultmann, miraculous conceptions of a Divine Being or Son of God, demon possession, angels, resurrection, voices from heaven, etc. are first century man's primitive understanding of the world that needs to be reinterpreted (demythologized) in twentieth century terms.[151] He sought to "demythologize" the gospels and recast the material in modern form according to twentieth century understanding of world: "*Man's knowledge and mastery of the world* have advanced to such an extent through science and technology that it is no longer possible for anyone seriously to hold the New Testament view of the world—in fact, there is no one who does."[152] This naturally focused the attention on literary forms in the gospel and the desire to discover the "essence of the gospel apart from these 'forms' (e.g. miracle stories)."[153]

To Bultmann, the form critic must discover the historical- or life-situation (Sitz im Leben) that gave rise to the literary materials in the gospels. Bultmann asserted that the gospel material, rather than reflecting the historical situation of Jesus, owed its present shape to the practical needs of the community, i.e. the gospels reflect the post-Easter beliefs of the Christian community rather than the pre-Easter period.[154]

---

[146] For more information on such philosophical presuppositions, see the chapter on "The Philosophical and Theological Bent of Historical Criticism."

[147] Guthrie, New Testament Introduction, 212.

[148] S.v. "Myth" by M. J. A. Horsnell, ISBE, 3:455-463 (especially note pp. 461-463).

[149] For an overview of Butlmann's view of mythology and the need to demythologize the New Testament, see Bultmann, "New Testament and Mythology" and "Demythologizing in Outline," in Kerygma and Myth I, 1-44; "The Message of Jesus and the Problem of Mythology" and "The Christian Message and the Modern World-View," in Jesus Christ and Mythology, 11-21, 35-59.

[150] Bultmann, Kerygma and Myth I, 10 footnote 2.

[151] Bultmann, Kerygma and Myth I, 1-2.

[152] Bultmann, Kerygma and Myth I, 4

[153] Guthrie, New Testament Introduction, 212.

[154] For further information, see Rudolf Bultmann, "The Study of the Synoptic Gospels," in Form Criticism, Two Essays on New Testament Research." Translated by Frederick C. Grant (New York: Harper, 1962), 11-76.

At the heart of Bultmann's method was the removal of any supernatural elements in the Gospels because of his presuppositional conclusion of a closed-continuum of cause-effect as advocated by Troeltsch's historical-critical approach.[155] The effect of all these presuppositions shows acutely on the Bultmann when he asserts, "I do indeed think that we now can know almost nothing concerning the life and personality of Jesus, since the early Christian sources show no interest in either, are moreover fragmentary and often legendary; and other sources about Jesus do not exist."[156]

Two strategic differences existed between Dibelius and Bultmann. First, Dibelius started with the activity of the early church ("In the sermon the elements of the future Christian literature lay side by side as in a mother cell")[157] and traced the history of forms from this early church tradition to their final incorporation in the gospels. Butlmann, however, worked back from the Gospel material toward alleged earlier forms, trying also to determine the "original" form and what later accretions were made to the tradition that eventually resulted in the Gospels.[158]

Secondly, Bultmann ascribed a greater element of creativity (fabricative embellishment) to the tradition of the early church than did Dibelius.[159] Dibelius saw the evangelists as collectors of material and hence a greater possibility of determining the original form and function in the community's life while Bultmann saw a much more radical working of the material so that the tradition did not reflect a historical core, i.e. the voice of Jesus was lost. Taylor's words are pertinent: "Dibelius is liberal rather than radical; Bultmann is radical to the point of skepticism, and it is not strange that he has been looked upon as *Strauss Redivivus.* If Bultmann is right, we have not only lost the Synoptic framework but also much the greater

---

[155] Bultmann writes, "The historical method includes the presupposition that history is a unity in the sense of a closed-continuum of effects in which individual events are connected by the succession of cause and effect . . . .

This closeness means that the continuum of historical events cannot be rent by the interference of the supernatural, transcendent powers and that therefore there is no 'miracle' in this sense of the word." Bultmann, "Is Exegesis Possible Without Presuppositions?, in Existence and Faith, 291-292.

[156] Bultmann goes on, "we can, strictly speaking, know nothing of the personality of Jesus. I am personally of the opinion that Jesus did not believe himself to be the Messiah." See Rudolf Bultmann, Jesus and the Word. Translated by Louise Pettibone Smith and Erminie Huntress Lantero (New York: Charles Scribner's Sons, 1958), 8-9.

[157] See Dibelius, From Tradition to Gospel, 70. See Perrin, What is Redaction Criticism?, 15 foonote 19.

[158] See Bultmann, The History of the Synoptic Tradition, 1-7; Perrin, What is Redaction Criticism?, 15.

[159] Perrin notes, "The difference in emphasis between Bultmann and Dibelius, however, is not only that the former ascribes a greater element of free creativity to the early church in her work on the tradition, but also that he is much more interested than is Dibelius in the actual details of that work. He is concerned with writing a history of the synoptic tradition, and, in the course of doing this, he is forced to attempt to describe and to understand the details of the processes at work in the creation and transmission of that tradition in a way that Dibelius, who is more concerned with a description of the original forms and their functions in the community's life, is not." Perrin, What is Redaction Criticism?, 18-19.

part of the material."[160] Yet, common to both was a rejection of the miraculous and therefore, they both rejected the historicity of the gospel in such areas. Their rejection, as was the case with the historical rise and development of form criticism, centered in philosophical and theological presuppositions.

Yet, "this difference is one of emphasis rather than essence."[161] However, because "Bultmann submitted the entire synoptic tradition to a searching analysis" Bultmann's "name and method of analysis have been more closely associated with form criticism than has the name of Dibelius."[162] Furthermore, Butlmann's approach was more radical and far more influential and widespread than Dibelius.

Thus, the historical and presuppositional background for the development of form criticism was virulent antisupernaturalistic presuppositions: deism, rationalism, historical skepticism, and evolution are only the most salient examples. Taylor, although favoring form critical analysis, candidly remarks, "Before the nineteenth century the investigation of the formation of the Gospel tradition was almost impossible."[163] The history just traced is termed by McKnight as "The Necessity for the Discipline."[164] Without the impact of such hostile presuppositions, form criticism may not have developed as a discipline. They provided the fertile background for its emergence. After a thorough analysis of form criticism, Benoit insightfully comments, "all the principles of Form-criticism . . . seem to have little real foundation and to be instead instruments in service of a cause. The idea is to withdraw all historical value from the gospel tradition in so far as it enshrines the supernatural." He goes on to note,

> When we become aware of the spirit which inspires all these proceedings [i.e. form criticism and its historical antecedents] we pass from the less to the better known. Behind all these relatively new methods . . . we discover one fundamental thesis which is not itself new at all. This is the denial of the supernatural which we are so accustomed to meeting in works of modern rationalist criticism. It is a thesis which, once it is stripped of its various masks, literary, historical or sociological analysis, reveals its true identify—*it is a philosophical one* [italics added].

---

[160] Vincent Taylor, The Formation of the Gospel Tradition. Second Edition (London: Macmillan, 1935), 14.

[161] Perrin relates that the difference in emphasis "should certainly not be overstressed; but it is nonetheless there and it is the reason why redaction criticism has developed more directly from the work of Bultmann than from that of Dibelius." Perrin, What is Redaction Criticism?, 18-19.

[162] Schmidt did groundwork in Mark, while Dibelius subjected varying parts of the gospel tradition to form-critical analysis. Yet, Bultmann analyzed the entire synoptic tradition. McKnight notes, "Bultmann submitted the entire Synoptic tradition to a searching analysis; and, although Dibelius was the first of the two writers, Bultmann's name and method of analysis have been of analysis have been more closely associated with form criticism than has the name of Dibelius." McKnight, What is Form Criticism?, 16.

[163] Taylor, The Formation of the Gospel Tradition, 2.

[164] McKnight also views Gunkel's ground-breaking work in form criticism as making New Testament form criticism possible, McKnight, What is Form Criticism?, 3, 10.

For it is the philosophy of the 17th and 18th century which has left his denial of the supernatural embedded in the minds of today, particularly the philosophy of Hegel which has had a dominant influence on German thought, and still holds sway today.

This it is which as a matter of cold fact lies at the root of rationalist biblical criticism, beginning with David Strauss, a disciple of Hegel, and his theory of myth, whose faithful heirs Dibelius and Bultmann are.[165]

Conservative evangelicals must ever keep the historical and presuppositional developments that lead to form criticism in mind whenever discussions of its legitimacy as a hermeneutical methodology arise no matter how far evangelicals choose to "modify" the discipline (i.e. "those who do not learn the lessons of history are doomed to repeat them"). Form criticism is a product of virulent antisupernaturalism encrusted with evolutionary dogma. Moreover, negative philosophical presuppositions led to a dismantling of the pericopes of the gospels. Since a credible case can be built for the historical, chronological and geographical integrity of the Gospel pericopes apart from the influence of these negative presuppositions, then any dismantling of them into isolated pericopes via form criticism is tenuous.[166]

Classification of Forms

Space limitations prevent a detailed discussion of various systems of form classification.[167] Instead, this section will summarize various critiques of form analysis.

In dealing with form criticism as historically developed and expressed, systems of form classification reveal the acute subjectivity and antisupernatural basis of the discipline. Moreover, form critics spend most of their time in this area. For example, Bultmann, in his History of the Synoptic Tradition, spends 306 pages of the work (parts I-II) in attempting to categorize and classify forms. Yet, although similar categories may appear frequently, no universally agreed-upon list of forms exists.[168]

Furthermore, often classification of form does not center on form but on content, especially when miraculous or supernatural elements are present. A few examples of this must suffice due to space limitations. Bultmann's category of "Historical Stories and Legends" demonstrates a pronounced antihistorical and

---

[165] Benoit, Jesus and the Gospel, 1:39.

[166] As Guthrie remarks, "the gospels themselves bear testimony to many connected sequences (e.g. Mk. 1:21-39; 2:1-3:6). If the passion narrative existed in continuous form, as is generally conceded, why not

[167] Apart from the work of Dibelius and Bultmann, for further summary details regarding classification see McKnight, What is Form Criticism?, 20-33; Taylor, The Formation of the Gospel Tradition, 44-167; Redlich, Form Criticism, Its Value and Limitation, 50-55; Stephen H. Travis, "Form Criticism," in New Testament Interpretation, 155-157; Bock, "Form Criticism," in New Testament Criticism and Interpretation, 181-188; Guthrie, New Testament Introduction, 213-223.

[168] Blomberg, "Form Criticism," in Dictionary of the Gospels and Jesus, 243.

antisupernatural bias. These are stories about extraordinary events in the lives of well-known people, e.g., Jesus's baptism, temptation, transfiguration, and resurrection narratives, the ministry of John the Baptist, etc. that serve as examples to avoid or follow. Bultmann argues that "instead of being historical in character are religious and edifying."[169] They are not properly miracle stories (which Bultmann separates) but often contain miraculous element.[170] Even though he uses the alternate name "Historical Stories," this does not indicate that he believes the stories to be historically true. Bultmann remarks, "If at the same time I naturally do not deny that historical happenings may underlie legends, I mean that 'unhistorical' applies to the idea of legend negatively in the sense that legends not only 'have no special interest in history' (Dibelius) but that they are not, in the modern scientific sense, historical accounts at all."[171]

Dibelius category of "myth" designates "*stories which in some fashion tell of many-sided doings of the gods.*"[172] These are narratives where the supernatural invades the human scene to authentic Jesus. Dibelius's category overlaps with Bultmann's category of legend here since Bultmann did not have a corresponding "myth" category thus subtly revealing the acute subjectivity and identification difficulty of form-critical systems of classification.

Although Dibelius allows for more a more historical basis for the story of Jesus, he asserts: "The only narratives in the Gospels which really describe a mythological event, i.e. a many-sided interaction between mythological but not human persons, are the records of the Baptismal miracle [Mark 1:9-11 and //], the Temptation of Jesus [Mark 1:12-13 and //], and the Transfiguration[Mark 9:2-8 and //]."[173] However, in spite of this qualification, Dibelius also rejected the resurrection and ascension of Jesus relegating such stories to myth, i.e., unhistorical.[174]

However, Dibelius goes on to assert that a Christ mythology arose late in the process of the traditions formation evidenced in the letters of Paul:

> The letters of Paul are an unambiguous proof that there once was a *Christ mythology*. At the same time, they are proof that this

---

[169] Bultmann, The History of the Synoptic Tradition, 244.

[170] Bultmann, History of the Synoptic Tradition, 244-274. Bultmann notes that historical stories should be classified with legends since they "are so much dominated by the legends that they can only be treated along with them" (p. 245). His separate treatment of miracle stories occurs on pages 209-244.

[171] Bultmann, The History of the Synoptic Tradition, 244-245, footnote 1.

[172] Dibelius, From Tradition to Gospel, 266.

[173] Dibelius, From Tradition to Gospel, 271.

[174] Dibelius reveals his anti-supernatural bias when he writes, "A thoroughgoing mythological presentation of the life of Jesus, it is true, would have had to extend to the events which the heavenly origin of the Master came to decisive expression. We should, therefore, have had to expect a mythological formulation of His descent upon the earth; and also of His death and of His liberation from death by resurrection and return to heaven . . . . It is, however, significant for our tradition that this thoroughgoing mythical formulation has not been carried out. This shows how firmly at bottom this tradition kept is feet upon the ground." Dibelius, From Tradition to Gospel, 269.

mythology could not be supported directly from the tradition of the life of Jesus. For Paul knew this tradition to some extent (I Cor. xi, 15), and if he had needed it he could have made its acquaintance much more closely but the Christ-myth through which for his churches he explains the great act of Divine redemption, had no need of the data handed down. This myth told the story of the Son of God who abandoned his cosmically intermediate place; in obedience to the Will of God he suffered a human fate, even to death on the Cross; he was finally raised by the power of God form the deepest humiliation to the status of "Lord" to whom all the world owed honour till He should come to conquer His enemies and to rule His Kingdom.[175]

For Dibelius, over time, miraculous elements were added to the historical Jesus (e.g. Jesus's descent from his heavenly realm to the earth, His resurrection, and ascension back to heaven) that did not constitute an original part of the gospel tradition but were later accretions from Hellenistic influences.[176]

Moreover, the category of "legend" or "myth" is quite artificial. Travis notes, "to describe 'legends' or 'myths' as forms when no common shape is discernible . . . is not form criticism."[177] Such categories indicate a presuppositional agenda and bias rather than form categorization.

The category of "miracle stories" (Bultmann) or "tales" (Dibelius) is another example where antisupernatural presuppositional biases affect form analysis. Importantly, the basis of the category is the nature of the miracle, not the form. Bultmann, affected by the religionsgeschichtliche schule ("history-of-religions school") and also by a pronounced negativity toward the miraculous, asserted,

> Yet it would not be right to consider the gospel miracle stories in the bounds of the NT only. The less the miracle stories as such are truly historical reports the more we need to *ask how they have found their way into the Gospel tradition.* And even if some historical events underlie some miracles of healing, it is still true that their narrative form has been the work of Tradition. And even if the motifs have grown up spontaneously in the early Church, there would be both central and peripheral motifs taken over from popular and even perhaps literary miracle stories . . . . The process of transferring some available miracle story to a hero (or healer or even a god) is frequently to found in the history of literature and religion.[178]

Bultmann, evidencing his evolutionary bias, argues that over time "an *increase of the miraculous element* is also to be found in particular features."[179] Reflecting this concept, in Mark 10:46-52 Bultmann asserts, "This story shows its secondary character in giving the name of the blind man . . . and it is the only name in any

---

[175] Dibelius, From Tradition to Gospel, 267-268.

[176] Dibelius, From Tradition to Gospel, 267-273.

[177] Travis, "Form Criticism," in New Testament Interpretation, 158.

[178] Bultmann, The History of the Synoptic Tradition, 228.

[179] Bultmann, The History of the Synoptic Tradition, 228.

miracle story in the synoptics, apart from Mark 5:22."180 However, as Guthrie remarks, "Both Dibelius and Bultmann reject the miraculous and therefore the historicity of the Gospel accounts of miracles. This is not so much on the basis of 'form' as on philosophical and theological grounds."181

Furthermore, pagan folklore tales of the miraculous are hypothesized to be parallel to the gospel material and also explain the rise of miraculous stories in the tradition. Working from the evolutionary presuppositional stance that dominated the history-of-religions School, Bultmann cites many pagan miracle stories in an attempt to justify this conclusion that gospel miracle stories of are the same type, and there must be regarded as unhistorical.182 Yet, the alleged parallels cited are qualitatively different in content. Even Bultmann must admit, "In general, however, the New Testament miracle stories are extremely reserved in this respect [in describing cures], since they hesitate to attribute to the person of Jesus the magical traits which were often characteristic of the Hellenistic miracle worker."183 Gospel miracle stories have no magical incantations and fanciful activities that markedly distinguish them from Hellenistic stories.

Furthermore, the folklore analogy, in reality, is fallacious since folklore took hundreds of years to develop. Only a maximum period of about 20-30 years hypothetically existed between Jesus and the Gospels, and reasonable evidence exists that the period may have been even shorter. Kenyon notes, "There is simply not time for elaborate processes of literary workmanship and development.184

In addition, Dibelius hypothesized that a special class of story-tellers and teachers were involved in the development of "tales."185 However, as Guthrie argues, "the distinction seems to have been created by Dibelius' analysis rather than being vouched for by independent historical testimony."186 Apart from the stories themselves, no evidence exists in the New Testament for those who told stories about Jesus without preaching.

Strategically, Redlich notes that much of the synoptic material defies classification according to form-critical categories:

> We conclude therefore that the assumption that the material can be classified according to their form is only true in part and in a very

---

180 Bultmann, The History of the Synoptic Tradition, 213.

181 Guthrie, New Testament Introduction, 217.

182 Bultmann argues, "The process of transferring some available miracle story to a hero (or healer or even a god) is frequently to be found in the history of literature and religion." For a complete discussion Bultmann, The History of the Synoptic Tradition, 209-244 (quote from p. 228).

183 Bultmann, "The Study of the Synoptic Gospels," in Form Criticism, 38.

184 Frederic G. Kenyon, The Bible and Modern Scholarship (London: John Murray, 1948), 52.

185 Dibelius argues, "For the further development of the evangelical tradition the story-teller and the teacher appear to have been of special significance." Dibelius, From Tradition to Gospel, 70.

186 Guthrie, New Testament Introduction, 214.

restricted manner. The only classification that can be made is that (a) as regards the sayings, there is a group with form, if we omit poetical form, namely the Parables, and (b) the narrative portions contains two groups which possess form, namely Apothegm-Stories and Miracle-Stories. The greater part of the material is "form"-less."[187]

Even after Bultmann's exhaustive analysis, Lightfoot echoed a similar statement in reference to Mark 1-13:

It is likely that the material will prove too complex and difficult for such rigorous treatment; and for the present at any rate it will suffice to draw attention to the two main kinds of stories about Jesus which are found in our earliest gospels ... a saying of his is the climax or at least the leading feature of the story; in the second, the emphasis is on an act of power done by him ... It seems at least possible that the new study has here achieved a valuable and lasting result, and that it has succeeded in distinguishing and classifying two types of stories, both of which are prominent in Mark.[188]

One may only wonder about the value of a method that has, according to Redlich, the capacity to identify clearly only two forms.

Furthermore, the types of form categories are not as distinct as suggested. Form critics often categorize with acute subjectivity resulting in curiously mixed forms that reflect their preconceived agendas rather than objective analysis. For example, in Mark 3:1-6, Dibelius identifies this story (the man with a withered hand) as a pure while he contends that Mark 10:46-52 (blind Bartimaeus) is a "less pure" paradigm and Mark 5:25-34 (the woman with the hemorrhage) a tale.[189] Yet, any such distinctions are quite artificial. Dibelius claims that didactic motives are central, and the healing is incidental in Mark 3:1-6 so that it can be classed as a paradigm, yet the pericope concludes with the miracle and its effect on the Pharisees rather than with a saying about the Sabbath.[190] To overcome this inconsistency, Dibelius can only assert that in this paradigm "the original ending in Mark iii, 6, is concealed." Mark 10:52 ends with a saying yet Dibelius says it is not a pure paradigm (most likely due to the miraculous healing), and Mark 5:34 ends in a saying but because of its miraculous nature Dibelius deprecates it as a "tale." Dibelius's conclusions reveal his subjective bias and antisupernaturalism.

Adding to the subjectivity of form-critical categories is the fact that a narrative may often be assignable to more than one form or are mixed in type. Bruce's comments are telling:

A narrative may be assignable to more than one "form"; thus the incident of the paralyzed man (Mk. 2:1-12) is a pronouncement story because the criticism that breaks out when Jesus forgives the man's sins is silenced by Jesus' pronouncement that "the Son of man has authority

---

[187] Redlich, Form Criticism, Its Value and Limitation, 55.

[188] Lightfoot, History and Interpretation in the Gospels, 43.

[189] Dibelius, From Tradition to Gospel, 51-52, 55, 71.

[190] Travis, "Form Criticism," in New Testament Interpretation, 158.

on earth to forgive sins" (Mk. 2:10); but it can also be classified as a miracle story, more specifically a healing story.[191]

Is Mark 2:1-12 a miracle story or a pronouncement story? The very idea of labeling it a "miracle" story draws special attention to the miraculous nature of the story and reflects the form critic's bias regarding miracles. Also, such a label is not based on form but content.

Contributing to this situation is that often judgment of classification is not based on form but entirely on the subjective prejudices of the form critic. For instance, in Bultmann's classification of the sayings of Jesus ("Dominical Sayings"), he divides them into several groups (Wisdom Sayings [i.e., *Logia*], Prophetic and Apocalyptic Sayings, Legal sayings and church rules, and "I" Sayings).[192] In the instance of the first class or Wisdom words, he divides them into three sub-classes based on the issue of his conception of genuineness: Jesus's use of existing sayings, Jesus's own creation of sayings, and the church's attribution of sayings to Jesus that he did not speak.[193] He assigns much to the third sub-class: "Actually many logia have been derived from the traditional wisdom and first taken into the Christian tradition by the Church, and treated as a saying of Jesus."[194] Bultmann continues, "It will only be in very few cases that one of the logia can be ascribed to Jesus with any measure of confidence."[195] He bases this decision on arbitrarily selected criteria for genuineness: a strong sense of eschatology (e.g., Mark 3:24-27), a summons to repentance (e.g., Mark 8:35; Luke 9:62), and those involving a new disposition of mind (e.g., Mark 7:15; Luke 14:11).[196]

Bultmann treats the "I" sayings of Jesus similarly. The "I" sayings of Jesus are sayings where he makes specific demands or special claims. They are interpreted not as Jesus's words but that which the community has produced, placing the sayings on the lips of Jesus, in order to meet the community's needs in the particular situation that the community finds itself. Regarding Matthew 10:34-36 and Luke 12:51-53, Bultmann contends, "The Church, putting Jesus in God's place as ruler of history, has made him proclaim that he will bring the time of terror, and had obviously experienced the fulfillment of the prophecy in its own life."[197] The Christian community's attribution of the saying to Jesus gives authoritative weight to the saying.

In the same manner, Bultmann interprets Prophetic and Apocalyptic sayings of Jesus as coming from the Christian community or as prophecies ex eventu. Regarding Matthew 5:11-12, he contends, "Matthew 5:11f. is a new element of the tradition ... arising *ex eventu* and for that reason created by the church" (compare

---

[191] S.v. "Criticism" by Bruce, ISBE, 1:823.

[192] For a complete discussion, see Bultmann, The History of the Synoptic Tradition, 69-179.

[193] Bultmann, *The History of the Synoptic Tradition*, 101.

[194] Bultmann, *The History of the Synoptic Tradition*, 101.

[195] Bultmann, *The History of the Synoptic Tradition*, 105.

[196] Bultmann, *The History of the Synoptic Tradition*, 105.

[197] Bultmann, *The History of the Synoptic Tradition*, 154-155.

also, for example, Bultmann at Matt. 10; 24; Mark 13).[198] He goes on to argue, "The church drew no distinction between such utterances of Christian prophets [e.g., Rev. 16:15] and the sayings of Jesus in the tradition, for the reason that even the dominical sayings in the tradition were not the pronouncements of a past authority, but sayings of the risen Lord, who is always a contemporary for the Church."[199]

As a result, Bultmann accepts only around forty sayings as genuinely attributable to Jesus. He also considers only the bare facts of life and death (not the resurrection) of Jesus to be authentic. The rest of the material is attributable to the fabrication or adaptation of the Christian community that had no biographical interest in the life of Jesus or desire for historical accuracy. In later life, Bultmann moderated his thinking but only very slightly.[200]

Not only may be classification be ambiguous but sometimes the same saying or discourse has been preserved in two different "forms." Bultmann contended, "it is no objection to form-critical approach, but rather a demonstration of its fruitfulness, to find that one piece of the tradition is seldom to be classified unambiguously in a single category." Yet, this statement subtlety reveals the acute bias and subjectivity in form analysis, for Bultmann just prior to this asserted, "The proper understanding of form criticism rests upon the judgment that the literature in which the life of given community . . . has taken shape, springs out of quite definite conditions and wants of life from which grows up a quite definite style and quite specific forms and categories." [201] Surely one cannot have it both ways, for the more the text resists such excessive systematization, the more form criticism is undermined.[202]

This discussion of form categorization stands as a warning to conservative evangelicals. Since Luther and the Reformation (1517), the grammatico-historical method consistently has demonstrated its ability and sufficiency to distinguish "forms" in the gospel material (parables, allegories, proverbs, types, poetry, etc.) rendering the need for any "form-critical" analysis highly suspect and unnecessary.[203] Current attempts at reforming form critical postures and labeled as "new" form criticism such as Klaus Berger's, Formgeschichte des Neuen Testaments only serve to underscore the inability of form criticism as a viable option for exegesis and partakes of many of the same weaknesses.[204] It also supplies a completely aberrant

---

[198] Bultmann, *The History of the Synoptic Tradition*, 110, 112-125.

[199] Bultmann, The History of the Synoptic Tradition, 127-128.

[200] Rudolf Bultmann, "Allgemeine Wahrheit und christliche Verkündigung," Zeitschrift für Theologie und Kirche 54 (1957): 244-254. See also J. M. Robinson's comments regarding Bultmann's moderation of his thinking, A New Quest of the Historical Jesus (London: SCM, 1959), 20 footnote 1.

[201] Bultmann, The History of the Synoptic Tradition, 4.

[202] Travis, "Form Criticism," in New Testament Interpretation, 159.

[203] An example of this would be the classic work of Milton S. Terry, Biblical Hermeneutics (Grand Rapids: Zondervan, n.d.) that was originally published in the nineteenth century (see pp. 161-600).

[204] For example, acute subjectivity is seen in the fact that Berger supplies four new and different form-critical categories (Sammelgattungen or "Collected Forms," Symbuleutische

understanding (presuppositionally, historically and practically) of form criticism, for the words of the Father and Systematizer of Form Criticism, Bultmann, must again be echoed:

> I am entirely in agreement with M. Dibelius when he maintains that form-criticism is not simply an exercise in aesthetics nor yet simply a process of description or classification; that is to say, it does not consist of identifying the individual units of the tradition according to their aesthetics or other characteristics and placing them in their various categories. It is much rather "to discover the origin and the history of the particular units and thereby to throw some light on the history of the tradition before it took literary form."[205]

Bultmann continues, "form criticism . . . not only presupposes judgements of facts alongside judgments of literary criticism, but must also lead to judgements about facts (the genuineness of a saying, the historicity of a report and the like)."[206] Bultmann's candor is refreshing about the true nature of form criticism. If Berger is attempting merely to describe the biblical phenomena in context, then much of what Berger attempts can be accomplished more effectively and accurately through the grammatico-historical hermeneutic that has consistently demonstrated its validity since the Reformation.

IV. Tradition Criticism/History[207]

An Overview of Tradition Criticism

Tradition criticism (traditionsgeschichte) is related closely to form criticism in that its principles were developed in conjunction with form criticism yet is now considered a separate discipline.[208] For many modern critics, especially those who

---

Gattungen or "Behavior Forms," Epideiktische Gattungen or "Demonstration Texts," and Dikanische Gattungen or "Decision Texts") and also assumes the Two Document Hypothesis. For further information, see Klaus Berger, Formgeschichte des Neuen Testaments (Heidelberg: Quelle & Meyer, 1984), 25-366.

[205] Bultmann, History of the Synoptic Tradition, 3-4.

[206] Bultmann, History of the Synoptic Tradition, 5.

[207] Catchpole prefers to translate the term traditionsgeschichte as "tradition history" instead of "tradition criticism" since the German word Geschichte better designates "meaningful process" or "changeful movement" rather than its usually translated meaning of "history": "the term 'tradition criticism' would be better abandoned and replaced by the term 'tradition history', interpreted in the sense of an on-going process of development in the form and/or meaning of concepts or words or sayings or blacks of material." Catchpole, "Tradition History," in New Testament Interpretation, 165.

[208] Guthrie, Catchpole and Osborne place tradition criticism (or, history) more closely in association with redaction criticism, while Blomberg includes the discussion of tradition criticism ("criteria of authenticity") under form criticism. Catchpole describes redaction criticism as a special case of tradition criticism. Stein closely associates form and tradition criticism but notes that the terms "technically . . . are not synonymous but in practice they essentially are." See Guthrie, New Testament Introduction, 243-247; David Catchpole, "Tradition History," in New Testament Interpretation, 165-180; Grant R. Osborne, "The Method of Redaction Criticism," in New Testament Criticism and Interpretation, 204-207;

advocate some hermeneutical role for form and redaction criticism, the most important task is to assess the authenticity of the units of Gospel tradition. Much of the effort centers in discovering the earliest form of the tradition unit through peeling away the layers of the narrative that allegedly accrued over time caused by the alleged *Sitz im Leben* of the church (or, Christian community) during the oral period. The application of these tradition criteria to the text are also considered a valid means for determining the relative antiquity and historical veracity of the Gospel units. The goal is to recover the "original" core of teaching in each Gospel pericope, i.e., the authentic teaching of Jesus versus what is non-authentic. In light of this, tradition criticism becomes the study of the origin, history, and development of a given saying especially in the Gospels but also throughout the New Testament.

Therefore, analysis and criticism of the traditions contained in the Gospels for the form critic takes essentially two tactics: The first is the recovery of the earliest and most authentic forms of the tradition by the application of certain laws of tradition. The second is to make critical judgments on the historicity of the saying by establishing certain "criteria of authenticity" whereby the origin of these traditions may be attributed directly to Jesus ("authentic") or be the creation or fabrication of the Christian communities (Palestinian, Hellenistic or Gentile).[209] In this latter area, tradition criticism finds its most prominent expression.

The Presuppositional Basis of Tradition Criticism

Importantly, these tradition criteria arose from the same virulent antisupernatural presuppositional foundation that gave rise to form criticism. At the heart of the method are negative historical presuppositions that are rooted in the radical skepticism of Enlightenment. In discussing the form-critical analysis of tradition material, Doty remarks, "The basic presuppositions for the modern historical-critical approach to the NT writings were set in the last part of the eighteenth century under the influence of deism and rationalism."[210] Moreover, for any conservative evangelical to treat tradition-critical principles in isolation from their negative presuppositional foundations carelessly overlooks their true nature, and, as a result, fails to consider properly their highly doubtful hermeneutical validity. If the history of modern interpretive methods demonstrates anything (see Chapter 2 on Presuppositions), it is that interpretive methods cannot be studied in isolation from historical, presuppositional, and intellectual developments without inviting disaster in hermeneutical methodologies. A hermeneutical method cannot be more valid than the validity of the foundation upon which it lies.

Blomberg, "Form Criticism," in The Dictionary of the Gospels and Jesus, 248-249; Robert H. Stein, "The 'Criteria' for Authenticity," in Gospel Perspectives. Edited by R. T. France and David Wenham (Sheffield: JSOT, 1980), 226, 254. Historically, since Bultmann and his followers provided the impetus for tradition criticism in seeking to determine allegedly authentic from inauthentic sayings of Jesus, the present article associates tradition principles here with form criticism.

[209] For further information on the nature of tradition criticism, consult R. S. Barbour, Traditio-Historical Criticism of the Gospels (London: SPCK, 1972).

[210] William G. Doty, "The Discipline and Literature of New Testament Form Criticism," Anglican Theological Review (October 1969), 286.

Taking a radically negative view of the historicity of the gospels sayings, Bultmann and his theological descendants (e.g., Käsemann, Conzelmann, Perrin) are responsible for the propagation of much of the criteria of authenticity, e.g., the principle of discontinuity (dissimilarity), multiple attestations and consistency of content (coherence).[211] They predicate the entire undertaking on the assumption that the Gospel traditions are inherently suspect unless good reasons can be advanced for accepting them. Tradition criticism places the onus probandi ("burden of proof") on the Gospels' claims to be authentic.

As expected, the inventors of these "criteria of authenticity" reflect this presupposition. In the History of The Synoptic Tradition, Bultmann himself accepted only about forty sayings as genuine and merely the event of Jesus life and death on the cross. The post-Bultmannian, Norman Perrin argues, "*the nature of the synoptic tradition is such that the burden of proof will be upon the claim to authenticity.*"[212] The instigator of the "New Quest" for the historical Jesus, Ernst Käsemann echoes a similar thought,

> Historical criticism has shattered this good faith [in the historical reliability of the gospels] as far as we ourselves are concerned. We can no longer assume the general reliability of the Synoptic tradition about Jesus . . . . our questioning has sharpened and widened until the obligation now laid upon us is to investigate and make credible not the possible unauthenticity of the individual unit of material but, on the contrary, its genuineness."[213]

As discussed, a primary task of tradition criticism is to apply laws of tradition to the material in order to discover an alleged "original" or earlier form of the tradition. Bultmann argued:

> [W]e may accurately observe how the Marcan material is altered and revised by Matthew an Luke, and how Matthew and Luke have presumably edited the text of Q (the Sayings-document). If we are able to deduce a certain regularity in this procedure, then we may certainly assume that the same laws held good even earlier, and we may draw conclusions as to the state of the tradition prior to Mark and Q.[214]

Bultmann, Dibelius, and other form critics also argued that the gospel traditions fell into the category of "folk tradition" ("characteristics of folk-tales,"

---

[211] For example, see Bultmann, The History of the Synoptic Tradition, 205; Ernst Käsemann, Essays on New Testament Themes (Philadelphia: Fortress, 1964), 34-37; Norman Perrin, Rediscovering the Teaching of Jesus (New York: Harper and Row, 1976), 39-43.

[212] Perrin, Rediscovering the Teaching's of Jesus, 39. Perrin also assumes that the early church placed words into the mouth of Jesus, so that "we must look for indications that the saying does not come from the Church, but from the historical Jesus."

[213] Käsemann, Essays on New Testament Themes, 34. While the "New Quest" for the historical Jesus is touted as an attempt to get away from the complete skepticism reflected in the Old Quest of Bultmann and others, it has faired little better in distancing itself from the radical skepticism anchored in the Enlightenment. For a survey of the New Quest, consult James M. Robinson, The New Quest of the Historical Jesus (London: SCM, 1959), 9-25.

[214] Bultmann, Form Criticism, Two Essays on New Testament Research, 29.

"folk-song," folk-anecdote," and "simple fairy-tales") and observations about how folk-lore traditions functioned would reveal the same rules or laws that the gospel traditions followed in their development.[215] Assumed parallels of development with German folklore, Greek literature, rabbinic literature, and the apocryphal gospels served as guides in the development of these laws as applied to the gospel material.[216]

However, as already demonstrated, the gospel material is qualitatively different than any assumed folklore parallels. In addition, not enough time would exist in any hypothesized "oral period." Folklore preservation takes many hundreds of years.

Another presuppositional basis that heavily influenced the development of the laws of tradition was the acceptance and predominance of the idea that Matthew and Luke used Mark and the hypothesized Q ("Quelle") source. By observing how Matthew and Luke allegedly used Mark and Q, form critics also extrapolated that Mark used the oral traditions available to him in a similar fashion.[217] However, such an assumption is based on another highly speculative hypothesis of the Two- and Four-Source approach (which itself was profoundly affected by the evolutionary Zeitgeist of the times). Since this highly questionable synoptic approach is coming under increasing suspicion and outright rejection, this emphasizes the tenuous nature and fallacious basis of such extrapolations.[218]

In dealing with tradition criticism, the form critic also inherently accepts an evolutionary viewpoint to the development of the tradition. This article already has discussed the profound influence that evolutionary concepts had upon the thinking of theologians such as Bultmann, Dibelius and others in the formulation, development and expression of form-critical principles during the latter half of the nineteenth and early part of the twentieth century. Both Bultmann's methodological analysis of the alleged "accretions" to the tradition and the resultant rules utilized to remove these accretions in order to uncover the "earliest" and most "authentic" core are replete with highly questionable evolutionary philosophical precepts. Only a mind thoroughly preconditioned by the virulent

---

[215] Bultmann, The History of the Synoptic Tradition, 67; Form Criticism, Two Essays on New Testament Research Dibelius, From Tradition to Gospel, 287-295.

[216] For example, in Bultmann's discussion of the feeding of the five thousand, he finds the Finnish fairy tale of a young girl feeding an army on three barley corns as a parallel to the feeding of the five thousand. See Bultmann, The History of the Synoptic Tradition, 236. Dibelius also cited analogies from rabbinical sources, and Greek and patristic literature. See Dibelius, From Tradition to Gospel, 133-177.

[217] Bultmann argues, "For the most part the history of the tradition is obscure, thought there is one small part which we can observe in our sources, how Marcan material is treated as it is adapted by Matthew and Luke." He goes on to note, "If we are able to detect any such laws, we may assume that they were operative on the traditional material even before it was given its form in Mark and Q, and in this way we can infer back to an earlier stage of the tradition than appears in our sources." Bultmann, The History of the Synoptic Tradition, 6.

[218] For an salient example of tenuous nature of the Marcan hypothesis, see Hans-Herbert Stoldt, History and Criticism of the Marcan Hypothesis (Macon, GA.: Mercer, 1980).

negative presuppositions of the age or Zeitgeist in which form criticism developed ("Spirit of the times") would give validity to such assumptions.

In accordance with these presuppositional axioms, form critics argued that the gospel narratives (i.e. in Mark) originally were single pictures in simple language, "the original tradition was made up almost entirely of brief single units (sayings and short narratives), and that almost all references to time and place which serve to connect up the single sections into a larger context are the editorial work of the evangelists."[219] In a chapter entitled, "The Laws Governing Popular Narrative and Tradition," Bultmann maintains,

> Narrators do not give us long unified accounts but rather small single pictures, individual scenes narrated with the utmost simplicity. These always occupy but a brief space of time; apart from the Passion Narrative no event or proceeding is narrated which covered more than two days. As a rule only two speaking characters appear in these scenes, or at the most three; involved proceedings are beyond the powers of the simple story teller. Where groups or crowds are present, they are treated as a unity. As such narratives pass from mouth to mouth, or when one writer takes them over from another, their fundamental character remains the same, but the detail are subject to the control of fancy and are usually made more explicit and definite.[220]

Thus, as time went on, for example, details were added. For example, while Mark used unnamed persons in his pericopes, the other Synoptics tended to identify these ("the tendency to characterize more definitely the dim figures in the tradition"). Thus, in Mark 14:13 unnamed disciples are sent to prepare for the last supper, while in Luke 22:8, their names are given as Peter and John; in Mark 7:17, "the disciples" are seen as posing the question to Jesus in general, while in Matthew 15:15, Peter asks the question of Jesus. Not only were figures identified by "later" tradition, but in Mark or Q while Jesus's opponents are unidentified, in Matthew and Luke the opposition "are almost invariably the scribes and Pharisees."

Bultmann also concludes that while some polemical words of Jesus addressed to scribes and Pharisees may be historical (e.g. Mark 12:38-40; and most of Matt. 23:1-31), "the schematic representation according to which the Pharisees and scribe are from the outset the sworn enemies of Jesus is certainly unhistorical."[221]

According to form critics like Dibelius, the length and ensuing "worldiness" of the narrative is a guide to the date, for "the fortune of primitive Christianity is reflected in the history of the Gospel-Form." Dibelius argues, "at the beginning of the history of primitive Christian literature; there stood a tradition of an unliterary nature, consisting of short narratives and striking sayings, which were repeated for practical purposes."[222] Then after time, "the mythological element take charge of the entire material of evangelical history." To him, paradigms, being the simplest

---

[219] Bultmann, Form Criticism, Two Essays on New Testament Research, 25.

[220] Bultmann, Form Criticism, Two Essays on New Testament Research, 32.

[221] Bultmann, Form Criticism, Two Essays on New Testament Research, 33, 35.

[222] Dibelius, From Tradition to Gospel, 287.

and shortest are "the earliest formal constructions." The distinct lack of miraculous elements, for Dibelius, also indicates their primitive historicity and, as a consequence, "trustworthiness." Also, Dibelius asserts that the paradigms narration in a "true, human, simple, and artless manner" indicates its primitive historicity. [223]

After that, "pleasure in the narrative for its own sake arose and seized upon literary devices." As a consequence, worldly elements that gave "a fully secular character" to the form were added as the Christian community began to imitate the surrounding techniques of the world's manner of story-telling. Thus, a lengthier form arose known as the "Tale" or "Wonder story" arose. Reflecting Greek and Oriental conceptions, these represented Jesus as a miracle worker. Thus, these foreign or miraculous elements in Tales indicate that "Tales are only to be used with great caution as historical sources" especially since "they were open to the invasion of foreign motives" and "by the pleasure of narrating the Tale."[224]

Next, legends or stories about Jesus and His associates developed as even more time passed. As a result, legends would be less trustworthy and, consequently, of a later date than paradigms or tales, i.e. legends were on the "periphery of the tradition." In Legends, "One told of these persons in the same way as similar narratives from the surrounding world spoke of other holy men." Through such legends, a complete "accommodation to the world and harmony with its relationships" predominated.[225]

According to form critics, observing distinctions between direct and indirect discourse is indicative of the original form. Thus, as time went on, indirect discourse became direct discourse, i.e. words were placed directly on the lips of gospel characters. For example, in Mark 8:32, when Jesus announced his impending crucifixion, the text states in general terms that Peter rebuked him, while in Matthew 16:22, the words that Peter used are reported (cf. Mark 14:23 vs. Matt. 26:27); the inarticulate cry from the cross in Mark 15:37 becomes specified in Luke 23:46.

According to form critics like Bultmann, Dibelus, and Taylor,[226] the presence of Semitisms, in distinction to Hellenistic elements, is often an indication of a tradition that is very early or even authentic. Two contemporary advocates for Semitisms as a test for antiquity are Joachim Jeremias and Matthew Black.[227] Bultmann typically argued, "since our gospels arose out of Greek Christianity, the

---

[223] Dibelius, From Tradition to Gospel, 288, 289-90.

[224] Dibelius, From Tradition to Gospel, 287, 291-292.

[225] Dibelius, From Tradition to Gospel, 287, 292-293.

[226] For further information, see Bultmann, The History of the Synoptic Tradition, 48, 55; Dibelius, From Tradition to Gospel, 34-35; Vincent Taylor, The Gospel According to St. Mark, 65.

[227] Jeremias was himself a major opponent of the History-of-Religions School in Germany. Yet, he too argued for the antiquity or genuineness of the saying based on the presence of Semitisms. See Joachim Jeremias, " The Parables of Jesus. Second Revised Edition (New York: Charles Scribner's Sons, 1972), 15. Matthew Black also supports the idea that Semitisms indicates antiquity. See Matthew Black, An Aramaic Approach to the Gospels and Acts. Third Edition (Oxford: The Clarendon Press, 1967), 271; "The Problem of the Aramaic Element in the Gospels, Expository Times LIX(1947-48), 171-176.

distinction provides us with a criterion which frequently enables us to determine whether this or that feature belongs to the older tradition or was composed later."[228]

Yet, the argument that formal Semitisms may establish the antiquity of the Gospels is tenuous for significant reasons. First, by the time period of the New Testament, Judaism and Hellenism had already experienced considerable interpenetration. This interpenetration is evidenced even in the terminology of the New Testament. For instance, the characteristic Palestinian institution of the Sanhedrin derived its name from the Greek word sunevdrion indicates the deep influence that Greek had even in the very heart of Palestinian Judaism.[229] The Talmud also indicates this penetration: Tosephta Sota XV 322.6 relates: "Permission was given to the House of Rabban Gamaliel to teach their children Greek owing to their relation with the (Roman) government." The Babylonian Talmud Sota 49b states that Rabbi Simeon related: "There were a thousand young men in my father's house, five hundred of whom studied the Law while the other five hundred studied Greek wisdom." Lieberman has demonstrated that Rabbis quoted not only from Jewish sources for their teachings but also from Greek sources (e.g. Greek proverbs).[230]

Second, studies indicate that Jesus's language environment was not exclusively Aramaic but also may have included considerable knowledge and use of Greek from the very start.[231] Gundry argued, "we can be sure that the tradition about Jesus was expressed from the very first in Hebrew, Aramaic, *and Greek* . . . . We cannot naively work on the assumption that everything was originally in Aramaic, that we should seek Aramaic equivalents wherever possible, and that wherever Aramaic equivalents cannot be traced we must reject authenticity."[232] Jesus, living in the city of Nazareth in the region of Galilee that was dominated by Gentiles, who spoke Greek (e.g. "Galilee of the Gentiles"—Matt. 4:15), would most likely have been familiar with Greek his whole life. Peter, Andrew, James and John would also probably have known Greek if they were to sell their fish in Gentile markets of Galilee. This factor, coupled with the missionary emphasis of the Gospel (cf. Matt. 28:19; Acts 1:8; 6:1) would ensure that the message occurred both orally and in writing from the very beginning in the *lingua franca* (i.e. Greek) of the civilized world as well as Aramaic. As Argyle notes, "If Jesus and his disciples were as familiar

---

[228] Bultmann, Form Criticism, Two Essays on New Testament Research, 18.

[229] For additional examples, consult Franz E. Meyer, "Einige Bermerkungen zur Bedeutung des Terminus 'Sanhedrion' in den Schriften des Neuen Testaments, New Testament Studies 14 (1967-68): 545-551.

[230] Saul Lieberman, Greek In Jewish Palestine. Second Edition (New York: Philipp Feldheim, 1965), 38-40.

[231] For a more detailed treatment of these points, consult Philip Edgcumbe Hughes, "The Languages Spoken by Jesus," in New Dimensions in New Testament Study. Edited by Richard N. Longenecker and Merrill C. Tenney (Grand Rapids: Zondervan, 1974), 127-143.

[232] Robert H. Gundry, "The Language Milieu of First-Century Palestine," Journal of Biblical Literature 83 (1964): 408.

with Greek as with Aramaic, the transition from the oral Aramaic stage to the Greek literary stage would have been natural and easy."[233]

Third, using the form critic's same logic, indications exist that Mark may be later rather than "earlier." For example, Mark's Latinisms (e.g. kenturivwn, xevsth", spekoulavtwr, iJkano;n poiei'n)[234] and his translation of Aramaic expressions (e.g. Mark 5:41; 15:22, 34) for the sake of those who did not know Aramaic may indicate that Mark was later rather than earlier as suggested by form critics.

To form critics, the writing style of the evangelist also is another indication of the earliness and trustworthiness of the tradition. Bultmann related, "While with Mark the art of the evangelist appears to be quite undeveloped, Luke displays a fine editorial artistry. Even the casual reader may note the difference if he observes the quite distinct manners in which Matthew and Luke introduce material from the Sayings-document into Mark" [in the composition of their own gospels].[235] Yet, as Redlich apply notes, "The stylistic methods of writers are no evidence of laws of tradition; they are indications of the standard of scholarship of the writers."[236]

Since the gospels were written by the apostles whose names they bear and who witnessed the events that they wrote concerning, then no substantial credibility exists to such laws. The most credible case, supported by consistent and unconvoluted testimony of church history, is that the gospels reflect either direct apostolic testimony (Matthew, John) or are based on eyewitness accounts (Mark (Peter), Luke [1:1-4]). The key to this is that only Bultmann's and Dibelius's (and any form critic's) presuppositions prevent the acceptance of this latter assertion. Instead of indicating any "development" of tradition or secondary elements, any comparison of individual gospel pericopes in Matthew, Mark, and Luke merely reveal selectivity in what the eyewitnesses chose to convey and also reflect the individual style of the writers.

Furthermore, forms critics, in their development of these "laws of tradition," are guilty of being selective in argumentation rather than thorough. They chose examples that only appeared to support their position while ignoring other tendencies and factors that convolute their hypotheses. Sanders, after examining

---

[233] Argyle notes: "Any Jewish tradesman who wished his business to prosper would be eager to make his range of customers as large as possible and so would welcome Greek-speaking Gentile customers as well as Jews. This would apply especially in Galilee of the Gentiles where the majority of the population was Gentile and Greek-speaking . . . . If Joseph and Jesus wanted their carpentry business to prosper, they would be happy to welcome Gentile as well as Jewish customers. They would therefore need to speak Greek as well as Aramaic if they were to converse with all their customers. Similarly Simon and Andrew, James and John would need to know Greek if they were to sell their fish in Gentile Markets. So would Levi, the inland revenue officer, the civil servant, engaged in government employ." A. W. Argyle, "Greek among the Jews of Palestine in New Testament Times," New Testament Studies 20 (1973), 88, 89.

[234] While additional Latin words appear in the other gospels (dhnavrion, kh'nso", kodravnth", kravbatto", legiwvn), the words listed here are exclusive to Mark. (vincent, Mark, 45.)

[235] Bultmann, Form Criticism, Two Essays on New Testament Research, 26

[236] Redlich, Form Criticism, 75.

these form-critical laws of tradition, concludes that the tradition does not follow assertions of simple to complex,

> There are no hard and fast laws of the development of the Synoptic tradition. On all accounts the tradition developed in opposite directions. It became both longer and shorter, both more and less detailed, and both more and less Semitic. Even the tendency to use direct discourse for indirect . . . was not uniform in the Synoptics themselves. For this reason, *dogmatic statements that a certain characteristic proves a certain passage to be earlier than another are never justified.*[237]

Caird concurs with this assessment. He cites, for example, in the triple tradition of the feeding of the five thousand that the "green grass" in Mark 6:39 disappears in Luke 9:14 which is the exact opposite of what one should expect if these laws of tradition were true. Caird concludes, "a law which tells us that tradition may either amplify or abbreviate, may either add details or omit them, is very little help in determining which of two accounts is the more original."[238]

Strategically, if central presuppositions of form criticism are rejected, such as antisupernaturalism, evolution, the Two-Document (or, Four-Document) Hypothesis, then these laws of tradition have no substantial basis for they operate on the tacit assumption of these presuppositions. If the gospels are accepted as eyewitness accounts (Matthew, John) or based on eyewitness accounts (Mark, Luke) as the unbroken testimony of early church history affirms, form critical assertions melt completely away. The specificity or lack of specificity merely reflects the personal choices of the eyewitness as to what they chose to include in the recounting of their stories. As a result, the tradition contained in the gospels is inherently stable.

Criteria of Authenticity for the Words of Jesus

The area of "authenticating" the sayings of Jesus consumes most of the effort in tradition criticism. Because form critics postulate that the gospels reflect the creative Christian community rather than preserving the actual words of Jesus, they inevitably became involved in attempting to identify "genuine" sayings of Jesus from those that were products of the Christian community. As a result, form critics developed "criteria of authenticity" to make such determinations. Such criteria inherently impugn the gospel record, placing the onus of proof on the gospels to demonstrate authenticity. Often, as will be seen, these principles are mutually contradictory and eliminate the vast majority of the sayings of Jesus as authentic.

The recent work by Funk, Hoover, and others of the so-called "Jesus Seminar" entitled, The Five Gospels: The Search for the Authentic Words of Jesus, represent the most recent pronouncement that uses the historical-critical method of tradition

---

[237] E. P. Sanders, The Tendencies of the Synoptic Tradition (Cambridge: At the University, 1969), 272. However, even Sanders is the product of the spirit of the time for supports the Four-Document Hypothesis typical of British scholarship.

[238] Caird, "The Study of the Gospels: II. Form Criticism," 140.

criticism to negate the authenticity of the Gospels.[239] Like Bultmann at the turn of the century, [240] who barely accepted approximately forty sayings as attributable to Jesus, the Jesus Seminar rejects 82% sayings of Jesus (analyzing more than 1500 sayings in their total inventory) with the remaining 18% as doubtfully authentic. Yet, the Seminar demonstrates its highly radical and prejudiced nature when it labels Bultmann as "neo-orthodox."[241]

The "Jesus Seminar" credits their analysis of the sayings of Jesus on the so-called "Seven Pillars of Scholarly Wisdom that serve as their basic presuppositional foundation: 1) a distinction between the Jesus of history and the Christ of faith, 2) a distinction in historical value between the Synoptic Gospels (containing some reflection of the historical Jesus) and the Gospel of John (containing only a "spiritual" Jesus and little historical value), 3) the priority of Mark, 4) recognition of a hypothetical "Q" (German, Quelle or "source") as the explanation for material common to Matthew and Luke but not found in Mark, 5) a distinction between Schweitzer's eschatological Jesus (the kingdom is entirely future and cataclysmic) and the Seminar's assertion of a non-eschatological view of Jesus's teaching (the kingdom is already here, i.e. "God's imperial rule"), 6) a fundamental contrast between Jesus's predominately oral culture and today's written culture, 7) the investigator's operating axiom for which no further demonstration is necessary is that the burden of proof for historical validity rests upon the Gospel's historical record. As a result, the investigator has "no final guarantees" as to what Jesus claimed and taught. The Seminar labels these axioms as "safeguards offered by the historical methodologies practiced by all responsible scholars."[242] As Carson relates, "The criteria by which so much gospel material ascribed to Jesus is dismissed as inauthentic are not much more than restatements of old fashioned form and redaction criticism."[243] Their final presupposition or "test" is "beware of finding a Jesus entirely congenial to you." Such an assertion, however, applies especially to the Jesus Seminar, who a priori determine the outcome of the "historical Jesus" by

---

[239] The "Jesus Seminar" includes the Gospel of Thomas in this count as a quasi-canonical Gospel as the number in the title of their work reflects. See Robert W. Funk, Roy W. Hoover, and the Jesus Seminar, The Five Gospels, What Did Jesus Really Say? (New York: Macmillan, 1993). The Seminar consists of 74 scholars, many of whom are listed in the back of the work in a section entitled, "Roster of the Fellows of the Jesus Seminar" (pp. 533-537). The exact selection process of the members of this "Seminar" is unknown.

[240] Funk attempts to distance himself from Bultmann. Funk prefers to echo the sentiments of the post-Bultmannian "New Quest for the historical Jesus" (inaugurated by Käsemann in 1953) that something can be known of the historical Jesus. However, the results of Funk's and the Seminar are essentially the same as that of Bultmann, i.e. little, if anything, is known of the "historical Jesus." See Charlotte Allen, "Away with the Manger," Lingua Franca 5 (Jan./Feb. 1995): 26.

[241] See The Five Gospels, 3, 5. For a succinct, critical analysis of the "Jesus Seminar," see D. A. Carson, "Five Gospels, No Christ," Christianity Today, April 25, 1994, 30-33.

[242] The Five Gospels, 3-5.

[243] Carson, "Five Gospels, No Christ," 32.

adopting such presuppositions that are far from neutral. Their Jesus of history is already decided before any examination of evidence.[244]

Claiming to be more "scientific" because the Seminar views the life of Jesus from "the new lens of historical reason and research rather than through the perspective of theology and traditional creedal formulations" the Jesus Seminar group is far from objectivity in its analysis. [245] Indeed, it cannot have the slightest hope of "scientific" objectivity since the Seminar admittedly anchors its research upon the same negative presuppositional foundation upon which historical criticism rests. The Seminar admits that, as a result, their underlying assumption is "the gospels are now assumed to be narratives in which the memory of Jesus is embellished by mythic elements that express the church's faith in him, and by plausible fictions that enhance the telling of the gospel story for first-century listeners who knew about divine men and miracle workers firsthand."[246]

Barbour, in his work Traditio-Historical Criticism of the Gospels, divides tradition-critical axioms into two broad categories: formal and material criteria. Formal criteria deal with the form in which the material was allegedly handed down or from the place which it occupies in the gospel tradition (e.g. multiple attestations, Aramaisms, poetic form, and parallelism). Material criteria deal with the actual content of the material itself (dissimilarity, coherence). Barbour terms this two-fold distinction a "rough-and-ready one" but says that "it has its usefulness."[247] Space for this article limits the discussion to only the most key criteria of these broad categories.

In analyzing these criteria, their methodological bankruptcy clearly is evident, i.e. they are neither valid nor capable of producing what they allege nor do they have any hope of being "objective" or "scientific" in approach. The Criterion of Multiple Attestation is one of the earliest formulated, being advocated by F. C. Burkitt.[248] Anchored upon the priority of Mark and the Two-Document Hypothesis as the solution to the synoptic "problem," this criterion suggests that when a saying or activity of Jesus appears in more than one of these sources the more likely that the saying would be authentic. British-trained tradition critics have tended to rely even more heavily on this principle than do Bultmannian-influenced tradition critics since it eventually centered upon the solution to the Synoptic Problem that the British, due to Streeter's influence (The Four Gospels–1924), heavily prefer (i.e. the Four-Source hypothesis–Mark, Q, M, L). [249] McArthur terms this criterion "the most

---

[244] The Five Gospels, 5.

[245] The Five Gospels, 2.

[246] The Five Gospels, 4-5.

[247] R. S. Barbour, Traditio-Historical Criticism of the Gospels (London: SPCK, 1972), 3.

[248] F. C. Burkitt was one of the earliest advocates of this principle. See F. C. Burkitt, The Gospel History and Its Transmission (Edinburg: T & T Clark, 1911), 147-148.

[249] Harvey K. McArthur, "Basic Issues, A Survey of Recent Gospel Research," Interpretation 18 (1964): 48. Streeter labeled the Four-Source hypothesis "The Fundamental Solution." See B. H. Streeter, The Four Gospels (London: Macmillan, 1953), 151-200.

objective of the proposed criteria."[250] This latter statement reveals the hopelessly subjective and biased nature of tradition criticism, for if this is the most "objective" criterion, then acute problems exist with the whole system.

Strategic flaws render this criterion as highly dubious: 1) The entire basis of the criterion centers in a highly questionable synoptic hypothesis. As a result, such a criterion automatically has a built-in bias. If, and it is very likely, that the Two- or Four-Source hypothesis is invalid, then this criterion proves nothing. Therefore, merely because several alleged "layers of tradition" contain, the saying or activity confirm nothing regarding authenticity. 2) No valid reason exists to deny the authenticity of a saying simply because it is found in only one alleged "source." This criterion is inherently negative since it implies that one witness is not sufficient. The Bible only has to record a saying or activity once for it to have been actually spoken or performed by Jesus.

Related to the Criterion of Multiple Attestation is the Criterion of Multiple Forms. C. H. Dodd was the first to suggest this principle as a tool for authenticity. Heavily influenced by form criticism, this principle suggests that a gospel motif may be authentic if it appears in multiple forms, i.e. in different form-critical categories (e.g. pronouncement and miracle stories).[251]

In reply, similar counter-arguments apply to this category as to the Criterion of Multiple Attestation. One witness is entirely sufficient to confirm what Jesus said or did. The acute subjectivity of form-critical categories (as noted in this chapter) also reveals the highly speculative nature of this criterion.

The Criterion of Aramaic Linguistic Phenomena asserts that the presence of Aramaisms in the gospel material suggests the "primitiveness" of a particular tradition and, hence indicates the increased likelihood that the tradition actually comes from Jesus. While Dalman, Burney, and Torrey were the earliest advocates of this hypothesis, Black and Jeremias have done the most extensive work.[252] Fuller goes so far as to say that "any saying of Jesus, if it is authentic, should exhibit Aramaic features, and if it has the structure of Aramaic poetry this increases the presumption that the saying is authentic."[253] Jeremias argues that the presence of Aramaisms "is of great significance for the question of the reliability of the gospel tradition," while Turner asserts, "the closer the approximation of a passage in the Gospels to the style

---

[250] McArthur relates, "Bultmannians do not display any great interest in this multiple-attestation criterion, apparently preferring more esoteric guides. Having indicated some scepticism of British tendencies in Gospel research I should comment that, in my judgment, their regular and faithful use of this criterion is to be commended." McArthur, "Basic Issues," 48.

[251] C. H. Dodd, History and the Gospel (London: Nisbet, 1938), 91-103.

[252] Gustav Dalman, Jesus-Jeshua, Studies in the Gospels (New York: KTAV, 1971[first published in 1929]), 1-30; C. F. Burney, The Poetry of Our Lord (Clarendon, 1925), 5-11; C. C. Torrey, Our Translated Gospels (New York and London: Harper, 1936), ix-lx; Black, An Aramaic Approach to the Gospels and Acts, 1-49; Joachim Jeremias, The Parables of Jesus. Second Revised Edition (New York: Charles Scribner's Sons, 1972), 25-27.

[253] Reginald H. Fuller, The New Testament in Current Study (Charles Scribner's Sons, 1962), 33.

and idiom of contemporary Aramaic, the greater the presumption of authenticity."[254]

In reply, some strategic considerations militate strongly against its validity: 1) This chapter has already demonstrated that the mere presence of Aramaisms is no real indication of primitiveness or earliness. On the contrary, Greek and Hellenism in general, as well as Aramaic, exercised a profound influence on the New Testament Palestinian environment, especially in terms of language and culture. Jesus and many of the disciples, being raised in Galilee or having contact with Gentiles, would also have spoken and taught in Greek as well as Aramaic. Jesus's use of uJpokrithv" in Matthew 6:2, 5, 16 is a case in point, for it retains the classical Greek meaning of "play actor," a meaning that is found in the papyri. As Argyle relates, "It is probable . . . that Jesus was really speaking Greek not only in his use of uJpokrithv" but in the other words of his teaching when doing so in Galilee of the Gentiles."[255] Therefore, something cannot be ruled out merely because it does not reflect an alleged Aramaic source. 2) The principle is hermeneutically misguided. Inerrancy and the grammatico-historical hermeneutic dictate that inspiration is grounded in the autographs and not in any hypothesized sources that allegedly lay behind them.

The Criterion of Palestinian Environmental Phenomena contends that if a tradition evidences Palestinian social, domestic, agricultural, religious or other customs, then the tradition originated in a Palestinian environment rather than being a creation of a Greek or non-Palestinian church. The assumption here is that if a tradition betrays the time and environment of Jesus, the higher the likelihood that the tradition is authentic. Jeremias argues that if the "pictorial element" of the tradition betrays Palestinian conditions, then a greater likelihood exists for the genuineness of the tradition.[256]

In reply, not all of Jesus teachings or incidents are exclusively Palestinian, especially since Jesus said things that indicate a Greek environmental influence also. For example, physicians served as models for sententious sayings in many cultures, and some serve as striking parallels to Jesus's words (Mark 2:17 cf. Meander, *Fragment 591 K*).[257] Traditions, therefore, should not be doubted merely because they do not indicate an exclusively Palestinian background.

In addition to these "formal criteria," two highly strategic "material criteria" exist: the Criteria of Dissimilarity and Coherence. Although its origin is uncertain, the Criterion of Dissimilarity (or, Distinctiveness) is among the most strategic

---

[254] Joachim Jeremias, New Testament Theology (New York: Charles Scribner's Sons, 1971), 8; Henry E. W. Turner, Historicity and the Gospel (London: A. R. Mowbray, 1963), 77-78.

[255] Argyle, "Greek Among Palestinian Jews in New Testament Times," 89. See also, Argyle, "'Hypocrites' and the Aramaic Theory, Expository Times LXXV(1963-64), 113-114 where he argues that "It is difficult to see how there can have been an Aramaic equivalent for this; for theatre was forbidden among the Jews" (p. 113).

[256] Jeremias, The Parables of Jesus, 11-12.

[257] Also, see Matt. 7:2 // Luke 6:37-38 // Mark 4:24 cf. Hesiod Works and Days, 349-350; Publilius Syrus, Sentences [A] 2. Taken from carlston 99.

tradition-critical factors used by its advocates and heralded as the most useful. France comments, "This is the essential criterion, around which all others revolve" and "All others [i.e. criteria] are extensions of it or are used only to check and confirm its findings."[258] It is deeply rooted in the form-critical approach of Dibelius, Schmidt, and Bultmann. Bultmann constantly subjected the gospel material to this criterion in his History of the Synoptic Tradition.[259] Käsemann describes it in the following terms, "In only one case do we have more or less safe ground under our feet [in determining authentic material]; when there are no grounds either for deriving a tradition from Judaism or for ascribing it to primitive Christianity."[260]

This criterion has come to its most fervent expression in the work of Perrin and Fuller. Fuller argues, "As regards the sayings of Jesus, traditio-historical criticism eliminates from the authentic sayings of Jesus those which are paralleled in the Jewish tradition on one hand (apocalyptic and Rabbinic) and those which reflect the faith, practice and situations of the post-Easter church as we know them from outside the gospels."[261] Perrin goes so far as to assert, "the criterion of dissimilarity . . . must be regarded as the basis for all contemporary attempts to reconstruct the teaching of Jesus."[262] The essence of this Criterion is that authenticity of a tradition about Jesus is established only when it does not fit within either the Christian community that transmitted it or the Jewish world in which Jesus lived and taught.

Several serious flaws render this Criterion tenuous. First, this criterion blatantly assumes the inauthenticity of the traditions as its operating principle. It automatically condemns the tradition to suspicion and unreliability ("guilty until declared innocent approach"). Second, by its very formulation, it eliminates the vast majority of the gospel material, especially since most does not conflict with Judaism or the early church. Third, this tool is based on an argument from silence. Our knowledge of Judaism during Jesus day and of the early church is limited. To eliminate material based on our limited knowledge of these periods is precarious. Fourth, acute subjectivity reigns in the application of this principle. Scholars constantly differ as to whether a particular item is more "natural" against the

---

[258] R. T. France, "The Authenticity of the Sayings of Jesus," in History, Criticism and Faith. Edited by Colin Brown (Downers Grove: InterVarsity, 1976), 108-109.

[259] For example, Bultmann argues, "We can only count on possessing a genuine similitude of Jesus where, on the one hand, expression is given to the contrast between Jewish morality and piety and the distinctive eschatological temper which characterized the preaching of Jesus; and where on the other hand we find no specifically Christian features." See Bultmann, History of the Synoptic Tradition, 205 (also 101, 104-105). The radical Schmiedel used this type of criterion even before Bultmann, see Paul W. Schmiedel, "Gospels," in Encyclopaedia Biblica. Edited by T. K. Cheyne and J. Sutherland Black (New York: Macmillan,1903), col. 1881-1883.

[260] Käsemann continues, "especially when Jewish Christianity has mitigated or modified the received tradition, as having found it too bold for its task." Käsemann, Essays on New Testament Themes, 37.

[261] Reginald H. Fuller, The Foundations of New Testament Christology (New York: Charles Scribner's Sons, 1965), 18.

[262] Norman Perrin, Rediscovering the Teaching of Jesus (New York: Harper & Row, 1976), 43.

background of primitive Christianity or against the background of Jesus ministry.[263] Fifth, this principle erroneously presupposes no connection between Jesus and contemporary Judaism to which he belonged, and especially also assumes no connection between Jesus and the Old Testament. A continuity would naturally have existed between Jesus and his contemporaries. To exclude such agreement would lead only to distortion of what Jesus taught and resulted in a minimalistic Jesus or what is euphemistically termed "a critically assured *minimum.*"[264] Fifth, this method directly conflicts with the Criterion of Palestinian Environmental Phenomena and Aramaic Criterion that an "authentic" saying of Jesus should reflect first century Palestine. The tradition critic eliminates material if it can be paralleled in contemporary Judaism and also if it has a background that cannot be positively shown to be consistent with Palestinian Judaism of the first century. At the outset, the critic has eliminated most, if not all, material.

The Criterion of Coherence functions as a buttressing corollary to that of Dissimilarity. Moreover, its essential validity is dependent upon the validity of the other principles discussed. If those principles are wrong or invalid, then any data accepted through coherence is also wrong and invalid. Although he not explicitly formulates this principle, Bultmann used this type of criterion in the course of his form-critical work on the synoptic tradition. Commenting on Matthew 12:28, he argues that the verse "can, in my view, claim the highest degree of authenticity which we can make for any saying of Jesus: it is full of that feeling of eschatological power which must have characterized the activity of Jesus."[265]

Perrin defines Coherence as follows, "material from the earliest strata of the tradition may be accepted as authentic if it can be shown to cohere with material established as authentic by means of the criterion of dissimilarity" and "once characteristics of Jesus teachings are established in this way [by the Criterion of

---

[263] The word "Abba" enforces this point. The word is Aramaic in form but no exact parallel is found in Judaism. It, however, was used by the early church (Rom. 8:15; Gal. 4:6). By strict application of Dissimilarity, it should be eliminated, but tradition critics seem to accept it almost universally. See Hooker, "On Using the Wrong Tool," Theology 75 (1972): 577. Perrin demonstrates his inconsistency when he comments on Mark 14:36 and Luke 11:2, "since . . . *abba* is . . . found in Rom. 8:15 and Gal. 4:6, it could be argued that the Jesus tradition is not here dissimilar to that of the early Church. But these may not be regarded as representing early Christian tradition as such. They are the only examples of it, and the Lord's Prayer is universally known with its Matthaean form of address . . . The most reasonable explanation is that it is characteristic of Jesus rather than the early Church . . . . All in all, therefore, we may regard it as established, on the basis of the criterion of dissimilarity, that Jesus addressed God as *abba.*" Perrin, Rediscovering the Teaching of Jesus, 41.

[264] Nils A. Dahl, "The Problem of the Historical Jesus," in Kerygma and History. Edited by Carl E. Braaten and Roy A. Harrisville (New York and Nashville: Abingdon, 1962), 156. See Barbour p. 50 footnote 11.

[265] Bultmann established the "feeling of eschatological power" as authentic through the Criterion of Dissimilarity. Bultmann subjectively deems authentic "such sayings as arise from the exaltation of an eschatological mood," "sayings which are the product of an energetic summons to repentance," or "sayings which demand a new disposition of mind." He accepts them because they "contain something characteristic, new, reaching out beyond popular wisdom and piety and yet are in no sense scribal or rabbinic nor yet Jewish apocalyptic." Bultmann, History of the Synoptic Tradition, 162; 105 cf. also p. 205

Dissimilarity], these characteristics can be used to validate sayings which themselves would not meet the requirements of the criterion of dissimilarity."[266] Thus, this principle contends that what is coherent with the material accepted as genuine by means of the Criterion of Dissimilarity can also be accepted as genuine.

Some strategic arguments also render this Criterion tenuous. First, and perhaps most obvious, since this principle depends so heavily upon the criterion of dissimilarity, it automatically inherits the same problems. The application of coherence will magnify errors in results derived by the application of dissimilarity. Second, acute subjectivity reigns in its formulation. What standards judge coherence? What may seem coherent to modern scholars may not have seemed coherent to a Jew or Christian in the first century. This is capriciousness at its most brazen form.

In sum, tradition critics have carefully chosen these criteria to ensure results. Minds already closed to the legitimacy of the tradition have devised principles designed to reinforce their preconceptions (perhaps better, misconceptions). Tradition critics never designed these principles to confirm, only to underscore their negativity about the reliability of tradition as a whole. At best, they conceive of only a bare minimum of credibility to the tradition, and they predetermined the results to confirm this a priori assumption by intentional design of criteria. It is circular reasoning in its most malignant form. They have guaranteed the results as meager. These tradition-critical principles betray a philosophically preconceived agenda buttressing the contention that a preconceived hostility to the text exists in tradition criticism that eliminates any hope of objectivity. Perhaps more significantly, these so-called tradition criteria are devoid of any concept of inspiration in regard to the biblical text. Their historical development stands as a salient testimony to this assertion. Critics formulated these principles entirely apart from such considerations, and, to a large degree, from a virulent hostility to such concepts.

V. The Growing Evangelical Practice of Form and Tradition Criticism

A recent article in Christianity Today, entitled "Who Do Scholars Say That I am?," decried with indignation the Jesus Seminar's wholesale purging of the words and works of Jesus.[267] In the past, other articles have also castigated the members of the Jesus Seminar for their "liberal theological persuasion" in deciding "what Jesus did and did not say."[268] Recent works, such as Jesus under Fire, The Jesus Quest— The Third Search for the Jew of Nazareth, Cynic Sage or Son of God? written by

---

[266] Perrin, Rediscovering the Teaching of Jesus, 43.

[267] James R. Edwards, "Who Do Scholars Say That I am?, Christianity Today, March 4, 1996, 15-20.

[268] See Walter W. Wessell, "Voting Out the Fourth Beatitude, The Jesus Seminar decides what Jesus did and did not say," Christianity Today, November 12, 1986, 34. See also, for example, Mark A. Kellner "Away with the Manger, The new Jesus seminar discounts the Virgin Birth," Christianity Today, November 14, 1994, 92-93;

prominent evangelicals, have also attempted to spotlight the negative pronouncements of the Seminar.[269]

This finger-pointing, however, by evangelicals is, to a very large extent, misleading, for sadly, many evangelicals are increasingly utilizing the same seriously flawed historical-critical hermeneutics and methodologies that they so strongly react against toward the Jesus Seminar. Evangelicals are operating from the same presuppositional grid as traced in this chapter. The result among evangelicals is the same type of dehistoricizing and rejection of the words and works of Jesus as reflected by the anathematized Jesus Seminar. Increasingly, the pertinent question for evangelicals no longer can be "who do the Jesus Seminar scholars say that Jesus is?" but "who do evangelicals say that Jesus is?" This growing evangelical practice that parallels the methodologies of the Jesus Seminar is also true in the employment of the historical-critical methods of form and tradition criticism. The following will highlight a mere sampling of evangelical usage of these methods.

For many years, among conservative evangelicals, a consistent, though not exclusive trend had tended toward rejection of form criticism. At one time Gundry argued,

> [I]t is obvious that a consistent, thorough-going form criticism will have no appeal to those who desire to recognize the inspiration of the Scriptures and the historical continuity between the Lord Jesus and the early church. And let all "conservatives" who are inclined to adopt some form critical terminology and viewpoints be apprised of the basic nature of that to which they are accommodating themselves.[270]

Unfortunately, many conservative evangelicals did not fully realize the pernicious basis of form-critical speculation, for Gundry asserted that the fundamental assumption of form criticism, i.e., "Gospel tradition first existed as brief, rounded units, circulating orally in the Christian community," could be "quite innocuous" without perhaps realizing that such a speculation has a tacit evolutionary presuppositional background as its motivating principle.[271] One cannot overstress that this fundamental assumption is extremely suspect in light of form criticism's presuppositional and historical development. It arose at a time in which evolutionary dogma was overwhelming not only the scientific but also the theological scene. One must not divorce form speculation from the history and presuppositions that led to its development. If the foundations of the method and the history that produced the discipline is highly questionable, then the practice and assumptions of the disciple must also be.

---

[269] Michael J. Wilkins and J. P. Moreland, gen. eds., Jesus Under Fire (Grand Rapids: Zondervan, 1995); Ben Witherington III, The Jesus Quest, The Third Search for the Jew of Nazareth (Downers Grove, IL.: InterVarsity, 1995); Gregory A. Boyd, Cynic Sage or Son of God (Wheaton, IL.: Victor, 1995).

[270] Stanley N. Gundry, "A Critique of the Fundamental Assumption of Form Criticism (Part Two)," Bibliotheca Sacra (April, 1966), 149.

[271] Stanley N. Gundry, "A Critique of the Fundamental Assumptions of Form Criticism (Part One)," Bibliotheca Sacra (January 1966), 32.

Moreover, this article has demonstrated that at the basis of this hypothesis of brief, rounded units also centers in the radical skepticism of K. L. Schmidt, who denigrated the contextual connections as unhistorical and embellished. If those connections are viewed, as they properly should be, as historically and chronologically trustworthy, then evangelicals should reject this "fundamental" assumption of form criticism. No form-critical dismantling of individual pericopes can be safely undertaken, for no one can with any accuracy or any certainty identify pericopes as isolated units that actually circulated independently. Instead, the pericopes are integral to the gospel and primarily reflect the personal reminiscences of the apostles and first-century eyewitnesses as they composed their work. The pericopes give no real proof of any circulation in terms of form critical speculation.

Conservative evangelicals must be careful in this regard to elucidate presuppositions and historical developments that gave rise form critical speculation, for as Linnemann has correctly identified, historical-critical practices are in essence ideologies rather than methodologies.[272] Similarly, Donald Guthrie's words are telling, "When all the limitations are taken into account the scope of a true form-critical approach will be seen to be severely restricted. Yet with such restrictions, it may well be asked whether such a movement can really make any effective contribution to gospel criticism."[273]

However, a growing trend among conservatives in this group appears to be a consensus toward engaging in various "modified" versions of historical criticism (e.g. form and tradition criticism) in hopes of engaging in "dialogue" with contemporary theological scholarship as a whole. This desire is evident in the comment of Kingsbury regarding the recently published work New Testament Criticism and Interpretation, produced by a variety of German and British-trained evangelical theologians, "*New Testament Criticism and Interpretation* constitutes a bold and imaginative undertaking: to bring American scholarship into dialogue with the contemporary guild of biblical scholarship."[274] Unfortunately, in this "dialogue" of evangelicals with "biblical scholarship," conservative evangelicals are the ones who have evidenced substantial change, not contemporary scholarship. Prominent evangelicals have been only too willing to adopt not only the terminology but also methodology of historical criticism.

Perhaps the assumed hope may be that some "modified" version of form criticism avoids the negative connotation that liberals and others have held toward conservative evangelicals as being "closed-minded" to current methodological practices (or, perhaps a better term is *ideologies*) and failing to engage in "dialogue" with contemporary scholarship as a whole.[275] Perhaps the desire to exhibit

---

[272] See Linnemann, Historical Criticism of the Bible: Methodology or Ideology?, 83-123.

[273] Guthrie, 233.

[274] See the back cover endorsements from the work edited by David A. Black & David S. Dockery, New Testament Interpretation (Grand Rapids: Zondervan, 1991), n.p.

[275] Two recent criticism have been Mark A. Noll, Between Faith and Criticism (Grand Rapids: Baker, 1986) and George Marsden, Reforming Fundamentalism (Grand Rapids: Eerdmans, 1987). Noll writes, "a combination of factors during the first third of the twentieth century—the loss of institutional bases within the older denominations, a shrinking corps of active Bible scholars, the spread of dispensationalism, the ascendency of activism, the distrust

scholarship has driven the growing evangelical consensus. Sadly, however, liberal conceptions of "scholarship" have driven evangelical perceptions of what scholarship really is. When liberal methodologies are unmasked for what they really are, philosophical agendas, the perception of genuine "scholarship" evaporates.

This current state of scholarship, however, also has produced another sad state of affairs among conservative evangelicals. Those who do not subscribe to form-critical suppositions are sometimes subjected to a variety of subtle ad hominem arguments and downright ostracism within the theological community for failing to dialogue and conform to such practices.[276] Theological, as well as political, correctness attempts to drown out dissenting voices that

Some impose a tactic like Davies. Davies writes, "all serious students of the New Testament today are to some extent Form Critics."[277] Davis not only uses the term "form criticism" in an aberrant sense in this sentence but does he really seek to imply by such a statement that those who question form criticism are not serious students of New Testament but only those who practice the method?

McKnight, follows a similar tactic, citing George Ladd as "an evangelical scholar who is the product of the American fundamentalism of the 1920's" who accepts form-critical analysis.[278] Again the thought appears to be that if George Ladd as a "fundamentalist" uses the method, "evangelical scholars" as a whole should adopt it. Apparently again, if someone is to be considered a "scholar" by the liberal community (and now increasingly the same ideas are touted by the evangelical community), then their methodologies must be adopted. If not, then the detractor is not a scholar. Such logic is non-sequitur as well as shameful!

McKnight emphasizes his point by citing Ladd's acknowledgment that form criticism contains "valid elements" and that it "has thrown considerable light on the nature of the gospels and the traditions they employ. Evangelical scholars should be willing to accept this light."[279] Besides McKnight's argument from authority being extremely weak in logic, just because some conservative theologians have accepted form criticism does not in any way legitimize its usage in the conservative evangelical camp. The issue must remain the validity of form-critical speculations rather than assuming validity based on a hand-count of what the "majority" decides.

Furthermore, does Ladd wish to imply by this statement that those who reject form criticism are ignorant fops when he asserts that "they should be willing to accept this light"? Perhaps the rejecters of form-critical method know full well the implications of the discipline and reject it upon that basis. Ladd begs the question when he argues that evangelical scholars should be willing to "accept the light." The

---

of the university, the disruption of the fundamentalist controversies—led to an eclipse of evangelical biblical scholarship" (pp. 60-61).

[276] Linnemann remarks that this ostracization also applies to limited opportunities to publish. See Eta Linnemann, Historical Criticism of the Bible, Methodology or Ideology?, 89.

[277] W. D. Davies, Invitation to the New Testament (Garden City, N.Y.: Doubleday, 1966), 97.

[278] McKnight, What is Form Criticism?, 2.

[279] George Eldon Ladd, The New Testament and Criticism (Grand Rapids: Eerdmans, 1967), 148, 168-69 cf. McKight, What is Form Criticism?, 2.

crucial issues must always center on whether form criticism demonstrates sound hermeneutical validity ("light"), or whether it destroys the perspicuity of the Word and plunges conservative evangelicals into deeper darkness in the interpretation of Scripture because of an already preconceived and biased agenda.

Ladd's form-critical approach adopts much questionable methodology. While rejecting the views of "extreme form critics," Ladd advocates a modified version of form criticism since, he contends, form criticism "contains valid elements."[280] He accepts the Two-Document Hypothesis as a presuppositional working basis for form criticism, arguing it is "to be accepted as a literary fact."[281] Yet, Ladd makes a telling admission: "The Solution to the Synoptic problem was not achieved by scholars who held a high view of the Bible but by men who were concerned primarily with historical and literary questions. These men felt that only because they had been set free from any dogmatic view of biblical inspiration were they able to deal fully with the Gospels as historical documents."[282] Perhaps that admission should make conservative evangelicals more cautious in accepting such "light." Ladd admits that an anti-supernatural bias led to the acceptance of Markan priority (Mark has no mention of Jesus's virgin birth, his infancy, etc.) but still prefers to adopt Markan priority apart from these considerations. However, the presuppositional and historical motives of the two- and four-source hypothesis are highly questionable and render Ladd's assertion of "literary fact" quite tenuous.

Ladd seeks to assert that traditional form criticism's "skepticism" is not a result of the method by itself but of form criticism coupled with a rationalistic view of the nature of history."[283] Yet, this article and a previous one ("The Philosophical and Theological bent of Historical Criticism") have demonstrated that form criticism's fundamental assumptions rest on a foundation of skepticism. That foundation produced the method and provided its working basis. How then can Ladd call the method valid? It can be no more valid than its presuppositions and historical developments!

Ladd advocates a modified approach. Yet, like other form critics, however, he advocates an exclusively oral period and categorically rejects out of hand any concept that that written documents could have existed early.[284] However, the idea of an exclusively oral period is an assumption that has become a dogma. Credible arguments exist that during Jesus's ministry his disciples may have written notes on the main aspects of his teaching.[285]

---

[280] Ladd, The New Testament and Criticism, 149

[281] Ladd, The New Testament and Criticism, 141.

[282] Ladd, The New Testament and Criticism, 141-142.

[283] Ladd, The New Testament and Criticism, 147-48.

[284] Ladd, The New Testament and Criticism, 148-149.

[285] This article has already cited some strategic works in this regard. For further investigation, consult Heinz Schürmann, "Die vorösterlichen Anfänge der Logientradition," in Der historische Jesus und der kerygmatische Christus: Beiträge zum Christusverständnis in Forschung und Berkündigung. Herausgegeben von Helmut Ristow und Karl Matthiae (Berlin: Evangelische Verlagsanstalt, 1962), 342-370.

Ladd argues: "A second valid contention of form criticism is that the Gospels are not 'neutral, objective, impartial' records but are witnesses to the faith of Christian believers."[286] Although he qualifies this statement, he concludes "the redemptive events recorded in the Gospels are 'objective' in the sense that they really happened in space and time, but their nature is such that they stand apart from merely human 'historical events' . . . for they cannot be understood by ordinary human observation but only by the response of faith."[287] However, one should not confine historicity in the Scripture only to acts of redemption. In Scripture, history is wedded to theology. If the foundational chapters of Genesis are not historical (e.g. Gunkel, Bultmann), then the redemptive acts addressed in the gospels have no validity. Geisler correctly notes,

> Evangelicals cannot look at historical and scientific affirmations in Scripture as purely symbolic or mythical. In short, we cannot separate science from the Scripture. When the Bible declares that Jesus was born of a virgin, then it affirms a biological truth as well as a spiritual one. And when Jesus answered the question about divorce by saying, 'Haven't you read that at the beginning the Creator 'made them male and female'" (Matt. 19:4), He not only laid down a moral principle but made a scientific pronouncement as well. The scientific cannot be separated from the spiritual without doing violence to the spiritual.[288]

Thus, if Adam was not a real person, if no actual Fall occurred in time and history, then the significance of Christ's death and all other redemptive acts are rendered suspect in the New Testament as well.

Ladd also accepts the analysis of forms according to "its setting in the early church" (<u>Sitz im Leben</u>) arguing "this is, to a certain extent, a valid position."[289] However, such a position forces him to admit that "such a study is highly hypothetical."[290] As part of his form analysis, he concludes that Mark was written in Rome to a Gentile audience and Matthew to a Jewish one. Yet, theologians have long reached such conclusions <u>without</u> the existence or need of form criticism.

Robert Stein is an example of an evangelical who reflects significant agreement with historical-critical and form-critical assumptions. Like other form critics, he assumes the British Four-Source hypothesis as a working presupposition.[291] He basis many of his interpretive conclusions on this hypothesis. Yet, more and more voices within the evangelical camp have identified significant reasons for the tenuous

---

[286] Ladd, The New Testament and Criticism, 153.

[287] Ladd, The New Testament and Criticism, 154.

[288] Norman L. Geisler, Biblical Errancy, An Analysis of Its Philosophical Roots (Grand Rapids: Zondervan, 1981), 21.

[289]Ladd, The New Testament and Criticism, 159.

[290] Ladd, The New Testament and Criticism, 161.

[291] Robert H. Stein, The Synoptic Problem (Grand Rapids: Baker, 1987), 129-138, 142-143. Stein does, however, qualify the fact that "Q" may be a layer of tradition rather than a single document.

nature of such a hypothesis.[292] To make any interpretive decisions on such a tenuous approach is ill-advised.

He also finds the primary assumption of form criticism positive: "One of the positive contributions of form criticism is the recognition that in general the Gospel traditions circulated as independent oral units before being incorporated into the Gospels. Some material, however, was collected into larger complexes such as Mark 1:21-39 (45); 2:1 to 3:6; and 4:1-34 before being incorporated into our Gospels."[293] As this article has noted, the Gospels offer no real proof for such form-critical assertions. Only by assuming historical-critical dogma can the assertion be buttressed. Because this period of church history is shrouded in mystery from approximately 30 to 50 or 60 C.E., dogmatic pronouncements concerning the nature of the tradition should make such dogmatic pronouncements merely speculative. The period of 20-30 years before the gospels were written is largely unknown. Guthrie writes, "the very fact that our historical data for the first thirty years of Christian history are so limited means that form critics inevitably had to draw a good deal on imagination."[294]

Stein also supports K. L. Schmidt's thesis that denigrates the historical, geographical, and chronological connections in the gospels:

> It would appear that there is a great deal to be said for Schmidt's thesis. When one looks at much of the material in the Gospel of Mark, it appears that the accounts were, for the most part, joined together on a non-chronological basis and that they indeed existed as independent units of tradition. . . . One can easily think of the pericopes as having begun with such introductions as "Once upon a time, Jesus . . . " or Once Jesus . . . ."[295]

Interestingly, Stein uses the traditional opening to fairy tales to describe an assumed early church introduction to these alleged isolated pericopes.

However, the particular identification of these independent units centers in the whim of the interpreter emphasizing the subjective nature of the selection. Instead of the evolutionary idea of independent units circulating in the church over a long period of time, evidence indicates that Mark may well reflect the personal recollections of the eyewitness and Apostle, Peter that he emphasized in his preaching. Eusebius records the words of Papias who was a personal acquaintance of the Apostle John in Ecclesiastical History 3.39: "'And John the Presbyter also said this, mark being the interpreter [eJrmhneuvte"] of Peter whatsoever he recorded he

---

[292] For example, see Bo Reicke, The Roots of the Synoptic Gospels (Philadelphia: Fortress, 1986). Eta Linnemann, Is There a Synoptic Problem? Translated by Robert W. Yarbrough (Grand Rapids: Baker, 1992); John Wenham, Redating Matthew, Mark, and Luke (Downers Grove, IL.: InterVarsty, 1992).

[293] Robert H. Stein, The Method and Message of Jesus' Teaching (Philadelphia: Westminster, 1978), 156 footnote 62.

[294] Guthrie, New Testament Introduction, 210.

[295] He further qualifies this by saying not all pericopes may have circulated as independent units (e.g., the passion narrative, Mark 1:21-39, 2:1-3:6; 4:1-34; 4:35-5:43; 7:1-23; 8:1-26; 12:13-37). Stein, The Synoptic Problem, 166-167.

wrote with great accuracy but not however in the order in which it was spoken or done by our Lord."[296]

Regarding the "Criterion of Multiple Attestation," Stein argues, "It is . . . true that this tool cannot provide historical certainty but only probability, but in historical matters this is all we can ever hope to achieve. Faith and belief may have unique access to historical certainty, but historical research can only deal with probabilities."[297] Does this mean that Jesus said and did can never be known for certain? Is certainty possible only through the eyes of faith? Is an existential leap required? Interestingly, he again basis probability of the historicity of the tradition upon multiple attestations within the Four-Source Hypothesis (i.e., Mark, Q, M, L). However, as noted, increasing evidence suggests the tenuous nature of this hypothesis, and thus the tenuous nature of Stein's assertions. Furthermore, as has been argued, these criteria place the burden of proof upon the tradition rather than allowing an objective approach to the historical accuracy of the tradition.

Regarding the "Criterion of Divergent Patterns from Redaction," he argues "materials in the Gospels that reflect an Evangelist's unique theological emphasis are probably less authentic or historical, especially if they appear only in his unique material (M in Matthew and L in Luke) or in his redactional work (summaries, explanatory clauses, seams, etc.)."[298] Thus, as with the more radical form and tradition critics, elements appearing in the Gospels to be historical can be demonstrated to be unhistorical.

Stein allows for the odd possibility of "inauthentic" but "authoritative" sayings attributed to Jesus:

> If a saying attributed to Jesus in the Gospels were inauthentic, its authoritative quality would remain, for the Evangelists not only recalled what the historical Jesus said and did but were taught by the Spirit and empowered by Him to interpret what the historical Jesus said and did (John 14:26; 16:14). Thus, in the Gospels the risen Christ also speaks through his Spirit by means of his prophets and apostles. These words are also authoritative even if not authentic. As a result, if the inauthenticity of a sayings should be demonstrated this should not be taken to mean that this saying lacks authority."[299]

In Matthew 5:31-32, Stein argues that the exception clause "is an interpretive comment added by Matthew" and that the version without the exception clause in Mark, Luke, and Q "is more authentic." Thus, according to Stein's logic, although Matthew placed these words directly on the lips of Jesus and although the exception clause is not authentic (Jesus did not speak the exception clause—it was really

---

[296] As Guthrie notes, evidence from Papias "cannot so easily be ignored." Guthrie, New Testament Introduction, 83.

[297] Stein, The Synoptic Problem, 142.

[298] Stein, The Synoptic Problem, 143.

[299] Robert H. Stein, "The 'Criteria' for Authenticity," in Gospel Perspectives, vol. 1. Edited by R. T. France and David Wenham (Sheffield: JSOT, 1980), 229.

Matthew's interpretation), it would still be authoritative.[300] In sum, however, this assertion actually results in attributing some quasi-concept of inspired deception to the gospel record. Furthermore, how would Matthew's readers recognize this interpretation in context? They would not. No indications exist that this exception clause is an interpretation.

For Stein, even if eyewitnesses of the events wrote the gospels, "it does not follow that eyewitness accounts of historical events are a priori accurate historical accounts . . . . We cannot . . . assume that we have proven the historicity of the gospel accounts even if we can that behind them stands the testimony of an eyewitness . . . . if eyewitness testimony of the gospel material should be established, then the burden of proof should rest upon those who would deny the historicity of the events reported."[301] For Stein, one can never be sure of the gospel events even if eyewitnesses are present. All that eyewitnesses can do is shift the burden of proof, but doubt always remains.

Stein supports the criterion of multiple forms, arguing "it would appear reasonable to suppose that the appearance of a tradition or motif in multiple forms is supportive, even if not conclusive, evidence for . . . authenticity."[302] Yet, as has been demonstrated, this criterion assumes so much form-critical subjectivity that it demonstrates nothing. He supports the Criterion of the Tendencies of the Developing Tradition, asserting that the gospel writers could change the original audience of the pericope. Thus, according to Stein, Luke 15:4-7 preserves the original audience to whom Jesus spoke the parable of the lost sheep, while Matthew, in 18:12-14, changed the original audience of this pericope from Jesus's opponents to the 'church." While Luke has the original audience, Matthew changed it for his own theological purposes to address the situation of his own audience, i.e. Sitz im Leben of the evangelist and his audience. Thus, for Stein, one can never be sure what the original audience of a pericope was, for the evangelist was free to change at will according to some hypothesized Sitz im Leben. By recognizing "certain of the 'laws' which the tradition experienced during the oral period, such as the changing of audience in the first and second/third Sitz im Leben" one can "be better able to ascertain what is authentic"[303] Being so thoroughly preconditioned by tradition-critical principles, he does not even consider the fact that as an itinerant preacher, Jesus may have repeated his parables to different audiences and adapted his message to those situations (thus, both audiences are original, and no postulating of fabrication on the part of the evangelists is needed). Instead, he allows subjective postulating of hypothetical Sitz im Lebens to control any determination of what is authentic and what is not.

Stein calls multiple attestation "a helpful tool for ascertaining the authenticity of the Gospel tradition." Indeed, he argues that "the multiple attestation of a tradition places the burden of proof upon those who would argue against the

---

[300] Robert H. Stein, The Synoptic Problem, 151-152. See also Robert H. Stein, Luke, vol. 24 in the New American Commentary. David S. Dockery, gen. ed. (Nashville, TN.: Broadman, 1992), 420.

[301] Stein, "The 'Criteria' for Authenticity," 226.

[302] Stein, "The 'Criteria' for Authenticity," 233.

[303] Stein, "The 'Criteria' for Authenticity," 238-239.

authenticity of a such a tradition."[304] Yet, since as has been seen, the underlying assumption of this criterion places the <u>onus propandi</u> on the tradition and has its basis in a highly doubtful synoptic hypothesis, one wonders how Stein has any confidence on a reversal of this burden of proof. The intent of the criterion is to cast suspicion on the tradition not to confirm the tradition. No amount of reform will overcome this built-in intent. Something predicated on acute skepticism cannot produce any positive results, no matter how much it is "reformed."

In Matthew 5:31-32, Stein advocates that Matthew placed upon the lips of Jesus the phrase "except on the ground of unchastity" as an interpretation. He bases this on his working presupposition of the Four Source hypothesis, "It seems reasonably clear in light of the threefold testimony of Mark, Q (Luke), and Paul, and by the difficulty of the saying when it lacks the exception for unchastity, that this form of the saying (without Matthew's 'exception clause') is more authentic."[305]

Stein also considers "[t]he Sermon on the Mount (Matt. 5:1-7:29) and the Sermon on the Plain Luke 6:20-49)" to be "literary creations of Matthew and Luke in the sense that they are collections of Jesus' sayings that were uttered at various times and places and have been brought together due to topical considerations, i.e. in order to have an orderly account ([Luke]1:3)." To Stein, although "there is no need, however, to deny that a historical event lies behind the scene," no "Sermon on the Mount" or "on the plain" ever took place as presented in the gospels but was a creative, fabricated embellishment of the evangelist.[306]

Stein supports the classification of forms, preferring Taylor's method. However, he admits that of three major classification systems (e.g., Bultmann, Dibelius, Taylor) "only two of the categories possess a distinct form–the pronouncement stories and miracle stories. The remaining types of material are essentially formless" and classification often "does not depend upon form as much as upon content."[307] He concludes that such "classification systems are helpful in that they provide convenient handles to refer to the various gospel traditions."[308] Yet, such admittedly meager abilities of form criticism serve to demonstrate that the vastly superior nature of the grammatico-historical hermeneutic renders form analysis tenuous as well as subjective. In addition, Stein, like other evangelical form critic, makes so many qualifications to an evangelical approach to form criticism that the validity and usefulness of the practice are entirely suspect in spite of claims to the contrary.

Robert Guelich, in his <u>The Sermon on the Mount</u> (1982) follows George Ladd's lead, his mentor, in asserting: "this commentary offers a *critical* exegesis in that it makes use of the literary and historical critical tools including text, source, form, tradition, redaction, and structural criticism" and goes on to assert "for many to whom the Scriptures are vital the use of these critical tools has historically been

---

[304] Stein, "The 'Criteria' for Authenticity," 232.

[305] Stein, The Synoptic Problem, 152.

[306] Stein, Luke, 198; Stein, The Synoptic Problem, 219-220.

[307] Stein, The Synoptic Problem, 171-172.

[308] Stein, The Synoptic Problem, 171-172.

more 'destructive' than 'constructive.' But one need not discard the tool because of its abuse."[309] Guelich prefers to ignore this history of abuse, for he asserts, contrary to historical evidence, "Like any other 'tool,' these of literary and historical criticism are basically neutral and often reflect the tendencies of the person using them . . . . But they have been refined to the extent that they offer the best instruments to date in exegeting the text."[310] Contrary to Guelich, as has been demonstrated in this article, literary and historical criticism are anything but "neutral" tools (see also chapter on "The Presuppositional and Theological Bent of Historical Criticism").

Like the early form critics, Guelich does not acknowledge the authorship of the Gospel as that of the tax-collector Matthew, in spite of the overwhelming historical attestation. He argues that his usage of the name "Matthew" in referring to the Gospel, "merely denotes the common traditional designation of the Gospel's author. The Gospel itself, of course, comes to us as anonymous in spite of the early church's assignment of it to the apostle Matthew."[311] As a result, Guelich prefers the "evangelist" in referring to the author of the Gospel of Matthew.

As with other form critics, Guelich assumes the four-source hypothesis.[312] This presupposition controls many of his hermeneutical decisions. Accordingly, based on this assumption ("The Sources of the Sermon on the Mount"), Guelich makes many extrapolations regarding the Sermon.[313] For Guelich, although the tradition "most likely" stem from Jesus's ministry, the Sermon on the Mount was not actually preached by Jesus as it is presented in Matthew (or Luke): "the Sermon on the Mount, as we know it, is ultimately the literary product of the first evangelist."[314] Instead, "as Dibelius suggested, even this underlying tradition resulted from the early community's compilation of various traditional units to meet their own catechal needs."[315] In light of this, "the actual 'Sermon' as such came into being when the tradition was combined into its present form in the post-Easter community, a process that makes moot the question of when and where Jesus 'preached' the Sermon."[316] Thus, according to Guelich, although both Matthew and Luke portray Jesus as preaching the "Sermon on the Mount," the sermon is not actually from Jesus but the product of the Christian community and the evangelists. Guelich contends that "Matthew has considerably changed the extent and profile of the Sermon tradition."[317]

---

[309] Robert A. Guelich, The Sermon on the Mount, A Foundation for Understanding (Waco, TX.: Word, 1982), 23.

[310] Guelich, The Sermon on the Mount, 23.

[311] Guelich, The Sermon on the Mount, 26.

[312] Guelich, The Sermon on the Mount, 33-34.

[313] Guelich, The Sermon on the Mount, 33-36.

[314] Guelich, The Sermon on the Mount, 33.

[315] Guelich, The Sermon on the Mount, 35.

[316] Guelich, The Sermon on the Mount, 35.

[317] Guelich, The Sermon on the Mount, 36.

He asserts that originally the Beatitudes were three (see Luke 6:20-21 // Matt. 3-4, 6). A fourth Beatitude (Luke 6:22-23 // Matt. 5:11-12) was "a separate traditional saying" that also goes back to Jesus.[318] According to Guelich,

> These four Beatitudes underwent further modification in the tradition with the change of person, with the expansion in number to eight in Matt. 5:5, 7-9, the first relating to the Beatitude of 5:3 and the other three corresponding in context to the three admonitions that followed in the tradition, and with the formulation of the antithetically parallel Woes in Luke 6:24-26, either in the tradition or by Luke. Therefore, Matthew found eight beatitudes in his Sermon tradition which he then adapted redactionally for his own purposes.[319]

The evangelist created one beatitude (Matt. 5:10), while four more (Matt. 5:5, 7-9) are the later products of the Christian community.[320] Guelich encapsulates his thesis,

> The Beatitudes of Matt. 5:3-12 indicate several stages of development. First, the core (5:3, 4, 6 par. Luke 6:20-21) had roots extending to Jesus' ministry to the desperate ones of his day . . . The fourth Beatitude (5:11-12, par. Luke 6:22-23) depicts the continuing struggle in this age for God's people. . . . Second, these four Beatitudes, brought together to make a clear declarative statement as the opening of the Sermon tradition, were later expanded by the use of the Psalms and Jesus' sayings to form four additional Beatitudes (5:5, 7-9) commensurate with Jesus' teachings and preaching as found in the tradition. Third, Matthew expressly adapted these Beatitudes (5:3, 4, 5, 6, 10) to Isaiah 61 in order to underline Jesus' person and work . . . Throughout the entire process of development, these nine Beatitudes remain consistent with the Jesus of the tradition.[321]

For Guelich, the Sermon on the "Mount" never happened as presented.

Such "extensive modification" not only leaves the bewildering question of how many beatitudes Jesus originally spoke (3, 4, 8?) but even what kind of "Sermon" took place. Would the original readers of the gospel be able to determine that such was the case? Such ephemeral and esoteric clues centering in the four-source hypothesis and cited by Guelich as to the compositional nature of the tradition do not accord with the grammatico-historical emphasis on the perspicuity of Scripture. Sadly, Guelich's assertions are based not on any objective analysis, but by the subjective whim of the interpreter utilizing, as Guelich terms them, the "neutral tools" of historical criticism (e.g., form and redaction criticism). Many have decried the Jesus Seminar's decision to vote out the fourth beatitude ("The Jesus Seminar

---

[318] Guelich, The Sermon on the Mount, 35.

[319] Guelich, The Sermon on the Mount, 35-36.

[320] Guelich, The Sermon on the Mount, 35-36;116-118.

[321] Guelich, The Sermon on the Mount, 117-118.

decides what Jesus did and did not say"), but evangelicals like Guelich do the very same thing.[322]

Guelich contends that "Matthew's Gospel and the Sermon in particular reflect the portrait artist's freedom to modulate, modify, relocate, rearrange, restructure, and restate as exercised by the community in the traditional process and by the evangelist's redaction."[323] This comment reveals that, for Guelich, not only does the Sermon often not reflect what Jesus said, but that the tradition was considerably modified by Christian community and the evangelist. All three Sitz im Lebens (i.e. Jesus, the Christian community, and the evangelist) exist for Guelich, so that not only the words but even the thoughts of Jesus are obscured by layers of life situations originating in the community and through the redaction of the evangelist. His conclusions result in a hopeless quagmire of seeking to determine whether Jesus actually said what is written in the gospel or whether it was reshaped by the Christian community or the evangelist. Under Guelich's system one can never be sure what was originally said by Jesus, if indeed, it was spoken at all by him or where it actually took place.

Guelich asserts that "the references to persecution and suffering, the deliberate contrast with 'the scribes and Pharisees' and 'hypocrites,' and the use of the Old Testament passages and types suggest an apologetic and polemical tone commensurate with a community that now found itself separated from and at odds with a Jewish community that now stood under the judgment of having rejected Jesus Messiah and his followers."[324] Yet, such factors are presented contextually in Matthew 5-7 as an integral whole within the Sermon and as coming from the lips of Jesus as he spoke to the disciples and multitudes present at the actual, historical occasion of the Sermon. The most natural understanding of these factors is that they reveal the historic situation of Jesus (i.e., His tensions and conflicts with the Jewish community as a whole during His lifetime) rather than any esoteric and subjective revelation of the situation of the evangelist's community. Any assertions to the contrary exist more in the form and redactional imagination of Guelich rather than being actually or clearly discernible in the Gospel.

Guelich also claims that the evangelist addressed a threat "of a strict Jewish-Christian attempt to maintain the Law of Moses by using the Jesus tradition as its basis and doubtless raised questions anew regarding the nature of the gospel and Gentile mission."[325] Guelich contends, "Matthew saw their presence as a threat so serious that he reshaped their Jesus tradition (e.g. 5:17-19) to counter and warn his community about these 'false prophets' (7:15-23). Thus the sermon must be read within the context of Judaism and a rigorous Jewish-Christianity."[326] He goes on to contend regarding Matthew 5:17-20 that "In no other section of the Sermon does

---

[322] Wessell decries the Jesus Seminar's methods, but Guelich does something very similar. Walter Wessell, "Voting Out the Fourth Beatitude, The Jesus Seminar decides what Jesus did and did not say." Christianity Today, November 12, 1986, 34-35.

[323] Guelich, The Sermon on the Mount, 25.

[324] Guelich, The Sermon on the Mount, 26.

[325] Guelich, The Sermon on the Mount, 26.

[326] Guelich, The Sermon on the Mount, 26.

the meaning of the passage depend so much on the use of tradition and redaction . . . . Consequently, the primary focus of the exegesis of 5:17-20 centers on the literary questions of form, source, and redaction." He contends that "one can attempt to delineate the various stages in the development of this unit with its differing, at times conflicting, meanings."[327] Furthermore, Guelich contends that the evangelist sometimes adds to the tradition "on the basis of 'an unconscious association of ideas' with little or no theological basis."[328]

Guelich blurs interpretation and application, for while warnings of persecution may have application to Christians at any time, a grammatico-historical interpretation of the passage legitimately must link the Sermon to only one Sitz im Leben: the earthly life of Jesus. This latter thought receives reinforcement by the fact that the life situations proposed for isolated units of tradition centers in pure speculation. No beliefs of the period when the synoptic gospels were produced can be or should be distinguished from the teachings of Jesus. Alleged Sitz im Lebens of the Christian community or evangelist is entirely based in acute subjectivity and imagination of the interpreter. No adequate proof that the material owed its present shape to the practical needs of an assumed community. The Book of Acts and Paul's epistles actually give very little information on the history of the early church. How can we reconstruct the church situation of the gospels when nothing of the church community history is given? To an overwhelmingly large degree, form critics have invented a Sitz im Leben of the church.

To Guelich, the evangelist displays authorial ineptitude with the tradition in 5:17-20 for "By *adding or the Prophets* to this context, the evangelist alters the saying from being a reference to Jesus' coming related specifically to the Law to being a reference to Jesus's coming related generally to the Scriptures. This modification has resulted in the blurring of the antithesis between the verbs *kataluvw* and *plhrovw*."[329] He goes on to argue that the evangelists reworking of the antithesis of 5:17 "has lost its sharpness since *kataluvw* and *plhrovw* no longer express a clear antithesis with reference to the object *Scriptures.* Whereas Jesus' coming *to fulfill the Scriptures* makes good sense, *to annul* or *to destroy* is awkward at best both lexically and materially. Jesus was hardly viewed as *annulling* or *destroying the Scriptures* in general."[330] Guelich explains this authorial ineptitude by "the differentiation between the pre-Matthean and Matthean forms of 5:17."[331] He also bases "modification" of the tradition in 5:17 upon his assumed "Jewish-Christian misuse of the saying for their purposes" of promoting legalism.[332]

Sadly, after Guelich's analysis, one is left wondering whether Jesus actually spoke 5:17-20, whether or to what extent the tradition actually existed in the community, or to what extend the imagination of the evangelist was working and how poorly it was operating. Again, would Matthew's readers have been capable

---

[327] Guelich, The Sermon on the Mount, 135.

[328] Guelich, The Sermon on the Mount, 138.

[329] Guelich, The Sermon on the Mount, 138.

[330] Guelich, The Sermon on the Mount, 142-143.

[331] Guelich, The Sermon on the Mount, 143.

[332] Guelich, The Sermon on the Mount, 142-143.

of detecting the esoteric signals that indicated the substantial modification of the material by the "pre-Matthean tradition?" The evangelist presents 5:17-20 as coming exactly from the lips of Jesus which are the most natural reading and understanding of the passage. Was the early church so devoid of historical interest (e.g., 1 Cor. 7:10, 12)? Importantly, should such conclusions be reached based upon the tenuous and extremely subjective nature of Guelich's hypothesized historical situation existing for Matthew and his audience? Once again, Guelich's imagination is at work rather than a grammatico-historical analysis of the Sermon.

Guelich also appears to support Schmidt's contention for the artificial nature of geographical and chronological connections. Indeed, for Guelich one cannot ever be sure that "the tradition" reflects "a theological tendency to localize events such as with calling of the Twelve, the Sermon, the Transfiguration, and the Olivet Discourse on a mountain" and "to what extent was this a historically accurate description of the location of the events . . . or . . . both?" He continues, "the ultimate answer to this question lies beyond our historical control . . . . the combination of the Sermon tradition with the traditional mountain setting for the calling for the Twelve may have resulted merely from the Church's catechetical interest in the Q Sermon material for new 'disciples' in the early church."333 In other words, the church's primary interest in the tradition may reflect "the Church's catechetical interests" and be a creation of the Christian community and the redaction of the evangelist.334 To Guelich, was the early church so devoid of historical interest that a literary device was used as a means to an end of instructing disciples? For Guelich, the ultimate question of where the Sermon on the "Mountain" took place is obscured by the early church's lack of interest in such details.335 Guelich's analyses throughout reveals a mind that is thoroughly preconditions by the negative presuppositions of historical criticism.

Mounce serves as another example of this tendency to dehistoricize the gospel tradition. He argues, "We are not to think of the Sermon on the Mount as a single discourse given by Jesus at one particular time. Undoubtedly, there was a primitive and actual sermon, but it has been enlarged significantly by Matthew."336 Thus, for Mounce, what appears in Matthew 5-7 is not what actually took place as presented in Matthew. The Sermon is a creation or fabrication ("enlarged significantly") of Matthew where words and sayings are placed onto the lips of Jesus that he did not speak on the occasion presented.

He cites several reasons as the basis for his postulating a synthetic creation known as the "Sermon on the Mount:" 1) "As a master teacher Jesus would not expect his listeners to be able to absorb this much ethical instruction at one time." "Even if Jesus cold have delivered the entire Sermon at one sitting, that would have been pedagogically unsound and psychologically unwise." 2) "Certain sections appear disconnected from what precedes and follows (e.g. 5:31, 32; 7:7-11);" 3)

---

333 Guelich, The Sermon on the Mount, 58-59.

334 Guelich, The Sermon on the Mount, 58-59.

335 Guelich, The Sermon on the Mount, 58-59.

336 Robert H. Mounce, Matthew, vol. 1 in the New International Biblical Commentary. Edited by W. Ward Gasque (Peabody, MA.: Hendrickson, 1991), 36.

"More importantly" . . . "thirty-four of the verses found in Matthew's sermon (which totals 107 verses) are not found in Luke's record of the event (Luke 6:20-49)."[337]

Mounce's first reason has no basis in reality, for, unlike modern teaching techniques, Jewish teachers of Jesus's time stressed content and memorization.[338] Moreover, Jesus addressed the Sermon primarily to his disciples, so content would naturally be expected (5:1); both Mounce's first and second reason completely ignore the beginning and concluding formulas (5:1; 7:28-29 cf. 11:113:53:19:1) that indicate not only authenticity but one single occasion. Matthew gives no clues in the immediate context that this was not what Jesus spoke on one occasion so that Matthew's readers would naturally have understood the Sermon as delivered on one historical occasion. Mounce's third reason assumes that Jesus spoke these sayings only once and did not consider that as an itinerant preacher Jesus may well have uttered these sayings on more than one occasion, and this would account for the scattering of sayings in Luke (e.g. Luke 12:22-31 cf. Matthew 6:25-34).

Hagner appears to echo an assessment somewhat like that of Bultmann regarding the negative portrayal of the Pharisees in the gospel tradition, especially Matthew 23:13-39. While Bultmann argues that "the schematic presentation according to which Pharisees and scribes are from the outset the sworn enemies of Jesus is certainly unhistorical," Hagner comments,

> Taken at face value Matthew 23:13-39 represents anything but an attractive picture of the Pharisees. Jesus accused them of hypocrisy and pretentiousness, and pronounced upon them a succession of woes (seven in all) culminating in the terrible climactic exclamation: 'You serpents, you brood of vipers, how are you to escape being sentenced to hell?' (23:33). It is a tragedy that from this ch. in Matthew the word 'Pharisee' has come to mean popularly a self-righteous, hypocritical pig. Unfortunately, not even Christian scholarship was able over the centuries to rid itself of an unfair bias against the Pharisees.[339]

Hagner relates that much of this negative assessment stems partly from anti-Semitism and especially from neglecting rabbinic literature, and only by considering the rabbinic literature can a balanced picture of the Pharisees be developed ("it will do not good to shut the eyes to the positive qualities of Pharisaism as revealed in the rabbinic literature").[340] Wyatt goes so far as to propose that "studies have demonstrated that an accurate portrayal of the Pharisees can be attained only by a comparison of the three major sources."[341]

---

[337] Mounce, Matthew, 36; S.v. "Sermon on the Mount," by R.H. Mounce, International Standard Bible Encyclopedia, vol. 3, 411-416.

[338] For example, Gerhardsson, The Origins of the Gospel Traditions, 15-24, 67-77.

[339] S.v. "Pharisees" by Donald Hagner, in the Zondervan Pictorial Encyclopedia of the Bible. Edited by Merrill C. Tenney, et. al. (Grand Rapids: Zondervan, 1975), 5:750 cf. Bultmann, Form Criticism, Two Essays on New Testament Research, 35.

[340] Hagner, "Pharisees," 750.

[341] S.v. "Pharisees," by R. J. Wyatt in The International Standard Bible Encyclopedia. Fully Revised. Geoffrey W. Bromiley, gen. ed. (Grand Rapids: Eerdmans, 1986), 3:823

Westerholm concurs with this thinking. He argues, "Gospel texts depicting certain Pharisees, when detached from their historical context and seen as portraying Jewish piety as a whole, have prevented Christians from arriving at a sympathetic understanding of Judaism. The concern of much contemporary scholarship to portray Judaism (and Pharisaism) in its own terms represents an important corrective." According to Westerholm, this negativity in Matthew owes its existence to a hypothetical Sitz im Leben that assumes some type of tension between Matthew's community and Jews: "Matthew's community, which includes both Jewish and Gentile Christians, clearly lives in an environment with a noticeable Jewish presence. Relations are tense, and the Matthean community perceives itself to be the object of persecution (cf. 5:10-12; 10:17-18; 23:34)."[342] One is left wondering whether Matthew's portrayal is actually reflecting Jesus's historical situation and true condition of the Pharisees or whether the evangelist Matthew has a hidden agenda and selectively distorts the "true" picture of the Pharisees in reaction to some hypothetical situation of persecution because of Pharisaical dominance. According to Westerholm's logic, the latter is the real case and responsible for this distortion of an accurate portrait of the Pharisees.

Yet, contrary to this kind of thinking, surely one must consider Jesus's (and the Scripture's) own portrayal of the spiritual condition of the Pharisees in Matthew as the true and consistently accurate assessment since he knew the hearts of men (cf. John 2:24; Matt. 5:20) and the disciples, under inspiration of the Holy Spirit, were conveying that correct, historical assessment rather than rabbinical literature or Josephus.

An evangelical form critic, Bock, contends, "In the hands of a skilled exegete who uses the tools of interpretation in a way that fits what they are capable of, Form Criticism can be a fruitful aid to understanding and to exposition."[343] Bock appears to favor Klaus Berger's form-critical approach,[344] but he admits "This surgery on Form Criticism probably strikes some as no longer being Form Criticism, but what it represents is a slimmed down version that allows the tool to do what it does best, which is to describe."[345] This admission is telling. Assuming, for the sake of argument, that Berger's approach merely describes without reaching a negative conclusion regarding historicity, labeling this version as "form criticism" supplies an aberrant definition and understanding of form criticism both presuppositionally and historically. Moreover, if the role of form criticism is "to describe" then it is entirely

---

[342] S.v. "Pharisees," in the Dictionary of the Gospel and Jesus. Edited by Joel B. Green, Scot McKnight and I. Howard Marshall (Downers Grove, IL.: InterVarsity, 1992), 613.

[343] Darrell L. Bock, "Form Criticism," in New Testament Criticism and Interpretation. Edited by David A. Black and David S. Dockery (Grand Rapids: Zondervan, 1991), 192.

[344] Bock relates concerning Berger, "Many strengths are seen here. There is an absence of traditional historical speculation. The account is related in terms of form to other similar texts. There is a willingness to recognize mixed types. He prioritizes the parts to each other. He recognized the problem with the title miracle story,' though there may be an overreaction here. There is much here to work with in terms of exegesis." See Bock, "Form Criticism," in New Testament Criticism and Interpretation, 191 cf. Berger, Formgeschichte des Neuen Testaments, 366.

[345] Bock, "Form Criticism, in New Testament Criticism and Interpretation, 187.

unnecessary.[346] One must also remember the words of Bultmann, " I am entirely in agreement with M. Dibelius when he maintains that form-criticism is not simply an exercise in aesthetics nor yet simply a process of description or classification; that is to say, it does not consist of identifying the individual units of the tradition according to their aesthetics or other characteristics and placing them in their various categories. It is much rather 'to discover the origin and the history of the particular units and thereby to throw some light on the history of the tradition before it took literary form.'"[347] Form criticism by its origin and design was intended to do more than merely describe. Bock supplies an aberrant definition that those who originated and designed the practiced would most likely not accept and which is foreign to the historical and presuppositional development. From the outset, Bultmann, Dibelius, and others who originated the discipline, declared that form criticism involves much more than classification but also makes inherent judgments on historicity, for it views the gospels as the product of the Christian community rather than eyewitness accounts by the apostles whose names they bear. Evangelicals must not enervate terminology and definition as a pretext for demonstrating "scholarly" involvement in historical-critical disciplines (e.g. a text without a context is a pretext) in attempting to invite broad-based appeal.

Since the Reformation, the grammatico-historical hermeneutic, in the hands of a skillful exegete, has successfully supplied genre descriptions without the negative conclusions in terms of historicity and the miraculous than has form-critical analysis. Only the grammatico-historical method supplies the necessary checks and balances against the predilections of form criticism to eisegete rather than exegete the text. Moreover, the grammatico-historical hermeneutic operates from the presupposition of the inerrancy of Scripture, while form criticism does not.

In contradistinction to Bock, Grant correctly and honestly contends that the negative evaluations of form criticism concerning historicity is integral to the discipline and must not be separated:

> It was maintained . . . that form criticism had nothing to do with the historicity of events whose purported records had been handed down orally, but only with the outward form of the tradition; but this was an impossible view. All literary criticism of the New Testament is ultimately historical criticism.[348]

This conclusion is more intellectually honest with its assessment of historical-critical disciplines and is confirmed by the high incidence of the negation of historicity of the tradition by those evangelicals who are linked to the more conservative evangelical camp and yet practice historical-critical methods.

---

[346] Hooker notes: "First, and most obviously, it is a literary tool. It tells us about the form of the material; it examines the shape of a piece of tradition and classifies it. This may be interesting to those who like doing that sort of thing, but I do not think it is particularly illuminating to be told that a miracle story is a miracle story, or that a paradigm is a paradigm—or an apophthegm—nor even that such stories take on certain shapes; one can learn that by watching TV commercials." Hooker, "On Using the Wrong Tool," 571.

[347] Bultmann, The History of the Synoptic Tradition, 3-4.

[348] Frederick C. Grant, The Earliest Gospel (New York: Abingdon, 1943), 41.

Bock goes on to assert that "As long as one does not deny that the origins of the tradition go back to the participants, this search for the *Sitz im Leben* in the church need not be a problem and in fact can help show the way to methods one might use to teach the account today."[349] This statement ignores the subjective nature of determining some alleged Sitz im Leben beyond that of the historical situation of Jesus. It allows the imagination of the interpreter to roam with few checks and balances. Importantly, the interpreter has no actual way of determining the sitz in Leben in the church beyond acute speculation that has no place in exegesis. The aim of the Gospel writers is to write a Gospel about Jesus, not a church addressing some esoteric problem that few readers of the Gospel could even begin to identify or decode. The early church was interested in the historical Jesus and would naturally want to know what he taught and why. No evidence exists for any hypothesized Christian community and its alleged Sitz im Leben(s) apart from the gospels themselves. Unchecked imagination drives the engine of the hypothesized community situation.

Hooker, although somewhat favorable to form analysis, correctly identifies the subjective nature of determining a *Sitz im Leben* in the church,

> We have no independent knowledge of the groups which formed the pericopes which we are discussing, and we can only deduce the needs and interests of the community which shaped the material from the material itself. The *Sitz im Leben* to which a pericope is assigned—often with great confidence—is only a hypothesis, and sometimes one feels that the hypotheses demonstrate an excessive endowment of imaginative ability on the part of those who put them forward . . . whether or not the early Church was adept at thinking up stories about Jesus to fit Church situations, the form-critics are certainly adept at thinking up Church situations to fit the stories of Jesus.[350]

The "life-situation" (or, Sitz im Leben) proposed for isolated units of tradition centers in pure speculation. The goal of sound hermeneutics must be to avoid subjectivity as much as possible not to add layers of additional speculation. Sound exegesis demands the maintenance of objectivity on the part of the interpreter and the suppressing of speculative imagination regarding an assumed "*Sitz im Leben* in the church." Only the grammatico-historical hermeneutic supplies the time tested and necessary checks and balances to avoid eisegesis. Certainly form criticism has demonstrated the exact opposite. Form criticism, whose very nature centers in a speculative, subjective, and questionable hermeneutic hypothesis should not be labeled as "a fruitful aid to understanding and to exposition." Form criticism, regardless of whatever "modified" form is pursued, is inherently inclined to assume without adequate proof that the gospel material owed its present shape to practical needs of the Christian community. Furthermore, the form-critical tendency to dehistoricize or discount the Gospel narratives centers in assuming some sort of dichotomy between the post-Easter and Pre-Easter periods based upon

---

[349] Bock, "Form Criticism, in New Testament Criticism and Interpretation, 187.

[350] Hooker, "On Using the Wrong Tool," 572.

hypothesizing separate Sitz im Lebens for these two periods. Evangelicals continue to court hermeneutical disaster by embracing form-critical directions.

Contrary to Bock's assertions, form criticism is also hermeneutically misguided. Inspiration and inerrancy extends to the written text not the period behind the gospel. Form criticism is not necessary to discover what Jesus taught, nor is form criticism necessary to understand the gospels adequately. The Gospels are not reinterpretations of the life of Christ to fit the historical situation of some later Christian community. Most importantly, the grammatico-historical hermeneutic recognizes only one *Sitz im Leben* as legitimate: that of the earthly life of Jesus as presented in the Gospels. Evangelicals must also recognize the gospels for what they are: apostolic eyewitness (or acquaintances of eyewitnesses) reporting of what actually took place. To go beyond this invites hermeneutical disaster.

This tendency toward hermeneutical disaster is seen in Bock's proposal that Matthew 13 and Mark 4 are most likely anthologies or collections of sayings. To Bock, these See Thomas, page 21 and Bock, p. 718, 742-743.

The evangelical concern for multiple Sitz im Lebens extends even to preaching. According to Greidanus, one needs to remember two horizons in preaching: that of the historical Jesus and that of the evangelist. Moreover, one should preach mainly from the horizon of the evangelist, not that of Jesus. Greidanus argues,

> Many preachers almost automatically opt for the horizon of the historical Jesus, preaching sermons on Jesus calling his disciples, Jesus healing the sick, Jesus challenging the Pharisees, etc. and applying the message from that original horizon to the church today. The question may be raised, however, if this aproach does full justice to the written text . . . . The Gospels, however, are not transparent windowpanes but distinctly colored presentations of the historical Jesus. To look right through the written text to Jesus' historical horizon is to miss the kerygmatic point made by the Gospel writer in a later horizon.[351]

Greidanus continues, "Which horizon has priority, that of the historical Jesus or that of the Gospel writer? Although the horizon of Jesus is chronologically prior, one learns about the historical Jesus only through the later Gospel writer. Hence, one's interpretation needs to begin with the horizon of the Gospel writer."[352] Thus, the superimposition of acute subjectivity of some assumed Sitz im Leben of the evangelist or his community becomes the starting point for teaching and proclaiming the Scripture. This position renders the historical situation of Jesus as secondary and the superimposition of the creative imagination of the interpreter as a primary starting point in the understanding of the meaning of Scripture. Consequently, eisegesis reigns in the interpretation of Scripture rather than a proper exegesis that must originate from the historical situation of Jesus as contained in the Gospels.

---

[351] S.v. "Preaching from the Gospels" by S. Greidanus, in the Dictionary of the Gospels and Jesus. Edited by Joel B. Green, Scot McKnight and I. Howard Marshall (Downers Grove, IL.: InterVarsity, 1992), 625.

[352] S. Greidanus, "Preaching from the Gospels," 625.

Catchpole, in New Testament Interpretation, advocates the use of tradition critical principles. Catchpole asserts, "the gospel tradition itself compels us to engage in tradition-historical inquiry." He goes on, "we can hardly avoid attributing to the later post-Easter stage both the redaction of material and, on occasion, its creation."[353]   Arguing from a tradition-historical basis, Catchpole asserts that Matthew 18:17 could not have been spoken by Jesus. He contends:

> This saying has in mind a disciplinary purification of the community, which is somewhat discordant with the message of the two parables of the two parables of the wheat and the tares (Mt. 13:24-30), and the dragnet (Matt. 13:47f.). Moreover, the saying presupposes an audience which is Jewish, and which also deprecates and excludes Gentiles and tax collectors. This seems most unlike the historical Jesus. The exclusion of Gentiles was hardly his approach: quite the contrary, he announced in word (18:11ff.) and action (Mk. 11:15-17) their acceptance and continually held them up as those whose example the Jews should follow in responding to the appeal or word of God (Lk. 7:9; 10:12-14; 11:31f.). And what applies to the Gentiles applies even more forcefully to the tax collectors. It was their inclusion, their joyful participation in his fellowship meals, their genuine repentance, which Jesus was prepared to defend with vigour and in the teeth of scathing criticism (Lk. 7:34; 15:1ff.; Mark 2:15-17).[354]

In light of this logic, he concludes, "So it appears to be unlikely that Matthew 18:17 is authentic; indeed, it seems to represent a later acceptance of attitudes which Jesus himself had resisted."[355] Yet, Catchpole's conclusion is not based on any convincing evidence but what he subjectively perceives to be an inconsistency in the Gospel at this point. Catchpole basis his argument not upon objective criteria, but only a subjective opinion (perhaps a better word is "whim") that it "seems" like Matthew 18:17 does not belong here or that such an action "seems most unlike the historical Jesus." It allows great subjective bias to determine what is authentic and what is not. Therein lies the danger of picking and choosing what the interpreter deems is authentic from what is not.

On the contrary, a very cogent case can be made that the overall contextual outworking of Matthew reveals that Matthew, the Jewish tax collector, and eyewitness of these events, places great emphasis on the primacy of Jesus's mission to the Jews. The focus of Matthew is upon the primacy of the offer of the kingdom to the Jews (Matt. 4:17, 23) that was promised in the Old Testament (Is. 42:1-3). Jesus warns his disciples not to go to the Gentiles or Samaritans in proclaiming the message of the kingdom (10:5-6). In 15:24, Jesus states to the Canaanite woman "I was sent only to the lost sheep of the house of Israel" yet still heals her son due to her expression of faith. This stress is consistent with the Old Testament promises that Messiah would first offer salvation to Israel and also be a light to the Gentiles (Is. 42:5-9; 61:1-3 cf. John 4:22). Paul also stressed the primacy of the Jews role in

---

[353] Catchpole, "Tradition History," in New Testament Interpretation, 168.

[354] Catchpole, "Tradition History," in New Testament Interpretation, 167-168.

[355] Catchpole, "Tradition History," in New Testament Interpretation, 168.

salvation and first hearing the message of the Gospel (Rom. 1:16; 2:9-10) and such a conviction governed his own early missionary efforts (Acts 13:5, 44-48; 14:1-2).

Furthermore, the focus of 18:17 is not so much upon deprecating Gentiles and tax-gatherers as it centers on the prevailing Jewish attitudes toward such groups in terms of exclusion. Jesus's point is that in the same way that Jews exclude Gentiles and tax-collectors, so should the church (or, assembly) treat the sinning members who do not repent. The focus of the comparison is upon the manner of exclusion not deprecation.

If such a statement in Matthew 18:17 ("let him be to you as a Gentile and a tax-gatherer") were produced by the post-Easter church, then would not statements centering on the universal ministry of Jesus to the Gentiles be placed more likely onto the lips of Jesus by the post-Easter Church than statements centering in ministry exclusive to Jews? That this and other sayings like it were preserved is a manifest testimony to the authenticity of the tradition rather than its inauthenticity. For conservative evangelicals, the best way to proceed is to operate solely on the basis of the authenticity of the saying and allow the text to speak for itself.

Catchpole also doubts the authenticity of Matthew 23:2-3. He argues that "such a saying undergirds Pharisaic traditional teaching with Mosaic authority and accepts Moses as the final court of appeal . . . . But this historic Jesus does not seem to have adopted so conservative an attitude to either tradition or law." Catchpole concludes regarding these verses, "we would have to ask whether an alternative post-Easter setting is available for Matthew 23-2f. In view of the Pharisaic membership and theological influence within the church, which is attested in Acts 15:5, 21:10 (cf. Gal. 2:4f., 12), the answer might not be hard to reach."[356] For Catchpole, as well as the radical form and tradition critics sighted in this article, the Christian community attributed words and sayings to Jesus that he did not say, and a distinction must be drawn between what the historical Jesus said and did and the post-Easter activity of the early church that attributed words and deed to Jesus that he did not really say.

In addition, Catchpole dismisses the idea that Jesus spoke Matthew 11:19. Instead, "the form of Matthew 11:19 is the product of the evangelists intervention." Relying heavily on the two-Gospel hypothesis, he dismisses sayings in Matthew that equate Jesus with "wisdom" because "Q and Luke are witnesses to the existence of a christology which does not go beyond the view that Jesus is a messenger of Wisdom." Instead, sayings of Jesus where he is equated with wisdom is a later product of the early church and "Matthew's community." In terms of the gospel tradition developments, Catchpole thinks in evolutionary terms: "we have to learn to live with a greater degree of raggedness at the edges and a less neat evolutionary process than would emerge if we envisaged a straight and consecutive development from Jesus to the Aramaic-speaking and Hellenistic Jewish-Christian outlooks and ultimately to the Gentile Christian position." For Catchpole, this evolutionary development produced "varied" and competing theologies within the Christian

---

[356] Catchpole, "Tradition History," in New Testament Interpretation, 168.

community.[357]   He also affirms the basic distinction between the form-critical concept of <u>historie</u> and <u>geschichte</u>:

> The gospels do belong to Jesus and also to the churches. For Jesus this means that he is seen as not merely *historisch*, a figure of the past, but also one whom we can see within the developing tradition as truly *geschichtlich*, that is, a person whose relevance is explored and exploited ever and again in places far removed from Galilee and Jerusalem and in times long after A.D. 30.[358]

Osborne also supports "a positive reappraisal of criteria for studying development tradition." He argues that "criteria should build on a positive foundation and seek to authenticate rather than disprove genuineness."[359] Once again, Osborne tries to reform principles that <u>inherently</u> make the tradition suspect no matter how one attempts reforms them. Ultimately the question centers in this: to whom is he attempting to demonstrate authenticity? If he attempts to demonstrate authenticity to a group (historical critics) that ultimately do not want to accept his <u>a priori</u> assumption of the genuineness of the tradition, then no matter how much he attempts to reform tradition critical principles, such critics will not be moved in the slightest to accept his conclusions. The massive shift in biblical scholarship as a whole (apart from evangelicals) has been toward inherent suspicion of the tradition. No amount of attempted "positive" spin of these inherently negative principles will carry weight with the vast majority. If he is attempting to demonstrate the authenticity of the tradition to those evangelicals already inclined to accept the tradition as genuine, then at best, all that Osborne's tradition-critical principles might offer is a tenuous possibility that the tradition might be from Jesus. Even Osborne admits that his criteria "can do no more than show probability" and are "so tentative." He can only decry the fact that this conclusion is "unwarranted pessimism."[360] Yet, one sees little value in such tentative judgments through such subjective principles. Such pessimism regarding Osborne's principles, however, actually centers not so much in pessimism but on a sober understanding of the true nature of these tradition-critical principles as presuppositionally and historically developed. Osborne's concludes,

> [T]here is no reason to ignore or repudiate *Traditionsgeschichte* as a positive tool for investigating the life and unfolding theology of the early Church. When he controls the negative dangers and wield the tool with honesty and sensitivity, the results will magnify the Word of God and continue the exciting discovery of ultimate truth in our time.[361]

However, even Osborne himself has not been able to control the "negative dangers" inherent in historical-critical methods, for at one time he advocated that Matthew had expanded the wording of the Great Commission: "it seems most likely

---

[357] Catchpole, "Tradition History," in <u>New Testament Interpretation</u>, 170.

[358] Catchpole, "Tradition History," in <u>New Testament Interpretation</u>, 178.

[359] Grant R. Osborne, "The Evangelical and Traditionsgeschichte," <u>Journal of the Evangelical Theological Society</u> 21 (June 1978): 122.

[360] Osborne, "The Evangelical and Traditionsgeschichte," 126.

[361] Osborne, "The Evangelical and Traditionsgeschichte," 130.

that at some point the tradition or Matthew expanded an original monadic formula."[362] Thus, for Osborne, Jesus did not speak the Great Commission as it appears in Matthew's Gospel. Jesus originally told the disciples to baptize in the name of the Father but that monadic stipulation was expanded into the "triadic baptismal formula of Matt 28:19" in order to "interpret the true meaning of Jesus' message for his own day . . . . However, we can know that Matthew has faithfully reproduced the intent and meaning of what Jesus said.[363] "Due to "widespread dissatisfaction," Osborne later attempted to revise his explanation.[364]

Osborne also appears to think in evolutionary terms in the development of the gospel.

Carson, Moo, and Morris, in a section entitled, "*the Evolution of the Synoptic Gospels*," discuss form criticism.[365] They decry the work of Bultmann and Dibelius for negating the historicity of the Gospels and assert that "Radical historical judgements . . . are not intrinsic to form criticism" and "form criticism entails no a priori judgment about the historicity of the material that it analyzes." Yet, as this article has shown, the very the presuppositions and history that led to the tenets of form criticism center in virulent antisupernaturalism (e.g. K. L. Schmidt's denegration of the chronological and geographical framework led to the hypothesizing of individual pericopes). The development form criticism was not possible without such factors. To say that form criticism entails no a priori judgment about historicity either ignores form criticism's history or attempts to supply an aberrant understanding to the term at the very least ("defined narrowly"). As has been demonstrated in this article, even evangelical from critics make such a prior judgment about historicity. Carson himself supplies another example of the tendency of evangelicals to dehistoricize the gospels accounts. In the pericope of the commissioning of the twelve (Matt. 10:5-42 //, reflecting Wenham's position, he argues, "it is possible that some sayings of Jesus, repeated by him often and on diverse occasions, were jotted down in a sort of amalgam form encapsulating their substance and then used by the evangelists in different contexts and adapted accordingly." For Carson, the door is now open to assume that what appears in the Gospels may not be what actually was, and in the case of the commissioning of the twelve in Matthew 10, the sermon may have come from a variety of sources (i.e. "Q") rather than on one historical occasion.[366]

In addition, Carson, Moo, and Morris accept several key evolutionary-driven assumptions, including the concept of "small units" of gospel material circulating

---

[362] Grant R. Osborne, "Redaction Criticism and the Great Commission: A Case Study Toward A Biblical Understanding of Inerrancy," Journal of the Evangelical Theological Society 19 (Spring 1976): 80.

[363] Osborne, "Redaction Criticism and the Great Commission, 80, 85.

[364] Grant R. Osborne, "The Evangelical and Redaction Criticism: Critique and Methodology," Journal of the Evangelical Theological Society 22 (December 1979): 311.

[365] See D. A. Carson, Douglas J. Moo, and Leon Morris, An Introduction to the New Testament (Grand Rapids: Zondervan, 1992), 20-25; D. A. Carson, "Matthew, vol. 8 in Expositor's Bible Commentary (Grand Rapids: Zondervan, 1984), 16.

[366] Carson, "Matthew," Expositor's Bible Commentary, 241-243; David Wenham, "The 'Q' Tradition Behind Matthew X," New Testament Studies

orally in the Christian community and "the two-source hypothesis" as "the best overall explanation for the relationship among the Synoptic Gospels."[367]

CONCLUSION

Several conclusions ensue from this discussion: First, the practice of form and tradition criticism must be considered in light of their historical and presuppositional developments. Form and tradition criticism are no more valid than the presuppositional and historical foundations that led to their development. If the foundations of a methodology are tenuous, then so is any practice of that methodology. The presuppositions and history of form and tradition criticism lead to the obvious conclusion that a radical and virulent antisupernaturalism along with evolutionary dogma led to their development

Second, evangelicals who attempt to practice "modified" versions of these disciplines either must attempt to ignore the presuppositional and historical impetuses that produced fundamental assumptions or supply an aberrant definition of the practice. In either case, the high failure rate of evangelicals to avoid the negative presuppositions of these disciples decisively demonstrates that these negative presuppositions are wedded to the practice and cannot be separated.

Third, since the gospels were written by apostles and eyewitnesses, they reflect an eyewitness account of what happened, i.e. only one Sitz im Leben truly exists– that of the period of the earthly life, death, and resurrection of the Messiah. Moreover, the Holy Spirit supernaturally guided and aided the formation of the gospel records (John 14:26; 16:13). The practice of these disciplines by evangelicals completely ignores and impugns this work of the Holy Spirit by positing errors and outright falsehoods in the gospels. Although the Gospels convey theology and are selective not exhaustive (John 21:30), this factor does not militate against the fact they are accurate historical and biographical works of Jesus life.

Fourth, since the Reformation (1517), the grammatico-historical hermeneutic has been the time-proven safeguard in hermeneutics that actively downplays subjectivity, and, instead, emphasizes objectivity in interpreting the written documents plainly and normally, according to the rules of grammar and the facts of history. Evangelicals who depart from this foundational hermeneutic and practice form and tradition criticism are courting hermeneutical disaster. Inspiration and inerrancy extend to the documents themselves, not to any hypothesized oral period or sources behind the gospels. The grammatico-historical hermeneutic alone is capable of identifying all literary genres without the negative presuppositions of form and tradition criticism. Any one of these four factors alone are entirely sufficient reasons for rejecting form and tradition criticism.

Sadly, in this evangelical dialogue with liberals and their methodologies, the liberals have not changed their essential practice. Evangelicals are the ones who have demonstrated such a willingness to change through compromise with

---

[367] Of course, a possible reply could be that the term "evolution" merely means development. However, the use of this term and the adoption of evolutionary principles clearly shows how saturated evangelicals have become to evolutionary concepts.

106

dangerous hermeneutical methodologies. They have done all of the changes to the detriment of the Word. The price necessary to dialogue is not worth the cost to the Word. The time has come to expose these hypotheses as tenuous and philosophically-motivated agendas rather than their masquerade as objective purveyors of truth. An iron to all of this is that evangelicals are using principles inherently hostile to the Word to "confirm" the authenticity of the Scripture; principles that cannot possibly lead to any form of certainty regarding the gospels; principles that were inherently designed not to lead to any form of objectivity. How then may they possibly be used as effective weapons against the liberal charge of non-historicity especially since they are being used for purposes that they were not intended?

The liberal theological world at large has squeezed evangelicals into its mold in the practice of form and tradition criticism. This sad situation has resulted from an incessant desire by some evangelicals to "dialogue" with their liberal counterparts in hopes of demonstrating "scholarship" and perhaps also to obtain a voice of influence or recognition in the liberal camp. While a host of evangelicals may be sighted as to the adverse influence of form and redaction, few, if any, liberals have been influenced by evangelicals to adopt a more conservative stance in this attempt at dialogue. Sadly, in the evangelical drive to keep up with the "theological Jonses," evangelicals are the ones who have adversely changed not their liberal counterparts. As a result, evangelicals, as well as liberals now, impugn the integrity and authority of Scripture through the practice of these methodologies.

Robert Yarbrough, in an article entitled "Evangelical Theology in Germany," has catalogued an interesting development: a significant trend ("of considerable moment") in current German scholarship from "a dissenting voice, small but hardly still" is toward abandoning historical-critical methods as bankrupt methodologies. They call "for spiritual renewal and biblical fidelity in a land which has done much to undermine, or at least radically redefine, both of these in recent generations."[368] According to Maier, historical-criticism "has arrived at the end of a blind alley."[369]

The evangelical drive to keep up with the "theological Jones" and dialogue with current methodologies should perhaps catch up to this trend: rejection of historical-critical methods. Only in this way would they fulfill their desire of being truly on the cutting edge of scholarship. Evangelicals dance on the edge of hermeneutical and, as a result, theological disaster, with historical-critical methods such as form and tradition criticism, for they have pushed the Scriptures over the dangling precipice that is historical criticism.

---

[368] Robert W. Yarbrough, "Evangelical Theology in Germany," in Evangelical Quarterly LXV (October 1993): 329, 353 cf. Gerhard Maier, The End of the Historical-Critical Method. Translated by Edwin W. Leverenz and Rudolf F. Norden (St. Louis: Concordia, 1977): 8-10; 11-92.

[369] Maier, The End of the Historical-Critical Method, 49.

CHAPTER 4 Historical Criticism

F. David Farnell

How Heterodoxy Becomes Orthodox Through Psychological Operations, i.e. how heresy infiltrates God's People

Introduction

What is the true nature of the historical-critical method of liberal biblical scholars that has been so whole-heartedly adopted by critical, evangelical scholars? How can one place its true nature on a practical level of understanding for the average reader of the Scriptures? How should the layperson or serious Bible student understand the impact of historical criticism on their understanding of Scripture? These questions go to the very heart of understanding historical criticism in its impact, both ideological and psychological, on the Bible interpreter when it is applied to the exegesis of the biblical text. Indeed, few exegetes understand this very important principle that is involved in historical criticism. Historical Criticism is the gold-standard for "magic" used by liberal and evangelical critical scholars to make the biblical text conform to modernistic, popular fads that now rule the biblical scholarly world. Indeed, true magic does exist, and it is found in historical criticism!

In its essential nature, historical criticism is a psychological operation that is conducted on the mind to control thinking and/or behavior. Psychological operation may be defined as planned operations to convey selected information and indicators to audiences in order to influence their emotions, motives, objective reasoning, and ultimately the behavior of groups, and individuals. Its aim is to control people's thinking in a desired way for a desired outcome. Integral to perception management, psychological operations are designed to induce or reinforce attitudes and behavior favorable to the originator's objectives.

The British were one of the first major military powers to use psychological warfare in both World Wars in a very scientific manner through, although many of the principles used go back to ancient times. The British Tavistock Institute of Human Relations (TIHR) may be considered the most prominent of such endeavors.[370] Indeed, this institute may be considered the leading center for manipulating belief and behavior. They have perfected the science of manipulating minds.

A central concept of any psychological operation is *to use accepted terms but to change their meaning to one that is desired by someone conducting the operation. The essence of a psychological operation is to confuse meaning of words and infiltrate the mind with conflicting concepts* to change one's thinking toward a desired goal of those who are conducting the operation. It uses misleading language to manipulate any person to produce in them a desired outcome. Each word claims

---

[370] http://www.tavinstitute.org/ (accessed on 4/22/2014).

to be something that in reality it is not or at least not to be understood in its original, tradition sense. It creates confusion in the person regarding the original intent of the term so as to establish a desired, changed definition or understanding, i.e. infiltrate the mind with conflicting concepts so as to produce the desired change in thinking.

A prominent example of this change in definitions is found in the book *1984*, written in 1949 by famed British writer George Orwell (whose real name was Eric Arthur Blair), the writer warned of the manipulation of words and their meanings as an important key to controlling what people think about someone or something. He called "newspeak" defined by Merriam-Webster as a noun, often capitalized, for propagandistic language marked by euphemism, circumlocution, and the inversion of customary meanings. Newspeak was a language "designed to diminish the range of thought," in the novel 1984. Words were imbued with meaning in "Newspeak" that were totally emptied of their original meaning to serve the purposes of those in control. Also employed is "doublethink," another term that Orwell popularized through his work, although he did not use the terms. "Doublethink" used terms that could be used in conflicting ways so language that deliberately disguises, distorts, or reverses the meaning of words from its normative, original sense. Its goal is to confuse the meaning of words for a desired outcome.[371]

Why bring up such a subject? Because one can only truly understand the nature of historical criticism by viewing it in this manner. At its heart, historical criticism is neither "historical" or "critical" in the traditional sense of the term. It may be viewed like the popular commercial cereal "Grape Nuts." The product is neither grapes nor nuts. It is plant based instead. In a way, the term is Doublespeak and Newspeak. So also is the term "historical criticism." It does not genuinely believe Biblical revelation contains history in the sense of what actually happened in a time-space continuum. Instead, historical criticism is post-modernistic that asserts all history is by nature a subjective interpretation of surviving traces of events. Hence, Scripture does not convey what actually happened. Even when the Bible presents itself in its plain, normal sense as conveying historical information, historical criticism *a priori* rejects its history outright. It is already biased against history in any tradition sense of the term. So, it is not "historical" in the normal understanding of the term "history" or "what happened in the past."

Moreover, it is not criticism, for "criticism" for criticism, in its traditional, normative sense, refers to applying criteria to any of various methods of studying texts or documents for the purpose of dating or reconstructing them, evaluating their authenticity, analyzing their content or style. In other words, criticism to be truly "criticism" seeks an objective outcome of true understanding of any literature. Historical criticism does not seek an objective, authentic (i.e. true to the text) outcome of the biblical writings. The goal of its criticism is to change the plain, normal sense of the text to an already predetermined outcome that is acceptable to the critic's whims and/or desires. What is "acceptable" to him or her, rather than evaluating any text for what it truly is. The historical critics goal to interpret the biblical text according to the current fads of the time. Traditional meaning or

---

[371] http://orwell.ru/library/novels/1984/english/en_app (accessed on 4/22/2014).

understanding is not its goal. The goal is conformity of the text to the subjective "sensibility" of the critic.

Herein lies the "magic" of historical criticism. When the text of Scripture offends current sensibilities or perceptions, i.e. "fads" and "popular ideas" of the critics day, the biblical critic can apply historical criticism in any way desired to the text to guarantee the interpretive outcome. For instance, Genesis 1-3 presents itself as historic events in a time-space continuum as recording the creation of the universe as well as the earth. Yet, modern historical-critics, having been conditioned by current scientism override the plain, normal sense of Scripture and dismiss the account as either non-historical, figurative, or false. Such an action is hardly objective or seeking to understand the literature as the original author expressed in the text. Another instance would be found in Matthew 23 wherein Jesus excoriated the Pharisees of his day in what is now considered "politically incorrect" and shocking terms. In light of holocaustic hermeneutics, i.e. the post-World War II prevalent thinking of the day even evangelical critics are dismissive of this chapter as being historically inaccurate. Jesus' words are dismissed as not spoken by him since one might the accusation of being "anti-semitic" through acceptance of the chapter as genuine. Instead, the cause of these tensions between Jesus and the Pharisees is attributed to an alleged conflict between Matthew's assumed community and the Jews of Matthew's day in the synagogue. Indeed, Westerholm attributes these sayings in the following terms, "The Gospels' depiction of Pharisees reflect both memories from the career of Jesus and subsequent development in the Christian communities."[372] Donald Hagner similarly writes, "It is a tragedy that from this ch.in Matthew [ch. 23] that the word 'Pharisee' has come to mean popularly a self-righteous, hypocritical prig. Unfortunately, not even Christian scholarship was able over the centuries to rid itself of an unfair bias against the Pharisees."[373] R. J. Wyatt suggests that the only accurate way to understand the Pharisees is to bring in rabbinic literature's and Josephus's information about them as an equal contribution to the Gospels. Here, second temple Judaistic literature is brought into equal authority with the Gospels in determining what the Pharisees were actually like in history.[374] Apparently, the Gospels only give part of the perception in Wyatt's mind.

Interestingly, Hagner admits in another one of his works, *The Jewish Reclamation of Jesus*, that historical criticism invented by German and British scholars was used by modern Jewish interpreters to remove this bias against the Pharisees that the Gospels portrayed in Jesus' actions and of Jesus' negative attitude toward Judaism in general as indicated in the Gospels: "[t]o the extent that the conclusions of nineteenth-century critical scholarship supported Jewish claims concerning Jesus, they were gladly accepted. Jesus became the reformer of Judaism; Paul, the creator of Christianity. In short, for Jewish modern scholarship the

---

[372] For example, see S. Westerholm, "Pharisees," *Dictionary of Jesus and the Gospels*. Eds. Joel N. Green and Scot McKnight (Downers Grove, ILL: InterVarsity, 1992), 613.

[373] D. A. Hagner, "Pharisees," Zondervan Pictorial Encyclopedia of the Bible. Gen. Ed. Merill C. Tenney (Grand Rapids: Zondervan, 1975): 4:750.

[374] R. J. Wyatt, "Pharisees," NISBE. Ed. Geoffrey W. Bromiley (Grand Rapids: Eerdmans, 1986): 3:823.

modern period is best characterized as the phrase, 'the Jewish reclamation of Jesus.'"[375] How could Jesus be now seen by both modern Christian scholars as well as Jewish scholars in a more acceptable, less hostile attitude toward Judaism that is portrayed in the Gospels? Liberal application of historical-critical ideologies to erase the plain, normal sense of the Gospels. Historical criticism is what enables the Gospel portrayal of Jesus and his attitudes toward Judaism to be radically modified by the motivations of second temple Judaism as well as the New Perspective on Paul accomplished by E. P. Sanders, James D. G. Dunn, N. T. Wright, all of whom seek to make Jesus more acceptable to Jewish sensibilities, to mention only a few.[376]

Historical criticism magically makes the politically incorrect problem disappear by being dismissive of the historical accuracy of the Gospels in recording the words and deeds of Jesus. Hence, it is neither historical or critical in the traditional sense of the terms. Historical critics, liberal and evangelical, constantly use this magic of historical criticism to remove anything in the Biblical record that affronts their biases and subjective sensibilities. Should a critic dislike the creation account of Genesis 1-3, especially in light of current evolutionary fads that predominate in academic university, historical criticism can be judiciously applied to negate the plain, normal sense of the biblical creation account. The same thing goes for Job, Jonah, prophetic announcements in Isaiah, etc. Importantly, historical criticism is ideologically based in philosophies of the Enlightenment, deism, romanticism, evolution, existentialism. It is far from neutral.[377] Historical criticism is the preferred psychological operation that is employed on the biblical text to remove any plain, normal sense that would offend the sensibilities of the interpreter. This basis provides the predominant reason that liberal critics apply it so generously to the biblical text because their personal biases and sensibilities reject the obvious or plain, normative assertions or implications of the text. This also most likely explains why evangelical critical scholars so whole-heartedly embrace it since they operate in a world of academia that would reject them if these evangelical critical scholars embraced the natural sense of the text, for academia would have little patience with them, thereby risking professional reputations as scholars.[378] Historical criticism can be applied to remove anything that the interpreter finds objectionable due to subjective bias against the text, all the while the interpreter can maintain the façade of his interpretation being critically proper and having the outward appearance of "neutral" or "scientific," when, it in fact, both he/she and historical criticism is hopelessly biased before any genuine criticism of the biblical text has begun.

---

[375] Donald A. Hanger, The Jewish Reclamation of Jesus (Eugene,OR: Wipf and Stock, 1997), 71; see also 92-94.

[376] See F. David Farnell, "The Problem of Philosophy in New Testament Studies," and Searching for the Historical Jesus: The Rise of the Searches," The Rise of the Three Searches," in The Jesus Quest. Eds. Norman L. Geisler and F. David Farnell (Maitland, FL: Xulon, 2014), 86-142; 361-420.

[377] See Norman L. Geisler, "The Philosophical Roots of Modern Biblical Criticism, The Jesus Quest The Danger From Within. Eds. Norman L. Geisler and F. David Farnell (Maitland, FL: Xulon, 2014) 65-85.

[378] See F. David Farnell, "Historical Criticism vs. Grammatico-Historical Criticism: Quo Vadis Evangelicals?," The Jesus Quest, 503-520.

THE GOAL OF THE ICBI STATEMENTS ON INERRANCY AND HERMENEUTICS

Historically, the overarching goal of The ICBI Statements of on Inerrancy (1978) and Hermeneutics (1982) was to prevent this psychological operation and assault of historical criticism on the biblical text. These documents arose as hard-won victories, as well as warnings to future generations of evangelicals, from previous decades of attacks on the trustworthiness of the Bible. Significantly, these documents affirm "grammatico-historical" rather than "historical-critical" hermeneutics as employed by these critically trained evangelicals. Why? Because the authors and those who signed their affirmation to these documents knew the ruinous impact that historical-critical ideologies had upon God's Word in church history. However, these British and European critically trained evangelicals who now advocate the adoption of some form of historical-criticism have effectively annulled the ideas framed in these two hard-won documents because they have forgotten history, especially the reasons why these articles were formulated.

First, the ICBI developers knew that historical criticism dehistoricizes the plain, normal reading of the text. Article XVIII reads:

> We affirm that the text of Scripture is to be interpreted by grammatico-historical exegesis, taking account of its literary forms and devices, and that Scripture is to interpret Scripture. We deny the legitimacy of any treatment of the text or quest for sources lying behind it that leads to relativizing, dehistoricizing, or discounting its teaching, or rejecting its claims to authorship.

What is the true essence of this term "historical criticism" which arose from the days of Spinoza? It is the ingredient that is used to make the Bible say whatever the researcher wants it to say. It is the acid dissolvent that destroys the plain, normal sense of Scripture and, in turn, can make the Bible reflect any prejudice of the interpreter that is imposed on the text. When Bible "scholars" want to make the Bible say something that it does not naturally say, they apply judiciously and generous portions of historical criticism to accomplish that magic! When Bible "scholars" are a priori in conflict, either presuppositionally or subjectively, by something in the OT or NT, i.e. find it unacceptable to them for a variety of their own prejudices, it allows the scholar to remake anything in Scripture to their own liking–either by negating it entirely or manufacturing an entirely different sense or meaning for a particular portion of Scripture. It allows the Bible to be REMOLDED into something acceptable to the "critical" scholar's whims. The philosophical pedigree of historical criticism guarantees that magic of transforming the Bible into something more acceptable to the modern, critical mind. This has been most prominent in "historical Jesus" research in which historical-critical criteria are the tools that German- and British-trained critical scholars use (borrowed from Spinoza) to find a Jesus that their critical presuppositions have already decided on in order to determine how they think He must really, truly be—a Jesus they find acceptable to them. These authenticity criteria tools are the "solvent" that allows critical scholars to dissolve the canonical Gospels and the information therein in order to find a Jesus that they prefer through the genius of an *a priori* application of historical criticism. *However, no two critical scholars agree on the same list of criteria or their*

112

exact definition and nature—proof positive that great evangelical confusion exists over terminology and the practice of interpretation

In contrast, the goal of the grammatico-historical method is to find the meaning which the authors of Scripture intended to convey, and the meaning comprehended by the recipients. Special allowance/provision is made for (1) inspiration, (2) the Holy Spirit, and (3) inerrancy. It may be understood as *the study of inspired Scripture designed to discover under the guidance of the Holy Spirit the meaning of a text dictated by the principles of grammar and the facts of history.*

"Grammatico-historical" criticism, advocated by the both the Reformers as well as the signers of the ICBI statements of 1978 and 1982, allows the Bible to say what it naturally says plainly and normally without an *a priori* agenda as with historical-critical ideologies. As more recent evangelicals receive their education from schools that advocate some form of historical criticism, an unstable blending of these two approaches is occurring. Much confusion exists in current evangelical circles regarding grammatico-historical and historical-critical approaches to exegesis.[379] These two hermeneutical disciplines are distinct and must not be confused by evangelicals. In contrast to the Reformation roots of the grammatico-historical method, the historical-critical hermeneutic has its roots in deism, rationalism, and the Enlightenment. Edgar Krentz, favorable to the practice, readily admits in his *The Historical-Critical Method* that "Historical method is the child of the Enlightenment."[380] Maier, opposed to historical criticism, argued, "historical criticism over against a possible divine revelation presents an inconclusive and false counterpart which basically maintains human arbitrariness and its standards in opposition to the demands of revelation."[381]

The Magic of Genre Criticism as a Sub-Discipline of Historical Criticism

Another way that historical criticism, used especially by critical evangelical scholars, is assaulting the Scripture through genre criticism. The word "genre" is French term for "style of literature types." Very basically, two literary types exist: either that which is prose (plain, normal understanding)/to be understood in some literal sense) or that which is poetry (to be understood in some non-literal, or symbolic, figurative sense). Thus, literal or figurative. Other terms can be used, but these two basics are the dividing line in genre. Critical evangelical scholars, borrowing heavily from their critical counterparts for academic recognition and influence, often use technical terminology in genre criticism that signals their desire to dehistoricize the Gospels, such as "midrash" or "apocalyptic Judaism" genre. In 1982, Robert Gundry in his Matthew, *A Commentary on His Literary and Theological Art*, is famous for using "midrash" genre to dismiss much of the historical

---

[379] See Robert L. Thomas, "Current Hermeneutical Trends: Toward Explanation or Obfuscation?, *JETS* 39 (June 1996): 241-256.

[380] Edgar Krentz, *The Historical-Critical Method* (Philadelphia: Fortress, 1975), 55.

[381] Gerhard Maier, *The End of the Historical-Critical Method* (St. Louis, MO: Concordia Publishing House, 1974), 25.

content of Matthew 1-3. Much of the contents of these infancy narratives struck Gundry a historically objectionable or untrue, i.e. he believed that these events surrounding Jesus' life did not happen in the time-space continuum of history since they had no extra-biblical confirmation in outside historical sources other than Matthew. Gundry used the "magic" of genre to remove his bias against the infancy narratives. Here are some examples of Gundry's use of the "magic" of genre or style to dehistoricize the text of Matthew 1-3 that he found objectionable:

(1) "Clearly, Matthew treats us to history mixed with elements that cannot be called historical in a modern sense. All history writing entails more or less editing of materials. But Matthew's editing often goes beyond acceptable bounds . . . Matthew's subtractions, additions, and revisions of order and phraseology often show changes in substance; i.e., they represent developments of the dominical tradition that result in different meanings and departures from the actuality of events" (p. 623). 382

(2) "Comparison with the other gospels, especially with Mark and Luke, and examination of Matthew's style and theology show that he materially altered and embellished historical traditions and that he did so deliberately and often" (p. 639).

(3) "We have also seen that at numerous points these features exhibit such a high degree of editorial liberty that the adjectives 'midrashic' and 'haggadic' become appropriate" (p. 628). Midrash means it did not happen in history as it was presented in the Gospels.

(4) "We are not dealing with a few scattered difficulties. We are dealing with a vast network of tendentious changes" (p. 625). This means it did not happen in history as it was presented in the Gospels.

(5) "Hence, 'Jesus said' or 'Jesus did' need not always mean that in history Jesus said or did what follows, but sometimes may mean that in the account at least partly constructed by Matthew himself Jesus said or did what follows" (p. 630). This means it did not happen in history as it was presented in the Gospels.

(6) "Semantics aside, it is enough to note that the liberty Matthew takes with his sources is often comparable with the liberty taken with the OT in Jubilees, the Genesis Apocryphon, the Targums, and the Midrashim and Haggadoth in rabbinic literature" (p. 628). This means it did not happen in history as it was presented in the Gospels.

(7) "These patterns attain greatest visibility in, but are by no means limited to, a number of outright discrepancies with the other synoptics. At least they are discrepancies so long as we presume biblical writers

---

382 The list of 9–13 as well as page numbers cited are from Robert Gundry, *Matthew A Commentary on His Literary and Theological Art* (Grand Rapids: Eerdmans, 1982) as well as *A Commentary on His Handbook for A Mixed Church under Persec*ution (Grand Rapids: Eerdmans, 1994). The latter note: an updated version of the 1982 commentary.

were always intending to write history when they used the narrative mode" (p. 624).

(8). "Matthew selects them [the Magi] as his substitute for the shepherds in order to lead up to the star, which replaces the angel and heavenly host in the tradition" (p. 27). The Magi, the star and the heavenly hosts did not happen as is presented in the Gospels.

(9). "That Herod's statement consists almost entirely of Mattheanisms supports our understanding Matthew himself to be forming this episode out of the shepherd's visit, with use of collateral materials. The description of the star derives from v. 2. The shepherds' coming at night lies behind the starry journey of the magi" (p. 31).

(10). "He [Matthew] changes the sacrificial slaying of 'a pair of turtledoves or two young pigeons,' which took place at the presentation of the baby Jesus in the Temple (Luke 2:24; cf. Lev 12:6–8), into Herod's slaughtering the babies in Bethlehem (cf. As. Mos. 6:2–6" (pp. 34, 35). This means these did not happen in history as it was presented in the Gospels.

What proof did Gundry have for these assertions? None. He found these areas personally objectionable to his own subjective sense of "history," so he used the magic of genre to dismiss the biblical text. When one examines the text of Matthew, the context clearly presents these as events that happened historically in the time-space continuum. The reader of this article is highly encouraged to examine the surrounding context of Matthew 1-3. Contextual clues and markers abound in these chapters to give every impression in the plain, normal reading of the text that historical events were being related by the writer Matthew (genealogical records of births in the time-space continuum in Matthew 1:1--17; historical events of the Jewish Babylonian deportation are mentioned in Matthew 1:17; the account of Jesus' birth into human existence is recounted in Matthew 1:18-25, including engagement of Jewish couples as well as the scandal of birth out of wedlock that occurred in the culture in Matthew; historical figures are mentioned who interacted with the birth of the child, such as Herod and the Magi from the East are detailed, including the child's early childhood and flight down into the country of Egypt in Matthew 2:1-23, with many temporal markers noted such as "when Jesus was born," "days of Herod," "magi arrived from the East," "the exact time the star appeared," "after coming into the house," "they left for Egypt," "when Herod died," etc. etc. etc. No clear signals exist to the reader of the text that anything in the overall text should not be understood as non-historical. Unfortunately, this did not deter Gundry from being quite dismissive of the text historically. Why? Perhaps the text just didn't existentially "feel" somehow right to him subjectively. However, genre and historical criticism allowed him to dismiss history and appear to readers of the commentary that he had objectivity on his side. He did not.

Similarly, Craig Blomberg, used genre criticism when he found something in the text of Matthew as personally somehow objectionable, i.e. Jesus' command to Peter of the coin in the fish's mouth is not historical, it did not happen (Matt. 17:24–27). Craig Blomberg asserts in reference to the story of the coin in the fish's mouth in Matthew 17:24–27, "It is often not noticed that the so-called miracle of the fish with the coin in its mouth (Matt 17:27) is not even a narrative; it is merely a command from Jesus to go to the lake and catch such a fish. We don't even know if Peter obeyed the command. Here is a good reminder to pay careful attention to the literary form."[383] To him, this story is not literal, it is figurative. In other words, even if from the early church to the 21st century, the orthodox church understood this as an actual event that happened with Jesus and Peter, Blomberg knows the read nature of the text since he is an evangelical critical scholar who is well respected in academia. The very weight of his reputation must mean that he is correct, at least one assumes. How the reader of Matthew would discern this lack of historicity here is not made clear by Blomberg. However, his "magic" use of historical criticism obfuscates his arbitrary, selective judgment, the reader of his assertions. No substantive evidence is provided, just psychological impact Blomberg's reputation has is all that suffices for such arbitrary decisions. The reader of this article is highly encouraged to examine the context surrounding Matthew 17:24-27. The narrative in Matthew 17 is presented with historical markers, "When they came to Capernaum," "those who collected the two-drachma tax said to Peter," Jesus issues a command to go depart and fish, Jesus predicts a coin is predicted to be found. The only thing lacking is a resolution statement that says, "and Peter fished and found the coin and paid the tax." All the other events in Matthew 17, both before and after, are presented as historical developments in the life of Jesus, why should this one be different? Because they somehow subjectively impacted Blomberg negatively. He warns the reader of his assertions to pay attention to the literary form. This is good advice for Blomberg that Blomberg himself does not follow. Both before and after, the genre is relating historical events. No signal is given to the reader that this event in the midst of Matthew 17 should not be taken otherwise. It flows naturally in Matthew's relating of the events before as well as in Matthew 18. The reasonable conclusion is that Blomberg is arbitrary, capricious in his exegetical assertions, and without any true warrant or substance in his assertions in any close examination of the context of the narrative in Matthew 17. Moreover, Blomberg defended Robert Gundry's midrashic approach to the Gospels in the following terms, so part of the magic of historical criticism is the "group-think" of the psychological operation that critical evangelical scholars employ. They are a very united voice for each other, defending each other's decisions. They move as a group, and only rarely disagree with each other for academic respectability among them is a strong motivating factor against criticism:

> Is it possible, even inherently probable, that the NT writers at least in part never intended to have their miracle stories taken as historical or factual and that their original audiences probably recognized this? If this sounds like the identical reasoning that enabled Robert Gundry to adopt his midrashic interpretation of Matthew while still affirming inerrancy, that is because it is the same. The problem will not disappear simply because one author [Gundry] is dealt with *ad hominem* . . . how should evangelicals react? Dismissing the sociological view on the grounds that the NT miracles present themselves as historical gets us nowhere. So do

---

[383]Blomberg, "A Constructive Traditional Response to New Testament Criticism," 354 fn. 32

almost all the other miracle stories of antiquity. Are we to believe them all?[384]

Michael Licona, in his work *The Resurrection of Jesus: A New Historiographical Approach,*[385] used a genre based criticism known as *bios* as a means of de-historicizing parts of the Gospel (i.e. the resurrection of the saints after Jesus crucifixion in Matthew 27:51–53 is non-literal genre or apocalyptic rather than an actual historical event). Although Michael Licona's work defends Jesus' bodily resurrection, the assumption of genre hermeneutic known as apocalyptic or eschatological Jewish texts whereby Licona dismisses the historicity of Matthew 27:51-53 (and its recording of the resurrection of saints) results effectively in the complete evisceration and total negation of His strong defense of Jesus' resurrection. His logic is self-defeating for his main assertion of Jesus' resurrection.

Licona argued "*Bios* offered the ancient biographer great flexibility for rearranging material and **inventing speeches . . . and they often included legend.** Because *bios* was a flexible genre, **it is often difficult to determine where history ends and legend begins.**"[386] Licona labels it a "strange little text"[387] and terms it "special effects" that have no historical basis.[388] Apparently, his subjective bias reacted negatively to this text as a historical event. His apparent concern also rests with only Matthew as mentioning the event. He concludes that "It seems best to regard this difficult text in Matthew a poetic device added to communicate that the Son of God had died, and that impending judgment awaited Israel."[389] Hence, once again the "magic" of historical criticism and genre removes the problem for Licona. If the events in Matthew 27:51-53 are held that way, nothing—absolutely nothing—stops critics from applying a similar kind of logic to Jesus' resurrection and reject its historicity. Licona's logic here is self-defeating and undermines his entire work on defending the resurrection. Would the average reader have detected this in reading Matthew 27 as the narrative unfolds? One would hope that Licona would take the events both before and after the resurrection of the saints as historically happening in Matthew, such as Jesus' cry from the cross, the ripping of the temple veil that happened prior to the event he rejects, as well as the soldier's exclamation regarding Jesus afterward as historical. Somehow, however, the story in the middle strikes him subjectively strange, and he uses the magic of historical criticism and genre to make it more reasonable to him by dismissing the resurrection of the saints as historical. Problem solved? No. For all these events surrounding Jesus' crucifixion both before and after are connected by a series of "and," i.e. this happened, "and" this happened, "and" this happened. It is highly, highly dubious to suggest any reader of Matthew 27 would have taken this resurrection of the

---

[384] Craig L. Blomberg, "New Testament miracles and Higher Criticism: Climbing Up the Slippery Slope," *JETS* 27/4 (December 1984) 436.

[385] Michael R. Licona, *The Resurrection of Jesus, A New Historiographical Approach* (Downers Grove: InterVarsity, 2010).

[386] Ibid., 34.

[387] Ibid., 548.

[388] Ibid., 552.

[389] Ibid., 553.

saint's event as any different in "genre" than the surrounding historical events delineated to the reader.

Another example is Darrell Bock and Robert Webb. They use the "magic" of historical criticism to appear as critical scholars who defend the Gospel by assuming a distinction between the Jesus of history and the Christ of faith, a distinction made popular by radical liberalism. IF such a distinction were true, and it is NOT, then nothing in the Gospels could be trusted. Under the guise of defending the Gospel accounts, they actually accomplish the opposite, i.e. cast grave suspicion on its historical veracity. Here are some of their assertions:

(1) Jesus' resurrection "probably" happened is the best we can say about this event and others historically because evangelicals must operate under post-modernistic historiography as a premise.

My Reply: (a) If they "probably" happened, then they might not have happened! Please tell us which ones, in your "evangelical critical opinion, might not have happened or did not happen or what aspects of them did not occur; (b) probability in the mind of the beholder!; (c) What enemies or even skeptics would be convinced by such logic—please name those you won over by your "logic."

(2) The Gospels only give us the "footprints" of Jesus or the "surviving traces" of his life:

My Reply: (a) If all we have is "footprints" then what can you tell about Jesus? Not much! (b) Is the word that these "critical evangelicals" use, i.e. "surviving traces" in reference to the Gospel text a term that honors the Word of God, and in this instance, canonical Gospels? (c) Who judges what is a surviving trace and what is not? Are these more "inspired" than other elements in the Gospels?

(3) The Jesus of the Bible and the Jesus of history are not necessarily the same. This category is fully legitimate for evangelicals to assert.

My Reply: Then tell us how Jesus was different in history and in faith? Only God's Holy Spirit is capable of truly presenting a matter as to how it actually was in a time-space continuum; (b) Since when are Faith and history in conflict, unless one capitulates to alien, philosophical and unbiblical assumptions?

(4) We must search for the historical Jesus to find out how Jesus was actually in history and what he really said and did.

My reply: (a) NO WE DON'T. The Gospels tell us that; (b) This tacitly, if not very explicitly, blasphemes God's Spirit in the process of inspiration of the Gospel text.

(5) All history is interpretation. The Gospels are historical interpretations. The Gospels contain surviving traces of Jesus' life but, they have been placed into historical narratives that have been interpreted according to the writers' perspectives. In order to discover the "surviving traces" of Jesus' life, we must apply criteria of authenticity

based in critical methods to determine if the events actually happened as they are portrayed.

My Reply: The God of Scripture does not "interpret." He is the ground of all reality. Therefore, the Gospels are the objective account of Jesus' life without "spin" or bias but God's account of what really happened as well as what he reveals through special revelation.

(6) A scale of probability, possibility or not historically verifiable must be used for the 100s of Gospel events.

My reply: (a) Please produce the "critical evangelical" study Bible with various color shades to show where each one of the 100s of Gospel stories fall into their scale. The pages would mostly be white with nothing verifiable in their logic.

Conclusion of the "Magic" of Historical Criticism

Admittedly, Part of this I article has been brief. Historical Criticism is *a psychological operation designed by men to cast doubt the Word of God*. That is its very intent historically and presuppositionally. It can never lose that detrimental impact no matter how hard critical evangelical scholars try to reform or deform it.[390] Whose critical evangelical scholars form of it should we accept since they ALL disagree on its characteristics when they modify it?

A few more points needs to be said. First, conservative evangelicals like myself who hold to inerrancy, i.e. the writer of this article, believe in criticism of the Bible, but it is the kind, quality, and presuppositions of criticism that is employed that must be the central question. Please do not use the aged canard or straw man that evangelical critical scholars use that conservative evangelicals like myself don't believe in criticism of the Bible. This charge is specious.

Second, who would be convinced of the surety of the Gospels or God's Word? While giving the assertion of affirming God's Word, these evangelical critical scholars instead assault it and undermine it. I can think of no better way of undermining God's Word in the eyes of God's people than what is being perpetrated through critical evangelical scholars use of historical criticism.

Finally, perhaps most strategically, the son of Thunder, John the Apostle and an eyewitness to Jesus' life, ministry, resurrection, and ascension, gives believers a clear indication of what to think of historical criticism and its magic or any other type of criticism. John is clear that the Holy Spirit is the Witness to the truth of God's Word. The genuine impact of the Holy Spirit on a truly born-again person is an affirmation, not doubt, of God's Word as composed by the Apostles who were eyewitnesses of His majesty. 2 Peter 1:19-21.

---

[390] See F. David Farnell, "Philosophical and Theological Bent of Historical Criticism," *The Jesus Crisis*, 85-131.

John 14:26 Updated American Standard Version (UASV)

26 But the Helper,391 the Holy Spirit, whom the Father will send in my name, that one will teach you all things and bring to your remembrance all that I have said to you.

John 16:13-14 Updated American Standard Version (UASV)

13 But when that one, the Spirit of truth, comes, he will guide you into all the truth; for he will not speak from himself, but whatever he hears, he will speak; and he will declare to you the things that are to come. 14 That one will glorify me, for he will take what is mine and declare it to you.

1 John 2:19-22 Updated American Standard Version (UASV)

19 They went out from us, but they were not of us; for if they had been of us, they would have continued with us; but they went out, so that they would be revealed that they all are not of us. 20 But you have been anointed by the Holy One, and you all have knowledge. 21 I have not written to you because you do not know the truth, but because you do know it, and because no lie is of the truth. 22 Who is the liar but the one who denies that Jesus is the Christ? This is the antichrist, even the one who denies the Father and the Son.

Historical Criticism and its "magic" casts doubt on God's Word. For a genuine, born again believer, the Holy Spirit affirms God's Word. His precious Spirit does not cast doubt. Would God's Spirit be involved in such a process as critical, evangelical scholars involve themselves in historical criticism as detailed here that raises up speculation and doubt? The net result of Historical criticism is that it subtlety and not so subtly blasphemes God's Spirit and His written testimony in His Word that He inspired. I call on evangelical, critical scholars for personal, spiritual introspection of what they are sowing in the seeds of their use of historical criticism. If critical, evangelical scholars deem this statement to be "unscholarly," then this present writer affirms the Lordship of Jesus Christ over any form of pseudo-scholarship and encourages critical, evangelical scholars to seek another line of work than ministry for the Word of God, for too much damage is done within the church through advocacy of historical criticism from those professing to know the Lord and Savior, Jesus Christ.

How "Errancy" Masquerades as "Inerrancy"

As the above has expressed, psychological operations are a central force in the historical-critical method, i.e. ideology. It is neither "historical" since its assumption of pot-modernistic historiography (i.e. post-modernism) does not believe that real knowledge of history is possible, or even desirable, since only surviving traces of events remain, nor is it critical since it seeks a preconceived, a priori outcome since its focus is not upon "truth" but upon preconceived conclusions that it desires to reach. The essence of any psychological operation is to change definitions and affect the mind of those who would be the object of that operation. Such an operation

---

391 Or, *Advocate*. Or, *Comforter*. Gr., *ho ... parakletos*, masc.

has occurred especially in the area of the orthodox definition of inerrancy as defined by the Chicago Statements on Inerrancy (1978) and Hermeneutics (1982) by critically-trained neo-evangelicals who now hold sway in academia.

Such operations are vastly more effective than outright assaults on ideas and concepts. Outright assaults often, if not almost exclusively, receive immediate opposition and rejection of any opposing idea that attempts replacement. Psychological operations against current thinking are much more effective because they are (1) more subtle and careful, indirect rather than direct. To replace an idea effectively time must be taken to replace concepts without awareness of that process being realized. This is the "magic" of historical-critical ideologies. (2) Another reason is that historical-criticism, at heart, is parasitic, adaptive and pliable in its approach. That is, historical criticism's indirect assault on the biblical text is adoptive of standard, even orthodox terminology but changes those meanings elusively over time, i.e. it is in no hurry, for the goal or ends justifies the means of changing normative terminology into that which is acceptable to the preconceived notions of the interpreter.

Importantly, a subtle and gradual movement away from orthodox concepts of the integrity of the Scripture in terms of its historical accuracy and meaning is occurring among evangelicals, especially by what is now known as evangelical, critical scholars.[392] A significant portion of evangelicalism no longer adheres to the nascent beliefs of the Christian church of the plenary (complete), verbal (word for word) inspiration (God-breathed) of Scripture and its resultant concomitant inerrancy. This is not the first time that the church has drifted away from these foundations. This writer has catalogued such a drift that historically occurred in his article, "Those Who Do Not Learn From The Lessons of History: Inerrancy Under Fire." It catalogues the eerily similar drifts among Christian denominations in the early part of the 20th Century when one examines current events among critical, evangelicals scholars in the 21st Century.[393] Similar historical events that caused the former drift away from the inerrancy and inspiration of the biblical texts now are shaking the foundations of orthodox belief once again.

How Inerrancy No Longer Means What It Says

In order to understand this momentous shift that is now re-occurring in the church, especially in terms of orthodox views of inerrancy, must revisit history, for God's people so quickly forget. In 1978 and 1982, evangelicals met under the

---

[392] For examples of this dangerous drift among evangelicals, see F. David Farnell, "Part Four: Beware of 'Critical' Post-Modern History," in The Jesus Quest The Danger from Within, Eds. Norman L. Geisler and F. David Farnell (Maitland, FL: Xulon, 2014), 359-520. See also F. David Farnell, "Can We Still Trust Critical Evangelical Scholars," http://inerrantword.com/180015375/blog/180004060/220000031/Can_We_Still_Trust_Critical_Evangelical_Scholars (accessed on May 4, 2014).

[393] F. David Farnell, "Those Who Do Not Learn From the Lessons of History," defendinginerrancy.com http://defendinginerrancy.com/learn-lessons-history/ accessed on 8/29/2014) and "Can We Still Trust Critical Evangelical Scholars" (http://defendinginerrancy.com/can-still-trust-critical-evangelical-scholars/ accessed on 8/29/2014).

auspices of the International Council on Biblical Inerrancy. Its purpose was "the defense and application of the doctrine of biblical inerrancy as an essential element for the authority of Scripture and a necessity for the health of the church. It was created to counter the drift from the important doctrinal foundation by significant segments of evangelicalism and the outright denial of it by other church movements."[394] ICBI reflects a long history, stretching back to The Fundamentals written in 1915 and reflex the thinking of the vast majority of conservative, orthodox theologians well back into the 20th Century that saw so much denial toward the dehistoricizing of the plain, normal sense of Scripture. This article is strategic for this discussion of the "magic" of historical criticism since historical criticism' aim is not to understand the text in its plain, normal sense but to make it pliable to contemporary trends of scholarship, no matter what the era or time. In contrast, grammatico-historical criticism seeks to discover the meaning of the text that the text conveys, plainly, normally, i.e. letting the text and its context convey the meaning rather than imposing foreign philosophical concepts upon the text.

INERRANCY AFFIRMS THE PLAIN, NORMAL SENSE OF SCRIPTURE: WHEN THE PLAIN SENSE OF SCRIPTURE MAKES SENSE SEEK NO OTHER SENSE

Article XVIII becomes very pertinent to this discussion of the "magic" of historical criticism that is now being advocated by evangelical critical scholars. History is being forgotten. Article XVIII states:

> *We affirm* that the text of Scripture is to be interpreted by grammatico-historical exegesis, taking account of its literary form and devices, and that Scripture is to interpret Scripture. *We deny* the legitimacy of any treatment of the text or quest for sources lying behind it that leads to relativizing, dehistoricizing, or discounting its teaching, or rejecting its claims to authorship.

In commenting on this article, R. C. Sproule, one of the founding and principle members of ICBI, made the following comments in his *Explaining Inerrancy: A Commentary*, that explained the committee's reasoning what grammatico-historical exegesis' goal is ("*We affirm*" and what it also was trying to prevent ("*We deny*")

> Article XVIII touches on some of the most basic principles of biblical interpretation. Though this article does not spell out in detail a vast comprehensive system of hermeneutics, it nevertheless gives basic guidelines on which the framers of the confession were able to agree. *The first is that the text of Scripture is to be interpreted by grammatico-historical exegesis* (italics added—not in original]. Grammatico-historical is a technical term that refers to the process by which we take the structures and time periods of the written texts seriously as we interpret them. Biblical interpreters *are not given the license to spiritualize or*

---

[394] ICBI Catalogue, International Council on Biblical Inerrancy, 1983; R. C. Sproul, *Explaining Inerrancy* (Orlando, FL: Ligonier, 1996 [1980 International Council on Biblical Inerrancy].

allegorize texts against the grammatical structure and form of the text itself [italics added—not in the original].[395]

In this first part is revealed that ICBI, and its heritage reflected in *The Fundamentals* going back into history of the twentieth century attacks on the biblical text, rejected historical critical hermeneutics for that very reason that it disregarded the historicity of what the text was communicating. ICBI rejected historical-criticism's attempt to dehistoricize the plain, normal reading of the text. Sproule continued,

> The Bible is not to be reinterpreted to be brought into conformity with contemporary philosophies but is to be understood in its intended meaning and word usage as it was written at the time it was composed. To hold to grammatico-historical exegesis is to disallow the turning of the Bible into a wax nose that can be shaped and reshaped according to modern conventions of thought. The Bible is to be interpreted as it was written, not reinterpreted as we would like it to have been written according to the prejudices of our own era.[396]

Here ICBI emphasized the (1) grammatico-historical exegesis in direct contrast to the historical-critical method, either combined with grammatico-historical or modified in its more radical form, now maintained by neo-evangelicals.[397] Why did they commend the grammatico-historical approach? Because the men who expressed these two watershed statements had experienced the history of interpretive degeneration among mainstream churches and seminaries ("As go the theological seminaries, so goes the church")[398] in terms of dismissing the Gospels as historical records due to historical-critical ideologies. Any attempt at dismissing the grammatico-historical, plain sense of Scripture is contrary to the orthodox inerrancy view.

Evangelical Historical Critics Embrace Historical Criticism to Remove the Plain, Normal Sense Involved in Orthodox Inerrancy

Many critical-evangelical scholars, especially the large number of those trained in British and Continental European Schools, believe that Historical Criticism can be "*modified*" in some way to produce positive results for understanding Scripture, both in the OT and NT, i.e. the negative presuppositions can be removed to allow for miraculous. Evangelicals modify or call for modifying the "definition" of HC to make it compatible to evangelical sensibilities as follows. I. Howard Marshall, mentor to many evangelical critical scholars today that are achieving such prominence, such as Craig Blomberg and Darrell Bock, in his "Historical Criticism," article introduced evangelicals influenced by him to his take on the discipline in 1977, "the study of any narrative which purports to convey historical information

---

[395] Sproule, 54.

[396] Sproule, *Explaining Inerrancy*, 54.

[397] For instance, Craig Blomberg advocates a combining of historical-criticism and the grammatico-historical in while other evangelicals like Bock

[398] J. Gresham Machen, *The Christian Faith in the Modern World* (Grand Rapids: Eerdmans, 1936) 65.

in order to determine what actually happened and is described or alluded to in the passage in question."[399] Marshall goes on to note, "Because the Bible is a divine-human book, it must be treated as both equal to and yet more than an ordinary book. To deny that the Bible should be studied through the use of literary and critical methodologies is to treat the Bible as less than human, less than historical, and less than literature."[400] This stands in direct contrast to ICBI 1978 that affirmed that that warned against dehistoricizing the plain, normal sense of Scripture due to human authorship as noted in Article IX: "We deny that the finitude or fallenness of these writers, by necessity or otherwise, introduced distortion or falsehood in God's Word." Furthermore, his view of the authorship of NT books allowed false attribution, i.e. pseudepigraphy. Marshall expressed his view on "pseudonymous" writings in the New Testament: In order to avoid the idea of deceit, he coined the words "allonymity" and "allepigraphy" in which the prefix *pseudos* ("false") is replaced with *allos* ("other") which gives a more positive concept to the writing of a work in the name of another person.[401]

Craig Blomberg, in his article on "The Historical-Critical/Grammatical" hermeneutic in the work, Biblical Hermeneutics Five Views,[402] asserts that historical criticism can be "shorn" of its "antisupernatural presuppositions that the framers of that method originally employed" and eagerly embraces "source, form, tradition and redaction criticism" as "*all essential* [italic and bold added—not in the original] tools for understanding the contents of the original document, its formation and origin, its literary genre and subgenres, the authenticity of the historical material it includes, and its theological or ideological emphases and distinctives."[403] Blomberg advocates "The Historical-Critical/Grammatical View"[404] of hermeneutics for evangelicals that constitutes an alarming, and especially unstable, blend of historical-critical ideologies with the grammatico-historical hermeneutic. Blomberg argues for a "both-and-and-and" position of combining grammatico-historical method with that of historical-critical ideologies.[405] As will be seen, Blomberg's utilization of historical criticism causes him to start changing his own understanding of the term "inerrancy."

He labels the "The Historical-Critical/Grammatical" approach "the necessary foundation on which all other approaches must build."[406] However, history is replete with negative examples of those who attempted this unstable blend, from

---

[399] I. Howard Marshall, "Historical Criticism," in *New Testament Interpretation*. Ed. I. Howard Marshall (Grand Rapids: Eerdmans, 1977) , p. 126.

[400] Marshall, "Historical Criticism," p. 126.

[401] See I. Howard Marshall, A Critical and Exegetical Commentary on the Pastoral Epistles (2004), 84.

[402] *Craig L. Blomberg, "The Historical-Critical/Grammatical View," in Biblical Hermeneutics Five Views (Downers Grove: IVP, 2012): 27-47.*

[403] Blomberg, "The Historical-Critical/Grammatical View," 46-47.

[404] *Craig L. Blomberg, "The Historical-Critical/Grammatical View," in Biblical Hermeneutics Five Views (Downers Grove: IVP, 2012): 27-47.*

[405] Blomberg, "The Historical-Critical/Grammatical View," 28.

[406] Ibid.," 47.

the neologians in Griesbach's day to that of Michael Licona's book currently under discussion (see below).[407] Baird, in his *History of New Testament Research*, commented: "The neologians of the 18th century did not deny the validity of divine revelation but assigned priority to reason and natural theology. While faith in God, morality, and immortality were affirmed, older dogmas such as the Trinity, predestination, and the inspiration of Scripture were seriously compromised...The neologians...appropriated the results of the historical-critical work of Semler and Michaelis."[408] Little difference exists between today's evangelical historical critics and the neologians of Griesbach's day in terms of intent to combine popular methods of their day with faith.

Interestingly, Blomberg blames books like Harold Lindsell's *Battle for the Bible* (1976) and such books as *The Jesus Crisis* for people leaving the faith because of their strong stance on inerrancy as a presupposition. In an online interview conducted by Justin Taylor in 2008, Blomberg responded this way to books that hold to a firm view of inerrancy. The interviewer asked, "Are there certain mistaken hermeneutical presuppositions made by conservative evangelicals that play into the hands of liberal critics?" Blomberg replied,

> Absolutely. And one of them follows directly from the last part of my answer to your last question. The approach, famously supported back in 1976 by Harold Lindsell in his *Battle for the Bible* (Zondervan), that it is an all-or-nothing approach to Scripture that we must hold, is both profoundly mistaken and deeply dangerous. No historian worth his or her salt functions that way. I personally believe that if inerrancy means "without error according to what most people in a given culture would have called an error" then the biblical books are inerrant in view of the standards of the cultures in which they were written. But, despite inerrancy being the touchstone of the largely American organization called the Evangelical Theological Society, there are countless evangelicals in the States and especially in other parts of the world who hold that the Scriptures are inspired and authoritative, even if not inerrant, and they are not sliding down any slippery slope of any kind. I can't help but wonder if inerrantist evangelicals making inerrancy the watershed for so much has not, unintentionally, contributed to pilgrimages like Ehrman's. Once someone finds one apparent mistake or contradiction that they cannot resolve, then they believe the Lindsells of the world and figure they have to chuck it all. What a tragedy![409]

To Blomberg, apparently anyone who advocates inerrancy as traditionally advocated by Lindsell is responsible for people leaving the faith.

---

[407] For Griesbach and his association with Neologians as well as its impact on his synoptic "solution," see F. David Farnell, "How Views of Inspiration Have Impacted Synoptic Problem Discussion," *TMSJ* 13/1 (Spring 2002) 33-64.

[408] William *The History of New Testament Research: From deism to Tübingen* (Philadelphia: Fortress, 1992) 116.

[409] See http://thegospelcoalition.org/blogs/justintaylor/2008/03/26/interview-with-craig-blomberg/ Accessed on 5/25/2013.

Darrell Bock, another student of Marshall, concurs with Marshall's definition of historical criticism, whom Bock also studied under at Aberdeen, "I need to introduce these methods because of their importance to the contemporary discussion about Jesus, as well as the *potential merit their judicious use* brings to an understanding of the Gospels. Any approach that helps us to understand better the nature of the Gospels and how they might work is worth considering."[410] Bock fails to define or explain what he means by "a judicious use," so one is left wondering what such use may involve. He hints at the use of form criticism for evangelicals, however, with his statement, "In the hands of a skilled exegete who uses the tools of interpretation in a way that fits what they are capable of, Form Criticism can be a fruitful aid to understanding and exposition."[411] The Jesus Crisis has already catalogued the bankruptcy of this hubris in that no evangelical scholar who practices historical criticism has been able to separate the skeptical nature of the discipline in exegetical decisions.[412]

Graham N. Stanton writes about the unifying factor historical criticism has been as a reproachment between Protestants and Roman Catholics in hermeneutical approaches, "[t]here is now considerable agreement among Protestants and Roman Catholic scholars about the appropriate tools and methods to be used in exegesis. Stanton continues, "Presuppositions adopted either consciously or unconsciously by the interpreter are far more influential in New Testament scholarship than disagreements over method."[413] Here Stanton reveals that the thin-line between Romanism and Protestantism holds merely at the line of presupposition. If those presuppositions disappear, then so will the hermeneutical and exegetical differences.

Peter H. Davids also extols the virtue of historical criticism practiced by evangelicals, "The sum of this discussion is that critical study of Scripture can clarify the message that the authors were trying to communicate either by showing how the author came to produce his or her work (through examining sources) or by clarifying the content in which the message was communicated. And while critical methodologies have undoubtedly led to a doubting of biblical authority by some, that is not their necessary conclusion, but one resulting from assumptions connected to them or perhaps even a misuse of them."[414]

Donald Hagner, like his evangelical counterparts, admits the danger inherent in historical criticism when it is practiced, "The way out of the quandary [concerning critical method] is neither to continue to use the historical-critical method as classically conceived nor to abandon it outright because of its destructive past, but rather to modify it so as to make it more appropriate to the material being

---

[410] [italics added—not in original]. See Darrell L. Bock, Studying the Historical Jesus A Guide to Sources and Methods (Grand Rapids: Baker, 2002), 139.

[411] Darrell L. Bock, Form Criticism, in *New Testament Criticism and Interpretation*. Eds. David Alan Black and David S. Dockery (Grand Rapids: Zondervan, 1991), 192.

[412] F. David Farnell, "Form and Tradition Criticism," *The Jesus Crisis*, 185-232.

[413] Graham H. Stanton, Presuppositions in New Testament Criticism," in *New Testament Interpretation*, 60.

[414] Peter Davids-- "Authority, Hermeneutics and Criticism," in *New Testament Criticism and Interpretation*. Eds. Black and Dockery (1993), pp. 31-32.

questioned . . . . The historical-critical method is indispensable to any adequate and accurate understanding of the Bible, but only where it is tempered by an openness to the possibility of supernatural causation in the historical process. Without this tampering of method, it is clearly inappropriate and ineffective, given the fact that the Bible is after all the story of God acting in history. In short, without this tampering, the method can only be destructive. One of the great challenges facing evangelical scholarship is precisely that of modifying the historical-critical method so that it becomes productive and constructive."[415] Hagner does not indicate whether biblical critics as a whole, such as those in the Society of Biblical Literature, would accept this evangelical "tampering" or whose tampered version of historical criticism would be adopted among evangelicals as a whole.

Errancy Now Masquerades As Inerrancy Among Critical Evangelical Scholars

These evangelical quotes about their adoption and definition, or perhaps better, the redefinition of historical criticism to accommodate evangelical beliefs, bring to focus the destructive skepticism that this ideology contains. Because critical evangelical scholars seek to adopt some form of historical criticism, the inevitable result is skepticism regarding biblical revelation. This is the unavoidable fruit of such recombination or hybridization of the grammatico-historical and historical-critical. The skepticism of historical criticism will always manifest itself in their exegetical decisions that drive their modified hermeneutic that encompasses some form of historical criticism. The core of the critical evangelical scholars' attempt to redefine inerrancy is the driving reason why new versions, heterodox version of "inerrancy," now are emerging. In other words, historical criticism cannot encompass any orthodox view of inerrancy. Inerrancy views must be shifted to accommodate the skepticism of historical criticism, with the resulting heterodox views of errancy among evangelical critical scholars that masquerade as under the false rubric of "inerrancy." That is, they have changed the definition of inerrancy to errancy to accommodate the skepticism of historical criticism. The following are merely a few examples of the critical evangelical scholars who now stand in prominence in the Evangelical Theological Society, which Society has "inerrancy" as its sole core statement.

CRAIG BLOMBERG'S VIEW OF INERRANCY IS REALLY _ERRANCY_

The Good News: Blomberg Says He Believes in "Inerrancy"

One of his most recent works, _Can We Still Believe the Bible?_ constitutes an outstanding example of the psychological operational change in understanding of inerrancy that is now occurring among evangelicals through adoption of historical criticism that ICBI in 1978 opposed as Article XVIII affirms: "*We affirm* that the text of Scripture is to be interpreted by grammatico-historical exegesis, taking account of

---

[415] Donald Hagner, "The New Testament, History, and the Historical Critical Method," in _New Testament Criticism and Interpretation_ (Grand Rapids: Baker, 2013), 86, 88.

its literary form and devices, and that Scripture is to interpret Scripture."[416] Blomberg's take on these issues in relationship to inerrancy does not correspond to the definition of "inerrancy" that hundreds of evangelical scholars formulated in 1978 and 1982. While Blomberg says he believes in "inerrancy," one is left wondering after reading his very recent works, what he means by the term, for his statements indicate he does not hold to an orthodox definition of the term as expressed by ICBI in 1978 and 1982.

His publisher, Baker Books, hails the book in the following terms, "Challenges to the reliability of Scripture are perennial and have frequently been addressed. However, some of these challenges are noticeably more common today, and the topic is currently of particular interest among evangelicals. In this volume . . . Craig Blomberg offers an accessible and nuanced argument for the Bible's reliability in response to the extreme views about Scripture and its authority articulated by both sides of the debate. He believes that a careful analysis of the relevant evidence shows we have reason to be more confident in the Bible than ever before. As he traces his own academic and spiritual journey, Blomberg sketches out the case for confidence in the Bible in spite of various challenges to the trustworthiness of Scripture, offering a positive, informed, and defensible approach." He dialogues in questions of textual criticism, canon issues, translations, inerrancy, genre interpretation, and miracles, offering various solutions to various problems that center in these topics. This book is highly commended by Scot McKnight (Northern Seminary), Darrell Bock (Dallas Theological Seminary), Paul Copan (Palm Beach Atlantic University), Craig S. Keener (Asbury Theological Seminary) and Leith Anderson (National Association of Evangelicals). Bock himself encourages the reader to "read and consider anew how to think about Scripture" on the back cover.

Blomberg immediately tips his hand regarding the true nature of this work when the dedication page says, "To the faculty, administration, and trustees of Denver Seminary who from 1986 to the present have created as congenial a research environment as a professor could hope for, upholding the inerrancy of Scripture without any of the watchdog mentality that plagues so many evangelical institutions."[417] (p. v). So clearly he relates these issues to the topic of inerrancy throughout his work. This statement also reveals the dual nature of this work in that it not only reveals Blomberg's aberrant take on inerrancy. While Blomberg says he believes in inerrancy, he works hard to redefine any orthodox understanding of it.

The Bad News: Craig Blomberg Denies Orthodox View of Inerrancy in Practice

Perhaps the term most summarizing the book is "angry rant" against anyone who would disagree with his take on these subjects in his work. He less than subtly decries "A handful of very conservative Christian leaders who have not understood the issues adequately" as having "reacted by unnecessarily rejecting new developments (pp. 7-8). The scholars that Blomberg depreciates come from a wide variety of theological positions on Scripture, but what binds them together is their unity of agreement on ICBI statements of 1978 on Inerrancy and 1982 on

---

[416] For a more extensive review of this work, see F. David Farnell, "Review of Craig Blomberg's Can We Still Believe The Bible? An Evangelical Engagement With Contemporary Questions." MSJ 25.1 (Spring 2014) 99-104.

[417] Craig Blomberg

Hermeneutics. In his logic, disagreeing with Blomberg or perhaps also those in his fraternity of critical, evangelical scholarship means being too labeled ignorant as well as Nazi-like since he tells of a teacher's warning to avoid "the far left or the far right" as being related to "Nazism and Communism." This also indicates that Blomberg thinks that he has found the proverbial Goldilocks position of perfect middle ground of understanding of biblical issues, especially inerrancy.

One is reminded in reading Blomberg's work verbiage here of that of Jack B. Rogers, and Donald K. McKim took a similar position in 1979 when they wrote about the 20th Century, "In this century both fundamentalism and modernism sometimes took extreme positions regarding the Bible,"[418] except that Rogers and McKim refrained from name-calling.

In terms of Blomberg's conception of inerrancy, he attacks "extremely conservative Christians" who continue to insist on following their modern understandings of what should or should not constitute errors in the Bible and censure fellow inerrantists whose views are less anachronistic.[419]" Blomberg identifies himself as a "fellow inerrantist" but hints that other conservative views are "anachronistic" on inerrancy.

Blomberg's understanding of inerrancy, however, involves an unusual take on what he terms "genre."[420] He relates something that immediately causes the reader to take pause: "Most important, simply because a work appears in narrative form does not automatically historical or biographical in genre. History and biography themselves appear in many different forms, and fiction can appear identical to history in form."[421] He relates that "the way in which the ancients wrote history is clearer now than ever before. Once again, the result is that we know much better what we should be meaning when we say we 'believe the Bible,' and therefore such belief is more defensible than ever."[422]

These statements stand in direct contradiction to the ICBI statements on inerrancy as well as hermeneutics. First, Blomberg here is at odds with ICBI on inerrancy when it states in Article XVIII emphatically that "We deny the legitimacy of any treatment of the text or quest for sources lying behind it that leads to relativizing, dehistoricizing, or discounting its teaching, or rejecting its claim to authorship. This, however, is exactly where Blomberg goes in his work a very recent chapter that he contributed to

The official ICBI commentary on this Article adds, **"It is never legitimate, however, to run counter to express biblical affirmations"** (emphasis added). Further, in the ICBI commentary on its 1982 Hermeneutics Statement (Article 13) on inerrancy, it adds, **"We deny that generic categories which negate historicity may rightly be imposed on biblical narratives which present themselves as factual. Some,**

---

[418] Jack B. Rogers and Donald K. McKim, The Authority and Interpretation of the Bible, An Historical Approach (New York et al: Harper & Row, 1979), xxiii.

[419] Blomberg, *Can We Still Believe?*, p. 10.

[420] Blomberg, *Can We Still Believe?*, p. 10-11.

[421] Blomberg, Can We Still Believe, p. 11.

[422] Blomberg, *Can We Still Believe?*, p. 11.

for instance, take Adam to be a myth, whereas in Scripture he is presented as a real person. Others take Jonah to be an allegory when he is presented as a historical person and [is] so referred to by Christ" (emphasis added). Its comments in the next article (Article 14) add, "We deny that any event, discourse or saying reported in Scripture was invented by the biblical writers or by the traditions they incorporated" (emphasis added). Clearly, the CSBI Fathers rejected genre criticism as used by Robert Gundry, Mike Licona, and many other evangelicals.

He attacks "ultraconservatives" who do not abide by his assessment in the following terms, "once again, unfortunately, a handful of ultraconservatives criticize all such scholarship, thinking that they are doing a service to the gospel instead of the disservice that they actually render."[423] Apparently, anyone who would be firm in commitment to the integrity of Scripture constitute the real enemy to evangelical critical scholarship.

Because of limited space in a review, Chapter 4, "Don't These Issues Rule Out Biblical Inerrancy" (pp. 119-146) and Chapter 5, "Aren't Several; Narrative Genres of the Bible Unhistorical" (pp. 147-178) deserve special scrutiny for anyone who would affirm belief, and especially inerrancy, in the Bible. Blomberg here addresses the "fundamentalist-modernist controversy." He claims that the idea of inerrancy as understood by American efforts is largely an American phenomena: "Other branches of evangelicalism, especially in other parts of the world not heavily influenced by American missionary efforts, tend to speak of *biblical authority, inspiration*, and even *infallibility*, but not inerrancy."[424] He relates that some have "consciously rejected inerrancy as too narrow a term to apply to Scripture."[425] He relates that these misunderstandings about inerrancy emerge especially "among those who are noticeably more conservative or those who are noticeably more liberal in their views of Scripture than mainstream evangelicalism."[426] He mentions the following who, in his misunderstood inerrancy because they are too conservative: "from the far right of the belief, have evangelical spectrum, Norman Geisler, William Roach, Robert Thomas, and David Farnell attack my writings along with similar ones by such evangelical stalwarts as Darrell Bock, D. A. Carson, and Craig Keener as too liberal, threatening inerrancy, or denying the historicity of Scripture."[427] In response to this, the writer of this review would urge the reader to examine the latest book from Geisler and Farnell, *The Jesus Quest The Danger From Within* (Xulon, 2014) to make up their own mind as to the interpretative approaches of Blomberg and these scholar especially in terms of inerrancy (we report, you decide). Blomberg addresses the effect that creeds and confession of Christendom especially in terms of inerrancy.[428]

---

[423] Blomberg, Can We Still Believe, p. 11.

[424] Blomberg, *Can We Still Believe*, p. 119.

[425] Blomberg, *Can We Still Believe*, p. 119.

[426] Blomberg, *Can We Still Believe*, p. 119.

[427] Blomberg, *Can We Still Believe*, p. 120.

[428] Blomberg, *Can We Still Believe*, p. 120-21.

He relates that "[t]here are two quite different approaches [to inerrancy], moreover, that can lead to an affirmation that Scripture is without error."[429] These two approaches are "inductive approach" that "begins with the phenomena of the Bible itself, defines what would count as an error, analyzes Scripture carefully from beginning to end, and determines that nothing has been discovered that would qualify as errant."[430] The "deductive approach" that begins with the conviction that God is the author of Scripture, proceeds to the premise by definition that God cannot err, and therefore concludes that God's Word must be without error."[431] He reacts negatively against the deductive approach of "evidentialists and "presuppositonalist" by noting that these two terms "ultimately views inerrancy as a corollary of inspiration, not something to be demonstrated from the texts of Scripture itself. If the Bible is God-breathed (2 Tim. 3:16), and God cannot err, then the Bible must be errant. Hence, the inductive approach to Blomberg requires that the Bible prove that it is inerrant through critical investigation of the texts themselves rather than the others that just assume the texts are inerrant. Thus, he shifts the burden of proof from the Bible to that of the scholar. It is the critical investigator that must establish whether the text is truly inerrant. Importantly, Blomberg believes that the real debate on inerrancy is one of "hermeneutics."[432] Thus, under this logic, one could hold to inerrancy but believe that a particular event in Scripture is really symbolic and not to be taken as literally an event in the time-space continuum (creation in six days).[433] As a result, "Genesis 1 can be and has been interpreted by inerrantist as referring to a young earth, and old earth, progressive creation, theistic evolution, a literary framework for asserting God as the creator of all things irrespective of his methods, and a series of days when God took up residence in his cosmic temple for the sake of newly created humanity in his image. Once again, this is a matter for hermeneutical and exegetical debate, not one that is solved by the shibboleth of inerrancy."[434] (p. 126). One must note, however, that Blomberg reveals his startling differences with inerrancy as defined by ICBI in 1978: "We affirm that the text of Scripture is to be interpreted by grammatico-historical exegesis, taking account of its literary forms and devices, and that Scripture is to interpret Scripture. We deny the legitimacy of any treatment of the text or quest for sources lying behind it that leads to relativizing, dehistoricizing, or discounting its teaching, or rejecting its claims to authorship. "Here Blomberg's position is neither grammatical, historical, or literal, for Blomberg argues, "defenders of inerrancy do not reflect often enough on what it means to say that nonhistorical genres are wholly truthful."[435] He also reflects a *deja vue* mantra of Rogers and McKim, who wrote in 1979, "But often without realizing it; we impose on ancient documents twenty-first century standards that are equally inappropriate." Rogers and McKim said, "To erect a standard of modern, technical precision in language as the hallmark

---

[429] Blomberg, *Can We Still Believe*, p. 121.

[430] Blomberg, *Can We Still Believe*, p. 121.

[431] Blomberg, *Can We Still Believe*, p. 121.

[432] Blomberg, *Can We Still Believe*, p. 125.

[433] Blomberg, *Can We Still Believe*, p. 126.

[434] Blomberg, *Can We Still Believe*, p. 126.

[435] Blomberg, *Can We Still Believe*, p. 128.

of biblical authority was totally foreign to the foundation shared by the early church" (Rogers and McKim, *The Authority and Intepretation of the Bible An Historical Approach*, p. xxii). Blomberg also supports elements of speech-act theory also maintains that "Vanhoozer's work is indeed very attractive, but it is scarcely at odds with the Chicago Statement."[436]   One wonders at this statement of Blomberg, since Van Hoozer denies the grammatico-historical approach, and as Geisler/Roach conclude, "[Van Hoozer] also claims to affirm much of the ICBI statement as he understands it. But that is precisely the problem since the way he understands it is not the way the framers meant it, as is demonstrated from the official commentaries on the ICBI statements."[437]

The practical result is genre can be used to deny anything in the bible that the interpreter finds offensive as a literal sense. The allegorical school did such a thing; the Gnostics did it to Scripture, and now Blomberg applies his updated version of it with genre being applied to hermeneutics. Blomberg's use of genre, to this present review, smacks of an eerie similarity to Rogers'/McKim's deprecation of literal interpretation when they noted Westerner's logic that viewed "statements in the Bible were treated like logical propositions that could be interpreted quite literally according to contemporary standards" (Rogers and McKim, *The Authority and Interpretation of the Bible*, xviii). In Chapter 5, Aren't Several Narrative Genres of the Bible Unhistorial," his use of hermeneutics continues to be the means by which he can redefine what normal definition of inerrancy would be, and he uses it to deny the plain, normal sense of Genesis 1-3 (p. 150),[438] while advocating that we must understand the author's intent in such passages, with the key question from Article 13 of ICBI, "standards of truth and error that are alien to its usage or purpose." Applying a completely wrong understanding of this clause of ICBI as well as the original intent of the founders of ICBI, Blomberg advocates that idea that "the question is simply one about the most likely literary form of the passage."[439] From there, he proceeds to allow for non-literal interpretation of Genesis 1-3 that are, in his view, fully in line with inerrancy, e.g. Adam and Eve as symbols for every man and woman,[440] evolutionary and progressive creation,[441] a non-historical Jonah,[442] the possibility of three Isaiah's (p. 162),[443] Daniel as Apocalyptic genre rather than prophetic,[444] fully embracing of midrash interpretation of the Gospels (non-literal) as advocated by Robert Gundry as not impacting inerrancy[445] as well

---

[436] Blomberg, *Can We Still Believe*, p. 136. The reader is referred here to Geisler/Roach evaluation of Van Hoozer for a different perspective, "Kevin Vanhoozer on Inerrancy," in *Inerrancy Defended* (Grand Rapids: Baker, 2011) p. 132-159.

[437] Geisler and Roach, Defending *Inerrancy*, 159.

[438] Blomberg, *Can We Still Believe*, p. 150.

[439] Blomberg, *Can We Still Believe*, p. 150.

[440] Blomberg, *Can We Still Believe*, p. 152.

[441] Blomberg, *Can We Still Believe*, p. 151-153.

[442] Blomberg, *Can We Still Believe*, p. 160.

[443] Blomberg, *Can We Still Believe*, p. 128.

[444] Blomberg, *Can We Still Believe*, p. 163-164.

[445] Blomberg, *Can We Still Believe*, p. 165-168.

as pseudepigraphy as fully in line with inerrancy in NT epistles under the guide of a "literary device" or "acceptable form of pseudonymity."[446] He argues that we don't know the opinions of the first century church well-enough on pseudepigraphy to rule it out: "[B]arring some future discovery related to first-century opinions, we cannot pontificate on what kinds of claims for authorship would or would not have been considered acceptable in Christian communities, and especially in Jewish-Christian circles when the New Testament Epistles were written. As a result, we must evaluate every proposal based on its own historical and grammatical merits, not on whether it does or does not pass some pre-established criterion of what inerrancy can accept."[447]

The response of other critical evangelical scholars to Blomberg's book has been warm and embracing. In a "blog tour for Blomberg's book, critical evangelical scholar at Dallas Theological Seminary, Darrell Bock warmly embraces Chapter 4 ("Don't These Issues Rule Out Biblical Inerrancy") that is currently under discussion in this article:

> Craig Blomberg's fourth chapter in *Can We Still Believe the Bible*, examines some objections to inerrancy from both the right and the left. Yes, there is a position to the right of holding to inerrancy. It is holding it in a way that is slow to recognize solutions that fit within the view by undervaluing the complexities of interpretation. People are far more familiar with those who challenge inspiration and doubt what Scripture declares on the left, but others attempt to build a fence around the Bible by being slow to see where legitimate discussion exists about how inerrancy is affirmed. To make the Bible do too much can be a problem, just as making it do too little.[448]

President of the Evangelical Theological Society for 2013-2104, Robert W. Yarborough also praised Blomberg's book in his Presidential Address in the following glowing terms, placing it at the top of his list of new books,

> Excellent recent books demonstrate the cogency and vitality of a reverent and indeed an inerrantist stance. Two such books were made available to me in pre-publication form for this address.

> Craig Blomberg, Can We Still Believe the Bible? The first is by Craig Blomberg, Can We Still Believe the Bible? An Evangelical Engagement with Contemporary Questions. Blomberg takes up six issues that he finds foundational to an affirmation of the Bible's comprehensive credibility like that affirmed by this society. In each of these categories, Blomberg cites the literature of those who reject a high view of the Bible's veracity or authenticity. As he points out, those critical of the Bible's truth do not return the favor, stonewalling evangelical arguments and publications as if that class of scholarship did not even exist. Blomberg calls attention to

---

[446] Blomberg, *Can We Still Believe*, p. 168-172.

[447] Blomberg, *Can We Still Believe*, p. 172.

[448] http://canwestillbelieve.com/ accessed on October 7, 2014; See also Bock's Blog, http://blogs.bible.org/bock/darrell_l._bock/craig_blombergs_can_we_believe_the_bible-_chapter_4 accessed on October 7, 2014.

the best studies he can find that reject his viewpoint. He then argues for the position from his inerrantist standpoint. He notes, "Not a single supposed contra- diction" in Scripture "has gone without someone proposing a reasonably plausible resolution." He also notes the irony that some are abandoning inerrancy today when "inerrantists have the ability to define and nuance their understanding of the doctrine better than ever before." This book is refreshing and important not only because of its breadth of coverage of issues, viewpoints, and literature. It is evenhanded in that both enemies of inerrancy and wrong-headed friends are called on the carpet. Blomberg revisits incidents like Robert Gundry's dismissal from this society and the kerfuffle over a decade ago surrounding the TNIV and inclusive language. He does not mince words in criticizing those he sees as overzealous for the inerrancy cause. Nor is he bashful in calling out former inerrantists who, Blomberg finds, often make their polemical arguments against what they used to believe with less than compelling warrant. I predict that everyone who reads the book will disagree strongly with the author about something. At the same time, the positive arguments for inerrancy are even more substantial. It is clear that Blomberg is not content with poking holes in non-inerrantist arguments. He writes, "I do not think one has to settle for anything short of full-fledged inerrantist Christianity so long as we ensure that we employ all parts of a detailed exposition of inerrancy, such as that found in the Chicago Statement."

Or again: "These Scriptures are trustworthy. We can still believe the Bible. We should still believe the Bible and act accordingly, by following Jesus in discipleship." I am skimming some of his concluding statements, but the real meat of the book is inductive demonstration of inerrancy's plausibility based on primary evidence and scholarship surrounding that evidence. If only a book of this substance had been available when I was a college or grad school student![449]

One is left wondering what view of inerrancy not only Blomberg affirms, but also what form Bock and Yarborough affirm since they so warmly embrace Yarborough's book. Clearly ICBIs view of inerrancy does not appear to be what they affirm when they make such comments. Perhaps a better title for this Baker book should be *Can We Still Believe Evangelical Critical Scholars?* Why? Critical evangelical scholars, like Blomberg, say that they believe in inerrancy, but Blomberg's book leave much doubt as to whether they really do believe it the way the church has traditionally maintained that doctrine throughout the millennia. Indeed, the present review challenges all to re-read Rogers' and McKim's work (1979), as well as Rogers, *Biblical Authority* (1977) to discover startling parallels in many thoughts between their position and that of critical evangelical scholars like Blomberg today. It is painfully obvious in this book that Paul's warning of not to be taken captive by philosophy has been totally overlooked, ignored and disregarded by Blomberg (Col. 2:8--See to it that no one takes you captive through philosophy and empty deception, according to the tradition of men, according to

---

[449] Robert Gundry - Defending Inerrancy, http://defendinginerrancy.com/robert-gundry-declares-peter-apostate/ (accessed October 28, 2015).

the elementary principles of the world, rather than according to Christ.) as well as Paul's warning to take every thought captive (2 Cor. 10:5—"*We are* destroying speculations and every lofty thing raised up against the knowledge of God, and *we are* taking every thought captive to the obedience of Christ."

JOHN H. WALTON'S AND D. BRENT SANDY'S VIEW OF INERRANCY IS REALLY *ERRANCY*

The Good News: Walton and Sandy Say They Believe in "Inerrancy"

The present writer has extensively reviewed John D. Walton and D. Brent Sandy, The Lost World of Scripture previously.[450] The writers state that their "specific objective is to understand better how both the Old and New Testaments were spoken, written and passed on, especially with an eye to possible implications for the Bible's inspiration and authority."[451] (p. 9). They add, "part of the purpose of this book is to bring students back from the brink of turning away from the authority of Scripture in reaction to the misappropriation of the term *inerrancy*" (p. 9).

They assert that as Wheaton University professors, they work "at an institution and with a faculty that take a strong stand on inerrancy but that are open to dialogue" and that this openness "provided a safe context in which to explore the authority of Scripture from the ground up."[452] John Walton wrote the chapters on the Old Testament while D. Brent Sandy wrote the chapters on the New Testament. W/S have written this book especially for "Christian students in colleges, seminaries and universities" with the hopes that they will find their work "useful," as well as writing for "colleagues who have a high view of Scripture, especially for those who hold to inerrancy."[453] The book is also "not intended for outsiders; that is, it's not an apologetic defense of biblical authority. Rather, "we're writing for insiders, seeking to clarify how best to understand the Bible."[454] The writers also assure the readers that they have a "very high view of Scripture; "[w]e affirm inerrancy" and that they "are in agreement with the definition suggested by David Dockery that the 'Bible properly interpreted in light of [the] culture and communication developed by the time of its composition will be shown to be completely true (and therefore not false) in all that it affirms, to the degree of precision intended by the author, in all matters relating to God and his creation" (David S. Dockery, *Christian Scripture: An Evangelical Perspective on Inspiration, Authority and Interpretation* (Nashville: B & H, 1994, p. 64).

The Bad News: Walton's and Sandy's View of Inerrancy is Really Errancy.

---

[450] F. David Farnell, "A review of John H. Walton and D. Brent Sandy. The Lost World of Scripture, Ancient Literary Culture and Biblical Authority (Downers Grove: IVP, 2013," *MSJ* 25.1 (Spring 2014), 121-129.

[451] John H. and D. Brent Sandy. *The Lost World of Scripture, Ancient Literary Culture and Biblical Authority* (Downers Grove: IVP, 2013), p. 9.

[452] Walton and Sandy, *The Lost World of Scripture*, p. 10.

[453] Walton and Sandy, *The Lost World of Scripture*, p. 10.

[454] Walton and Sandy, *The Lost World of Scripture*, p. 9..

The central thrust of the book is that the world of the Bible (both Old and New Testament) is quite different from modern times: "Most of us a probably unprepared . . . for how different the ancient world is from our own . . . We're thousands of years and thousands of miles removed. It means we frequently need to put the brakes on and ask whether we're reading the Bible in light of the original culture or in light of contemporary culture. While the Bible's values were very different from ancient cultures', it obviously communicated in the existing languages and within cultural customs of the day."[455] (p. 13). Such a recognition and the "evidence assembled in this book inevitably leads to the question of inerrancy." (p. 13). [T]he truth of the matter is, no term, or even combination of terms, can completely represent the fullness of Scripture's authority" (p. 13). W/S then quote the Short Statement of the Chicago Statement on Biblical inerrancy of 1978 (p. 14). This creates the impression that they are in agreement with the statement. However, this is deceptive because book constitutes an essential challenge to much of what the Chicago Statements asserted. This uneasiness with the Chicago Statement can also be seen in those who are listed as endorsers of the work, Tremper Longmann III who chairs the Robert H. Gundry professor of Biblical Studies, as well as Michael R. Licona who recently, in his *The Resurrection of Jesus*, used genre criticism to negate the resurrection of the saints in Jerusalem in Matthew 27:51-53 at Jesus crucifixion as apocalyptic genre rather than indicating a literal resurrection, and Craig Evans, Acadia Divinity College, who is not known for his support of the Chicago Statements.

The book consists of 21 propositions that seek to nuance biblical authority, interpretation and an understanding of inerrancy, with the essential thought of these propositions flowing basically from 2 areas: (1) their first proposition, "Ancient Near Eastern Societies were *hearing dominant* (italics added) and had nothing comparable to authors and books as we know them" [in modern times since the printing press] while modern societies today are "*text dominant*"[456] and (2) speech-act theory that they frequently refer to in their work (pp. 41-46, 48, 51, 200, 213-218, 229, 288). They qualify their latter acceptance of speech-act theory:

> We do not agree with many of the conclusions with speech act theory, but we find its foundational premise and terminology helpful and have adopted its three basic categories. The communicator uses *locutions* (words, sentences, rhetorical structures, genres) to embody an *illocution* (the intention to do something with those locutions—bless, promise, instruct, assert) with a *perlocution* that anticipates a certain response from the audience (obedience trust, belief) (p. 41).

They go on to assert that God accommodated his communication in the Scripture: "[a]ccomodation on the part of the divine communicator resides primarily in the locution, in which the genre and rhetorical devices are included." (p. 42). And,

---

[455] Walton and Sandy, *The Lost World of Scripture*, p. 9

[456] Walton and Sandy, *The Lost World of Scripture*, (italics added) (p. 19, see also pp. 17-28).

[G]enre is largely a part of the locution, not the illocution. Like grammar, syntax and lexemes, genre is a mechanism to convey an illocution. Accomodation takes place primarily at the louctionary level. Inerrancy and authority related to the illocution; accommodation and genre attach at the locution. Therefore, inerrancy and authority cannot be undermined, compromised or jeopardized by genre or accommodation. While genre labels may be misleading, genre itself cannot be true or false, errant or inerrant, authoritative or nonauthoritative. Certain genres lend themselves to more factual detail and others more toward fictional imagination." (p. 45).

While admittedly the book's propositions entail many other ideas, from these two ideas, an oral dominated society in ancient times of the OT and NT vs. a written/text dominant society of modern times and the implications of speech-act theory cited above, flow all that W/S develop in their assertions to nuance their take on what a proper view of inerrancy and biblical authority should be. The obvious implication of these assertions is that Robert Gundry, who was removed from ETS due to his dehistoricizing in 1983, was wronged because value judgments about genre do not impact the doctrine of inerrancy. Gundry was perfectly in the confines of inerrancy to dehistoricize because, according to W/S, it was ETS that misunderstood the concept of inerrancy as not genre driven. It is the illocution (purpose or intent), not the wording that drives inerrancy. Gundry's theorizing of a midrashic genre, according to this idea, had nothing at all to do with inerrancy. Gundry believed sincerely in inerrancy but realized the midrashic, not historical, nature of Matthew 2.

Walton's and Sandy's work are reminiscent of Rogers and McKim, in their now famous, *The Authority and Interpretation of the Bible* (1979), *An Historical Approach*, who made a similar error in their approach to Scripture. They also spoke of "the central Christian tradition included the concept of accommodation;" that today witnesses a "scholastic overreaction to biblical criticism;" "the function and purpose of the Bible was to bring people into a saving relationship with God through Jesus Christ"; "the Bible was not used as an encyclopedia of information on all subjects;" and "to erect a standard of modern, technical precision in language as the hallmark of biblical authority was totally foreign to the foundation shared by the early church." (R/M, xxii). W/S similarly assert in their implications of an oral society that "The Bible contains no new revelation about the material workings and understanding of the Material World" (Proposition 4, pp.49-59) so that the

Bible's "explicit statements about the material world are part of the locution and would naturally accommodate the beliefs of the ancient world. As such they are not vested with authority. We cannot encumber with scriptural authority any scientific conclusions we might deduce from the biblical text about the material world, its history or its regular processes. This means that we cannot draw any scientific conclusions about such areas as physiology, meteorology, astronomy, cosmic geography, genetics or geology from the Bible. For example, we should believe that God created the universe, but we should not expect to be able to derive from the biblical texts the methods that he used or the time that it took. We should believe that God created humans in his image and that through the choices they made sin and death came into the world. Scientific conclusions, however, relating to the material processes of human origins (whether from biology in general or genetics in particular) may be outside the purview of the Bible. We need to ask whether the Bible is making those sort of claims in its illocutions" (p. 55).

They continue,

> The Bible's claims regarding origins, mechanics or shape of the world are, by definition of the focus of its revelation, mechanics or shape of the world are, by definition of the focus of its revelation in the theological realm. (p. 55).

According to W/S, what the Bible says plainly in the words of Genesis 1 may not be what it intends. Immediate special creation cannot be read into the text; rather the door is open for evolution and the acceptance of modern understandings of science. Thus, Genesis 1 and 2 may well indicate God's creation but not the means of how he created, even when the locutions say "evening and morning"; "first day" etc. Much of what is in Genesis 1 reflects "Old World Science": "one could easily infer from the statements in the biblical text that the sun and moon share space with the birds (Gen. 1). But this is simply a reflection of Old World Science, and we attach no authority to that conclusion. Rather we consider it a matter of deduction on the part of the ancients who made no reason to know better." (p. 57). For them, "[t]he Bible's authority is bound into theological claims and entailments about the material world. For them, since the Bible is not a science textbook, its "authority is not found in the locution but has to come through illocution" (p. 54). Genesis 1-2, under their system, does not rule out evolution; nor does it signify creation literally in six "days." Such conclusions press the text far beyond its purpose to indicate God's creation of the world but not the how of the processes involved. They conclude, "we have proposed that reticence to identify scientific claims or entailments is the logical conclusion from the first two points (not a science textbook; no new scientific revelation) and that a proper understanding of biblical authority is dependent on recognizing this to be true" (p. 59). They assert that "it's safe to believe that Old World Science permeates the Old Testament" and "Old World Science is simply part of the locution [words, etc.] and as such is not vested with authority" (p. 300).

Apparently, W/S believe that modern science has a better track record at origins. This assumption is rather laughable. Many "laws" of science for one generation are overturned in other generations. Scientific understanding is in constant flux. Both of these authors have failed to understand that modern science is predominated overwhelmingly by materialistic philosophies rather than presenting any evidence of objectivity in the area of origins. Since Science is based on observation, testing, measurement and repeatability, ideas of origins are beyond the purview of modern science too. For instance, the fossil record indicates the death of animals, but how that death occurred and what the implications of that fossil record are, delves more into philosophy and agendas rather than good science. Since no transitional forms exist between species in the fossil record, evolution should be rendered tenuous as an explanation, but science refuses to rule it out due to a dogmatic *a priori*.

While W/S quote the ICBI "short statement" their work actually is an assault on the articles of affirmation and denial 9f the 1978 Chicago Statement on Inerrancy. In article IX, it noted that "**We affirm** that inspiration, though not conferring omniscience, guaranteed true and trustworthy utterance on all matters of which the biblical authors were moved to speak and write" and Article XII, "**we deny** that biblical infallibility and inerrancy are limited to spiritual, religious, or redemptive themes, exclusive of the fields of history and science. We further deny that scientific hypotheses about earth history may properly be used to overturn the teaching of Scripture on creation and the flood." Article XI related, "far from misleading us; it is true and reliable in all matters in addresses."

Another area that is troubling is in their theorizing of text-canonical updating. W/S adoption of multiple unknown redactor/editors who updated the text over long periods of time in terms of geography, history, names, etc. actually constitutes an argument, not for inerrancy, but for deficiency in the text of Scripture and hence an argument for errancy, not inerrancy. Due to the OT being an oral or ear dominated society, W/S also propose a text-canonical updating hypothesis: "the model we propose agrees with traditional criticism in that it understands the final literary form of the biblical books to be relatively late and generally not the literary product of the authority figure whose words the book preserves (p. 66). This while Moses, Isaiah, and other prominent figures were behind the book, perhaps multiple, unknown editors were involved in any updating and final form of the books in the OT/NT that we have. For them, in the whole process of Scripture, "[t]he Holy Spirit is behind the whole process from beginning to end" in spite of the involvement of unknown hands in their final development (p. 66). W/S negate the central idea of inerrancy that would center around original autographs that were inerrant, or that such autographs even existed: "Within evangelical circles discussing inerrancy and authority, the common affirmation is that the text is inerrant in the original autographs . . . since all copies were pristine, inerrancy could only be connected with the putative originals ("p. 66). Modern discovery of the Dead Sea Scrolls has made it "clear that there was not only one original form of the final literary piece" of such books as Samuel and Jeremiah (p. 67). Which version is original cannot be determined. Under W/S it does not make any difference because "in the model that we have proposed here, it does not matter. The authority is associated with Jeremiah, no matter which compilation is used. We cannot be dependent on the 'original autographs,' not only because we do not have them, but also because the very concept is anachronistic for most of the Old Testament" (p. 67). For W/S, "inerrancy and authority are connected initially to the figure or the authoritative traditions. We further accept the authority represented in the form of the book adopted by faith communities and given canonical status" (p. 67). "Inerrancy and authority attach to the final canonical form of the book rather than to putative original autographs" (p. 68). Later on in their work, W/S assert that "inerrancy would then pertain to the role of the authorities (i.e. the role of Moses or Isaiah as dominant, determinative and principle voice), not to so-called authors writing so-called books—but the literature in its entirety would be considered authoritative" (p. 281). For them, "[a]uthority is not dependent on the original autographs or an author writing a book. Recognition of authority is identifiable in the beliefs of a community of faith (of whom we are heirs) that God's communications through authoritative figures and traditions have been captured and preserved through a long process of transmission and composition" (p. 68). For them, Mosaic authorship of the Pentateuch "does not decide the matter" regarding its authority, for many may have been involved in the final form of the first five books of Moses (p. 69). The final form involved perhaps many unknown editors and updaters: "Our interest is in the identity of the prophet as the authority figure behind the oracles, regardless of the composition history of the book" (p. 72). Thus, while Moses, Jeremiah, for instance, were the originator of the tradition or document and names are associated with the books, this approach of many involved in the product/final form of the book and variations, "allows us to adopt some of the more important advances that critical scholarship has offered" (p. 74). For them, unknown editors over long periods of time would have updated the text in many ways as time passed. They argue "it is safe to believe that some later material could be added and later editors could have a role in the compositional history of a canonical book" (p. 299). Their positing of such a scheme, however, is suggestive that the text had been corrected, updated, revised all which smacks of a case for errancy more than inerrancy in the process.

Again, orthodox views of inerrancy, like the 1978 Chicago Statement, were not so negative about determining the autographs as article X related, "**We affirm** that inspiration, strictly speaking, applies only to the autographs of Scripture, which in the providence of God can be ascertained from available manuscripts with great accuracy."

W/S also assert that "exacting detail and precise wording were not necessary to preserve and transmit the truths of Scripture" (p. 181) because they were an "ear" related culture rather than a print related culture (Proposition 13).

In reply to W/S, while this may be true that the New Testament was oral, such a statement needs qualification by W/S in their propositions throughout. No matter what the extent of orality in the OT and NT as posed by W/S, the reportage in these passages is accurate though it may not be, at times precise. While they are correct that "exacting detail and precise wording were not necessary to preserve and transmit the truths of Scripture, two competing views need to be contrasted in that oral reportage that was written down in the text of Scripture: an orthodox view and an unorthodox view of that reportage. This important distinction is lost in W/S's discussion (see Norman L. Geisler, "Evangelicals and Redaction Criticism, Dancing on the Edge" [1987] for a full discussion):

ORTHODOX VIEW	UNORTHODOX VIEW
REPORTING THEM	CREATING THEM
SELECTING THEM	CONSTRUCTING THEM
ARRANGING THEM	MISARRANGING THEM
PARAPHRASING THEM	EXPANDING THEM
CHANGE THEIR FORM (Grammatical Change)	CHANGE THEIR CONTENT (Theological Change)
CHANGE THEIR WORDING	CHANGE THEIR MEANING

TRANSLATE THEM	MISTRANSLATE THEM
INTERPRET THEM	MISINTERPRET THEM
EDITING	REDACTING

Article XIII of the 1978 Chicago Statement was careful to note that inerrancy does not demand precision at all times in reportage. Any criticism of the Chicago Statements in this area is ill-advised, "We further deny that inerrancy is negated by biblical phenomena such as a lack of modern technical precision, irregularities of grammar or spelling, observational descriptions of nature, the reportage of falsehoods, the use of hyperbole and round numbers, the topical arrangement of material, variant selections of material in parallel accounts, or the use of free citations. W/S's caveat on harmonization needs qualification: "it is not necessary to explain away the differences by some means of harmonization in order to it fit modern standards of accuracy" (p. 151). While anyone may note many examples of trite harmonization, this does not negate the legitimacy or need for harmonization. Tatian's *Diatessaron* (c. 160-175) is a testimony to the ancient church believing that the Gospels could be harmonized since they were a product of the Holy Spirit. From the ancient Christian church through to the time of the Reformation, the church always believed in the legitimacy and usefulness of harmonization. It was not until modern philosophical presuppositions (e.g., Rationalism, Deism, Romanticism, etc.) that created the historical-critical ideology arose that discredited harmonization. The orthodox position of the church was that the Gospels were without error and could be harmonized into a unified whole. The rise of modern critical methods (i.e. historical criticism) with its accompanying low or no views of inspiration discredited harmonization, not bad examples of harmonization. For harmonization during the time of the Reformation, see Harvey K. McArthur, "Sixteenth Century Gospel Harmonies," in *The Quest Through the Centuries: The Search for the Historical Jesus* (Philadelphia: Fortress,1966) 85 -101).

On page 274, W/S assert "[o]ur intention is to strengthen the doctrine of biblical authority through a realistic application of knowledge of the ancient world, and to understand what inerrancy can do and what it can't do." They believe that the term inerrancy is a term that "is reaching its limits" and also that "the convictions it sought to express and preserve remain important" (p. 274). "Inerrancy" is no longer the clear, defining term it once was and that "has become diminished in rhetorical power and specificity, it no longer serves as adequately to define our convictions about the robust authority of Scripture" (p. 275). They cite several errors of inerrancy advocates in the past. Most notably are the following: inerrancy advocates, "have at times misunderstood 'historical' texts by applying modern genre criteria to ancient literature, thus treating it as having claims that it never intended." Apparently, this position allows W/S to read the findings of modern "scientism" into the ancient text that often conflicts with today's hypothesis of origins (i.e. creation). "They have at times confused locution [words, sentences, rhetorical structures, genres] and illocution [the intention to do something with those locutions—bless, promise, instruct, assert"]. Inerrancy technically applies on to the latter, though of course, without locutions, there would be no illocution." W/S here confuse inerrancy with interpretation and understanding of a text with this supposition. Each word is inspired but the understanding or interpretation of those words may not be considered "inerrant" but a process of interpretation of those words in the context in which those words occur. If Genesis 1 says "evening and morning" and "first," "second" day, it is tenuous to imply that these terms are so flexible in interpretation to allow for long periods of time to accommodate evolutionary hypotheses. "They have been too anxious to declare sections of the Old Testament to be historical in a modern sense, where it may not be making those claims for itself." Here, this principle allows W/S to negate any part of the Old Testament that does not accord with modern sensibilities. It creates a large opening to read into the text rather than allow the text to speak for itself. They assert that positions such as "young earth or premillennialism may be defensible interpretations, but they cannot invoke inerrancy as a claim to truth" (p. 282). For W/S, "the Israelites shared the general cognitive environment of the ancient world . . . . At the illocutionary level, we may say that traditions in the early chapters of Genesis, for example, served the Israelites by offering an account of God and his ways and conveying their deepest beliefs about how the world works, who they are and how it all began. These are the same questions addressed by the mythological traditions of the ancient world, but the answers given are very different" (p. 303-304).

One other area where the elasticity of W/S's concept of history centers in that they allow for the hyperbolic use of numbers in the Old Testament: "It is safe to believe that the Bible can use numbers rhetorically with the range of the conventions of the ancient world" (p. 302). For them, "[w]e may conclude that they are exaggerated, or even that contradictory amounts are given in sources that report the same event" (p. 302). These may well be inaccuracies or contradictions according to our conventions, but that doesn't mean that they jeopordize inerrancy. Again, numerical quantity is locution. Authority ties to the illocution and what the narrator is *doing* with those numbers" (p. 302). Whatever he is doing, he is doing wit the accepted conventions of their world" (p. 302).

Finally, W/S argue that "our doctrine of authority of Scripture has become too enmeshed in apologetics . . . . If we tie apologetics and theology too tightly together, the result could be that we end up trying to defend as theology what are really just apologetic claims we have made" (p. 306).

Finally, W/S contend: "ill-formed versions of inerrancy have misled many people into false understandings of the nature of Scripture, which has led to poor hermeneutics for interpreting Scripture and to misunderstandings of Bible translations. Even more serious, certain views of inerrancy have led people away from the Christian faith. Such views can also keep people from considering more important matters in Scripture. If there is a stumbling block to people coming to the faith, should it not be Christ alone rather than a wall that we inadvertently place in the way of spiritual pilgrimages?" (p. 308). This reviewer has one reply to the illogic of W/S. If the documents are cannot be trusted in their plain, normal sense (e.g. creation), then how can their testimony about Christ be trusted? If the documents have as much flexibility as hypothesized by W/S, how can they be trusted to give a reliable, accurate and faithful witness to Him? While W/S have wrapped their work in an alleged improvement of current concepts of inerrancy and its implications, they have actually presented a system that is (1) quite inferior to that of the ICBI statements of 1978 and 1982 and (2) one that really is designed to undermine the years of evangelical history that went into the formulation of those documents against the onslaught of historical-critical ideologies that W/S now embrace. They treat that history and reasons of the formulation of ICBI statements in a dismissive fashion that is perilous for those who do not remember the events of the past are doomed to repeat its mistakes as evidenced in this work of W/S. A better title for this book would have been "The Lost World of Inerrancy" since W/S's system undermines the very concept. One is left wondering what form of "inerrancy" is really advocated by Walton and Sandy. It is not any stretch to say that their view really masquerades "errancy" in the form of "inerrancy."

CONCLUSION TO THE MAGIC OF HISTORICAL CRITICISM

The present writer could multiply the examples of critical evangelical scholars who "say" that they believe in "inerrancy." However, their practice and assertions in biblical interpretation really support unorthodox errantist views. The present writer has reviewed the following additional works and invites the reader to examine his reviews of these works, for all of the following scholars assert a belief in inerrancy, but their works actually affirm errancy:

(1) Christopher M. Hays and Christopher B. Ansberry, *Evangelical Faith and The Challenge of Historical Criticism.* London: SPCK, 2013 cf. F. David Farnell, "A Review of" in *MSJ* 25.1 (Spring 2014), 107- 113. Sadly, Ansberry is a Master's College graduate who should have known better through his training.

(2) James K. Hoffmeier and Dennis R. Magary, Eds. *Do Historical Matters Matter To Faith?, A Critical Appraisal of Modern and Post Modern Approaches to Scripture.* James K. Hoffmeier and Dennis R. Magary, Eds. Wheaton, IL: Crossway, 2012 cf. F. David Farnell, "A Review of" in MSJ 24.2 (Fall 2013) 149-157. Sadly, this work constitutes a MASSIVE ASSAULT ON ORTHODOX INERRANCY.

Evangelicals are in very deep difficulty at the beginning of the 21st Century. Many critical evangelical scholars say that they believe in "inerrancy," while their views assault tradition views of inerrancy. Importantly, from this point in evangelical history, when someone says that they believe in inerrancy, one must now ask, "what do you mean by the term 'inerrancy' since the orthodox definition of inerrancy has now been hijacked and changed.

CHAPTER 5 Rhetorical Criticism

Thomas Marshall

Hebrews 1:1-2a Updated American Standard Version (UASV)

[1] Long ago God spoke to the fathers by the prophets at different times and in many ways, [2] in these last days he has spoken to us by a Son ...

Introduction

As our coverage of the various forms of Biblical Criticism in this book has been showing, scholars seek to view the biblical texts as having human rather than supernatural origins. This grew out of the rationalism of the 17th and 18th centuries. The use of this so-called scholarly research asks when and where a particular text originated; how, why, by whom, for whom, and in what circumstances it was produced; what influences were at work in its production; what sources were used in its composition; and what message it was intended to convey.

In the 19th century, Biblical Criticism became divided between Higher Criticism – the study of the composition and history of biblical texts, and Lower Criticism – the close examination of the text to establish their original or "correct" readings. These terms, for a large part, are no longer used, and contemporary criticism has seen the rise of new methods of study which draw on literary and multidisciplinary sociological approaches to address the meaning(s) of texts and the wider world in which they were conceived. The various forms of study of the Scriptures (Textual, Form, Source, Traditional-Historical, Redaction, Canonical, Narrative, etc.) all claim to be ways to validate (or invalidate) the truth of the written words that we have today.

Historical criticism was the dominant form of criticism until the late 20th century when biblical critics became interested in questions aimed more at the meaning of the text than its origins and sought out methods used in mainstream literary criticism of the day. The reader may come upon the terms diachronic and synchronic forms of criticism. The diachronic form of criticism is concerned about the development of the scriptural texts over time. The other form (synchronic) focuses upon the text, as it exists at a particular moment – meaning the text we have today.[457]

This concept of focusing on the text's form and content is called New Criticism, or Formal Criticism.[458] While this direction of formal criticism became prominent in the 1920's, it flourished in the United States during the 1940's – 60's, becoming the dominant form in many scholastic circles in the 1970's.

Rhetorical criticism became a separate, distinct approach to Scripture in 1968, when James Muilenburg described the need for it and named the discipline in his

---

[457] This is often referred to as the "final form" in many scholarly works.

[458] (Tate 2012)

Society of Biblical Literature's presidential address delivered at the University of California, Berkley. His address (and subsequent article in the *Journal of Biblical Literature*), was entitled Form Criticism and Beyond.[459] Although various rhetorical-critical techniques were already in use regarding Scripture, Muilenburg's speech helped provide definition, direction and impetus for this critical approach to the study of the Scriptures. His students then provided a nucleus of practitioners for this sub discipline, and others, in turn, joined in the research.

This chapter will attempt to provide the reader with a definition of what is *Rhetorical Criticism*, the historical background, the presuppositions that are involved, the fundamental components and contradictions of this form of Higher Criticism.

Definition and Description

Rhetoric (more explanation can be found in the section on Presuppositions) is the use of available means of persuasion on the part of an author (speaker) wishing to influence the response of one or more readers (hearers) to their point of view.[460] Concerning rhetorical criticism, this form of analysis asks how the text *functions* for its audience, including especially its original audience. It is an analysis of how the author utilizes certain means of persuasion to advance their agenda for the people involved in a particular situation.

Whereas we find *historical criticism* seeking to discover the impact of text in its historical setting, the *rhetorical criticism* advocate seeks to insert himself into the situation. Therefore, by using a contemporary/historical interpretation, the scholar works to discover the author's (speaker's) presentation of the text to affect the hearer's (reader's) identification of the challenges presented and then to respond to these challenges in the way that the author (speaker) so determines.

Originally called *stylistic criticism* the followers of Muilenburg have sought bold, sophisticated attempts of bringing out the meaning of the texts in consideration.[461] Since *form criticism* appeared to become scholastic in its approach of assigning passages to traditional genres thus stereotyping them and forcing them into referring to nothing outside of the sanctuary, it was important to bring some semblance of usefulness to real life usage. The objective of this type of analysis was to delineate the individual units and their structure.[462] More can be said in the next section dealing with the Historical and Presuppositional Background of this critical method.

---

[459] (Muilenburg 1969)

[460] (McKenzie 2013)

[461] (Patrick and Scult 1990)

[462] (Patrick and Scult 1990)

Historical and Presuppositional Background

To begin this section of study on this critical method, let us begin by defining what is meant by the term Rhetoric. Rhetoric is the study of effective speaking and writing. Rhetoric is the art of persuasion. In its extensive history, rhetoric has enjoyed many definitions, accommodated many different purposes, and varied widely in what it included. Still for most of its history, it has maintained its fundamental character as a discipline for training students to perceive how language is at work orally and in writing, in addition to becoming proficient in applying the resources of language in their own speaking and writing.

Because rhetoric examines so attentively the <u>how</u> of language, the methods, and means of communication, it has sometimes been written off as something only concerned with style or appearances, and not with the quality or content of the communication. Rhetoric is an art that is just as much concerned with what one could say as how one might say it. Indeed, a basic premise for rhetoric is the indivisibility of means from meaning; how one says something conveys meaning as much as what one says. Rhetoric studies the effectiveness of language comprehensively, including its emotional impact, as much as its propositional content.

To continue our insight into rhetoric, we need to understand the three major parts of persuasion that this system incorporates. The three major parts are *Ethos, Pathos,* and *Logos. Ethos* means the good character and credibility of the speaker. You may want to think of *ethos* as related to "ethics," or the moral principles of the writer: ethos is the author's way of establishing trust with his or her reader, establishing his credibility. Questions we could ask in line with this could include: Why should I (the reader or listener) pay attention to what the person has communicated? How does the communicator provide examples or support that she has something valid and important for me to listen or read? Does the communicator provide evidence of their education or professional experience to convince me that he or she is a valid, educated, and experienced source? The arguments[463] presented in this form of rhetoric are designed to appeal to the credibility of the presenter.

Ethos concerns the appeal to the emotions of the listener/reader. You may want to think of *pathos* as empathy (the psychological identification with or vicarious experiencing the feelings, thoughts, or attitudes of another), which pertains to the experience of or sensitivity toward emotion. It is the quality or power in literature or speech, of arousing feelings of pity, sorrow, etc. Some questions that we could ask in accordance with this mode of rhetoric could include: How is the communicator trying to make one feel, or what has been communicated that makes me want to do something? What specific parts of the writer or speaker's message make me feel happy, sad, inspired, dejected, and so on? In other words, what emotions are triggered by the message being considered?

---

[463] "Argument" in these explanations are used in the sense of Logic – i.e. a statement, reason, or fact   for or against a point, an address or composition intended to convince or persuade; a persuasive discourse.

Finally, *Logos* appeals to the intellect as it seeks to furnish clear and persuasive proof for the argument being presented. You may want to think of *logos* as "logic," because something that is logical "makes sense"—it is reasonable. It comes from the Greek, which can be translated word, reason, or discourse; from the Greek root *legein* "to speak." In philosophy, *logos* can be understood as reason or the rational principle expressed in words and things, arguments, or justifications; it is personified as the source of order in the universe. In Christian Theology, it is the divine word or reason incarnate in Jesus Christ (John 1:1–14). Some questions that may arise in connection with this mode of rhetoric could include: What evidence does the person communicating provide that convinces one that his or her argument is logical—that it makes sense? What proof is the speaker/writer offering the listener/reader? How does this mode of rhetoric of the communicator appeal to the intellectual side of the receiver?

Rhetoric also takes on three forms according to Aristotle. These three forms are forensic, deliberate, and epideictic.[464] The first, forensic (or judicial) rhetoric is speech or writing that considers the justice or injustice of a certain charge or accusation. Today lawyers in trials decided by a judge or jury primarily employ forensic rhetoric. The next, deliberate rhetoric is speech or writing that attempts to persuade an audience to take (or not take) some action. Whereas judicial rhetoric is primarily concerned with past events, deliberative discourse, according to Aristotle, always advises about things to come. Political speeches and debates fall under the category of deliberative rhetoric. The final form or epideictic rhetoric is speech or writing that praises or blames. Also known as ceremonial discourse, epideictic rhetoric includes funeral orations, obituaries, graduation and retirement speeches, letters of recommendation, and nominating speeches at political conventions. Interpreted more broadly, epideictic rhetoric may also include works of literature.[465]

Rhetoric has a long history and has been codified in detail in many Greek writings. The Mesopotamians and Ancient Egyptians both valued the ability to speak with eloquence and wisdom. However, it wasn't until the rise of Greek democracy that rhetoric became a high art that was studied and developed systematically. Many historians credit the ancient city-state of Athens as the birthplace of classical rhetoric. Because Athenian democracy assembled free men into politics, these Athenian men had to be ready to speak in the Assembly and seek to persuade his countrymen to vote for or against a particular piece of legislation. A man's influence in ancient Athens depended on upon his rhetorical ability. Thus, small schools dedicated to teaching rhetoric began to form. The first of these schools began in the 5th century B.C. among an itinerant group of teachers called the Sophists. Sophists prided themselves on their ability to win any debate on any subject even if they had no prior knowledge of the topic through the use of confusing analogies, flowery metaphors, and clever wordplay. In short, the Sophists focused on style and presentation even at the expense of truth.[466]

---

[464] (Kostenberger 2011)

[465] (Nordquist n.d.)

[466] (McKay and McKay n.d.)

This manipulation of the truth brought about a negative connotation for the name Sophist, and in fact, we find that the Athenians executed Socrates for being a Sophist. Both Plato and Aristotle condemned the Sophists for relying solely on emotion to persuade an audience and for their disregard for truth. In his treatise, *The Art of Rhetoric*, Aristotle established a system for understanding and teaching rhetoric.

In *The Art of Rhetoric*, Aristotle defined rhetoric as "the faculty of observing in any given case the available means of persuasion." While Aristotle preferred persuasion through the use of reason alone, he recognized that at times an audience would not be capable of following arguments based solely on scientific and logical principles. If this was the case, the use of persuasive language and techniques were necessary for truth to be taught. According to Aristotle, sometimes you had to fight fire with fire.

The Art of Rhetoric had a tremendous influence on the development of the study of rhetoric for the next 2,000 years. Roman rhetoricians Cicero and Quintilian frequently referred to Aristotle's work, and universities required students to study *The Art of Rhetoric* during the 18th and 19th centuries.

Rhetorical criticism of the Bible can be dated back to at least St. Augustine. Augustine, the Church's foremost teacher in the classical art of Christian preaching, a master rhetorician, and former teacher of oratory, was convinced that the pagan rhetorical tradition, so important to the ancient cultures of Greece and Rome, had great insights to offer Christian preachers about the art of good preaching. From this, the church has utilized the concepts codified by the Greeks and Romans as a part of their hermeneutical methods. In the 4th century A.D., epistolary theory (an epistle is a narrative addressed to someone - as in the form of a letter) became part of rhetorical theory.

Thus, we have come to see that the modern application of techniques of rhetorical analysis to biblical texts begins with James Muilenburg in 1968 as a corrective to form criticism, which he saw as too generalized and insufficiently specific. For Muilenburg, rhetorical criticism emphasized the unique and unrepeatable message of the writer or speaker as addressed to his audience, including especially the techniques and devices which went into crafting the biblical narrative as it was heard (or read) by its audience.

"What Muilenburg called rhetorical criticism was not exactly the same as what secular literary critics called rhetorical criticism, and when biblical scholars became interested in "rhetorical criticism," they did not limit themselves to Muilenburg's definition...In some cases, it is difficult to distinguish between rhetorical criticism and literary criticism, or other disciplines".[467] Rhetorical criticism (at least as defined by Muilenburg) takes a special interest in the relationship between the biblical text and its intended audience within the context of the communal life setting. Rhetorical criticism seeks to ascertain how the text functions for its audience, including its original audience: to teach, persuade, guide, exhort, reproach, or inspire. It concentrates on identifying and elucidating unique features of the situation,

---

[467] (Morrision n.d.)

including both the techniques, manifest in the text itself and the relevant features of the cultural setting, through which this purpose is pursued.

So, we can ascertain that Muilenburg saw Rhetorical Criticism as an attempt to move beyond form criticism. It was not only looking at the form and genre of the piece but also the rhetorical devices employed to win over the reader/hearer. The *Sitz in leben* (German, roughly translated as "setting or situation in life") is expanded to include the response intended by the author.[468]

Fundamental Components

This brings us to discuss the fundamental components of this critical view. In this section of our analysis, we will discuss the areas of the assumptions that this critical method is based upon, the three types of rhetorical criticism (as given by David Goodwin[469]), rhetorical criticism of the Hebrew Bible, rhetorical criticism of the New Testament, and steps to application of this method (as described by George Kennedy[470]).

Beginning with the basic assumptions of this methodology we see that there are two. The first of these assumptions is that language is adequate, even being imperfect, to communicate human intentions. The second assumption that is accepted in this view is that a communicative act includes an intentional use of language, a response, and a rhetorical situation.[471] Both of these assumptions seem highly plausible and acceptable. It is only through language that man is able to communicate thoughts, feelings, ideas, and concepts. Often (sometimes intentional, sometimes unintentional) the ability to communicate can deliver a flawed or incorrect message.

In the field and study of communication, in a very simplistic explanation, there is a sender and a receiver. Without both of these components, no communication is produced. The sender/author is the one who initiates the message, and the receiver/reader (hearer) is the one who interprets the message. In between these two main functionaries, there are various filters (both good and bad) that can distort the message. In a perfect situation, the receiver hears (reads) and accurately interprets the message that the sender says (writes). Therefore, the sender/author utilizes language to produce a message that he/she intends for the hearer/reader to respond in a prescribed and intended method. Given this understanding of a simplistic model of communication, the two assumptions that we view here show that the concept of rhetorical criticism is interested in the process, the product, and the effect of the communication (spoken or written).[472]

---

[468] (Law 2012)

[469] (Goodwin 1991)

[470] (Kennedy 1984)

[471] (Tate 2012)

[472] (Tate 2012)

David Godwin proposes that there are three types of rhetorical criticism – traditional (Neo-Aristotelian), transitional, and contemporary.[473] The traditional method, also called the Neo-Aristotelian method is the first formal method of rhetorical criticism, and the most widely applied method. It deals with persuasive discourse, both in written and oral form. It looks through the lens of the three kinds of appeal (logos, ethos, and pathos) that we have previously discussed. The critic also will employ the two types of proof – artistic and inartistic. By artistic proofs, we mean those that may be discovered through rhetorical invention, arguments that the speaker must invent: definition, comparison, relationships, circumstances, testimony, notation, and conjugates. By inartistic proofs, we are speaking of the proofs which are not supplied by the writer's efforts, but existed beforehand, such as witnesses, admissions under torture, written contracts, and the like. The latter type needs only to be used; the first type has to be invented. Finally, in Neo-Aristotelian rhetorical criticism, the critic works through the five major divisions of research, invention, arrangement, style, memory, and delivery. Invention is the location and creation of ideas and materials for the speech/writing, arrangement is the structure/organization of the speech/writing, style is the language of the speech/writing, memory is the mastery of the subject matter of the speech/writing, and finally, delivery is of the management of the voice, gestures or genre in the presentation of the speech/writing.

The next type of rhetorical criticism given by Goodwin is the transitional method. This methodology looks at and examines the transactions between the rhetorical situation, the rhetorical strategies, and the rhetorical effects. The rhetorical situation is the context of the rhetorical undertaking, made up (at a minimum) of the communicator, the issue at hand, and an audience. The rhetorical strategies are an analogy, argument, persuasion, cause-and-effect, description, narration, illustration, process, division/classification, comparison/contrast, and definition. Finally, rhetorical effects are how the receivers (readers/hearers) react to the intended purpose of the writer/speaker.

The final form of rhetorical criticism as outlined by Goodwin is the contemporary method. Mark Klyn and Wayne Booth speak of a single method of critical analysis. Others consider a pluralistic approach to rhetorical criticism. They work from post-modern assumptions and place the critic as central to the method of critical analysis. In the general consensus, the methodology used can and is very fluid. In simple words, there is no right or wrong method. Post-modernism roots itself in the postulate that there are no foundational truths, and as such all methods and considerations are equally acceptable. Thus, the historical-critical components hold no place in this branch of rhetorical criticism.

From Goodwin's views and analysis let us move into a reflection upon the rhetorical criticism of the Hebrew Bible (the Old Testament). The tasks, as defined by Muilenburg, would distinguish this approach from that of *form criticism* and *source criticism*. In the methodology of source criticism, the critic reads the text searching for indications of earlier texts and traditions. The goal seems to be to discover the history and culture of the community at the time of the earlier texts. This differs from rhetorical criticism because in rhetorical criticism the critic reads the

---

[473] (Goodwin 1991)

text as an intentional communication reflecting the needs, interests, and challenges that were facing the persons it was delivered to.[474] This creates a difference in the way that features such as, repetition, changes in the poetic design, etc. The rhetorical critic seeks to discover any signs of the internal composition in its communication purposes before researching the possibly of faulty editing or flaws in the existence of the communication.[475]

Form critics also study a text to discover what it can yield about the prehistory of traditions, the social settings, and the typical literary patterns and the circumstances that make the communication useful for that particular text. The rhetorical critic analyzes the particular text in its final distinctive form without paying any particular attention to the variations or changes from the typical use of that form.[476]

Considering the rhetorical analysis of the Hebrew Bible, the critic generally starts by identifying the start and finish of each rhetorical unit – i.e. the identification of the various literary devices employed.[477] The determination of the cohesion of these units helps establish the "boundaries"[478] of the unit. When these "boundaries" are established provisionally, the critic then seeks to identify the internal structures[479], rhetorical devices[480], and any indication of "movement" inside of the text.[481] Often a painstaking process of re-writing and schematically organizing the unit being examined accomplishes this.[482] Sometimes the critic's focus on the text remains at the level of style and composition; some go beyond this to questioning how and in what direction does the communication move the audience – how is the dynamics of persuasion utilized.

The use of rhetorical criticism is not refined to the Hebrew Bible (Old Testament) alone. The use of this methodology is not a new form of interpretation of the New Testament teachings. In his work *On Christian Doctrine*, Augustine in the fourth century directly addresses this topic. Others who have used this methodology of research and teaching include Philip Melanchthon and Erasmus.[483] While many of the modern applicants of this method utilize the new methods of rhetorical critical study, the criticism of the New Testament generally utilize the classical Greco-Roman handbooks on rhetoric as their heuristic tools. This assists them in discovering the ethos, pathos, and logos of traditional rhetoric to explain the approach and appeals made in the communications. We will consider the

---

[474] (Watson and Hauser 1994)

[475] (Meynet 1998)

[476] (Trible 1994)

[477] These devices would include, but not be limited to acrostics, repetition, inclusio, etc.

[478] (Muilenburg 1969)

[479] The smaller units within the larger units.

[480] Such as, parallelism, alliteration, chiasm, and other such features.

[481] (Muilenburg 1969)

[482] (Trible 1994) (Meynet 1998)

[483] (Watson 1988) (Mack 1990)

problems incorporated in today's approach to rhetorical criticism of the New Testament in the following section of our topic.

One practical approach to utilizing the rhetorical method of critical study has been developed by George Kennedy,[484] although this is not the only method used today.[485] Kennedy's methodology (presented in the following from his work, *New Testament Interpretation Through Rhetorical Criticism*) generally is a five-step process to research and develop the critical analysis of the book (or passage). The first step is that one needs to determine the boundaries of the rhetorical unit for analysis. This might be a complete book or multiple units within that book. The units might be found by transitional words, distinctive words or phrases, a change of mode or genre, or any other markers discovered in the text.

Once the units have been discerned, the critic must describe the rhetorical situation and the issue, problem, or situation that causes or prompts this unit of communication that calls forth the response discovered in the rhetorical unit. Sometimes this is easy to see, other times it makes the critic delve too deeply into the passage. Even in these early stages, the critic must be attentive to discern the author's agenda that is at work in this situation.

The next stage (step) is that the critic needs to determine the rhetorical problem or the point of the issue, and determine the rhetorical genre of the unit (which form is used for the agenda – forensic, deliberative, or epideictic). Determining what is the main point in the discourse is often involved because of other rhetorical situations that intersect with the main communicative discourse. The determination of the rhetorical problem is closely akin to determining the rhetorical genre being used in the text. The genre is closely affiliated with the kind of goal the presenter is seeking to elicit. The form of rhetoric used will utilize certain strategies common to that form.

The fourth step that Kennedy places before the reader is to analyze the invention[486], arrangement, and style. When studying the finished work, the critic must look at the appeals used, not all that were available to the communicator. The use of classical rhetorical criticism gives the researcher three kinds of appeals to look for. We have already discussed these – ethos, pathos, and logos. The researcher needs to consider the invention – the choice of appeals utilized in the finished piece of communication.

The rhetorical critic must also study the arrangement of the communication. How did the creator line up his arguments and appeals? How would these produce the optimal effects sought? They also need to consider the style that the communicators choose. The proper tone and level of argumentation used to attempt to achieve the communicator's purpose. The classical rhetorical criticism

---

[484] (Kennedy 1984)

[485] An alternative to Kennedy's method can be seen in deSilva's work. (deSilva 2009)

[486] Invention is the first step in constructing an oration. It is here that the orator gathers together the possible arguments available to address the various segments of the rhetorical situation.

methodology also included two more areas – memory and delivery. These are not readily applicable to the New Testament texts that are studied.

The fifth and final stage (step) that Kennedy chose was to evaluate the rhetorical effectiveness of the unit in its employment of invention, arrangement, and style in meeting the rhetorical issue, problem, or situation that causes or prompts this unit of communication that calls forth the response. In other words, is the rhetoric of the text up to the challenge of persuading the audience in the situation?[487] It is this step that challenges the critic to determine the answers to questions dealing with the original presentation and response of the audience. Did the communicator provide evidence of his credibility? Did she provide answers to what the audience needed to know to respond according to the projected outcome? Were the needs of the ethos, pathos, and logos appear to be able to produce the intended response from the hearer/reader?

Thus, in this short consideration of the fundamental components of this methodology, we started with the two basic assumptions, reviewed the three types of rhetorical criticism as given by David Goodwin, a brief overview of rhetorical criticism of the Hebrew Bible, followed by a study of the rhetorical criticism of the New Testament, and ended with the suggested steps to applying this method as was described by George Kennedy. Next, we will briefly touch upon some of the fundamental issues negatively impacting this Critical methodology of Biblical study.

Fundamental Contradictions

Kostenberger has stated, "Application of rhetorical criticism to the study of the Paul's letters and those of other New Testament writers is of doubtful merit."[488] And so, in this section, let us consider some of the negative aspects of this field of biblical research.

In some areas, questions have been broached on whether the use of rhetorical criticism applies to written communication. Particularly the question as to whether this form of study can be used with Paul's letters. Should the ancient rhetorical handbooks be used, or would the also ancient handbooks on epistolary be better used? The epistolary handbooks catalog the various types of letters with statements on why a writer would choose one over another. They also provide examples of the various letters. The objection given against the epistolary handbooks is that much of the New Testament writings are of an oral nature. Several books are not letters at all (i.e. First John and Hebrews as well as the Gospels). In addition, even the true letters have an oral/public aspect to them. They were designed to be read aloud at the gathering of the church. Some believe that they represent the sermon or speech that the author would have delivered if he could have been present to do it.

One aspect that seems to be the problem is that the rhetorical critics apply the Greco-Roman stylism of rhetoric to manuscripts older than the development of this form. David deSilva in the *Oxford Encyclopedia of Biblical Interpretation* uses the

---

[487] (McKenzie 2013)

[488] (Kostenberger 2011, page 468)

example of Yehoshua Gitay using this rhetorical method as a framework for the study of Isaiah 40-48[489]. Gitay (one who accepted the Deutero-Isaiah authorship) did so, not assuming that the author had access to this methodology, but that using this tool can help the researcher to uncover the strategies of persuasion and find the text's deeper rational, emotional, and ethical appeals to the reader.

One danger that is possible with this form of biblical study is in allowing the text freely to overflow the bounds of the intended purpose – overflowing to the point of flooding – and is becoming very apparent in the followers of this discipline. The task is to discover what is in the text, not to seek to make the text conform to the tradition reflected in the Greco-Roman handbooks. The critic can easily slip into eisegesis instead of exegesis. In fact, probably the area that the most criticism is leveled against this form of biblical study is in the area of the scholars seeking to force the texts into the genres of rhetoric. Very few of the New Testament texts fit the basic patterns of rhetoric (an example is Galatians which comes very close to fitting the forensic form of rhetoric) most do not. The scholar and researcher must take care in the heuristic use of the ancient handbooks in the analysis of the biblical texts.

Conclusion

Therefore, having spent this time in this chapter considering the definition of what is *Rhetorical Criticism*, the historical background, the presuppositions that are involved, the fundamental components and contradictions of this form of Higher Criticism, we now provide a few concluding statements and considerations.

Rhetorical Criticism gives invitation to study and research the text of the Bible in its final form as a very well thought out and presented composition. It invites the critic to see the passages as vehicles for creating an influence upon the readers to be challenged and come to see how they apply to their situations and lead to a response to these situations.

Rhetorical Criticism has brought attention back to the text and its composition rather than focusing on the pre-history of the text as form and source criticism does. In a sense, this has accomplished the desire and goal of Muilenburg as put forth in his address to the Society of Biblical Literature in 1968. Rhetorical Criticism has provided a new form of framing the way one observes the literary unit within the text. Whether it is a large unit (such as an entire book of the Bible) or a micro-unit (such as a verse of paragraph), one is called to determine the intentions of the originator, the intentional use of the chosen language and the response anticipated.

Rhetorical Criticism focuses the scholar on the sender/receiver connection. One seeks to discover the rhetorical situation, the process of the communication, and the effect that it has had and will have upon the reader/listener. While providing a method of understanding the biblical passages, it also is vulnerable to misuse by substituting eisegesis in place of exegesis. From the time of Augustine (perhaps even earlier), the study of the Scriptures through the use of rhetoric has been around. We ascertained that Muilenburg saw Rhetorical Criticism as an

---

[489] (McKenzie 2013)

attempt to move beyond form criticism. It was not only looking at the form and genre of the piece but also the rhetorical devices employed to win over the reader/hearer. The *Sitz in leben* (German, roughly translated as "setting or situation in life") is expanded to include the response intended by the author.[490]

While having a place in the study of the Holy Scriptures, rhetorical criticism is both helpful and possibly a harmful way of maintaining the valid understanding of the truth as Peter wrote, "for no prophecy was ever produced by the will of man, but men carried along by the Holy Spirit spoke from God."[491]

---

[490] (Law 2012)

[491] 2 Peter 1:21 UASV

CHAPTER 6 Reader-Response and Narrative Criticism

Thomas Howe

Introduction

At the very beginning of his monumental work, *A History of Literary Criticism and Theory*, M. A. R. Habib declares, "In our world it has become more important than ever that we learn to read critically."[492] What does it mean to "read critically"? What, in fact, is criticism? The term is tossed around and employed by everyone, and yet there are few who take the time to define the term. This may be because its meaning is thought to be so obvious that no one thinks it necessary to define. Like many academic terms, it is used so often, and so often with reference to views that conflict, it may be in danger of losing all meaning. A term that becomes so broad in its use is in danger of becoming useless. *When* the term first came to life is perhaps a question not likely to be answered with any certainty. It certainly seems, *prima facie*, to be a term that indicates a method of doing something. One dictionary defines the term thus: "the scientific investigation of literary documents (as the Bible) in regard to such matters as origin, text, composition, character, or history."[493] There can be no doubt that the term acquired global currency when adopted by Immanuel Kant in the title of several of his works: *Kritik der reinen Vernunft*, that is, *Critique of Pure Reason*.[494] Kant employed the term to characterize his philosophical methodology. It was a rational investigation and presentation of Kant's notion of what it means to know and how knowledge occurs. As Christopher Kaiser has observed, "A strict methodology can suffocate the spirit of open inquiry."[495] Unfortunately, it seems that criticism in general, and biblical criticism in particular, has developed such a methodology that, as we shall see, other forms of open inquiry are *a priori* ruled unscholarly.

A Short History of Biblical Criticism

Leading Up

The Renaissance had provided the Reformers with the tools needed to challenge the institutional organization of the Catholic Church. At least since Augustine, the Roman Catholic Church had used the Latin Vulgate as the Bible from

---

[492] M. A. R. Habib, *A History of Literary Criticism and Theory from Plato to the Present* (Malden, Massachusetts: Blackwell Publishing, 2008), 1.

[493] *Merriam-Webster Unabridged Dictionary* (2002), s.v. "Criticism."

[494] Immanuel Kant, *Kritik der reinen Vernunft* (Hamburg: Felix Meiner Verlag, 1998); *Critique of Pure Reason*, tran. Paul Guyer and Allen W. Wood. Cambridge: Cambridge University Press, 1998).

[495] Christopher B. Kaiser, *Creational Theology and the History of Physical Science: The Creationist Tradition from Basil to Bohr* (Leiden: Brill, 1997), 11.

which theology and piety were extricated and systematized. With the Renaissance cry, *ad fontes* ("to the sources"), the European world of scholarship began to develop a historical awareness. During the Middle Ages, biblical studies were designed to use the text in such a manner as to provide insights on the present. There was no sense of the historical context or the historical situatedness of biblical passages or biblical books. The historical awakening of the Renaissance forced the scholar to view the Bible as a book composed in an ancient historical setting that must be studied in its own right to be able properly to interpret the text.

Also, the return to the sources meant that the Reformers could sidestep the Vulgate and go directly to the documents themselves. Yet the warnings of the Scholastics that uncontrolled access to the Bible would garner more harm than good did not sway the Reformers from working diligently to make the Bible available in the vernacular. And, precisely as the Roman Catholic apologists has admonished, movements, and isms, and cults, and various brands of reformers multiplied as each leader or group approached the text and interpreted it independently. Closely following upon the growth of religious groups came conflict and war that ravaged Europe so that there was not a moment's peace or an unaffected mother. The critics of religion soon became aware that there seemed to be no non-circular way of interpreting the Bible. Everyone claimed that the Bible was their authoritative source, yet their conflicting and contradictory conclusions seemed to indicate that one could appeal to the Bible on the basis of his own interpretative method. As Michael Legaspi observes, "For each group, the presence of the *other* Christian confession, which also claimed fidelity to the Bible made it necessary for each group to defend its distinctive mode of biblical interpretation."[496] As Legaspi goes on to explain, "the Bible proved 'an insufficient basis for distinguishing between Protestant and Catholic'; as a result, 'the shared language of Scripture' could not be the 'primary source of theological precision and judgment.'"[497] Approaching the biblical text meant viewing it from one's confessional perspective, and Legaspi points out, "Reading or hearing the Bible was not sufficient for understanding it. One first had to choose where to stand."[498]

By the time Jean Astruc (1684–1766) published his conclusions about Mosaic authorship, there already existed a tradition of scholarship in which the figure of Moses was analyzed and examined from many different perspectives. Moses had been presented as the originator of Israelite religion, the founder of the nation, and the victim of assassination at the hands of Joshua and Caleb. Legaspi describes Astruc's claims. Although the quote is long, it is necessary to include all of it for getting a sense of his presentation:

> To Astruc, Moses was the keeper of earlier documents, the *mémoires*. Moses had at his disposal twelve written documents, two major and ten minor ones, which he organized into four distinct columns. His two main sources, A and B, maintained an unvarying preference for a particular divine name: *Elohim* in the A source and

---

[496] Michael C. Legaspi, *The Death of Scripture and the Rise of Biblical Studies* (Oxford: Oxford University Press, 2010), 17 (emphasis in original).

[497] Ibid.

[498] Ibid., 18.

Jehovah in the B source. The use of divine names as a source-critical criterion was the cornerstone of his theory, an innovation that would become, through the work of Eichhorn, the basis for modern Pentateuchal criticism. The bulk of the *Conjectures* is simply a division of Genesis (and Exodus 1-2) into the four putative columns. Astruc aimed to reproduce, line by line, the very documents that at one time lay before Moses. To this synopsis he added several *remarques* describing the advantages of his system. It explained away many infelicities: the puzzling alternation in the use of divine names, troubling repetitions in the narrative, and discrepancies in the chronological perspectives of the narrator *(antichronismes)*. The sources that Moses inherited not only used different names for God, they also originated in different time periods. The source divisions thus saved Moses from charges of negligence and stupidity. Can it be imagined, Astruc asked, that Moses is responsible for faults, repetitions, and bizarre variations which are better and more naturally explained by the existence of multiple underlying sources? Astruc's *Conjectures* was an apologetic work. It was not simply a vague, skeptical discussion of Mosaic authorship. Rather, it was a clear, constructive, and highly detailed presentation of Pentateuchal sources calculated to deflect criticism of the Bible. It was intended to acquit the biblical *text* of anachronisms and irregularities by showing that the reader of Genesis is actually dealing with disparate *texts*. How these came together to form Genesis—when Moses did not intend to join them in this way—is not entirely certain. Clearly aware that he had come to a weakness in his theory, Astruc guessed that some kind of scribal negligence or mistake was to blame for the disordered appearance of Genesis. The blame, then, lay with unnamed copyists. Moses remained, for Astruc, the revered *Auteur* whose unique wisdom, education, and political experience demanded the highest respect.[499]

Rise of Modern Natural Science

The rise of modern natural science created a whole new way of understanding scholarship: "It was no longer possible, as was the case in the Middle Ages, to appeal to God as a kind of Aristotelian *prima causa* ["first cause"]. The scholar was forced to find the *natural cause*, and explanation kept within the Kantian categories of time and space. It was assumed that any phenomenon has a natural cause, meaning that it should be traceable for human investigators."[500] An example of this is the passage in Deuteronomy 34 that recounts the death of Moses. Scholars whose labors were expected to be "scientific" concluded that Moses certainly did not write this material. As Lemche explains, "When Deuteronomy concludes with the story about Moses's death, it might be reasonable to assume that Moses at least did not write

---

[499] Ibid., 136–37.

[500] Niels Peter Lemche, *The Old Testament Between Theology and History: A Critical Survey* (Louisville: Westminster John Knox Press, 2008), 33–34.

that chapter (Deuteronomy 34)."[501] A "scientific" conclusion could not propose that this information was supernaturally revealed to Moses before his death since that would not be an explanation in terms of natural causes, that is, a "scientific" explanation. It was reasonable to conclude that Moses did not write this material because people do not generally know the details of how they died, or at least they are not around to write them down. So, it is perfectly natural, "scientific," to believe that Moses did not write the material about how he died.

The antisupernatural bias is evident in such observations as: "The book [of Daniel] reflects political and religious events that belong to the middle of the second century BCE, the Maccabean period. Here the references to acts that took place in 165 BCE, the Seleucid King Antioch IV's desecration of the temple of Jerusalem, are decisive for the date of Daniel."[502] There is no acknowledgment of even the possibility of supernatural prophecy. In fact, Lemche refers to Daniel's prophetic material as, "This piece of 'prophetic' literature . . ." As is representative of historical-critical "scholars," by placing the word 'prophetic' in quotation marks, Lemche indicates the complete rejection of the possibility of actual prophecy. Lemche emphatically declares, "The history of reality happens within the confines of space and time. There is no room for miracles. The supernatural has no say."[503]

The Nature of Biblical Criticism

Biblical criticism is usually thought to be synonymous with historical criticism, or what is frequently referred to as higher criticism or the historical-critical method. However, whereas biblical criticism is an umbrella term that refers to the many kinds of critical method used in biblical studies, historical criticism, or the historical-critical method, can actually refer to a group of techniques that are supposedly used to study the historical, social, and cultural background of the Bible. Unfortunately, the literature often subsumes the findings of some other critical method under the heading of historical-criticism. For example, the Documentary Hypothesis is usually referred to as the application of the historical-critical method when in fact the claims of the hypothesis are the results of the application of several critical methods or techniques, including source criticism, redaction criticism, as well as historical criticism. According to Richard and Kendall Soulen, Biblical Criticism "refers in the broadest sense to the use of rational judgment in understanding the Bible."[504] Concerning the term 'biblical criticism,' John Barton says, "The term 'biblical criticism' is now somewhat outmoded. It is common to speak of 'biblical studies' and of 'biblical interpretation,' but for the older term 'biblical criticism' it has become more usual to say 'the historical-critical method' (occasionally 'historico-

---

[501] Lemc Niels Peter Lemche, *The Old Testament Between Theology and History: A Critical Survey* (Louisville: Westminster John Knox Press, 2008), 33–34.he, *The Old Testament*, 37.

[502] Ibid., 97.

[503] Ibid., 261.

[504] *Handbook of Biblical Criticism*, 3d ed (2001), s.v. "Biblical Criticism."

critical')."[505] Because of this terminological confusion, we will use the term 'biblical criticism' as an umbrella term to refer to the totality of criticisms or critical approaches. The specific methods or techniques will be referred to by their specific titles.

Edgar Krentz reports the "critical steps" that came out of The Ecumenical Study Conference at Wadham College, Oxford in 1949: "(1) the determination of the text; (2) the literary form of the passage; (3) the historical situation, the *Sitz im Leben*; (4) the meaning which the words had for the original author and hearer or reader; (5) the understanding of the passage in the light of its total context and the background out of which it emerged."[506] This sounds very much like the steps prescribed in any contemporary course on exegesis. There is, however, a critical assumption that is not identified in the listing of these steps. Soulen and Soulen identify the underlying perspective of the practice of biblical criticism: "More narrowly, however, it ['Biblical Criticism'] refers to an approach to the study of scripture that is centrally concerned with searching for and applying neutral, i.e., scientific and nonsectarian, canons of judgment in its investigation of the biblical text."[507] Not all biblical critics agree that criticism is a scientific method. According to John Barton, "Even if biblical critics did generally believe their own work to be the application of historical-critical *method* understood in a scientific way, they would be wrong. Biblical criticism is not, in fact, the application of method to the biblical text."[508] Nevertheless, James Kugel points out, "Stating around 150 years ago, a major effort was launched in universities and divinity schools in different countries— principally in Germany and Scandinavia, Holland, England, and the United States—to understand the Bible afresh, reading it 'scientifically' without any presuppositions."[509]

However, it seems that the standard books on introduction to Biblical Criticism generally employ some reference to a scientific method in defining it. According to Krentz, Ulrich Wilckens provides the reader with a "formal definition of scientific biblical interpretation,"[510] by which he means biblical criticism: "The only scientifically responsible interpretation of the Bible is that investigation of the biblical texts that, with a methodologically consistent use of historical understanding in the present state of its art, seeks via reconstruction to recognize and describe the meaning these texts have had in the context of the tradition history of early

---

[505] John Barton, *The Nature of Biblical Criticism* (Louisville, Kentucky: Westminster John Knox Press, 2007), 1.

[506] A. Richardson and W. Schweitzer, ed., *Biblical Authority for Today* (Philadelphia: Westminster Press, 1951), 241–44; quoted in Edgar Krentz, *The Historical-Critical Method* (Philadelphia: Fortress Press, 1975), 2.

[507] *Handbook of Biblical Criticism*, 3d ed (2001), s.v. "Biblical Criticism."

[508] Barton, *Biblical Criticism*, 57.

[509] James L. Kugel, *How to Read the Bible: A Guide to Scripture, Then and Now* (New York: Free Press, 2008), xiii.

[510] Edgar Krentz, *The Historical-Critical Method* (Philadelphia: Fortress Press, 1975), 33.

Christianity."[511] In the opening statement of his book on the history and problems of the New Testament, Werner Kümmel refers to the "scientific view of the New Testament."[512] This scientific method, if indeed it is a scientific method, grew out of the conflicts during the Enlightenment between what was believed to be rational biblical study and the hegemony Catholic church. To understand the presuppositions upon which Biblical Criticism are still based, it will be important to look briefly and its origins.

Descartes

Crucial to the critical approach to the Bible is the claim to encounter the text without any theological bias or confessional attachments. This approach grew out of the Enlightenment effort to investigate reality without bias, prejudice, or any preconceived notion of what reality must be. This was particularly an assumption of natural science that developed as a result of Descartes' influence. Descartes had influenced not only philosophy but all branches of inquiry to begin any intellectual pursuit by doubting all that was supposedly known. "In terms of his use of God to solve the fundamental problems of epistemology, Descartes' heritage was not his solution but the difficulties which he raised and, perhaps most importantly, the way in which he raised them. His grandiose attempt to ground all knowledge on God was not successful, but in posing the issue as he did he boosted the possibilities for science to exist as an activity autonomous from all theological and ecclesiastical interference."[513]

The sixteenth century was focused on the need for certain knowledge in all branches of inquiry, especially in theology. The centuries of religious wars had devastated the land and exhausted the people, and certain knowledge seemed the only way to bring peace and rest. As James Byrne goes on to point out, "There is, moreover, no more convincing example of this passionate search for certainty which became one of the great, dominant ideas around the middle of the century than the work of Descartes. The purpose of the Meditations was to provide proofs for the existence of God, which equaled or even surpassed geometrical proofs in certainty and self-evidence. Descartes' whole philosophy was motivated by the question of the possibility of certain knowledge, and its success would be incomprehensible had this not also been the question of this time."[514]

Descartes' method begins, as is well known, with doubt by which he ultimately arrives at the undoubtable assertion, "I think, therefore I am." Descartes concludes that while he is attending his mind upon this indubitable assertion, he sees that this

---

[511] Ulrich Wilckens, "Über die Bedeutung historischer Kritik in der modernen Bibelsexegese," in *Was heisst Auslegung der Heiligen Schrift?* (Regensburg: Friedrich Pustet, 1966), 133; quoted in Krentz, *Historical-Critical Method,* 33.

[512] Werner Georg Kümmel, *The New Testament: The History of the Investigation of Its Problems,* trans. S. McLean Gilmour and Howard C. Kee (Nashville: Abingdon Press, 1970), 13.

[513] James M. Byrne, *Religion and the Enlightenment from Descartes to Kant* (Louisville, Kentucky: Westminster John Knox Press, 1996), 65.

[514] Ibid., 11.

is a clear and distinct perception. As Delahaunty puts it, "he then picks out a feature of his state of mind when he is attending to that proposition (that it is a state of clear and distinct perception); he infers that it is the possession of this feature which causes his state of mind to be one of knowledge; and he is tentatively extrapolating the general rule that any conscious state which exhibits the mark of clear and distinct perception will be knowledge."[515] Descartes will then apply this criterion to any additional propositions as a test for truth or falsehood. As Delahaunty goes on to say, "In the last step, he seems covertly to assume the causal axiom that if a state is F because it is Y, then any Y-state will also be F."[516] But Descartes' quest goes further than simply a question of the existence of God. That truth had not been widely questioned as yet. Rather, Descartes' quest was for a certainty that would ultimately and finally resolve the conflicts between confessions. Descartes hoped that he would be able to deduce from his first principles a system of philosophy and religion that would, having the certainty of geometry, force all sides to accept the force of the demonstration.

Another of Descartes' assertions that becomes an assumption universally accepted is that extra-mental reality is constituted of body extended in space. There is no sense of anything metaphysical in extra-mental reality. Consequently, during the Enlightenment, the assumptions that are imbibed by all are (1) one must begin any intellectual endeavor by doubting everything that cannot be demonstrated to be true; (2) truth is demonstrated by the characteristic of being a clear and distinct perception after the manner of Descartes' Cogito; (3) extra-mental reality is ultimately constituted of body extended in space.

Spinoza

Spinoza, who is generally held to be the father of modern biblical criticism, was highly influenced by Descartes' method even though he argued strongly against much of Descartes' system and conclusions. "The challenge of modernization was forced on the church by the emergence of liberal political philosophy in the seventeenth century. Figures such as Baruch Spinoza are among the first to practice what we recognize today as modern historical criticism of the Bible."[517] And Spinoza's *Theological-Political Treatise* was "the first extended treatise on biblical criticism to employ recognizably modern methods of analysis. 'In our time,' writes Leo Strauss (1899–1973), 'scholars generally study the Bible in the manner in which they study any other book. As is generally admitted, Spinoza more than any other man laid the foundation for this kind of Biblical study.' To understand Spinoza's views on the Bible, one must know his politics."[518] Spinoza was also influenced by the rise of modern natural science, which, according to Travis Frampton, led

---

[515] R. J. Delahaunty, *Spinoza: Arguments of the Philosophers* (London: Routledge & Kegan Paul Books, 1985), 16.

[516] Ibid.

[517] Roy A. Harrisville and Walter Sundberg, *The Bible in Modern Culture: Theology and Historical-Critical Method from Spinoza to Käseman* (Grand Rapids: William B. Eerdmans Publishing Company, 1995), 25.

[518] Ibid., 37.

Spinoza to the conclusion that natural law, and "natural science and mathematics . . . [were] the only way to ascertain reliable knowledge of the universe, humankind, and true ideas."[519] But to understand his methodology, one must understand his principles of interpretation. The following quote, although very long, is necessary in order to have a better understanding of how Spinoza approached the biblical text.

1. It should inform us of the nature and properties of the language in which the Bible was written and which its authors were accustomed to speak. Thus, we should be able to investigate, from established linguistic usage, all the possible meanings of any passage. And since all the writers of both the Old and the New Testaments were Hebrews, a study of the Hebrew language must undoubtedly be a prime requisite not only for an understanding of the books of the Old Testament, which were written in that language but also for the New Testament. For although the latter books were published in other languages, their idiom is Hebraic.

2. The pronouncements made in each book should be assembled and listed under headings so that we can thus have to hand all the texts that treat of the same subject. Next, we should note all those that are ambiguous or obscure, or that appear to contradict one another. Now here I term a pronouncement obscure or clearer according to the degree of difficulty with which the meaning can be elicited from the context, and not according to the degree of difficulty with which its truth can be perceived by reason. For the point at issue is merely the meaning of the texts, not their truth. I would go further: in seeking the meaning of Scripture, we should take every precaution against the undue influence, not only of our own prejudices but of our faculty of reason in so far as that is based on the principles of natural cognition. In order to avoid confusion between true meaning and truth of fact, the former must be solved simply from linguistic usage, or from a process of reasoning that looks to no other basis than Scripture.

For further clarification, I shall give an example to illustrate all that I have here said. The savings of Moses, "God is fire," and "God is jealous," are perfectly clear as long as we attend only to the meanings of the words; and so, in spite of their obscurity from the perspective of truth and reason, I classify these sayings as clear. Indeed, even though their literal meaning is opposed to the natural light of reason, this literal meaning must nevertheless be retained unless it is in clear opposition to the basic principles derived from the study of Scripture. On the other hand, if these statements in their literal interpretation were found to be in contradiction with the basic principles derived from Scripture, they would have to be interpreted differently (that is, metaphorically) even though they were in complete agreement with reason. Therefore, the question as to whether Moses did or did not believe that God is fire must in no wise be decided by the rationality or irrationality of the belief, but solely from other pronouncements of Moses. In this particular case, since there are several other instances where Moses clearly tells us that God has no resemblance to visible things in heaven or on the earth or in the water, we must hence conclude that either this statement or all those others must be explained metaphorically. Now since one should depart as little as possible from the literal

---

[519] Travis L. Frampton, *Spinoza and the Rise of Historical Criticism of the Bible* (New York: T&T Clark, 2006), 8.

meaning, we should first inquire whether this single pronouncement, 'God is fire,' admits of any other than a literal meaning; that is, whether the word 'fire' can mean anything other than ordinary natural fire. If the word 'fire' is not found from linguistic usage to have any other meaning, then neither should this statement be interpreted in any other way, however much it is opposed to reason, and all other passages should be made to conform to it, however much they accord with reason. If this, too, should prove impossible on the basis of linguistic usage, then these pronouncements would have to be regarded as irreconcilable, and we should, therefore, suspend judgment regarding them. However, since the word 'fire' is also used in the sense of anger or jealousy (Job ch. 31 v. 12), Moses' pronouncements are easily reconciled, and we can properly conclude that these two statements, 'God is fire' and 'God is jealous' are one and the same statement.

Again, as Moses clearly teaches that God is jealous and nowhere tells us that God is without passions or emotions, we must evidently conclude that Moses believed this, or at least that he intended to teach this, however strongly we may be convinced that this opinion is contrary to reason. For, as we have shown, it is not permissible for us to manipulate Scripture's meaning to accord with our reason's dictates and our preconceived opinions; all knowledge of the Bible is to be sought from the Bible alone.

3. Finally our historical study should set forth the circumstances relevant to all the extant books of the prophets, giving the life, character and pursuits of the author of every book, detailing who he was, on what occasion and at what time and for whom and in what language he wrote. Again, it should relate what happened to each book, how it was first received, into whose hands it fell, how many variant versions there were, by whose decision it was received into the canon, and, finally, how all the books, now universally regarded as sacred, were united into a single whole. All these details, I repeat, should be available from a historical study of Scripture; for in order to know which pronouncements were set forth as laws and which as moral teaching, it is important to be acquainted with the life, character and interests of the author. Furthermore, as we have a better understanding of a person's character and temperament, so we can more easily explain his words. Again, to avoid confusing teaching of eternal significance with those which are of only temporary significance or directed only to the benefit of a few, it is also important to know on what occasion, at what period, and for what nation or age all these teachings were written down. Finally, it is important to know the other details we have listed so that, in addition to the authenticity of each book, we may also discover whether or not it may have been contaminated by spurious insertions, whether errors have crept in, and whether experienced and trustworthy scholars have corrected these. All this information is needed by us so that we may accept only what is certain and incontrovertible, and not be led by blind impetuosity to take for granted whatever is set before us

Now when we possess this historical account of Scripture, and all are firmly resolved not to assert as the indubitable doctrine of the prophets anything that does not follow from this study or cannot be most clearly inferred from it, it will then be time to embark on the task of investigating the meaning of the prophets and the Holy Spirit. But for this task, too, we need a method and order similar to that which we employ in interpreting Nature from the facts presented before us. Now in examining natural phenomena we, first of all, try to discover those features that are most universal and common to the whole of Nature, to wit, motion-and-rest and the rules and laws governing them which Nature always observes and through which she constantly acts, and then we advance gradually from the two other less universal features. In just the same way we must first seek from our study of Scripture that which is most universal and forms the basis and foundation of all Scripture; in short, that which is commended in Scripture by all the prophets as doctrine eternal and most profitable for all mankind. For example, that God exists, one alone and omnipotent, who alone should be worshiped, who cares for all, who loves above all others those who worship him and love their neighbors as themselves. These and similar doctrines, I repeat, are taught everywhere in Scripture so clearly and explicitly that no one has ever been in any doubt as to its meaning on these points. But what God is, in what way he sees and provides for all things and similar matters, Scripture does not teach formally, and as eternal doctrine. On the contrary, we have clearly shown that the prophets themselves were not in agreement on these matters, and therefore on topics of this kind we should make no assertion that claims to be the doctrine of the Holy Spirit, even though the natural light of reason may be quite decisive on that point.[520]

Harrisville provides a very good summary of these three principles:

> In the pivotal seventh chapter of the Treatise, Spinoza offers three basic rules for critical study of the Bible (see 142–44). First, such study 'should inform us of the nature and properties of the language in which the Bible was written and which its authors were accustomed to speak.' Biblical study is based on language study. Second, the 'pronouncements' of each book should be organized by subject matter for the purpose of comparison and contrast with special attention paid to those that are obscure or contradictory. Finally, the circumstances of each book and author must be set forth so that various historical settings of Scripture are taken into account and clarified. Spinoza's method is one that the contemporary reader will readily recognize as common to scholarly literature on the Bible. The accent is on historical understanding; religious claims are studiously avoided.[521]

Frampton takes exception to Harrisville and Sundberg's assessment of Spinoza's motivation as an effort to eviscerate the core theology of the Bible: ". . . it was not the political philosophies of the seventeenth century, with representative figures like Spinoza, Thomas Hobbes, or John Locke, that were solely responsible for developing methods of historical criticism of the Bible later taken up, modified and used by eighteenth- and nineteenth-century liberal Protestants. This view is oversimplified."[522] Spinoza had, according to Frampton, distilled the message of Scripture to the injunctions to love God and love one's neighbor.

---

[520] Baruch Spinoza, *Theological-Political Treatise*, in *Complete Works*, trans. Samuel Shirley, ed. Michael L. Morgan (Indianapolis: Hackett Publishing Company, 2002), 458–60.

[521] Harrisville and Sundberg, *The Bible in Modern Culture*, 39.

[522] Frampton, *Spinoza*, 14.

For from Scripture itself we learn that its message, unclouded by any doubt or any ambiguity, is in essence this, to love God above all, and one's neighbour as oneself. There can be no adulteration here, nor can it have been written by a hasty and errant pen; for if doctrine differing from this is to be found anywhere in Scripture, all the rest of its teaching must also have been different. For this is the basis of the whole structure of religion; if it is removed, the entire fabric crashes to the ground, and then such a Scripture would not be the sort of thing we are now discussing, but a quite different book.[523]

Frampton explains, "In other words, those who called themselves faithful adherents of God's Word and defenders of the Bible, but who did not *practice* the universal tenets of the faith (loving God, loving neighbor), were, according to the outcast Jew, devoted instead to doctrines and human superstitions — but not to the true worship of God as commanded in the Old and New Testaments."[524] Apparently neither Frampton and certainly Spinoza did not understand that message of the Gospel, that there is none righteous (Rom. 3:10), and those who live by the law will die by the law since by the law no flesh will be justified in His sight (Rom. 3:20). Frampton goes on to object to the characterization by Dungan that of historical criticism and Spinoza eviscerated the Bible's core theology: "Spinoza simplified the content of the Bible's theological and ethical message: love God and love one's neighbor. How, then, did he eviscerate the Bible's core theology?"[525] Of course, the way Spinoza and the historical-critical method eviscerated the Bible's core theology was to pervert it from a gospel of salvation by grace through faith to a reductionistic moral precept of life by the law. That Spinoza missed the entire message of the New Testament is evident by his declaration: "First, faith does not bring salvation through itself, but only by reason of obedience; or, as James says (Ch. 2 v. 17), faith in itself without works is dead."[526]

Spinoza's method develops out of his experience of persecution as a Jew. This experience propels him to discover a view of reality that will force the world to see every other person as part of a unity which all men together compose, thus preventing persecution and marginalizing because no man will persecute or marginalize himself. This unity, of course, is Spinoza's thesis that all is one: *Deus sive Natura*. As Gilson puts it, "While all of reality, then, is one massive substance, the distinction between attributes and modes of substance makes it possible to conceive within the unity of reality a kind of bi-polarity, distinguishing and uniting the

---

[523] Spinoza, *Tractatus Theologico-Politicus*, 508–9.

[524] Frampton, *Spinoza*, 16.

[525] Ibid., 17. The quote from Dungan is, "Speaking for myself, I had always thought that the historical-critical study of the Bible had nothing to do with politics. . . . I never knew that I was a foot soldier in a great crusade to eviscerate the Bible's core theology, smother its moral standards under an avalanche of hostile historical questions, and, at the end, shove it aside so that the new bourgeois could get on with the business at hand." David Laird Dungan, *A History of the Synoptic Problem: The Canon, the Text, the Composition, and the Interpretation of the Gospels* (New York: Doubleday, 1999), 148.

[526] Spinoza, *Tractatus Theologico-Politicus*, 161.

creating and the created"[527] With the imagination man can perceive a world of particular things, and with the reason man can grasp the unity of all particular things in the reality of the One. As Gilson goes on to say, "When one grasps the unity of reality in the necessity of the one substance, it becomes evident that everything has to be as it is and that no reality ever really passes away into nothingness but merely goes through modal changes. *Sub specie aeternitatis*, every isolated thing is quasi-divine; nothing is to be despised; everything is to be honored with an almost religious devotion, as emanations and modes of the divine substance."[528]

One major factor in disunity and persecution is the factionalization based on conflicting religious commitments and fanaticism. The mutual destruction that characterizes the various institutionalized religions over the past couple of centuries prior to Spinoza is for Spinoza, indicative of the division and persecution that has characterized his own experience and the experience of his countrymen. Therefore, Spinoza must demonstrate that the true sense of Scripture reflects the unity of Nature. The passions that fuel the destructive behavior of religious fanaticism is actually a confused cognition, as Gilson points out:

> A passion is a confused idea to which we seem to submit because we do not possess the means to dominate it. That "means" can only be a clear and distinct idea that unveils the real sense of the confused representation—an active affect counteracting the passive one. "An affection which is a passion," reads the Third Proposition in Part V [of Spinoza's Ethics], "ceases to be a passion as soon as we form a clear and distinct idea of it." For to understand an affection clearly and distinctly is to replace it in its ontological background and recognize it as a modal moment of the divine attribute itself. Such an understanding permits the soul to see that "all things are necessary," because determined by the conatus[529] to play a part in the structuring of reality in and by "an infinite chain of causes." The necessity of each and of all things understood, the conflicting desires or the sadness that might otherwise accompany such things are eliminated.[530]

As Harrisville said, quoted above, "To understand Spinoza's views on the Bible, one must know his politics,"[531] Spinoza's politics is grounded upon the oneness of God such that no one person can be marginalized or persecuted, that all men should be free to believe as they choose without fear of persecution, so long as one's beliefs and practices do not rob another of his freedom. This political "oneness" is supported by Spinoza's understanding of the principal teaching of the Bible, namely, "that God exists, one alone and omnipotent, who alone should be worshiped, who cares for all, who loves above all others those who worship him

---

[527] Etienne Gilson and Thomas Langan, *Modern Philosophy: Descartes to Kant* (New York: Random House, 1963), 132.

[528] Ibid., 132–33.

[529] In Spinoza, the "conatus" is the force in every animate creature toward the preservation of its existence.

[530] Gilson and Langan, *Modern Philosophy*, 138–39.

[531] Ibid., 37.

and love their neighbors as themselves."[532] If every man can enjoy freedom without fear, and if every man loves his neighbor as himself, then all persecution and war will be eliminated.

Spinoza did not accept the Bible as the Word of God. The Word of God may be something that an individual may experience through reading the Bible, but they are not the same thing: "I then pass on to indicate the prejudiced beliefs that originate from the fact that the common people, prone to superstition and prizing the legacy of time above eternity itself, worship the books of Scripture rather than the Word of God. Thereafter I show that the revealed Word of God is not to be identified with a certain number of books, but is a simple conception of the divine mind as revealed to the prophets; and that is — to obey God with all one's heart by practising [sic] justice and charity."[533] Also, Spinoza bequeathed to modern academia the basic approach that the true student of the Bible does not accept inerrancy as a viable theological assumption: "And this is further evident from the fact that most of them assume as a basic principle for the understanding of Scripture and for extracting its true meaning that it is throughout truthful and divine — a conclusion which ought to be the end result of study and strict examination; and they lay down at the outset as a principle of interpretation that which would be far more properly derived from Scripture itself, which stands in no need of human fabrications."[534] The assumptions that the Bible is not the "Word of God" and that the student must not assume that the Bible is true and accurate in anything unless it can be substantiated by objective historical-critical investigation and the application of reason are two of the basic assumptions of modern Biblical Criticism. As Harrisville puts it, "Historical-critical method is the child of enemies of Christianity and the Augustinian tradition. They are, to be sure, opponents whose bill of particulars against Christianity, especially as an established political force of the state, was, for the most part, entirely just. But these critics of the Bible were nonetheless engaged in unrelenting warfare, and they used historical criticism as their most devastating weapon."[535]

Modern Era

The spirit of independence from any predetermined theological perspectives is still a basic assumption of contemporary Biblical Criticism. Spinoza and those who followed in his footsteps mounted an all-out war on the supernatural, as noted by Delahaunty: "Spinoza, trained in the Jewish schools, remained complicatedly loyal to the tradition; but in subjecting even the Bible to the rule of reason, he carried the war on supernaturalism into the most sacred places."[536] Christian Hartlich has articulated 8 theses with associated rationales delineating the historical-critical method that, although not specifically denying the supernatural, characterizes the

---

[532] Spinoza, *Theological Political Treatise*, 460.

[533] Ibid., 392.

[534] Ibid., 391.

[535] Harrisville and Sundberg, *The Bible in Modern Culture*, 60.

[536] Delahaunty, *Spinoza*, 1.

spirit that energized Spinoza. Some of the Rationales are quite long, so we reproduce only the theses.

Thesis 1: Under no conditions can the historian presuppose the truth of statements regarding events in documents from the past; he must ascertain the truth with critical procedures.

Thesis 2: "Sacred history" is characterized by the fact that beings which are not ascertainable in the context of ordinary experience — beings of divine, demonic, and supernatural origin — are active in an otherwise empirical and natural sequence of events. Statements concerning such "sacred history" are fundamentally unverifiable, and in this sense, from the perspective of that which has in fact taken place, without value for the historian.

Thesis 3: The mediation of the truth of statements concerning events in documents from the past is only possible by means of the historical-critical method. This is rooted in the way human knowledge is constituted, and the stipulations for the mediation of such knowledge, therefore, are not arbitrarily chosen, but necessary and generally mandatory for all persons who desire historical truth.

Thesis 4: There is no other criterion for determining whether an event referred to in a document from the past actually took place than the possibility of locating it in the context of the framework of experience constituted by the discipline in its present state of knowledge. Whether other frameworks of experience were present yesterday, or might be present tomorrow — these conceivable possibilities do not abrogate the validity of this thesis.

Thesis 5: The writers of "sacred history" have at their disposal no "higher capability of knowledge" that places them in a position to make truthful statements concerning events which lie outside the boundaries drawn by the constitution of knowledge common to all human beings.

Thesis 6: The concept of factuality (Tatsächlichkeit) was unknown to the writers of sacred history. Their way of narrating is naive, insofar as it takes place without thorough critical reflection on the conditions underlying statements about events with claims of truth. In their narrations of events, they thus allow heterogeneous elements to flow together, which the historian today must fundamentally separate.

Thesis 7: The writers of sacred history, like that found in the Bible, make use of history as a form in order by this means an indirect appeal — to call forth faith. Whoever is misled by a misunderstanding of their form of expression and thus conceives the statements of sacred history to be assertions of facts commits a fundamental hermeneutical error.

Thesis 8: A disastrous theological error arises as a consequence of this false hermeneutical perspective, namely, when this "sacred history," which wants to serve and be understood as a means of expression, is itself made the primary object of faith. Faith in the forgiveness of God is something essentially different from holding a story about the forgiveness of God to be true.[537]

The final statement of the Rationale for Thesis 8 captures the spirit of modern Biblical Criticism: "And that means it is understood not as a rendering of objective events, but as an indirect appeal for authentic faith making use of history as a form."[538] In other words, when preaching and teaching the Bible, the preacher/teacher should not operate on the assumption that the events recorded in the Bible refer to actual, historical events. Rather, the authors/redactors/ editors used the historical, literary form to communicate a spiritual message in order to generate faith in his hearers. We can certainly believe in the forgiveness of God, but we dare not believe that any biblical stories depicting God's forgiveness are true. This is the legacy of the Enlightenment.

Over the last twenty years, there has developed in the discipline of Biblical Criticism a division separating two basic approaches or assumptions about what constitutes Biblical Criticism. As McKenzie and Haynes describe it,

> The division between critical methods that adhere to a historical paradigm for understanding texts and those that embrace a literary paradigm has been well documented in recent literature . . . One fundamental disagreement between "historical" and "literary" methods of biblical criticism is found in their assumptions about the relationship between texts and history. This disagreement can be expressed in simple terms by saying that historical methods such as source criticism, form criticism, tradition-historical criticism, and redaction criticism emphasize the historical, archaeological, or literary *backgrounds* or roots of a text, and the development of the text *through time.* Thus historical-critical methods are sometimes referred to as "diachronic." On the other hand, literary methods such as structural criticism, narrative criticism, reader-response criticism, and poststructuralist criticism tend to focus on the *text itself* in its final form (however the final form might have been achieved), the relationships between a variety of textual elements (both surface and deep), and the interaction between texts and *readers.*[539]

McKenzie and Haynes also remind the reader that these kinds of distinction often fail to represent the real picture and that there are critical approaches that are not easily made to fit into one or the other camp. Notwithstanding these problems, we will attempt to follow this distinction to form the structure of our treatment of the nature of biblical criticism.

---

[537] Christian Hartlich, "Historical-Critical Method in its Application to Statements Concerning Events in the Holy Scriptures," trans. Darrell J. Doughty (Madison, New Jersey: Institute for Higher Critical Studies), [Online], available: <http://daniel.drew.edu./~ddoughty/ hartlich.html.> [30 September 1996].

[538] Ibid.

[539] Steven L. McKenzie and Stephen R. Haynes, ed. *To Each Its Own Meaning: An Introduction to Biblical Criticisms and Their Applications* (Louisville, Kentucky: Westminster John Knox Press, 1999), 7.

The historical-critical method has come under serious criticism in recent years to the point that many scholars are talking about the demise of the method altogether. The move away from the traditional application of Historical Criticism to the Old Testament may have been fostered by the work of a Scandinavian scholar, Ivan Engnell (1906–1964). Ivan Engnell built his claims on the basis of the work of another Scandinavian scholar, H. S. Nyberg (1889–1974). Walter Rast summarized the significance of Nyberg's contribution as "the emphasis it placed for the first time on the priority of oral tradition in the composition of the Old Testament Literature."[540] Working with this assumption, Engnell rejected the claims of the Documentary Hypothesis and declared that there never were any such documents as J and E. As Rast explains,

> He contended that no written sources such as J and E ever existed, as the source critics of the Pentateuch thought of them. Nor did the process of composition occur, as they believed, by means of essentially written collections, additions, duplications, interpolations, and redaction. Rather, he held that the Old Testament literature was produced and circulated by groups of people concerned with preserving and developing certain traditions, and that this was done through long periods of oral transmission. In fact most of the questions of the composition of the Old Testament have to do with oral tradition, which had the most formative role in the production of that literature.[541]

Therefore, what was for many years thought to be the sure and certain findings of the Historical-Critical Method were virtually destroyed by the speculations of these two Scandinavian scholars. One wonders, then, if the sure and certain findings of the Uppsala School, the name applied to those who followed in the footsteps of Nyberg and Engnell, will also one day be destroyed by the speculations of other "scholars." This demonstrates the fact that these claims are merely speculation not being based on any sound foundation. In fact, no sooner did the claims of these Scandinavian scholars become translated and accessible to scholars in other countries than these very claims came under serious attack. Other scholars claimed that Nyberg, Engnell, and others had overestimated the place of oral transmission in the Ancient Near East and with reference to the Old Testament. The primary complaint was that, according to Nyberg, the Old Testament literature was put into written form only after the Babylonian exile: "Only at this time did the conditions occur which necessitated the writing down of the literature."[542] The critics of this claim demonstrated that written literature had been an important part of religious belief in many cultures prior to the time of Israel's exile. For example, Roland de Vaux (1903–1971) argues that there are many examples of writing predating Israel's exile: "He cites as evidence various written documents now known to have originated in the Mesopotamian and Syro-Phoenician regions in very early times, as well as references in the Old Testament itself to such ancient

---

[540] Walter E. Rast, *Tradition History and the Old Testament* (Philadelphia: Fortress Press, 1972), 10.

[541] Ibid., 11.

[542] Ibid., 10.

writings as the Book of the Wars of Yahweh (Num. 21:14) or the Book of Yashar (Josh. 10:13; 2 Sam. 1:18)."[543]

Reader-Response Criticism

Nature of the Approach

The modern notion of reader-response is not completely new. As an integral part of his definition of tragedy, Aristotle included the effects that tragedy should produce in the hearer: "Tragedy is, then, a representation of an action that is heroic and complete and of a certain magnitude—by means of language enriched with all kinds of ornament, each used separately in the different parts of the play: it represents men in action and does not use narrative, and through pity and fear it effects relief to these and similar emotions."[544] Habib recognizes this aspect to Aristotle's definition: "Finally, his consideration of audience reaction as a crucial factor in the composition of tragedy presages much reader-response criticism."[545]

A Reader-Response approach to the text of the Bible is not necessarily a critical approach. All teachers, preachers, and students of the Bible have a "reader-response" approach to some degree. That is, as readers of the Bible, we all want to respond to what the text is saying, and, as teachers and preachers, we want those to whom we teach and preach to respond to the claims of the Bible. In this non-technical sense, we all employ a reader-response approach to the text.

Richard and Kendall Soulen give a very succinct depiction of Reader-Response Criticism:

> **Reader-Response Criticism** refers to a literary approach that is centrally concerned with the reader and the process of reading rather than with the author or the text as a self-contained unity. Although similar in many respects to the movement known as RECEPTION THEORY, from which it in part derives, reader-response criticism is a much more pluralistic phenomenon that lacks a single focused methodology. Nevertheless, practitioners generally subscribe to two key premises. First, the meaning of a literary text does not reside "within" the text as a self-contained unity but is actualized or created by the interaction of the reader and the text. Literature is like a performative art, analogous to the performance of a musical work or the staging of a drama. Second (and accordingly), the meaning of a text can differ from reader to reader and indeed from "performance" to "performance," as

---

[543] Ibid., 14–15.

[544] Aristotle, *Poetics*, trans. W.H. Fyfe., vol. 23, *Aristotle in 23 Volumes* (Cambridge, Massachusetts: Harvard University Press;, 1932) VI.1449b. Aristotle, *Aristotelis Opera Omnia* (Parisiis: Editoribus Firmin-Didot et Sociis, 1927), VI.1449b.

[545] Habib, *A History of Literary Criticism and Theory*, 61.

different readers perform the text in different circumstances to different ends.[546]

The two key premises refer to the assumptions that Reader-Response critics have when they come to interpreting the text. Once again, there is a matter of degree when it comes to the assumption that the meaning is *not* in the text. The simple graphic illustrates the continuum from simple response to the meaning in the text to the creating of meaning by the reader.

Response to the meaning in the text

Creating the meaning of the text

Reader-Response Continuum

Although most scholars would object to the characterization of the Reader-Response approach in this manner, nevertheless it is the case that there are degrees of commitment to the first key assumption. Those who are proclaiming the meaning of the Word of God and looking to generate in his hearers a response to God's Word would, in the eyes of most critics, not qualify as a Reader-Response approach.

Edgar McKnight gives an interesting synopsis of Radical Reader-Response Criticism:

> Reader-response criticism approaches biblical literature in terms of the values, attitudes, and responses of readers. The reader, therefore, plays a role in the "production" or "creation" of meaning and significance. This attitude toward the role of the reader relativizes the conventional view that the meaning of a text is like the content of a nut, simply awaiting its extraction by a reader. Radical reader-response approaches also challenge conventional views concerning the autonomy of the critic and the scientific and objective nature of the process of reading and criticism.[547]

It is important to notice that in the above quote, McKnight points out that the reader plays a role not only in the significance of the text, assuming the meaning/significance distinction introduced by E. D. Hirsch, but the reader also plays a role in the production of the meaning of the text. As Edgar McKnight puts it, "The postmodern perspective which allows readers to use the Bible today is that of a radical reader-oriented literary criticism, a criticism which views literature in terms

---

[546] John C. Holbert and Alyce M. McKenzie, What Not to Say: Avoiding the Common Mistakes that Can Sink Your Sermon (Lousiville: Westminster Knox Press, 1972), 175

[547] Edgar V. McKnight, "Reader-Response Criticism," *To Each Its Own Meaning*, 230.

of readers and their values, attitudes, and responses. . . . A *radical* reader-oriented criticism is postmodern in that it challenges the critical assumption that a disinterested reader can approach a text objectively and obtain verifiable knowledge by applying certain scientific strategies."[548] Tremper Longman, in his helpful historical survey, identifies the reader-centered theories as proposing, "Meaning resides in the reader, not in the text."[549]

The notion that the reader constitutes the meaning of the text is not *always* a radical reader-response approach. Sometimes when the critic talks about the reader constituting the meaning, it is with reference to the gaps and ambiguities of the text. As Jerome Walsh puts it, "How do gaps and ambiguities work as narrative devices? What effects do they have that more complete and straightforward writing would fail to achieve? There are at least two. The first is fairly obvious: Gaps and ambiguities require the reader to put much more effort into *making sense* (that is, *creating the meaning)* of the story."[550] In this sense, reader-response means that the reader must attempt to fill in the gaps or clear up the ambiguities in the text. There is no sense in this approach, even though he uses the phrase "creating the meaning," that the reader-creates the meaning of the text itself. What he means is that the reader must "make sense" of the gaps and ambiguities. These gaps and ambiguities can have a powerful impact upon the reader as Walsh says, "This not only increases the investment of the reader in the story;"[551]

An example of a narrative gap can be found in the account of God's testing of Abraham in Genesis 22: "¹Now it came about after these things, that God tested Abraham, and said to him, 'Abraham!' And he said, 'Here I am.' ²He said, 'Take now your son, your only son, whom you love, Isaac, and go to the land of Moriah, and offer him there as a burnt offering on one of the mountains of which I will tell you.' ³So Abraham rose early in the morning and saddled his donkey, and took two of his young men with him and Isaac, his son, and he split wood for the burnt offering, and arose and went to the place of which God had told him" (Gen. 22:1–3). Notice that the narrator says nothing about Abraham's immediate response to God's command. There is a gap between God's command to Abraham and the morning when Abraham prepares to depart. The reader must fill in this gap according to the context. Gaps in the text are not accidental. They have a function in the narrative that the reader is left to surmise. It appears to be the case in the testing of Abraham that the lack of any mention of Abraham's immediate response is designed to depict the faithful determination of Abraham to fulfill God's directive. Many people attempt to depict Abraham's response as shock and despair at such a command.

Also, notice how the gap and the disengaged account of Abraham's preparation, departure, and ultimate arrival at the appointed place have no

---

[548] Edgar V. McKnight, *Postmodern Use of the Bible: The Emergence of Reader-Oriented Criticism* (Nashville: Abingdon Press, 1988), 14–15 (emphasis in original).

[549] Tremper Longman, III, *Literary Approaches to Biblical Interpretation* (Grand Rapids: Zondervan Publishing House, 1987), 38.

[550] Jerome T. Walsh, *Old Testament Narrative: A Guide to Interpretation* (Louisville: Westminster John Knox Press, 2009), 76.

[551] Ibid.

emotional content. It is a stark description of the events. There is no account of any conversation between the participants along the way. However, when they arrive at the place of sacrifice, the author hits the reader with the emotional content in the give and take between Abraham and Isaac: "⁶Abraham took the wood of the burnt offering and laid it on Isaac, his son, and he took in his hand the fire and the knife. So the two of them walked on together. ⁷Isaac spoke to Abraham, his father and said, 'My father!' And he said, 'Here I am, my son.' And he said, 'Behold, the fire, and the wood, but where is the lamb for the burnt offering?' ⁸Abraham said, 'God will provide for Himself the lamb for the burnt offering, my son.' So the two of them walked on together" (Gen. 22:6–8). Twice the author notes that the walked "together." This intimate father and son interaction is a stark contrast to the straightforward description of Abraham's preparation and departure, and the gap in the narrative concerning Abraham's immediate response set up the reader for the impact of the intimate and emotion filled interaction of the father and son. There are certainly other ways to understand this narrative material, but this should demonstrate that a reader-response analysis of this type is not a "creation" of meaning in the radical sense, which we will now briefly discuss.

There is, nevertheless, that more radical approach of Reader-Response criticism. Even Walsh implies this when he says, talking about the reader filling in the gaps and clearing up the ambiguities, "also makes the story that results in some measure a reflection of each reader's unique, personal approach to people and to life."[552] According to Schuyler Brown, the assumption that linguistic meaning resides in a text "is certainly not intuitively obvious."[553] Brown proposes to demonstrate that "meaning exists formally only in human beings."[554] How does Brown suppose meaning can be communicated? He asserts, "meaning is generated by a reader reading a text."[555] It seems, however, that Brown is advocating a self-contradictory position. Surely Brown is counting on his text to communicate his proposition that meaning exists formally only in human beings. Brown seems to be asserting that the meaning of a text originates in the mind of the reader and is not determined by the text, in which case, the meaning of Brown's own text is not found in his text but in those who read his text. But this leaves no objective standard of verifying the interpretation of textual meaning. Of course for radical reader-response advocates, textual meaning is in no need of being verified since there is no textual meaning.

In their book *Linguistics & Biblical Interpretation*, Peter Cotterell & Max Turner assert that the Reader-Response interpretation proposes that "meaning is merely potential in any text; it only becomes actual in relation to a reader."[556] Now, either the author is counting on the text actually to mean that texts have only potential meaning, or, since the text has only potential meaning, it does not actually mean

---

[552] Ibid.

[553] Schuyler Brown, "Reader Response: Demythologizing the Text," *New Testament Studies* 34 (April 1988): 232.

[554] Ibid.

[555] Ibid.

[556] Peter Cotterell and Max Turner, *Linguistics & Biblical Interpretation* (Downers Grove, Illinois: InterVarsity Press, 1989), 55.

that texts have only potential meaning. Consequently, it is a potentiality that some texts do have actual meaning. In either case, this assertion is self-defeating.

Practice of the Approach: Responding to the Message of Job

When taking a reader-response approach to the text, it will often be necessary to refer to the underlying language: Hebrew in this instance. Many literary techniques that an author employs are difficult to capture in an English translation. In addition, it is inevitable that any reader-response approach must necessarily begin with the text and its meaning. Therefore, for all their protests that the meaning is not in the text, even the reader-response critic must begin with what the text means.

We are all familiar with the story of Job and his three companions. The literary techniques of the author are designed to have a profound impact upon the reader. Early in the story we are given a description that characterizes the piety of Job: "Job . . . was blameless, upright, fearing God and turning away from evil" (Job 1:1). But, this material also gives a clue to an understanding of the unfolding events. In verse 4 we are told that Job's sons and daughters would have a feast each day of the week at the homes of his sons. There is no hint of any immorality, yet Job would offer sacrifices for each just in case, as the text describes: "When the days of feasting had completed their cycle, Job would send and consecrate them, rising up early in the morning and offering burnt offerings the number of them all; for Job said, 'Perhaps my sons have sinned and cursed God in their hearts'" (Job 1:5). In Job's statement, he says something that is not usually captured in an English translation. A literal translation of the Hebrew text says, "Perhaps my sons have sinned and *blessed* (*ûbērᵃcû*). Now who would offer sacrifices for someone who "blessed" God? This is called an antithetic-euphemisms. Job did not simply have reverence for God. He was terrified that if he or his family did anything offensive, God would destroy him, his family, and all that he owned. In fact, in 3:23 Job declares, "For the dread I dreaded has come upon me, and what I feared has befallen me." The very thing Job was trying to avoid is the very thing that happened to him. At least this is the way Job saw it.

Beginning at verse 6 of chapter 1, the reader is given a behind the scenes look at the arrangement between Satan and God. God challenges Satan, "Have you considered My servant Job?" (Job 1:8). Satan then challenges God, "Does Job fear God for nothing?" By this Satan means that Job fears God only because he expects something from God in return. So Satan challenges God to remove His protection around Job and let Satan afflict him, and Job would curse God. Of course, we know that Job does not curse God. Then at the second meeting between God and Satan, Satan again challenges God, "However, put forth Your hand now, and touch his bone and his flesh; he will curse You to Your face" (Job 2:4).

From this point on, the dialogues between Job and his three companions unfolds. The reader, however, has knowledge that none of the participants in the dialogues has. As readers, we know that the challenge brought by Satan is the cause of all of Job's suffering. Therefore, the author builds into the mind of the reader a sense of superior knowledge and a "God's eye view" so to speak. The reader feels that he has an understanding that transcends the understanding of the characters.

The author then develops in the reader an expectation of the point at which the behind-the-scenes knowledge that the reader has will be revealed to Job and his companions, and then they will understand as the reader understands; the characters will be given the light that the reader has had all along.

That expectation and suspense are heightened by the delay tactic of the author who introduces the speech of Elihu beginning in 32:2. Elihu adds no new insight or understanding to the discussions that have already taken place. Elihu's speech drones on, and the reader is aggravated. The author has created in the reader an intensity of expectation, as if to say, "Get on with it! Let God tell all of you what is really going on, please!" Yet when God finally begins His monologue, the reader is suddenly slapped in the face with the realization that, even with the behind-the-scenes knowledge, the he does not understand the working of God any better than any of the characters. God does not explain to Job the challenge that led to Job's suffering. God basically tells Job, "There are many things that take place of which you may have no understanding. Nevertheless, I have given you sufficient evidence that I can be trusted, and in those times of trouble, when you don't understand, trust Me that I am in control, and all that transpires is ultimately for the good of all those who trust Me." The reader is hit with the realization that he cannot lean on his own understanding. Even when he thinks he has that behind-the-scenes knowledge, he may still not be able to understand. And like Job, the impact on the reader is powerful, and the speeches of God tear down in the reader any sense of superiority and humbles the reader bringing him down from his supposed lofty heights to the same level as Job and his companions.

However, God gives us the evidence that He will make things right. In the last chapter, God restores to Job all that he had lost and double the amount. But there is a curious gap in the descriptions of Job's situation. There is no mention of Job's wife. There is, however, a recognition of Job's three daughters. The text names these daughters and reports that they were each given an inheritance; something that was almost unheard of in this culture. In the narrative, the three daughters fill the gap left by the lack of any mention of Job's wife. All of this is designed to give the reader a sense of resolution. All will ultimately be set right. Justice will finally be done. God will leave no loose ends. And the reader is comforted, by the personal encounter with God. This is precisely what Job experienced. Job had heard of God, but did not know God on a personal level, as he says, "I have heard of You by the hearing of the ear; but now my eye sees You" (Job 42:2). Job is transformed by this personal encounter, and so is the reader. The reader is brought from his sense of superior sight to the realization that God is much more than we can ever understand. However, I can trust Him. He will ultimately make all things right.

This is perhaps an oversimplification of the reader-response methodology, but it does give a sense of how the critic focuses on the response that the reader has to the gaps and implications in the text. The meaning that is ultimately derived from the text is, in one sense, created by the reader. When God begins to speak, that feeling in the reader of superiority that is crushed and that humbles the reader is not specifically stated in the text, but, by the techniques of the author, the impact comes out of the text and is developed in the mind and heart of the careful reader.

Critique of Reader-Response Criticism

It is important to note that Reader-Response Criticism, in its more radical forms, has been influenced by modern philosophy especially in terms of epistemology (the study of knowledge), as McKnight notes:

> Reader-response criticism has been directly influenced by fields of study intimately related both to textual interpretation and to the epistemological revolution. These include hermeneutics, structuralism and poststructuralism, and phenomenology. Long before the advent of reader-response criticism on the American scene, hermeneutics transformed the question of interpretation into the question of knowledge ("How do we know?") and the question of being ("What is the mode of being of that being who only exists through understanding?"). Rudolf Bultmann and the New Hermeneutic utilized the relationship between being, language, and humankind postulated by Martin Heidegger. The New Hermeneutic was unable to establish a satisfying coordination between the role and function of the Bible, the language of the Bible, and specific strategies designed to allow the biblical text to carry out the postulated role. As a result, the hermeneutical tradition in biblical studies stagnated. Some forms of reader-response criticism, however, move back to the idea of Heidegger, that the understanding of a text does not simply involve the discovery of an inner meaning contained in the text, that to understand a text is to unfold the possibility of being, which is indicated by that text.[557]

McKnight specifically states that Reader-Response Criticism is based on the claims of modern epistemology:

> When criticism questioned the status of the language of literature, the knowledge involved in literature, and the nature of the self or the subject in the reading process, a revolution took place. Thrust squarely into the field of literature were the philosophical questioning of the intrinsic limits of knowledge (epistemology) and the reaction to such questioning by movements such as hermeneutics, structuralism, and poststructuralism, and phenomenology. Parallel to the conclusion of reader response criticism that there is no absolutely neutral language of literature to serve as a foundation for readers' responses is the conclusion of philosophy that there is no absolute foundation that can be used in the determination of knowledge. The foundationalist approach in philosophy would assume the possibility of advancing a proposition whose truth is demonstrable without any sort of assumptions and from which further theories could be strictly developed. In place of such a foundationalist theory of knowledge came a circular theory, whereby knowledge is justified in nonlinear, or circular, fashion through the relationship of the results obtained to the beginning point.[558]

---

[557] McKnight, *Post-Modern Us of the Bible*, 19.

[558] Ibid., 17–18.

One conclusion of modern epistemology as it relates to Reader-Response Criticism is the rejection of the possibility of what McKnight calls "absolutely neutral language of literature" and consequently "there is no absolute foundation that can be used in the determination of knowledge." In other words, to the question of knowledge and objectivity, modern epistemology and Reader-Response Criticism reject the possibility of having objective knowledge. The two basic questions of epistemology then are 1) is it possible to know, and 2) is it possible to have certainty. These two questions are addressed below.

Is It Possible to Know?

The primary question in epistemology concerns the nature of knowledge and is characterized by the question, "What is knowledge?" This question is often involved with a related question, "Is it possible to know?" Many believe that before one can ask what it is we know, one must first establish the fact that knowledge is possible. A response to the question, "Is it possible to know?" prior to beginning the study of epistemology is not only possible but critical. It must be admitted at the outset that it is possible to know. To assert that knowledge is not possible is to assert a contradiction. Either one knows that knowledge is not possible, in which case the original assertion is false because at least this knowledge is possible, or one does not know that knowledge is not possible, in which case the original assertion cannot be maintained. Many have questioned the possibility of knowledge with a question like this: "If you do not understand the nature of human cognition [i.e., knowledge], how and to what extent can you put confidence in what it makes you aware of in other things?" or "How can one be sure of one's knowledge about anything in particular, if one does not first know what knowledge itself is?"[559]

The essential problem with these questions is, if one must know what knowledge is before one can know anything in particular, how can one ever come to know what knowledge is? One would have to both know and not know in the same sense. As Joseph Owens puts it, "Here cognition itself is the topic for the inquiry, while it is also the examiner. On that account, the charge of circularity might arise, with the reliability of cognition resting on cognition's own reliability."[560] Not only is the claim that knowledge is not possible contradictory, but the agnostic form of the question is contradictory. The agnostic form of the question is something like this: "Because there is no possibility of objective knowledge, we should suspend all judgments on whether or not it is possible to know." If it is not possible to know anything in particular unless one knows what knowledge is, then one is doomed never to know. Likewise, if we suspend judgment on whether or not we can know, then we are equally doomed never to know because precisely the same faculty that is doubted is the faculty one must employ to remove doubt.

The fact of the matter is, we do know some things, and the inquiry is to discover how we know, not whether we know. The first question, then, "What is

---

[559] Both of these questions are posed in Joseph Owens, *Cognition: An Epistemological Inquiry* (Houston, Texas: The Center for Thomistic Studies, 1992), 16.

[560] Ibid., 20.

knowledge?" assumes the fact of knowledge and aims at discovering how knowledge is possible and explainable. There is an analogy here to any physical activity. It is not necessary to understand the physiology of walking before one can walk. Rather, the fact that one can walk gives rise to the investigation of how such activity is possible and explainable. Unless we acknowledge the fact that we do know, we will never come to know. When McKnight claims that there is no absolutely neutral knowledge he is presenting his case as if it is an absolutely, universal, and neutral fact of knowledge. But this proposition is self-defeating. To the degree that Reader-Response Criticism, by McKnight's own lights, is based on modern epistemology, to that degree Reader-Response Criticism is also self-defeating.

Therefore, the framing of the basic task of epistemology will shape how one approaches the task. It cannot be the case that epistemology is the quest to discover whether it is possible to know since the very faculty whose reliability is in question is the only faculty we possess to address the question. The basic task of epistemology must be the quest to discover how it is that we know.

Is it Possible to Have Certainty?

The second problem in epistemology concerns epistemic criteria and involves the basic question, "How do we justify claims of knowledge?" This problem is often addressed in terms of the question, "Is it possible to have certainty?" Once again we must affirm, prior to our investigation, the fact that it is possible to have certainty. To assert that no one can be certain about anything is to assert a contradiction. Either one is certain that there is no certainty, in which case the original assertion is false because at least this is certain, or one is not certain that certainty is not possible, in which case the original assertion cannot be maintained.

Criticisms of this question are similar to the criticisms of the previous question. Views and proposals differ among philosophers about what constitutes certainty, whether certainty is a necessary criteria of knowledge, and whether certainty admits of degrees. Minimally we may employ the definition of certainty provided by *The Oxford Companion to Philosophy*: "A proposition is said to be certain when it is indubitable. A person is certain of a proposition when he or she cannot doubt it."[561] If it cannot be doubted that certainty is not possible, then the assertion is self-defeating. If it can be doubted that certainty is not possible, then the original assertion cannot be maintained. Even if we attempt to suspend judgment on the possibility of certainty, we cannot escape the criticism, for either we cannot doubt that judgment ought to be suspended, or we can doubt that it should. The same consequences follow.

The fact of the matter is, we can be certain about some things. For example, we can be certain that a proposition cannot be both true and false in the same sense. To deny the law of contradiction is to affirm it. It is in fact indubitable. Although we may have certainty about a very small number of things, certainty is undoubtedly possible. Once again the task of epistemology must not be framed in

---

[561] C. J. Hookway, "certainty," in *The Oxford Companion to Philosophy*, ed. Ted Honderich (Oxford: Oxford University Press, 1995), 129.

terms of whether certainty is possible, but how it is possible, and how it can be explained.

Once again McKnight's claim that there is no absolutely neutral knowledge defeats itself. McKnight presents his claim as if it were absolutely neutral knowledge. In other words, he presents his case of if he is absolutely certain that it is true that there is no absolute certainty. To the degree that Reader-Response Criticism is based on a rejection of certain knowledge, to that degree Reader-Response Criticism is self-defeating and therefore false.

Critique of Reader-Response Criticism

One of the most serious issues with Reader-Response Criticism is seemingly uncritical assumption of modern epistemology. Having retreated from reality into the mind, modern epistemology has ultimately led to the rejection of any objective knowledge. According to this perspective, all knowledge is inescapably laden with the perspective of the interpreter. No one has a neutral point of view; as Thomas Nagle says, there is no such thing as a view from nowhere.[562] By this, he means that everyone views the world from some point of view. Since everyone has his or her own point of view, there is no such thing as a view from nowhere. Since there is no such thing as a view from nowhere, then there can be no objectivity or neutrality. Everything must be viewed from one's own perspective or point of view. This ultimately leads to the rejection of any absolute truth, and the tolerance of all perspectives. This perspective of modern epistemology has been a major factor in the development of Radical Reader-Response criticism, and McKnight attests.

> When criticism questioned the status of the language of literature, the knowledge involved in literature, and the nature of the self or the subject in the reading process, a revolution took place. Thrust squarely into the field of literature were the philosophical questioning of the intrinsic limits of knowledge (epistemology) and the reaction to such questioning by movements such as hermeneutics, structuralism, and poststructuralism, and phenomenology. Parallel to the conclusion of reader-response criticism that there is no absolutely neutral language of literature to serve as a foundation for readers' responses is the conclusion of philosophy that there is no absolute foundation that can be used in the determination of knowledge. The foundationalist approach in philosophy would assume the possibility of advancing a proposition whose truth is demonstrable without any sort of assumptions and from which further theories could be strictly developed. In place of such a foundationalist theory of knowledge came a circular theory, whereby knowledge is justified in nonlinear, or circular, fashion through the relationship of the results obtained to the beginning point.[563]

---

[562] Thomas Nagel, *The View from Nowhere* (New York: Oxford University Press, 1986).

[563] McKnight, *Post-Modern Use of the Bible*, 17–18.

McKnight claims that modern epistemology has led us to the realization that there is "no absolute foundation that can be used in the determination of knowledge." Yet this very statement is an absolute foundation which McKnight uses in the determination of what can and cannot be counted as knowledge. McKnight assumes that his readers will take his assertions as absolute truth about what can be counted as absolute truth. Also, McKnight has assumed that there can be only one sense of a foundationalist theory of knowledge, when in fact there is another foundationalist theory that does not succumb to McKnight's criticisms. The foundationalist theory that McKnight and most modern philosophy rightly rejects is a Cartesian foundationalism.

Cartesian foundationalism asserts that there is one undeniable truth from which all knowledge can be deduced. For Descartes, this was the *cogito ergo sum*, "I think therefore I am." Supposedly, this was an undoubtable truth as the starting point of all knowledge. From this indubitable starting point, Descartes believed he could deduce all knowledge. This project was soon abandoned by modern philosophy.

However, another foundationalism holds that there are undeniable, self-evident first-principles of thought and being. But, this approach does not argue that all knowledge can be or even should be deduced from these self-evident principles. Rather, all knowledge must be *reduceable* to first principles. The first principles of thought and being include the three laws of thought: the principle of noncontradiction, which means that a truth-claim cannot be both true and false in the same sense. The principle of non-contradiction is true in thought because it is true in reality. A thing cannot both be and not be in the same sense; the principle of identity, which means that A is A, a thing is what it is. Again, this is the case because it is based on reality. Anything is what it is; and the principle of excluded middle, which means either A or non-A, there is no middle between these. This principle is also based on reality. There is no middle between being what something is and not being that. A tree is a tree, and anything that is not a tree is a non-tree. There is no middle-something between these.

Anyone who denies these principles must employ them in order to make his denial. Any knowledge claim cannot ultimately deny any one of these first principles. For a very brief example, let us consider those who claim that God, as a spirit-being has a spirit-body, having legs, arms, a head, a mouth, etc., just as we do.[564] However, when this claim is reduced to first principles, it becomes contradictory.

> As a being with a spirit body, God is circumscribed to a location in space.
> As a being located in space, God moves from planet heaven to planet earth.
> Anything that is located and moves partakes of befores and afters.
> Moving from here to there.
> Before the move and after the move.
> Anything that partakes of befores and afters is temporal.

---

[564] An example of someone who holds this belief is Finis J. Dake, *Dake's Annotated Reference Bible: The New Testament* (Grand Rapids: Zondervan Publishing House, 1961), 97, John 4:24, note r.

Therefore, God is temporal.

God is spirit and omnipresent (orthodox Christian doctrine).
Anything that is spirit and omnipresent must be eternal (rational demonstration).
Therefore, God is eternal.

God is temporal and eternal in the same sense.
The temporal is the eternal.
But, this is a contradiction.
Therefore, it must not be the case that God is both temporal and eternal.

But it is irrational to conclude that the Cause of the universe is temporal
Therefore, God, the Cause of the universe, must be eternal and not temporal
Therefore, it must not be the case that God is located in space.
Therefore, it must not be the case that God has a spirit body.
Consequently, passages that speak of God having body parts must be figurative.[565]

Although this is perhaps a crude example, it does illustrate the idea of reducing a claim to first principles. Any truth-claim that violates one of these first principles cannot be true. This foundationalism is not the kind of foundationalism that is rejected by McKnight and others because it is not based on a modern epistemology. As a result, it is, in fact, possible to have an absolute foundation upon which can be based a certainty of knowledge, as we have already demonstrated above. It necessarily follows from this that a Radical Reader-Response Criticism cannot produce true results. The meaning is in fact in the text. McKnight's own book assumes that the meaning he put into his text is what he believes the reader will get out of his text. So his own claims contradict his enterprise. We must indeed respond to the text, but we must respond to the meaning that is in the text, not a meaning that is supposedly supplied by the reader.

Narrative Criticism

Nature of the Approach

With Narrative Criticism, we come to the approach that has had the most impact on my own approach to the Old Testament. Narrative Criticism is often referred to as Literary Criticism, but it should not be confused with Source Criticism which also sometimes goes by the title Literary Criticism. Whereas Source Criticism is part of the overall approach known as the Historical-Critical Method, Narrative Criticism is a decidedly different approach. Mark Powell gives a helpful explanation of the basic distinctions between the Historical-Critical Method and Narrative Criticism:

---

[565] Thomas A. Howe, *Objectivity in Biblical Interpretation* (Charlotte, NC: Thomas A. Howe, 2015), 224–25.

The dominant mode of biblical studies for more than a century has been the historical-critical method. Actually a conglomeration of approaches, this method seeks to reconstruct the life and thought of biblical times through an objective, scientific analysis of biblical material. Source criticism, for example, attempts to delineate the sources that the evangelists used in the composition of their Gospels. Form criticism concentrates on defining the *Sitz im Leben* (setting in life) that individual units of tradition may have had before they came to be incorporated into the Gospels. Redaction criticism seeks to discern the theologies and intentions of the evangelists themselves by observing the manner in which they edited their sources and arranged the individual units of tradition. These disciplines share a common desire to shed light upon significant periods in the transmission of the Gospels: the period of the historical Jesus, the period of oral tradition in the life of the early church, or the period of the final shaping of the Gospels by the evangelists.[566]

Powell goes on to point out that the major limitations of the Historical-Critical Method, including all its sub-disciplines, "is that they fail to take seriously the narrative character of the Gospels."[567] Powell also expressed this difference as four basic principles:

1. … Literary-critical analysis is not to discover the process through which a text has come into being but to study the text that now exists.
2. *Literary criticism emphasizes the unity of the text as a whole.* Literary analysis does not dissect the text but discerns the connecting threads that hold it together.
3. *Literary criticism views the text as an end in itself.* The immediate goal of a literary study is to understand the narrative.
4. *Literary criticism is based on communication models of speech-act theory.* The philosophical bases for literary criticism are derived from theories about communication.[568]

This is not the place to undertake a study of speech act theory, but a brief description of it from *An Introduction to Language and Linguistics*, edited by Ralph Fasold and Jeff Connor-Linton will provide a working knowledge of the basic principles of speech act theory:

[John Austin (1962–Present)] pointed out that when people use language, they are performing a kind of action. He called these actions speech acts. It's easy to see the "act" nature of language when a minister says, "I now pronounce you husband and wife" in a wedding ceremony. By virtue of this sentence being said by an appropriate person, the engaged couple becomes a married couple. Most speech acts are not so "official," but they all rely on the speaker using an utterance to signal his/her intention to accomplish some action and the hearer inferring that action from the utterance. When people make bets and threats and

---

[566] Powell, *Narrative Criticism*, 2.

[567] Ibid.

[568] Ibid., 7-10.

promises, offer congratulations and apologies, or issue orders or challenges, they are using language to accomplish actions.[569]

These four basic principles distinguish between Historical Criticism and Narrative Criticism. Narrative Criticism has both an Old Testament and a New Testament approach, and although they are similar enough to warrant the same broad classification, they can be very different in assumptions and in conclusions. And these differences are not because of the differences in the Testaments themselves. David Gunn summarizes these differences:

> More specifically the term [narrative criticism] has been used of formalist analysis,[570] especially in a New-Critical vein, where the critic understands the text to be an interpretable entity independent of both author and interpreter. Here meaning is to be found by close reading that identifies formal and conventional structures of the narrative, determines plot, develops characterization, distinguishes point of view, exposes language play, and relates all to some overarching, encapsulating theme. Unlike historical criticism, which in practice has segmented the text, formalist narrative criticism has often been an exercise in holism. . . . While developments in New Testament narrative studies over the past tthree [*sic*] decades could be said in general terms to parallel work on the Hebrew Bible, the two fields have also remained distinct. Narrative criticism of the Gospels and Acts has tended to be relatively conservative in its methodology, concerned with observing the mechanics or artistry of literary construction, the conventions of ancient rhetoric, and often still haunted by historical criticism's need to know the author's "intention" and the text's "original" readership if it is to speak legitimately of the text's meaning. While centering interest on the story, especially its plot and characters as elements of an artistic whole, Gospel critics have been reluctant to take a literary approach that unravels unity and/or places the reader in an ideologically exposed position in relation to the text.[571]

By the expression "relatively conservative in its methodology," Gunn is not referring to theological conservatism, but rather to the tendency not to allow the imagination to take flight in interpreting the narrative aspects of the text. Rather, New Testament practitioners are more conservative in that they stick closer to the more traditional forms of criticism and to a more "scientific" approach. As Gunn points out, they tend to want to ground their interpretive conclusions in historical-critical findings. Gooder's definition of Narrative Criticism is from the perspective of a New Testament practitioner: "Narrative criticism interprets New Testament

---

[569] Ralph Fasold and Jeff Connor-Linton, ed. *An Introduction to Language and Linguistics* (Cambridge: Cambridge University Press, 2006), 162.

[570] Often referred to as a scientific approach to literature, Formalist analysis emphasizes the objective and literal interpretation of a literary text in terms of its tone, theme, and style. It is considered scientific because its approach is unembellished and literal. Like New Criticism, Formalist Criticism does not consider elements outside of the text itself, such as politics or history or culture. Formalist Criticism focuses on the form of a text rather than its content.

[571] David M. Gunn, "Narrative Criticism," in *To Each Its Own Meaning*, 201–2.

narratives as literary texts, using categories that are applied in interpreting all other forms of literature, for example, plot, characterization, setting, and so forth."[572]

Practice of the Approach: Literary Techniques in Genesis 1

The creation account in Genesis 1 has been the focus of an enormous amount of analysis and commentary; perhaps more than any other single chapter in the Old Testament. Nevertheless, this passage does contain many of the techniques for which one searches as a Narrative critic. Not everyone would agree that this chapter is narrative, and in the strict sense, they are perhaps correct. Even so we will use this chapter to illustrate some of the characteristics of narrative primarily because they are so easily recognized. In order to point out and discuss these characteristics, it will be necessary for you, as a reader, to read through Genesis chapter 1 several times. Also, there will be several instances in which we will need to talk about the Hebrew text.

CREATION WEEK						
	Day 1	Day 2	Day 3	Day 4	Day 5	Day 6
Verses	3–5	6–8	9–13	14–19	20–23	24–31
Beginning	And God said	And God Said	And God Said	And God Said	And God Said	And God Said
God Spoke	v. 3 - And God said	v. 6 - And God said	v. 9 - And God said v. 11 - And God said	v. 14 - And God said	v. 20 - And God said	v. 24 - And God said v. 26 - And God said v. 28 - And God said v. 29 - And God said
Work	• Light created • Division between light and darkness	• Expanse • Division between waters above and waters below	• Collection of waters • Appearance of dry ground • Sprouting of the land with herbage and trees with fruit and seeds	• Creation of luminaries • Creation of sun, moon, and stars • Division of light and darkness	• Creation of swarming things in the sea • Creation of birds of the heavens • Creation of great sea monsters	• Creation of land creatures • Creation of man
Work	SUBDUING ⟶ FILLING					
Work		SUBDUING ⟶ FILLING				
Work			SUBDUING ⟶ FILLING			
Naming	Called the light "day" and called the darkness "night"	Called the expanse "heavens"	Called the dry ground "land" and called the collection of waters "seas"			
Evaluating	v. 4 - God saw that it was good		v. 10 - God saw that it was good v. 12 - God saw that it was good	v. 18 - God saw that it was good	v. 21 - God saw that it was good v. 25 - God saw that it was good	v. 31 - And God saw all which He made, and behold it was very good
Ending	And it was evening, and it was morning, the first day	And it was evening, and it was morning, the second day	And it was evening, and it was morning, the third day	And it was evening, and it was morning, the fourth day	And it was evening, and it was morning, the fifth day	And it was evening, and it was morning, the sixth day

Overall Structure of Genesis 1

The graphic in above sets out the overall structure of the passage. Repeating phrases are often a good indicator of structure, and there are several in this chapter. The most obvious are the repeating statements at the end of each creation day: "And it was evening, and it was morning, the X day," where X stands for the number of each day. This clearly sets the overall structure, each section ending with this phrase. These sections correspond to each of the six creation days.

---

[572] Paula Gooder, "Narrative criticism," in *Searching for Meaning*, 80.

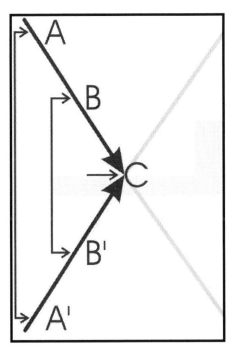

Illustration of Chiasm

Also, there is the repetition of the declaration, "And God said . . ." This occurs in verses 3, 6, 9, 11, 14, 20, 24, 26, 28, and 29. There are ten times that the text states that "God said." The author wants the reader to capture the repetition of this phrase. God did not go to war against some opposing force. God simply spoke, and it was done, ten times. This is very important once we realize that later in Exodus God again spoke, and Gods words were written on stone tablets. In fact, what is almost always translated as the "ten commandments" are in fact never referred to as the time commandments. Rather the author referred to them as "the ten words" (*asereth haddebārim*). As God had established the cosmic order in the ten words of creation, so God established the national order of His people with the ten words on the stone tablets.

The chapter also has an introduction; "In beginning God created the heavens and the earth." That this is an introductory statement is indicated by the beginning of the next verse: "Now the earth was empty and uninhabitable . . ." In Hebrew, the most often used conjunction is the *waw* (pronounced *vav*). This is a single letter that is attached to a word. The *waw* conjunction has a wide range of meanings depending on the context and on the word to which it is prefixed. Generally, when the *waw* is prefixed to a verb it serves as a conjunction usually translated "and." However, when the *waw* is prefixed to a noun or pronoun at the beginning of a sentence, it usually indicates a disjunction. The disjunction can be strong, translated "but," or it can be a literary indicator being translated "now." This is the case in verse two. The *waw* is prefixed to the word "earth" which is the first word in the Hebrew text. So, I have translated it to give the sense of the literary disjunction. This structure sets off the first verse from the following material indicating that verse 1 functions as an introduction and a summary statement, so to speak, of what God did in the creation week.

So verse 1 is an introductory statement, and verse 2 gives us an introductory setting. This can be represented by the graphic in . The graphic also reveals another literary device called a chiasm. A chiasm is the organizing of the text so that the author can direct the reader's attention on the important material. This device is called a chiasm because it follows the shape of the Greek letter *chi*, which looks like the English capital X. The chiasm follows on side of the letter so that the parts correspond, A with A', B with B', and so on, and it focuses in on the point of the structure (see).

In this instance there are three parts that form the chiastic structure, A, B, and A'. Usually when a chiasm has one center point, the focus of emphasis is on this center point. In this case, the author indicates that the important material on which to focus our attention is the material describing the six creation days.

It is important to consider the three words that are used by the author (whom I believe was Moses) employed to describe the condition of the earth: *tōhû*, meaning "uninhabitable," and *bōhû*, meaning "empty," and *hōšek*, meaning "darkness." The six creation days are grouped into three units. These unites are indicated by the relation of creating/subduing and filling. The three groups of creation days are designed to answer to the three words used to describe the condition of the earth. On the first day, God creates light and divides between the day and night. The creation of light addressed the condition of darkness that was over the earth. The creation of light subdues the darkness. On the fourth day, God fills the heavens with light giving bodies, the sun, moon, and stars. This is the first group expressing the subduing—filling work of God.

On the second day God separates the waters above from the waters below. On the fifth day God fills the waters with sea creatures and the heavens with flying creatures. Again, expressing the subduing—filling work of God.

On the third day God the subduing—filling work is again expressed. God collects the waters and dry ground appears. God causes herbage to grow and trees having fruit and seed. God subdued the waters and the land, and then filled it up on the sixth day by creating land creatures and man.

God's creation activity was designed to address the three conditions of the earth. Darkness was subdued by the creation of light. The land was uninhabitable, and God subdued this condition by separating the waters above from the waters below and collecting the waters so that dry ground appeared. God subdued the emptiness of the earth by filling it, first with luminaries in the heavens, then with sea creatures and flying creatures, and third by filling the land with land creatures and man.

The literary structure has directed the reader to see God's activity of subduing and filling. In verse 28, God commands the couple, "Be fruitful and multiply, and fill the earth, and subdue it; and rule over the fish of the sea and over the birds of the sky and over every living thing that moves on the earth" (Gen. 1:28). As God subdued and filled, He commands the couple to fill and subdue. In other words, God created the couple to mimic God's actions; to be like God. The man and the woman were representatives of God on the earth.

Critique of Literary Criticism

Approaching the biblical text according to its literary characteristics is an important development in Bible study. The literary techniques that the authors used were designed to lead the reader to see the important aspects of the literary piece. The authors of the biblical text did not have the tools that are available to some who is speaking to an audience. A speaker can raise his voice, pound on the pulpit, project images to aid in communication and many other techniques that are available to a speaker. It was necessary for the authors of Scripture to use their literary skills to communicate, to emphasize, to cause the reader to respond. Approaching the biblical text as literature enables the interpreter to discover these techniques and to get out of the text what the author wanted the reader to get.

However, a literary approach can also go to the extreme of approaching the Scripture as only another literary piece that needs to be analyzed in order to get the story. Walsh is a good example of taking the approach so far that it loses sight of the fact that Scripture is first of all the revelation of God to us. When the text makes a reference to God or when God speaks, Walsh treats "God" in the text as merely another character in the story.

> As in the case of telling, the narrator also shows us God speaking and acting. And just as with any other character, it is up to the reader to infer the qualities of the Deity that are revealed in what God says or does. It is inevitably a temptation to the modern reader to interpret the character of God in the story in accord with one's own theological understandings of the Deity. But this is clearly inappropriate: we have no guarantee that *our* understanding of God is identical to the one the implied author expects the implied reader to bring to the text. Furthermore, as I mentioned above, it is not impossible for an implied author to create a story world in which the character called "God" speaks or acts in a way different from what the author would expect of the Deity the author worships in the real world.[573]

Walsh informs the reader that it is inappropriate to bring to the text "one's own theological understanding of the Deity." However, Walsh does this very thing when he says, "it is not impossible for an implied author to create a story world in which the character called "God" speaks or acts in a way different from what the author would expect of the Deity the author worships in the real world." This statement reveals at least two theological assumptions that Walsh brings to the text: 1) That the text is not the Word of God. If it is the case that an author can depict God differently from the God whom the author actually worships indicates that Walsh does not believe that the text is designed to reveal the true nature of God whom we worship. 2) Walsh does not believe that the text presents God as the immutable and eternal God Who is worshiped in classical, orthodox Christianity. An observation by Walsh reveals this assumption: "Yhwh says that he will delay the punishment for Solomon's sin and punish Solomon's son instead (11:12). This does not square with our theology or our notions of justice, divine or human; however, it would not bother the ancient Israelite implied reader. Transgenerational reward and punishment was a theological axiom for preexilic Israel (see Exod. 34:6–7)" (Walsh, 36–37). If it is possible, as Walsh indicates, for the author to create a character "God" in his story Who does not bear the qualities of the God of the real world, then God, character or real, is subject to characterization just as any other character. As he says earlier,

---

[573] Walsh, *Old Testament Narrative*, 36

It is important to remember that God, too, is a character in the story and that the narrator can use the same techniques to construct God's character out of words. The narrator *tells* us, for instance, that Yhwh was "pleased" (3:10), and later that he was "angry" (11:9). There is another implication to the statement that God is a character in the story world. Just as the story world (the secondary world) is separate from the world of the reader (the primary world), so too the characters (human or divine) in the story world need not be mirror images of beings in the real world that bear the same names. . . . Literary license is not a modern invention! This warning is equally true of the character "God." Nothing would prevent an author from creating a narrative world in which the character "God" has traits different from those of the God the author worships.[574]

The reason Walsh brings these assumptions to the text, and the reason why his "warnings" are themselves "inappropriate" is because it is not possible to come to the text without some metaphysical assumptions whether or not (and in this case Walsh is not) aware of them. God has revealed His true nature in His creation, and Paul says,

Romans 1:18-23 Updated American Standard Version (UASV)

[18] For the wrath of God is revealed from heaven against all ungodliness and unrighteousness of men, who suppress the truth in unrighteousness, [19] because that which is known about God is evident among[575] them; for God made it evident to them. [20] For his invisible attributes are clearly seen from the creation of the world, being perceived through what has been made, even his eternal power and divine nature, so that they are without excuse. [21] For although they knew God, they did not honor him as God or give thanks, but they became futile in their reasoning, and their foolish hearts were darkened. [22] Claiming to be wise, they became fools, [23] and exchanged the glory of the incorruptible God for an image in the form of corruptible man and of birds and four-footed animals and creeping things.[576]

As the revelation of God, the text is designed to reveal the true nature of God and to overturn many of our assumptions about Him and ourselves. One of the pitfalls of Narrative Criticism is treating the text as merely narrative that is no more than a fascinating story to analyze, not as divine revelation. As we noted above, Walsh demonstrates his assumptions about God in such statements as, "In his last speech, Yhwh says that he will delay the punishment for Solomon's sin and punish Solomon's son instead (11:12). This does not square with our theology or our notions of justice, divine or human; however, it would not bother the ancient Israelite implied reader. Transgenerational reward and punishment were a theological axiom for preexilic Israel (see Exod. 34:6–7)" (Walsh, 36–37). This is an example in which the text reveals to us our assumption about God and is designed to teach us how God actually is. If this action by God is in fact contrary to our theology and notions of justice, as Walsh, notes, then we must find out why this is

---

[574] Ibid., 34–35

[575] Or *in*; or *within*

[576] Or *reptiles*

so. Walsh sees this as merely an interesting aspect of the narrative, whereas it is, in fact, a revelation of God that is designed to overturn our assumptions about God by His actions which are contrary to our presumptions about how God should act. This is not simply an exercise of the interpretation of a narrative. Rather, it is an opportunity to grow in our understanding of who God is.

Conclusions

It is evident that the conclusions of biblical criticism, though having the appearance of a "scientific" enterprise, are produced on the basis of the subjective evaluations of the critic. Such statements as the following evidence this: "The presence of a second literary hand is sometimes evident in a distinctive way of thinking or theological stance. When a definite change in theological approach is accompanied by other indications of a different literary hand the likelihood of a second literary source is greatly increased."[577] It is the subjective opinion by which the critic concludes that there is a change in theological approach. The subjective nature is brilliantly expressed by Habel: "Difference in literary style are sometimes easier to feel than to define."[578] Often, the critic completely misses the meaning of the passage which would if discerned, eliminate the notion that there is a change in theological approach. However, if there is a change in theological approach, there is no reason proposed on the basis of which to conclude that there is a different literary tradition. Is not one and the same author capable of changing theological approaches? For the critic, the expression "change in literary approach" is equivalent to "a contradictory or conflicting theological approach." However, the conclusion that theological approaches are contradictory, or conflicting is also due to the critics inability to have any real insight into the text. The biblical critic is trained to jump immediately to the conclusion that distinct theological approaches are a clue to distinct literary traditions. Because he is trained this way, there is no interpretive effort to understand the text in terms of a unity. Distinct theological approaches, or other "evidence," automatically signal distinct literary traditions and are therefore interpreted that way. The biblical critic has presupposed the validity of his approach and does not allow for the possibility that the text can be explained any other way. So, any contrary evidence or argument is rejected out of hand on the basis the subjective judgment that any other approach is naive or uninformed or unscholarly.

There is an important principle that is seemingly lost on the critical scholar, a principle expressed by Jesus in His dialogue with Nicodemus. After having explained to Nicodemus the principles of the new birth, Nicodemus expressed his doubts, "How can these things be?" Jesus responded with a statement that captures the principle that was true for Nicodemus and is true with reference to the claims of modern criticism: "If I told you earthly things and you do not believe, how will you believe if I tell you heavenly things?" (Jn. 3:12). The point is, if we cannot believer the Word of God when it tells us about things that we have the capacity to verify or falsify, then how can we trust it when it tells us about things that we have no

---

[577] Norman Habel, *Literary Criticism of the Old Testament* (Philadelphia: Fortress Press, 1971), 15.

[578] Ibid., 18.

capacity to investigate? This principle is illustrated by the claims of Tradition History as expressed by Rast:

> Martin Noth's well-known work on the Deuteronomic History pays attention to features which can be said to belong to a redaction history of that work. Like Engnell, Noth contended that the books of Joshua through Kings do not represent the continuation of certain of the sources isolated by documentary criticism in the Tetrateuch. Rather, these books are made up of an amalgam of traditions, to which Noth also gave the name Deuteronomic History. As they now lie before us, they are held together by the theological viewpoint of the Deuteronomic historian. Writing at the time of the exile of Jehoiachin to Babylon, the Deuteronomist attempted to present Israel's history from the time of Moses to the calamity of the exile as a history in which God's faithfulness to the promise given to the patriarchs continues, even though Israel is often wayward in her deeds.[579]

The problem that seems to escape the notice of the critic is if the history of Israel from the time of Moses did not, in fact, occur in the way in which the "Deuteronomist" portrayed, then there is no real basis upon which to trust his claims concerning the supposed faithfulness of God. If this account is not real history, meaning it did not really occur the way the text portrays it, then God did not, in fact, demonstrate faithfulness to Israel, and in fact, there is no reason to believe He would demonstrate any faithfulness to Israel during the exile. If we cannot trust the text to tell us the truth about earthly matters, then we cannot trust it to tell us about heavenly matters. The critic destroys the historical reliability of the text while trying to retain the spiritual message, but in the end, the critic destroys both the text and the message of the text.

---

[579] Rast, *Tradition History*, 17.

CHAPTER 7 Feminist Criticism of the Bible

Dianna Newman

Introduction

Emerging in the academic literature in the nineteenth and twentieth centuries, feminist theology has captivated the interests of men and women involved in theological studies over the last several decades due, in part, to the widespread acceptance that the biblical text is nothing more than a tool of oppression used to oppress women systematically. In today's culture, no longer does there exist a majority who believes the biblical text to be the whole counsel of God or who hold to its authority as a legitimate tool to inform the lives everyday people live. Instead, the vast majority today relegates the biblical text and Christianity, in general, to the mire—they consider it a vestige from an undesirable and primordial past. The way forward, many opines, involves deconstructing the text to find new meanings that thousands of years of church history have been too obtuse to uncover.

Those who live in feminist theological circles are a diverse group of women; so much so, that it would be a mistake to think feminist theology is monolithic. At one end of the spectrum, there are radical and/or post-Christian feminist theologians whose work belies the notion that Christianity cannot be redeemed since it cannot meet the standards of the feminist critique of the text. These feminists are content to reconstruct Christianity with a hermeneutic that honors women's experiences *of* and location *within* the biblical text. Other feminist theologians—those of a more liberal and/or reformist-leaning—believe that some aspects of Christianity are salvageable and can, therefore, be redeemed.[580] In *Women-Church: Theology and Practice of Feminist Liturgical Communities*, Rosemary Radford Ruether writes from the perspective of "religious feminists who seek to reclaim aspects of the biblical tradition, Jewish and Christian, but who also recognize the need both to go back *behind* [italics mine] biblical religion and to transcend it."[581]

Even with such widespread differences, however, feminist theologians are unified by several key ideas, not the least of which is the one echoed by Letty M. Russell, that "the Bible needs to be liberated from its captivity to one-sided white, middle-class, male interpretation. [In addition it] needs liberation from privatized and spiritualized interpretations that avoid God's concern for justice . . ."[582]

The last two hundred years have seen a good number of women whose work set the stage for feminist theology as it's studied and taught today. And while it would be far reaching to suppose that those who lived near the beginning of the

---

[580]Linda Woodhead, "Spiritualising the Sacred: A Critique of Feminist Theology," *Modern Theology* 13, no.2 (April 1997): 197.

[581]Rosemary Radford Ruether, *Women-Church: Theology and Practice of Feminist Liturgical Communities* (San Francisco: Harper and Row, 1986), 3-4.

[582]Letty M. Russell ed., *Feminist Interpretation of the Bible* (Philadelphia: Westminster Press, 1985), 12.

theological shift were themselves feminist[583], their work absolutely set the stage for the type of scholarship that proliferates today. Antoinette Brown (*d. 1921*), for instance, was the first woman to be ordained a minister by a recognized congregation in the United States. Brown was an avid believer in God and in the Scriptures and fought for women's equality, abolition, and temperance. Sarah Grimke (*d. 1873*) was a Quaker and woman's rights advocate whose understanding of Scripture set the stage for the abolition of slavery in the United States and brought attention to the idea of women's equality with men. On the other end of the spectrum was Elizabeth Cady Stanton whose scholarship resulted in *The Women's Bible*—a book where she served as both editor and contributing author. *The Woman's Bible* was published in 1895 and was written on the premise that religion served as the ideological justification for the continued oppression of women. The differences between the early suffragists (like Brown and Grimke) and early feminist theologians like Stanton are strikingly apparent just by looking at Stanton's views of the Bible in relation to women. In the introduction of *The Women's Bible* Stanton writes:

> The Bible teaches that woman brought sin and death into the world, that she precipitated the fall of the race, that she was arraigned before the judgement seat of Heaven, tried, condemned and sentenced. Marriage for her was to be a condition of bondage, maternity a period of suffering and anguish and in silence and subjection, she was to play the role of dependent on man's bounty for all her material wants, and for all the information she might desire . . . Here is the Bible position of woman briefly summed up.[584]

The primary purpose of this chapter is to offer a critique of the feminist critical method. I will argue that the feminist critical method is an inadequate one, as it is burdened with unavoidable difficulties. This critique falls into two parts. I will begin the first by locating feminist theology within its broader context of Liberation Theology. Tethering feminist theology to liberation theology serves to reveal the former's ideological assumptions. Following this will be a discussion on Hermeneutics, which will lead into a discussion of feminist theory's hermeneutic with which critical analysis is employed.

The second part will focus exclusively on, arguably, the most contentious topic in feminist theology today—God language. It is argued that the language used to describe God is distinctly and intentionally male language and its use throughout Christian history, feminist theologians argue, has caused both theological and psychological oppression of women that manifest itself in a myriad of ways. Here I will incorporate an analysis of the reforms suggested by feminist theologians they believe will curtail the effects of oppression. I will demonstrate how such reforms will ultimately prove ineffective.

---

[583] *In A Scripture of Their Own: Nineteenth-Century Bible Biography and Feminist Bible Criticism,* Rebecca Styler makes the important point that the suffragists maintained a belief that women and men were essentially different, that they had differentiated gender roles, and they also took as true that the whole Scriptures were the words of God.

[584] Elizabeth Cady Stanton, *The Women's Bible* (Boston: Northeastern University Press, 1993), 7.

One word of caution is in order before we begin. In no way should this chapter be taken to suggest that Christian history is absent of woman oppression at the hands of men. To suggest such a thing would be patently dishonest and ignorant. *All* religions, not just Christianity, have been guilty of some form of oppression. In fact, history has shown that religion is not a necessary ingredient for woman oppression or any other type of oppression to occur. Throughout all of the human history oppression has happened at the hands of *ir*religious men, *ir*religious governments, and *ir*religious institutions. It seems to be the case that humans will find a way to oppress other humans, whether religion is involved or not.

Gary Deddo, echoing the same sentiments in *This is My Name Forever: The Trinity & Gender Language For God* writes, "that Christianity in general terms has been used to justify wrongdoing is not in question. This is a matter of record, and of regret, which ought to lead to a repentance embodied in action by all those who give their allegiance to the Christian faith."[585] Yet Deddo goes on to rightly point out that "the problem of the abuse of good and true things is not just a problem confined to Christianity . . . It is a universal problem facing humanity as a whole in all its existence. This wider issue is . . . fully acknowledged in Christianity . . . [and] is a primary tenet of Christian conviction about the perennial fallen state of humanity."[586] That said, when it comes to Christianity *as* Christianity, there exists (and rightly so) a reasonable expectation that man and woman ought to exist together in mutually constructive and complementary ways, as they both love and serve the One who created them both in his image and his likeness. Yet, the reality of the situation lurks ominously in our consciousness that Christians do not *always* form their beliefs and practices congruent with the biblical Christian ethic that they claim.

Suffice to say that as we begin to discuss feminist criticism of the Bible, we must remember to acknowledge the credible reasons that feminist theology exists today, and understand the forces that inspired women to launch their valiant endeavor to begin with.

Feminist Theology as Liberation Theology

What is liberation theology? And why should a discussion of feminist theology be set in its context? Liberation Theologies began to take shape in the United States in the 1960s as theologians of the time wrestled to reconcile the social realities of the day with their theological commitments and expectations. As a result, these theologians came to believe that true faith was immediately and actually redemptive—not just eschatologically so. They began to promote the view that *true* theology must have "as a point of reference the experience of the poor and their struggle for liberation."[587] Liberation theologians hold that the *sine qua non* of true

---

[585]Alvin F. Kimel Jr., ed., This Is My Name Forever: The Trinity & Gender Language for God (Downers Grove: InterVarsity Press, 2001), 9.

[586]Ibid.

[587]Stanley J. Grenz and Roger E. Olsen, *20ᵗʰ Century Theology: God & the World in a Transitional Age* (Downers Gove, IL: Intervarsity Press, 1992), 211.

faith is liberation from all forms of oppression. Therefore, any faith that lacks this as its *telos*, by definition, must be reinterpreted or abandoned altogether.

For instance, *Latin American Liberation Theology* has as its central focus the experience of the poor classes in Latin America who have been subjected to institutionalized social and economic oppression resulting in gross levels of poverty.[588] *Black Liberation Theology* has as its central focus the socio-historical experience of black people in America—a people who possess a history riddled with the most malicious forms of racial oppression. *Feminist Theology*, properly speaking, is also a liberation theology because it focusses on the experiences of women as an oppressed sex. Feminist theologians call for a theological framework that liberates women from the oppressive ways the Bible has traditionally been interpreted and reinforced by Christian tradition.

All liberation theologies focus on a particular group within a given society that have been oppressed and/or marginalized, and they proceed by taking the experience of oppression in these groups to craft a theology that aims to end the experienced oppression and alter the structures in place that give oppressors their power. Feminist theology emerged on the heels of the broader feminist movement and just like the feminist movement, feminist theology identifies men as the oppressor and male-dominated structures as men's vehicle.

One salient note to be made at this juncture is to highlight the fact that the culture is eerily silent about women's experiences of oppression, not the hands of men, but from other *women*. The culture fails to treat systems/institutions that advantage females in the same way that it treats systems/institutions that advantage males.[589] For instance, while the academic literature has been addressing for some time now the inconsistencies between feminism and the beauty industry, it's interesting to note that the culture has not picked up on this, causing the beauty industry to proceed with very little cultural resistance.[590] Outside of the beauty industry United States culture is deafeningly silent about the justice system, which is a system that advantages women on the basis of their sex, while disadvantaging men on the basis of theirs.[591]

---

[588]Ibid., 210.

[589]*In Feminism and Pop Culture: Seal Studies*, Andi Zeisler makes the point that the culture is quite content to perpetuate actions that are ultimately damaging to women. Zeisler refers to a beauty industry—dominated, consumed, and maintained by women—that survives only through the perpetuation of women's' insecurity.

[590]For further reading on how culture manifests oppression, see Paula Black's article, "Discipline and pleasure: the uneasy relationship between feminism and the beauty industry" in *Feminism in Popular Culture*, edited by J Hollows and R Moseley. In addition to this, Chapter 5 of Stacy Malkan's book, *Not Just a Pretty Face: The Ugly Side of the Beauty Industry*, Malkan writes about the ways in which corporations are knowingly using toxic chemicals in beauty products that have unquestionably been linked to various cancers and diseases. It is largely women who buy into the beauty standards created by a multi-billion-dollar beauty industry. And it is women, in most cases, who judge *other* women on the basis of those same standards.

[591]See *Estimating Gender Disparities in Federal Criminal Cases* by Sonja B. Star, University of Michigan Law and Economics Research Paper, No. 12-018.

The feminist movement, broadly, and feminist theology, specifically, rarely performs the reflexive task—one in which scholars apply the standards they use to critique others on *themselves*. The reflexive task is one that insulates academicians from the charge of hypocrisy—from the charge of faulting others for doing the very thing being done. It will be interesting to see whether feminist theologians and writers ever take up the charge of addressing this reflexive void.

Returning to liberation theology, Anthony Bradley (writing on black liberation theology) comments about the self-assumed and often loudly proclaimed identity[592] that members of oppressed groups typically adopt. He writes, "victimology is the adoption of victimhood as the core of one's identity."[593] It is important to emphasize what Bradley is *not* saying in this sentence just as much as what he *is* saying. He is not making the point that the recognition of victimhood is the thing that ought to be discouraged. Nor is he making the claim that oppression does not work in powerful ways to impact how the oppressed view themselves. No serious scholar would dare suggest that the experiences of oppression by marginalized groups do not impact their collective cognitive psychological state. Instead, Bradley is making a more nuanced claim by bringing light to the idea that victimhood, in liberation theology, becomes the core of one's *identity* in the world; it becomes essential to one's humanity.

However, in reality, the exact opposite is true. Expressions of oppression are accidental, not essential. [594]

The reason for that is this: here in the United States some women experience oppression in certain contexts but at the very same time are not oppressed in other contexts. Some women experience oppression in ways that other women do not. The presence or absence of oppression is not core to what it is to *be* a woman. Feminist theology seems to suggest otherwise by making the bold claim that part and parcel of what it means to *be* a woman is to *be* oppressed. To make this point even clearer: women over the past several hundred years have been fighting long and hard to rid society of oppression against women. And because of their efforts, some forms of oppression have been removed. The very fact that forms of oppression have disappeared over time proves that oppression is accidental. Because if it was essential to woman, woman would have disappeared along with the oppression. In the end, feminist theology commits the classic confusion between essence/accident categories; and in doing that, their discussion of oppression's centrality to womanhood becomes a philosophically absurd one.

---

[592]Bradley takes his cues from John McWhorter, author of *Losing the Race: Self-Sabotage in Black America*, whose description of victimology broaches upon member's self-assessment of victimology.

[593]Anthony B. Bradley, *Liberating Black Theology: The Bible and the Black Experience in America* (Wheaton: Crossway, 2010), 19.

[594] The term *essential* is here used in a philosophical sense. It refers to "what" a thing is, or its essence. When philosophy refers to *accidents*, *accidents* are things, that if absent, do not in any way affect "what" a thing is—*accidents* don't affect *essence*. So, for instance, my hand is an accident in the sense that, if I lose it, the loss in no way affects what I am—a human. A person can lose (and every year many people *do*) a limb and still be human persons. What persons cannot lose is their humanity and still remain human. This is because one's humanity is *essential*.

Bradley goes on to say that "it [victimology] is a subconscious, culturally inherited affirmation that life . . . has been in the past and will be in the future a life of being victimized by . . . oppression.[595] Feminist theology is no different from black liberation theology in this regard. It, too, begins with oppression and "tries to articulate adequately the Christian witness of faith from the perspective of women as an oppressed group."[596]

In his book, Bradley highlights several key problems with tethering a victimhood identity to racial identity.[597] Suffice to say here that in the context of feminist theology the resultant problems are equally problematic. Number one, to have as one's view that women's experiences are identical to oppressive experiences is to "suggest that *women have a vested interest in maintaining victimhood* [italics mine]; without it both women's identity and their ability to do theology . . . collapse."[598] Number two, tethering victimhood to one's core identity ignores the fact that women have a myriad of experiences by which they form their self-identities as human persons in the world. And number three, self-identifying as a victim suggests women are incapable *of* and helpless *to* produce their own meaning in the world. Instead, they are reliant on the meanings imposed on them by the men who run patriarchal society.

Prima facie, it seems that such a view of woman proves contrary to the entirety of the feminist movement premise that woman are just as capable as men to live "fully human."

Feminist Criticism

So far, we have been speaking about feminist theology as if it and feminist criticism are two sides of the same coin. In addition, this is true, inasmuch as wherever feminist theology exists, feminist criticism has been present to inform the theological conclusions reached. Be that as it may, very few are familiar with the working assumptions of feminist criticism; they are unaware of the principles of interpretation used by feminist theologians as part of their process. That being the case, before we delve into feminist criticism, let us first give attention to the vitally important subject of hermeneutics.

Hermeneutics

When a person picks up a book and aims to read it in order to understand what it means, they first must be able to interpret the book. This is because in all communication, both verbal and written, interpretation precedes meaning, which then leads to understanding. People who have been reading books in their native

---

[595] *Liberating Black Theology*, 19.

[596] Pamela Dickey Young, *Feminist Theology/Christian Theology: In Search of Method* (Eugene, OR: Wipf and Stock, 1990), 60.

[597] For those interested in the parallels between feminist theology and black liberation theology, Bradley's book will be essential reading.

[598] Linda Woodhead, "Spiritualising The Sacred: A Critique of Feminist Theology," *Modern Theology* 13:2 (April 1997): 199.

language for many years easily lose sight of this interpretive process—they rarely are conscious of the thought, "what rules or judgments am I going to make in order to interpret what I am about to read?" This is because of their familiarity with the process, due to their repeated experiences with reading texts in their native language. Yet the interpretive process can be easily seen in small children as they are learning to read. As children struggle to interpret the words in storybooks, they quickly learn the benefits of sounding words out that they've never seen before. They tend to read long sentences with short words or short sentences with long words over and over again so that they get the "thought" of the sentence. Not only that, they often read the same books repeatedly. Children learn to do these things as a means of interpreting their storybook, and they are motivated to do these things because of a desire to understand what their storybook means.

In *all* communication interpretation precedes meaning, which then leads to understanding.

As adults who have learned how to navigate this, we still apply certain principles in an effort to interpret things we read. The interpretive process for adults is more complicated as texts become more complicated—but adults still undergo the interpretive process.

Properly understood, hermeneutics is the "term used to identify the study of the *principles* [italics mine] of interpretation"[599] and it assumes, without controversy, that a text *means* something. Things that lack meaning need not be interpreted. For instance, the sentence "her ingbatosh cried over the orange showaniyat arewisopate" need not be interpreted since it means nothing. But if a text can be interpreted, the act of interpretation itself *assumes* the text has meaning. This is because texts consist of grammatical sentences, which are the most fundamental units of meaning. In turn, sentences are made up of words that have their own definitions and or grammatical functions. Textual objectivity simply means that a text has a singular meaning precisely because words strung together in grammatically correct ways convey singular meaning.

Objectivity, in turn, assumes that reality is a *real thing*. That is to say, communication between persons occurs because reality is *real*, and people wish to interact with one another about it.[600] When the passenger in a vehicle gently reminds the driver that a police car is behind them, the passenger is communicating to the driver that something real exists—the police car. When the passenger communicates to the driver "a police car is behind us," the statement has a singular meaning; it may hold several implications and/or be significant to the driver on different levels, but the statement itself has *one singular meaning*. Words, in this sense, act as symbols and they point to *real* things—whether those things are conceptually real or actually real.

Again, children in the process of learning to read, illustrate this idea perfectly. Because of their lack of exposure to English words—and in many cases, their lack of

---

[599]Thomas A Howe, *Objectivity in Biblical Interpretation*, (CreateSpace, 2015), 2.

[600]The term *real* is not to be equated with the term *material*. I am not here espousing a Materialist worldview which claims the material world is all that exists. As one committed to Theism, I am making the point that immaterial realities can be just as actual as material realities can be. I am saying that tangibility is not a necessary condition for actuality.

exposure to things in reality—children have to make as many connections as possible between words and reality in order to obtain the meaning of a story. Therefore, for instance, an insightful adult will point to a picture of a cow and then point to the word *cow* so that the child can make the connection and understand that the word *cow* has a referent—in this case, the reference is the picture of the cow. Or an adult will point to a picture of a red streak and then point to the word *red* so that the child can make the connection and understand what *red* is. The whole enterprise of learning how to read assumes reality is *real*, and it involves making connections between words and the objects or concepts they point to.

No longer children, adults who have been reading English for quite some time bring to interpretation their understanding of how words work in relationship to one another and to reality. The principles of interpretation can often be a more involved process when it comes to complex pieces of literature, but the process is, in some respects, still the same. Adults, for instance, bring their understanding of English grammar rules and the principles that govern metaphor, simile symbols, etc. They also bring their principles of how to distinct between materiality and immateriality when reading. All of these hermeneutical aids are part of the interpretive process—they help one find meaning in the text, which hopefully leads to understanding.

It is important to say that hermeneutics, in this case, *biblical* hermeneutics, is not an option—it is necessary in order to ascertain meaning. To this end, Thomas Howe notes "theologians and philosophers through the centuries have studied the practice of interpretation and endeavored to establish principles that would lead the interpreter to *the* meaning of the text."[601]

Meaning

It has already been stated that hermeneutics concerns itself with the principles of interpretation, but to be sure interpretation, by itself, is not the ultimate goal. The ultimate goal of interpretation is meaning. Hermeneutics has in view this question: "what does this text *mean*?" For decades now, literary theorists, hermeneutic theorists, and philosophers of language have had lively discussions on the topic of meaning. What does meaning *mean*? For the purposes of this discussion, the question is a pointed one: *Where* is meaning found? When two people communicate, where is meaning located? Is it in the mind of the person speaking (or writing)? Is it in the mind of the person listening (or reading)? Or is it in neither, could meaning be located in what's being said or the thing being read?[602]

For instance, as you read this chapter on Feminist Criticism, ask yourself: is the meaning of this chapter in the mind of the author (Dianna) or is it in *your* mind, the reader? If it is neither of those things—neither the author or the reader—could it actually be located in the text of the chapter itself. Is the meaning of this chapter somehow "in" the text?

---

[601]Ibid.

[602]For insightful commentary on hermeneutics, see Thomas A. Howe, *Objectivity in Biblical Interpretation*

There is no consensus among linguists today *where* the locus of meaning is to be found. Those who hold to the traditional view of meaning have understood it to be found in the text. They have opined that texts have objective meaning and words point to objective realities outside any one person's mind. Reality, they say, makes texts meaningful—without it, texts would be meaningless. Therefore, for instance, when the passenger says "a police car is behind us" that statement means something because there *is* a police car behind the vehicle, and that statement remains objectively true as long as the police car remains behind the vehicle.

Since meaning has traditionally been understood to be in texts, principles of interpretation have traditionally proceeded via historical- critical methods. Historical-critical methods are all predicated on the belief that, one, the biblical text has objective meaning and two, people who approach the biblical text can find out what that meaning is. Historical-critical methods seem intuitively true; it seems intuitive that literature has objective meaning, but as we will soon see, most modern minds are doubtful of this very notion.

Literary Criticism

Literary Criticism of the biblical text began to become popular in the latter part of the twentieth century as scholars began to implement the insights of literary theory into interpretation. Literary theory, when applied to the biblical text, led to biblical scholars attending to the processes of a text's production and interpretation." Christina Bucher notes,

> Influenced by reader-response approaches, biblical interpreters have for the most part abandoned the position that there is a single, correct interpretation of a biblical text, which can be discovered if one employs correctly the tools of the historical-critical method. . . . [reader response] interpretation depends upon both readers and texts and, therefore, interpretation is multivalent.[603]

With the advent of literary criticism, the traditional view that biblical interpretation was objective slowly began its demise within biblical scholarship. Today, most biblical scholarship employs methods of interpretation that stem wholly from literary theory and its reader-oriented approach. Reader-oriented approaches are ones in which "readers do not *search* for a text's meaning; they *create* meaning through the act of reading. . . . [literary critics] argue . . . biblical texts are processes, not products."[604] Feminist literary criticism, or **feminist criticism**, is one of the many approaches to textual interpretation using literary theory. Biblical feminist criticism is an approach to biblical interpretation that employs a particular feminist method to critique the biblical text. Because of its views of objectivity, feminist criticism challenges the idea of an objective method of biblical interpretation and questions that objective biblical truth is possible.

---

[603]Christina Bucher, "New Directions in Biblical Interpretation Revisited," Bretheren Life and Thought 60, no. 1 (Spring 2015), 36.
[604]Ibid.

Dr. Norman Geisler notes that all forms of biblical criticism (including literary criticism) in the late twentieth century questioned seriously the notion of authority generally, and *biblical* authority specifically.[605] Having been influenced by Immanuel Kant's views that objective reality was inaccessible to the human mind, literary criticism's main focus was a concern for the sources the biblical authors were alleged to have used, and it also dealt with questions relating to authorship unity and dating.[606]

While the guiding philosophical assumptions of literary criticism are outside the scope of this chapter to discuss in detail, suffice to say here that it ultimately led to biblical scholarship either outright ignoring or downplaying the text's cultural and historical context;[607] eventually, literary critics embraced the idea that pieces of literature were *not* in the business of making truth claims about reality.

This rejection of historical-critical methods of interpretation led to the view that meaning was found in a reader's response to the text. Reader response theories of meaning are ones which posit that meaning is located in the mind of the person reading a text—or the mind of the person receiving the verbal communication. Feminist theologian Barbara Brown Zikmund writes "in current biblical study it is almost as important to examine the contemporary situation *of the reader* [italics mine] as it is to know the particular milieu that produced a text many centuries earlier."[608] Christina Bucher summarizes the shift well, pointing out that

> Biblical interpreters have for the most part abandoned the position that there is a single, correct interpretation of a biblical text, which can be discovered if one employs correctly the tools of the historical-critical method. Rather, interpretation depends upon both readers *and* [emphasis added] . . . interpretation is multivalent. . . . Readers do not search for a text's meaning; they create meaning through the act of reading.[609]

Feminist theologians admit their rejection of textual objectivity. In *Beyond God the Father: Toward a Philosophy of Liberation*, Mary Daly clarifies her methodology through which she hopes to deal with questions surrounding "religious symbols and concepts."

> I will begin my description with some indications of what my method is *not*. First of all it obviously is not that of a "kerygmatic theology," which supposes some unique and changeless revelation peculiar to Christianity or to *any* religion. Neither is my approach that of a disinterested observer who claims to have an "objective knowledge about" reality. Nor is it an attempt to correlate with the existing cultural situation certain "eternal truths" which are presumed to have been

---

[605]Norman L. Geisler and William E. Nix, *A General Introduction to the Bible: Revised and Expanded* (Chicago: Moody Press, 1986), 434.

[606]*A General Introduction to the Bible*, p. 434-436.

[607]*New Directions*, 35.

[608]Letty M. Russel, ed., *Feminist Interpretation of the Bible* (Philadelphia: Westiminster, 1985), 22.

[609]*New Directions*, 36.

captured as adequately as possible in a fixed and limited set of symbols [words]. None of these approaches can express the revolutionary potential of women's liberation for challenging the forms in which consciousness incarnates itself and for changing consciousness.[610]

One may be wondering why a discussion of hermeneutics and meaning have been inserted into a discussion of feminist criticism of the Bible. The reason is because it's important to know that feminist criticism of the Bible, as evidenced by Mary Daly's remarks above, embraces a reader response view of the text, rather than the traditional historical-critical method of interpretation. As we begin to discuss the feminist hermeneutic, as expressed by some of the most notable feminist scholars, it is instructive to remember that reader response theories of meaning are treated as incontrovertibly correct in feminist criticism of the Bible.

Before we turn to feminist hermeneutics, the author's opinion in this matter should be clear. It is the opinion of the author that all reader response approaches to meaning are both philosophically and intuitively insufficient. A comprehensive philosophical critique cannot be given at this time, but think about the complications—practical and otherwise—that result from the view meaning is *not* objectively found in a text.

Number one, imagine being in a bookstore and upon perusing all the different sections, you land in the Astrology section—a topic you enjoy. As you walk down the aisle, a book with a very attractive cover catches your eye, so you decide to pick it up. After skimming through it very quickly, you come to realize the book is entirely about a very remote astrophysical thesis, and that there are whole chapters in it about the complex mathematical and chemical equations that make the remote astrophysical thesis a very probable one. What do you do? Do you continue skimming the book with the intent to purchase, or do you not? The vast majority of people will do the latter. They will place the book back on the shelf *not* because it isn't attractive and not because they aren't interested in Astrology; most people will put the book back where they found it because they know the chances are slim to none that the book will be meaningful to them—they don't believe they'll be able to understand all of the math and chemistry to make sense of anything. This is because, intuitively, people know that they derive meaning from text; this is why they flip through the book and skim the pages. People intuitively know a reader does not decide the meaning. Rarely will a person purchase a book she knows she has no chance of understanding but buys anyway because she plans to assign her own meaning to it. Practically speaking, we order our lives on this concept every day. Practically, we think the text has objective meaning every time we read cookbooks in the kitchen, traffic signs on the road, or poison warning labels on bottles.

Number two, we can also think about this in the context of verbal communication. When one person speaks to another person, she uses the words that she thinks are sufficient to convey a precise and specific meaning. In other words, people make deliberate choices about the words they use in order to convey the specific meaning they intend. When person A accuses person B of

---

[610] Mary Daly, *Beyond God the Father: Toward a Philosophy of Liberation* (Boston: Beacon Press, 1973), 7.

miscommunicating, the accusation being made by A is that B has failed to use words adequately, and doing that has resulted in a meaning that was never meant by B. Doing this creates the need for a clarifying conversation between A and B. It is never acceptable in verbal communication for person B to tell person A that her communication was altered by B to fit B's internal motivations. On the other hand, when person C and person D are talking with one another, it is never acceptable for person C to assume that D has access to her mind, and can, therefore, read C's intentions. If person C wants person D to understand her, C will do well to learn how to communicate meaningfully by using appropriately meaningful words.

The simple point being made is that we sense every day that meaning resides in words. Any time *mis*communication takes place; people lay blame on the misuse of *words* (or not using enough of them) for the mixed messages that cross between people. If this were *not* the case, then no one could ever be charged with "sending mixed messages," "mis-speaking, ""being mean, rude, insensitive, etc., with their words."

In addition, number three, notice the self-defeating position that feminist critics place themselves in when they proceed off the premise that texts lack objective meaning. Feminist critics go to great lengths to write commentaries and/or books on various scripture passages or aspects of Christianity because they feel those things are detrimental to women. Feminists throughout the ages have worked long and hard to present their views intelligently and articulately, hoping that their perspectives are understood and accepted as viable in the wider community. Feminist theologians hope that people will read their work and amend their perspectives about the Bible based on the persuasiveness of the arguments. It is hard to imagine a feminist theologian using valuable resources (time, money, effort) to write something that she has no expectation will be persuasive to other people.

Nevertheless, the question that arises from that desire is a poignant one, given their view that texts do not have objective meaning: why take the time to write if literature (*their* books and *their* articles) has no objective meaning? Are feminist critics the only ones who write objectively and meaningfully about their topic? Feminist critics of the Bible expect, and they should, that their words will be read and interpreted in a way that is consistent with the meaning they wished to convey when they wrote. So, for instance, when someone reads Rosemary Radford Ruther's *Sexism and God-Talk: Toward a Feminist Theology* and they come away from it with the understanding that her *critical principle of feminist theology* refers to her views on locomotion, for example, that would be an *in*correct understanding—[611] an objectively incorrect understanding of what Reuther meant by the concept. In fact, it is quite likely that if Reuther had the opportunity to correct someone's misunderstanding of her critical principle, she would say her critical principle has been *misunderstood*, or that her work has been *misinterpreted*.

Mary Daly's comment above from *Beyond God the Father* displays this self-defeating phenomenon just as well as Reuther's does. She writes, "neither is my approach that of a disinterested observer who claims to have an "objective

---

[611] What should be understood about Reuther's critical principle of feminist theology when she uses the term is that it's a hermeneutic principle whose only concern is the full humanity of woman.

knowledge about" reality. Yet, Daly *does* have an objective view of reality. Her working assumptions as a feminist theologian *assume* an objective view of reality that insists traditional Christianity is both patriarchal and abusive. Her views about traditional Christianity being patriarchal are not just true for her; Daley thinks they are true even if one chooses to ignore them.

Though feminist critics go to great lengths to oppose textual objectivity, the notion is not as easy to get rid of as they imagine.

The Feminist Hermeneutic

The issues taken up by feminist theologians, just as the issues taken up by feminist philosophers, are varied. What unites the assumptions of both is recognition that (1) history has not been favorable to the acknowledgment of woman, and (2) men have had a direct role in shaping that history. In *Sexism and God-Talk* Ruether's overall premise is that patriarchy has dominated all aspects of society, not the least of which is Christian theology; the book is her attempt to redeem basic biblical principles that are appropriate to feminist theology. Right in line with the thoughts of liberation theologians, Ruether believes any theology that diminishes the full humanity of women (and other oppressed groups) is *not* a divine revelation. That being the case, she wishes to extract from biblical principles alternative principles that are appropriate for the promotion of the full humanity of women.

Across a representative sample of feminist theologians, the thing that diminishes the full humanity of women is the same—it is the lack of recognition of *women's experiences.* Ruether writes, "the uniqueness of feminist theology lies not in its use of the criterion of experiences but rather in its use of *women's* experience, which has been almost entirely shut out of theological reflection in the past. The use of women's experience in feminist theology, therefore, explodes as a *critical force* [italics mine]."[612] Feminist theology is extremely committed to the notion of the value of experience as that relates to its essential role in the acquisition of human knowledge. The accusation levied against classical theology is that it has denigrated the role of experience, preferring to elevate "objectivity" instead. Ruether notes the disdain for objectivity well when she writes:

> It is generally assumed by traditional theology that any experience let alone "women's experience," is merely a subjective and culture-bound source of ideas and cannot be compared with the objectivity of scripture, which discloses the "word of God" outside of, over, and against the subjectivity and sinful impulses of human experience. As a narrow and contemporary source, experience cannot compare with the accumulated weight of theological tradition. It is sheer impertinence to suggest that "women's experience" can be used to judge scripture and theological tradition,"[613]

---

[612]Rosemary Radford Reuther, *Sexism and God-Talk: Toward a Feminist Theology* (Boston: Beacon Press, 1983), 13.

[613]*Feminist Interpretation of the Bible*, 111.

Classical theology—with its claim to special revelatory experiences, its canonization of certain scriptures that are based on a hierarchy of acceptable experiences, its stance that adherents of the faith can "experience the divine"— imbibes, for feminist theology, the notion that human experience is infused within the Christian tradition at all levels of its existence. Since the interpretation of a text both begins and ends with human experience, she proposes the critical principle upon which Christian texts and traditions should be judged.

> The critical principle of feminist theology is the promotion of the full humanity of women. *Whatever denies, diminishes, or distorts the full humanity of women is, therefore, appraised as not redemptive* [italics mine]. Theologically speaking, whatever diminishes or denies the full humanity of women must be presumed *not to reflect* [italics mine] the divine . . . This negative principle also implies the positive principle: what does promote the full humanity of women is of the Holy.

She goes on to say that:

> This principle is hardly new. . . . the correlation of original, authentic human nature (*imago dei*/Christ) and diminished, fallen humanity provided the basic structure of classical Christian theology. The uniqueness of feminist theology is not the critical principle, fallen humanity, but the fact that women claim this principle for themselves. Women name themselves as subjects of authentic and full humanity. . . . [it has been the] naming of males as norms of authentic humanity [that] has caused women to be scapegoated for sin and marginalized in both original and redeemed humanity.

There is a lot that can be said about Ruether's claims since they are fraught with unavoidably problematic conclusions and difficulties that undermine the veracity of feminist critical studies of the Bible. The first difficulty is a logical one; specifically, the self-defeating nature of the claim that experience is both the starting point and ending point of interpretation. Do you see it?

Ruether's belief in a hermeneutical circle entails the notion that all knowledge begins is amended and ends with experience. Yet it seems Ruether fails to see how such a hermeneutical circle undermines her own objectives—as she advances all of her scholarly knowledge by critically assessing Christian texts and traditions and as she writes books and articles aiming to legitimate *her* experience of Christian texts and tradition as objectively true for everyone. Presumably, Reuther expects that those who do not share her experience of a particular data set—presumably, should accept her views she thinks her views should be accepted even by those who do not share in her experiences of "woman's experience." Yet at the very same time, she claims everyone's knowledge of things begins with one's personal experience.

Yet even with that said, Ruether's position is not an unredeemable one since it turns out to be half-way correct. That is to say; the Christian tradition *has* been delivered through the experiences of certain individuals. Reuther says as much when she writes "what have been called the objective sources of theology; Scripture and tradition, are themselves codified collective human experience;"[614] her point is that

---

[614] *Sexism and God-Talk*, 12.

subjectivity has driven the formation of Christian tradition and canonization. Specifically, it has been *male* subjectivity that has driven the formation of Christian tradition and canonization.

Yet what Ruether misses is this: the *entire* process is not one that begins and ends in subjectivity simply because "Scripture and tradition" always refer *back* to some data that exists *independent* of the experience. Scripturally, the validity of reported experiences derives from whether they reflect and/or whether they focus back to an objective truth about a *real* reality. In a sense, it can be said that Scriptural tradition communicates real truth via human experience—authentically biblical revelation is never quite content communicating human experience just for the sake of communicating human experience.[615]

At the base of this issue is category confusion between *experience* and *propositional truth claims.* Experiences, in themselves, are neither true nor false—they just *are.* If person A reports his experience of a thing to person B, B has no access to the experience and is consequently unable to verify it for herself. All she can do is either trust or distrust that A is reporting accurately of an experience that is meaningful to him; she makes a choice whether to act or not act on said experience based on her trust of A. But if person A makes a truth claim—claims that something is true or that it is false—tied to an experience, person B has the ability corroborate the claim since she has access to reality, enough to conclude that A's statement (and probable/improbable experience) of it is "true" or "false." Experiences, by themselves, are neither true nor false, they just *are*—unless said experiences are somehow tethered to reality in a meaningful way.

One caveat should be made at this point: an experience, which cannot be tethered to objective truth (reality), can still be a meaningful experience. But only for the one who experienced it. Individuals can and do have subjectively meaningful experiences; there are biblical instances in which individuals had experiences that were deeply meaningful to them.[616] Notwithstanding, individual experiences are not the grounds upon which Christian theology or tradition rest—experiences serve, in some sense, as evidence and/or supplements to claims that assert themselves as objective truths.

This, then, leads to the next point, which is this: an experience of an event is not true or false by virtue of it being expressed by a certain gender. In other words, feminist theology sees it as very problematic that the Scriptures appear to codify *male* experiences as if male experiences are intrinsically false or illicit by virtue of being male. On the opposite side, feminist theology sees women's experiences as inherently valuable and legitimate just by virtue them belonging to women.

---

[615]Here, I am only speaking about Christian scripture, since Reuther's comments are directed to Christian scripture. One should note as well that Scriptures *do* include experiences (such as dreams/visions) that are subjectively experienced and solely meaningful to the person who experienced it. individuals external to subjective experience are never required to appropriate the experience for themselves—they *are* expected, however, to acknowledge the *objective truth* said experiences often allude to.

[616]In 2 Cor. 12, Paul speaks of a personal revelation experience in which he was "caught up" to paradise. Such an event impacted Paul greatly, yet there is no indication that Paul's experience had to be appropriated by the community of believers in his day.

It bears repeating: an experience of an event is not true or false by virtue of it being expressed by a certain gender.

In fact, the very notion of *women's experience* is arguably the most contested concept of feminist criticism. There simply is no consensus among feminist theologians what constitutes "women's experience." Reuther's view is that it describes more than just the biological differences between men and women; she sees it as that which is "free" from male bias and/or patriarchal influence given that patriarchal society continuously imposes a male hermeneutic upon women causing women to interpret their experiences *as* women through male dominated culture."[617] (Notice once again the portrayal of women as "victims" unable to move as free agents in the world except for the guiding force of patriarchal culture to "help" them sort through their experiences as women. One might even suggest their perpetual references to women as "helpless" and "dominated" effects the very treatment/image that feminists are fighting against!) Even within the ranks of feminist theologians, there is no consensus concerning the concept of women's experience. Grace Jantzen (*d. 2006*), a feminist philosopher and theologian, had "little time for the work of the pioneering feminist theologians . . . [because of their] philosophically naïve appeals to "women's experience' as privatized and . . . [their failure] to acknowledge the "irreducibly diverse" nature of the many variables in women's lives (race, class, sexual orientation).[618] Linda Woodhead notes that the "uncritical dependence upon 'women's experience' gives the impression that the nothing is unproblematic and uncontested. Nothing, I think, could be further from the truth."[619] Further critiquing the notion of women's experience, Woodhead goes on to say:

> Feminist theologians assume that religion comes *after* experience. They believe this to be true of language too. Both, they say, represent the process whereby concepts and symbols are imposed upon experience in an attempt to understand and to communicate it. . . . Moreover, concepts and symbols have authority primarily for the individual who imposed them—other individuals must be free to 'concretise' (*sic*) their experience in their own ways and to 're-image' concepts and symbols at will. But this conception of experience as private and pre-linguistic fails to account for the complex and diverse ways in which knowledge is actually acquired, and it ignore the essentially social (or 'textualised') (*sic*) nature of the process. It is by being members of communities and by being formed by texts and traditions that we come to knowledge: contrary to the belief of much feminist theology, we do not have pre-social, pre-linguistic and pre-cultural 'experiences' and then shape tradition, texts and community of them. I do not spin God out of my own private experience of the divine; I know God because he was manifest in Jesus Christ, and because the scripture, tradition and community which formed me bear witness to Him. I may indeed be

---

[617] *Feminist Interpretation*, 113-114.

[618] William J Wainwright, ed., *The Oxford Handbook of Philosophy of Religion* (New York, Oxford University, 2005), 498.

[619] *Spiritualising the Sacred*, 197.

blessed with 'a religious experience,' but I only know it to be such . . . because I am able to 'test the Spirit' against what tradition and community tell me of God. Never could the latter [experience] be entirely private in the way which feminist theology suggests.[620]

All this notwithstanding, feminist theology remains content to implement women's experience as the basis of its textual critique. Aware of the elusiveness of the concept, feminist theologian Margaret A Farley attempts to offer another means of criticizing the biblical text. She writes,

> for those who are reluctant to bring to scripture what seems to be a measure for its meaning and authority,[621] [women's experiences] one solution suggests itself in the face of a seeming dilemma. That is, it might be argued that *scripture itself* [italics added] provides the basis for feminist consciousness. True discernment of the biblical witness yields feminist insights, which in turn become principles of interpretation for the rest of scripture. In other words, *convictions regarding the full humanity of women emerge precisely from the bringing of women's experience to the address of scripture* [italics added].[622]

Yet Farley's attempt to validate the methodological efficacy of "women's experience" fares no better than Reuther's. The first problem with her solution is this: if interpretation of scripture is necessary in order to know what the text means—and it *is* necessary—then it cannot be true that "scripture itself" provides a basis since "scripture itself" is the very thing that needs interpreting. In other words, how would one know which scriptures provide a basis for feminist consciousness without first interpreting the scripture to make sure they are sufficient? Farley's argument is a circular one. The second problem with her solution is equally problematic since it begs the question.[623] "Women's experience," as a critical method, entails the idea woman has been excluded from full humanity. So it comes as no surprise that when one *brings* women's experience to Scripture, one will emerge with convictions regarding her full humanity. Begging the question *always* brings the expected conclusions, but those conclusions are not in any way logically compelling—since they have been brought about by committing a logical fallacy in the argument.

Thus far we have seen the failure of feminist criticism to produce a viable methodology, since it falls short on multiple grounds: (1) its inability to reach methodological consensus on what *woman's experience* is, (2) its inability to produce a body of work free from the objectivity it claims has tainted the western

---

[620]Ibid., 198.

[621]Here in *Feminist Interpretation of the Bible*, Farley is making the case that interpretation of the Bible is necessary in order for the Bible to be understood. She attempts to make the case that a feminist interpretation of the Bible calls for a *standard* by which to perform the interpretational (hermeneutical) task. This standard is women's experiences.

[622]*Spiritualising the Sacred*, 48.

[623]The informal fallacy known as begging the question is committed when the conclusion of an argument is used as one of the promises in the argument. In other words, the conclusion is as a premise to drive the argument to its (obvious) conclusion.

theological tradition, and (3) its inability to avoid lines of argumentation that are fraught with informal fallacies. These are all legitimate reasons that ought to give pause to the discipline as an academically valid one.

What is His Name?

In the previous section, it was demonstrated that the hermeneutic employed by feminist theologians is driven by a number of working assumptions including but not limited to: (1) a belief that texts communicate subjective experiences rather than objective knowledge (2) a belief that meaning is primarily driven by how readers respond to a text given their subjective points of view and (3) the inherent oppressive structures of religion work to promote patriarchy and the oppression of women in male dominated society.

Granting these beliefs, it stands to reason that the most contentious issue in feminist theology today concerns language; specifically, the male-dominated images and words traditionally used to describe God promote both social and psychological woman oppression. Biblical references to God such as King, Son, Father, Master, Ruler etc. further demonstrate a tacit approval of patriarchy and oppression. In *Beyond God the Father* Mary Daly writes

> The symbol of the Father God, spawned in the human imagination and sustained as plausible by patriarchy, has in turn rendered service to this type of society [patriarchal society] by making its mechanisms for the oppression of women appear right and fitting. If God in "his" heaven is a father ruling "his" people, then it is in the "nature" of things and according divine plan and the order of the universe that society be male-dominated.[624]

Those committed to the idea that biblical language engenders intrinsic patriarchal structures believe that by replacing male dominated God-language with new metaphors and images, woman oppression can be reversed.

Such reformers come with four types of proposals: (1) all references to the Divine should reflect a female deity; (2) female imagery should be incorporated along with male imagery when talking about God; (3) non-gender images and/or language should be used exclusively of God and (4) a composite of the former two options.[625] Before we begin our discussion of male-dominated language, we would do well to unpack more this notion of oppression, since inherent within the very notion of the idea is an observation that derails the feminist cause from the outset.

Oppression

Broadly speaking, two ideologies stand behind the notion oppression, such that looking at the ideologies themselves allow for a thorough understanding of the

---

[624] *Beyond God the Father*, 13.

[625] Mary Stewart Van Leeuwen, ed., *After Eden: Facing the Challenge of Gender Reconciliation* (Grand Rapids: Eerdmans, 1993), 153.

concept. The two ideologies that stand in the back of the concept are what may largely be construed as (1) Humanistic or Darwinian ideologies and (2) a Christian theistic ideology. By looking at each of these, the goal is to find out whether one, both, or neither promote the feminist claim that Christian Scriptures and tradition endorse female oppression.

I will begin by looking at the issue of oppression through the lenses of Humanism/Darwinism. Roughly speaking, Darwinism is a collection of ideas, which posit that in any given environment the strong survive to future generations while those who are weak in that given environment do *not* survive to future generations. Known by the moniker, "survival of the fittest," Darwinism hinges on the notion that not only is this "weeding out" of the weak a natural process, but it is also a necessary one. Social Darwinism posits the same idea that biological Darwinism does—that in the social world, those who "rise to the top" of the social ladder do so because they possess something inherently stronger that the weak don't.

On a Darwinian view, those who rise to the top are to be *expected* to rise to the top.

Yet when stated this way, immediately one sees the difficulty that Darwinists run into. If, according to Darwinism, it is natural and necessary that one group will "outlast" another group or one group will become "subject" to a stronger one, then what basis do the weak have for complaining that they are being outlasted? In the context of social Darwinism, why would there be angst when Darwinian principles run their course and a certain group experiences oppression? Darwinians should *expect* for a group in society to be oppressed, and truth be told they should expect *female* oppression since history has shown that, as a group, men are stronger than women to the extent that they can effect change by force, if necessary.

The irony is that most Darwinists *do* have a problem with oppression. They believe—and rightly so!—that oppression is wrong and that women should not be oppressed.

A Christian theistic view envisions the nature of oppression differently. A Christian theist perspective believes that all forms of oppression are wrong and that people ought not to use or abuse other people for personal gain. The differences between men and women are clear—there are emotional, psychological, cognitive, behavioral and biological ones—but those differences are meant to be complementary. Differences, in themselves, do not entail oppression. And while feminist theologians eschew Christian theism, in theory, it is not always easy to ascertain which aspects of Christian theology they accept and which aspects they question. It seems "common," notes Woodhead, "for feminist theologians to hold it [their feminist commitments] as a more basic commitment than their commitment to Christianity . . . [where their critique] becomes a rather formalistic exercise in weighing up Christianity *against* [italics mine] an externally imposed, externally derived and unquestionable standard."[626]

What does all this mean for feminist theologians who propose that by changing the ways in which we talk about God, oppression will be eradicated? The Christian theistic view seems to suggest that because sinful nature is the cause of

---

[626] *A Critique of Feminist Theology*, 197.

oppression—and every human person has a sinful nature—the subjugation of another for one's own benefit is likely to continue. If on the chance men lose the ability to oppress, the task is likely to be taken up by women. But surely the oppression of men is no better than the oppression of women. With all this being said, I will now consider the proposal offered by feminist theologians that the exclusively male language used to talk about God promotes oppression and if changed, will lead to its extinction.

Is Israel's God a Man?

According to feminist theology, the gender of Israel's God is decidedly male. Number one, the divine name YHWH is consistently translated into English in the masculine gender; and number two, the imagery and titles used of God in the biblical text are decidedly masculine. For instance, God is referred to as a heavenly father, not a heavily *mother.*

Any discussion on the consistent practice of translating God's name using male language requires a working knowledge of linguistics and how language works. The Hebrew language, just like Latin and French, is grammatically gendered languages—in other words, the nouns in Hebrew are assigned a grammatical gender—either masculine, feminine, or neuter. In gendered languages, it is customary that nouns indicating male beings are masculine in grammatical gender, and nouns indicating female beings are feminine in grammatical gender. However, outside of this, there exists no *necessary* relationship between the grammatical gender of a word and the sex of the object. In other words, there is no relationship between actual gender and grammatical gender in Hebrew or any other gendered language.[627] By way of example, French is a moderately gendered language; its nouns are either grammatically masculine or feminine. The term *le chien* is masculine, and it means "the dog." But dogs are sexed, and in reality exist as either male or female. This illustrates the point that in a gendered language, grammatical gender is not ever a statement about an object's biological sex.

English, unlike Hebrew, is *not* a gendered language. While English recognizes the same three genders that Hebrew does (masculine, feminine, and neuter) the gender of a noun in English is notional as opposed to grammatical. The sex of a noun usually coincides with the sex of the object. To this end, English employs certain words (3rd person pronouns) to indicate a noun's sex and has grammar rules that reinforce the idea. So for instance, we all remember the grammar rule which states that the gender of a pronoun must agree with the gender of the noun it replaces. We know this rule so well that we immediately notice when it's violated. The sentence "Mark and *her* friend John went to the library" is noticed by the ear because a pronoun (*her*) and noun (*Mark*) are in disagreement with one another and the sentence forces us to wonder if Mark is female. We immediate know that a grammatically correct sentence should read "Mark and *his* friend went to the library."

---

[627]Frederic M. Wheelock and Richard A. Lafleur, *Wheelock's Latin,* 7th ed. (New York: Harper Collins, 2011), 15.

Suffice to say that in English there are a group of words (her, his, him, he, she, it) that have no content on their own; instead, they grammatically point to their noun-antecedent.

What does all this mean for feminist theology? The first thing that must be acknowledged is grammatically masculine words do not entail actual sex. This is a simple linguistic rule of all gendered languages. The fact that the word for *God* in Hebrew (YHWH) is grammatically masculine does not in any way entail that God's sex is male. Responsible translation *requires* that a word of a certain grammatical gender in one language be translated with personal pronouns that agree with the grammatical construction in the original language. And it isn't controversial to say that translation should never be violated to conform to ideological and/or political commitments.[628]

Yet even while this is the case, it is glaringly true that the Scriptures portray God as masculine, and that when feminine imagery is used of God, such imagery is subordinate to the masculine characterizations.[629] While that is uncompromisingly true, feminist theologians would do well to remember that the clear theological teaching of the church has never been obfuscated by the linguistic necessities of written language. Both Scriptures and Christian tradition assert that God is not a man and that he transcends biological classification.[630]

Feminist Theology and Jesus

Many feminists reject the Trinity on the grounds that it exemplifies another instance of predominately male imagery. Equally problematic for feminist theology is that Christian theology images the Trinity as a hierarchical ordering where the Father is "over" the Son and the Son and Father are "over" the Spirit.[631] Both of these things, in feminist theological circles, promote patriarchy and the continued existence of institutional structures of oppression so that men can continue to exert authority "over" others.

Feminist theology is divided when it comes to the second person in the Trinity, Jesus. Feminist theologians acknowledge there are instances in which he treated women well,[632] but there are also instances in which he acts less than "divine" in his treatment of women.[633] No matter what end of the spectrum one places themselves on, it does not go beyond notice to feminist theologians that Jesus' sex reinforces the charge of patriarchy in Christianity, given that a *male* is "sent" to save woman, redeem her, and "name" her as part of the new Christian community.

---

[628] *This Is My Name Forever*, 67-69.

[629]Ibid., 71.

[630]Ibid.

[631] *After Eden*, 148.

[632]For instance, his treatment of the Samaritan woman he met at the well.

[633]An example would be Mark 7:24-29 where Jesus seemingly refers to a woman as a dog.

The fact of Jesus's maleness is often viewed as a negative. Some wonder if God is beyond male and female, why could Jesus not come to Earth as a woman to show that both male and female are accounted for in divinity? In my final point of this chapter, I would like to suggest that Jesus' maleness holds implications that are in the *interests* of women, and communicate something about the worth and value that God ascribes to them.

It is a historical truth that the second person of the Trinity came to the Earth as a male baby who grew into a man. Throughout his life, Jesus was committed to performing the works he was sent to do. His ultimate assignment was to secure salvation by way of his substitutionary death. In the last week of his life, an all-male Jewish council condemned him to death, and he was subsequently stripped, brutally beaten, whipped, and adorned with a crown made of thorns, all this done by men of the Roman guard. Forced to carry a cross that he ultimately could not bear the burden of, Jesus arrived at the crucifixion site where soldiers methodically and expertly drove nails through his wrists and feet. Hanging on the cross for several hours, one last death blow was felt when a spear was plunged into his side.

The interesting and relevant question to ask is this: what if Jesus had been a woman? Would feminist theologians today *really* be content with a female Jesus enduring the type of suffering seen above? For the sake of gender equality in the Trinity, would they support the idea that a *woman's* brutal death and victorious resurrection now serves as a sign of redemption? I humbly submit the answer is a resounding "no." I contend that feminist theologians would be united in the view that no woman should have to endure the type of suffering and agonizing death that Jesus endured. Charges of Christianity instantiating the most horrific forms of misogyny would abound if Jesus had been a woman, not to mention the message it would send as that relates to violence against women and all that that entails. In the end, feminist theology leaves itself in a "no-win" situation as that relates to the gender of God incarnate.

In this chapter, I have shown that feminist criticism of the Bible creates problems that are impossible to solve given the working assumption of its critical method. It is my contention that these working assumptions are too faulty to be of any redeemable value. As noted by Linda Woodhead, "feminist theology has failed to be sufficiently theological" and only time will tell whether feminist theology will orient itself to the problems of its working assumptions, or ultimately surrender its viability as a functional option. The hope is that it will be the former and that feminist theologians everywhere would find the life-giving meaning and significance in what is held to the unabated Word of God.

CHAPTER 8 The Synoptic Gospels in the Ancient Church: The Testimony to the Priority of the Gospel of Matthew

F. David Farnell

Introduction[634]

The Gospel of Matthew was the church's most popular Gospel in the decades up to the time of Irenaeus (ca. A.D. 180). After an extensive analysis of Matthew's influence on early Christianity, Massaux relates,

> Of all the New Testament Writings, the Gospel of Mt. was the one whose literary influence was the most widespread and the most profound in Christian literature that extended into the last decades of the second century. . . .

> Until the end of the second century, the first gospel remained the gospel par excellence . . . .

> The Gospel was, therefore, the normative fact of Christian life. It created the background for ordinary Christianity.[635]

Moreover, the unanimous and unquestioned consensus of the church Fathers was that Matthew was the first gospel written, and almost without exception, the early church placed the Gospel of Matthew first in the canon of the New Testament. Petrie observes, "Until the latter half of the eighteenth century, the apostolic authorship of 'the Gospel according to Matthew' seems to have been generally accepted."[636]

However, the Enlightenment and its spawning of historical-critical methodologies—particularly that aspect of the system called "Source Criticism"—marked the beginning of the end of that viewpoint.[637] Most New Testament scholars at the turn of the twenty-first century resoundingly reject the unanimous

---

[634] This article appeared in the Master's Seminary Journal, vol 10/1 (Spring 1999) 53-86 as a Festschrift for Robert L. Thomas.

[635] Édouard Massaux, *The Influence of the Gospel of Saint Matthew on Christian Literature Before Saint Irenaeus*, trans. by Norman J. Belval and Suzanne Hecht, Arthur J. Bellinzoni, ed., 3 vols. (Macon, Ga.: Mercer University, 1993), 3:186-87.

[636] C. Steward Petrie, "The Authorship of 'The Gospel According to Matthew': A Reconsideration of the External Evidence," *New Testament Studies* 14 (1967-1968): 15. Stonehouse, a leading advocate of Markan priority, admitted, "[T]he tradition concerning the apostolic authorship of Matthew is as strong, clear, and consistent and . . . the arguments advanced against its reliability are by no means decisive . . . the apostolic authorship of Matthew is as strongly attested as any fact of ancient church history" (Ned B. Stonehouse, *The Origins of the Synoptic Gospels* [Grand Rapids: Eerdmans, 1963], 46-47, cf. 76-77).

[637] Bernard Orchard and Harold Riley, *The Order of the Synoptics, Why Three Synoptic Gospels?* (Macon, Ga.: Mercer, 1987), 111.

testimony of the early church regarding Matthean priority in favor of the Two- or Four-Source Theory[638] of how the Synoptic Gospels came into existence.[639] That rejection characterizes not only those of a liberal-theological perspective. It also extends to include many who probably would classify themselves as conservative evangelicals, men such as Hill, Carson along with Moo and Morris, Martin, and France who explain away the evidence from Papias and church tradition regarding Matthean priority in deference to a theory of modern vintage that requires the priority of Mark.[640] Few conservative evangelicals today dare to challenge the "findings" of Source Criticism.

The theory of Mark's being written first flies in the face of what is quite clear from the writings in the early church, as Massaux has pointedly demonstrated:

> The literary influence of the Gospel of Mk. is practically nil of these writings [i.e., the church writings of the first two centuries up to Irenaeus]. This characteristic of the early tradition constitutes a strange phenomenon. How can we explain this silence of tradition, if, as is generally believed, Mk. was the first of the canonical gospels? How can we explain the first Christians hardly resorted to it, so that it appeared almost nonexistent? Did it not respond, perhaps to the exigencies and concrete needs of the community of the time? Or have we been wrong to elevate it to the detriment of the Gospel of Mt.?[641]

Someone besides Massaux needs to set the record straight. The church fathers must have their hearing, apart from a dogmatism that bases itself on a late-blooming theory regarding gospel sequence. They lived much closer to the composition of the gospels than anyone associated with the Enlightenment. Also, they were scholars in their own right, so it is a grave mistake to dismiss their testimony so casually as moderns have tended to do. They bear a unified testimony against critical assumptions of the last two centuries that have supported the priority of Mark and the associated Two- (or Four-) Source Theory. The discussion of their

---

[638] The Two-Source Theory contends that Mark was written first, then Matthew and Luke wrote in dependence on Mark and a document called "Q," which contained material common to Matthew and Luke but not found in Mark. The Four-Source Theory adds documents called "M"—used by Matthew in addition to the others—and "L"—used by Luke in addition to the others.

[639] See Bernard Orchard and Thomas R. W. Longstaff, *J. J. Griesbach: Synoptic and text-critical studies 1776-1976* (Cambridge: Cambridge University, 1978), 134; William R. Farmer, *The Synoptic Problem* (Macon, Ga.: Mercer University, 1976), 48-49; Burnett Hillman Streeter, *The Four Gospels, A Study of Origins* (Macmillan and Co., 1924), 151-98. Orchard and Longstaff cite Griesbach as an example of one who criticized the early fathers. Farmer cites the lack of evidence supporting the Two- (or Four-Source) Theory.

[640] David Hill, *The Gospel of Matthew*, in The New Century Bible Commentary (Grand Rapids: Eerdmans, 1972), 28; D. A. Carson, Douglas J. Moo, and Leon Morris, *An Introduction to the New Testament* (Grand Rapids: Zondervan, 1992), 70-71; R. T. France, *Matthew*, Tyndale New Testament Commentary (Grand Rapids: Eerdmans, 1985), 34-38; Ralph P. Martin, *New Testament Foundations*, vol. 1 of *The Four Gospels* (Grand Rapids: Eerdmans, 1975), 139-60, 225.

[641] Massaux, *Gospel of Saint Matthew*, 3:188.

writings will also evidence the shortcomings of the avenue of Source Criticism that results in the Two-Gospel Theory.[642]

Papias

Early in the first half of the second century A.D., Papias was bishop of Hierapolis in the Phrygian region of the province of Asia—a city about 20 miles west of Colosse and 6 miles east of Laodicea.[643] Nothing much is known of Papias's life beyond the comment of Irenaeus that he was "one of the ancients" (ajrcai'o" ajnhvr, *archaios aner*).[644] His writing activity dates between ca. A.D. 95 and 110.[645] That early dating makes his works crucial, for he is one of only a few witnesses to a very early period of church history.

Papias (along with his friend and contemporary, Polycarp) was a disciple and personal acquaintance of the Apostle John, because Irenaeus wrote that Papias was "the hearer of John."[646] Unfortunately, Papias's writings are no longer extant. Only

---

[642] The Two-Gospel Theory holds that Matthew was written first, then Luke wrote depending on Matthew, and finally Mark wrote in dependence on Matthew and Luke.

[643] See Eusebius *Ecclesiastical History* 3.36.1-2.

[644] Irenaeus *Against Heresies* 5.33.3-4; cf. Eusebius *Ecclesiastical History* 3.39.1-2.

[645] Yarbrough gives five convincing arguments supporting this date: First, Papias's position in Eusebius's *Ecclesiastical History* (Book 3) places him with young Polycarp, Ignatius and even Clement, i.e. those who were the immediate successors to the apostles. Moreover, in Book 3 Eusebius catalogues no matters latter than Trajan's reign (97-117), and Book 4 opens with the twelfth year of Trajan (ca. 109), indicating that Eusebius viewed Papias as flourishing before A.D. 109. Second, Eusebius's Chronicon places the aged Apostle John, Papias, Polycarp and Ignatius (in that order) in the same entry with the year "100" placed next to this entry as part of his running table of dates [see Helm, *Die Chronik des Hieronymus*, 7:193-194]; Third, Irenaeus called Papias "one of the ancients" (ajrcai'o" ajnhvr-Irenaeus *Against Heresies* 5.33.3-4; cf. Eusebius *Ecclesiastical History* 3.39.1-2). Since Irenaeus most likely had personal contact with Polycarp, who was a companion of Papias (Eusebius *Ecclesiastical History* 5.20.4-8; Irenaeus *Against Heresies* 5.33.4; cf. Eusebius *Ecclesiastical History* 3.39.1), he is not liable to be mistaken in his opinion of Papias's connections with earliest apostolic origins. Fourth, Irenaeus confirms that Papias was a hearer of John (Eusebius *Ecclesiastical History* 3.39.1). Fifth, neither Eusebius nor Irenaeus identifies Papias as an anto-gnostic witness, thus placing Papias much earlier than such gnostics as Valentinus, Basilides and Marcion. whose teachings both Irenaeus and Eusebius were trying to refute. See Yarbrough, "The Date of Papias," 186-187. For a more complete review of the strong evidence linking Papias to the date of ca. 95-110, see Robert W. Yarbrough, "The Date of Papias: A Reassessment," *Journal of the Evangelical Theological Society* 26 (June 1983): 181-91; Robert H. Gundry, *Matthew, A Commentary on His Handbook for a Mixed Church Under Persecution*, 2nd ed. (Grand Rapids: Eerdmans, 1994), 611-13.

[646] See Irenaeus *Against Heresies* 5.33.4; also quoted by Eusebius *Ecclesiastical History* 3.39.1. Regarding Eusebius' skeptical attitude about whether Papias ever heard the apostle John (*Ecclesiastical History* 3.39.1-2) see William R. Schoedel, *Polycarp, Martyrdom of Polycarp, Fragments of Papias*, vol. 5 of *The Apostolic Fathers*, Robert M. Grant, ed. (Camden, N. J.: Thomas Nelson, 1967), 89-92; Rudolf Helm, *Eusebius Werke*, vol. VII of *Die Chronik des Hieronymus*, in Die Griechischen Christlichen Schriftsteller der Ersten Jahrunderte (Akademie-Verlag: Berlin, 1956): 193-94; 412-13. For persuasive evidence that Papias *did* have direct contact with the apostle, see Robert H. Gundry, *Matthew, A Commentary on His*

fragments of his works remain and are largely known through quotations by later Fathers, especially Eusebius. Papias wrote a series of five treatises entitled *Interpretation of the Oracles of the Lord* (Logivwn kuriakw'n ejxhghvsew", *Logiōn kuriakōn exegeseōs*) in which he draws information from the remaining, living-eyewitness sources, i.e., the Apostle John himself and another original disciple of Jesus named Ariston, concerning what the apostles had said or done.[647] In essence, Papias's assertions had their foundation in direct "eyewitness" (i.e., firsthand) reports.[648] If Papias wrote ca. A.D. 95-110, then the information that he imparts reaches well back into the first century and is an invaluable source of information regarding the gospels.

Papias included a brief account in his *Expositions* regarding the composition of Matthew: "Matthew collected (sunetavxato, *sunetaxato*) the oracles (ta; lovgia, *ta logia*) in the Hebrew language (JEbrai?di dialevktw/, *Hebraidi dialektōi*), and each interpreted (hJrmhvneusen, *hermeneusen*) them as best he could."[649] A great deal of conflict, however, has raged around this short statement, especially regarding the meaning and significance of the words "the oracles" (ta; lovgia) and the phrase "in the Hebrew language" (JEbrai?di dialevktw/). An understanding of the latter expression has some impact on how one interprets the former.

Ta logia *as an independent collection of Jesus' sayings.* Regarding the meaning of "the oracles" (ta; lovgia), Scholars exhibit several major interpretations. Some

---

Handbook for a Mixed Church under Persecution, 2nd ed. (Grand Rapids: Eerdmans, 1994), 611-613. Eusebius' skepticism may have stemmed from his anti-chiliastic view as opposed to that of Papias (and Irenaeus) who strongly affirmed a physical reality of the millennium (see Eusebius, *Ecclesiastical History* 3.39.12-13). Or, it may have resulted from Papias' alleged preference for oral tradition rather than authorized books as his sources (see Eusebius, *Ecclesiastical History* 3.39.4; cf. also Robert M. Grant, ed., "An Introduction," in vol. 1 of *The Apostolic Fathers, A New Translation and Commentary* [New York: Thomas Nelson and Sons, 1964], 86).

[647] Eusebius denied that Papias was a direct hearer of the Apostle John by inferring that another John, John the Elder who was different from John the Apostle, lived in Ephesus at the time (*Ecclesiastical History* 3.39.5-6). A close reading of Papias's words, however, reveals that he neither affirmed nor denied that he was hearer or eyewitness of the apostles. He does not mention it in the passage. Petrie argues, "[T]here is nothing to justify the careless confidence with which Eusebius contradicts Irenaeus" (C. Stewart Petrie, "Authorship of 'The Gospel According to Matthew'," 15-32 [esp. 17-18]). Furthermore, even if Papias was not a personal disciple of John, as Lightfoot contended, "still his age and country place him in more or less close connection with the traditions of the Apostles; and it is this fact which gives importance to his position and teaching" (J. B. Lightfoot, *Essays on the Work Entitled Supernatural Religion* [London: Macmillan and Co., 1889], 142).

[648] Eusebius *Ecclesiastical History* 3.39.15-16. Papias's statement regarding John the disciple and the Elder John probably referred to one and the same person, i.e. John the Apostle (Petrie, "Authorship," 18-24; Gundry, *Matthew*, 611-13).

[649] Eusebius *Ecclesiastical History* 3.39.16. All quotes of Papias and Eusebius in Part 1 of this chapter are taken from the Loeb Classical Library Series. See Eusebius, *The Ecclesiastical History*, with an English translation by Kirsopp Lake, 2 vols. (London: William Heinemann, 1926).

think that it refers to an independent collection of Jesus' sayings, perhaps Q.[650] T. W. Manson popularized the view:

> In Eusebius we find a quotation from Papias stating that "Matthew composed the oracles (ta; lovgia) in the Hebrew language, and each one interpreted them as he was able." This obviously cannot refer to the first Gospel, which is essentially a Greek work based on Greek sources, of which Mark is one. It is, however, possible that what is meant is the document which we now call Q.[651]

Adding support to this conclusion was the fact that ta; lovgia is not usual way of referring to a "gospel" and would be rather unique, for the normal descriptive term already seen by the time of Papias and evidenced in early manuscripts of the gospels would be to; eujaggevlion (*to euaggelion*, "the gospel").[652]

That explanation of ta; lovgia, however, is dubious for several reasons. First, Papias does not use ta; lovgia to refer only to sayings but also to the deeds of Jesus. The title of Papias' work, *Interpretation of the Oracles of the Lord* (Logivwn kuriakw'n ejxhghvsew", *Logiōn kuriakōn exegeseōs*) implies that more than Jesus' words are encompassed in its meaning, for enough is known regarding this work that he did not restrict it in scope to an exposition merely of Jesus's words.[653]

Second, in Eusebius's *Ecclesiastical History* 3.39.15-16, Papias commented that in composing his gospel, Mark, being Peter's interpreter, "wrote accurately all that he remembered . . . of the things said *or done* by the Lord" [emphasis added] and immediately after this spoke of Peter as "not making, as it were, an arrangement of the Lord's oracles (suvntaxin tw'n kuriakw'n poiouvmeno" logivwn, *suntaxin tōn kuriakōn poiumenos logiōn*), so that Mark did nothing wrong in thus writing down single points as he remembered them." Since Mark's gospel included deeds as well as words, the expression tw'n. . . logivwn (*tōn . . . logiōn*, "the oracles") must include both too.

Third, the parallelism between these two phrases—"the things said or done" (ta; . . .h] lecqevnta h] pracqevnta, *ta . . . e lechthenta e prachthenta*) and "the oracles of the Lord" (tw'n kuriakw'n . . . logivwn)—in immediate juxtaposition

---

[650] According to most, the designation "Q" stands for the first letter of the German word for "source," *Quelle*. That position, however, is debated. See the discussion in John J. Schmitt, "In Search of the Origin of the Siglum Q," *Journal of Biblical Literature* 100 (1981): 609-11.

[651] T. W. Manson, *The Teaching of Jesus* (London: SCM Press, 1957), 18-20; cf. also *idem, The Sayings of Jesus* (London: SCM Press, 1949), 18-19; *idem*, "The Gospel of Matthew," in *Studies in the Gospels and Epistles*, Matthew Black, ed. (Manchester: Manchester University, 1962), 82-83.

[652] Lampe cites only two example of this phrase referring to "the gospels" contained in the *Chronicon Paschale* (seventh century A.D.) (see "lovgion, tov" in G. W. H. Lampe, *A Patristic Greek Lexicon* (Oxford: At the Clarendon, 1961), 806.

[653] Eusebius *Ecclesiastical History* 3.39.1.

demonstrates that the latter expression, i.e. "the oracles of the Lord" (i.e. tw'n kuriakw'n . . . logivwn), can encompass both the deeds as well as the words of Jesus.

Fourth, immediately after these statements regarding Mark's gospel, Papias applies the term ta; lovgia to Matthew's work, thus making it hard to avoid the conclusion that he refers to Matthew's gospel rather than some hypothetical sayings source like Q.[654] Therefore, the ta; lovgia is most naturally understood as a synonym for the gospel.[655]

No evidence exists that such a document as "Q" ever existed at Papias' time or any other time. The increasing skepticism of a wide spectrum of NT scholars regarding the nature (e.g., make-up and extent) of Q and whether such a document ever really existed in church history make this suggestion highly dubious.[656]

Ta logia *as a collection of OT proof texts.* A second view similar to the first is that ta; lovgia refers to an OT *testimonia* collection (i.e., a book of OT proof texts) compiled by Matthew from the Hebrew canon for use in Christian apologetics, one that eventually was incorporated into canonical Matthew. Hunt forcefully argues,

> ªLºovgia has nothing to do with the title of any book, but is a technical term meaning O.T. oracles. That is to say that lovgia was not the *name* of a book composed by St. Matthew, or by anyone else, but was a description of the contents of the book; it was composed of lovgia, which had been arranged by St. Matthew.[657]

For Hunt, those who would see the term lovgia as meaning "gospel" most likely "have been hypnotized by tradition" and "for whatever ta; lovgia may have been taken as meaning at a later period, it could not have meant *The Gospel*

---

[654] Kittel argues that Papias' use of the term lovgia (logia) cannot be confined to mere sayings or collections of sayings, but more likely has reference to the whole gospel, i.e., words and deeds of Jesus: "[I]t is just as clear and indisputable that in the light of the usage of the LXX, NT and early Church the more comprehensive meaning is also possible" Gerhard Kittel, "lovgion," *TDNT*, 4:141.

[655] See Lightfoot, *Essays on Supernatural Religion*, 172-76.

[656] See Stewart Petrie, "Q is Only What You Make It," *Novum Testamentum* 3 (1959): 28-33. Petrie points out that the wide variety and conflicting hypotheses concerning the nature and extent of Q have cast great suspicion on the validity of the hypothesis for its existence. Farrar, though holding to the idea that Matthew and Luke utilized Mark, nonetheless, argues that against the existence of Q (A. M. Farrar, "On Dispensing with Q," in *Studies in the Gospels*, Essays in Memory of R. H. Lightfoot, D. E. Nineham, ed. [Oxford: Blackwell, 1955]: 55-88). After an extensive analysis, Linnemann, a former post-Bultmannian who at one time was a staunch advocate of the Two-Source Hypothesis, concludes that any idea of Q is a "fantasy, is "based on error," and "proves untenable" (Eta Linnemann, "Gospel of Q." *Bible Review* XI [August 1995]: 19-23, 42-43).

[657] B. P. W. Stather Hunt, *Primitive Gospel Sources* (London: James Clarke & Co., 1951), 184; cf. also Rendel Harris, *Testimonies*, 2 vols. (Cambridge: University Press, 1920), 1:118-123, 130-131, 2:1-11, and F. C. Grant, *The Gospels: Their Origin and Their Growth* (New York: Harper, 1957): 65, 144.

according to St. Matthew when originally written; since nobody will maintain that a gospel was ever called ta; lovgia."[658]   Similarly, Grant asserts that that tw'n kuriakw'n . . . logivwn predominately refer to "divine utterances" like those contained in the OT.[659] Therefore, Papias seems to refer to Matthew's collection of OT prophecies of the Messiah, "a collection of the kind embedded in the Gospel of Matthew."[660]

Yet, this view seems unlikely for significant reasons. First, a similar criticism applies to this view as to the first view above, i.e., in the context of Papias' writings, ta; lovgia most likely refers to both deeds and sayings of Jesus and not to a hypothesized collection of OT proof-texts.   This view, therefore, supplies an aberrant meaning to Papias' words. It also makes Grant's assumption regarding tw'n kuriakw'n . . . logivwn as referring to OT oracles tenuous since Papias, in the context of Eusebius' discussion, refers to Jesus' sayings and deeds rather than OT sayings, the latter not being in view at all in that context.[661]

Second, the view cannot account for the diversity of text forms in OT quotations in Matthew and for the way he often parallels the LXX rather than the Hebrew OT (e.g., Matt. 1:23; 5:21, 27, 38, 43; 13:14-15; 21:16).[662]

Third, the most likely understanding of the term hJrmhvneusen refers to "translation" of a language, especially in light of his phrase "in the Hebrew language" (JEbrai?di dialevktw/), rather than "interpretation" of OT sayings, the latter being the sense required under this view.[663]   Furthermore, this Hebrew (i.e., Aramaic) *testimonia* collection may not need to be "translated" especially since the LXX would have been well-established.

Ta logia *as an error by Papias.*   Yet, if some scholars find neither of these two views satisfactory regarding ta; lovgia, then they often envision two alternatives in their discussion of its meaning: either Papias was inaccurate and his testimony should be discounted, or Papias was referring to some other composition of Matthew which is not now extant.

Carson, Moo, and Morris prefer the idea that Papias' statement was partially in error when he asserted a Semitic (i.e. Aramaic) original of Matthew, labeling it as

---

[658] Hunt, *Primitive Gospel Sources*, 184.

[659] Grant, *Gospels, Their Origin and Growth*, 65, 144; cf. Eusebius *Ecclesiastical History* 3.39.1, 14.

[660] Grant, *Gospels, Their Origin and Growth*, 65.

[661] Eusebius *Ecclesiastical History* 3.39.1, 14.

[662] Gundry notes, "Of the twenty formal quotations peculiar to Mt, seven are Septuagintal. Seven are non-Septuagintal. In six there is a mixture of Septuagintal and non-Septuagintal" (Robert H. Gundry, *The Use of the Old Testament in St. Matthew's Gospel* [Leiden: E. J. Brill, 1967], 149).

[663] Martin, *New Testament Foundations*, 1:239.

"an intelligent, albeit erroneous, guess."[664] From their point of view Papias spoke from ignorance, especially if he "had no real knowledge of just how much Greek was spoken in first-century Palestine, especially in Galilee."[665] At times, they are ambivalent as to who wrote the gospel bearing Matthew's name, for after discussing the evidence, both pros and cons, for apostolic authorship of the gospel, they conclude "at one level very little hangs on the question of the authorship of this [Matthew's] gospel. By and large, neither its meaning nor its authority are greatly changed if one decides that its author was not an apostle."[666] For them, apostolic, eyewitness origin ultimately carries little weight for the validity of this gospel. Martin holds the same perspective.[667]

Harrison deprecates Papias in a fashion similar to Carson, Moo and Morris, arguing that "Papias, like Jerome, confused the *Gospel according to the Hebrews* or something like it with an Aramaic Matthew."[668] Similarly, Hill comments, "[T]he tradition of Matthean priority rests . . . on a misinterpretation of Papias' statements, or on Papias' misunderstanding of the actual matter to which he was referring."[669]

Significantly, most of these evangelicals who dismiss the testimony of Papias apparently do so because of their acceptance of the historical-critical conclusion that Mark was the first gospel, as expressed in the Two- or Four-Source hypothesis.[670] For them, current (and dogmatic) source-critical conclusions are sufficient to override strong and ancient historical testimony.[671] Yet, in reply, apostolic origin of the gospels is vital for a document that purports to be a record of Jesus' historical ministry on earth. The anonymity of the Matthean gospel argues strongly for the validity of tradition that attached Matthew's name to it because such anonymity is inexplicable apart from its direct association with the apostle Matthew. Matthew was a relatively obscure figure among the Twelve, so no adequate reason exists to explain why the early church would have chosen his name rather than a better-known apostle if he had not indeed written it.

Furthermore, the more reasonable explanation is that Papias, possessing information from highly placed apostolic and eyewitness testimony regarding Matthew, was correct, and that attempts at deprecating Papias border on

---

[664] Carson *et al.*, *Introduction to the New Testament*, 70.

[665] Ibid., 71.

[666] Ibid., 74; cf. D. A. Carson, "Matthew," vol. 8 of *Expositor's Bible Commentary.* Frank E. Gaebelein, gen. ed. (Grand Rapids: Zondervan, 1984), 19.

[667] Martin, *New Testament Foundations*, 1:240.

[668] Everett F. Harrison, *Introduction to the New Testament* (Grand Rapids: Eerdmans, 1971), 169.

[669] Hill, *Gospel of Matthew*, 29.

[670] E.g., Carson, Moo and Morris, *Introduction to the New Testament*, 61-85 (esp. 68-69); Martin, *New Testament Foundations*, 1:139-60; 224-43; Hill, *Matthew*, 29-34.

[671] E.g., Carson, "Matthew," 13.

intellectual presumptuousness. Petrie describes such a casual dismissal of the evidence: "This is the kind of unintentional belittling guess that easily hardens from 'may be' to a firm statement and then becomes a dogmatic basis for further adventures in criticism."[672] Since Papias is not relating his own opinion but citing information derived from firsthand reports of the apostle John and the disciple Ariston, a supposition of Papias' confusion is unlikely. For as Gundry observes, "Possibilities of confusion decrease the closer we approach the time of writing. It is especially hard to think that one of the twelve apostles, John himself, fell into such an error."[673] Interestingly, Papias uses the imperfect tense (e[legen, elegen-"he was saying") to depict how John repeatedly transmitted information to him about Mark's arrangement of topics.[674] Theirs was not just a one-time conversation. Petrie best summarizes Historical Criticism's attack on Papias' credibility well:

> This testimony is on much firmer ground than the best speculative guesses of the twentieth century, and it must be fairly and fully reckoned with in the quest for Gospel backgrounds. Failing substantial evidence to contradict it or to turn its meaning, it is not to be dismissed because of its inconvenience for current hypotheses. If it does not accord with these hypotheses, it is the hypotheses that must be considered anew. For the one is tangible evidence from a competent, informed, and credible witness; the rest, however attractive or even dazzling they appear, lack its substantiality.[675]

Ta logia *as a canonical Greek Matthew.* A fourth view of Papias' meaning takes ta; lovgia to refer to the canonical Greek version of Matthew's gospel and exonerates Papias as an accurate reporter, but says his readers misunderstood him. Reflecting a concept similar to Kürzinger,[676] Gundry asserts that rather than a linguistic sense Papias' expression "in the Hebrew dialect" (JEbrai?di dialevktw/) has a literary sense, referring to a Semitic style: "In describing Matthew, then, 'a Hebrew dialect' means a Hebrew way of presenting Jesus' messiahship."[677] With this approach, the verb hJrmhvneusen had the sense of "explain" rather than "translate."

Moreover, Kürzinger points out that immediately before Papias' statement regarding Matthew, he describes Mark's composition of his gospel as reflecting

---

672 Petrie, "Authorship of 'The Gospel According to Matthew,'" 29.

673 Gundry, *Matthew, A Commentary,* 618.

674 Eusebius *Ecclesiastical History* 3.39.15.

675 Petrie, "The Authorship of Matthew," 32. Strangely, Hagner, a Markan prioritist, agrees: "[I]t seems better to take this early piece of evidence seriously rather than to dismiss it as being dead wrong. Papias had reason for saying what he did . . . we do well to attempt to make sense of his testimony" (Donald A. Hanger, *Matthew 1-13,* vol. 33A of *Word Biblical Commentary,* David A. Hubbard and Glenn W. Barker, eds. (Waco, Tx.: Word, 1993), xlvi.

676 Josef Kürzinger, "Das Papiaszeugnis und die Erstgestalt des Matthäusevangeliums," *Biblische Zeitschrift* 4 (1960): 19-38; cf. *idem,* "Irenäus und sein Zeugnis zur Sprache des Matthäusevangeliums," *New Testament Studies* 10 (1963), 108-15.

677 Gundry, *Matthew: A Commentary,* 619-20.

Peter's testimony. There Papias calls Mark the "interpreter" (eJrmhneuth;", herme neutes [—Eusebius *Ecclesiastical History* 3.39.15]) of Peter. Kürzinger insists that this cannot mean that Mark was Peter's "translator," but must have been the "interpreter" of that preached or spoken by Peter.[678] Thus, Papias' statement regarding Matthew must mean that everyone "passed on" or "interpreted" Matthew's Greek gospel to the world as he was able.

A first response to that analysis notes that although the sense of argumentational style is a possible meaning of dialevktw/,[679] it is a more remote and secondary sense. The most natural understanding of dialevkto" (dialektos) is "language," not "interpretation."[680] Also, the term in combination with the noun JEbrai?di (*Hebraidi*, lit. "Hebrew" but most likely a reference the Aramaic language) and the verb eJrmhneuvein (*hermeneuein*, "to interpret") points to the latter's natural meaning of "translate (a language)" rather than to an alleged Semitic style.

Second, the church fathers understood Papias' statement as referring to language. Without exception they held that the apostle Matthew wrote the canonical Matthew and that he wrote it first in a Semitic language.[681]

Third, all six occurrences of the word dialevkto" in the NT refer to human languages rather than to a particular style of argument (Acts 1:19; 2:6, 8; 21:40; 22:2; 26:14).[682] These arguments render the view of Kürzinger and Gundry as very improbable.

A significant observation notes that the common thread of all four viewpoints of Papias' words discussed so far is an *a priori* assumption of validity of the Two-Document Hypothesis. As a result, they all attempt to find a way either to diminish

---

[678] Cf. Kürzinger, "Das Papiaszeugnis," 22-23, 27-30.

[679] E.g., cf. Liddell and Scott, *A Greek English Lexicon*, rev. and augmented by Henry Stuart Jones, with a 1968 Supplement (Oxford: At the Clarendon, 1940), 401.

[680] E.g., *BAGD*, 185; James P. Louw and Eugene A. Nida, *Greek-English Lexicon of the New Testament Based on Semantic Domains* (New York: United Bible Societies, 1988), 1:389 (33.1).

[681] E.g., Irenaeus *Against Heresies* 3.1.1 (quoted in Eusebius *Ecclesiastical History* 5.8.2); Tertullian (*Against Marcion* 4.2); Pantaenus, cited by Eusebius (*Ecclesiastical History* 5.10.3); Origen (quoted by Eusebius in *Ecclesiastical History* 6.25.3-6); Eusebius himself (*Ecclesiastical History* 3.24.5-6); and Jerome *Preface to the Commentary on Saint Matthew*; *Lives of Illustrious Men* 2.3.

[682] Gundry argues that these NT occurrences of diavlekto" (*dialektos*, "language" or "dialect") are articular (and thus definite) so that human language is clearly in mind in these passages. In contrast, Papias's reference does not have the article (i.e. JEbrai?di dialevktw/, Hebraidi dialektôi, "Hebrew dialect"). He concludes that Papias's reference should be considered indefinite ("a Hebrew way of presenting Jesus' messiahship" or Semitic style of argument) rather than definite ("the Semitic language"). See Gundry, *Matthew*, 629-20. Yet, in reply, the article is not necessary for Papias to mean "language." The force of JEbrai?di ("Hebrew") with dialevktw/ is sufficient to make the term definite without the article. For instances where the article is not necessary to make a noun definite, consult Daniel B. Wallace, *Greek Grammar Beyond the Basics* (Grand Rapids: Zondervan, 1996), 245-54.

the force of Papias' words, dismiss his information as inaccurate or wrong, or superimpose a totally foreign understanding. Survival of the cherished synoptic hypothesis drives them to pursue such tactics as Gundry illustrates in his discussion of Papias' words: "[I]t is the currently prevalent and well-substantiated opinion that our Greek Matthew shows many signs of drawing in large part on the Gospel of Mark, also written in Greek."[683]

Gundry goes one step further in his analysis of Papias' words. He takes them to indicate that Matthew deliberately corrected Mark. Immediately before Papias' comments about Matthew (Eusebius *Ecclesiastical History* 3.39.16), Eusebius quotes Papias' description of the composition of Mark:

> "And the Presbyter [John] used to say this, 'Mark became Peter's interpreter and wrote accurately all that he remembered, not, indeed, in order, of the things said or done by the Lord. For he had not heard the Lord, nor had he followed him, but later on, as I said, followed Peter, who used to give teaching as necessity demanded but not making, as it were, an arrangement of the Lord's oracles, so that Mark did nothing in wrong in writing down single points as he remembered them. For to one thing he gave attention, to leave out nothing of what he had heard and to make no false statements in them.'" This is related by Papias about Mark.[684]

Since the statements come before Papias' comments about Matthew's gospel, Gundry contends that they prove that Mark wrote before Matthew. In a nutshell, he argues that the sequence and nature of discussion in this section indicate that Matthew should be understood as a deliberate corrective to Mark. He notes that Papias' statements that Mark's gospel was written "not, indeed, in order" and "not making . . . an arrangement of the Lord's oracles" comes immediately before Papias' discussion of Matthew and how he "collected" (sunetavxato) his oracles. Gundry contends, Matthew did it "for the precise purpose of bringing order out of the chaos in Mark."[685]

However, a few observations show Gundry's contentions to be tenuous. First, Eusebius is quoting *detached* statements of Papias regarding Mark and Matthew so that the sequence of the gospels means nothing nor does any alleged dependence among the gospels surface in the order of discussion in the text.[686]

---

[683] Gundry, *Matthew: A Commentary*, 618.

[684] Eusebius *Ecclesiastical History* 3.39.15.

[685] Gundry, *Matthew: A Commentary*, 614.

[686] Gundry contends that the ou\≥n in Ecclesiastical History 3.39.16 refers back "to the statement about Mark" and therefore ties the thought about Mark and Matthew together. As a result," ou\≥n contains an immmensely important implication for synoptic studies . . . Matthew's reason for writing is in view . . . Matthew wrote his gospel for the precise purpose of bringing order out of the chaos in Mark." Gundry, *Matthew: A Commentary*, 614. However, contrary to Gundry, his contention of a link through ou\≥n is dubious. The ou\≥n grammatically draws an inferential conclusion to the discussion about Mark, going back by 3.39.14. Furthermore, peri; de; occurs after the ou\≥n and functions to introduce a new,

225

Second, such a theory indicates the absolute paucity of evidence for the Two-Document Hypothesis in ancient tradition. Its proponents must attempt to make something out of nothing in a desperate attempt at proving their *a priori* and *dogmatic* assumption that colors everything they analyze.

Papias' words (and Eusebius' citation and discussion) do not constitute any type of proof for Markan priority or literary dependence between Matthew and Mark. They add absolutely nothing to an understanding of any relationship between Matthew or Mark (or the other gospels for that matter). Eusebius' disjointed citation of Papias' words about Mark coming before that same historian's citation of Papias' words about Matthew's gospel have no relevance to that issue. Such alleged evidence goes far beyond what the statements indicate and is blatantly *non sequitur.* As a matter of fact, Papias' statements here actually constitute evidence against an assumed literary dependence, for he remarked that Mark depended on Peter for the contents of his gospel!

Ta logia as an early edition of Matthew's gospel. A final view, distinct from the others (and also from their synoptic hypotheses) is that Papias referred to an earlier edition of Matthew written entirely in Hebrew (i.e., Aramaic) that Matthew wrote first. That was perhaps a proto-Matthew, i.e., a shorter version that eventually came to be incorporated into (not necessarily translated from but contained within) an expanded Greek version, i.e., the canonical Gospel of Matthew.[687] Thus, Papias indicated that Matthew wrote first (prior to the other gospels) and that in so doing, he produced an initial Aramaic edition. The Aramaic edition served as a model and/or source for some of the contents of his Greek edition that he most likely produced as a fresh work soon after he wrote the Aramaic one.[688]

Several arguments support this proposal. First, it permits Papias to speak for himself and allows for an understanding of his words in their natural sense. Since

---

unrelated information concerning Matthew's gospel (cf. Paul's introduction of new subject matter in 1 Cor. 7:1, 25; 8:1; 12:1; 16:1, 12), thus demonstrating that these two thoughts of Papias about Mark and Matthew most likely are not linked together nor in any way indicative of Gundry's contention for Matthew as a corrective of Mark.

[687] The canonical Greek Version shows no signs of being translated from Aramaic. For example, in certain places it transliterates Aramaic into Greek before giving a Greek translation—e.g., Matt. 1:23, ΔEmmanouh/l, oζ e΄stin meqermhneuo/menon meqΔ hJmwθn oJ qeo/ß (*Emmanouḗl, ho estin methermēneuomenon meth' hēmōn ho theos*—"Immanuel, which is interpreted 'God with us'"); Matt. 27:33, Golgoqaθ, oζ e΄stin Kraniːou To/poß lego/menoß (*Golgotha, ho estin Kraniou Topos legomenos*, "Golgotha, which is called 'the Place of the Skull'"); cf. also Matt. 27:46. Also, the Greek Matthew provides explanations of local customs among the Jews that would have been unnecessary for an Aramaic-speaking audience (e.g., Matt. 27:15). Though the Greek Matthew is not a translation, Matthew may have produced an expanded version of the life of Christ that incorporated much of the original Aramaic without being a direct translation of it. Such an entirely reworked version would have suited the needs of the Diaspora Jews and others.

[688] Louis Berkhof, *New Testament Introduction* (Grand Rapids: Eerdman-Sevensma, 1915), 64-71; Henry Clarence Thiessen, *Introduction to the New Testament* (Grand Rapids: Eerdmans, 1943), 137.

he was closest to the events and relied on excellent sources, his information must have priority over speculative modern hypotheses.

Second, an expanded Greek version would have been quickly helpful among Matthew's targeted Jewish audience, especially those hellenized Jews who no longer spoke Hebrew (the *Diaspora* [Acts 6:1]). Although Matthew concentrated his efforts at first among Hebraistic Jews who spoke Aramaic, such a gospel would have limited appeal outside of the land of the Jews. Tradition has it that Matthew eventually left the environs of Jerusalem to minister among non-Aramaic-speaking peoples.[689] The dominance of Greek in the Hellenistic world would have impelled him to produce another edition. Because he was a former tax-collector for the Romans, he would most likely have been conversant in Greek as well as Aramaic,[690] thus facilitating the writing of both versions. Once the Greek Matthew became current in the church, the limited appeal of Aramaic caused that edition to fall into disuse. Papias' statement that "each interpreted" Matthew's gospel [Aramaic version] "as best he could" probably hints at the reason why Matthew would have quickly produced a Greek version: to facilitate the understanding of his gospel in the universal language of Greek.

Third, this view accords with the very early and consistent manuscript ascription of the Gospel to Matthew (KATA MAQQAION, *KATA MATHTHAION*, "According to Matthew").[691] The title is not a part of the original text, but no positive evidence exists that the book ever circulated without this title. Moreover, the ascription has a very early date, approximately A.D. 125.[692] As Guthrie notes, "the title cannot be dismissed too lightly, for it has the support of ancient tradition and this must be the starting point of the discussion regarding authorship."[693] Very early and consistent ascription of the Greek gospel to Matthew would indicate that the transfer of connection from Matthew's Aramaic version mentioned by Papias to

---

[689] Eusebius *Ecclesiastical History* 3.24.5-6; Hippolytus *On the Twelve Apostles* 7; cf. D. A. Hagner, "Matthew," in vol. 3 of *ISBE*, Geoffrey W. Bromiley, gen. ed. (Grand Rapids: Eerdmans, 1986), 280.

[690] Matt. 9:9-14; Mark 2:13-17; Luke 5:27-32; cf. Gundry, *Use of the Old Testament*, 183; Edgar J. Goodspeed, *Matthew, Apostle and Evangelist* (Philadelphia: John C. Winston, 1959), 42-47.

[691] Davies and Allison try to explain away the title in light of their assumption of that Mark wrote first and the Matthean gospel could not have been written by an apostle. Their case lacks persuasiveness in light of consistent manuscript evidence, however (cf. W. D. Davies and Dale C. Allison, *The Gospel According to Matthew*, International Critical Commentary [Edinburgh: T & T Clark, 1988], 1:58).

[692] Ropes reasons, "Probably as early in the second century as the year 125, someone, in some place, or some group of persons, assembled for the use and convenience of the churches the only four Greek books describing the life and teachings of Jesus Christ which were then believed to be of great antiquity and worthy of a place in such a collection" (J. H. Ropes, *The Synoptic Gospels*, 2nd Impression with New Preface [Cambridge, Ma.: Harvard University, 1960], 103).

[693] Donald Guthrie, *New Testament Introduction*, 2nd Edition (Downers Grove, Ill.: InterVarsity, 1990), 156-57.

the Greek gospel occurred at a very early stage well into the first century. Such a very early stage would have placed Greek Matthew into a period when people, such as surviving apostles, eyewitnesses and other who possessed first-hand knowledge regarding the Gospel would have linked the Aramaic and Greek versions together as coming from the hand of Matthew. Moreover, during this strategic early period the prevention of such linkage could also have occurred if such attempts at linkage were inaccurate.

This early ascription coordinates well with the very early and widespread influence of Greek Matthew in the early church in the period before Irenaeus. Signficant Matthean influence can be seen in such early second century works as 1 Clement (ca. A.D. 81-96), Barnabas (ca. A.D. 70-135), the Letters of Ignatius of Antioch (ca. A.D. 98-117), 2 Clement (ca. A.D. 138-142), Polycarp (*to thePhilippians* ca. A.D. 98-117; d. ca. 156 or 167), Aristedes of Athens (fl. A.D. 123), Justin Martyr (d. ca. 165), Tatian (fl. ca. A.D. 160-170) and the Didache (ca. A.D. late first century to mid-second century), to mention only a few.[694] Such influence finds its most reasonable explanation in Matthean authorship of the Greek Gospel as well as the Aramaic version discussed by Papias. Furthermore, this unbroken stream of tradition indicates that Matthew was responsible for both versions of the Gospel that bears his name. While the Aramaic version was helpful for Matthew's work among Jews, his departure to work with gentiles resulted in his issuance of the Greek version in the lingua franca of the day in order to facilitate the spread the good news regarding Messiah among gentiles.

Fourth, though patristic witnesses like Papias uniformly spoke of an Aramaic original for the gospel, they accepted the Greek Matthew as unquestionably authoritative and coming from the apostle Matthew himself.[695] They offered no explanation concerning the change in language.[696] Most likely, that indicates their regard for the Greek Matthew as authoritative and substantially representative of the Hebrew ta; lovgia.[697] Besides, all references to the Gospel of Matthew in the early church fathers reflect the Greek Matthew rather than the Hebrew. They never viewed the Greek Gospel of Matthew as inferior but as equal or better than the other Greek canonical gospels in terms of its authority and influence.

The Matthean authorship of both the Greek and Aramaic versions is strengthened by the unlikelihood of such a transfer occurring between documents that differed significantly in language and in content unless Matthew himself did produce both versions. The traditions of Matthean authorship for both versions are

---

[694] The reader is once again directed to Massaux's excellent cataloguing of Matthew's extensive influence in Christian literature during this early period (consult Massaux, *The Influence of the Gospel of Saint Matthew*, Books 1-3. For the composition dates of some of these works, consult Robert M. Grant, gen. ed. *The Apostolic Fathers. A New Translation and Commentary* (New York: Thomas Nelson & Sons, 1964): 1:38, 46-48, 64, 71; 3:42-43, 76-77; 5:4.

[695] See note 48 for a list of fathers who supported this.

[696] Jerome who wrote, "who afterwards translated it into Greek is not certainly known," is a possible exception (Jerome *Lives of Illustrious Men* 2.3).

[697] Hiebert, *Introduction to the New Testament*, 1:53.

so significantly early and consistent that authorship by Matthew himself constitutes the most reasonable explanation for both streams of tradition.

Fifth, the universal ascription of the Greek Matthew to the apostle Matthew and the failure of tradition to mention any other possible author except Matthew renders unconvincing any suggestion that the early church forgot the true author of the work. Only a brief span of 50 to 60 years passed between its composition and the statements of Papias. A less-prominent apostle such as Matthew would not have been a likely candidate to receive credit for such an important and influential document as the Greek Matthew unless he did indeed write it. As indicated earlier in this chapter, "of all the New Testament Writings, the Gospel of Mt. was the one whose literary influence was the most widespread and the most profound in Christian literature that extended into the last decades of the second century. . . . [T]he first gospel remained the gospel par excellence. . . . The gospel was, therefore, the normative fact of Christian life. It created the background for ordinary Christianity."[698]

The only adequate explanation for the gospel's influence and overwhelming popularity in the early church is its apostolic authorship. That one of the Twelve wrote it soon after writing his Aramaic ta; lovgia and before Mark and Luke wrote their gospels is far and away the most satisfactory explanation for the facts that remain from early church history.

In light of the evidence, unless someone feels compelled to embrace historical-critical scholarship's *a priori* assumption of Markan priority, the testimony of Papias is credible and supportive of Matthean priority and Matthean authorship of the gospel that bears Matthew's name.

Irenaeus

Irenaeus (b. ca. A.D. 115-120 and martyred ca. A.D. 200), an immigrant from Asia Minor, was presbyter of the church at Lyons in Gaul. He was one of the early church's most able apologists and theologians, writing against Marcion and the Gnostics with His work *Refutation and Overthrow of Knowledge Falsely So-called* which tradition has more conveniently labeled *Against Heresies* (completed ca. A.D. 185).[699]

In his youth he claims to have been a disciple of Polycarp (b. ca. A.D. 70 and d. ca. A.D. 155-160). He writes, "Polycarp . . . was not only instructed by apostles and conversed with many who had seen the Lord, but was also appointed bishop by apostles in Asia in the church in Smyrna."[700] Irenaeus continues, "We also saw him [i.e., Polycarp] in our childhood. . . . He [i.e., Polycarp] constantly taught those things which he had learnt from the apostles, which also are the tradition of the

---

[698] Massaux, *Influence of the Gospel of Saint Matthew*, 3:186-187.

[699] Eusebius *Ecclesiastical History* 5.7.1. Two major writings of Irenaeus have survived. In addition to *Against Heresies*, he also wrote *Demonstration of the Apostolic Preaching*, the latter being an instructional book demonstrating that the Christian faith fulfills the OT, first published in the twentieth century.

[700] Eusebius *Ecclesiastical History* 4.14.3.

church, which alone are true."[701] As reported by Eusebius, Polycarp, in turn, was a disciple of the Apostle John:

> "I [i.e. Irenaeus] remember the events of those days more clearly than those which happened recently, for what we learn as children grows up with the soul and is united to it, so that I can speak even of the place in which the blessed Polycarp sat and disputed, how he came in and went out, the character of his life, the discourses which he made to the people, how he [Polycarp] reported his intercourse with John and with the others who had seen the Lord, how he remembered their words, and what were the things concerning the Lord which he had heard from them . . . and how Polycarp had received them from the eyewitnesses of the word of life."[702]

Besides Polycarp, Irenaeus also had met and conversed with many apostolic and sub-apostolic fathers of Asia Minor and obtained information from them about the life and teachings of the Lord and the activities of the early church.[703] He thus reflected information from many sources and not only from his own childhood memories. He also had traveled extensively (e.g., from Asia Minor to Gaul and also the church in Rome), so that his information is not from an isolated region but widespread.

Irenaeus writes the following regarding the gospels:

> Now Matthew published among the Hebrews a written gospel also in their own tongue, while Peter and Paul were preaching in Rome and founding the church. But after their death, Mark also, the disciple and interpreter of Peter, himself handed down to us in writing the things which were preached by Peter, and Luke also, who was a follower of Paul, put down in a book the gospel which was preached by him. Then John, the disciple of the Lord, who had even rested on his breast, himself also gave forth the gospel, while he was living in Ephesus in Asia.[704]

Proponents of the Two-Document Hypothesis dismiss Irenaeus' assertion as useless because they assert he was merely repeating Papias. Filson argues, "But note this: Papias is the key witness. Irenaeus, for example, obviously knows and uses Papias as an authority. No tradition demonstrably independent of Papias exists."[705] Nineham does the same: "The testimony of early Christian writers subsequent to Papias, such as Irenaeus, Clement of Alexandria, Origen, and Jerome, need not be discussed at length, for it is not clear that these writers had any trustworthy source

---

[701] Ibid., 4.14.3-4; 5.20.5-6; cf. Irenaeus *Against Heresies* 3.3.4.

[702] Eusebius *Ecclesiastical History* 5.20.5-6

[703] Irenaeus *Against Heresies* 2.22.5; 4.27.1; 4.32.1; 5.36.2.

[704] Ibid., 3.1.1-4; cited also in Eusebius's *Ecclesiastical History* 5.8.1-4.

[705] Floyd Filson, *A Commentary on the Gospel According to Matthew*, 2nd ed. (London: Adam & Charles Black, 1971), 16.

of information other than the Papias tradition."[706] Streeter, the great advocate of the Four-Document Hypothesis, deprecates Irenaeus' ability to testify regarding Polycarp's connection to John, dismissing the evidence because of Irenaeus' youth. He says he was too young to tell to which "John" Polycarp referred.[707]

Petrie drives to the heart of their problem, noting, "There is in the document [i.e., the writings of Irenaeus] no hint of dependence [i.e., on Papias]. Indeed, Irenaeus was sufficiently close to the authorities of Papias to have gathered this information on his own."[708] In addition, Irenaeus was more than likely at least 15 years old, old enough "to understand the meaning of Polycarp's words and also to distinguish between the Apostle John and any other John."[709] As Lightfoot reasoned, "A pupil of Polycarp, at all events, was not likely to be misinformed here."[710] Besides nullifying the Two- or Four-Source Theory's view of Markan priority, Irenaeus' testimony also negates literary dependence of Mark on Matthew as proposed by the Two-Gospel Hypothesis, because it states that Mark depended on Peter's preaching, not on the other written gospels of Matthew or Luke, for his information.

In sum, proponents of Two-Document Hypothesis must either reject, ignore, or explain away much of the evidence by any means possible, because acceptance of its credibility would reinforce the fact of Matthew's gospel being written prior to the other gospels. That constitutes a strong testimony either against their assumption of the priority of Mark or, for that matter, against the idea that Mark depended on Matthew instead of Peter's preaching as held by the Two-Gospel Hypothesis. The belittling of Irenaeus by advocates of the Two-Document Hypothesis notwithstanding, Irenaeus' testimony is credible and important in its own right, constituting an independent and reliable witness for information regarding Matthew as the first gospel.

Worthy of observation also in this section is Irenaeus' failure to make a substantial distinction between the Aramaic and Greek versions as coming from Matthew.[711] For example, in *Against Heresies* 3.1.1 Irenaeus discusses all four gospels. In this discussion, he mentions only the Hebrew Matthew. Yet, in the work he shows a close familiar with Greek Matthew by referring to it frequently.[712]

---

[706] D. E. Nineham, *St. Mark* (Philadelphia: Westminster,1963), 39 n.

[707] Streeter apparently held that the Apostle John and the Elder John to whom Papias referred were two different individuals (Streeter, *Four Gospels*, 444).

[708] Petrie, "Authorship of 'The Gospel According to Matthew,'" 29.

[709] A. C. Perumalil, "Are not Papias and Irenaeus competent to report on the Gospels?," *Expository Times* 91 (August 1980): 336.

[710] J. B. Lightfoot, *Supernatural Religion*, 142.

[711] Irenaeus *Against Heresies* 3.1.1; also cited by Eusebius *Ecclesiastical History* 5.8.2.

[712] To cite only a few random examples, cp. Irenaeus *Against Heresies* "Preface" 2 with Matt. 10:26; cp. 1.1.3 with Matt. 20:1-16; cp. 1.3.5 with Matt.10:21, 34; cp. 1.6.1 with Matt. 5:13-14; cp. 1.8. with Matt. 26:38-39; 27:46; cp. 3.8.1 with Matt. 6:24.

That indicates that he equated the Aramaic Matthew with the Greek Matthew and intimately connected them with each other.

Although the statement cited follows the order Matthew, Mark, Luke and John, the sequence in this passage is unique to Irenaeus.[713] He generally follows the order of Matthew, Luke, Mark and John at other places which, as Campenhausen notes, "would seem therefore to be the order most familiar to Irenaeus himself."[714] Yet, in another place, he follows the sequence John-Luke-Matthew-Mark (*Against Heresies* 3.2.8) perhaps because of theological rather than historical, reasons.[715] Since Irenaeus follows a variety of sequences when mentioning the gospels, he is not of much help in establishing a sequence of composition, but he does offer support for the priority of Matthew as first to be composed and apparent support for the composition of Luke before Mark.

Clement of Alexandria

The origins of Christianity in Alexandria are obscure. The movement must have appeared there at a relatively early date since it appears firmly established at least as early as ca. late second century.[716] According to Eusebius, Pantaenus was the earliest leader of the catechetical school in Alexandria ca. A.D. 185. He as a converted Stoic philosopher whom Eusebius describes as "especially eminent."[717] Eventually, Pantaenus was "appointed as a herald for the gospel of Christ to the heathen in the East, and was sent as far as India."[718] Upon arrival, Pantaenus allegedly discovered that the Hebrew version of Matthew's gospel had preceded him there, being left by the Apostle Bartholomew.[719] That tradition corroborates information from both Papias and Irenaeus about Matthew writing originally in Hebrew (or Aramaic).

Clement of Alexandria (ca. A.D. 150-215) located in Alexandria and became a pupil of Pantaenus.[720] In time, he distinguished himself as a scholar and became a

---

[713] Irenaeus in this context appears to be setting forth an apologetic regarding the content of each gospel as being inspired by the Holy Spirit and united in testimony about the true contents of the gospel in contrast to the teaching of heretics. He is not necessarily setting forth a strict compositional order (cf. *Against Heresies* 3.2.1).

[714] Hans von Campenhausen, *The Formation of the Christian Bible* (Philadelphia: Fortress, 1972), 195 n. 243; cf. e.g., Irenaeus *Against Heresies* 3.9.1-11.8; 4.6.1.

[715] Campenhausen explains this order of John-Luke-Matthew-Mark as corresponding "to the various epochs of salvation history" from Irenaeus's perspective (Campenhausen, *Formation of the Christian Bible*, 195 n. 243).

[716] Williston Walker and Richard A. Norris, David W. Lotz and Robert T. Handy, *A History of the Christian Church*, 4th ed. (New York: Charles Scribner's Sons, 1985), 87.

[717] Eusebius *Ecclesiastical History* 5.10.1-2.

[718] Ibid., 5.10.2.

[719] Ibid., 5.10.2-3.

[720] Ibid., 5.11.1-2.

teacher for over twenty years in Alexandria, succeeding Pantaenus as the leader of the school. At the outbreak of persecution under Severus in A.D. 202, he left Alexandria, never to return. In spite of periods of intense persecution, the school gained great prominence and importance. Beyond that, few facts regarding Clement are available. Nothing certain is known concerning his parentage or early training.[721] Most likely, he was not a Christian during his early years. According to Eusebius, however, he was "the namesake of the pupil of the apostles who had once ruled the church of Rome"[722] while his name reflects his connection with the Egyptian city of Alexandria where he accomplished all his important works. His extant works are *Exhortation to the Greeks*, *Pedagogue*, *Stromateis* or *Miscellanies*, *Who is the rich man that shall be saved?* and some fragments from *Selections from the Prophets* which is a brief commentary on portions of the Scripture.

Information from Clement is of basic importance in determining the order of composition of the gospels, for not only was he a preeminent early church scholar as head of the Alexandrian school but was also in personal contact with a number of church elders from different parts of the Mediterranean world and their information regarding that order. The following quotation of Clement by Eusebius reveals Clement's widespread network of information:

> This work [i.e. *Stromateis*] is not a writing composed for show, but notes stored up for my old age, a remedy against forgetfulness, an image without art, and a sketch of those clear and vital words which I was privileged to hear, and of blessed and truly notable men. Of these one, the Ionian, was in Greece, another in South Italy, a third in Coele-Syria, another in Egypt, and there were others in the East, one of them an Assyrian, another in Palestine of Hebrew origin. But when I had met the last, and in power he was indeed the first, I hunted him out from his concealment in Egypt and found rest.[723]

The last elder in Egypt referred to is most likely Pantaenus. Since he probably met Pantaenus in the latter part of the second century, the testimony that the various elders passed on would reflect well back into the first half of that century.[724]

What is important for the present study is that Clement's widespread information furnishes important additional information about the order of the synoptics. Eusebius quotes him as follows regarding this order:

---

[721] Butterworth says he may have been an Athenian by birth (G. W. Butterworth, "Introduction," *Clement of Alexandria*, trans. by G. W. Butterworth, The Loeb Classical Library [London: William Heinemann, 1919], xi).

[722] Eusebius, *Ecclesiastical History* 5.11.1

[723] Ibid., 5.11.3-4; Clement *Stromateis* 1.1.1.11; cf. also J. Stevenson, *The New Eusebius*, rev. by W. H. C. Frend (London: SPCK, 1987), 180 [*Stromateis* 1.1.11.1-3; *Ecclesiastical History* 5.11.3-5].

[724] William R. Farmer, "The Patristic Evidence Reexamined: A Response to George Kennedy," in *New Synoptic Studies*, William R. Farmer, ed. (Macon, Ga.: Mercer University, 1983), 7.

And again in the same books Clement has inserted a tradition of the primitive elders with regard to the order of the Gospels, as follows. He said that those Gospels were first written which include the genealogies, but that the Gospel according to Mark came into being in this manner: When Peter had publicly preached the word at Rome, and by the Spirit had proclaimed the Gospel, that those present, who were many, exhorted Mark, as one who had followed him for a long time and remembered what had been spoken, to make a record of what was said; and that he did this, and distributed the Gospel among those that asked him. And that when the matter came to Peter's knowledge he neither strongly forbade it nor urged it forward. But that John, last of all, conscious that the outward facts had been set forth in the Gospels, was urged on by his disciples, and, divinely moved by the Spirit, composed a spiritual Gospel. This is Clement's account.[725]

Several important features emerge from those words. First, Clement supplies *unique* information when revealing that the gospels with genealogies (Matthew and Luke) originated before Mark. A scholar of his stature was not likely merely to repeat information without careful investigation. Though Clement does not reveal whether Matthew was first and Luke second or Matthew second and Luke first, he does clearly indicate Mark's third position after Matthew and Luke and not before them as modern historical-critical theories such as Two- and Four-Document Hypotheses maintain.

Moreover, the information from Clement does not contradict Matthew's being first but is an important supplement to information gleaned from other church fathers (e.g., Papias, Irenaeus, Tertullian). The others make plain that Matthew was first, thereby placing Luke second in sequence when combined with Clement's information. Like Irenaeus, Clement places the apostle John's gospel last, saying John wrote it with full awareness of the other three and designed it to supplement the "synoptic" accounts as a "spiritual Gospel." The order of composition, then, was Matthew first, Luke second, Mark third, and John last.

Third, very important in evaluating Clement's information in regard to any proposed solution to the Synoptic Problem is that the tradition he passed on did not come just from a single elder in a single locality but from "a tradition of the primitive elders" (paravdosin tw'n ajnevkaqen presbutevrwn, *paradosin tōn anekathen presbuterōn*) scattered widely throughout the Christian community. That indicates that it was a tradition known and received in different places some time in the early to mid-second century. Clement's wide travels made this information all the more significant, because it represents a strong tradition in the early church, not merely a fanciful whim of Clement and a few others. As a result, one cannot easily dismiss such information.

---

[725] Eusebius *Ecclesiastical History* 6.14.5-7; Clement *Hypotyposeis* 6. The quotation comes from Eusebius, *The Ecclesiastical History, Volume II*, trans. by J. E. L. Oulton, The Loeb Classical Library (Cambridge, Ma.: Harvard University Press, 1932), 46-59.

Fourth, according to Eusebius in *Ecclesiastical History* 2.16.1, Mark helped found the church at Alexandria and was its first overseer. For Clement to place Mark's gospel third in order of composition is, therefore, all the more important. Gamba notes, "He [Clement] would have no reason at all to place Mark's gospel after the other two that contain a genealogy of Jesus, unless it was for a definite and grounded persuasion of historical nature."[726] That reinforces the strength and reliability of Clement's testimony.

Tertullian

Tertullian (ca. A.D. 160-ca. 225), an exact contemporary of Clement of Alexandria, constitutes a prime witness to the faith of the African church regarding the authenticity of the gospels. Despite his eventual Montanist proclivities, he was the outstanding apologist of the Western church of his time.[727]

Little is known of his life except that he was a native of Carthage whose father had been a Roman centurion on duty in that city. He knew and used both Latin and Greek and loved the classics. He became a proficient lawyer and taught public speaking and law in Rome, where he became a convert to Christianity. His goal was the development of a sound Western theology and the defeat of all false philosophical and pagan forces opposed to Christianity.[728]

Tertullian's importance for gospel study lies especially in the fact that he witnessed to the tradition of all Western Christianity, especially the tradition of Rome. His treatise, *Against Marcion* (ca. A.D. 207-212), is especially relevant to the composition of the gospels, because he affirms that apostles wrote Matthew and John, that Mark's gospel reflects Peter's preaching, and that Paul was the sponsor of Luke.

Regarding the four gospels, Tertullian reported that "the evangelical Testament has Apostles as its authors."[729] Here Tertullian makes no distinction between an Aramaic and Hebrew Matthew but considers the Greek Matthew has come from the apostle Matthew himself. Since Tertullian was a lawyer and orator by profession and an outstanding apologist against the heretic Marcion in his *Treatise Against Marcion* where he mentions the gospels' composition, he most probably had his information correct concerning the traditions behind the four gospels. He saw no grounds at all for setting aside this tradition as he attacked Marcion's stance. Any possibility of the facts being wrong would have weakened

---

[726] Giuseppe Fiov. Gamba, "A Further Reexamination of Evidence from Early Tradition," in *New Synoptic Studies*, William R. Farmer, ed. (Macon, Ga.: Mercer University, 1983), 21 n. 10. For further discussion of other ancient documents that suppor Clement's tradition, see ibid., 21-29.

[727] Tertullian became a Montanist in the very early part of the third century A.D. (cf. Earle E. Cairns, *Christianity Though the Centuries* [Grand Rapids: Zondervan, 1996], 106-7].

[728] Cairns, *Christianity Through the Centuries*, p. 106.

[729] Tertullian *Against Marcion* 4.5.3; cf. ibid., 4.2.1-5.

his attack against Marcion. That his comments corroborate as well as supplement the traditions of Papias, Irenaeus, and Clement strengthens his case even more.

Origen

Origen (ca. A.D. 185-253) was born into a Christian family in Alexandria. At the age of eighteen, because of his renowned scholarship, he became Clement of Alexandria's successor as the principal Christian teacher in that city after Clement left due to the persecution under Septimus Severus in A.D. 202.[730] Although an eclectic Middle Platonism that was prevalent in Alexandria and in the East adversely affected his thought and gave him a strong propensity toward an allegorical hermeneutic, he was the most remarkable scholar of his time in depth and breadth of learning.

Origen's extant works evidence his profound scholarship. Unfortunately, most of his writings have perished, but he may have written over six thousand works. Several salient examples of his scholarship are representative of the rest. His *Hexapla*, in which several Hebrew and Greek versions of the OT are arranged in parallel columns, constitutes the beginnings of textual criticism. One of his greatest contributions was his work *De Principiis* (ca. A.D. 230), which exists only in a Latin version by Rufinus. It is the first Christian treatise of systematic theology. In the fourth book of that work, he set forth his allegorical method of interpretation. In *Against Celsus* he devised an apologetic defense against the anti-Christian Platonist Celsus. Yet, the majority of his writings took the form of an exegetical commentary on Scripture.

Origen was also widely traveled, having visited Rome (ca. A.D. 211-212), where he met Hippolytus, and Arabia (ca. A.D. 213-214). In ca. A.D. 215 when emperor Caracalla drove all teachers of philosophy from Alexandria, Origen traveled to Caesarea in Palestine. He resumed his teaching in Alexandria ca. A.D. 216 and continued there until ca. AD. 230-231. Therefore, the information that he imparts regarding the Synoptic Gospels is from a man not only of great learning and research but also one who was widely traveled.

Eusebius records the following from Origen's *Commentary on the Gospel of Matthew*:

> But in the first of his [*Commentaries*] on the Gospel According to *Matthew*, defending the canon of the Church, he gives his testimony that he knows only four Gospels, writing somewhat as follows: ". . . as having learnt by tradition concerning the four Gospels, which alone are unquestionable in the Church of God under heaven, that first was written that according to Matthew, who was once a tax-collector but afterwards an apostle of Jesus Christ, who published it for those who from Judaism came to believe, composed as it was in the Hebrew language. Secondly, that according to Mark, who wrote it in accordance with Peter's instructions, whom also Peter acknowledged as his son in the catholic epistle. . . . And thirdly, that according to Luke, who wrote,

---

[730] Cf. Eusebius *Ecclesiastical History* 6.1-8, 16, 29, 23-27, 32.

for those who from the Gentiles [came to believe], the Gospel that was the praise of Paul. After them all, that according to John.[731]

Here Origen's statement reflects an order of Matthew, Mark, Luke, and John, but nothing in the context requires this to be an assumed chronological order for Mark and Luke. His explicit statement is that Matthew wrote first and John last, but otherwise Eusebius' discussion centers in Origen's view of the exact number of the gospels rather than in the order of their composition.[732] Most likely, Eusebius included Origen's statement because of its bearing on the *number* (not the *order*) of gospels in the canon of the church. He probably accepted Origen's order as reflecting the *canonical* order of appearance in NT manuscripts. On the other hand, Eusebius included Clement's statement cited earlier in this chapter because it related directly to the *chronological* sequence of composition of the gospels (i.e., Matthew, Luke, Mark, and John).[733]

In another place, Origen stressed the apostolic origin of the four gospels and rejected numerous apocryphal gospels as spurious. Origen accepted only four gospels: "For Matthew did not 'take in hand' but wrote by the Holy Spirit, and so did Mark and John and also equally Luke."[734] In this quotation, he does not distinguish between Greek and Aramaic versions of Matthew but includes the Greek Matthew as written by the apostle himself along with the other three gospels (i.e., John, Mark, and Luke). Though he was aware that Matthew originally wrote in Hebrew (see earlier quotation from his *Commentary on the Gospel of Matthew*), this latter statement implies that he made no distinction between the Aramaic and Greek versions, but included the Greek as equally authoritative with the other three gospels and also stressed its origin from the Holy Spirit.

Just as with Tertullian and Clement, to doubt Origen's assertions that Matthew and John were written by apostles and that men associated with the apostles wrote the gospels that bear their names (i.e., Luke and Mark) would be to repudiate Origen's intelligence as a preeminent, careful scholar and also to question his integrity.

Eusebius

Eusebius of Caesarea (ca. A.D. 260-ca. 340), bishop of Caesarea in Palestine, was a pupil of the presbyter Pamphilus, who was himself a student of Origen. Many look to him as the Father of Church History, especially in light of his most famous work *Ecclesiastical History*, which surveyed the history of the church from apostolic times until A.D. 324.[735] His purpose was to compose a record of past trials of the

---

[731] Ibid., 6.25.3-6.

[732] The larger context deals with Origen's view of the number of sacred writings in the OT and NT (ibid., 6.25.1-14).

[733] Farmer, "Patristic Evidence Reexamined," 14.

[734] Origen *Homily in Luke* I; cf. also Orchard and Riley, *Order of the Synoptics*, 137.

[735] *Ecclesiastical History* consists of ten books, the first seven of which recount the history of the church from the beginning to A.D. 303 and the last three some events in

church at the end of its long struggle and the beginning of its era of prosperity. The work is particularly valuable since Eusebius had access to the excellent library housed at Caesarea and also the imperial archives. He also records that he exerted great effort, to be honest and objective in using the best and most reliable of the primary sources available to him.[736] Therefore, in many respects, Eusebius is an invaluable source of knowledge concerning the history of the church during her first three centuries of existence. Eusebius was also a participant in the Council of Nicaea (A.D. 325).

Much of the earlier information in this chapter has come from Eusebius' *Ecclesiastical History*. Much of *Ecclesiastical History* is a record of what others said and did, but at times, Eusebius appears to give his own personal views. He mentions that only two apostles, Matthew, and John, left their recollections and that they wrote under the pressure of necessity: "[T]hey took to writing perforce."[737] Though he mentions that Matthew first wrote in the Hebrew language, he also considers Greek Matthew to have come from the apostle's hand.[738] He notes that John was aware of Matthew, Mark, and Luke, and confirmed their accuracy when he composed his gospel.[739] He refers to sections of the Greek Matthew and ascribes them to the apostle as their author.[740]

In addition, according to Eusebius, Mark composed his gospel on the basis of Peter's preaching,[741] while Luke's gospel came about through his association "with Paul and his [Luke's] conversation with other apostles."[742]

Augustine

Augustine (ca. A.D. 354-430) was a younger contemporary of Jerome, who while young, studied grammar, Latin classics, and rhetoric with parental hopes for his becoming a lawyer or a high civil servant in the imperial government. After his conversion, he became a priest in A.D. 391 and in A.D. 396 the bishop of Hippo in North Africa. Some have acclaimed him as the greatest of the church fathers.[743] He left over one hundred books, five hundred sermons, and two hundred letters. His influence became pervasive not only in the African church but in the Western

---

Eusebius's own lifetime until the Council of Nicaea in A.D. 325. He wrote in a strict chronological order.

[736] Eusebius *Ecclesiastical History* 1.1.1-8

[737] Ibid., 3.24.6

[738] Ibid., 3.24.5-7

[739] Ibid., 3.24.7-8

[740] Ibid., 3.24.9-10

[741] Ibid., 2.15.1-2

[742] Ibid., 3.24.15

[743] Augustine's *Confessions* 1-10 give the story of his life until shortly after his conversion. He gives an account of his conversion in 8.12.

Church, even surpassing that of Jerome. His most widely known work is probably his *Confessions*, one of the great autobiographical works of all time. His *City of God* may be his greatest apologetic work. He also wrote many other significant works including *The Harmony of the Gospels* and *Christian Doctrine*.

Augustine's position on the order of gospels composition appears in his *Harmony of the Gospels*: "Now, these four evangelists . . . are believed to have written in the order which follows: first Matthew, then Mark, thirdly Luke, lastly John."[744] Augustine here passes on a tradition of the order of composition as in the present NT canon. His assignment of Matthew as first and John as last is in overall harmony with earlier tradition as reviewed above in this chapter.

Yet, the Augustinian order conflicts with Clement's sequence in reversing the order of Mark and Luke. Militating against assigning too much weight to the aspect of Augustine's order of Mark being prior to Luke is that he, in contrast to Clement, does not clearly identify the origin of his information or show how widespread or general was the acceptance of his sequence. He merely states that they "are believed to have written in the order which follows." Significant questions remain unanswered as to who held the views he espouses, how widespread was the belief, and what evidence was available for the information he imparts.

In contrast, Clement's information has better documentation, for it is much earlier, reaching back into the early part of the second century and reflecting a widespread consensus. Augustine's is much later and unspecified as to source. Overall, such factors make Clement's information decidedly more weighty in molding a decision regarding the order of composition of the synoptics.

Within the same context, Augustine continues,

[A]s respects the task of composing that record of the gospel which is to be accepted as ordained by divine authority, there were (only) two, belonging to the number of those whom the Lord chose before the passover, that obtained places,—namely, the first place and the last. For the first place in order was held by Matthew and the last by John. And thus the remaining two, who did not belong to the number referred to, but who at the same time had become followers of the Christ who spoke in those others, were supported on either side by the same, like sons who were to be embraced, and who in this way were set in the midst between these twain.[745]

Here Augustine implicitly accepts that the Greek Matthew came from the apostle Matthew as its author and that John was written by the apostle John. This latter quotation, however, appears most likely to deal with the order of the gospels

---

[744] Augustine *The Harmony of the Gospels* 1.2.3. Quotations from Augustine's *Harmony* come from Philip Schaff, ed., vol. 6 of *The Nicene and Post-Nicene Fathers*, here after designated *NPNF*.

[745] Ibid.

within the canon and is not necessarily helpful for giving the order of composition. Neither does it specify whether Luke was prior to Mark or Mark prior to Luke.[746]

Augustine goes on to note that prior to the Greek version of Matthew the Apostle wrote first in the Hebrew language, once again confirming the tradition set forth by the other church fathers: "Of these four, it is true, only Matthew is reckoned to have written in the Hebrew language; the others in Greek." Yet as with other church fathers, he does not explain the transition from Aramaic to Greek but accepts without question that the Greek version was from the apostle.[747] He confirmed that latter point by following up his comments on the order of the gospels and on Matthew's composition of his gospel in Greek before the others with his analysis of the Greek Matthew (as well as the other Greek gospels) as to their themes and character, thereby leaving the strong impression that he saw no significant difference between the Aramaic and Greek versions of Matthew's gospel.[748]

At another place, Augustine commented that "Mark follows him [i.e. Matthew] closely and looks like his attendant and epitomizer."[749] That statement, however, appears not to be based on tradition but on Augustine's personal analysis of Matthew in comparison with Mark. Hence, no reveal significance attaches to it beyond the fact of reflecting Augustine's personal reflections and observations in explaining agreements between Matthew and Mark. Moreover, as the next section of this chapter will reveal, the church fathers viewed the gospels as being composed independently of one another. Augustine's *Harmony of the Gospels* evidences no indications to the contrary. As a matter of fact, it indicates just the opposite.

At another place, Augustine discusses the canonical order as follows:

> Now the whole canon of Scripture on which we say this judgment is to be exercised, is contained in the following books. . . . That of the New Testament, again, is contained within the following:—Four books of the Gospel, according to Matthew, according to Mark, according to Luke, according to John.[750]

Here again he apparently reflects the compositional order of Matthew, Mark, Luke and John.

---

[746] Cf. David Peabody, "Augustine and the Augustinian Hypothesis: A Reexamination of Augustine's Thought in De Consensu Evangelistarum," in *New Synoptic Studies*, William R. Farmer, ed. (Macon, Ga.: Mercer, 1983), 38.

[747] Augustine *The Harmony of the Gospels* 1.2.4. Augustine refers to the Hebrew Matthew at least two other times in his Harmony (2.66.128 and 2.80.157), in both of which places he refers to or quotes the Greek Matthew while talking about a Hebrew original. He never denies that the Greek version came from Matthew himself.

[748] Ibid., 1.2.5-6

[749] Ibid., 1.2.4.

[750] Ibid., 2.8.13.

One other place deserves mention as possibly significant, for Augustine relates the following distinguishing characteristics of the contents of the gospels:

> [I]t is a clearly admitted position that the first three—namely, Matthew, Mark and Luke—have occupied themselves chiefly with the humanity of our Lord Jesus Christ. . . . And in this way, Mark . . . either appears to be preferentially the companion of Matthew . . . or else, in accordance with the more probable account of the matter, he holds a course in conjunction with both [the other synoptists]. For although he is at one with Matthew in a large number of passages, he is nevertheless at one rather with Luke in some others.[751]

Peabody, who favors the Two Gospel Hypothesis, argues from this statement that Augustine has changed his mind regarding his relegation of Luke to third position in order of composition, reasoning that after Augustine's extensive analysis of the gospels "Augustine's new, more probable view of Mark is that Mark is literarily dependent upon both Matthew and Luke" and "Augustine had not one but two views of the relationships among the Gospels."[752] That conclusion is not warranted, however. Peabody has a strong desire to explain away the apparent Augustinian order of composition of Matthew, Mark, Luke, and John in hopes of establishing him as supportive of the Two-Gospel Hypothesis and its order of Matthew, Luke, Mark, and John. As a result, he reads too much into Augustine's statement. Augustine, in context, is merely describing the similarities and differences between the Gospel of John and the three Synoptic Gospels. Furthermore, in the immediate context, he refers to the gospels in the order Matthew, Mark, and Luke, thus giving a strong indication that he has not changed his mind regarding his assumed order of composition. Another explanation for Augustine's assertions is that he may have identified any established canonical order (Matthew, Mark, Luke, and John) with the order of composition, but demonstrating that beyond a reasonable doubt is impossible.

Above all, one point is important. Regardless of the difference of opinion between Clement and Augustine on the order of composition of the gospels, neither Augustine nor Clement place Mark first in order of composition as the Two-Document Theory supposes. Virtually *all* church fathers place Matthew earliest. Although they may mention a Hebrew or Aramaic original of Matthew, the fathers accepted without any serious question that the Greek Matthew came from the apostle Matthew, the Gospel of Luke from Luke's association with Paul, Mark from his association with Peter's preaching, and the apostle John's Gospel came last in order of composition.

Conclusion regarding Order of Composition

An analysis of data from the church fathers results in one conspicuous conclusion: they do not support either the Two-Document Hypothesis or the Two-Gospel Hypothesis. The assumed dependence of Matthew and Luke on Mark is totally without historical foundation as is the assumed dependence of Mark on

---

[751] Ibid., 4.10.11

[752] Peabody, "Augustine and the Augustinian Hypothesis," 61-62.

Matthew and Luke instead of on Peter's preaching. Strained and desperate interpretations by proponents of the Two-Document Hypothesis as well as by those of the Two-Gospel Hypothesis stand as a monumental testimony to their dismal failure in mustering any support among the fathers.

Papias' testimony answers the question as to whether Mark was in any sense dependent on Matthew as the Two-Gospel Theory would require, for Mark wrote on the basis of Peter's preaching, not on the basis of literary dependence on Matthew. Besides, the church fathers were not merely unthinkingly reflecting Papias, because they (e.g., Irenaeus, Clement, Tertullian, Origen) were renowned scholars in their own right who had information from widespread and independent sources. They did not need to rely solely on Papias for their information.

A newly released work, *Mark*, vol. II from the Ancient Christian Commentary on Scripture buttresses these contentions. This work, by appealing to the ancients, circumnavigates such sacrosanct, as well as highly erroneous, historical-critically cherished icons originating out of source, form, tradition and redaction criticism, revealing some interesting contradictions with post-Enlightenment assertions. For instance, the volume on Mark reveals that the early church fathers overwhelmingly neglected Mark, rarely produced a sustained commentary on Mark. Instead, Matthew and John received the most attention. While one could argue that they held Matthew and John in high esteem because they were apostolic, one still wonders why, if Mark was really the first written gospel as so ardently maintained by source criticism (contra the Two-Document Hypothesis), did the fathers so persistently neglect it. Moreover, the volume also reveals that the fathers consistently maintained that Mark actually wrote Mark (not some unknown "evangelist" as maintained by historical criticism) and that it reflected Peter's preaching rather than being a condensation of Matthew and Luke (contra the Two-Gospel Hypothesis). The conclusion the work reaches is astoundingly refreshing: "It had always been evident that Mark presented a shorter a shorter version of the gospel than Matthew, but the premise of literary dependency was not generally recognized. The view that Matthew and Luke directly relied on Mark did not develop in full form until the nineteenth century,"[753] Such a perspective also indicates that the fathers regarded Matthew, not Mark, as the first gospel to be written. From this reviewer's perspective, only by *a priori* reading into the church fathers of these two recent synoptic hypotheses move from acute speculation to enslaving dogma.

Far from contradicting each other, the information that these fathers supply is largely complementary, consistent, and congruent: the apostle Matthew wrote first, the apostle John last, with Luke and Mark writing between these two. Some difference of opinion exists as to whether Luke or Mark wrote second, but the probability is on the side of Luke's being second. Mark derived his material from the preaching of Peter, not from Matthew and Luke.

Sadly, the overarching reason why modern scholarship rejects or explains away their testimony is adherence to an assumed hypotheses of literary dependence, which is the basic assumption of Historical Criticism (hereafter HC).

---

[753] Thomas C. Oden & Christopher A. Hall, *Mark*, vol. II of Ancient Christian Commentary on Scripture (Downers Grove, IL: InterVarsity, 1998), xxix.

The church fathers stand solidly against the stultifying dogma of modern Source Criticism that blindly upholds the Two- (or Four-) Document Hypothesis and the Two-Gospel Hypothesis, theories that suppress, dismiss, or ridicule any evidence contrary their assumed tenets. Instead of being blindly rejected, explained away, or enervated by a pre-conceived agenda or predilection toward a particular synoptic hypothesis, the statements of the fathers should have their full weight in any discussion of the synoptic issue. Their voices objectively analyzed constitute a united witness against the concept of the priority of Mark based on literary dependence, and in turn, provide a cogent testimony for the chronological priority of the writing of Matthew. Could it be that Enlightenment-spawned historical-criticism has so systematically ignored the early fathers because they stand as manifest contradictions to its cherished dogmas or might it also reflect intellectual arrogance displayed by much of modern scholarship?

CHAPTER 9 Contemporary 21st Century Evangelical NT Criticism: Those Who Do Not Learn From the Lessons of History

F. David Farnell

At the Turn of the Twentieth Century . . .

In 1909, God moved two Christian laymen, wealthy California oil magnates who were brothers named Lyman and Milton Stewart, to set aside a large sum of money for issuing twelve volumes that would set forth the fundamentals of the Christian faith and which were to be sent free of charge to ministers of the gospel, missionaries, Sunday School superintendents, and others engaged in aggressive Christian work through the English-speaking world. A committee of twelve men who were known to be sound in the faith was chosen to have the oversight of the publication of these volumes. Entitled, *The Fundamentals*, they were a twelve-volume set published between 1910 and 1915 that set presented the fundamentals of the Christian faith. Three million individual volumes were distributed. R. A. Torrey related his own personal knowledge and experience with these volumes in the following terms,

> Rev. Dr. A. C. Dixon was the first Executive Secretary of the Committee, and upon his departure for England Rev. Dr. Louis Meyer was appointed to take his place. Upon the death of Dr. Meyer the work of the Executive Secretary developed upon me. We were able to bring out these twelve volumes according to the original plan. Some of the volumes were sent to 300,000 ministers and missionaries and other workers in different parts of the world. On the completion of the twelve volumes as originally planned the work was continued through The King's Business, published at 536 South Hope St., Los Angeles, California. Although a large number of volumes were issues than there were names on our mailing list, at last the stock became exhausted, but appeals for them kept coming in from different parts of the world. [754]

Its purpose was to combat the inroads of liberalism that had been experienced by the church during the latter half of the nineteenth and early twentieth centuries (1885-1910) with the denominational conflict that resulted (1910-1930). In essence, it was the early twentieth century's witness to future Christian generations of their Scriptural beliefs as well as a record detailing a crisis in biblical belief and authority for their time, constituting a warning to a future generation to avoid what they had experienced among the denominations of their day. During this time, modernists, or what is now known as "critical scholarship," had refused to give voice to

---

[754] "Preface," in *The Fundamentals: A Testimony to the Truth*, R. A. Torrey, A. C. Dixon and others, eds. (Grand Rapids Baker Reprint, 1972), vol. 1. Reprinted without alteration or abridgment from the original, four-volume edition issues by the Bible Institute of Los Angeles in 1917.

anything approaching the trustworthiness of Scripture. Conservatives were isolated and shunned within mainline denominations. They decided to fight back. The 1925 Scopes Trial regarding evolution also marked a watershed issue for fundamentalists during this period.[755] The New Testament Gospels were being dismissed as historically defective, resulting in what Schweizer called the "quest" for the historical Jesus. Fundamentalists refused to participate in the First Search for the "historical Jesus," because they realized it's *a priori* destructive presuppositional foundations and its intent to destroy the influence of the Gospels and Christianity on society.[756]

Higher Criticism Devastates American Churches and Schools

In 1915, the Bible Institute of Los Angeles sponsored a four-volume edition of *The Fundamentals* that included all but a few of the original 90 articles. Again, Torrey, who served as the Dean of the Bible Institute of Los Angeles from 1912 to 1924, as well as the first pastor of the Church of the Open Door in downtown Los Angeles, gave the following information in the "Preface" to the 1917 edition:

> As the fund [supplied by the Lyman brothers] was no longer available for this purpose, the Bible Institute of Los Angeles, to whom the plates were turned over when the Committee closed its work, have decided to bring out the various articles that appeared in The Fundamentals in four volumes at the cheapest price possible All the articles that appeared in The Fundamentals, with the exception of a very few that did not seem to be in exact keeping with the original purpose of The Fundamentals, will be published in this series.[757]

In this four-volume series, the following subjects were highlighted as problems that had plagued the church during that time. First and foremost was the very negative impact that higher criticism was having on Old and New Testament interpretation and inspiration in biblical training centers and churches of the day. The very first article in the four-volume series, *The History of the Higher Criticism*, by Dyson Hague, set the tone for all the volumes and provided the overall context or framework for the rest of the articles. The fundamentalists who produced these volumes were not anti-critical in terms of scriptural issues, for they declared that the term can mean "nothing more than the study of the literary structure of the various books of the Bible. Now this in itself is most laudable. It is indispensable."[758] They were, however, very wary of the kind of criticism that scholarly endeavors might employ in the analysis of the text with an anti-supernatural bias. While it embraced

---

[755] See George Marsden, *Understanding Fundamentalism and Evangelicalism* (Grand Rapids: Eerdmans, 1991), 36-37.

[756] For more information, see F. David Farnell, "Searching for the 'Historical' Jesus: The Rise of the Three Searches," in *The Jesus Quest*. Eds. Norman L. Geisler and F. David Farnell (Maitland, FL: Xulon, 2014), 361-420; Albert Schweitzer, *The Quest of the Historical Jesus*. Translated by W. Montgomery from the first German edition, *Von Reimarus zu Wrede* (1906). Introduction by James M. Robinson (New York: MacMillan, 1968).

[757] "Preface," in *The Fundamentals*, vol. 1.

[758] Dyson Hague, "The History of the Higher Criticism," in *The Fundamentals*, 1:9.

"a higher criticism which is reverent in tone and scholarly in work"[759] that dealt with "author, date, circumstances, and purpose of writing,"[760] it rejected higher criticism based on the facts that (1) its experts were without a true "spiritual insight," (2) were those who "go far in the realm of the conjectural," and (3) the dominant men of the movement were men with a strong bias against the supernatural," adding that "[s]ome of the men who have been the most distinguished in the higher critical movement have been men who have no faith in the God of the Bible, and no faith in either the necessity or the possibility of a personal supernatural revelation."[761] This form of higher criticism was penetrating the American mainline denominations and causing great problems in Christian seminaries and schools that were once faithful.

European critical scholarship received special negative targeting in Hague's opening article, calling the popular German theories of the day as "German Fancies" and "some of the most powerful exponents of the modern Higher Critical theories have been the Germans, and it is notorious to what length the German fancy can go in the direction of the subjective and of the conjectural. For hypothesis weaving and speculation, the German theological professor is unsurpassed."[762] Hague also commented that "German thinkers are men who lack in a singular degree the faculty of common sense and knowledge of human nature."[763] Hague noted that "the dominant minds [of higher criticism] which have led and swayed the movement, who made the theories that the others circulated, were strongly unbelieving."[764]

The article also centered the origin of this form of negative higher criticism impacting his day to the scholarship of (1) The French-Dutch, (2) the Germans and (3) the British-Americans.[765] He traced the beginnings of modern criticism on these groups for a marked influence away from the inspiration of Scripture, with Spinoza, the rationalist Dutch philosopher, as the father of modern biblical criticism. Hague insightfully noticed, "Spinoza was really the fountain-head of the movement, and his line was taken in England by the British philosopher Hobbes. He went deeper than Spinoza, as an outspoken antagonist of the necessity and possibility of personal revelation."[766]

After spreading from Spinoza and Hobbes, he identified the strong German influence of his day that had spread to American schools and churches. Hague sounded the alarm over the latest or "third stage" of the higher critical movement in America as the "British-American Critics" that were now active in theological schools.[767] He noted a particularly alarming trend among these British and American

---

[759] Ibid., 1:10.

[760] Ibid., 1:9.

[761] Ibid., 1:12-14.

[762] Ibid., 1:12.

[763] Ibid.

[764] Ibid., 1:14-15.

[765] Ibid., 1:14.

[766] Ibid., 1:15.

[767] Ibid., 1:17.

scholars, a piety that was combined with radical European skepticism. He identified Robertson Smith, a Scotchman, as "a man of deep piety and spirituality," who "combined with a sincere regard for the Word of God a critical radicalism that was strangely inconsistent, as did the scholar "George Adam Smith, the most influential of the present leaders, a man of great insight and scriptural acumen who in his works . . . adopted some of the most radical and least demonstrable of the German theories."[768]

Hague saw three areas as core beliefs of the "Continental Critics" influencing America that "can be confidently asserted of nearly all": (1) denial of "the validity of miracle, and the validity of any miraculous narrative. What Christians consider to be miraculous they considered legendary or mythical;" (2) "they . . . denied the reality of prophecy and the validity of any prophetical statement;" and (3) they . . . denied the reality of revelation, in the sense in which it has ever been held by the universal Christian church . . . Their hypotheses were constructed on the assumption of the falsity of Scripture."[769] Hague summed up the whole of the higher criticism assault on the church "in one word" as "rationalistic" and "men who had discarded belief in God and Jesus Christ Whom He had sent. The Bible, in their view, was a mere human product."[770] The crescendo of Hague's lament centered in the fact that their views "have so dominated modern Christianity and permeated modern ministerial thought."[771]

Hague analyzed "English-writing Higher Critics" as "a more difficult subject" because "The *British-American Higher Critics* represent a school of compromise," commenting that

> On the one hand they practically accept the premises of the Continental school with regard to the antiquity, authorship, authenticity, and origins of the Old Testament books. On the other hand, they refuse to go with the German rationalists in altogether denying their inspiration. They still claim to accept the Scriptures as containing a Revelation from God. But may they not hold their own peculiar views with regard to the origin and date and literary structure of the Bible without endangering their own faith or the faith of Christians? This is the very heart of the question.[772]

Hague also catalogued the impact of higher criticism on the discrediting of the Old Testament, e.g., the JPED hypothesis was rampant with its idea of unknown "redactors," noting that "[i]n the redactory process no limit apparently is assigned by the critic to the work of the redactors who compiled the Pentetuech "[w]ith an utterly irresponsibility of freedom" expressed by "leading theological writers of and professors of the day."[773] Moreover, the entire Old Testament had been called into

---

[768] Ibid., 1:18.

[769] Ibid., 1:19-20.

[770] Ibid., 1:20.

[771] Ibid., 1:21.

[772] Ibid., 1:21-22.

[773] Ibid., 1:24.

question, relating that "[t]he time-honoring traditions of the Catholic Church are set at naught, and its thesis of the relation of inspiration and genuineness and authenticity derided," e.g., Deutero-Isaiah, Daniel as "purely pseudeonymous" of the second century B. C.

In reference to the New Testament, historical criticism's assault was just beginning:

> With regard to the New Testament: The English writing schools have hitherto confined themselves mainly to the Old Testament, but if Professor Sanday, who passes as a most conservative and moderate representative of the critical school, can be taken as a sample, the historical books are 'yet in the first instance strictly historical, put together by ordinary historical methods, or , in so far as the methods on which they are composed, are not ordinary, due to the peculiar circumstances of the case, and not to influences, which need be specially described as supernatural.'[774]

Interestingly, Hague refers to the famous scholar William Sanday who would also rise to New Testament fame, especially in regard to synoptic hypotheses. This full quote is from the Bampton lectures of 1893 on Inspiration at Oxford University where the full quote of Sanday is as follows:

> We observe too that the Historical Books of the New Testament, like those of the Old Testament, whatever the sanctity attaching to them from their contents, are yet in the first instance strictly histories, put together by ordinary historical methods, or in so far as the methods on which they are composed are not ordinary, due to rather their peculiar circumstances of the case, and not to influences, which need specially described as supernatural."[775]

Here, Sanday immediately reduces the inspired nature of the canonical Gospels and Acts as not being composed by any "supernatural" influences, confirming Hague's view of British scholarship as compromising on vital issues. Sanday's limited or inconsistent view of "inspiration" distinguished between the "Traditional" approach of inspiration as viewed by the faithful, i.e., deductive, preferring what he called the "inductive approach" to inspiration.[776] It also demonstrated that the last vestiges of the orthodox view of inspiration were rapidly disappearing from the British scene at the end of the nineteenth century. Sanday argued,

> To sum up then, we may compare the Traditional and Inductive theories of Inspiration thus. The inspiration implied by both is real and no fiction, a direct objective action of the Divine upon the human. Nay, in one sense, if the inductive conception of Inspiration is not more real than the other, it is at least more thoroughly realized, because it is not

---

[774] Ibid., 1:26.

[775] William Sanday, *Inspiration: Eight Lectures on the Early History and Origin of the Doctrine of Inspiration. Being the Bampton Lectures for 1893* (New York Longmans, Green and Co, 1893), 399.

[776] See Norman L. Geisler, *Systematic Theology*, vol. 1, chapter 12.

something which is simply taken for granted but comes freshly and spontaneously, in such a way that the mind can get a full and vigorous impression of it, from the study of the documents themselves. The danger of the traditional view is lest inspiration should be thought of as something dead and mechanical; when it is arrived at inductively it must needs be conceived as something vital and organic. It is a living product which falls naturally into its place in the development of the purpose of the Living God. It is not therefore in the least degree inferior in quality to traditional inspiration. So far as they differ it would be rather in quantity, inasmuch as on the inductive view inspiration is not inherent in the Bible as such, but is present in different books and parts of books in different degrees. More particularly on this view—and here is the point of greatest divergence—it belongs to the Historical Books rather as conveying a religious lesson than as histories, rather as interpreting than as narrating plain matter of fact. The crucial issue is that in this last respect they do not seem to be exempted from possibilities of error.[777]

From this Hague correctly concluded that Continental and British scholarship in his day were outside the realm of orthodoxy regarding inspiration, "the difficulty presents itself to the average man of today is this: How can these critics still claim to believe in the Bible as the Christian Church has ever believed it?"[778] At best, scholarship in his day was claiming some form of partial inspiration with a redefinition of orthodox understanding of the concept that was held from the nascent church, arguing "[t]heir theory of inspiration must be, then, a very different one from that held by the average Christian" and "its most serious feature is this: It is a theory of inspiration that completely overturns the old-fashioned ideas of the Bible and its unquestioned standard of authority and truth. For whatever this so-called Divine element is, it appears quite consistent with the defective argument, incorrect interpretation, if not what the average man would call forgery or falsification. It is, in fact, revolutionary."[779]

Hague viewed these ideas of higher criticism in his day as threatening "the Christian system of doctrine and the whole fabric of systematic theology."[780] He alluded to name-calling among advocates of historical criticism toward Bible-believing people as being "ignorant alarmists" and "obscurantists,"[781] yet noted that these critical scholars were "irreverent in spirit" and must "certainly be received with caution."[782]

Even more interesting, however, was his following comment about the views of the "younger men" in his generation of scholars toward higher criticism:

---

[777] Sandy, *Inspiration*, 399-400.

[778] Hague, "The History of Higher Criticism," 1:27.

[779] Ibid., 1:29-30.

[780] Ibid., 1:32.

[781] Ibid., 1:36-37.

[782] Ibid., 1:37.

There is a widespread idea especially among younger men that the critics must be followed, because their scholarship settles the questions . . . There is also a widespread idea among the younger men that because scholars are experts in Hebrew that, therefore, their deductions as experts in language must be received. This, too, is a mistake . . . If we have any prejudice, we would rather be prejudiced against rationalism. If we have any bias, it must be against a teaching which unsteadies the heart and unsettles faith. We prefer to stand with Our Lord and Savior Jesus Christ in receiving the Scriptures as the Word of God, without objection and without a doubt. A little learning and a little listening to rationalistic theorizers and sympathizers may incline us to uncertainty; but deeper study and deeper research will incline us, as it inclined other scholars, to the profoundest conviction of the authority and authenticity of the Holy Scriptures."[783]

Hague noted that the younger scholars insisted that the critical scholars be followed as the "experts." Repeatedly, Hague addressed name-calling by the young scholars toward more conservative, Bible-believing scholarship was being conducted. He lamented that "[t]he old-fashioned conservative views are no longer maintained by men with pretension to scholarship. The only people who oppose the higher critics views are the ignorant, the prejudiced, and the illiterate."[784] Yet he crystalized the real cause of concern regarding the higher criticism of his day,

What the conservative schools oppose is not Biblical criticism, but Biblical criticism by rationalists. They do not oppose the conclusions . . . because they [i.e. higher critics] are experts and scholars; they oppose them because the Biblical criticism of rationalists and unbelievers can be neither expert or scientific. A criticism that is characterized by the most arbitrary conclusion from the most spurious assumptions has no right to the word scientific. And further. Their [the faithful of Hague's day] adhesion to the traditional views is not only conscientious but intelligent. They believe that the old-fashioned views are as scholarly as they are Scriptural. It is the fashion in some quarters to cite the imposing list of scholars on the side of the German school, and to sneeringly assert that there is not a scholar to stand up for the old views of the Bible.[785]

Hague concluded his article by affirming that "we desire to stand with Christ and His Church . . . A little learning, and a little listening to rationalistic theorizers and sympathizers may incline us to uncertainty; but deeper study and deeper research will incline us . . . to the profoundest conviction of the authority and authenticity of the Holy Scriptures, and to cry 'Thy word is very pure; therefore Thy servant loveth it.'"[786]

Hague's first article set the tone and direction for the entire rest of the four volumes of *The Fundamentals* of 1917. The first volume of the four issued in 1917

---

[783] Ibid., 1:39.

[784] Ibid., 1:39-40.

[785] Ibid., 1:40.

[786] Ibid., 1:42.

included the following subjects that upheld the factual, historical basis of the material in each Testament and revealed where higher critical attacks were occurring at the turn of the twentieth century. The names in parenthesis reveal the "roll-call of the faithful" who defended Scripture in the articles that are listed and provide the reader with a sweeping overview of the variegated assault from higher criticism within the Church at the turn of the twentieth century. Sadly, *many orthodox English theologians participated in the articles, but as the twentieth century would progress, higher criticism's influence on the British Empire would render its national church and evangelistic influence almost completely null and void.*[787]

I. The History of Higher Criticism (Dyson Hague)

II. The Authorship of the Pentateuch (i.e., Denial of Mosaic Authorship) (George F.   Wright)

III. The Fallacies of the Higher Criticism (Franklin Johnson)

IV. The Bible and Modern Criticism (F. Bettex)

V. The Holy Scriptures and Modern Negations (James Orr)

VI. Christ and Criticism (Robert Anderson)

VII. Old Testament Criticism and New Testament Christianity (W. H. Griffith Thomas)

VIII. The Tabernacle in the Wilderness: Did It Exist? (David Heagle)

IX. The Internal Evidence of the Fourth Gospel (G. Osborne Troop)

X. The Testimony of Christ to the Old Testament (William Caven)

XI. The Early Narratives of Genesis (James Orr)

XII. One Isaiah (George L. Robinson)

XIII. The Book of Daniel (Joseph D. Wilson)

XIV. The Doctrinal Value of the First Chapter of Genesis (Dyson Hague)

XV. Three Peculiarities of the Pentateuch which are Incompatible with the Graf-   Wellhausen Theories of Its Composition (Andrew Craig Robinson)

XVI. The Testimony of the Monuments to the Truth of the Scriptures (George Frederick   Wright)

XVII. The Recent Testimony of Archaeology to the Scriptures (M. G. Kyle)

XVIII. Science and the Christian Faith (James Orr)

XIX. My Personal Experience with the Higher Criticism (J. J. Reeve)

---

[787] See Dennis M. Swanson, "The Downgrade Controversy and Evangelical Boundaries: Some Lessons from Spurgeon's Battle for Evangelical Orthodoxy," in *The Jesus Quest*. Eds. Norman L. Geisler and F. David Farnell (Matiland, FL: Xulon, 2014), 229-298.

The second volume of the four defended the following and revealed where other attacks on Scripture were occurring, especially against orthodox views of inspiration and theology:

I. The Inspiration of the Bible—Definition, Extent and Proof (James M. Gray)

II. Inspiration (L. W. Marshall)

III. The Moral Glory of Jesus Christ, A Proof of Inspiration (William G. Moorehead)

IV. The Testimony of Scripture to themselves (George S. Bishop)

V. Testimony of the Organic Unity of the Bible to Its Inspiration (Arthur T. Pierson)

VI. Fulfilled Prophecy a Potent Argument for the Bible (Arno C. Gaebelein)

VII. Life in the Word (Philip Mauro)

THEOLOGY

VIII. Is There a God? (Thomas Whitelaw)

IX. God in Christ the Only Revelation of the Fatherhood of God (Robert E. Speer)

X. The Deity of Christ (Benjamin W. Warfield)

XI. The Virgin Birth of Christ (James Orr)

XII. The God-Man (John Stock)

XIII. The Person and Work of Jesus Christ (Bishop Nuelsen)

XIV. The Certainty and Importance of the Bodily Resurrection of Jesus Christ from the   Dead (R. A. Torrey)

XV. The Personality and Deity of the Holy Spirit (R. A. Torrey)

XVI. The Holy Spirit and the Son of God (W. J. Erdman)

XVII. Observations on the Conversion and Apostleship of St. Paul (Lord Lyttelton)

XVIII. Christianity No Fable (Thomas Whitelaw)

The third volume of the four continued the defense of orthodox views of theology and evangelism against higher criticism's attacks as well as Roman Catholicism's infiltration:

I. The Biblical Conception of Sin (Thomas Whitelaw)

II. Paul's Testimony to the Doctrine of Sin (Charles B. Williams)

III. Sin and Judgment to Come (Robert Anderson)

IV. What Christ Teaches Concerning the Future Resurrection (William C. Proctor)

V. The Atonement (Franklin Johnson)

VI. At-One-Ment, By Propitiation (Dyson Hague)

VII. The Grace of God (C. I. Scofield)

VIII. Salvation by Grace (Thomas Spurgeon)

IX. The Nature of Regeneration (Thomas Boston)

X. Regeneration, Conversion, Reformation (George W. Lasher)

XI. Justification by Faith (H. C. G. Moule)

XII. The Doctrines that Must Be Emphasized in Successful Evangelism (I. W. Munhall)

XIII. Preach the Word (Howard Crosby)

XIV. Pastoral and Personal Evangelism, or Winning Men to Christ One by One (John Timothy Stone)

XV. The Sunday School's True Evangelism (Charles Gallaudet Trumbull)

XVI. The Place of Prayer in Evangelism (R. A. Torrey)

XVII. Foreign Missions, or World-Wide Evangelism (Robert E. Speer)

XVIII. A Message from Missions (Charles A. Bowen)

XIX. What Missionary Motives Should Should Prevail? (Henry W. Frost)

XX. Consecration (Henry W. Frost)

XXI. Is Romanism Christianity? (T. W. Medhurst)

XXII. Rome, the Antagonist of the Nation (J. M. Foster)

XXIII. The True Church (Bishop Ryle)

XXIV. The Testimony of Foreign Missions to the Superintending Providence of God (Arthur T. Pierson)

XXV. The Purpose of the Incarnation (G. Cambell Morgan)

XXVI. Tributes to Christ and the Bible by Brainy Men not Known as Active Christians

The final volume issued warnings to beware of philosophies, modern thought and "isms" that had infiltrated the thinking of the church:

MODERN THOUGHT

I. Modern Philosophy (Philip Mauro)

II. The Knowledge of God (David James Burrell)

III. The Wisdom of This World (A. W. Pitzer)

IV. The Science of Conversion (H. M. Sydenstricker)

V. The Decadence of Darwinism (Henry H. Beach)

VI. The Passing of Evolution (George Frederick Wright)

VII. Evolution in the Pulpit (an Occupant in the Pew)

VIII. The Church and Socialism (Charles R. Erdman)

"ISMS"

IX. Millennial Dawn: A Counterfeit of Christianity (William H. Moorehead)

X. Mormonism: Its Origin, Characteristics and Doctrines (R. G. McNiece)

XI. Eddyism, Commonly Called "Christian Science" (Maurice E. Wilson)

XII. Modern Spirtualism Briefly Tested by Scripture (Algernon J. Pollock)

XIII. Satan and His Kingdom (Jessie Penn-Lewis)

FURTHER TESTIMONY TO THE TRUTH

XIV. Why Save The Lord's Day (Daniel Hoffman Martin)

XV. Apologetic Value of Paul's Epistles (E. J. Stobo)

XVI. The Divine Efficacy of Prayer (Arthur T. Pierson)

XVII. The Proof of the Living God, as Found in the Prayer Life of George Muller, of   Bristol (Arthur T. Pierson)

XVIII. Our Lord's Teaching about Money (Arthur T. Pierson)

XIX. The Scriptures (A. C. Dixon)

XX. What the Bible Contains for the Believer (George F. Pentecost)

XXI. The Hope of the Church (John McNicol)

XXII. The Coming of Christ (Charles R. Erdman)

XXIII. The Testimony of Christian Experience (E. Y. Mullins)

XXIV. A Personal Testimony (Howard A. Kelly)

XXV. A Personal Testimony (H. W. Webb-Peploe)

XXVI The Personal Testimony of Charles T. Studd (Charles T. Studd)

XXVII. A Personal Testimony (Philip Mauro)

In sum, *The Fundamentals* constitute a startling witness left as a testimony by the faithful to the early twentieth century churches experience of the attack on orthodox Protestant beliefs, conducted aggressively by higher criticism, liberal theology, Catholicism (also called Romanism in the work), socialism, Modernism, atheism, Christian Science, Mormonism, Millennial Dawn, Spiritualism, and evolutionism that had infiltrated its ranks and subsequently caused great damage within the church with regard to its vitality and theology. Above all, they left it as

254

a warning to future generations in hopes of preventing a similar occurrence among God's people in the future.

In 1958, at its fiftieth year celebration, the Bible Institute of Los Angeles published a new edition of *The Fundamentals*, called *The Fundamentals for Today*, supervised by Charles Lee Feinberg and a committee of professors from Talbot Theological Seminary.[788] This reissue consisted of 64 selected and updated articles from the original 90 whereby Biola/Talbot affirmed their commitment at that time to the founding fathers views of the full inspiration and authority of both the Old and New Testaments.

The Resulting Call to God's People to Gather in Defense of the Faith

An immediate impact of *The Fundamentals* was the alerting of God's people regarding the worsening spiritual condition that the church was experiencing. God's people issued a call to assemble throughout America, rallying in defense of God's inerrant Word. Warren Wiersbe related, "[a]t that time in history, Fundamentalism was become a force to reckon with, thanks to effective preachers, popular Bible conferences and the publications that taught 'the fundamentals' and also exposed the growing apostasy of that day . . . It was a time of growth and challenge."[789] On May 25–June 1, 1919, six thousand Christians met in Philadelphia at "The World Conference on Christian Fundamentals." W. H. Griffith Thomas chaired the Resolutions Committee, while popular, well-known fundamentalist preachers spoke for those days, such as W. B. Riley, R. A. Torrey, Lewis Sperry Chafer, James M. Gray and William L. Pettingill. Delegates came from 42 states in America, most of the Canadian provinces as well as seven foreign countries to rally against the infiltration of destructive higher criticism and liberalism of the day in the church. The Conference issued *God Hath Spoken* (Philadelphia: Bible Conference Committee, 1919) that consisted of 25 addresses that were delivered at the conference and stenographically recorded for posterity.[790] The work described two outstanding phenomena as leading to the assembly in Philadelphia in 1919 that are very telling:

> On the one hand, the Great Apostasy was spreading like a plague throughout Christendom. A famine was everywhere—"not a famine of bread, nor a thirst for water, but of hearing the words of Jehovah." Thousands of false teachers, many of them occupying high ecclesiastical positions, were bringing in damnable heresies, even denying the Lord ' that bought them, and bringing upon themselves swift destruction. And many were following their pernicious ways, by reason of whom the way

---

[788] *The Fundamentals For Today, The Famous Sourcebook of Foundational Biblical Truths*. R. A. Torrey, Ed. Updated by Charles L. Feinberg. Biographical introductions by Warren Wiersbe (Grand Rapids: Kregel,1958, 1990).

[789] Warren Wiersbe, "Foreword," in *The Fundamentals for Today*.

[790] *God Hath Spoken (Hebrews 1:1-2) Twenty-five Addresses Delivered at the World Conference on Christian Fundamentals*. Stenographically reported under the direction of a Biblically trained expert (Philadelphia: Bible Conference Committee, 1919).

of truth was evil spoken of. The Bible was wounded in the house of its friends. The great cardinal doctrines of Scripture were set at naught. The Virgin Birth of our Lord, His Sacrificial Death and Bodily Resurrection, these and similar truths were rejected as archaic and effete. The Consensus of Scholarship, the Assured Results of Modern Research, New Light from Original Sources, the Findings of Science, all these high-sounding phrases, and others like them, became popular slogans calculated to ensnare the simple, and to deceive if possible the very elect. People generally accepted the so-called Findings of Science at their face value, never suspecting that they were only the inventions of "false apostles, deceitful workers, transforming themselves into the apostles of Christ." To "the man whose eyes are open," of course, all this was "no marvel; for Satan himself is transformed into an angel of light."

On the other hand, parallel with the deepening apostasy, and probably actually stimulated by it, there was a widespread revival-not a revival in the sense of great ingatherings resulting from evangelistic effort, but a revival of interest in, and hunger for, the Word of God. This hunger, I say, was probably stimulated by the apostasy; for what will increase hunger like a famine? The sheep of Christ began to look up to their Shepherd for food, even for "every word that proceedeth out of the mouth of God." Men and women began insistently to ask, "Hath God really spoken? And, if so, what hath He said? What saith the Scriptures?"[791]

This quote reveals that God's people realized the crisis, not only did the faithful wrote apologetic defenses against what was occurring, such as *The Fundamentals*, to expose the grave danger but they also gathered the faithful together in defense of the orthodox faith (Phil. 1:3; Jude 3). W. B. Riley, a well-known Baptist leader of the time, declared in his sermon, "The Great Divide, or Christ and the Present Crisis," that

The future will look back to the World Conference on Christian Fundamentals . . . as an event of more historical moment than the nailing up, at Wittenberg, of Martin Luther's ninety-vive theses. The hour has struck for the rise of a new Protestantism . . . But now the very denominations, blessed by the Reformation, are rapidly coming under the leadership of a new infidelity, known as "Modernism," the whole attitude of which is inimical both to the church and the Christ of God.[792]

The assembly issues a doctrinal declaration as follows:

THE DOCTRINAL STATEMENT OF THE WORLD CONFERENCE ON CHRISTIAN FUNDAMENTALS. MAY 25–31, 1919, IS AS FOLLOWS:

"Your committee on resolutions herewith submits the following report:

We regard it timely and altogether essential that this World Conference on Christian Fundamentals in Philadelphia should give expression to the faith

---

[791] *God Hath Spoken*, "Introduction," 7-9.

[792] William B. Riley, "The Great Divide, or Christ and the Present Crisis," in *God Hath Spoken*, 27.

for which it stands and we unite in declaring the following as our Doctrinal Statement:

I. We believe in the Scriptures of the Old and New Testaments as verbally inspired of God, and inerrant in the original writings, and that they are the supreme and final authority in faith and life.

II. We believe in one God, eternally existing in three persons, Father, Son and Holy Spirit.

III. We believe that Jesus Christ was begotten by the Holy Spirit, and born of the Virgin Mary, and is true God and true man.

IV. We believe that man was created in the image of God, that he sinned and thereby incurred not only physical death, but also that spiritual death which is separation from God, and that all human beings are born with a sinful nature, and, in the case of those who reach moral responsibility, become sinners in thought, word, and deed.

V. We believe that the Lord Jesus Christ died for our sins according to the Scriptures as a representative and substitutionary sacrifice; and that all who believe in Him are justified on the ground of his shed blood.

VI. We believe in the resurrection of the crucified body of our Lord, in His ascension into heaven, and in His present life there for us, as High Priest and Advocate.

VII. We believe in "that blessed hope," the personal, premillennial and imminent return of our Lord and Saviour Jesus Christ.

VIII. We believe that all who receive by faith the Lord Jesus Christ are born again of the Holy Spirit, and thereby become the children of God.

IX. We believe in the bodily resurrection of the just and the unjust, the everlasting blessedness of the saved, and the everlasting, conscious punishment of the lost."[793]

As a result of such warnings, the faithful broke away from mainline denominations and established their own Bible colleges and seminaries to preserve a faithful remnant. In subsequent years, scores of Bible schools and seminaries were launched by fundamentalists across America during this period of denominational decay. Moody Bible Institute was founded in 1886 by evangelist Dwight L. Moody. Lyman Stewart funded the production of *The Fundamentals* which heralded the founding of the Bible Institute of Los Angeles. By 1912, Torrey, coming from Moody Bible Institute, became Dean of the Bible Institute of Los Angeles. The warning of J. Gresham Machen that "as go the theological seminaries, so goes the church" struck deep at the heart of Bible-believing scholars everywhere: "many seminaries today *are* nurseries of unbelief; and because they are nurseries of unbelief the churches that they serve have become unbelieving churches too. As go the theological

---

[793] The Bible Conference Committee, *God Hath Spoken* (Philadelphia: Bible Conference Committee, 1919), 11-12.

seminaries, so goes the church."[794] In 1929, Machen was influential in founding Westminster Theological Seminary as a result of Princeton's direction.[795] Dallas Theological Seminary was founded in 1924[796] and Fuller Theological Seminary was founded in 1947 by Biola graduate, Charles E. Fuller along with Harold Ockenga. These are just a select few of the many schools founded by faithful men in this period. Many today in evangelicalism can trace their educational and denominational roots to this period of time wherein the church was in a period of severe decline among mainstream groups.

At the Turn of the Twenty-first Century . . . LESSONS SOON FORGOTTEN

After this strategic withdrawal by fundamentalists of the first generation who fought the battle to preserve Scripture from the onslaught of historical criticism as well as its subsequent searching for the historical Jesus, subsequent generations from fundamentalist groups became discontent with their isolation from liberal-dominated mainstream biblical scholarship.

Sadly, by the mid-1960s, history was repeating itself. Prominent voices were scolding fundamentalists for continued isolation and dialogue and interaction once again became the rallying cry.[797] Carl F. H. Henry's criticisms struck deep, "The preoccupation of fundamentalists with the errors of modernism, and neglect of schematic presentations of the evangelical alternative, probably gave neo-orthodoxy its great opportunity in the Anglo-Saxon world...If Evangelicals do not overcome their preoccupation with negative criticism of contemporary theological deviations at the expense of the construction of preferable alternatives to these, they will not be much of a doctrinal force in the decade ahead."[798]

Echoing similar statements, George Eldon Ladd (1911-1982) of Fuller Theological Seminary became a zealous champion of modern critical methods, arguing that the two-source hypothesis should be accepted "as a literary fact" and that form criticism "has thrown considerable light on the nature of the Gospels and the traditions they employ" adding, "Evangelical scholars should be willing to accept

---

[794] J. Gresham Machen, *The Christian Faith in the Modern World* (Grand Rapids; Eerdmans, 1965 [1936]), 65.

[795] For a revealing look at Machen's struggle, see J. Gresham Machen, *Christianity and Liberalism* (Grand Rapids: Eerdmans, 1946 [1923]); idem. *The Virgin Birth of Christ.* Second Edition (New York and London: Harper & Brothers, 1932 [1930]); idem. *What is Faith?* (Grand Rapids: Eerdmans, 1946 [1925]).

[796] For a recent recounting of the history of Dallas Theological Seminary, see John D. Hannah, *An Uncommon Union: Dallas Theological Seminary and American Evangelicalism* (Grand Rapids: Zondervan, 2009).

[797] This section on the 21st Century is excerpted from F. David Farnell, "Searching for the Historical Jesus: Does History Matter to Neo-Evangelicals?," in *The Jesus Quest*, 421-466.

[798] Carl F. H. Henry, *Jesus of Nazareth, Savior and Lord* (London: Tyndale, 1970 (1966), 9.

this light."[799]   Indeed, for Ladd, critical methods have derived great benefit for evangelicals, "it has shed great light on the historical side of the Bible; and these historical discoveries are valid for all Bible students even though the presuppositions of the historical-critical method have often been hostile to an evangelical view of the Bible. Contemporary evangelicals often overlook this important fact when they condemn the critical method as such; for even while they condemn historical criticism, they are constantly reaping the benefits of its discoveries and employing critical tools."[800] Ladd asserts, "One must not forget that . . . everyday tools of good Bible study are the product of the historical-critical method."[801] George Ladd catalogued the trend of a "substantial group of scholars" whose background was in the camp of "fundamentalism" who had now been trained "in Europe as well as in our best universities" and were "deeply concerned with serious scholarship."[802] He also chided fundamentalists for their "major preoccupation" with defending "inerrancy of the Bible in its most extreme form," but contributing "little of creative thinking to the current debate."[803]   Although Ladd acknowledged that historical-critical ideology was deeply indebted for its operation in the Enlightenment and the German scholarship that created it openly admitted its intention of "dissolving orthodoxy's identification of the Gospel with Scripture,"[804] Ladd sent many of his students for subsequent study in Britain and Europe in order to enlarge the influence of conservatives, the latter of which influence was greatly responsible for the fundamentalist split at the turn of the twentieth century.[805]

Today, Ladd serves as the recognized paradigm for current attitudes and approaches among evangelical historical-critical scholarship in encouraging evangelical education in British and Continental institutions as well as the adoption and participation in historical criticism to some form or degree, actions which

---

[799] George Eldon Ladd, *NT and Criticism* (Grand Rapids: Eerdmans, 1967), 141, 168-169.

[800] Ibid., 10.

[801] Ladd offers two examples: Kittel and Friedrich, *Theological Dictionary of the New Testament* and Arndt, Gingrich, Bauer and Danker, *A Greek-English Lexicon of the New Testament*; Ladd, *NT and Criticism*, 11.

[802] George E. Ladd, "The Search for Perspective," *Interpretation* XXV (1971), 47.

[803] Ladd, "The Search for Perspective," 47. In a hotly debated book, Harold Lindsell in the mid-1970s detailed the problems facing Fuller, the Southern Baptist Convention and other Christian institutions due to the encroachment of historical criticism from European influence. See Harold Lindsell, "The Strange Case of Fuller Theological Seminary," in *The Battle for the Bible* (Grand Rapids: Zondervan, 1976), 106-121. Marsden's book also covers this period in *Reforming Fundamentalism* (Grand Rapids: Eerdmans, 1987).

[804] Ladd, "The Search for Perspective, 49 cf. Ladd's citing of this admission by Ernst Käsemann may be found in the latter's, *Essays on New Testament Themes* (London: SCM, 1964), 54-62.

[805] An example of one of Ladd's students is the late Robert Guelich who wrote *The Sermon on the Mount, A Foundation for Understanding* (Waco, TX: Word, 1982). Guelich promoted an exegesis "that . . . makes use of the literary critical tools including text, source, form, tradition, redaction, and structural criticism" and goes on to assert "for many to whom the Scriptures are vital the use of these critical tools has historically been more 'destructive' than 'constructive.' But one need not discard the tool because of its abuse."

previously were greatly responsible for the fundamentalist-modernist split.[806] Lessons from what caused the last theological meltdown had long been forgotten or carelessly disregarded.[807]

Yet, significantly, Ladd had drawn a line for his scholarly participation that he would not cross. Ladd (d. 1982) lived during the second "search for the 'historical Jesus'" and had correctly perceived, "The historical-critical method places severe limitations upon its methodology before it engages in a quest for the historical Jesus. It has decided in advance the kind of Jesus it must find—or at least the kind of Jesus it may not find, the Jesus portrayed in the Gospels" and "If the Gospel portrait is trustworthy, then 'the historical Jesus' never existed in history, only in the critical reconstructions of the scientific historians. A methodology which prides itself in its objectivity turns out to be in the grip of dogmatic philosophical ideas about the nature of history."[808] Ladd countered, "[i]n sum, the historical-critical method is not an adequate method to interpret the theology of the New Testament because its presuppositions limit its findings to the exclusion of the central biblical message." Instead, Ladd recognized the contribution of a "historical-theological" method of theology based on the *Heilsgeschichte* ("salvation history") approach that takes the New Testament as serious history and said, "[m]y own understanding of New Testament Theology is distinctly *heilsgeschichtlich*."[809]

In 1976, a book came on the scene that sent massive shock waves throughout the evangelical movement: *The Battle for the Bible* by Harold Lindsell.[810] Lindsell catalogued what he perceived was and alarming departure from the doctrine of inerrancy among evangelicals. Around this same time, Francis Schaeffer had argued, "Holding to a strong view of Scripture or not holding to it is the watershed of the evangelical world."[811] Lindsell catalogued departures from inerrancy by the Lutheran Missouri Synod, the Southern Baptists, and other groups. He listed what he perceived as deviations that resulted when inerrancy is denied as well as how

---

[806] Mark Noll conducted a personal poll/survey among evangelicals and has, as a result, described Ladd as "the most widely influential figure on the current generation of evangelical Bible scholars." Ladd was "most influential" among scholars in the Institute for Biblical Research and was placed just behind John Calvin as "most influential" among scholars in the Evangelical Theological Society. See Noll, 97, 101, 112-114 [note especially p. 112 for this quote], 116, 121, 159-163, 211-226. Moreover, Marsden described Noll's book, *Between Faith and Criticism*, as making "a major contribution toward understanding twentieth-century evangelical scholarship." See George M. Marsden, *Reforming Fundamentalism* , 250 fn. 9. Since Noll marked out Ladd as the outstanding figure influencing the recent paradigm shift in twentieth-century evangelical scholarship toward favoring historical-critical methods and since Marsden promotes Noll's book as making "a major contribution toward understanding twentieth-century evangelical scholarship," this paper uses Ladd as the outstanding paradigmic example, as well as typical representative, of this drift among evangelicals toward historical-critical ideologies that favor literary dependency hypotheses.

[807] For further historical details, see F. David Farnell, "The Philosophical and Theological Bent of Historical Criticism, in *The Jesus Crisis*, 85-131.

[808] George E. Ladd, "The Search for Perspective," *Interpretation* XXV (1971) 51.

[809] Ladd, "The Search for Perspective," 47.

[810] Harold Lindsell, *The Battle for the Bible* (Grand Rapids: Zondervan, 1976).

[811] Francis A. Schaeffer, *The Great Evangelical Crisis* (Wheaton, IL: Crossway, 1984) 51.

the infection of denial spreads to other matters within evangelicalism. Because Lindsell was one of the founding members at Fuller Seminary, he especially focused on what he felt were troubling events at Fuller Seminary regarding the "watershed" issue of inerrancy.[812] Most strategically, Lindsell attributed the "use of historical-critical method" as a foundational cause of the destruction of inerrancy among denominations. He noted, "there are also those who call themselves evangelicals who have embraced this [historical-critical] methodology. The presuppositions of this methodology . . . go far beyond mere denial of biblical infallibility. They tear at the heart of Scripture, and include a denial of the supernatural."[813] In *The Bible in the Balance*, Lindsell dedicated a whole chapter to historical criticism, labeling it "The Bible's Deadly Enemy":

> Anyone who thinks the historical-critical method is neutral is misinformed . . . It appears to me that modern evangelical scholars (and I may have been guilty of this myself) have played fast and loose with the term because they wanted acceptance by academia. They seem too often to desire to be members of the club which is nothing more than practicing an inclusiveness that undercuts the normativity of the evangelical position. This may be done, and often is, under the illusion that by this method the opponents of biblical inerrancy can be won over to the evangelical viewpoint. But practical experience suggests that rarely does this happen and the cost of such an approach is too expensive, for it gives credence and leads respectability to a method which is the deadly enemy of theological orthodoxy.[814]

As an interpretive ideology, Lindsell noted that both form and redaction criticism are destroying the historical trustworthiness of the Gospels. He noted: "When the conclusion is reached that the Gospels do not reflect true history the consequences are mind-boggling. We simply do not know who the real Jesus was. This undermines Scripture and destroys the Christian faith as a historical vehicle. It opens the door wide to a thousand vagaries and brings us right back to trying to find the canon within a canon."[815]

Reaction to Lindsell's first book was exceedingly swift.[816] Some praised it while others vilified it. In response to the book, many concerned evangelicals began to form what would become known as the "International Council on Biblical Inerrancy" in 1977 that would produce the Chicago Statements on Biblical Inerrancy (1978) and Hermeneutics (1982) as a response.[817] Lindsell himself catalogued the reaction in a second companion volume, *The Bible in the Balance*. Donald Dayton

---

[812] Lindsell, *The Battle for the Bible*, 23.

[813] Ibid., 204.

[814] Lindsell, *The Bible in the Balance*, 283.

[815] Ibid., 297

[816] For a more detailed history on this period, see chapters 1-3 detailing the developmental, historical details surrounding the International Council on Biblical Inerrancy, Norman L. Geisler and William C. Roach, *Defending Inerrancy* (Grand Rapids: Baker, 2011), 17-42.

[817] "Taking a Stand on Scripture," *Christianity Today* (December 30, 1977), 25.

recounted the fear that it produced among evangelicals in the following terms, "Evangelicals are jittery, fearing Lindsell's book might herald a new era of faculty purges and organizational splits—a reply of earlier conflicts, this time rending the evangelical world asunder."[818]   Dayton later wrote that "'Evangelical' and 'fundamentalist' controversies over scriptural authority and biblical inerrancy seem endless" citing Lindsell's works as continuing to disturb the evangelical world.[819]

In 1979, then Fuller professor Jack B. Rogers and Donald K. McKim responded directly to Lindsell's assertion that plenary, verbal inspiration was the orthodox position of the church in their *The Authority and Interpretation of the Bible* by attempting to argue that Lindsell's position on inerrancy was inaccurate.[820]   They argued, "The central Christian tradition included the concept of accommodation"[821] and that modern views of inerrancy did not reflect the church's historic position, but resulted from "extreme positions" taken both from fundamentalism and modernism" "regarding the Bible."[822] Lindsell's and many others' views of inerrancy, Rogers and McKim alleged, were from "the old Princeton position of Hodge and Warfield" who had drunk deep from "Scottish common sense realism" rather than reflecting the historic position of the church.[823]   They noted, "Our hypothesis is that the peculiar twists of American history have served to distort our view of both the central Christian tradition [concerning inerrancy] and especially of its Reformed Branch."[824] They went on to note:

> The function, or purpose, of the Bible was to bring people into a saving relationship with God through Jesus Christ. The Bible was not used as an encyclopedia of information on all subjects. The principle theological teachers of the church argued that the Bible not be used to judge matters of science, for example, astronomy. Scripture's use was clearly for salvation, not science. The forms of the Bible's language and its cultural context were open to scholarly investigation. The central tradition included the concept of accommodation . . . God had condescended and adapted himself in Scripture to our ways of thinking and speaking . . . To erect a standard, modern technical precision in language as the hallmark of biblical authority was totally foreign to the foundation shared by the early church."[825]

---

[818] Donald W. Dayton, "'The Battle for the Bible': Renewing the Inerrancy Debate," *Christian Century* (November 10, 1976), 976.

[819] Donald W. Dayton, "The Church in the World, The 'Battle for the Bible' Rages On," *Theology Today* (January 1, 1980), 79.

[820] Jack B. Rogers and Donald K. McKim, *The Authority and Interpretation of the Bible: An Historical Approach* (San Francisco: Harper & Ro2, 1979). Rogers and McKim relied heavily upon the work of Ernest R. Sandeen, *The Roots of Fundamentalism: British and American Millenarianism 1800-1930* (Chicago: University of Chicago, 1970).

[821] Rogers and McKim, "Introduction," xxii.

[822] Ibid," xxiii.

[823] Ibid., 289-298.

[824] Ibid., xxii.

[825] Ibid., xxii.

The Bible was to be viewed as reliable in matters of faith and practice but not in all matters. In 2009, as an apparent result of his approach to Scripture, Rogers released *Jesus, The Bible and Homosexuality*, that calls for evangelical tolerance and acceptance of homosexuality, gay, lesbian, and transgender issues not only for church membership but for ordination in ministry.[826]

As a direct response to Rogers and McKim, John Woodbridge published his *Biblical Authority: A Critique of the Rogers/McKim Proposal* as an effective critique of their proposal.[827] Lindsell's negative historical take on problems has received counter-balancing by Marsden's *Reforming Fundamentalism* produced in 1987. By 1978, conservative evangelicals who knew the importance of inerrancy as a doctrinal watershed felt the need to produce *The Chicago Statement on Biblical Inerrancy* and produced another on *Hermeneutics* in 1982 to reaffirm their historical positions in these areas as a response to Rogers' and McKim's work.[828]

As a direct consequence of these events, Robert Gundry asked to resign from membership of ETS in 1982 due to his involvement in alleged de-historicizing of Matthew as reflected in his commentary *Matthew: A Commentary on His Literary and Theological Art*.[829] His removal, as will be seen, still raises strong feelings among evangelical scholarship. Gundry contended that Matthew's story of the slaughtering of the babies in Bethlehem should not be seen as historical but as a type of allegorical, midrashic device or illustration.[830] Genre was now being used by evangelicals as an excuse or hermeneutic to de-historicize the plain, normal sense of the Gospels. Using redaction critical hermeneutics centering in genre issues about Matthew 2:7-8, he argued that the theological editor of Matthew redacted/edited the offering of two turtledoves or two young pigeons in the temple (Luke 2:24) and transformed it into Herod's slaughter of the babies in Bethlehem.[831] As another example, Gundry also asserted that Matthew transformed the Jewish shepherds that appear in Luke 2 into Gentile Magi[832] and had also changed the traditional manger into a house. For Gundry, then, the nonexistent house was where the nonexistent Magi found Jesus on the occasion of their non-visit to Bethlehem. Gundry's use of genre issues based in historical-critical ideology (redaction criticism) as a means to negate the historicity of events that were always considered genuine historical events by the orthodox community from the beginnings of the church alarmed the vast majority (74%) of evangelicals in the Evangelical Theological Society.

---

[826] Jack Rogers, *Jesus, the Bible, and Homosexuality*. Revised and Expanded Edition (Louisville, KY: Westminster John Knox, 2009).

[827] John D. Woodbridge, *Biblical Authority, A Critique of the Rogers/McKim Proposal* (Grand Rapids: Zondervan, 1982).

[828] "Chicago Statement on Biblical Inerrancy," *JETS* 21/4 (December 1978) 289-296 and "The Chicago Statement on Biblical Hermeneutics," *JETS* 25/4 (December 1982) 397-401.

[829] Robert H. Gundry, *Matthew: A Commentary on His Literary and Theological Art* (Grand Rapids: Eerdmans, 1982).

[830] Ibid., 34-35.

[831] Ibid.

[832] Ibid., 31.

Another result of Lindsell's works in addition to the formation of ICBI was James Barr's response as penned in his two strategic works *Fundamentalism* and *Beyond Fundamentalism*. In 1977, Barr composed his *Fundamentalism* as a direct reaction against the "fundamentalism" of Lindsell, noting in his foreword: "It is not surprising that, in a time of unusual ferment and fresh openness among evangelicals, there should appear a book like Harold Lindsell's *The Battle for the Bible* . . . insisting on a hard position of total inerrancy of the Bible."[833] Instead, Barr praised Jack Rogers' work, *Confessions of a Conservative Evangelical,*[834] as "a work indicating an openness to new trends among evangelicals" and characterized it as "an interesting expression of a search for an evangelical tradition different from the dominant fundamentalist one."[835]

In *Fundamentalism*, Barr urged evangelicals to separate from and reject fundamentalism's characteristics in three specific areas:

(a) A very strong emphasis on the inerrancy of the Bible, the

absence from it of any sort of error.

(b) A strong hostility to modern theology and methods, results and

implications of modern critical study of the Bible.

(c) An assurance that those who do not share their religious

viewpoint are not really 'true Christians' at all.[836]

In his 1984 work, *Beyond Fundamentalism*, Barr again continued to urge evangelicals to continue separation from fundamentalism in these areas: "This [work] seeks to offer help to those who have grown up in the world of fundamentalism or have become committed to it but who have in the end come to feel that it is a prison from which they must escape."[837]

Lindsell's work, as well as ICBI, continued to send shockwaves through evangelical society. In 1982, Alan Johnson in his presidential address to ETS asked through analogy whether higher criticism was "Egyptian gold or pagan precipice" and reached the conclusion that "the refinement of critical methodologies under the

---

[833] James Barr, "Foreword to the American Edition," in *Fundamentalism* (Philadelphia: Westminster, 1977), vi.

[834] Jack Rogers, *Confessions of a Conservative Evangelical* (Philadelphia: Westminster 1974).

[835] Barr, "Foreword to the American Edition," in *Fundamentalism*, iv.

[836] Ibid., 1.

[837] James Barr, "Preface," in *Beyond Fundamentalism* (Philadelphia: Westminster, 1984), vii.

magisterium of an inerrant scriptural authority can move us gently into a deeper appreciation of sacred Scripture."[838]

Craig Blomberg, in 1984, soon after the ICBI statements, raised questions regarding biblical interpretation in the Gospels, arguing for genre distinctions. In reference to the story of the coin in the fish's mouth in Matthew 17:24-27, Blomberg defended Robert Gundry's midrashic approach to the Gospels in the following terms:

> Is it possible, even inherently probable, that the NT writers at least in part never intended to have their miracle stories taken as historical or factual and that their original audiences probably recognized this? If this sounds like the identical reasoning that enabled Robert Gundry to adopt his midrashic interpretation of Matthew while still affirming inerrancy, that is because it is the same. The problem will not disappear simply because one author [Gundry] is dealt with *ad hominem* . . . how should evangelicals react? Dismissing the sociological view on the grounds that the NT miracles present themselves as historical gets us nowhere. So do almost all the other miracle stories of antiquity. Are we to believe them all?[839]

Barr's criticisms also stung deeply among evangelicals. At an annual Evangelical Theological Society meeting in Santa Clara, California, in 1997, Moisés Silva, who himself had studied under Barr ("my admiration for Barr knows no bounds"), chided conservative scholarship for their lack of openness to methods of modern critical in his presidential address entitled, "Can Two Walk Together Unless They Be Agreed? Evangelical Theology and Biblical Scholarship."[840] Silva took his mentor, Barr, to task for misrepresenting evangelicals by failing to notice that many evangelicals were open to historical-critical hermeneutics, citing not only recent evangelicals who espoused critical methods but also earlier evangelicals like Machen, who took "seriously the liberal teachings of his day."[841] Silva asserted that "there is the more direct approach of many of us who are actually engaged in critical Biblical scholarship."[842] Thus, by 1997, many evangelicals were openly disregarding Lindsell's warning about historical criticism.

The next year, in 1998, Norman Geisler, took quite the opposite approach and warned evangelicals regarding the negative presuppositions of historical-critical ideologies in his "Beware of Philosophy," citing lessons from history as

---

[838] Alan F. Johnson, "Historical-Critical Method: Egyptian Gold or Pagan Precipice," *JETS* 26/1 (March 1983) 3-15. See also, Carl F. H. Henry, "The Uses and Abuses of Historical Criticism," vol. IV: God Who Speaks and Shows, in *God Revelation and Authority* (Waco, TX: Word, 1979), 385-404.

[839] Craig L. Blomberg, "New Testament miracles and Higher Criticism: Climbing Up the Slippery Slope," *JETS* 27/4 (December 1984): 436.

[840] Moisés Silva, "Can Two Walk Together Unless They Be Agreed? Evangelical Theology and Biblical Scholarship "*JETS* 41/1 (March 1998): 3-16 (quote from p. 4).

[841] Ibid., 8.

[842] Ibid., 10.

demonstrating their negative consequences.[843]   In his address, Geisler featured a 1998 work entitled, *The Jesus Crisis*, that detailed growing evangelical involvement in historical-critical ideologies like questing for the "historical Jesus."   Just like Lindsell's books, *The Jesus Crisis* stirred up a hornet's nest of controversy among evangelicals.   To say the least, Geisler's address, as well as his praise for The Jesus Crisis, revealed a significant cleavage within evangelicalism that had developed since ICBI.   While some praised *The Jesus Crisis* as needing to be written,[844] other evangelicals disdained the work as strident, fundamentalist rhetoric that was closed-minded to a judicial use of historical criticism.[845]   Darrell Bock reacted to *The Jesus Crisis* with the following: "As a whole, *The Jesus Crisis* displays a lack of discernment about the history of Gospels study.   The book should have given a more careful discussion of difficult details in the Gospels and the views tied to them, especially when inerrantists critiqued by the book are portrayed as if they were denying the accuracy of the Gospels when in fact they are defending it."[846]   Bock contended, "Careful consideration also does not support the claim that even attempting to use critical methods judiciously leads automatically and inevitably to denial of the historicity of the Gospels. Unfortunately, this work overstates its case at this basic level and so places blame for the bibliological crisis at some wrong evangelical doorsteps."[847]

In a highly irregular move for the Evangelical Theological Society that disallowed book reviews in the form of journal articles, Grant Osborne was given an opportunity in the next issue of *JETS* to counter Geisler's presidential address, wherein Geisler's address as well as *The Jesus Crisis* were criticized, saying, "the tone is too harsh and grating, the positions too extreme."[848]   In 2004, Geisler, a world-renown Christian apologist and long-time member of ETS, decried the society's acceptance of open theists among its ranks and withdrew his membership, perceiving a drift in the wrong direction for the Evangelical Theological Society of which he was a founding member.   Grant Osborne, however, in his use of redaction-critical hermeneutics, advocated that the Great Commission was not originally spoken by Jesus in the way that Matthew had recorded it, but that "It

---

[843] See also Norman L. Geisler, Ed. *Biblcal Inerrancy An Analysis of its Philosophical Roots* (Grand Rapids: Zondervan, 1981).   The book gives the philosophical background to ideas that lead inevitably to a denial of inerrancy and result in a supposition of errancy regarding Scripture.

[844] See the back cover page of the work where some called it "a blockbuster" and "the best up-to-date analysis in print of the dangerous drift of evangelical scholarship into negative higher criticism"— Robert L. Thomas and F. David Farnell, *The Jesus Crisis: The Inroads of Historical Criticism into Evangelical Scholarship* (Grand Rapids: Kregel, 1998).

[845] Osborne's article constitutes a criticism of not only Geisler but *The Jesus Crisis*, Grant Osborne, "Historical Criticism and the Evangelical," *JETS* 42/2 (June 1999): 193-210.

[846] Darrell L. Bock, "Review of The Jesus Crisis," *Bibliotheca Sacra* 157 (April-June 2000): 232.

[847] Bock, "Review of *The Jesus Crisis*," 236.

[848] Osborne, "Historical Criticism and the Evangelical," 209.

seems most likely that at some point the tradition or Matthew expanded an original monadic formula."[849] He later reversed his position in the following terms:

A misunderstanding of my position with respect to this, in fact, has led to widespread dissatisfaction regarding my approach to the triadic baptismal formula of Matt 28:19. There I posited that Matthew had possibly expanded an original monadic formula in order "to interpret the true meaning of Jesus' message for his own day . . . However, Matthew has faithfully reproduced the intent and meaning of what Jesus said."[23] In my next article mentioned above I clarified this further by stating, "The interpretation must be based on the original words and meaning imparted by Jesus."[24] Here I would like to clarify it further by applying the implications of my second article to the first. I did not mean that Matthew had freely composed the triadic formula and read it back onto the lips of Jesus. Rather, Jesus had certainly (as in virtually every speech in the NT) spoken for a much longer time and had given a great deal more teaching than reported in the short statement of Matt 28:18-20. In it I believe that he probably elucidated the trinitarian background behind the whole speech. This was compressed by Matthew in the form recorded. Acts and Paul then may have followed the formula itself from the commission speech, namely the monadic form.[850]

In 2001, Craig Blomberg, in his article "Where Should Twenty-First Century Biblical Scholarship," decried *The Jesus Crisis*: "It is hard to imagine a book such as Thomas and Farnell's *The Jesus Crisis* ever appearing in Britain, much less being commended by evangelical scholars as it has been by a surprising number in this country. Avoiding Thomas's and Farnell's misguided separatism and regular misrepresentation of others' works, a higher percentage of us need to remain committed to engaging the larger, scholarly world in contextually sensitive ways that applaud as much as possible perspectives that we do not adopt while nevertheless preserving evangelical distinctives."[851] Blomberg went on to praise his own brand of scholarship: "It still distresses me . . . how many religious studies departments in the U.S. (or their libraries) are unaware of the breadth and depth of evangelical biblical scholarship. This situation need not remain this way, as witnessed by the fact that this is an area in which our British counterparts have made considerably more progress in, at times, even less-promising contexts."[852]

---

[849] Grant Osborne, "Redaction Criticism and the Great Commission: A Case Study Toward a Biblical Understanding of Inerrancy," *Journal of the Evangelical Theological Society* 19/2 (March 1, 1976): 80.

[850] Grant R. Osborne, "The Evangelical and Redaction Criticism: Critique and Methodology," *Journal of the Evangelical Theological Society* 22/4 (December 1979): 311; cf. idem. "Great Commission," 80, 85; idem. "The Evangelical and *Traditionsgeschichte*," *Journal of the Evangelical Theological Society* 21/2 (June, 1978): 128.

[851] Craig Blomberg, "Where Should Twenty-First Century Scholarship Be Heading?," in *Bulletin for Biblical Research* 11.2 (2001): 172. This article was also published in "The past, present and future of American Evangelical theological scholarship," in *Solid Ground* (Leicester: Apollos, 2000) 314-315.

[852] Craig Blomberg, "Where Should Twenty-First Century Scholarship Be Heading?, 172.

Such a response by Blomberg serves as an illustration of the startling erosion of inerrancy among New Testament scholars, especially those who have been schooled on the European continent. Many of these European-trained scholars ignore the lessons of history learned by evangelicals at the turn of the twentieth century and as highlighted in the Chicago Statements of 1978 and 1982. Significantly, Blomberg and those agreeing with him exemplify the significant, substantive shift in hermeneutics that these evangelicals are now engaging in. The Chicago Statement on Inerrancy in 1978 expressly commended the grammatico-historical approach in Article XVIII:

> We affirm that the text of Scripture is to be interpreted by grammatico-historical exegesis, taking account of its literary forms and devices, and that Scripture is to interpret Scripture. We deny the legitimacy of any treatment of the text or quest for sources lying behind it that leads to relativizing, de-historicizing, or discounting its teaching, or rejecting its claims to authorship.

Why did they commend the grammatico-historical approach? Because the men who expressed these two watershed statements had experienced the history of interpretive degeneration among mainstream churches and seminaries ("As go the theological seminaries, so goes the church")[853] in terms of dismissing the Gospels as historical records due to historical-critical ideologies. Blomberg, instead, now advocates "The Historical-Critical/Grammatical View"[854] of hermeneutics for evangelicals that constitutes an alarming, and especially unstable, blend of historical-critical ideologies with the grammatico-historical hermeneutic. Blomberg argues for a "both-and-and-and" position of combining grammatico-historical method with that of historical-critical ideologies.[855]

Blomberg chose to ignore *The Jesus Crisis* (1998) that has already catalogued the evangelical disaster that such a blend of grammatico-historical and historical-critical elements precipitates in interpretive approaches.[856] Stemming from this blending of these two elements are the following sampling of hermeneutical de-historicizing among evangelicals: The author of Matthew, not Jesus, created the Sermon on the Mount; the commissioning of the Twelve in Matthew 10 is a compilation of instructions collected and gathered but not spoken on a single occasion; Matthew 13 and Mark 4 are collections or anthologies not spoken by Jesus on a single occasion; Jesus did not preach the Olivet Discourse in its entirety as presented in the Gospels; the scribes and Pharisees were good people whom Matthew portrayed in a bad light; the magi of Matthew 2 are fictional characters; Jesus did not speak all of the parables in Matthew 5:3-12.[857]

---

[853] J. Gresham Machen, *The Christian Faith in the Modern World* (Grand Rapids: Eerdmans, 1936) 65.

[854] Craig L. Blomberg, "The Historical-Critical/Grammatical View," in *Biblical Hermeneutics Five Views (Downers Grove: IVP, 2012): 27-47.*

[855] Blomberg, "The Historical-Critical/Grammatical View," 28.

[856] See Robert L. Thomas and F. David Farnell, *The Jesus Crisis*, noting especially the "Introduction The Jesus Crisis: What is it?," 13-34.

[857] Ibid., 15.

This section also tellingly reveals Blomberg's "both/and" approach of combining grammatico-historical with historical-critical, a telling admission of the strong impact of British academic training on evangelical hermeneutics, as well as his willingness to create a bridge between Christian orthodoxy and Mormonism. While Blomberg is irenic and embracing with Mormons, he has great hostility toward those who uphold the "fundamentals" of Scripture.

In his article on "The Historical-Critical/Grammatical" hermeneutic, he asserts that historical criticism can be "shorn" of its "antisupernatural presuppositions that the framers of that method originally employed" and eagerly embraces "source, form, tradition and redaction criticism" as "*all essential* tools for understanding the contents of the original document, its formation and origin, its literary genre and subgenres, the authenticity of the historical material it includes, and its theological or ideological emphases and distinctives."[858] He labels the "The Historical-Critical/Grammatical" approach "the necessary foundation on which all other approaches must build."[859] However, history is replete with negative examples of those who attempted this unstable blend, from the neologians in Griesbach's day to that of Michael Licona's book currently under discussion (see below).[860] Baird, in his *History of New Testament Research*, commented: "The neologians did not deny the validity of divine revelation but assigned priority to reason and natural theology. While faith in God, morality, and immortality were affirmed, older dogmas such as the Trinity, predestination, and the inspiration of Scripture were seriously compromised . . . The neologians . . . appropriated the results of the historical-critical work of Semler and Michaelis."[861]

Interestingly, Craig Blomberg blames books like Harold Lindsell's *Battle for the Bible* (1976) and such books as *The Jesus Crisis* for people leaving the faith because of their strong stance on inerrancy as a presupposition. In an online interview conducted by Justin Taylor in 2008, Blomberg responded this way to books that hold to a firm view of inerrancy. The interviewer asked, "Are there certain mistaken hermeneutical presuppositions made by conservative evangelicals that play into the hands of liberal critics?" Blomberg replied,

> Absolutely. And one of them follows directly from the last part of my answer to your last question. The approach, famously supported back in 1976 by Harold Lindsell in his *Battle for the Bible* (Zondervan), that it is an all-or-nothing approach to Scripture that we must hold, is both profoundly mistaken and deeply dangerous. No historian worth his or her salt functions that way. I personally believe that if inerrancy means "without error according to what most people in a given culture

---

[858] Blomberg, "The Historical-Critical/Grammatical View," 46-47. Italics and bold added.

[859]Ibid.," 47.

[860] For Griesbach and his association with Neologians as well as its impact on his synoptic "solution," see F. David Farnell, "How Views of Inspiration Have Impacted Synoptic Problem Discussion," *TMSJ* 13/1 (Spring 2002): 33-64.

[861] William *The History of New Testament Research: From deism to Tübingen* (Philadelphia: Fortress, 1992) 116.

would have called an error" then the biblical books are inerrant in view of the standards of the cultures in which they were written. But, despite inerrancy being the touchstone of the largely American organization called the Evangelical Theological Society, there are countless evangelicals in the States and especially in other parts of the world who hold that the Scriptures are inspired and authoritative, even if not inerrant, and they are not sliding down any slippery slope of any kind. I can't help but wonder if inerrantist evangelicals making inerrancy the watershed for so much has not, unintentionally, contributed to pilgrimages like Ehrman's. Once someone finds one apparent mistake or contradiction that they cannot resolve, then they believe the Lindsells of the world and figure they have to chuck it all. What a tragedy![862]

To Blomberg, apparently anyone who advocates inerrancy as traditionally advocated by Lindsell is responsible for people leaving the faith.

It is also the hermeneutic of historical criticism through which Blomberg developed his globalization hermeneutical approach. In a very telling article of Blomberg's historical-grammatical hermeneutical approach, he advocates "The Globalization of Biblical Interpretation: A Test Case— John 3-4."[863] This "hermeneutic" clearly has an *a priori* agenda that is imposed on the text when Blomberg summarizes the approach as "asking new questions of the text, particularly in light of the experiences of marginalization of a large percent of the world's population."[864] From Blomberg's perspective "[s]tudents of scripture . . . have realized that the traditional historical-critical interpretation has been disproportionately Eurocentric and androcentric . . . and various new methodologies have been developed to correct this imbalance."[865] That such a conclusion has any substantial basis in fact, beyond opinion, is not substantiated by the article. Apparently, for Blomberg, the goal of exegesis and interpretation is not to understand the text as was originally intended but to search the biblical text for an already prescribed agenda of "globalization." This is telling, for under this scheme the meaning and significance of the biblical text would be its usefulness in promoting an agenda that is already predetermined, i.e., subjecting Scripture to the shifting sands of interpretation that Blomberg identifies as follows: "issues of liberation theology, feminism, religious pluralism, the disparity between the world's rich and poor, and contextualization of biblical material."[866]

---

[862] See http://thegospelcoalition.org/blogs/justintaylor/2008/03/26/interview-with-craig-blomberg/ Accessed on 5/25/2013.

[863] Craig L. Blomberg, "The Globalization of Biblical Interpretation: A Test Case John 3-4," *Bulletin of Biblical Research* 5 (1995): 1-15.

[864] Ibid., 1.

[865] Ibid.

[866] Blomberg, "The Globalization of Biblical Interpretation," 2; cf. Craig L. Blomberg, "The Implications of Globalization for Biblical Understanding," in *Globalization*. Eds. Frazer Evans, Robert A. Evans, and David A. Roozen (Maryknoll: Orbis, 1993), 213-28; 241-45.

In response to Blomberg's assertions regarding such newly developing issues, one cannot help but be reminded of Paul's own warning to the Ephesian church about the purpose of teaching and preaching by God's shepherd's over the church:

> And He gave some *as* apostles, and some *as* prophets, and some *as* evangelists, and some *as* pastors and teachers, for the equipping of the saints for the work of service, to the building up of the body of Christ; until we all attain to the unity of the faith, and of the knowledge of the Son of God, to a mature man, to the measure of the stature which belongs to the fullness of Christ. As a result, we are no longer to be children, tossed here and there by waves and carried about by every wind of doctrine, by the trickery of men, by craftiness in deceitful scheming; but speaking the truth in love, we are to grow up in all *aspects* into Him who is the head, *even* Christ. (Eph 4:11-15)

Here Paul clearly warns the Church against subjecting the Word of God to "waves" and "winds" of every doctrine and by application, whatever trends may predominate society through the centuries until Jesus' return. A question left unanswered by Blomberg is what happens to the imposition of such interpretation of the text when the next fade or "ism" replaces these emphases. Nor have these emphases necessarily been subjected to Scripture to form any biblical basis whatsoever that they should be imposed on the text of Scripture *a priori* as interpretive principles. Second Corinthians 10:5 warns believers to take every thought captive.

Yet, where he teaches at Denver Seminary, the seminary has such an interpretive approach that it has embraced reflecting "a more central place in its [Denver Seminary's] curriculum . . . focusing on historical Christianity's mandate to worldwide mission" and "goes on to elaborate 'an empathetic understanding of the different genders, races, cultures, and religions to be able to contextualize the gospel more effectively,' 'increased application and promotion of biblical principles to such global issues as economic development, social justice, political systems, human rights, and international conflict,' and related concerns."[867] Blomberg argues "it is perhaps best to think of the globalization of biblical interpretation as the processes either of asking questions of the biblical passage which are not traditionally asked within a particular interpretive community or of allowing new answers, more supportive of the world's oppressed, to emerge from old questions out of a more careful exegesis of the text itself."[868] He asserts that "these new questions and answers are often suggested as we read the Bible through the eyes of the individuals quite different from ourselves."[869] How one can subjectively view the Bible through the eyes of other individuals is not explained but it does highlight the existentialist basis of the new hermeneutic (Ebeling, Fuchs) where truth rests, not in the text, but in the interpreter's subjective experience. Here also Blomberg makes a telling omission that his goal in globalization hermeneutics is not necessarily to elucidate

---

[867] "Final Report on the Globalization Project at Denver Seminary" (Denver: Denver Seminary, 1993), 2.

[868] Blomberg, "The Globalization of Biblical Interpretation," 3.

[869] Ibid.

original intent of the authors of Scripture but to devise interpretive decisions that are "more supportive of the world's oppressed."[870]

What is even more concerning is his application of these principles to the biblical text. One example must suffice in John 4 with the woman at the well. Here Blomberg's concern for reading feminist issues causes him to see the woman as a "victim rather than a whore" where he dismisses the idea that the woman was sexually promiscuous, which he terms "an unfounded assumption." Instead, Blomberg asserts that "[t]he fault could well have resided more with the men than with the woman; we simply have no way of knowing. That she was currently living with a man to whom she was not legally married might just as easily have stemmed from her fifth husband having abandoned here without a legal divorce and from her need to be joined to a man for legal and social protection."[871] Such an interpretation requires Blomberg to ignore the woman's summoning of the men of the village with the following words: "So the woman left her waterpot, and went into the city and said to the men, 'Come, see a man who told me all the things that I *have* done; this is not the Christ, is it?'" This latter confession is best understood as an admission that Jesus correctly knew the spiritual condition of her immoral lifestyle (cf. 4:18 where Jesus knows how many husbands she had. Otherwise, it is an empty statement apart from its moral implications.

What is patently obvious is that Blomberg's concern for sociological and political correctness greatly clouds his exegesis of John 3-4. Fortunately, Blomberg realizes that the passage remains "fundamentally Christocentric; Jesus is the principle personage in both passages" and that "the person and work of Christ subordinates all liberationist, feminist, and postmodernist readings, important as they may be."[872] Nevertheless, his assertion that "Biblical scholarship which does not yet acknowledge such 'metacriticism' lags behind the social sciences in this respect" is quite disturbing, for it opens up the proverbial "Pandora's box" for a host of foreign elements to be imposed on the biblical text, resulting in Scripture being reduced to a tool for the promotion of globalist and/or fleeting agendas that are not anchored to a grammatico-historical understanding of the Scriptures' content or meaning.

Evangelicals Join in the Third Quest

After decrying Geisler's presidential address as well as the warnings set forth in *The Jesus Crisis*, in 1999 evangelicals who embraced historical-critical ideologies began a significant endeavor at joining in a Third Quest for the "historical Jesus." Most evangelicals up to that time did not participate in the first or second quests, but this evangelical corroboration in searching was a decade-long process of engaging in the effort. In 2010, Darrell Bock and William Webb produced *Key Events in the Life of the Historical Jesus* that recorded the research of scholars associated with the Institute of Biblical Research (IBR). Operating from the position of post-modernistic historiography, this work asserted that only twelve events in the Gospels had the best chance of probably happening in history. In examining

---

[870] Ibid.

[871] Ibid., 12.

[872] Ibid., 14.

this work, one wonders whether Harold Lindsell's warning regarding historical-critical ideologies was not very prescient: "the use of the historical-critical method . . . leads, as night follows day, to the need for finding the canon within the canon." Lindsell labeled such a result as a "requirement" of historical criticism.[873] Interestingly, in 2010, Scot McKnight withdrew from the Third Search, citing similar reasoning: "a fundamental observation about all genuine historical Jesus studies: *Historical Jesus scholars construct what is in effect a fifth gospel.* The reconstructed Jesus is not identical to the canonical Jesus or the orthodox Jesus. He is the reconstructed Jesus, which means he is a 'new' Jesus." [874]

In a recent IBR article, "Faith and the Historical Jesus," Bock "defends the value of having mediated presentations of Jesus" as exhibited in the third search for the historical Jesus.[875] Bock comments, "For many evangelicals, especially lay evangelicals, the skepticism surrounding much of historical-Jesus work is to be shunned as a rejection of the Bible as the Word of God."[876] Apparently Bock believes that while some Bible students are limited in understanding and ability and, as a result of their educational deficiencies, might not appreciate Jesus research, some New Testament scholars who are as highly trained as he is can engage in the discussion, so long as "one must appreciate the nature of what historical-Jesus work seeks to achieve as well as the limitations such a historically oriented study operates under when it seeks to cross thousands of years to do its work."[877] The problem, for Bock, lies not in the historical-critical approach but in the skill, or lack of skill, of a researcher and realizing that such studies have limitations "in understanding and ability" in making a case for the New Testament traditions tied to Jesus.[878]

What is, however, even more fascinating is Robert Miller's reply to Bock's article supporting evangelical participation in searching for the "historical Jesus": "When It's Futile to Argue about the Historical Jesus."[879] Miller is an active member of the Society of Biblical Literature and a critic of evangelical participation in historiographical questions that the latter attempt to marginalize or limit in searching for the "historical Jesus." He argues that evangelicals who participate in these studies aren't consistent or critical enough in the historiographical principles needed for answers that academic scholarship is seeking: "I maintain that the arguments about the historical Jesus can be productive only among those who already agree on a number of contested questions about historiographical method and the nature of the Gospels. Therefore, debates about the historical Jesus that

---

[873] Lindsell, *The Bible in the Balance*, 292-293.

[874] Scott McKnight, "The Jesus We'll Never Know, Why scholarly attempts to discover the 'real' Jesus have failed. And why that's a good thing," *Christianity Today* (April 2010): 25.

[875] Darrell L. Bock, "Faith and the Historical Jesus: Does A Confessional Position and Respect for the Jesus Tradition Preclude Serious Historical Engagement?," *Journal for the Study of the Historical Jesus* 9 (2011): 3.

[876] Ibid., 4.

[877] Ibid.

[878] Ibid.

[879] Robert J. Miller, "When It's Futile to Argue about the Historical Jesus: A Response to Bock, Keener, and Webb," *Journal for the Study of the Historical Jesus* 9 (2011): 85-95."

occur between the 'evangelical' camp (which sees the canonical Gospels as fully reliable historically) and the 'traditional' camp (which sees the Gospel as blends of fact and fiction) are futile."[880] Furthermore, he argues that the idea that the Gospels are to be compared to ancient *bios* genre is wrong, for he asserts that ancient *bios* genre was more historically accurate than the Gospels, i.e., the comparison is wrong! Miller asserts that no camp is persuaded by the other in their assertions: "Scholarship from one camp is unavoidably unpersuasive to the other camp . . . That's why debates about basic issues in our field never change people's minds in any fundamental way."[881] For evangelicals, the critical scholars go too far in their denigration of the Gospels; for the critical scholars the evangelicals do not go far enough in allowing de-historicizing of the Gospel material. The end result of such an impasse would appear to be that the Gospels are subject to a scholarly tug-of-war and that, in the process, are denigrated as historically trustworthy, i.e. the Gospels are undermined as reliable historical documents rather than affirmed as is insisted by Bock, Webb, and Keener.

Miller's argument, interestingly, is similar to Perrin's argument against Eldon Ladd that Ladd refused to allow his acceptance of historical criticism to move him too far. Norman Perrin regarded Ladd's passion for approval among liberals as a motivation that led to Ladd's misconstruing some of the more liberal scholars' positions in order to make them support his own views.[882] Perrin bluntly argued,

> We have already noted Ladd's anxiety to find support for his views on the authenticity of a saying or pericope, and this is but one aspect of what seems to be a ruling passion with him: the search for critical support for his views altogether. To this end he is quite capable of misunderstanding the scholars concerned . . .

> Ladd's passion for finding support for his views among critical scholars has as its counterpart an equal passion for dismissing contemptuously aspects of their work which do not support him. These dismissals are of a most peremptory nature.[883]

Perrin labeled Ladd's support for the credibility of the Gospels as accurate historical sources for the life of Jesus as "an uncritical view" and that Ladd was guilty of eisegesis of liberals' views to demonstrate any congruity of their assertions with his brand of conservative evangelical. Marsden continues:

> [Ladd] saw Perrin's review as crucial in denying him prestige in the larger academic arena. . . . The problem was the old one of the neo-evangelical efforts to reestablish world-class evangelical scholarship.

---

[880] Ibid., 85.

[881] Ibid., 89-90.

[882] Perrin commented, "One aspect of Ladd's treatment of sayings and pericopes which the reviewer [Perrin] found annoying is his deliberately one-sided approach to the question of authenticity." Norman Perrin, "Against the Current, A Review of *Jesus and the Kingdom: The Eschatology of Biblical Realism*," by George Eldon Ladd, 229; cf. Marsden, *Reforming Fundamentalism*, 250.

[883] Ibid., 230.

Fundamentalists and conservatives did not trust them . . . and the mainline academic community refused to take them seriously.

Perhaps Perrin had correctly perceived a trait of the new evangelical movement when he described Ladd as torn between his presuppositional critique of modern scholarship and his eagerness to find modern critical scholars on his side . . . No one quite succeeded philosophically in mapping the way this was to be done, though. The result was confusion, as became apparent with subsequent efforts to relate evangelical theology to the social sciences at the new schools. For . . . Ladd, who had the highest hopes for managing to be in both camps with the full respect of each, the difficulties in maintaining the balance contributed to deep personal anxiety.[884]

As a direct result of Bock's and Webb's *Key Events* and its support for post-modernistic historiography, Geisler and Roach dedicated a whole chapter of their work to analyzing its efforts in their recently released *Defending Inerrancy* (2011).[885] Geisler's and Roach's book arose out of concern for a perceived drift away from the concerns for inerrancy of the ICBI movements in 1978 and 1982. They noted their concern especially in relationship to the Evangelical Theological Society: "many young evangelicals trained in contemporary higher criticism have grown increasingly dissatisfied with the traditional view of unlimited inerrancy that was embraced by Warfield, the ETS founders, and the ICBI."[886] They noted that two camps now existed within ETS: those who adhered to the Chicago Statements and their view of unlimited inerrancy and those who did not. They wanted, therefore, evangelicals to remember recent problems surrounding inerrancy in the history of evangelicals that led to the founding of ETS as well as the events that created the Chicago Statements on Inerrancy (1978) and Hermeneutics (1982).

Geisler and Roach counter Bock's claim that historical criticism allows "serious historical engagement" decidedly in the negative: It is *not* serious historical engagement but "bristles" with presuppositions that Bock and Webb choose to ignore; in post-modernistic historiography the term "history" "bristles with presuppositions."[887] While commending Bock and Webb for their response to the Jesus Seminar, as well as their sincere efforts in seeking to know the actual Jesus of history, Geisler and Roach listed several significant concerns that directly impact the doctrine of inerrancy, among which are: (1) late dating of New Testament books; (2) the use of evangelical redaction criticism that denigrates the role of eyewitnesses involved in the composition of the canonical Gospels; (3) the assumption of methodological naturalism, especially in terms of their assumptions of post-modernistic historiography; (4) failing to account for the fact that the idea of a "quest" for the "historical Jesus" constitutes a de facto denial of inerrancy and impugns the Gospels as historical records; and (5) disregarding the Spinozian impact of dealing with alleged sources behind the text rather than the inspired text itself;

---

[884] Marsden, *Reforming Fundamentalism*, 250.

[885] Norman L. Geisler and William C. Roach, *Inerrancy Defended Affirming the Accuracy of Scripture for a New Generation* (Grand Rapids: Baker, 2011).

[886] Ibid., 13.

[887] Ibid., 209.

and (6) neglecting the role of the Holy Spirit in the production of the Gospels (John 14:26; 16:13).[888] Their conclusion was that such participation by Bock, Webb, and other participants in *Key Events* undermine the doctrine of inerrancy as well as the trustworthiness of Scripture. Geisler and Roach argue, "Bock-Webb wrongly believe that they have cleansed the critical-historical method of its naturalistic biases and purified it for appropriate use by evangelicals to find the historical Jesus . . . this is as naïve as the belief that methodological naturalism as a science, to which they compare their approach (KE, 45) will escape the web of naturalistic conclusions . . . Many young scholars seem slow to learn that methodology determines theology. And a naturalistic methodology will lead to a naturalistic theology."[889] As a result, their adoption of "an unorthodox methodology . . . undermines the inerrancy of Scripture."[890]

An Evangelical Crisis of Attitude toward Inspiration and Inerrancy

A very recent work reflecting current thinking among evangelicals who received training and/or influence from British and European continental schools, *Do Historical Matters Matter to the Faith?*, (2012)[891] highlights changing views regarding inerrancy and historicity issues centering in the Bible. The work relates its purpose as follows:

> We offer this book to help address some of the questions raised about the historicity, accuracy, and inerrancy of the Bible by colleagues within our faith community, as well as those outside it. There will be a special emphasis placed on matters of history and the historicity of biblical narratives, both Old and New Testaments, as this seems presently to be a burning issue for theology and faith. Hence, we begin with a group of essays that deal with theological matters before moving on to topics in the Old Testament, the New Testament, and archaeology."[892]

In reacting against those critical of evangelical scholarship's refusal to embrace historical-critical ideologies, such as James Barr and, more recently Kenton Sparks in his *God's Word in Human Words*,[893] the work boasts about the academic degrees of the contributors: "(The contributors of this book who did their doctoral work in British universities—Aberdeen, Oxford, and Cambridge—would hardly agree with

---

[888] Ibid., 193-211.

[889] Ibid., 201.

[890] Ibid., 211.

[891] For a more complete review of this work, see F. David Farnell, "Review of *Do Historical Matters Matter to the Faith?*" Eds. Hames K. Hoffmeier and Dennis R. Magary (Wheaton IL: Crossway, 2012) in *The Master's Seminary Journal* 24/1 (Spring 2013): 149-157.

[892] "Preface," in *Do Historical Matters Matter to Faith?*," 23.

[893] Kenton Sparks, *God's Word in Human Words: An Evangelical Appropriation of Critical Biblical Scholarship* (Grand Rapids: Baker Academic, 2008).

this assessment!) The readers need only to review the list of contributors to see where they completed their PhDs, and it will be abundantly clear that the vast majority worked in secular and critical contexts and had to deal directly with critical issues. In fact, even in the context of Near Eastern studies, the critical approaches of *Altstestamentlers* were a part of the curriculum" [parenthetical marks in original].[894] Because the focus of the present chapter is on New Testament issues, not every chapter in this work will be discussed, but only those that focus on inerrancy and New Testament issues that demonstrate this crisis of attitude among evangelicals.

In Chapter One, "Religious Epistemology, Theological Interpretation of Scripture, and Critical Biblical Scholarship," Thomas McCall sets forth a philosophy of biblical scholarship for the group. McCall advocates a type of "methodological naturalism": "MN holds only that the method of CBS [critical biblical scholarship] 'can be followed and may be valuable for historians' but do not give the only or final word on all matters (historical or otherwise)."[895] What McCall fails to consider in his discussion is that often a "methodology" is really an ideology with an underlying agenda in its presuppositional foundations (Col. 2:8; 2 Cor. 10:5). This chapter suggests a Hegelian/Fichtian dialectic: Fundamentalism (i.e. Reformed Epistemology) is too dismissive or critical of critical biblical scholarship (thesis) and critical biblical scholarship in its historic form is too "binding and obligatory" (antithesis), so the synthesis is expressed by evangelicals who use critical methods to engage in dialogue because "critical biblical scholarship can be 'appropriated' in a way that is both intellectually and spiritually healthy."[896] Acceptance of critical biblical scholarship in various, limited ways is the only way to have influence in the larger marketplace of ideas in biblical criticism.

McCall's idea of influencing, however, is attenuated by 1 Corinthians 1:18-2:14, where Paul sets forth the myth of influence, i.e. the fact that the default response of anyone who does not have the Spirit of God (i.e. unbelievers) is to conclude that the things of God are "foolishness" or "an offense" (1 Cor 1:23) and that God deliberately has planned that wisdom of unsaved men is inherently unable to arrive at a true understanding of the truth of God's Word (1 Cor 2:8-14). This places "critical biblical scholarship" in a tenuous light, for it operates decidedly on foundational unbelief. Only those with the Spirit of God can understand the thoughts of God, for no one will boast before God concerning his own wisdom (1 Cor 1:30).

In Chapter Three, "The Divine Investment in Truth, Toward a Theological Account of Biblical Inerrancy," Mark Thompson asserts a belief in inerrancy but argues strongly that suspicion regarding inerrancy "stems from the way that some have used assent to this doctrine [inerrancy] as a shibboleth. Individuals and institutions have been black-listed for raising doubts about the way the doctrine has been construed in the past. Only those who are able to affirm biblical inerrancy

---

[894] "Preface," in *Do Historical Matters Matter to Faith?*, 22.

[895] Thomas H. McCall, "Theological Interpretation and Critical Biblical Scholarship," in *Do Historical Matters Matter to Faith?*," 52.

[896] Ibid., 54.

without qualification are to be trusted." [897] Thompson singles out Harold Lindsell as "one of the most conspicuous examples" of those who cause this distrust. For Thompson, the greatest suspicion against inerrancy is as follows, "[m]ost serious of all . . . is the way still others, reared in the strictest form of the doctrine of biblical inerrancy, have abandoned the faith under the intense questioning of biblical criticism. Forced to choose between a perfect, unblemished text and seemingly incontrovertible evidence of error in Scripture, such people begin to lose confidence in the gospel proclaimed throughout Scripture. In light of such cases, the doctrine of biblical inerrancy might even be deemed dangerous." [898] These evangelicals have apparently forgotten that it was Harold Lindsell who was a great impetus in the ICBI discussion of both 1978 and 1982. History is now being forgotten. He blames people who hold to a strong view of inerrancy for causing people to depart from the faith. Apparently, for Thompson, inerrancy is a cause of defection especially if one holds to it strongly.

Thompson argues instead that, "the doctrine should not be judged by the abuse of it or by inadequate explanations." [899] He argues for a solution in the following terms: "Strong convictions about the inerrancy of Scripture need not mean that this aspect of Scripture is elevated above all others in importance. Biblical inerrancy need not entail literalism and a failure to take seriously the various literary forms in which God's words come to us, nor need it repudiate genuine human authorship in a Docetic fashion." [900] Such a statement clearly indicates that Thompson places Scripture on the same level as any other book and is, therefore, subject to the same assault that historical-critical ideologies, far from neutral, have perpetrated upon it. Thompson concludes that a solution toward resolving any distortions in the doctrine of inerrancy is as follows: "the doctrine of inerrancy almost inevitably becomes distorted when it becomes the most important thing we want to say about Scripture." [901] He affirms Timothy Ward's solution, "Timothy Ward's assessment that inerrancy is 'a true statement to make about the Bible but is not in the top rank of significant things to assert about the Bible' is timely." Thus, Thompson's solution appears to downplay the significance of inerrancy for biblical issues as a way of overcoming difficulties regarding the doctrine as well as recognizing that not all statements in the Bible are to be taken as literal in terms of genre.

In Chapter Fourteen, "God's Word in Human Words—Form-Critical Reflections," Robert W. Yarbrough argues for seeing a value to historical-critical approaches such as form critical studies by evangelicals even if in a limited way: "Form criticism did call attention to the important point that the Gospels comprise units of expression that may be sorted into discernible categories. Admittedly, form critics approached Gospel sources with premises and convictions that created blind spots in their observations. Limitations to the method as typically practiced

---

[897] Mark D. Thompson, "The Divine Investment in Truth, Toward a Theological Account of Biblical Inerrancy," in *Do Historical Matters Matter to the Faith?* (Wheaton, IL: Crossway, 2012) 71 fn 2.

[898] Ibid., 72.

[899] Ibid.

[900] Ibid.

[901] Ibid., 97

amounted to built-in obsolescence that would eventually doom it to irrelevancy in the estimation of most Gospels interpreters today."[902] However, Yarbrough argues that "to study works from the form-critical era is to be reminded that literary sub-units—even sacred sources—can be grouped and analyzed according to the type of discourse they enshrine and the clues to the cultural surroundings they may yield."[903] He acknowledges that Eta Linnemann "renounced her lifelong professional and personal commitment to what she called historical-critical theology . . . she tested the claims of historical-critical views that she had been taught as a student and then as a professor had inflicted on hapless university undergraduates in an attempt to disabuse them of their Christian faith in Jesus and the Bible, the better to equip them for service in enlightened post-Christian German society."[904]

Yet, Yarbrough, delving into his perceived psychoanalysis of Linnemann's perceptions of biblical scholarship, labels her as someone among evangelicals who overreacted to the historical-critical approaches. He noted that "In academic mode, whether lecturing or writing, Linnemann tended toward overstatement and polemics. It is as if a couple of decades of vehement rejection of the Gospels' trustworthiness created a corresponding zeal for their defense once she rejected the 'critical' paradigm she embraced in Bultmann's heyday and under the spell of her identity as one of his students. Her scholarly pro-Bible writings are not a model of balanced scholarship, cautious investigation, and measured, gracious interaction with those she viewed as soft on the question of the Bible's inaccuracy."[905]

However, Yarbrough's psychoanalysis of Linnemann is directly challenged by Linnemann's own story as a former post-Bultmann who witnessed first-hand the dangerous nature of historical criticism, for she based it on a thorough understanding and analysis of the approach as an ideological one. Eta Linnemann, herself a student of Rudolf Bultmann, the renown *formgeschichtliche* critic, and also of Ernst Fuchs, the outstanding proponent of the New Hermeneutic, notes regarding Historical Criticism,

> [I]nstead of being based on God's Word . . . it [historical criticism] had its foundations in philosophies which made bold to define truth so that God's Word was excluded as the source of truth. These philosophies simply presupposed that man could have no valid knowledge of the God of the Bible, the Creator of heaven and earth, the Father of our Savior and Lord Jesus Christ."[906]

She stresses that the Enlightenment laid not only the atheistic staring point of the sciences but that of biblical criticism as a whole.[907] One comment is especially insightful that in the practice of the historical-critical methods, "What is concealed

---

[902] Robert W. Yarbrough, "God's Word in Human Words: Form-Critical Revelations," in *Do Historical Matters Matter to Faith*, 328.

[903] Ibid.

[904] Ibid., 332.

[905] Ibid.

[906] Eta Linnemann, *Historical Criticism of the Bible* (Grand Rapids: Baker, 2001), 17-18.

[907] Ibid., 29.

from the student is the fact that science itself, including and especially theological science, is by no means unbiased and presuppositionless. The presuppositions which determine the way work is carried on in each of its disciplines are at work behind the scenes and are not openly set forth."[908] Linnemann notes, "a more intensive investigation [of historical criticism] would show that underlying the historical-critical approach is a series of prejudgments which are not themselves the result of scientific investigation. They are rather dogmatic premises, statements of faith, whose foundation is the absolutizing of human reason as a controlling apparatus."[909] Her rejection stemmed not from psychological motives but years of academic research into its dangers.

In Chapter Fifteen, "A Constructive Traditional Response to New Testament Criticism," Craig Blomberg sets forth "constructive" solutions to problems in the New Testament text that he believes would be in line with inerrancy and solve difficulties that evangelicals face. In Blomberg's article, he decries the Evangelical Theological Society's dismissal of Robert H. Gundry in 1982 and reaffirms his support for Gundry to be allowed to make a midrashic approach to de-historicizing (i.e. allegorizing) the story of Herod's killing of babies in Bethlehem in Matthew 2 as consistent with a belief in inerrancy:

> For Gundry, inerrancy would only be called into question if Matthew were making truth claims that were false. But if Matthew were employing a different style, form of genre that was not making truth claims about what happened historically when he added to his sources, then he could not be charged with falsifying the truth. Preachers throughout church history have similarly added speculative detail, local color, possible historical reconstruction, and theological commentary to their retelling of biblical stories. As long as their audiences know the text of Scripture well enough to distinguish between the Bible and the preacher's additions, they typically recognize what the preacher is doing and do not impugn his or her trustworthiness.
>
> A substantial number of voting members of the Evangelical Theological Society present at the annual business meeting of its annual conference in 1983 disagreed that Gundry's views were consistent with inerrancy, at that time the sole tenet in the Society's doctrinal statement, and requested his resignation from the society. I voted with the minority. Following the papers and writings of my own professors from seminary, especially D. A. Carson and Douglas Moo, I believed Gundry had shown how his view could be consistent with inerrancy, even though I did not find his actually approach to Matthew convincing. in other words, the issue was a hermeneutical one, not a theological one. The trustees of Westmont College, where Gundry taught, agreed, and he continued his illustrious teaching and writing career there until his retirement.[910]

---

[908] Ibid, 107.

[909] Ibid., 111.

[910] Craig L. Blomberg, "A Constructive Traditional Response to New Testament Criticism," in *Do Historical Matters Matter to Faith?*, 349.

In accordance with Gundry, one of Blomberg's solution for difficult problems in New Testament in relationship to inerrancy is to allow for a genre of non-historicity to be considered: "Though not a panacea for every conceivable debate, much more sensitive reflection over the implications of the various literary and rhetorical genres in the Bible would seem an important first step that is not often taken enough . . . in some contexts it may take some careful hermeneutical discernment to determine just what a text is or is not affirming. Style, figures of speech, species of rhetorical and literary form and genre all go a long way toward disclosing those affirmations."[911] For Blomberg, difficulties can be resolved at times by realizing the non-historical nature of some portions of the New Testament.

In a 1984 article, Blomberg uses this as an explanation of the story of the coin in the fish's mouth in Matthew 17:21-24: "Is it possible, even inherently probable, that the NT writers at least in part never intended to have their miracle stories taken as historical or factual and that their original audiences probably recognized this? If this sounds like the identical reasoning that enabled Robert Gundry to adopt his midrashic interpretation of Matthew while still affirming inerrancy, that is because it is the same. The problem will not disappear simply because one author [Gundry] is dealt with *ad hominem*...how should evangelicals react? Dismissing the sociological view on the grounds that the NT miracles present themselves as historical gets us nowhere. So do almost all the other miracle stories of antiquity. Are we to believe them all?"[912] Blomberg noted, "It is often not noticed that the so-called miracle of the fish with the coin in its mouth (Matt 17:27) is not even a narrative; it is merely a command from Jesus to go to the lake and catch such a fish. We don't even know if Peter obeyed the command. Here is a good reminder to pay careful attention to the literary form."[913] Unfortunately, this solution would seem to be at odds with the ICBI statement on Hermeneutics when it states in Article XIII: "We deny that generic categories which negate historicity may rightly be imposed on biblical narratives which present themselves as factual."

Blomberg offers another solution toward solving problems surrounding pseudonymity in relation to some New Testament books whereby the "critical consensus approach could . . . be consistent with inerrancy, 'benign pseudonymity.'"[914] Blomberg also uses the term "ghost-writer" to describe this activity.[915] Another more common name for this would be pseudepigraphy (as some scholars claim for Ephesians, Colossians, and the Pastoral Epistles) but Blomberg desires to change normally used terminology:

> A *methodology* consistent with evangelical convictions might argue that there was an accepted literary convention that allowed a

---

[911] Ibid., 351.

[912] Craig L. Blomberg, "New Testament Miracles and Higher Criticism: Climbing Up The Slippery Slope," *Journal of the Evangelical Theological Society* 27/4 (December 1984): 436.

[913] Blomberg, "A Constructive Traditional Response to New Testament Criticism," 354 fn. 32

[914] Ibid., 353, 360.

[915] Ibid.

follower, say, of Paul, in the generation after his martyrdom, to write a letter in Paul's name to one of the churches that had come under his sphere of influence. The church would have recognized that it could not have come from an apostle they knew had died two or three decades earlier, and they would have realized that the true author was writing thoughts indebted to the earlier teaching of Paul. In a world without footnotes or bibliographies, this was one way of giving credit where credit was due. Modesty prevented the real author from using his own name, so he wrote in ways he could easily have envisioned Paul writing were the apostle still alive today. *Whether or not this is what actually happened*, such a hypothesis is thoroughly consistent with a high view of Scripture and an inerrant Bible. We simply have to recognize what is and is not being claimed by the use of name 'Paul' in that given letter.[916]

For Blomberg, the key to pseudonymity would also lie in motive behind the writing. Blomberg argues that "One's acceptance or rejection of the overall theory of authorship should then depend on the answers to these kinds of questions, not on some *a priori* determination that pseudonymity is in every instance compatible or incompatible with evangelicalism."[917] He argues, "[i]t is not the conclusion one comes to on the issue [of pseudonymity] that determines whether one can still fairly claim to be evangelical, or even inerrantist, how one arrives at that conclusion."[918] Yet, how could one ever know the motive of such ghostwriters? Would not such a false writer go against all moral standards of Christianity? Under Blomberg's logic, Bart Ehrman's *Forged* (2011) only differs in one respect: Blomberg attributes good motives to forgers, while Ehrman is honest enough to admit that these "benign" writings are really what they would be in such circumstances: *FORGED WRITING IN THE NAME OF GOD—WHY THE BIBLE'S AUTHORS ARE NOT WHO WE THINK THEY ARE.*[919] Is either one of these scholars able to read the proverbial "tea leaves" and divine the motives behind such perpetrations? Not likely!

Blomberg also carries this logic to the idea of "historical reliability more broadly." He relates, "Might some passages in the Gospels and Acts traditionally thought of as historical actually be mythical or legendary? I see no way to exclude the answer *a priori*. The question would be whether any given proposal to that effect demonstrated the existence of an accepted literary form likely known to the Evangelists' audiences, establishes as a legitimate device for communicating theological truth through historical fiction. In each case it is not the proposal itself that should be off limits for the evangelical. The important question is whether any given proposal has actually made its case."[920]

Blomberg evidences the strong leanings of evangelical critical scholarship toward historical-critical ideologies when he applies his historical-critical/grammatical hermeneutic to the Gospel texts. He notes regarding his *The*

---

[916] Ibid., 352.

[917] Ibid., 353.

[918] Ibid., 352.

[919] See Bart Ehrman, *Forged* (New York: One, 2011).

[920] Blomberg, "A Constructive Traditional Response to New Testament Criticism," 354.

Historical Reliability of the Gospels that "Christians may not be able to prove beyond a shadow of a doubt that the Gospels are historically accurate, but they must attempt to show that there is a strong likelihood of their historicity. Thus the approach of this book is always to argue in terms of probability rather than certainty, since this is the nature of historical hypotheses, including those that are accepted without question."[921] Again, Blomberg argues, "[A] good case can be made for accepting the details as well as the main contours of the Gospels as reliable. But...even if a few minor contradictions genuinely existed, this would not necessarily jeopardize the reliability of the rest or call into question the entire basis for belief."[922]

The fact, however, is that "probability" logically rests in the "eye of the beholder" and what is probable to one may be improbable to another. For instance, what Blomberg finds "probable" may not be to critics of the Gospels who do not accept his logic. This also places Scripture on an acutely subjective level where the logical impact of this approach is to reduce the Gospels to a shifting sand of "one-upmanship" in scholarly debate as to who accepts whose arguments for what reasons or not. Blomberg argues that "an evenhanded treatment of the data [from analysis of the Gospel material] does not lead to a distrust of the accuracy of the Gospels."[923] But this is actually exceedingly naïve, for who is to dictate to whom what is "evenhanded?" Many liberals would think that Blomberg has imposed his own evangelical presuppositions and is *very far* from being "evenhanded." He convinces only himself with this assertion. Blomberg admits "critical scholarship is often *too* skeptical."[924] The phrase "*too* skeptical" is relative to the critic. Who is to judge whether something is too critical when evangelicals adopt the same ideologies? Yet, since he has chosen to play with the rules of the critical scholars' game concerning the Gospels (however much he modifies their approach—they remain its inventors), they may reply on an equally valid level that Blomberg is too accepting. This is especially demonstrated when Blomberg accepts "criteria of authenticity" that are used to determine whether or not portions of the Gospels are historically reliable. He argues, "Using either the older or the new criteria, even the person who is suspicious of the Gospel tradition may come to accept a large percentage of it as historically accurate."[925] One would immediately ask Blomberg to cite an example, any example, of someone who was previously skeptical but has now come to a less skeptical position, but he does not. Criteria of authenticity are merely *a priori* tools that prove what one has already concluded.[926] If one is skeptical regarding tradition, one can select criteria that enforce the already conceived position. If one is less skeptical, then one can apply criteria that will enforce the already accepted less-skeptical conclusion. Each side will not accept the

---

[921] Craig L. Blomberg, *The Historical Reliability of the Gospels* (Downers Grove: InterVarsity, 2007) 36.

[922] Ibid., 37.

[923] Ibid., 297.

[924] Ibid., 310.

[925] Ibid., 312.

[926] For this see, F. David Farnell, "Form Criticism and Tradition Criticism," in *The Jesus Crisis*, 185-232.

data of the other. What does suffer, however, is the Gospel record as it is torn apart by philosophical speculation through these criteria. For Blomberg, one may speak only of the "general reliability" of the Gospels since he has deliberately confined himself to these philosophically-motivated criteria.

Very telling with Blomberg is that he sees two "extreme positions" on historical reliability: the first being those who affirm the Gospels reliability "simply because they believe their doctrine of the inspiration of Scripture requires them to" and the second being "the other end of the confessional spectrum" consisting of "many radical critics" who "would answer the question [regarding reliability] negatively, thinking that proper historical method requires them to disbelieve any narrative so thoroughly permeated by supernatural events, theological interpretation and minor variation among parallels as are in the four Gospels."[927] Blomberg instead asserts his position as in-between: "the Gospels must be subjected to the same type of historical scrutiny given to any other writings of antiquity but that they can stand up to such scrutiny admirably."[928] The naiveté of this latter position is breath-taking, since historical criticism has been shown to be replete with hostile philosophical underpinnings that apparently Blomberg is either unaware of or choosing to ignore.[929] These presuppositions always control the outcome. Moreover, would those who use such radical ideologies in approaching Scripture be convinced of Blomberg's moderation of them? Most likely, they would interpret his usage as biased. What does suffer, however, is the Gospels' historical credibility in the process.

Blomberg argues that "[i]f it is unfair to begin historical inquiry by superimposing a theological interpretation over it, it is equally unfair to ignore the theological implications that rise from it."[930] A much more pertinent question, however, for Blomberg to answer is, "Is it fair for the Gospel record to be in turn subjected to historical critical ideologies whose purpose was to negate and marginalize the Gospel record?" Blomberg is so willing and ready to remove the former but very welcoming in allowing the latter in his own subjective approach to the Gospels.

Finally, Blomberg, seemingly anticipating objections to many of his ideas, issues a stern warning to those who would oppose the proposals that he has discussed:

> [L]et those on the 'far right' neither anathematize those who do explore and defend new options nor immediately seek to ban them from organizations or institutions to which they belong. If new proposals...cannot withstand scholarly rigor, then let their refutations proceed at that level, with convincing scholarship, rather than with the kind of censorship that makes one wonder whether those who object have no persuasive reply and so have to resort simply to demonizing and/or silencing the voices with which they disagree. If evangelical

---

[927] Blomberg, *Historical Reliability*, 322-323.

[928] Ibid., 323.

[929] See F. David Farnell, "The Philosophical and Theological Bent of Historical Criticism," in *The Jesus Crisis*, 85-131.

[930] Blomberg, *Historical Reliability*, 325.

scholarship proceeded in this more measured fashion, neither inherently favoring nor inherently resisting 'critical' conclusions, whether or not they form a consensus, then it might fairly be said to be both traditional *and* constructive.[931]

Blomberg had earlier received strong criticism due to his involvement in co-authoring a book with Stephen E. Robinson, a New Testament professor at Brigham Young University, entitled *How Wide the Divide? A Mormon and an Evangelical in Conversation.*[932] As a result, he states, "Many of us who were trained at seminaries that were vigorously engaged in labeling (rightly or wrongly) other historically evangelical seminaries as no longer evangelical and who then came to the UK for doctoral study found the breadth of British definitions of evangelicalism and the comparative lack of a polemical environment like a breath of fresh air."[933] Yet, this desire for lack of criticism and just an irenic spirit in Christian academics hardly finds legitimacy in terms of the biblical model displayed in the Old and New Testaments. Much of the Old Testament castigated God's people for their compromising on belief or behavior (e.g. Numbers 11-14; Psalm 95). Under today's sentiments, the Old Testament might be labeled anti-Semitic due to its criticism of Jewish people. In the New Testament, whole books were composed to criticize false teaching and wrong behavior on the part of God's people, such as Galatians, 1-2 Corinthians, the Pastoral Epistles, the Johannine Epistles, and chapters two and three of Revelation. Jesus himself fearlessly castigated powerful groups of important people (Matt 21-23). One is reminded of the satirical pieces that have been done on the fact that if Paul wrote Galatians today, he would have been vilified in many popular Christian magazines.[934]

In Chapter Sixteen, "Precision and Accuracy," Bock asserts that the genre of the gospels is a form of ancient Greco-Roman biography known as *bios*: "[w]hen we think about the Gospels, there sometimes is a debate about the genre of this material. There was a time when this material was considered unique in its literary orientation. However, recently a consensus has emerged that the Gospels are a form of ancient *bios*."[935] He echoes the thinking of Charles Talbert and British theologian Richard Burridge who popularized this view.[936] This assertion that the Gospels are a form of ancient *bios* is fraught with dangers regarding historical

---

[931] Ibid., 364.

[932] Craig L. Blomberg and Stephen E. Robinson, *How Wide the Divide? A Mormon and an Evangelical in Conversation* (Downers Grove, IL: InterVarsity, 1997).

[933] Carl R. Trueman, Tony J. Gray, Craig L. Blomberg, Eds., *Solid Ground: 25 Years of Evangelical Theology* (Leicester: IVP and Apollos, 2000), 315.

[934] For a wonderful satire of this very issue, see "If Paul's Epistle to the Galatians was published in Christianity Today," in http://sacredsandwich.com/archives/2781. Acccessed on 5/27/2013.

[935] Darrell L. Bock, "Precision and Accuracy," in *Do Historical Matters Matter to Faith?*, 368.

[936] See Charles H. Talbert, *What is a Gospel? The Genre of the Canonical Gospels* (Philadelphia: Fortress, 1977); Richard A. Burridge, *What Are the Gospels? A Comparison with Graeco-Roman Biography.* Second Edition (Cambridge: Cambridge University, 2004).

matters surrounding the Gospels since it can readily lead to de-emphasizing the Gospels as historical documents.

This growing opinion among evangelical scholars that the Gospels are *bios* recently created a storm of controversy when Michael Licona, in his work *The Resurrection of Jesus A New Historiographical Approach*,[937] used *bios* as a means of de-historicizing parts of the Gospel (i.e. Matthew 27:51-53 with the resurrection of the saints after Jesus crucifixion is non-literal genre or apocalyptic rather than an actual historical event). Licona argued "*Bioi* offered the ancient biographer great flexibility for rearranging material and **inventing speeches . . . and they often included legend.** Because *bios* was a flexible genre, **it is often difficult to determine where history ends and legend begins.**"[938]

Licona's work exhibits many commendable items, such as a strong stance, on the historical basis for Jesus' bodily resurrection, from the dead. One might be encouraged that in light of historical criticism's assault on the miraculous since Spinoza and the Enlightenment, Licona has maintained the historical, orthodox position of the church. However, like Robert Gundry before him in 1983, Licona (2010) uses genre issues in historical criticism to negate portions of Scripture that have always been considered historical by orthodox Christianity from the earliest times. He has stirred up much controversy that parallels that of the Gundry/ETS circumstance that resulted in the ICBI documents of 1978 and 1982. Being influenced by historical criticism, Licona has accepted a consensus that has emerged among critically-trained historical-critical scholars that the Gospels are a form of ancient "*bios.*"[939]

Bock argues, "[i]n ancient biography actions and sayings are the focus of the portrayal. The timing of the events is of less concern that the fact that they happened. Sometimes figures from distinct periods can be juxtaposed in ways that compare how they acted. The model of the figure that explains his greatness and presents him as one worthy of imitation stands at the core of the presentation. The central figure in a *bios* often is inspiring. The presentation of Jesus in the Gospels fits this general goal . . . This genre background is our starting point."[940]

Operating from this consensus of the gospel as *bios*, Bock argues that the Olivet Discourse may have an "updated" saying. Comparing the disciples' question in Mark 13:4 ("'Tell us, when will these things be, and what *will be* the sign when all these things are going to be fulfilled?" with Luke 21:7 ("Teacher, when therefore will these things be? And what *will be* the sign when these things are about to take place?") and Matthew 24:3 ("Tell us, when will these things be, and what *will be* the sign of Your coming, and of the end of the age?"), Bock notes that "something is going on between the versions in Mark and Luke in comparison to Matthew."

---

[937]Michael R. Licona, *The Resurrection of Jesus, A New Historiographical Approach* (Downers Grove: InterVarsity, 2010).

[938] Ibid., 34.

[939]Bock also accepted this basic genre classification, see Darrell L. Bock, "Precision and Accuracy: Making Distinctions in the Cultural Context," in *Do Historical Matters Matter to Faith?* (Wheaton: Crossway,2012), 368.

[940] Ibid.

Bock continues, "Matthew has taken the question as it was in Mark and Luke and has presented what the disciples essentially were asking, even if they did not appreciate all the implications in the question at the time . . . Whether the disciples say the end is in view or Matthew is drawing that out as inherent in the question asked, the point is that Matthew is drawing that out as inherent in the question asked, the point is that Matthew has made the focus of the question clearer than the more ambiguous way it is asked in Mark and Luke." Bock asserts that "Matthew may actually be giving us the more precise force and point of the question, now paraphrased in light of a fuller understanding of what Jesus's career was to look like." Apparently, Bock allows for the possibility that the disciples may not have asked the question as is set forth in Matthew 24:3 but that Matthew updated the question by adding this comment to the lips of the disciples regarding the "end of the age: "Matthew has simply updated the force of the question, introducing the idea of the end [of the age] as the topic Jesus implied by his remark about the temple."[941] One is left wondering with Bock's postulation whether the disciples actually asked the question as Matthew presented ("end of the age") or did Matthew add words to their lips that they did not say? Bock's approach here is essentially a subtle form of de-historicizing the Gospels at this point. Equally plausible, however, is that the disciples did ask the question in the way in which Matthew phrased it and that a harmonization of the passage could be postulated that would not require such creative invention on the part of Matthew.

Echoing the same kind of thinking in this book, Darrell Bock states in a self-review of his own work in *Do Historical Matters Matter?*: "I do not often note books to which I have contributed on this blog, but this work is an exception. *Do Historical Matters Matter to Faith?: A Critical Appraisal of Modern and Postmodern Approaches to Scripture* (Edited by James Hoffmeier and Dennis Magary) explores issues tied to the authority and inspiration of Scripture. This series of essays covers an array of issues from the Old and New Testaments."[942] Yet, this book clearly maintains that inerrancy is not a critical issue in Biblical studies.

In Bock's own review of his *Key Events* work as co-editor with Robert Webb, Bock distances himself not only from inerrancy but also from the subject of inspiration as alien to Third Search evangelical critical scholars like himself:

> As a co-editor of this volume, I should explain what this book is and is not. It is a book on historical Jesus discussion. It is not a book that uses theological arguments or categories (as legitimate as those can be) to make its case. This means we chose as a group to play by the rules of that discussion, engage it on those terms, and show even by those limiting standards that certain key events in the life of Jesus have historical credibility. So in this discussion one does not appeal to inspiration and one is asked to corroborate the claims in the sources before one can use the material. This is what we did, with a careful look

---

[941] Ibid., 372.

[942] http://blogs.bible.org/bock/darrell_l._bock/do_historical_matters_matter_t o_faith_a_critical_appraisal_of_modern_and_postmodern_approaches_to_scriptur e. Accessed on 5/27/2013.

at the historical context of 12 central events. To be accurate, the article by Webb accepts the resurrection as a real event, but argues for a limitation on what history (at least as normally practiced today) can say about such events. The problem here is with what history can show, not with the resurrection as an event. Many working in historical Jesus study take this approach to the resurrection. I prefer to argue that the best explanation for the resurrection is that it was a historical event since other explanations cannot adequately explain the presence of such a belief among the disciples. Webb explains these two options of how to take this in terms of the historical discussion and noted that participants in our group fell into each of these camps. Some people will appreciate the effort to play by these limiting rules and yet make important positive affirmations about Jesus. Others will complain by asking the book to do something it was not seeking to do.[943]

What is most remarkable is that nowhere in such evangelical collaborative works as *Key Events* or *Who Is Jesus?*[944] Does Bock (or any other evangelical involved) mention how such principles stand presuppositionally opposed to affirming the Scriptures, especially its inerrancy, nor does Bock issue any warnings in these works that the searchers are conducting their search apart from any consideration of inerrancy? Apparently, critical-evangelical scholars may have personal, subjective beliefs about inerrancy or inspiration, but in Third Search activities that they conduct such ideas are shunned as not a part of this scholarly endeavor. Nowhere in any of Bock's searching books does he mention that this all is an effort to use the arguments of the historical-critics against them. He merely assumes these ideas and it results in a weakening of the Gospels. No apologetic is ever offered in countering such things; no history or presuppositions are mentioned. He treats historical-critical principles such as source, form, redaction, tradition criticism and post-modernistic historiography as fully valid. Indeed, at the expense of both inspiration and inerrancy, he has succeeded in making the term "historical Jesus" normal when it is truly aberrant from an orthodox understanding. It is founded on a German critical scholarship of *historie* (actual history) versus *geschichte* (faith interpretation of those events); a concept that at its foundation rejects the Jesus of the Bible. He nowhere even hints that these principles are flawed or inconsistent when he writes these works and apparently buys into them substantially. One cannot tell qualitatively where any of these critical evangelical scholars substantively disagrees with any of these "searching" principles. They wrote no caveat about post-modernistic historiography; no counter-chapter or alternative to it was presented. It was treated as normative for these books and not even so much as a footnote was written that would indicate that not all the authors agree with post-modernistic historiography. Bock and those allied with him appear to assume historical-critical validity of the principles as if they completely accept these concepts. He treats searching as normative, standard and as if all evangelical scholars do this kind of thing.

---

[943] Amazon review at http://tinyurl.com/9p7r99j. Accessed on 5/27/2013.

[944] Darrell L. Bock and Robert W. Webb, *Key Events* (Grand Rapids: Eerdmans, 2009); Darrell L. Bock, *Who is Jesus? Linking the Historical Jesus with the Christ of Faith* (New York et al: Howard, 2012).

In another work, evangelical Daniel Wallace also plays down the importance of inspiration and inerrancy. In a statement from his chapter entitled "*Who's Afraid of the Holy Spirit? The Uneasy Conscience of a Non-Charismatic Evangelical*," Wallace admits a personal struggle:

> **(3) This emphasis on knowledge over relationship can produce in us bibliolatry.** For   me, as a New Testament professor, the text is my task--but I made it my God. The text   became my idol. Let me state this bluntly: The Bible is not a member of the Trinity. One   lady in my church facetiously told me, "I believe in the Trinity: the Father, Son and Holy   Bible." Sadly, too many cessationists operate as though that were so. One of the great   legacies Karl Barth left behind was his strong Christocentric focus. It is a shame that too   many of us have reacted so strongly to Barth, for in our zeal to show his deficiencies in   his doctrine of the Bible, we have become bibliolaters in the process. Barth and Calvin   share a warmth, a piety, a devotion, an awe in the presence of God that is lacking in too   many theological tomes generated from our circles.[945]

The present writer finds this kind of statement not in accordance with the assertions of Scripture itself. Scripture presents its foundational importance of inspiration and inerrancy with hundreds of verses that present this constant truth. God's Words has exalted status, "I will bow down toward Your holy temple and give thanks to Your name for Your lovingkindness and Your truth; for You have magnified Your word according to all Your name" (Ps. 138:2). God's Word is a sanctifying force, "Sanctify them in the truth; Your word is truth" (John 17:17). Jesus affirmed "the Scripture cannot be broken" (John 10:35) and 2 Timothy 3:16-17 states, "All Scripture is inspired by God and profitable for teaching, for reproof, for correction, for training in righteousness, so that the man of God may be adequate, equipped for every good work." Wallace's logic here is startlingly poor. If the documents cannot be trusted—if they are not inspired and inerrant—then one cannot have a "Christocentric" anything. Apparently, however, good critical scholars are obliged never to bring these verses up in scholarly discussions or risk being labeled unscholarly.

In seeking to counter the damage to the determination of the wording of Scripture by Bart Ehrman's work *Misquoting Jesus*, Wallace is more than willing to surrender inerrancy as an issue:

> Second, what I tell my students every year is that it is imperative that they pursue truth rather than protect their presuppositions. And they need to have a doctrinal taxonomy that distinguishes core beliefs from peripheral beliefs. When they place more peripheral doctrines such as inerrancy and verbal inspiration at the core, then when belief in these doctrines starts to erode, it creates a domino effect: One falls down, they all fall down. It strikes me that something like this may be what happened to Bart Ehrman. His testimony in *Misquoting Jesus* discussed inerrancy as the prime mover in his studies. But when a glib comment

---

[945] Daniel Wallace, "Who's Afraid of the Holy Spirit? The Uneasy Conscience of a Non-Charismatic Evangelical," in *Who's Afraid of the Holy Spirit? An Investigation into the Ministry of the Spirit of God Today*, edited by M. James Sawyer and Daniel B. Wallace (Dallas, TX: Biblical Studies, 2005), 8.

from one of his conservative professors at Princeton was scribbled on a term paper, to the effect that perhaps the Bible is not inerrant, Ehrman's faith began to crumble. One domino crashed into another until eventually he became "a fairly happy agnostic." I may be wrong about Ehrman's own spiritual journey, but I have known too many students who have gone in that direction. The irony is that those who frontload their critical investigation of the text of the Bible with bibliological presuppositions often speak of a "slippery slope" on which all theological convictions are tied to inerrancy. Their view is that if inerrancy goes, everything else begins to erode. I would say rather that if inerrancy is elevated to the status of a prime doctrine, that's when one gets on a slippery slope. But if a student views doctrines as concentric circles, with the cardinal doctrines occupying the center, then if the more peripheral doctrines are challenged, this does not have a significant impact on the core. In other words, the evangelical community will continue to produce liberal scholars until we learn to nuance our faith commitments a bit more, until we learn to see Christ as the center of our lives and scripture as that which points to him. If our starting point is embracing propositional truths about the nature of scripture rather than personally embracing Jesus Christ as our Lord and King, we'll be on that slippery slope, and we'll take a lot of folks down with us.[946]

Even more startling is Wallace's assertions regarding evangelical theological views like inerrancy or inspiration that apparently reflect a similar view to Rogers and McKim (mentioned earlier in this article): "our theology is too often rooted in Greek philosophy, rationalism, the Enlightenment, and Scottish Common Sense realism" which he defines as "a philosophical departure from that of the sixteenth-century Reformers, though it was a handmaiden of Princetonian conservative theology in the nineteenth century."[947] For Wallace, evangelicals operate on a "docetic bibliology" regarding Scripture when they insist on the *ipsissima verba* or similar ideas.[948] Thus, Wallace's view encompasses such ideas as Luke altering the meaning of Jesus' words in Luke 5:32 (cf. Mark 2:17; Matt 9:13) so that he asserts that "To sum up: There seems to be evidence in the synoptic gospels that, on occasion, words are deliberately added to the original sayings of Jesus" and "[i]n a few instances, these words seem to alter somewhat the picture that we would otherwise have gotten from the original utterance; in other instances, the meaning seems to be virtually the same, yet even here a certain amount of exegetical spadework is needed to see this. On the other hand, there seem to be examples within the synoptics where the words are similar, but the meaning is different."[949]

---

[946] Daniel B. Wallace, "The Gospel according to Bart, A Review of Bart D. Ehrman's *Misquoting Jesus: The Story Behind Who Changed the Bible and Why* (Bible Studies Foundation, 2006 Bible.org); http://bible.org/article/gospel-according-bart. Accessed on 5/27/2013. Note: this quote is from the full version of Wallace's review of Ehrman.

[947] Daniel B. Wallace, "An Apologia for a Broad View of Ipsissima Vox," Presented at the 51st Annual Meeting of the Evangelical Theological Society, November 18, 1999, 1 (also note p. 1 ft. 2).

[948] Ibid., 10

[949] Ibid., 12.

These statements leave one to wonder if Jesus truly said what is recorded in the Gospels or that the substance has been changed redactionally. Wallace concludes, "it seems that our interpretation of inspiration is governing our interpretation of the text. Ironically, such bibliological presuppositions are established in modern terms that just might ignore or suppress the data they are meant to address and which are purportedly derived. And there is an even greater irony here: the fact of the Incarnation—an essential element in orthodox Christology-*invites* (italics in original) rigorous historical investigation. But what if our bibliological presuppositions *reject* (italics in original) that invitation?"[950] What "rigorous historical investigation" entails is not clearly specified, except that it involves at least the utilization of the criteria of authenticity and dissimilarity.[951]

In a recent blog entry, Wallace related: "I am unashamedly a Protestant. I believe in *sola scriptura, sola fidei, solus Christus*, and the rest. I am convinced that Luther was on to something when he articulated his view of justification succinctly: *simul iustus et peccator* ("simultaneously justified and a sinner")."[952] However, he laments the lack of unification on Protestant theology, and says that three events in his life are having an impact on his thinking: (1) His attendance of Greek Orthodox worship services: "I have spent a lot of time with Greek Orthodox folks. It doesn't matter what Orthodox church or monastery I visit, I get the same message, the same liturgy, the same sense of the 'holy other' in our fellowship with the Triune God. The liturgy is precisely what bothers so many Protestants since their churches often try very hard to mute the voices from the past. 'It's just me and my Bible' is the motto of millions of evangelicals." (2) His own personal experience of seeing a personal friend of his in Protestantism deny Jesus' deity, where he laments the lack of an ecclesiastical hierarchy: "This cancer could have been cut out more swiftly and cleanly if the church was subordinate to a hierarchy that maintained true doctrine in its churches. And the damage would have been less severe and less traumatic for the church." (3) His realization on ecclesiastical hierarchy involved in canon formation: "What is significant is that *for the ancient church, canonicity was intrinsically linked to ecclesiology.* It was the *bishops* rather than the congregations that gave their opinion of a book's credentials. Not just any bishops, but bishops of the major sees of the ancient churches." He relates, "we Protestants can be more sensitive about the deficiencies in our own ecclesiology rather than think that we've got a corner on truth. We need to humbly recognize that the two other branches of Christendom have done a better job in this area. Second, we can be more sensitive to the need for doctrinal and ethical accountability, fellowship beyond our local church, and ministry with others whose essentials but not necessarily particulars don't line up with ours. Third, we can begin to listen again to the voice of the Spirit speaking through church fathers and embrace some of the liturgy that has been used for centuries." Wallace's hinting at a unified ecclesiastical hierarchy superseding the local church appears to reveal his persuading toward seriously contemplating

---

[950] Ibid., 19.

[951] Ibid., 15.

[952] http://danielbwallace.com/2012/03/18/the-problem-with-protestant-ecclesiology/ (Accessed on 5/10/2013).

membership in the Anglican Church.[953] In a reply to a comment on the blog entry, Wallace writes:

> Russ, I have thought about the Anglican Church quite a bit actually. I love the liturgy, the symbolism, the centrality of the Eucharist, the strong connection with the church in ages past, and the hierarchy. And yes, I have seriously considered joining their ranks–and still am considering it. There are some superb Anglican churches in the Dallas area. Quite surprising to me has been my choice of academic interns at Dallas Seminary in the last few years. Over half of them have been Anglican, and yet when I picked them for the internship I didn't know what their denominational affiliation was. Exceptional students, devoted to the Lord and his Church, and committed to the highest level of Christian scholarship. And they have respect for tradition and the work of the Spirit in the people of God for the past two millennia.[954]

Sadly, what Wallace fails to discern is that such overwhelming ecclesiastical hierarchy is what caused the need of reformation. The Church had rotted from the top down with the rise of Romanism and even later with Anglicanism. Infection spreads much more rapidly in "top-down" hierarchies. Independent local churches such as those exhibited in Protestantism generally preserve a greater safeguard against spreading heresy.

Interestingly, William Craig, professor of apologetics at Talbot School of Theology, uses historical criticism to question the veracity of guards being at Jesus' tomb. In a recent Ankerberg interview, Craig negates the guards in the following manner. In response to Ankerberg's question, "Were there guards at the tomb?" Craig replied:

> Well now this is a question that I think is probably best left out of the program, because the vast, vast majority of New Testament scholars would regard Matthew's tomb story, or guard story as "unhistorical". Um, I can hardly think of anybody who would defend the historicity of the guard at the tomb story and the main reasons for that are two: one is because it's only found in Matthew, and it seems very odd that if there were a Roman guard or even a Jewish guard at the tomb that Mark wouldn't know about it, and there wouldn't be any mention of it. The other reason is that nobody seemed to understand Jesus' resurrection predictions. The disciples who heard them most often had no inkling of what he meant, and yet somehow the Jewish authorities were supposed to have heard of these predictions, and understood them so well that they were able to set a guard around the tomb. And again, that doesn't seem to make sense. So, most scholars regard the Guard at the Tomb

---

[953]Wallace cites a work by Dungan that strongly influenced his belief in an ecclesiastical hierarchy. See David Laird Dungan, *Constantine's Bible: Politics and the Making of the New Testament* (Minneapolis: Fortress Press, 2007). Dungan's work highlights Eusebius' record (*Ecclesiastical History*) of the influence of ancient bishops in canon formation. Dungan, however, records the formation of canon prior to the onslaught of Romanism as well as Greek Orthodoxy.

[954]http://danielbwallace.com/2012/03/18/the-problem-with-protestant-ecclesiology/ (accessed on 5/10/2013).

story as a legend or a Matthean invention that isn't really historical. Fortunately, this is of little significance for the empty tomb of Jesus, because the guard was mainly employed in Christian apologetics to disprove the conspiracy theory that the disciples stole the body—but no modern historian or New Testament scholar would defend a conspiracy theory because it's evident when you read the pages of the New Testament that these people sincerely believed in what they said. So, the conspiracy theory is dead, even in the absence of a guard at the tomb. The true significance of the guard at the tomb story is that it shows that even the opponents of the earliest Christians did not deny the empty tomb, but rather involve themselves in a hopeless series of absurdities trying to explain it away, by saying that the disciples had stolen the body. And that's the real significance of Matthew's "Guard at the Tomb" story.[955]

In reply to this "logic" of Craig, note that *if* evangelicals accepted what the early church always and consistently witnessed—that Matthew was the first Gospel written—instead of accepting historical-critical presuppositions, then Mark actually left out Matthew's guard story. Moreover, if Matthew made up guards around Jesus' tomb, then what stops Craig's reasoning from being extended to the fact that the writers made up the "sincere" response of belief, or for that matter, the whole idea of the resurrection? To start throwing out parts of the Gospels because they aren't recounted in Mark or because "no modern historian or New Testament scholar" thinks they are is not only illogical but dangerous to Christianity.

In another place, Craig seems to give credence to the guards:

So although there are reasons to doubt the existence of the guard at the tomb, there are also weighty considerations in its favor. It seems best to leave it an open question. Ironically, the value of Matthew's story for the evidence for the resurrection has nothing to do with the guard at all or with his intention of refuting the allegation that the disciples had stolen the body. The conspiracy theory has been universally rejected on moral and psychological grounds, so that the guard story as such is really quite superfluous. Guard or no guard, no critic today believes that the disciples could have robbed the tomb and faked the resurrection. Rather the real value of Matthew's story is the incidental -- and for that reason all the more reliable -- information that Jewish polemic never denied that the tomb was empty, but instead tried to explain it away. Thus the early opponents of the Christians themselves bear witness to the fact of the empty tomb.[956]

The impression one might receive from this is that Craig believes the guards at the tomb story but, at the same time, is not sure of its validity since he leaves it an

---

[955] Transcribed from Youtube video of Ankerberg interview of Craig on May 25, 2010. Accessed and transcribed on June 22, 2013 (http://www.youtube.com/watch?v=b8UMb7NlxkU).

[956] William L. Craig, "The Guard at the Tomb" *New Testament Studies* 30 (1984): 273-81(quote from page 80).

open question. If Matthew said guards were there, can it be left an "open question" for those who believe in the trustworthiness, let alone, inerrancy of Scripture?

At another point, he echoed a similar statement to Michael Licona regarding the resurrection of the saints in Matthew 27:51-53. In a YouTube video of Craig debating in 2007 at the University of Sheffield, in the United Kingdom against James Crossley on the bodily resurrection of Jesus, Craig sets forth the idea that admitting to legendary elements in the Gospels (i.e. the resurrection of the saints) "does nothing to undermine the remaining testimony of the gospels to things like the crucifixion of Jesus, the empty tomb, the resurrection appearances" (citing Dale Allison as his authority for this statement). When asked directly by a questioner in the audience if he believed in the story of the resurrection of the saints in Matthew 27:51-53, "I'm not sure what to think." He also says "it could be part of the apocalyptic imagery of Matthew which isn't meant to be taken in a literal way. That this would be part of the typical sort of apocalyptic symbolism to show the earth-shattering nature of the resurrection and need not to be taken historically literally." He goes on to conclude, "this is not attached to a resurrection narrative. This story about the Old Testament saints is attached to the crucifixion narrative. So that if you try to say that because Matthew has this unhistorical element in his crucifixion account, that, therefore, the whole account is worthless, you would be led to deny the crucifixion of Jesus, which is one indisputable fact that everyone recognizes about the historical Jesus. So it really doesn't have any implications for the historicity of the burial story, the empty tomb story or the appearance accounts. It's connected to the crucifixion narrative." Notice that his adoption of historical criticism drives him toward allowing for non-historicity in narrative accounts in the Gospels.[957] The key question for Craig to answer must be that if they made up stories of the saints' resurrection, what would stop them from making up stories about Jesus' resurrection? One cannot have it both ways by saying that one story is historical, but the other may be made-up fiction due to apocalyptic imagery.

This view is not uncommon among evangelicals. Craig Evans, an active participant in British-influenced searching for the 'historical' Jesus, when commenting on the resurrection of the saints in Matthew 27:51b-53, argues:

> I do not think the tradition in Matthew 27:51b-53, which describes at the time of Jesus' death the resurrection of several saintly persons, has any claim to authenticity. This legendary embellishment, which may actually be a late-first century or early-second-century gloss, is an attempt to justify the Easter appearances of Jesus as resurrection, in the sense that Jesus and several other saints were the "first fruits" of the general resurrection. This is, of course, exactly how Paul explains the anomaly (1 Cor. 15:23).[958]

---

[957] http://www.youtube.com/watch?v=3SNuhjRZZI4 (accessed on September 30, 2013).

[958] Craig A. Evans, "In Appreciation of the Dominical and Thomistic Traditions: The Contribution of J. D. Crossan and N. T. Wright to Jesus Research," in *The Resurrection of Jesus, John Dominic Crossan and N. T. Wright in Dialogue*, Ed. Robert B. Stewart (Minneapolis, MN: Fortress, 2006), 195 fn 30.

Similarly, Michael Green, while Senior Research Fellow at Wycliffe Hall, Oxford University, in his *Message of Matthew*, is abruptly dismissive of the resurrection of the saints in Matthew 27:51-53. Green comments,

> Does Matthew mean us to take this literally? Does he mean that the tombs were broken open, and that the bodies were somehow clothed with flesh and brought to life, as in Ezekiel's vision? It is possible, but unlikely that this is how Matthew intended us to read it. After all, he says that these bodies of the saints went into the holy city *after* Jesus' resurrection. By that phrase he is guarding the primacy of the resurrection of Jesus, "the firstfruits of those who have fallen asleep," yet he presents us with these resuscitated bodies at the cross itself, long before the resurrection. If Matthew meant us to think of these people from a bygone age walking into Jerusalem that Friday evening, how would that accord with his plain insistence throughout this chapter (especially 40-50) that no compelling proofs of Jesus' deity were given at this time of his death any more than they were during his life?
>
> No, Matthew seems to be giving us a profound meditation on what the crucifixion of Jesus means for the destiny of humankind. His death is an eschatological event; it is a foretaste of the end of the world.[959]

Again, citing his agreement with Donald Hagner,[960] Green comments in a footnote on this passage,

> I agree with Donald Hagner that in recording this story [of the saints' resurrection] Matthew wanted, at the very point when Jesus died, to draw out its theological significance. A straightforward historical reading of these verses is hard to contemplate. Who were these people? Were they resurrected or resuscitated? Why did they go into the holy city? What happened to them subsequently? Indeed, what happens to the priority of Jesus' resurrection? And if they *appeared to many people (53)*, why is there no reference to this event elsewhere, either inside or outside the New Testament?[961]

Donald Hagner, after an extensive discussion of the passage, dismisses any substantial historicity to the saints' resurrection, and remarks that,

> I side, therefore, with recent commentators . . . in concluding that the rising of the saints from the tombs in this passage is a piece of theology set forth as history . . . It is obvious that by the inclusion of this material Matthew wanted to draw out the theological significance of the death (and resurrection of Jesus). That significance is found in the establishing of the basis of the future resurrection of the saints. We may thus regard the passage as a piece of realized and historicized apocalyptic

---

[959] Michael Green, *The Message of Matthew*. Ed. John R. W. Stott (Downers Grove, IL: InterVarsity, 2000), 302-303.

[960] Donald A. Hagner, Matthew 14-28, vol. 33b in the Word Biblical Commentary (Waco, TX: Word, 1995),

[961] Green, *The Message of Matthew*, 302-303 fn 18.

depending on OT motifs found in such passages as Isa 26:19; Dan 12:2; and especially Ezek 37:12-14.[962]

Interestingly, Hagner wrongly attributes this dehistoricized view to Gundry. While Gundry did dehistoricize, a careful examination of his commentary on *Matthew: A Commentary on His Handbook for a Mixed Church under Persecution* reveals that while Gundry attributed Old Testament motifs to the passage, he believed that the saints resurrection actually happened.[963]

Finally, Leon Morris, in his *Gospel According to Matthew*, also appears to place significant doubt on the historicity of this section. Morris notes,

> Nobody else mentions this, and we are left to conclude that Matthew is making the point that the resurrection of Jesus brought about the resurrection of his people. Just as the rending of the temple curtain makes it clear that the way to God is open for all, so the raising of the saints shows that death has been conquered. Those so raised went into Jerusalem and *appeared to many*. Since there are no other records of these appearances, it appears to be impossible to say anything about them. But Matthew is surely giving expression to his conviction that *Jesus* is Lord over both the living and the dead.

Instead, Morris prefers to see it as possibly being linked to an idea of general resurrection of God's saints at the end of the age: "It seems that here Matthew has the great death-and-resurrection in mind and links his raising of the saints to the whole happening. Thus he mentions it when he speaks of the death of Jesus but goes on to what he says happened at the time of the resurrection."[964] He concludes that one thing is certain in the passage, "Matthew is surely giving expression to his conviction that Jesus is Lord over both the living and the dead."[965]

The Honesty of Bart Ehrman

Interestingly, Bart Ehrman directly blames historical criticism as a large reason for his departure from the faith. Ehrman is very honest and open to note that an important, strategic factor in his loss of confidence in his faith was explicitly that of historical-critical ideologies and their impact on seminary students' thoughts:

> The approach taken to the Bible in almost all Protestant (and now Catholic mainline seminaries) is what is called the 'historical-critical" method . . .

---

[962] Donald A. Hagner, *Matthew 14-28*, vol. 38b in the Word Biblical Commentary (Waco, TX: Word, 1995), 851-852.

[963] Hagner identifies his view of non-historicity as being also Gundry's view; see Hagner, 851. However, Gundry nowhere in commenting on this passage negates its historicity. See Robert H. Gundry, *Matthew A Commentary on His Handbook for a Mixed Church Under Persecution*. 2nd Edition (Grand Rapids: Eerdmans, 1995), 576-577.

[964] Leon Morris, *The Gospel According to Matthew* (Grand Rapids: Eerdmans, 1992), 725.

[965] Ibid.

The historical-critical approach has a different set of concepts and therefore poses a different set of questions . . .

A very large percentage of seminaries are completely blind-sided by the historical critical method. They come in with expectations of learning the pious truths of the Bible so that they can pass them along in their sermons, as their own pastors have done for them. Nothing prepares them for historical criticism. To their surprise they learn, instead of material for sermons, all the results of what historical critics have established on the basis of centuries of research. The Bible is filled with discrepancies, many of them irreconcilable contradictions . . .

But before long, as students see more and more of the evidence [of contradictions], many of them find that their faith in the inerrancy and absolute historical truthfulness of the Bible begins to waver. There simply is too much evidence, and to reconcile all of the hundreds of differences among the biblical sources requires so much speculation and fancy interpretive work that eventually it gets to be too much for them.[966]

He goes on to note that "I came to see the potential value of historical criticism at Princeton Seminary. I started adopting this new (for me) approach, very cautiously at first, as I didn't want to concede too much to scholarship. But eventually I saw the powerful logic behind the historical-critical method and threw myself heart and soul into the study of the Bible from this perspective." He then immediately goes on to note, "It is hard for me to pinpoint the exact moment that I stopped being a fundamentalist who believed in the absolute inerrancy and verbal inspiration of the Bible."[967] The cause of Bart Ehrman's fall from faith came when he embraced historical criticism! Not one of his mentors at the Bible-believing schools he attended had prepared him for historical-criticism's massive assault on Scripture by pointing out the presuppositional biases that anchor historical criticism's assault on Scripture. Bart Ehrman is a tragic figure in that none of his "evangelical" mentors had properly prepared him for the onslaught of historical-critical ideologies.

Judging by Ehrman's comments, perhaps he should not be seen so much as a defector, but as an example of the tragic failure of mentoring in evangelical biblical education. He began his training in a conservative theological school (Moody Bible Institute), but somewhere along his path at Wheaton College someone encouraged him to attend a more prestigious "critical" school (i.e., Princeton) to study. It was at Princeton Seminary, which had abandoned any sense of faithfulness to God's Word long ago, that Ehrman was exposed to historical criticism.[968] Moreover, the evangelical institutions that had previously trained him apparently did not prepare him for the onslaught of historical criticism that would impact his thinking. Erhman should serve as a salient and very recent example that Hagner is wrong both

---

[966] Bart D. Ehrman, "A Historical Assault on Faith," in *Jesus Interrupted* (New York: Harper One, 2009), 4-6

[967] Ibid., 15.

[968]See Ehrman, "Preface," in *Jesus Interrupted*, x-xii.

academically and especially spiritually to encourage students to dabble in historical criticism. When seminaries become degree mills focused on maximizing headcounts and prestigious academia at the expense of quality spiritual formation of the individual students through careful mentoring, disaster always ensues. Notice that while Marshall, Hagner, and other evangelicals call pseudepigraphy by a euphemism and accept it as in line with inspiration, Ehrman recognized this complete inconsistency and was honest enough to call such activity what it truly is: FORGED! [969]

While Ehrman is honest, evangelicals who are involved in historical-critical research are not quite as open and frank. Yarborough feels that Linnemann went too far. Ehrman would find commonality in Linnemann's assessment that historical-critical ideologies are an overwhelmingly strategical, negative influence. Harold Lindsell, in his *The Battle for the Bible* (1976) as well as his subsequent work, *The Bible in the Balance* (1978), was instrumental in sounding the warning among Bible-believing people of historical criticism's destruction of inerrancy and infallibility. Lindsell warned "The presuppositions of this methodology . . . go far beyond a mere denial of biblical infallibility. They tear at the heart of Scripture, and include a denial of the supernatural."[970] In *The Bible in the Balance*, Lindsell devoted an entire chapter to the issue, entitled "The Historical Critical Method: The Bible's Deadly Enemy" in which he argued,

> Anyone who thinks that the historical-critical method is neutral is misinformed. Since its presuppositions are unacceptable to the evangelical mind this method cannot be used by evangelicals as it stands. The very use by the evangelical of the term, the historical-critical method, is a mistake when it comes to his own approach to Scripture . . . . It appears to me that modern evangelical scholars (and I may have been guilty of this myself) have played fast and loose with the term perhaps because they wanted acceptance by academia. They seem too often to desire to be members of the club which is nothing more than practicing an inclusiveness that undercuts the normativity of the evangelical theological position. This may be done, and often is, under the illusion that by this method the opponents of biblical inerrancy can be won over to the evangelical viewpoint. But practical experience suggests that rarely does this happen and the cost of such an approach is too expensive, for it gives credence and lends respectability to a method which is the deadly enemy of theological orthodoxy. [971]

Yet, these current critically-trained evangelicals apparently believe that they themselves are somehow immune to its subversive power that Linnemann, Lindsell, and others warned of. Is this the case, or is this hubris on the part of these critically-

---

[969] Bart D. Ehman, *Forged and Counterforgery: The Use of Literary Deceit in Early Christian Polemics* (Oxford: Oxford University, 2013) and *Forged Writing in the Name of God—Why the Bible's Authors are Not Who We Think They Are* (New York: Harper One, 2011).

[970] Harold Lindsell, *The Battle for the Bible* (Grand Rapids: Eermans, 1976), 204.

[971] Harold Lindsell, *The Bible in the Balance* (Grand Rapids: Zondervan, 1978), 283.

trained evangelicals? Church history stands as a monumental testimony against any such boldness on their part.

In Craig Blomberg's more recent work, *Can We Still Believe the Bible?*,[972] he moves away from orthodox understandings of inerrancy and champions the case of Robert Gundry who used a non-historical genre argument to dismiss much of the infancy narratives in Matthew and attacks people who defend orthodox views of inerrancy as being linked to "Nazis" and "Communists."[973] As Norman Geisler has shown in an insightful review article regarding Blomberg's work, it does NOT support any orthodox concept of inerrancy like ICBI, "even though Blomberg says that he affirms and understands these documents . . . one thing is certain: his views are contrary to the clear statements of the ICBI."[974] Since Geisler was a founding member of ICBI, he would recognize whether Blomberg understands the ICBI documents as intended by its authors. Geisler constitutes a powerful witness against this evangelical drift away from inerrancy.

Blomberg also champions Sanday's viewpoint of an inductive approach to Scripture. He relates that "[t]here are two quite different approaches [to inerrancy], moreover, that can lead to an affirmation that Scripture is without error."[975] These two approaches are "inductive approach" that "begins with the phenomena of the Bible itself, defines what would count as an error, analyzes Scripture carefully from beginning to end, and determines that nothing has been discovered that would qualify as errant."[976] The "deductive approach" that begins with the conviction that God is the author of Scripture proceeds to the premise by definition that God cannot err, and therefore concludes that God's Word must be without error."[977] He reacts negatively against the deductive approach of "evidentialists and "presuppositonalists" by noting that these two terms "ultimately views inerrancy as a corollary of inspiration, not something to be demonstrated from the texts of Scripture itself." If the Bible is God-breathed (2 Tim. 3:16), and God cannot err, then the Bible must be errant. Hence, the inductive approach to Blomberg requires that the Bible prove that it is inerrant through a critical investigation of the texts themselves rather than the others that just assume the texts are inerrant. Thus, he shifts the burden of proof from the Bible to that of the scholar. It is the critical investigator who must establish whether the text is truly inerrant. Importantly, Blomberg believes that the real debate on inerrancy is one of "hermeneutics."[978] Thus, under this logic, one could hold to inerrancy but believe that a particular event in Scripture is really symbolic and not to be taken as literally an event in the

---

[972] Craig L. Blomberg, *Can We Still Believe The Bible?* (Grand Rapids: Baker, 2014).

[973] Two reviews of Blomberg should be noted, Norman L. Geisler, A Response to Craig L. Blomberg's Can We Still Believe the Bible? April 11, 2014 accessed at http://defendinginerrancy.org/ on April 13, 2014; F. David Farnell, A Review of Craig L. Blomberg's *Can We Still Believe the Bible?*, The Master's Journal Spring 2014, XXX.

[974] Geisler, "A Review of Craig Blomberg's *Can We Still Believe the Bible?*,

[975] Blomberg, *Can We Still Believe?*, 121.

[976] Ibid., 121.

[977] Ibid.

[978] Ibid., 125.

time-space continuum (such as creation in six days).[979] As a result, "Genesis 1 can be and has been interpreted by inerrantists as referring to a young earth, an old earth, progressive creation, theistic evolution, a literary framework for asserting God as the creator of all things irrespective of his methods, and a series of days when God took up residence in his cosmic temple for the sake of newly created humanity in his image. Once again, this is a matter for hermeneutical and exegetical debate, not one that is solved by the shibboleth of inerrancy."[980] Under the inductive approach, a Christian would never be able to assert the whole inerrancy of the Bible, for the Bible would need to be constantly re-examined in its parts according to the shifting sands of critical evangelical scholarship's usage of historical-critical ideologies.

One must note, however, that Blomberg reveals his startling differences with inerrancy as defined by ICBI in 1978: "We affirm that the text of Scripture is to be interpreted by grammatico-historical exegesis, taking account of its literary forms and devices, and that Scripture is to interpret Scripture. We deny the legitimacy of any treatment of the text or quest for sources lying behind it that leads to relativizing, dehistoricizing, or discounting its teaching, or rejecting its claims to authorship." Here Blomberg's position is neither grammatical, historical, or literal, for Blomberg argues, "defenders of inerrancy do not reflect often enough on what it means to say that nonhistorical genres are wholly truthful."[981] He also reflects a *deja vu* mantra of Rogers and McKim who wrote in 1979, "But often without realizing it, we impose on ancient documents twenty-first century standards that are equally inappropriate." Rogers and McKim, said, "To erect a standard of modern, technical precision in language as the hallmark of biblical authority was totally foreign to the foundation shared by the early church."[982] Blomberg also supports elements of speech-act theory also maintains that "Vanhoozer's work is indeed very attractive, but it is scarcely at odds with the Chicago Statement."[983] The reader is referred here to Geisler and Roach evaluation of Vanhoozer for a different perspective, "Kevin Vanhoozer on Inerrancy," in *Inerrancy Defended*.[984] One wonders at this statement of Blomberg, since Vanhoozer denies the grammatico-historical approach, and as Geisler and Roach conclude, "[Vanhoozer] also claims to affirm much of the ICBI statement as he understands it. But that is precisely the problem since the way he understands it is not the way the framers meant it, as is demonstrated from the official commentaries on the ICBI statements."[985]

The practical result is genre can be used to deny anything in the bible that the interpreter finds offensive as a literal sense. The allegorical school did such a thing,

---

[979] Ibid., 126.

[980] Ibid., 126.

[981] Ibid., 128.

[982] Rogers and McKim, *The Authority and Intepretation of the Bible: An Historical Approach*, xxii.

[983] Blomberg, 136.

[984] Norman L. Geisler and William C. Roach, *Inerrancy Defended* (Grand Rapids: Baker, 2012), 132-159.

[985] Geisler and Roach, *Inerrancy Defended*, 158.

the gnostics did it to Scripture as well, and now Blomberg applies his updated version of it with genre being applied to hermeneutics. Blomberg's use of genre, to this present reviewer, smacks of an eerie similarity to Rogers and McKim's deprecation of literal interpretation when they noted Westerner's logic that viewed "statements in the Bible were treated like logical propositions that could be interpreted quite literally according to contemporary standards."[986] In Chapter 5, "Aren't Several Narrative Genres of the Bible Unhistorial," his use of hermeneutics continues to be the means by which he can redefine what normal definition of inerrancy would be, and he uses it to deny the plain, normal sense of Genesis 1–3,[987] while advocating that we must understand the author's intent in such passages, with the key question from Article 13 of ICBI, "standards of truth and error that are alien to its usage or purpose." Applying a completely wrong understanding of this clause of ICBI as well as the original intent of the founders of ICBI, Blomberg advocates that idea that "the question is simply one about the most likely literary form of the passage."[988] From there, he proceeds to allow for non-literal interpretation of Genesis 1–3 that are, in his view, fully in line with inerrancy, e.g., Adam and Eve as symbols for every man and woman,[989] evolutionary and progressive creation,[990] a non-historical Jonah,[991] the possibility of three Isaiah's,[992] Daniel as Apocalyptic genre rather than prophetic,[993] fully embracing of midrash interpretation of the Gospels as advocated by Robert Gundry as not impacting inerrancy,[994] as well as pseudepigraphy as fully in line with inerrancy in NT epistles under the guide of a "literary device" or "acceptable form of pseudonymity.[995] He argues that we don't know the opinions of the first century church well-enough on pseudepigraphy to rule it out: "[B]arring some future discovery related to first-century opinions, we cannot pontificate on what kinds of claims for authorship would or would not have been considered acceptable in Christian communities, and especially in Jewish-Christian circles when the New Testament Epistles were written. As a result, we must evaluate every proposal based on its own historical and grammatical merits, not on whether it does or does not pass some pre-established criterion of what inerrancy can accept."[996]

Interestingly, the 2013 President of the Evangelical Society, Robert W. Yarborough praises Blomberg's work, *Can We Still Believe?* in the following terms. Although the quote is lengthy, it is necessary to show the degradation of inerrancy

---

[986] Rogers and McKim, *The Authority and Interpretation of the Bible*, xviii.

[987] Blomberg, *Can We Still Believe?*, 150.

[988] Ibid.

[989] Ibid., 152.

[990] Ibid., 151-153.

[991] Ibid., 160.

[992] Ibid., 162.

[993] Ibid., 163-164.

[994] Ibid., 165-168.

[995] Ibid., 168-172.

[996] Ibid., 172.

among the seminary teachers in America, for he addresses the future of the direction of evangelical academia toward the inerrancy of Scripture:

> This book is refreshing and important not only because of its breadth of coverage of issues, viewpoints, and literature. It is evenhanded in that both enemies of inerrancy and *wrong-headed friends* are called on the carpet. Blomberg revisits incidents like Robert Gundry's dismissal from this society and the kerfluffle over a decade ago surrounding the TNIV and inclusive language. He does not mince words in criticizing those he sees as overzealous for the inerrancy cause. Nor is he bashful in calling out former inerrantists who, Blomberg finds, often make their polemical arguments against what they used to believe with less than compelling warrant. I predict that everyone who reads the book will disagree strongly with the author about something.[997]

Please note that in Blomberg's book, these "wrong-headed" friends are those who hold to an orthodox view of inerrancy as well as the ICBI statements of 1978 and 1982.

Yarborough continues,

> At the same time, the positive arguments for inerrancy are even more substantial. It is clear that Blomberg is not content with poking holes in non-inerrantist arguments. He writes, "I do not think one has to settle for anything short of full-fledged inerrantist Christianity so long as we ensure that we employ all parts of a detailed exposition of inerrancy, such as that found in the Chicago Statement."

> Or again: "These Scriptures are trustworthy. We can still believe the Bible. We should still believe the Bible and act accordingly, by following Jesus in disciple- ship." I am skimming some of his concluding statements, but the real meat of the book is inductive demonstration of inerrancy's plausibility based on primary evidence and scholarship surrounding that evidence. *If only a book of this substance had been available when I was a college or grad school student!*[998]

If this is the future of their concept of "inerrancy" in evangelical seminaries, then all hopes of a firm foundation for Scripture are shipwreck.

Conclusion:

Historical Matters Don't Seem to Matter to Historical-Critical Evangelicals

In answering the question posed by the book, *Do Historical Matters Matter to Faith?*, an alarming trend has been noticed among these evangelicals who pursue such a *modus operandi* based in historical-critical ideologies as delineated above. A

---

[997] Robert W. Yarborough, "The Future of Cognitive Reverence for the Bible," *JETS* 57/1 (March 2014): 5-18 (quote from page 9). Italics added.

[998] Ibid. Italics added.

subtle and, at times, not so subtle de-historicizing of the Gospels is taking place. Such an evangelical trend dangerously impacts the ICBI statements crafted in 1978 (Inerrancy) and 1982 (Hermeneutics) for views of the inerrancy and interpretation of the Gospels as well as the entire Old and New Testaments. While the evangelicals involved are to be commended for their assertion that they affirm a belief in inerrancy, their practice seems to be at odds with such an assertion. This question of historical matters mattering would seem to need a negative answer in many instances. Because these evangelicals have a problematic view of the historical basis of the Gospels, many of them have joined together in the pursuit of what is termed "searching for the 'historical Jesus'" which is based on a philosophically-driven post-modernistic historiography.

It is now clear that the influence of European training upon American evangelicals has had a very deleterious impact on the trustworthiness of God's Word for a new generation of scholars. Sadly, these evangelicals apparently believe that they themselves are immune to the subversive powers of historical criticism that no one previously ever surmounted. By contrast, the ICBI Statements on Inerrancy (1978) and Hermeneutics (1982) were designed to be a warning and safeguard to future generations of evangelical scholars. History has repeated itself. As at the turn of the twentieth century, a call must go forth today to rally the faithful to expose doctrinal error to preserve a faithful remnant for the glory of our Lord Jesus Christ.

CHAPTER 10 The Documentary Hypothesis

Edward D. Andrews

It was in the latter half of the nineteenth century that higher criticism began to be taken seriously. These critics rejected Moses as the writer of the Pentateuch, arguing instead that the accounts in Genesis, Exodus, Leviticus, Numbers, and Deuteronomy were based on four other sources [writers] written between the 10th and the 6th centuries B.C.E. To differentiate these sources one from the other, they are simply known as the "J," "E," "D," and "P" sources. The letters are the initial to the name of these alleged sources, also known as the Documentary Hypothesis.

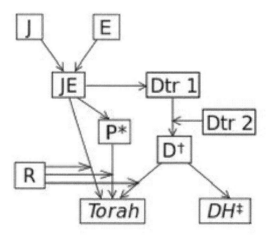

Diagram of the Documentary Hypothesis.

*   includes most of Leviticus

†   includes most of Deuteronomy

‡   "Deuteronomic history": Joshua, Judges, 1 & 2 Samuel, 1 & 2 Kings – Wikipedia

Source Criticism, a sub-discipline of Higher Criticism, is an attempt by liberal Bible scholars to discover the original sources that the Bible writer(s) [not Moses] used to pen these five books. It should be noted that most scholars who engage in higher criticism start with liberal presuppositions. Dr. Gleason L. Archer, Jr., identifies many flaws in the reasoning of those who support the Documentary Hypothesis; however, this one flaw being quoted herein is indeed the most grievous and lays the foundation for other irrational reasoning in their thinking. Identifying their problem, Archer writes, "The Wellhausen school started with the pure assumption (which they have hardly bothered to demonstrate) that Israel's religion was of merely human origin like any other, and that it was to be explained as a mere product of evolution."[999] In other words, Wellhausen and those who followed him begin with the presupposition that God's Word is *not* that at all, the Word of God, but is the word of mere man, and then they reason **into** the Scripture not **out of** the Scriptures based on that premise. As to the effect, this has on God's Word and those who hold it as such; it is comparable to having a natural disaster wash the foundation right out from under our home.

Liberal Christianity says that Moses did not pen every word from Genesis through Deuteronomy. They conclude that this is nothing more than a tradition that originated in the times that the Jews returned from their exile in Babylon in 537 B.C.E. and the destruction of Jerusalem in 70 C.E. These source critics reason that there was and is a misunderstanding of Deuteronomy 31:9, which says that Moses "[wrote] this law, and delivered it unto the priests the sons of Levi, that bare the ark of the covenant of Jehovah, and unto all the elders of Israel." They argue that Deuteronomy only implies that Moses wrote the laws of Deuteronomy chapters 12–28; moreover, this was extended into a tradition that encompassed the belief that the entire Pentateuch was *not* written by Moses.

In addition, these source critics put forth that the language of Deuteronomy chapters 12–18, as well as the historical and theological context, places the writing and completion of these five books centuries after Moses died. According to these critics, this alleged tradition of Moses being the author of the first five books of our Bible was completely accepted as fact by the time Jesus Christ arrived on the scene in the first-century C.E. These critics further argue that Jesus, the Son of God, was also duped by this tradition and simply perpetuated it when he referred to "the book of Moses" (Mark 12:26), which to the Jews at that time counted Genesis, Exodus, Leviticus, Numbers, and Deuteronomy as a book by Moses. In addition, at John 17:23, Jesus spoke of "the law of Moses," which he and all others Jews had long held to be the Pentateuch. Thus, for the critic, Jesus simply handed this misunderstood tradition off to first-century Christianity.

We have read much in previous chapters thus far about these critical scholars, but it will not hurt to review, before delving into discrediting their hypothesis. How has such extreme thinking as this Documentary Hypothesis come down to us, going from being a hypothesis to being accepted as *law* in secular universities and most seminaries? What is the relationship between a hypothesis, theory, and law? In the physical sciences, there are several steps before a description of a phenomenon becomes law.

(1) **Observation:** "I noticed that objects fall to the earth."

(2) **Hypothesis:** "I think something must be pulling these objects to the earth. Let me call it gravity."

(3) **Experimentation:** "Let me put this to the test by releasing different objects from that cliff. Umm, it seems that everything I let go falls. My hypothesis seems to be right."

---

[999] 999. Gleason L. Archer, A Survey of Old Testament Introduction (Moody Publishers, Chicago, 2007), 98.

(4) **Theory:** "I have noticed that every time I release an object, and wherever I do it, over the sidewalk, from the 32nd floor of that office building and even from the cruise ship—they fall to the earth as if pulled by something. It happens often enough to be called a theory."

(5) **Law:** "Well, this has consistently been occurring over the years. It must be absolutely true and therefore a Law."

Where does the "Documentary Hypothesis" fit into this scheme? Wellhausen *et al.* made certain **Observations** and then produced a **Hypothesis** to explain what they saw. I would argue that is as far as they made it in following the formula for the scientific method.

The Forefathers of Source Criticisms

Abraham Ibn Ezra (1089–1164) Ibn Ezra was, by far, the most famous Bible scholar of medieval times. True enough, he may have questioned the idea that Moses wrote the entire Torah; however, he chose not to do this in an outward way; he chose to be more subtle in presenting such an idea. For Ibn Ezra, several verses seemed not to have come from Moses, but one verse stood out above the others. Deuteronomy 1:1 reads: "These are the words that Moses spoke to all of Israel beyond the Jordan." The east side of the Jordan would be "this" side with the west side being the "other side." (Numbers 35:14; Joshua 22:4) The point of his contention here being the fact that Moses was never on the other side of the Jordan, the west side, with the Israelite nation. Therefore, the question begs to be asked, Why would Moses pen "beyond," a seeming reference to the west side? This will be answered soon enough.

Thomas Hobbes (1588–1679) writes, "It is therefore sufficiently evident that the five books of Moses were written after his time, though how long after it be not so manifest." Is Hobbes a friend or foe of Christianity? Like Francis Bacon before him, he deepened the crack in the acceptance of the Bible being a source of divine authority.[1000]

Benedict Spinoza (1632–1677) writes, "It is thus clearer than the sun at noon the Pentateuch was not written by Moses but by someone who lived long after Moses." Spinoza lays the groundwork for higher criticism based on logical or reasonable deduction, believing that thought and actions should be governed by reason, deductive rationalism.[1001] He writes that because "There are many passages in the Pentateuch which Moses could not have written, it follows that the belief that Moses was the author of the Pentateuch is ungrounded and irrational."[1002] Moses was not the only Biblical author to lose his writership at the chopping block of Spinoza. "I pass on, then, to the prophetic books ... An examination of these

---

[1000] Garrett, Don, *The Cambridge companion to Spinoza* (Cambridge: Cambridge University Press, 1996), 389.

[1001] Richard Elliot Friedman, *Who Wrote The Bible* (San Francisco: Harper Collins, 1997), 21.

[1002] R. H. M. Elwes, *A Theologico-political Treatise, and a Political Treatise* (New York, NY: Cosimo Classics, 2005), 126.

assures me that the prophecies therein contained have been compiled from other books ... but are only such as were collected here and there, so that they are fragmentary." Daniel did not fare so well either, he is only credited with the last five chapters of his book. Spinoza presents the notion that the 39 books of the Hebrew Old Testament were set down by none other than the Pharisees. Moreover, the prophets spoke not by God, being inspired, but of their own accord. As to the apostles, Spinoza wrote, "The mode of expression and discourse adopted by [them] in the Epistles show very clearly that the latter are not written by revelation and divine command, but merely by the natural powers and judgment of the authors." Did Matthew, Mark, Luke, and John, fare any better? Hardly! Spinoza states: "It is scarcely credible that God can have designated to narrate the life of Christ four times over, and to communicate it thus to mankind."

Spinoza had no respect for those he deemed fools because of their belief in miracles. He writes, "Anyone who seeks for the true causes of miracles and strives to understand natural phenomena as an intelligent being, and not gaze upon them like a fool, is set down and denounced as an impious heretic by those, whom the masses adore as the interpreters of nature and the gods. Such a person knows that, with the removal of ignorance, the wonder which forms their only available means for proving and preserving their authority would vanish also. . . . A miracle, whether a contravention to, or beyond nature is a mere absurdity."[1003] Such a dogmatic disbelief in miracles is a contributing factor to Spinoza being the father of modern-day higher criticism.

Richard Simon (1638–1712). This French Catholic priest accepted Moses as the author for most of the Pentateuch, but he is the first to notice repetition with certain portions that would come to be known as doublets.

- two different creation stories

- two stories of the Abrahamic covenant

- two stories where Abraham names his son, Isaac

- two stories where Abraham claims Sarah as his sister

- two stories of Jacob's journey to Haran

- two stories where God revealed himself to Jacob at Bethel

- two stories where God changes Jacob's name to Israel

- two stories of when Moses got water from a rock at Meribah

Jean Astruc (1684–1766) This French physician and professor of medicine would, by a rather naïve observation, get the Documentary Hypothesis underway. While Astruc never denied Mosaic writership, he had observed that there seemed to be two sources for Moses' penning the early chapters of Genesis: one that favored the title God (Elohim), and another that favored the personal name of God (Jehovah). This theory seemed to carry even more support by duplicate material, as Astruc viewed Genesis chapter one as one creation account and Genesis chapter

---

[1003] Norman L. Geisler, *Inerrancy* (Grand Rapids, MI: Zondervan, 1980), 318.

two as another. It should be kept in mind that Astruc credited Moses as the writer, but was simply looking for what Moses may have drawn on in penning the Pentateuch.[1004]

David Hume (1711–1776) was an eighteenth-century Scottish philosopher whose influence on the denial of divine authority, miracles, and prophecy has had a major impact that has reached down to the twenty-first century! Hume has three major pillars that hold up his refutation of divine authority. First, he writes, "A miracle is a violation of the laws of nature."[1005] The laws of nature have been with man since his start. If a person falls from a high place, he will hit the ground. If a rock is dropped into the sea, it will sink. Each morning our sun comes over the horizon and each night it goes down, and so on. Without a doubt, there are laws of nature that never fail to follow their purpose. Therefore, for Hume, there is nothing that would ever violate the laws of nature. This 'conclusive evidence,' Hume felt, "is as entire as any argument from experience" that there could never be miracles.

Hume's second pillar is based on his belief that humankind is gullible. Moreover, he reasons that the masses of 'religious persons' want to believe in miracles. In addition, there have been many who have lied about so-called miracles, which have been nothing but a sham. For his third pillar, Hume argues that miracles have occurred only in the time periods of ignorance; as the enlightenment of man grew the miraculous diminished. Hume reported, "Such prodigious events never happen in our days." Hume rejected the inspiration of Scripture on two grounds: (1) he denied the possibility of miracles and prophecy, and (2) he rejected the Bible's divine authority as a whole because, to him, it was based upon perception or feeling, rather than upon fact, nor could it be proved by observation and experiment. Thus, for Hume, the result is that the Bible "contains nothing but sophistry and illusion."[1006] As we can see, Hume's conclusion is obvious: Because the Bible is, in fact, not inspired, it could never be a true source of knowledge that it claims, and it is certainly not God's Word for humankind.

Johann Gottfried Eichhorn (1752–1827) took Jean Astruc's conjectures beyond Genesis to other books of the Pentateuch, arguing that the Pentateuch contained three primary sources that were distinct by vocabulary, style, and theological features. He also borrowed the phrase "higher criticism" from Presbyterian minister and scientist Joseph Priestly, and he was the first to name these alleged sources "E" (for Elohim) and "J" for Jehovah.[1007]

Karl Heinrich Graf (1815–1869), aside from Julius Wellhausen, was the person we look to most for the modern documentary hypothesis. For Graf the "J" source

---

[1004] Norman L. Geisler and William E. Nix, *A General Introduction to the Bible. Rev. and Expanded* (Chicago, IL: Moody Press, c.1986, 1996), 156.

[1005] David Hume, *An Enquiry Concerning Human Understanding* (Boston, MA: Digireads.com, 2006), 65.

[1006] Ibid., 90.

[1007] Norman L. Geisler and William E. Nix, *A General Introduction to the Bible. Rev. and Expanded* (Chicago, IL: Moody Press, c.1986, 1996), 157.

was the earliest, composed in the ninth century B.C.E.;[1008] the "E" source was written shortly thereafter. The author of Deuteronomy wrote shortly before Josiah's clearing away false worship in the seventh century B.C.E., and finally, the "P" source was written in the sixth century after the exile.

In 1878, the German Bible critic **Julius Wellhausen (1844–1918)**, writing in *Prolegomena zur Geschichte Israels* (*Prolegomena to the History of Israel*), popularized the ideas of the above scholars that the first five books of the Bible, as well as Joshua, were written from the 9th century into the 5th century B.C.E., over a millennium [1,000 years] after the events described.[1009]

The capital letter "J" is used to represent an alleged writer. In this case it stands for any place God's personal name, Jehovah, is used. It is argued that this author is perhaps a woman as it is the only one of their presented authors who is not a priest. (Harold Bloom, *The Book of "J"*) They date the portion set out to "J" to c.850 B.C.E. Some scholars place this author in the southern portion of the Promised Land, Judah.[1010]

Another writer is put forth as "E," for it stands for the portion that has Jehovah's title Elohim, God. Most higher critics place this author c.750–700 B.C.E. Unlike "J," this author "E" is said to reside in the northern kingdom of Israel. As stated earlier, this author is reckoned a priest, with his lineage going back to Moses. It is also proffered that he bought this office. In addition, it is argued that an editor combined "J" and "E" after the destruction of Israel by the Assyrians but before the destruction of Jerusalem by the Babylonians, which they date to about 722 BC.E.[1011]

These same critics hold out that the language and theological content of "D," Deuteronomy, is different from Genesis, Exodus, Leviticus, and Numbers. Thus they have another author. They argue that the priests living in the northern kingdom of Israel gathered "D" over several hundred years; however, it was not until much later that "D" was combined with the earlier works. It is also said that the "D" writer (source) was also behind Joshua, Judges, 1 and 2 Samuel and 1 and 2 Kings (Dtr). It is suggested strongly that, in fact, this is the book found in the temple by Hilkiah the high priest and given to King Josiah. (2 Kings 22:8) It is further put forth that J/E/D were fused together as one document in about 586 B.C.E.[1012]

The source critics use the capital letter "P" for Priestly. This is because this portion of the Pentateuch usually relates to the priesthood. For instance, things like the sacrifices would be tagged as belonging to this author. Many scholars suggest that "P" was written before the destruction of Jerusalem, which they date at 586

[1008] B.C.E. means "before the Common Era," which is more accurate than B.C. ("before Christ"). C.E. denotes "Common Era," often called A.D., for anno Domini, meaning "in the year of our Lord."

[1009] Ernest Nicholson, *The Pentateuch in the Twentieth Century: The Legacy of Julius Wellhausen* (New York: Oxford University Press, 1998), 36–47.

[1010] Mark F. Rooker, *Leviticus: The New American Commentary* (Nashville: Broadman & Holman, 2001), 23.

[1011] Ibid., 23.

[1012] Ibid., 23.

B.C.E. Others put forth that it was written during the exile of seventy years, the Priest(s) composing this holy portion for the people who would return from exile, while others say it was written after the exile, about 450 B.C.E. These liberal scholars find no consensus on when this supposed author "P" wrote this portion of the first five books. The critics tell us that the final form of J/E/D/P was composed into one document about 400 B.C.E.[1013]

The capital "R" represents the editor(s) who put it together and may have altered some portions to facilitate their social-circumstances of their day. The "R" comes from the German word *Redakteur* (Redactor), which is an editor or reviser of a work.

With all the focus on Wellhausen and the impetus he has given to the Documentary Hypothesis, one would conclude that he had made an enormous, critical investigation of the text, which, in essence, moved him to cosign with his predecessors. If that is your conclusion, you will have to regroup, for it was simply a feeling that something was not quite right that moved Wellhausen to accept a system of understanding without any evidence whatsoever. In his book *Prolegomena to the History of Israel,* first published in 1878, Wellhausen helps his readers to appreciate just how he came about his expressed interest in the Documentary Hypothesis:

> In my early student days I was attracted by the stories of Saul and David, Ahab and Elijah; the discourses of Amos and Isaiah laid strong hold on me, and I read myself well into the prophetic and historical books of the Old Testament. Thanks to such aids as were accessible to me, I even considered that I understood them tolerably, but at the same time was troubled with a bad conscience, as if I were beginning with the roof instead of the foundation; for I had no thorough acquaintance with the Law, of which I was accustomed to be told that it was the basis and postulate of the whole literature. At last I took courage and made my way through Exodus, Leviticus, Numbers, and even through Knobel's Commentary to these books. But it was in vain that I looked for the light which was to be shed from this source on the historical and prophetical books. On the contrary, my enjoyment of the latter was marred by the Law; it did not bring them any nearer me, but intruded itself uneasily, like a ghost that makes a noise indeed, but is not visible and really effects nothing. Even where there were points of contact between it and them, differences also made themselves felt, and I found it impossible to give a candid decision in favour of the priority of the Law. Dimly I began to perceive that throughout there was between them all the difference that separates two wholly distinct worlds. Yet, so far from attaining clear conceptions, I only fell into deeper confusion, which was worse confounded by the explanations of Ewald in the second volume of history of Israel. At last, in the course of a casual visit in Göttingen in the summer of 1867, I learned through Ritschl that Karl Heinrich Graf placed the law later than the Prophets, and, almost without knowing his reasons for the hypothesis, I was prepared to accept it; I readily acknowledged

---

[1013] Ibid., 23–24.

to myself the possibility of understanding Hebrew antiquity without the book of the Torah.[1014]

Martin Noth (1902–1968) A liberal twentieth-century German scholar who specialized in the pre-Exilic history of the Jewish people. Noth presented what he called the "Deuteronomic Historian." He argued that the language and theological outlook of Joshua, Judges, 1 and 2 Samuel and 1 and 2 Kings was the same as the book of Deuteronomy. Noth believed this writer lived during the exile because of a reference from 2 Kings to the exile. Modern critics, however, believed this writer lived before the exile, with 2 Kings 25:27 being a later addition.

Frank M. Cross, Jr., Hebrew and Biblical scholar' muddies the water even more with his proposition that there was not one Deuteronomistic history, but two. The first he proposed to be written during the reign of the Judean King Josiah to aid him in cleaning up the false worship going on within Judah. After the destruction of Jerusalem, Cross said the same writer or possibly another goes back to edit this work, to add in the destruction of Jerusalem and the exile to Babylon.

Redaction Criticism

I briefly address the Redaction Theory here because of its relationship to the Documentary Hypothesis. As stated above in our alphabet soup of alleged authors ("J," "E," "D," "P," and "R"), a redactor is an editor or reviser of a work. Redaction Criticism is another form of Biblical criticism that intends to investigate the Scriptures and draw conclusions concerning their authorship, historicity, and time of writing. This form of criticism as well as the others has really done nothing more than tear down God's Word. R. E. Friedman, the Documentary Hypothesis' biggest advocate, asserts that the "J" document was composed between 922–722 B.C.E. in the southern kingdom of Judah, while the northern kingdom of Israel was composing the "E" document during these same years. Friedman contends that sometime thereafter a compiler of history put these two sources together, resulting in "J/E," with the compiler being known as "RJE." Friedman states that shortly thereafter, the priesthood in Jerusalem put out yet another document, known today as "P," this being another story to be added to the above "J/E." Going back to their authors for the first five books of the Bible, Friedman and these critics claim a redactor, or editor put the whole Pentateuch together using "D," "P," and the combination of "J/E." For them this editor (Deuteronomist) used the written sources he had available to make his additions for dealing with the social conditions of his day. They claim this editor's express purpose was to alter Scripture to bring comfort and hope to those who were in exile in Babylon. Wellhausen's theories, with some adjustments, have spread like a contagious disease, until they have consumed the body of Christendom. However, the real question is, Do these higher critics have any serious evidence to overturn thousands of years of belief by three major religious groups (Jews, Christians, and Muslims) that the Pentateuch was written by Moses?

What these critics have are pebbles, each representing minute inferences and implications [circumstantial evidence at best] that they place on one side of a scale.

[1014] Julius Wellhausen, *Prolegomena to the History of Israel* (1878), 3–4

These are weighed out against the conservative evidence of Moses' authorship of the Pentateuch. As unsuspecting readers work their way through the books and articles written by these critics, the scales seem to be tilted all to one side, as if there were no evidence for the other side. Thus, like a jury, many uninformed readers; conclude that there is no alternative but to accept the idea that there are multiple authors for the Pentateuch instead of Moses, who is traditionally held to be the sole author.

Just what impact has the Documentary Hypothesis had on academia? Let us allow R. Rendtorf, professor Emeritus of the University of Heidelberg, to answer:

> Current international study of the Pentateuch presents at first glance a picture of complete unanimity. The overwhelming majority of scholars in almost all countries where scholarly study of Old Testament is pursued, take the documentary hypothesis as the virtually uncontested point of departure for their work; and their interest in the most precise understanding of the nature and theological purposes of the individual written sources seems undisturbed.[1015]

Let us take a moment to look at many of these pebbles and see which side of the scale they are to be placed on. As stated at the outset, we will address the major arguments as a case against the whole. Some of these pebbles are major obstacles for honest-hearted Christians.

Arguments of Higher Critics for the Documentary Hypothesis

We will address four areas of argumentation from the higher critics: (1) the divine names, (2) discrepancies, (3) repetition, known as "doublets," and (4) differences in language and style. We will give at least one example of each and address at least one example under the evidence for Moses' writership.

Divine Names

The higher critics argue that every Bible verse that contains the Hebrew word for God, ('*Elohim*), set off by itself has its own writer, designated by the capital "E" ("Elohist"). On the other hand, any verse that contains the Tetragrammaton, (Jehovah, Yahweh), God's personal name, is attributed to yet another writer, "J" ("Jawist"). (Cassuto, 18-21) Let us see how they explain this. The critics argue that "God" ('*Elohim*) is restricted in use exclusively in the first chapter of Genesis (1:1– 31) in relation to God's creation activity, and that starting in Genesis 2:4 through the end of the second chapter we find God's personal name.

R. E. Friedman speaks of a discovery by three men: "One was a minister, one was a physician, and one was a professor. The discovery that they made ultimately came down to the combination of two pieces of evidence: doublets and the names

---

[1015] R. Rendtorff, "The Problem of the Process of Transmission in the Pentateuch," *JSOT* (1990): 101.

of God. They saw that there were apparently two versions each of a large number of Biblical stories: two accounts of the creation, two accounts each of several stories about the patriarchs Abraham and Jacob, and so on. Then, they noticed that, quite often, one of the two versions of a story would refer to God by one name and the other version would refer to God by a different name." (R. E. Friedman, 50)

Different settings, however, require different uses. This principle holds true throughout the whole of the entire Old Testament. Moses may choose to use (*'Elohim'*) in a setting in which he wants to show a particular quality clearly, like power, creative activity, and so on. On the other hand, Moses may choose to use God's personal name (Jehovah, Yahweh) when the setting begs for that personal relationship between the Father and his children, the Israelites, or even more personable, a one-on-one conversation between Jehovah God and a faithful servant.

The Divine Names: The weakness of claiming multiple authors because of the different names used for God is quite evident when we look at just one small portion of the book of Genesis in the *American Standard Version* (1901). God is called "God Most High," "possessor (or maker) of heaven and earth," "O Lord Jehovah," "a God that seeth," "God Almighty," "God," "[the] God,"[1016] and "the Judge of all the earth." (Genesis 14:18, 19; 15:2; 16:13; 17:1, 3; 18:25) It is difficult to believe that different authors wrote these verses. Moreover, let us look at Genesis 28:13, which says, "And, behold, Jehovah stood above it, and said, I am Jehovah, the God ["Elohim"] of Abraham thy father, and the God of Isaac: the land whereon thou liest, to thee will I give it, and to thy seed." Another scripture, Psalm 47:5, says, "God is gone up with a shout, Jehovah with the sound of a trumpet."[1017] In applying their documentary analysis, we would have to accept the idea that two authors worked together on each of these two verses.

Many conservative scholars have come to realize that in a narrative format one will often find a ruler being referred to not only by name but also by a title, such as "king." M. H. Segal observes: "Just as those interchanges of human proper names and their respective appellative common nouns cannot by any stretch of the imagination be ascribed to a change of author or source of document, so also the corresponding interchanges of the divine names in the Pentateuch must not be attributed to such a literary cause."[1018] If one were to look up "Adolf Hitler" using Academic American Encyclopedia, within three paragraphs he will find the terms "Führer," "Adolf Hitler," and simply "Hitler." Who is so bold as to suggest that there are three different authors for these three paragraphs?

Dr. John J. Davis[1019] helps us to appreciate that there is "no other religious document from the ancient Near East [that] was compiled in such a manner; a documentary analysis of the Gilgameš Epic or Enūma Eliš would be complete folly.

[1016] The title *'Elo·him'* preceded by the definite article *ha*, giving the expression *ha·'Elo·him'*.

[1017] See also Psalm 46:11; 48:1, 8.

[1018] See also Psalm 46:11; 48:1, 8.

[1019] John J. Davis, *Paradise to Prison: Studies in Genesis* (Salem: Sheffield, 1975), 22–23.

The author of Genesis may have selected divine names on the basis of theological emphasis rather than dogmatic preference. Many divine names were probably interchangeable; Baal and Hadad were used interchangeably in the Hadad Tablet from Ugarit,[1020] and similar examples could be cited from Egyptian texts."[1021]

In fact, we now know that there were many deities in the ancient Near East that had multiple names. As stated above with the Babylonian Creation account, the Enuma Elish, the god Marduk (Merodach), chief deity of Babylon, also had some 50 different names.[1022] It would not even be thinkable to apply any of the Documentary Hypothesis analysis to any of these works. Why? Not only because we can see that ancient writers are no different than modern writers and are able to use different names and titles interchangeably within their work, but they were written on stone, so to speak. If one has one clay tablet that has both a personal name and two different titles for the same king, it would be difficult to argue that there were two or three different authors for the one tablet. Bible scholar Mark F. Rooker has the following to say about the use of Elohim and Yahweh in the Old Testament:

> Moreover, it is clear that throughout the Old Testament that the occurrence of the names of God as Elohim or Yahweh is to be attributed to contextual and semantic issues, not the existence of sources. This conclusion is borne out by the fact that the names consistently occur in predictable genre. In the legal and prophetic texts the name Yahweh always appears, while in wisdom literature the name for God is invariably Elohim. In narrative literature, which includes much of the Pentateuch, both Yahweh and Elohim are used.[1023] Yet consistently the names do not indicate different sources but were chosen by design. The name Elohim was used in passages to express the abstract idea of Deity as evident in God's role as Creator of the universe and the Ruler of nature. Yahweh, on the other hand, is the special covenant name of God who has entered into a relationship with the Israelites since the name reflects God's ethical character. (Cassuto, 31) Given the understanding of the meaning of these names for God, it is no wonder that the source which contains the name Yahweh would appear to reflect a different theology from a selected group of texts which contained the name Elohim."[1024]

[1020] G. R. Driver, *Canaanite Myths and Legends* (New York: T. & T. Clark, 1971), 70-72.

[1021] For example, see the "Stele of Ikhernofret" in James B. Pritchard, ed., *Ancient Near Eastern Texts*, 2nd ed. Princeton: Princeton University Press, 1955, pp. 329–30.

[1022] K. A. Kitchen, *On the Reliability of the Old Testament* (Grand Rapids: Eerdmans, 2003), 424–5.

[1023] Similarly, Livingston has pointed out that the cognate West Semitic divine names il and ya(w) appear to be interchangeable in the Eblaite tablets. (*The Pentateuch in Its Cultural Environment*, 224.)

[1024] Mark F. Rooker, *Leviticus: The New American Commentary* (Nashville: Broadman & Holman, 2001), 26–27.

Let us, on a small scale, do our own analysis of the divine names in the first two chapters of Genesis. The Hebrew word (*'elohim'*) is most often agreed upon to be from a root meaning "be strong," "mighty," or "power."[1025] It should be said too that by far, most Hebrew scholars recognize the plural form (*im*) of this title *'elo·him'* to be used as a plural of "majesty," "greatness," or "excellence." The Hebrew word (*'elo·him'*) is used for the Creator 35 times from Genesis 1:1 to 2:4a. Exactly what is the context of this use? It is used in a setting that deals with God's power, his greatness, his excellence, his creation activity, all of which seems appropriate, does it not?

Moving on to Genesis 2:4b–25, we find God now being referred to by his personal name, the Tetragrammaton (YHWH, JHVH), which is translated "Jehovah" (KJV, ASV, NW, NEB, etc.) or "Yahweh" (AT, NAB, JB, HCSB, etc.). It is found in verses 4b–25 eleven times; however, it comes before his title (*'elohim'*).[1026] Why the switch, and what is the context of this use? This personal name of God is used in a setting that deals with his personal relationship with man and woman. This is not a second creation account; it is a more detailed account of the creation of man, which was only briefly mentioned in chapter one in passing, as each feature of creation was ticked off. In chapter two, the Creator becomes a person as he speaks to his intelligent creation, giving them the prospect of an perfect eternal life in a paradise garden, which is to be cultivated earth wide, to be filled with perfect offspring. Therefore, we see a personal interchange between God and man as He lays out His plans to Adam, which seems very appropriate, does it not when switching from using a title in chapter one to using a personal name in chapter two? In chapter two, we have the coupling of the personal name "Jehovah" with the title "God," to show that we are still talking about this 'great,' 'majestic,' 'all powerful' Creator, but personalized as he introduces himself to his new earthly creation.

Thus, there is no reason to assume that we are talking about two different writers. No, it is two different settings in which a skilled writer would make the transition just as Moses did. It would be no different than if a modern-day news commentator was giving as a report about the United States President visiting Russia to meet with Dmitry Anatolyevich Medvedev, in which he used the title President predominately. The following week the same news commentator may be covering the President visiting a hospital with injured children who had survived a tornado, and refer to the President as President Obama. It isn't difficult to see that one is an official setting where the President needs to be portrayed as powerful, while in the other setting; he needs to be portrayed as personable. The same principles used herein apply to the rest of the Pentateuch and the Old Testament as a whole.

Discrepancies

Discrepancies, or should I say "perceived" discrepancies, are the critic's favorite pebble. These perceived discrepancies set off an alarm for the critic, and then he rushes off with his pebble like a child to add it to the multiple-authors side of the

---

[1025] Ibid., 27.

[1026] "Jehovah God." Heb., Yehwah´ 'Elohim´.

scale. To differentiate between the supposed different sources texts, I will lay them out as follows:

("J") will be used to represent an alleged writer. In this case, it stands for any place God's name Jehovah is used.

("E") will be for the portion that has Jehovah's title, *Elohim*, God.

("P") will be for the portion of priestly activities.

("D") Deuteronomy is different from Genesis, Exodus, Leviticus, and Numbers. Thus, it has another author.

("RJE") will represent the compiler who put "J" and "E" together.

("R") will represent the editor(s), who put it all together and may have altered some portions to express their social circumstances of their day.

("U") will represent the alleged "unknown independent texts."

"**Narrative Discrepancy**" (Genesis 12:1, ASV) Now Jehovah said unto Abram, Get thee out of thy country, and from thy kindred, and from thy father's house, unto the land that I will show thee: ("J") (after Terah, Abram's father, died, Abram is commanded to leave Haran)

> (**Genesis 11:26, ESV**) When Terah had lived 70 years, he fathered Abram, Nahor, and Haran ("U"). (When Terah was 70, Abram was born.)

> (**Genesis 11:32, ESV**) The days of Terah were 205 years ("U"): and Terah died in Haran ("R"). (Terah died at the age of 205, which would make Abraham 135 when he left Ur.)

> (**Genesis 12:4, ASV**) So Abram went, as Jehovah had spoken unto him; and Lot went with him ("J"): and Abram was seventy and five years old when he departed out ("P") of Haran ("R"). (12:4 has Abram being only 75 when he leaves Haran.)

Discrepancy: According to 11:32, Terah died at the age of 205; hence, Abram must have been 135 when he was called to leave Haran. However, 12:4 says that he was only 75 when he left Haran. The Source Critic informs us that this seeming contradiction is resolved if Genesis chapter 12 is of a different source from the genealogy of Genesis chapter 11.

The above need not be a contradiction at all. True enough, it was at the age of 70 that Terah began having children (Genesis 11:26), but does Abraham have to be the firstborn child simply because he is listed first? Consider, what weight does the names Nahor and Haran play in the Bible account? Now consider, what about the name Abraham? He is considered the father and founder of three of the greatest religions on this planet: Judaism, Christianity, and Islam. He is the third most prominent person named in God's Word. This practice, that of placing the most prominent son first in a list of sons even though they are not the firstborn is followed elsewhere in God's Word with other prominent men of great faith, for example, Shem and Isaac. (Genesis 5:32; 11:10; 1 Chronicles 1:28) Therefore, let us keep it simple. Genesis 11:26 does not say that Abram was the firstborn; it simply says that Terah began fathering children, and then it goes on to list his three sons, listing the most prominent one first. Thus, it is obvious that Terah fathered Abram at the age of 130. (Genesis 11:26, 32; 12:4) In addition, it is true that Sarah was Abram's half-sister, not by the same mother, but by having Terah as the same father. (Genesis 20:12) Therefore, in all likelihood, it is Haran who is the firstborn of Terah, whose daughter was old enough to marry Nahor, another of Terah's three sons. – Genesis 11:29.

"Narrative Discrepancy" (Genesis 37:25–28, 36; 38:1; 39:1, YLT)

> (Genesis 37:25–28, YLT) And they sit down to eat bread ("E"), and they lift up their eyes, and look, and lo, a company of Ishmaelites coming from Gilead, and their camels bearing spices, and balm, and myrrh, going to take [them] down to Egypt. 26 And Judah saith unto his brethren, 'What gain when we slay our brother, and have concealed his blood? 27 Come, and we sell him to the Ishmaelites, and our hands are not on him, for he [is] our brother—our flesh;' and his brethren hearken ("J"). 28 And Midianite merchantmen pass by and they draw out and bring up Joseph out of the pit ("E"), and sold him to the Ishmaelites for twenty shekels of silver. They took Joseph to Egypt ("J"). (Genesis 37:36) And the Medanites have sold him unto Egypt, to Potiphar, a eunuch of Pharaoh, head of the executioners ("E"). (Genesis 38:1) And it cometh to pass, at that time, that Judah goeth down from his brethren, and turneth aside unto a man, an Adullamite, whose name [is] Hirah ("J"). (Genesis 39:1) And Joseph hath been brought down to Egypt, and Potiphar, a eunuch of Pharaoh, head of the executioners, an Egyptian man, buyeth him out of the hands of the Ishmaelites who have brought him thither ("J").

Discrepancy: In Genesis 37:25 the Ishmaelites are passing by at the opportune time mentioned in verses 26 and 27, with Judah suggesting that instead of killing Joseph they sell him to the Ishmaelites. Yet, verse 28 switches in midstride to the Midianites, as they drew Joseph from the pit, selling him to the Ishmaelites. In verse 36, the Medanites (likely a scribal error; almost every translation has Midianites, so we will accept that as so) are selling Joseph to Potiphar in Egypt. Yet, the discrepancy pushes the envelope even further, for Genesis 39:1 says, it was the Ishmaelites who delivered and sold Joseph to Potiphar in Egypt. Was Joseph sold to Ishmaelites or to Midianites? In addition, who delivered and sold Joseph to Potiphar in Egypt? It seems that the higher critics are bent on using ambiguous passages (ambiguous at first glance to the casual reader) to facilitate their

Documentary Hypothesis. You might say that these discrepancies are fuel for the engine that drives their Documentary Hypothesis locomotive. E. A. Speiser writes:

> The narrative is broken up into two originally independent versions. One of these (J) used the name Israel, featured Judah as Joseph's protector, and identified the Ishmaelites as the traders who bought Joseph from his brothers. The other (E) spoke of Jacob as the father and named Reuben as Joseph's friend; the slave traders in that version were Midianites who discovered Joseph by accident and sold him in Egypt to Potiphar.[1027]

For Speiser, it is time to slice up the text and divide it up between our alleged "J"-Text and "E"-Text writers. It is also hypothesized that our "R"-Redactor edits the two and slips in some additional information as well, suggesting that the Midianites are the ones who were actually passing by, selling Joseph later to the Ishmaelites. Thus, it would be the Ishmaelites, who would deliver and sell Joseph to Potiphar in Egypt. Yes, at first glimpse, this would appear to make it all well, but we still have a problem: Genesis 37:36 states that it was the Midianites, who sold Joseph to Potiphar in Egypt.

Actually, when one looks below the surface reading, there is no discrepancy here at all. Ishmael (son of Hagar and Abraham) and Midian (son of Keturah and Abraham) were half-brothers. It is highly likely that there was intermarriage between the descendants of these two, allowing for an interchangeable use of the expression "Ishmaelites" and "Midianites." (Genesis 25:1–4; 37:25–28; 39:1) We see this in the days of Judge Gideon when Israel was being attacked, with both terms "Ishmaelites" and "Midianites" being used to describe the attackers. (Judges 8:24; 7:25; 8:22, 26) Alternatively, even still we could have an Ishmaelite caravan encompassing Midianite merchants that were passing by, with the Midianites brokering the deal and delivering Joseph from the pit to the Ishmaelite caravan, where Joseph would be under the Ishmaelites' custody even if he was being *detained* by the Midianites. Once they arrived at Potiphar's place in Egypt, it would be the Midianites to broker the deal with Potiphar. Thus, it can be stated either way, the Ishmaelites or the Midianites delivered and sold Joseph to Potiphar in Egypt.

Repetitions (Doublets)

What are doublets? It is the telling of the same story twice, making the same events appear to happen more than once. For example,

(1) there are two stories of the creation account,

(2) two stories of God's covenant with Abraham,

(3) two stories where Abraham names his son Isaac,

(4) two stories where Abraham claims Sarah is his sister, two stories of Jacob's journey to Haran,

---

[1027] E. A. Speiser, *Genesis,* Anchor Bible (Garden City, N.Y.: Doubleday, 1964), 293–4.

(5) two stories where God revealed himself to Jacob at Bethel,

(6) two stories where God changes Jacob's name to Israel,

(7) two stories of when Moses got water from the rock at Meribah, and a detailed description in Exodus 24–29 of how to build the tabernacle, then within five chapters a retelling of how they did it, repeating the details again in chapters 34–40.

The critic goes on to point out that, there is more to this "doublet" story than meets the eye; they argue that one of the doublets will contain the title for the Creator, God (*Elohim*); while the other doublet of the same story will contain the personal name for the Creator, Jehovah. Moreover, they argue that there are other defining features that are only within one side or the other.

(Genesis 1:27, ESV) So God created man in his own image, in the image of God he created him; male and female he created them.

(Genesis 2:7, ASV) And Jehovah God formed man of the dust of the ground, and breathed into his nostrils the breath of life; and man became a living soul.

Within two chapters, we have two verses where the writer, if one person, informs us of the creation of man twice, the second as though the first was never mentioned at all. Again, the source critic will argue that there were two sources of the same information on the creation of man and the compiler allowed both to remain. What the source critic fails to tell his reader is that there are sense breaks within the various accounts in these first three chapters. Genesis 1:1–2:3 is the basic creation account. Genesis 2:4–25 is the restating of day three (verses 5, 6) and the subsequent preparation of the earth for the settling of man and woman in the Garden of Eden. Genesis 3:1–24 is specifically about the temptation, the entry of sin and death into the world, the promise of a seed to save humankind, a description of the conditions of imperfection and of man's loss of the Garden of Eden.

Bible scholar Leon Kass, who supports the Documentary Hypothesis, had this to say about the creation account of Genesis chapters 1 and 2:

Once we recognize the independence of the two creation stories, we are compelled to adopt a critical principle of reading if we mean to understand each story on its own terms. We must scrupulously avoid reading into the second story any facts or notions taken from the first, and vice versa. Thus, in reading about the origin of man in the story of the Garden of Eden, we must not say or even think that man is here created in God's image or that man is to be the ruler over the animals. Neither, when we try to understand the relation of man and woman in the Garden, are we to think about or make use of the first story's account of the coequal coeval creation of man and woman. Only after we have read and interpreted each story entirely on its own should we try to integrate the two disparate teachings. By proceeding in this way, we will discover why these two separate and divergent accounts have been juxtaposed and how they function to convey a coherent, noncontradictory teaching about human life.[1028]

Let us look at another example in which the critic has argued that one source says forty days while the other speaks of 150 days:

(Gen 7:12, NET) And the rain fell on the earth forty days and forty nights.

(Gen 7:24, NET) The waters prevailed over the earth for 150 days.

Genesis 7:24 and 8:3 say the floodwaters lasted for 150 days, yet; Genesis 7:4, 12 and 17 say it was only forty days. Once again, the difference is solved with a simple explanation. Each is referring to two different time periods. Let us look at these verses again (italics mine):

(Gen 7:12, NET) And the rain fell on the earth forty days and forty nights. [Notice that the 40-days refer to how long the rain fell—"the rain fell."]

(Gen 7:24, NET) The waters prevailed over the earth for 150 days. [Notice that the 150-days refer to how long the flood lasted—"waters prevailed."]

(Gen 8:3, NET) The waters kept receding steadily from the earth, so that they had gone down by the end of the 150 days.

(Gen 8:4, NET) On the seventeenth day of the seventh month, the ark came to rest on one of the mountains of Ararat.

(Gen 7:11; 8:13, 14, NET) In the *six hundredth year of Noah's life*, in *the second month*, on the seventeenth day of the month, on that day all the fountains of the great deep burst open and the floodgates of the heavens were opened. *In Noah's six hundred and first year*, in the first day of the first month, *the waters had dried up* from the earth, and Noah removed the covering from the ark and saw that *the surface of the ground was dry.* And *by the twenty-seventh day of the second month the earth was dry.*

By the end of the 150 days, the water had gone down [Gen 8:3]. Five months from the beginning of the rain, the ark comes to rest on Mount Ararat [8:4]. Eleven months later the waters dried up [7:11; 8:13]. Exactly 370 days from the start (lunar months), Noah and his family left the ark and were on dry ground.

Yet another example is found in 2 Kings 24:10-16. Verses 10-14 say, "At that time the servants of Nebuchadnezzar king of Babylon came up to Jerusalem, and the city was besieged. And Nebuchadnezzar king of Babylon came to the city while his servants were besieging it, and Jehoiachin the king of Judah gave himself up to the king of Babylon, himself and his mother and his servants and his officials and his palace officials. The king of Babylon took him prisoner in the eighth year of his reign and carried off all the treasures of the house of the LORD and the treasures of the

---

[1028] Leon R. Kass, *The Beginning of Wisdom: Reading Genesis* (New York: Free Press, 2003), 56.

320

king's house, and cut in pieces all the vessels of gold in the temple of the LORD, which Solomon king of Israel had made, as the LORD had foretold. He carried away all Jerusalem and all the officials and all the mighty men of valor, 10,000 captives, and all the craftsmen and the smiths. None remained, except the poorest people of the land."

Verses 15-16 say, "And he carried away Jehoiachin to Babylon. The king's mother, the king's wives, his officials, and the chief men of the land he took into captivity from Jerusalem to Babylon. And the king of Babylon brought captive to Babylon all the men of valor, 7,000, and the craftsmen and the metal workers, 1,000, all of them strong and fit for war."

Here we have a repetition of the same events back-to-back. Why? Is it multiple sources and the redactor simply keeping both? In an attempt to stave off the conservative view of Moses' writership, scholar, and critic Richard Elliot Friedman writes:

> Those who defended the traditional belief in Mosaic authorship argued that the doublets were always complementary, not repetitive, and that they did not contradict each other, but came to teach us a lesson by their 'apparent' contradiction. But another clue was discovered that undermined this traditional response. Investigators found that in most cases one of the two versions of a doublet story would refer to the deity by the divine name, Yahweh . . . , and the other version of the story would refer to the deity simply as 'God.' That is, the doublets lined up into two groups of parallel versions of stories. Each group was almost always consistent with the name it used. Moreover, the investigators found that it was not only the names of the deity that lined up. They found various other terms and characteristics that regularly appeared in one of the other group. This tended to support the hypothesis that someone had taken two different old source documents, cut them up, and woven them together to form the continuous story in the Five Books of Moses.[1029]

Ancient Semitic literature has other similar examples of repetition. Moreover, the use of Elohim in one instance and Jehovah in another is due to context and semantic issues. Notice Friedman's use of the phrases "in most cases" and "almost always." Which is it? And as we will see, he is overstating his case to the point of exaggeration. Let us look at the most popular example in the "Matriarch in Danger." It has three occurrences in Genesis: Sarah in Egypt with Pharaoh (Genesis 12:10–20), Sarah in Gerar with Abimelech (Genesis 20:1–18), and Rebekah in Gerar with Abimelech (Genesis 26:7–11). Friedman would argue that we simply have one story with three different sources that had been maintained over time. The personal name of God, Jehovah, is used in the account of Sarah in Egypt with Pharaoh (vs. 17). The title Elohim is used in the account about Sarah in Gerar with Abimelech (vs. 3), but so is Jehovah (vs. 18). In the account of Rebekah in Gerar with Abimelech, neither Elohim nor Jehovah is used. Therefore, Friedman's case is really no case at all, because both Jehovah and Elohim appear in one account with Sarah in Gerar

---

[1029] Richard Elliot Friedman, *Who Wrote The Bible* (San Francisco: Harper Collins, 1997), 22.

with Abimelech and neither Jehovah nor Elohim appear in the account with Rebekah in Gerar with Abimelech. It should be noted that all three occurrences are in reference to Abimelech and Pharaoh, but both times that the name Jehovah is used, it is in reference to Jehovah executing a punishment of these rulers. If their best example does not even come close to their claims, then what are we to think of the others? Before moving on to the differences in language and style, we should close with one last point about the literature of the Ancient Near East (ANE). One of the features of ANE literature, which includes Hebrew, is its parallelism, repetition, the telling of stories that are similar to stress patterns that are important. Even in the book of Acts, you have three different accounts of Paul's conversion (Ac 9:3-8; 22:6-11; 26:12-18). It is repetition for emphasis. At the outset of this section, we mentioned that chapters 24-29 of Exodus give a detailed description of how the tabernacle was built, and chapters 34-40 repeat the very same information. Chapters 24-29 contain the directions, and chapters 34-40 show how they did it; thus, the repetition is emphasizing that they did exactly what Jehovah had asked them to do.

Differences in Language and Style

Supporters of the Documentary Hypothesis would argue that within the Pentateuch we see such things as preferences for certain words, differences in vocabulary, reoccurring expressions in Deuteronomy that are not found in Genesis, Exodus, Leviticus, and Numbers, all evidence for the higher critics and their multiple source theory. Also, there are individual characteristics in grammar and syntax. Further, the critic describes "P" as being very boring, completely lacking in interest or excitement, dry; while the writers of "J" and "E" are very vivid and lively, holding the reader's interest in their storytelling. Additionally, "D" uses expressions like 'with all your heart and all your soul,' which the rest of the Pentateuch lacks in those types of expressions. Their conclusion is that there is no alternative but to have multiple writers as the differences in language and style dictate.

If the alleged writers of the Pentateuch were so narrow in their vocabulary and writing abilities that they would use only one given word for a given idea and never use another when dealing with that idea, it would be easy to suggest a division of actual sources. Yet this is not the case at all. The writers of the Hebrew Scriptures throughout ancient Israel actually expressed a great variety of words in their work. Douglas K. Stuart (Ph.D., Harvard University), Professor of Old Testament at Gordon–Conwell Theological Seminary, is of the same opinion:

> In fact, the contrary situation appears to be true. In ancient Israel there were four demonstrable indications of a preference for variety in written expression rather than for desire for stylistic consistency. (1) If there were two different ways of spelling a word the Israelites chose to preserve both spellings as valid and to include both of them frequently in any document. Thus with regard to spelling (orthography), ancient Israelites had no commitment to consistency to style, but the free use of alternative spellings was regarded as not only proper, but desirable. (2) In the case of common expressions, a similar phenomenon can be

observed. Where variation was possible, it apparently was not avoided, but preferred. Alternative ways of forming a given multiword expression were employed commonly so that both alternatives were preserved. Thus, in the case of repeated phraseology in prose contexts, there was no commitment to consistency of style, but rather the alternative formulation was regarded not only proper, but desirable. (3) With regard to variation in grammatical forms, a similar phenomenon is observed. If there existed two different ways of saying something, even in the case of a common verb form, both ways were used so as to preserve both in the common discourse. Again, the preference appears to have been for inclusion of variety rather than for consistency of one form if two existed. (4) The Masoretic system of *Kethib-Qere* represents a fourth indicator of the tendency in past times to preserve variance rather than to select one option and to employ it consistently, a tendency that extended into the medieval period when the Masoretes worked. This system arose from a desire to include, not merely side-by-side, but actually within the same word, two variant readings rather than two select ones. The Masoretes provide the consonants of one text option in the vowels of another. They indicated their preferred reading, but did not omit the reading they regarded as inferior, they simply did not localize it.[1030]

Differences in Style and Vocabulary: An investigator would not be honest if he were simply to reject these differences out of hand, as though they did not exist. Therefore, rightly, we need to investigate these differences, giving an answer that has substance. I will cite one of their pillar examples, to demonstrate the principle that if they are so far off base here, then we can conclude their foundation in this area is really no foundation at all. Before we get started, let us do a little review of Biblical Hebrew, to be better able to address our example.

(Qal): Qal is the simple form of the verb, meaning "light" or "easy." This is the simple active stem of the verb.

(Hiphil): This is generally called the "*causative*" form because it reveals the *causative* action of the qal verb. The "*h*" is prefixed to the stem, which modifies the root.

Qal	yalad (to give birth)
Hiphil	holid (he caused to give birth)

[1030] Douglas K. Stuart, *The New American Commentary: An Exegetical Theological Exposition of Holy Scripture: EXODUS* (Nashville: Broadman & Holman, 2006). See pp. 30–31 for examples of the above four points.

Examples:

> **Gen. 14:18**: Irad begat (*yalad*) Mehujael

> **Gen. 5:4**: Adam after he begat (*holid*) Seth

The advocates of the Documentary Hypothesis argue that to find *yalad* in the genealogy of Cain in Genesis chapter 4, the Table of Nations in Genesis chapter 10, and Nahor's family line in Genesis chapter 22 (all being of the "J" author), while finding *holid* in Adam's history down to Noah in Genesis chapter 5 as well as the genealogy of Shem found in Genesis chapter 11 (being of the "P" author) is nothing more than proof positive that there are two authors: "J" and "P."

In short, we are not dealing with a word or phrase that is peculiar to an individual writer like "J" or "P." No, this is nothing more than an example of following the basic rules of Hebrew grammar and syntax. In many cases, it could not have been written in any other way, because it is the socially accepted usage of the Hebrew language. When those who support the Documentary Hypothesis pull Hebrew words or even phrases out of their setting (as I have done above), looking at them in isolation, their reasoning becomes based solely on personal wishes, feelings, or perceptions, rather than on linguistic rules, reasons, or principles of the language itself. Hebrew, like any other language, conforms to the socially accepted style, with the regular and specific order, or arrangement. The Hebrew language has its own rules and allowable combinations of how words are joined together to make sense to the Hebrew mind. Umberto Cassuto, also known as Moshe David Cassuto, (1883–1951), who held the chair of Biblical studies at the Hebrew University of Jerusalem had this to say concerning the usage of *yalad* and *holid:*

> It will suffice to note the fact that the verb *yaladh* occurs in the signification of *holidh* only in the *past tense* [perfect] and the *present* [participle]. We say, "so-and-so *yaladh* [mas. sing. perfect] so-and-so," and we say *yoledh* [participle mas. Sing.: "is begetting"]; but we do not say in the *future tense* [imperfect] so-and-so *yeledh* [to signify: "he will beget"] (or *wayyeledh* [imperfect with *waw* conversive, to connote: "and he begot"]) so-and-so." In the imperfect, the *Qal* is employed only with reference to the mother, for example, so-and-so *teledh* ["will give birth to"] (*watteledh* ["and gave birth to"]) so and so." In connection with the father one can only say, *yolidh* [*hiphil* imperfect; "he will beget"] or *wayyoledh* [*hiphil* imperfect with *waw* conversive; "and he begot"] (although we find in Prov. xxvii 1: what a day may bring forth ["*yeledh*"; *Qal* imperfect] the verb is used there not in connotation of "begetting" but actually in the sense of "giving birth"). Similarly, we do not say, using the infinitive, Aajare *lidhto* [to signify: "after his begetting"] but only Aajare *lidhtah* ["after her giving birth"]; with regard to the father we can only say Aajare *holidho* ["after his begetting"]. This is clear to anyone who is sensitive to the Hebrew idiom. In the genealogies from Adam to Noah and from Noah to Abraham, it would have been impossible to write anything else but *wayyoledh* and Aajare *hoilidho;* every Hebrew author would have had no option but to write

thus and not otherwise. It is not a question of sources but of the general usage of the Hebrew tongue.[1031]

Professor K. A. Kitchen, one of the leading experts on Biblical history, notes in his book *Ancient Orient and Old Testament:* "Stylistic differences are meaningless, and reflect the differences in detailed subject-matter." He says that similar style variations can also be found "in ancient texts whose literary unity is beyond all doubt."[1032]

A 1981 news report relates to this debate and provides some interesting facts.[1033]

TEL AVIV, Israel (UPI)—A five-year long computer study of the Bible strongly indicates that one author—and not three as widely held in modern criticism—wrote the book of Genesis.

"The probability of Genesis' having been written by one author is enormously high—82 percent statistically," a member of the research team said in an article published in Wednesday's *Jerusalem Post.*

Professor Yehuda Radday, a Bible scholar from the Technion, a Haifa university, said more than 20,000 words of Genesis were fed into a computer which conducted a painstaking analysis of its linguistic makeup.

Bible critics widely hold that Genesis had three authors—the Jawhist or "J" author, the Elohist or "E" author and a priestly writer, dubbed "P."

"We found the J and E narratives to be linguistically indistinguishable," Radday told a news conference today. But the P sections differ widely from them.

"This is only to be expected, since dramatic tales and legal documents must necessarily display different 'behavior,'" he said. "If you compared love letters and a telephone directory written by the same person, linguistic analysis would point to different authors."

The team combined statistical and linguistic methods with computer science and Bible scholarship to reach their conclusions. They used 54 analysis criteria, including word length, the use of the definite article and the conjunction "and," richness of vocabulary and transition frequencies between word categories.

[1031] Umberto Cassuto, *The Documentary Hypothesis* (New York, NY: Shalem Press, 2006), 55-56.

[1032] K. A Kitchen, *Ancient Orient and Old Testament* (Downers Grove, IL: InterVarsity Press, 1975), 125.

[1033] As published in the *St. Petersburg Times:* http://tinyurl.com/noke4m

"These criteria are a reliable gauge of authorship because these traits are beyond an author's conscious control and furthermore are countable," Radday said.

A mathematics expert on the team ran a computer check against classical German works by Goethe, Herder and Kant and found that the statistical probability of their being the sole authors of their own work were only 22 percent, 7 percent and 9 percent respectively.

As mentioned above, Jewish and Christian conservatives accept one writer for the first five books of the Bible, namely, Moses. The critics, however, argue that although Moses is definitely the main character of the Pentateuch because they are unable to find any *direct mention* within it of Moses having written these five books, it is for them simply a tradition that Moses is the writer. This author is certain that is not the impression you will have after reading the next chapter.

Internal and External Evidence for Moses Authorship

First, it is obvious that Moses did *not* write *every word* of the Pentateuch. Why? The section that relates his death would be something that Joshua could have added after Moses' death. (Deuteronomy 34:1–8) In addition, the critic would argue, it would hardly seem very meek to pen these words about oneself: "Now the man Moses was very meek, more than all people who were on the face of the earth." (Numbers 12:3, ESV) Nevertheless, consider that Jesus said of himself: "I am gentle and lowly in heart" (Matthew 11:29, *ESV*), which no one would fault Jesus with as though he were boasting. Both Moses and Jesus were simply stating a fact. The amount of possible material that may have been added by Joshua, another inspired writer is next to nothing and does not negate Moses' authorship.

What Does the Biblical Evidence from the Old Testament Report?

Exodus 17:14 (ASV)	Exodus 24:4 (ASV)	Exodus 34:27 (ASV)
14 And Jehovah said unto Moses, Write this for a memorial in a book, and rehearse it in the ears of Joshua: that I will utterly blot out the remembrance of Amalek from under heaven.	4 And Moses wrote all the words of Jehovah, and rose up early in the morning, and builded an altar under the mount, and twelve pillars, according to the twelve tribes of Israel.	27 And Jehovah said unto Moses, Write thou these words: for after the tenor of these words I have made a covenant with thee and with Israel.
Leviticus 26:46 (ASV)	Leviticus 27:34 (ASV)	Numbers 33:2 (ASV)
46 These are the statutes and ordinances and	34 These are the commandments, which	2 And Moses wrote their goings out according to

laws, which Jehovah made between him and the children of Israel in mount Sinai by Moses.	Jehovah commanded Moses for the children of Israel in mount Sinai.	their journeys by the commandment of Jehovah: and these are their journeys according to their goings out.
Numbers 36:13 (ASV) 13 These are the commandments and the ordinances which Jehovah commanded by Moses unto the children of Israel in the plains of Moab by the Jordan at Jericho.	**Deuteronomy 1:1 (ASV)** 1 These are the words which Moses spake unto all Israel beyond the Jordan in the wilderness, in the Arabah over against Suph, between Paran, and Tophel, and Laban, and Hazeroth, and Di-zahab.	**Deuteronomy 31:9 (ASV)** 9 And Moses wrote this law, and delivered it unto the priests the sons of Levi, that bare the ark of the covenant of Jehovah, and unto all the elders of Israel.
Deuteronomy 31:22 (ASV) 22 So Moses wrote this song the same day, and taught it the children of Israel.	**Deuteronomy 31:24 (ASV)** 24 And it came to pass, when Moses had made an end of writing the words of this law in a book, until they were finished,	**Joshua 1:7 (ASV)** 7 Only be strong and very courageous, to observe to do according to all the law, which Moses my servant commanded thee:
Joshua 8:31 (ASV) 31 as Moses the servant of Jehovah commanded the children of Israel, as it is written in the book of the law of Moses, an altar of unhewn stones, upon which no man had lifted up any iron: and they offered thereon burnt-offerings unto Jehovah, and sacrificed peace-offerings.	**1 Kings 2:3 (ASV)** 3 and keep the charge of Jehovah thy God, to walk in his ways, to keep his statutes, and his commandments, and his ordinances, and his testimonies, according to that which is written in the law of Moses, that thou may prosper in all that thou does, and whithersoever thou turn thyself.	**2 Kings 14:6 (ASV)** 6 but the children of the murderers he put not to death; according to that which is written in the book of the law of Moses, as Jehovah commanded, saying, The fathers shall not be put to death for the children, nor the children be put to death for the fathers; but every man shall die for his own sin.
2 Kings 21:8 (ASV) 8 neither will I cause the feet of Israel to wander any more out of the land	**Ezra 6:18 (ASV)** 18 And they set the priests in their divisions, and the Levites in their	**Nehemiah 13:1 (ASV)** 1 On that day they read in the book of Moses in the audience of the

which I gave their fathers, if only they will observe to do according to all that I have commanded them, and according to all the law that my servant Moses commanded them.	courses, for the service of God, which is at Jerusalem; as it is written in the book of Moses.	people; and therein was found written, that an Ammonite and a Moabite should not enter into the assembly of God for ever,
Daniel 9:13 (ASV) ¹³ As it is written in the law of Moses, all this evil is come upon us: yet have we not entreated the favor of Jehovah our God, that …	**Malachi 4:4 (ASV)** ⁴ Remember ye the law of Moses my servant, which I commanded unto him in Horeb for all Israel, even statutes and ordinances.	

To reject Moses as the writer of the Pentateuch is to reject these inspired writers and suggest they are not reliable; moreover, this would mean they were not inspired, because those under inspiration would not make such errors. If these critics are correct, then all the above is merely a great conspiracy. This author hardly thinks so!

What Does the Biblical Evidence from Jesus Christ Report?

Matthew 8:4 (ESV)	Matthew 11:23-24 (ESV)
⁴And Jesus said to him, "See that you say nothing to anyone, but go, show yourself to the priest and offer the gift that Moses commanded, for a proof to them."	²³And you, Capernaum, will you be exalted to heaven? You will be brought down to Hades. For if the mighty works done in you had been done in Sodom, it would have remained until this day. ²⁴ But I tell you that it will be more tolerable on the day of judgment for the land of Sodom than for you."
Matthew 19:4-5 (ESV)	Matthew 19:8 (ESV)
⁴He answered, "Have you not read that he who created them from the beginning made them male and female, ⁵and said, 'Therefore a man shall leave his father and his mother and hold fast to his wife, and the two shall become one flesh'?	⁸He said to them, "Because of your hardness of heart Moses allowed you to divorce your wives, but from the beginning it was not so.

Matthew 24:37 (ESV)	Mark 10:5 (ESV)
37 For as were the days of Noah, so will be the coming of the Son of Man.	5And Jesus said to them, "Because of your hardness of heart he wrote you this commandment.
Mark 12:26 (ESV)	Mark 1:44 (ESV)
26And as for the dead being raised, have you not read in the book of Moses, in the passage about the bush, how God spoke to him, saying, 'I am the God of Abraham, and the God of Isaac, and the God of Jacob'?	44and said to him, "See that you say nothing to anyone, but go, show yourself to the priest and offer for your cleansing what Moses commanded, for a proof to them."
Mark 7:10 (ESV)	Luke 5:14 (ESV)
10For Moses said, 'Honor your father and your mother'; and, 'Whoever reviles father or mother must surely die.'	14And he charged him to tell no one, but "go and show yourself to the priest, and make an offering for your cleansing, as Moses commanded, for a proof to them."
Luke 11:51 (ESV)	Luke 17:32 (ESV)
51from the blood of Abel to the blood of Zechariah, who perished between the altar and the sanctuary. Yes, I tell you, it will be required of this generation.	32 Remember Lot's wife.
Luke 24:27, 44 English Standard Version (ESV)	John 5:46 English Standard Version (ESV)
27And beginning with Moses and all the Prophets, he interpreted to them in all the Scriptures the things concerning himself. 44Then he said to them, "These are my words that I spoke to you while I was still with you, that everything written about me in the Law of Moses and the Prophets and the Psalms must be fulfilled."	46For if you believed Moses, you would believe me; for he wrote of me.
John 7:19 English Standard Version (ESV)	John 8:58 (UASV)
19 Has not Moses given you the law? Yet none of you keeps the law. Why do you seek to kill me?"	

		Jesus said to them, "Truly, truly, I say to you, before Abraham came to be I have been in existence."[1034]

How does one ignore the strongest evidence of Moses' writership of these five books, which is specifically referred to by Jesus Christ and numerous other inspired writers? Being on trial by the modern-day critic, I am certain Moses would appreciate the numerous witnesses that can be called to the stand on his behalf.[1035]

What Does the Biblical Evidence from the Apostles Report?

Acts 2:32 (ESV)	Acts 6:14 (ESV)	Acts 15:5 (ESV)
[32]This Jesus God raised up, and of that we all are witnesses.	[14]for we have heard him say that this Jesus of Nazareth will destroy this place and will change the customs that Moses delivered to us."	[5]But some believers who belonged to the party of the Pharisees rose up and said, "It is necessary to circumcise them and to order them to keep the law of Moses."
Acts 26:22 (ESV)	Acts 28:23 (ESV)	Romans 10:5 (ESV)
[22] To this day I have had the help that comes from God, and so I stand here testifying both to small and great, saying nothing but what the prophets and Moses said would come to pass:	[23]When they had appointed a day for him, they came to him at his lodging in greater numbers. From morning till evening he expounded to them, testifying to the kingdom of God and trying to convince them about Jesus both from the Law of Moses and from the Prophets.	[5]For Moses writes about the righteousness that is based on the law, that the person who does the commandments shall live by them.

[1034] K. L. McKay, A New Syntax of the Verb in New Testament Greek (New York: Peter Lang, 1994), p. 42.

[1035] Old Testament witnesses to Moses' writership of the Pentateuch: Joshua 1:7; 8:32–35; 14:10; 1 Kings 2:3; 1 Chronicles 6:49; 2 Chronicles 33:8; 34:14; 35:12; Ezra 3:2; 6:18; 7:6; Nehemiah 1:7, 8; 8:1, 14, 15; Daniel 9:11, 13; Malachi 4:4. New Testament witnesses to Moses' writership of the Pentateuch: Matthew 8:2–4; 19:7; Mark 1:44; 12:26; Luke 2:22; 16:29, 31; 24:27, 44; John 1:45; 7:22; 8:5; 9:29; 19:7 [Leviticus 24:16]; Acts 3:22; 6:14; 15:5; 26:22; 28:23; Romans 10:5; 1 Corinthians 9:9; Hebrews 9:19; 10:28.

1 Corinthians 9:9 (ESV)	Hebrews 9:19 (ESV)	Hebrews 10:28 (ESV)
[9]For it is written in the Law of Moses, "You shall not muzzle an ox when it treads out the grain." Is it for oxen that God is concerned?	[19]For when every commandment of the law had been declared by Moses to all the people, he took the blood of calves and …	[28] Anyone who has set aside the law of Moses dies without mercy on the evidence of two or three witnesses.

What Does the Internal Evidence Report?

If the writer(s) of the Pentateuch were, in fact, living from the ninth century into the fifth century B.C.E., more than a millennium [1,000 years] after the events described, they would have had to be thoroughly familiar with, even an expert in geology, geography,[1036] horticulture, archaeology, toponymy, onomatology (Archer, 1974), botany, zoology,[1037] climatology,[1038] and history. **Alternatively,** he would have to have been an eyewitness who walked through the events and situations detailed in the Pentateuch; thus, the writer. Here is how I defend these affirmations:

- He would need to have a thorough knowledge of Egyptian names and titles that match inscriptions.

- He would need to have been an expert in toponymy, the study of place-names.

- He would need to have been an expert in onomatology, the study of proper names of all kinds and the origin of names.

- He would need to be aware of the customs and cultures and religious practices of Egypt, desert dwellers, and life in Canaan 1,000 years into the past.

- He would need to have a thorough knowledge of the environment, climate, and the physical features of three regions.

- He would need to have a thorough knowledge of botany, being aware of naturally occurring plant life in three regions 1,000-years before his time.

- He would need to have a thorough knowledge of the environment, climate, and the physical features of three regions.

[1036] Genesis 13:10; 33:18; Numbers 13:22.

[1037] Leviticus 11 and Deuteronomy 14.

[1038] Exodus 9:31, 32; Exodus 16–Deuteronomy.

This internal evidence deals with the proof within the Pentateuch about Moses: the customs and culture of some 3,500 years ago, literary forms used as well as the language itself, and the unity of these five books. As to dating the Pentateuch based on literary forms, one needs look no further than the titles by which God is referred to within the Hebrew Scriptures. From the years of 850–450 B.C.E., we find the Hebrew expression *Yehowah´ tseva'ohth´*, "Jehovah of armies," being used in a significant way. It is found 243 times, with variations, in the Scriptures: 62 times in Isaiah, 77 in Jeremiah, 2 in Micah, 4 in Nahum, 2 in Habakkuk, 2 in Zephaniah, 15 in Haggai, 54 in Zechariah, and 25 in Malachi. This is the same time period, in which higher criticism places the writing of the books of the Pentateuch. If they were penned or constructed during this time period, one would expect to find a high number of occurrences of the expression "Jehovah of armies." Yet, we find just the opposite: there is not one occurrence of this expression to be found in the five books of the Pentateuch. This evidence demonstrates that these books were written prior to the book of Isaiah, before 800 B.C.E., which invalidates the Documentary Hypothesis. Moreover, many aspects of the priesthood that had been adjusted over the centuries, under inspiration, would have been evident if the Pentateuch were written after David[1039] and others had made such adjustments.

The building of the tabernacle at the foot of Mount Sinai fits in with the environment of that area. F. C. Cook stated, "In form, structure, and materials, the tabernacle belongs altogether to the wilderness. The wood used in the structure is found there in abundance."[1040] The external evidence validates names, customs, and culture, religious practices, geography, places and materials of the book of Exodus, which would have been privy only to an eyewitness. The geographical references by this writer are so vast, detailed, and tremendously precise that it is almost impossible to have him be anyone other than an eyewitness.

Deuteronomy reads, "Then we . . . went through all that great and terrifying wilderness." This region in which the annual rainfall is less than 25 cm./10 in. is not different even today, which puts the nomadic traveler on a constant search for water and pasture. In addition, we have meticulous directions as to the encampment of the Israelites (Numbers 1:52, 53), the marching orders (Numbers 2:9, 16, 17, 24, 31), and the signals of the trumpet (Numbers 10:2–6) that directed their every move as evidence that these accounts were written in the "great and terrifying wilderness." Numbers 13:22 makes reference to the time Hebron was built, using the city of Zoan as a reference point: "They went up into the Negeb and came to Hebron. Ahiman, Sheshai, and Talmai, the descendants of Anak, were there. (Hebron was built seven years before Zoan in Egypt.)" Moses "was instructed in all the wisdom of the Egyptians" (Acts 7:22); thus, he would have knowledge of the building of Zoan, an Egyptian city, and of Hebron, a city on one of the trade routes between Memphis in Egypt and Damascus in Syria.

From the internal evidence, it is clearly obvious that the writer must have had an intimate knowledge of the desert, being an eyewitness to that environment. (See

---

[1039] David organized the tens of thousands of Levites into their many divisions of service, including a great chorus of singers and musicians.—1 Chronicles 23:1–29:19; 2 Chronicles 8:14; 23:18; 29:25; Ezra 3:10.

[1040] F. C. Cook, *Exodus* (1874), 247.

Leviticus 18:3; Deuteronomy 12:9; 15:4, 7; Numbers 2:1; Leviticus 14:8; 16:21; 17:3, 9.) The evidence is such because it is something that cannot be retained for a thousand years, but must come from an eyewitness. The details are extremely exact, and some would not have existed hundreds of years later: "Then they came to Elim, where there were twelve wells of water and seventy palm trees, and they camped there by the water," and "ram skins dyed red, fine leather, acacia wood." – Exodus 15:27; 25:5

Again, it should be noted that Moses "was instructed in all the wisdom of the Egyptians." (Acts 7:22) It is also obvious that the writer was quite familiar with Egyptian names: Pithom, meaning "House of Atum;" On, meaning "City of the Pillar" (the Greeks called the city Heliopolis); Potiphera·[1041] meaning "He Whom Ra Has Given;" and Asenath, her name deriving from Egyptian, meaning: "Holy to Anath."

In addition, the writer used Egyptian words generously. "He had Joseph ride in his second chariot, and [servants] called out before him, '*Abrek!*' So he placed him over all the land of Egypt." (Genesis 41:43) The exact meaning of this expression transliterated from Egyptian into Hebrew has not yet been determined. Some feel that it is an Egyptian word meaning (*Attention!*) while others see it as a Hebrew word meaning *Kneel* or *Bow down!* One misstep and the writer will lose credibility. However, this is never the case with the writer of the Pentateuch. He mentions the acacia tree, which is found in Egypt and Sinai but not in the land of Canaan. Moreover, this writer refers to numerous animals that are to be found primarily in Egypt or Sinai. – See Deuteronomy. 14:5; Leviticus 16:11.

The old form of words in the Pentateuch are of the time frame of the fifteenth century B.C.E. as well, and had no longer been in use for centuries by the time of the supposed writer(s) and redactor(s) of the ninth to the sixth centuries B.C.E. Dr. John J. Davis gives us the most widely recognized example, "The pronoun *she,* which appears as *hiw'* instead of *hî'*. Another example is the word *young girl,* spelled *na'ar* instead of *na'ărâ*, the feminine form."[1042]

All who engaged in idolatry or prophesying falsely were to be stoned to death, no exceptions. (Deuteronomy 13:2–11) This included not only individuals but also entire communities, every person within a city (verses 12–17). One has to ask, why would a writer include this if it were penned during the time period of 850–450 B.C.E. when most of the time Israel was shoulder deep in idolatry and false prophets abounded? This would mean certain destruction for every city in the kingdom. It would have been mere foolishness to incorporate these laws, which could never be enforced and would cause nothing but resistance to the law. However, it makes perfectly good sense for laws such as these to be given to people living in the time of Moses who had just exited an idolatrous nation and who was preparing to go in and conquer a number of other nations who lived and breathed idolatry.

[1041] A funeral pillar (stele) discovered in 1935 and now in the Cairo Museum refers to a personage named Potiphare.

[1042] John J. Davis, *Paradise to Prison: Studies in Genesis* (Salem: Sheffield, 1975), 26.

What Does the External Evidence Report?

"The book of the law of Moses," as Joshua called the Pentateuch, was accepted by Jews, Christians, and Muslims as containing evidence of inspiration. The fact that Moses is the writer of these five books is not something that grew up out of tradition; it is something Moses himself claims, saying he wrote under the divine command of Jehovah God. Moreover, the Jewish communities throughout the Roman empire were in total harmony with the fact that Moses was the writer of the Pentateuch, this being supported by the Samaritan Pentateuch, the Palestinian Talmud, the Babylonian Talmud, the Apocrypha, Philo Judaeus (a contemporary of Jesus and Paul and the first century), and by Jewish historian Flavius Josephus (37–100 C.E.).[1043] What about the early Christian writers, who wrote about Christianity between 150 C.E. and 400 C.E.?

> Moses, the servant of God, recorded, through the Holy Spirit, the very beginning of the creation of the world. First he spoke of the things concerning the creation and genesis of the world, including the first man and everything that happened afterwards in the order of events. He also indicated the number of years that elapsed before the Deluge.– *Theophilus* (c. 180, E), 2.118.[1044]

> The origin of that know ledge should not, on that account, be considered as originating with the Pentateuch. For knowledge of the Creator did not begin with the volume of Moses. Rather from the very first it is traced from Adam and paradise.— *Tertullian* (c. 207, W), 3.278.[1045]

> What portion of scripture can give us more information concerning the creation of the world than the account that Moses has transmitted?– *Origen* (c. 225, E), 4.341.[1046]

> The destruction of Sodom and Gomorrah by fire on account of their sins is related by Moses in Genesis.-- *Origen* (c. 248, E), 4.505.[1047]

> Moses said, "And the Lord God saw that the wickedness of men was overflowing upon the Earth" [Gen. 6:5–7].-- *Novatian* (c. 235, W), 5.658.[1048]

> It is contained in the book of Moses, which he wrote about creation, in which is called Genesis.-- *Victorinus* (c. 280, W), 7.341.[1049]

[1043] See Ecclesiasticus 45:5; 2 Maccabees 7:30; Philo (*On the Life of Moses* II; III, 12–14; IV, 20; VIII, 45–48, pp. 93–95); Josephus (*The Antiquities of the Jews*, 3.8.10); Exodus 17:14; 24:4.

[1044] David W. Bercot, *A Dictionary of Early Christian Beliefs* (Peabody: Hendrickson, 1998), 599.

1045. Ibid., 600.
1046. Ibid., 600.
1047. Ibid., 600.
1048. Ibid., 601.
1049. Ibid., 601.

If you will look at the books of Moses, David, Solomon, Isaiah, or the Prophets who follow . . . . You will see what offspring they have left.--*Methodious* (c. 290, E), 6.333.[1050]

Let the following books be considered venerable and holy by you, both of the clergy and the laity. Of the Old Testament: The five books of Moses—Genesis, Exodus, Leviticus, Numbers, and Deuteronomy. . . .-*Apostolic Constitutions* (compiled c. 390, E), 7.505.[1051]

Archaeology and the Bible

Unlike higher criticism, archaeology is a field of study that has a solid foundation in physical evidence, instead of presenting only hypotheses, inferences, and implications. Within archaeology, one has both explicit and direct evidence as well as implicit evidence. There are many great publications that will undoubtedly go into this area in much greater detail, but suffice it to say that the Biblical events, the characters, geography, agriculture, plants and trees and settings are all in harmony with and accessible through archaeology.

While archaeology is not a total vindicator, it has defended God's Word. No one can argue against the fact that our understanding of ancient times has increased tremendously over the past 150 years and is being continuously refined. At present, one could list thousands of events within the Scriptures that are in complete harmony with the archaeological record. In fact, Wellhausen had nothing like what is available to the modern scholar. If he had, one would have to wonder if he would have come to the same conclusions. Conveying this exact point, Dr. Mark F. Rooker, Professor of Old Testament and Hebrew, stated:

Regarding the issue of differing divine names, it is now clear from archaeological data not available to Wellhausen and early critical scholars that deities in the ancient Near East often had multiple names. This fact is especially clear in the conclusion to the Babylonian Creation account, the *Enuma Elish,* where the god Marduk is declared to be preeminent and his fifty different names are mentioned in celebration of his conquest.[22] No one has suggested that each name represents a different source, as was done in biblical studies. On the contrary, it would have been impossible to attribute these different names to different sources that have been pasted or joined together in the literary account because the Mesopotamian writing system involved inscription in stone! Moreover, it is clear that throughout the Old Testament the occurrence of the names of God as Elohim or Yahweh are to be attributed to contextual and semantic issues, not the existence of sources. This conclusion is borne out by the fact that the names consistently occur in predictable genre. . . . Thus through scientific discovery and analysis the criterion of the differing divine names, which gave rise to the Documentary Hypothesis, has been found wanting. If this information would have been known in the last years of the nineteenth century, it is

---

1050. Ibid., 601.
1051. Ibid., 602.

safe to assume that the critical approach to the Pentateuch would never have seen the light of day.[1052]

Much archaeological evidence as well as other forms of evidence has been uncovered to reveal the accuracy of the record. The ziggurat located at Uruk (Erech) was found to be built with clay, baked bricks for stone, and asphalt (bitumen) for mortar.[1053] The Egyptian names and titles that Moses penned in the book of Exodus match Egyptian inscriptions. The book of Exodus shows that the Hebrew people were allowed to live in the land of Egypt as foreigners, as long as they kept separate from the Egyptians. Archaeology supports this custom. Likely, you will recall that Pharaoh's daughter bathed in the Nile (Exodus 2:5), which "was a common practice in ancient Egypt," according to Cook's *Commentary*. "The Nile was worshipped as an emanation . . . of Osiris, and a peculiar power of imparting life and fertility was attributed to its waters."

> The fact that a king's daughter should bathe in the open river is certainly opposed to the customs of the modern, Mohammedan East, where this is only done by women of the lower orders, and that in remote places (Lane, *Manners and Customs*); but it is in harmony with the customs of ancient Egypt,[1054]* and in perfect agreement with the notions of the early Egyptians respecting the sanctity of the Nile, to which divine honours even were paid (vid., Hengstenberg's *Egypt*, etc. pp. 109, 110), and with the belief, which was common to both ancient and modern Egyptians, in the power of its waters to impart fruitfulness and prolong life (vid., *Strabo*, xv. p. 695, etc., and Seetzen, *Travels* iii. p. 204).[1055]

In addition, history also testifies to the fact that magicians were a well-known feature of Egyptian life during the period of Moses.--Genesis 11:1-9; Exodus 8:22; 2:5; 5:6, 7, 18; 7:11.

Bricks have been found made with and without straw. The painting below was found in the private tomb of Vizier Rekhmire (the highest official under Pharaoh) on the west bank of ancient Thebes. Archaeology also supports "taskmasters--Egyptian overseers, appointed to exact labor of the Israelites,"[1056] as well as strictly controlled or enforced quotas that had to be met. (Exodus 5:6) Moreover, Egyptian papyri express serious concern for the needed straw (which was lacking at times) to be mixed with the mud to make these bricks. (Exodus

---

1052. Mark F. Rooker, *Leviticus: The New American Commentary* (Nashville: Broadman & Holman, 2001), 26–27.

[1053] (Genesis 11:3, *ESV*) "And they said to one another, 'Come, let us make bricks, and burn them thoroughly.' And they had brick for stone, and bitumen for mortar."

[1054] Wilkinson gave a picture of a bathing scene in which an Egyptian woman of rank is introduced, attended by four female servants.

1055. Carl Friedric Keil and Franz Delitzsch, *Commentary on the Old Testament* (Peabody, MA: Hendrickson, 2002), S. 1:278.

1056. Robert Jamieson, A. R. Fausset, and David Brown. *A Commentary, Critical and Explanatory, On the Old and New Testaments* (Oak Harbor: Scranton & Company, 1997), 51.

1:13, 14) The Papyri Anastasi, from ancient Egypt, reads, "There was no one to mould bricks, and there was no straw in the neighbourhood."[1057]

Furthermore, the historical conditions and surroundings are in accord precisely with the occasions and assertions in the book of Numbers. We have references to Edom, Egypt, Moab, Canaan, Ammon, and Amalek, which are true to the times, and the names of places are free from error.[1058] Archaeology is never absolute proof of anything, but it continues to add evidence, weighty at times to the fact that Moses had to be the writer of the Pentateuch. *Halley's Bible Handbook* writes, "Archaeology has been speaking so loudly of late that it is causing a decided reaction toward the conservative view. The theory that writing was unknown in Moses' day is absolutely exploded. And every year there are being dug up in Egypt, Palestine and Mesopotamia, evidences, both in inscriptions and earth layers, that the narratives of the Old Testament are true historical records. And 'scholarship' is coming to have decidedly more respect for the tradition of Mosaic authorship."[1059]

The Silver Amulet is one of many archaeological nails in the coffin of the Documentary Hypothesis. Why? This portion of Numbers is argued by the critics to be part of the "P" document that was supposedly penned between 550 and 400 B.C.E. However, initially, it was dated to the late seventh / early sixth centuries B.C.E.

Of course, this dating was subsequently challenged by Johannes Renz and Wolfgang Rollig (*Handbuch der Althebraischen Epigraphik*, 1995) because the silver was cracked and blemished to the point of making many words and a few lines unreadable. This allowed these critics to argue for a date in the third to second centuries B.C.E. period, which would remove this stain on the lifeless body of their Documentary Hypothesis.

Then it was shipped to the University of Southern California to be examined under photographic and computer imaging. The results? The researchers stated that they could "read fully and [had] analyzed with far greater precision," which resulted in the final analysis of being yet another vindication for Moses—the original dating stands: late seventh century B.C.E.

Exodus 14:6, 7 (*ESV*) reads, "So he [the Pharaoh] made ready his chariot and took his army with him, and took six hundred chosen chariots and all the other chariots of Egypt with officers over all of them." Pharaoh, being the god of the world and the supreme chief of his army, personally led the army into battle. Archaeology supports this custom.

Why are there no Egyptian records of the Exodus of the Israelites from Egypt? The critics may also ask why is there no archaeological evidence to support the Israelite's 215-year stay in Egypt (some of which was in slavery) and the devastation that was executed on the gods of Egypt. There is, in fact, one simple answer that archaeology has provided us: Any new Egyptian dynasty would erase any unflattering history prior to their dynasty, if such even existed, as it was their custom

1057. Adolf Erman and H. M. Tirard. *Life in Ancient Egypt* (Whitefish: Kessinger, 2003), 117.

1058. "Sirion . . . Senir." These names appear in the Ugaritic texts found at Ras Shamra, Syria, and in the documents from Bogazköy, Turkey.

1059. Henry Halley, *Halley's Bible Handbook* (Grand Rapids: Zondervan, 1988), 56.

never to record any defeats that might be viewed as embarrassing or critical, which could damage the dignity of their people, for they were an extremely prideful empire.[1060]

For example, Thutmose III ordered others to chisel Queen Hatshepsut out of the history books when he removed the name and representation of Queen Hatshepsut on a monumental stone record later uncovered at Deir al-Bahri in Egypt as well as from any other monuments she had built. Hatshepsut, daughter of Thutmose I, would eventually gain the throne upon her father's death even though Thutmose II (husband and half-brother to Hatshepsut) technically ascended the throne in name only. At best, Thutmose II lasted only three or four years before dying of a skin disease. Thutmose III was too young to rule, thus, Queen Hatshepsut simply held her own as the first female Pharaoh. Embarrassing for Thutmose III, indeed! Thus, as he grew, his hatred mounted for Hatshepsut and Senmut (her lover). After her death, Thutmose III worked vigorously to remove her name and the name of her lover from Egyptian history. If this was embarrassing, how much more so would be the ten plagues that had humiliated numerous gods of Egypt, including the Pharaoh himself? The exodus of 600,000 male slaves and their families, plus Egyptians who had chosen Jehovah as God instead of the Pharaoh of Egypt would have been quite embarrassing, indeed!

In 1925, discoveries of clay tablets were made at the ancient town of Nuzi in northeastern Mesopotamia; it was here that archaeologists found a tremendous number of legal contracts dating to the fifteenth-century B.C.E. These actually shed much light on the life of people of that time. Due to the slow-moving life condition of the ancient Near East, they reflect life conditions for many years on both sides of the fifteenth century. Thus, what we now possess and know from studies of these Nuzi Tablets is that there are numerous customs in the Patriarchal period that were very much in common practice among the ancient Hurrians who lived in northern Mesopotamia, encompassing Haran, which was the home of Abraham after he left Ur and where Isaac later found his wife Rebekah.

Abraham's Contract. Eliezer was to be the legal inheritor of childless Abraham's property and position after Abraham's death. In fact, Abraham referred to Eliezer when he said, "a slave born in my house will be my heir." (Genesis 15:2, 3) Tablets from Nuzi discovered by archaeologists help the modern-day reader understand how a servant could become heir to his master's household. Mesopotamian records from the time of Abraham (2018–1843 B.C.E.); makes mention of the tradition of a childless couple adopting a son in their old age to have him take care of them up unto their death, and thereafter inheriting the household property. But if for some reason the couple would end up having a child, the child would become the primary heir instead, with the adopted servant or son getting a minor portion of the property as well. (Wood, 1996) In a culture that passed history down orally through its generations, we find Moses being only three generations removed from Abraham's great-grandson Levi (Levi, Kohath, Amram, and Moses) while our alleged "J" was a thousand years removed from Abraham, and the redactor even further. It is only by means of modern-day archaeology that we are aware of just how accurate the Genesis account is with minor details such as

---

1060. Joseph P. Free, *Archaeology and Bible History* (Grand Rapids, MI: Zondervan Publishing, 1964).

the legal system of adoption rights in Mesopotamia from 2000 B.C.E. (time of Abraham) to 1500 B.C.E. (time of Moses), knowledge that would not be available to our alleged composers. Thus, archaeology puts the Genesis account right back into the hands of its true writer, Moses.

The Price of a Slave. Joseph was the son of Jacob by Rachel, the grandson of Isaac, and the great-grandson of Abraham, and was sold as a slave to some Midianite merchants for a mere 20 pieces of silver by his jealous brothers in about 1750 B.C.E. (Genesis 37:28; 42:21) Throughout the stream of time, we find inflation in the slave trade, and the Biblical account of the price for Joseph falls exactly where it should to be in harmony with secular archaeology, as you can see in chart 1. Again, our alleged "J," "E," "D," and "P" composers would be a thousand years removed from Abraham, and "R" (the redactor) even further; thus they would have no access to this information so as to have gotten it correct. Only the actual writer, Moses, would be aware of this information by family records or oral tradition.

The Inflation of the Slave Trade in Biblical Times (Wood, 1996)

SOURCE	DATE	PRICE OF A SLAVE IN SILVER
Akkad and 3rd Ur Dynasties	2000 B.C.E.	8–10 pieces of silver
Joseph (Genesis 37:2, 28)	1750 B.C.E.	20 pieces of silver
Hammurabi Code	1799–1700 B.C.E.	20 pieces of silver
Old Babylonian Tablets	B.C.E.	15–30 pieces of silver
Mari tablets	1799–1600 B.C.E.	20 pieces of silver
Exodus 21:32	1520–1470 B.C.E.	30 pieces of silver
Nuzi tablets	1499–1400 B.C.E.	30 pieces of silver
Ugarit tablets	1399–1200 B.C.E.	30–40 pieces of silver
Assyria	First millennium B.C.E.	50–60 pieces of silver
2 Kings 15:20	790 B.C.E.	50 pieces of silver
Persia	750–500 B.C.E.	90–120 pieces of silver

Seti I began much like his father Ramses, as a military commander. His military prowess led to many triumphs that are recorded on the walls of the temple of Amon-Ra at Karnak. Here Seti I recorded his military triumphs; captives are shown being seized by their hair. As was expressed earlier, victories were proudly recorded on Egyptian monuments, but embarrassing or critical events were ignored, that is, never chiseled into their annals of history.

Concluding Thoughts

I had given much thought to a conclusion that contained quotations from many reputable scholars who use thought-provoking points to support the writership of Moses for the Pentateuch, but what would that prove? Certainly, if you quote a reputable scholar you would add weight to an argument, but it does not make the case. It only validates that you are not alone in your reasoning. Therefore, I have added quotations of only two scholars to make just that point. One does not count the number of people who believe one thing as opposed to another and those with the most votes win. No, the results should be based on evidence. In fact, the higher critics will infer that they are in the right by saying, 'Today, you will hardly find one scholar in the world who will argue for the writership of Moses for the Pentateuch.' If that makes them in the right, it also makes them in the wrong. Why? Because for centuries, for millenniums, the majority of Bible scholars—in the Jewish world, the Christian world, and the Islamic world—accepted Moses' writership; that is, until the Age of Reason within the eighteenth and nineteenth centuries when people started to question not only the writership of Moses but the very existence of God.

Would any Christian living in 1700 C.E. have ever doubted the writership of Moses? Hardly! So how did the Documentary Hypothesis become Documentary Fact? All it took was for some leading professors at major universities to plant seeds of doubt within their students. Being at the entrance of the era of higher criticism and skepticism of the nineteenth century, this Documentary Hypothesis had a well-cultivated field in which to grow. It created a domino effect as a few scholars produced a generation of students, who would then be the next generation of scholars, and so on.

As we moved into the twentieth century, these questions had become "facts" in the eyes of many; in fact, it became in vogue to challenge the Bible. Leading schools and leading scholars of higher criticism were the norm, and soon the conservative Christian was isolated. The twentieth-century student received a lean diet from those few scholars who still accepted God's Word as just that, the Word of God, fully inerrant, with 40 writers of 66 books over a period of about 1,600 years. No, these students would now be fed mostly liberal theology, and any who disagreed were portrayed as ignorant and naïve. This planting of uncertainty or mistrust, with question after question bringing Moses' writership into doubt, with most literature focusing on this type of propaganda, would create the latest generation of scholars, and today they dominate the world of scholarship.

How did this progressive takeover come off without a hitch? The conservative scholarship of the early twentieth century saw these liberal naysayers as nothing more than a fly at a picnic. Most did not even deem it necessary to address their questions, so by 1950–1970, the Documentary Hypothesis machine was in full throttle. It was about this same time that the sleeping giant finally awoke to find that conservative scholarship had taken a backseat to this new creature, liberal scholarship. It is only within the last 30–40 years that some very influential conservative scholars have started to publish books in a move to dislodge this liberal movement.* Is it too little, too late?

*This is not to say that the 19th and early 20th century did not have any apologist defending against biblical criticism. There were some giants in this field, like R. A. Torrey.

It is possible to displace higher criticism, but many factors stand in the way. For one, any opposition is painted as uninformed and inexperienced regarding the subject matter. Moreover, the books that tear down the Bible with all their alleged critical analysis sell far better than those do that encourage putting faith in God's Word. In addition, many conservative scholars tend to sit on the sideline and watch as a few leading scholars attempt to do the work of the many. In addition, there are liberal scholars continually putting out numerous articles and books, dominating the market. Unlike the conservative scholars in the first part of the twentieth century, these liberal scholars in the first part of the twenty-first century are not slowing down. Moreover, they have become more aggressive.

The book *Introduction to the Bible*, by John Laux, explains just what the Documentary Hypothesis would have meant for the Israelites if it were true:

> The Documentary Theory is built up on assertions which are either arbitrary or absolutely false. . . . If the extreme Documentary Theory were true, the Israelites would have been the victims of a clumsy deception when they permitted the heavy burden of the Law to be imposed upon them. It would have been the greatest hoax ever perpetrated in the history of the world.[1061]

It goes much further than that; it would mean that the Son of God was either fooled by what these higher critics argue, that there was a tradition of Moses being the writer of the Pentateuch, which developed through time and was accepted as reality during Jesus' day, or that Jesus was a liar, because he had lived in heaven prior to his coming down to earth and was aware of the deception but had continued a tradition that he knew to be false. The truth is that the Son of God was well aware that Moses was, in fact, the writer of the Pentateuch and he presented Moses as such because he was there at the time!

So again, because Jesus taught that Moses was, in fact, the writer of the Pentateuch, we have three options:

- Jesus knew Moses was the writer because Jesus was there, in heaven, prior to his Virgin birth and observed Moses as the writer; or
- Jesus knew that Moses was not the writer and simply perpetuated a Jewish tradition that Moses was the writer; or
- Jesus possessed a limited knowledge and simply believed something that was a tradition because he was unaware of it being such.

So if Jesus knew Moses was *not* the writer and purposely conveyed misinformation for the sake of Jewish tradition, this makes Jesus a liar and therefore a sinner, which would contradict what Hebrews 4:15 says of him, that "he was without sin." If he was simply in ignorance and was mistakenly conveying misinformation, this certainly does away with Jesus having a prehuman existence. (John 1:1–2; 3:13; 6:38, 62; 8:23, 42, 58; Colossians 1:15–18; Revelation 3:14;

1061. John Laux, *Introduction to the Bible* (Chicago: Tan Books & Pub., 1992), 186.

Proverbs 8:22–30) Based on the scriptures and other evidence presented, we can conclude that Jesus was well aware that Moses was the writer, and that is what he truthfully taught.

Duane Garrett makes the following observation concerning the Documentary Hypothesis:

> The time has long passed for scholars of every theological persuasion to recognize that the Graf-Wellhausen theory, as a starting point for continued research, is dead. The Documentary Hypothesis and the arguments that support it have been effectively demolished by scholars from many different theological perspectives and areas of expertise. Even so, the ghost of Wellhausen hovers over Old Testament studies and symposiums like a thick fog. . . . One wonders if we will ever return to the day when discussions of Genesis will not be stilted by interminable references to P and J. There are indications that such a day is coming. Many scholars are exploring the inadequacies of the Documentary Hypothesis and looking toward new models for explaining the Pentateuch.[1062]

These world-renowned scholars who have gone left of center are witty and able to express thoughts, ideas, and feelings coherently, having conviction that leads unsuspecting ones who are not aware of the facts to accept ideas that are made to appear as smooth-fitting pieces in a large puzzle, thinking that they are nothing more than long-awaited answers. Sadly, many unsuspecting readers have taken their words as absolute truth.

Jesus quotes or alludes to 23 of the 39 books of the Hebrew Scriptures. Specifically, he quotes all five of the books attributed to Moses—the book of Deuteronomy 16 times alone, this obviously being one of his favorites. As we close this chapter, we are going to let our greatest witness take the stand. As you read Jesus' references to Moses and the Law you will undoubtedly notice that he viewed Moses' writership as historically true, completely authoritative, and inspired of God. If one does not accept, Moses, as the writer of the Pentateuch as Jesus did, is that not calling Jesus a liar.

As Christians, we accept what the Bible teaches as true. By way of common sense and sound reasoning, the vast majority of the issues of higher criticism's Social Progressive Christian and Christian Modernists have been answered quite easily by the conservative scholar in absolute terms: for example, F. David Farnell, Gleason L. Archer Jr., C. John Collins, K. A. Kitchen, Norman L. Geisler, and others. For the handful of issues left, we still have reasonable answers, which are not beyond a reasonable doubt at this time; we are quite content to wait until we are provided with the concrete answers that will make these few issues beyond all reasonable doubt. The last 150 years of evidence that has come in by way of archaeological discoveries, a better understanding of the original language, historical-cultural and contextual understanding, as well as manuscripts has answered almost all those

---

[1062] Garrett, Duane. *Rethinking Genesis: The Sources and Authorship of the First Book of the Pentateuch* (Grand Rapids: Baker Books, 1991), 13.

doubtful areas that have been called into question by the higher critics. Therefore, because we lack the complete answers for a few remaining issues means nothing.

Consider this: A critic raises an issue, but it is answered by a new archaeological discovery a few years later. The critic runs to another issue, and it is later answered by an improved understanding of the original languages. Then he runs to look for yet another issue, and it is answered by thousands of manuscripts that are uncovered over a period of two decades. This has been the case with thousands of issues. What are we to think the agenda is of those who continue scouring God's Word looking for errors, discrepancies, and contradictions? How many times must they raise objections and be proven wrong before we stop listening to their cries? If that is the case, why do their books still outsell those that expose their erroneous thinking? Does that say something about the Christian community and their desire for tabloid scholarship (sensationalized stories)? Would the average Christian rather read an article or book by Dan Brown on how Jesus allegedly married and had sexual relations with Mary Magdalene and fathered children (false, of course), or read an article or book on the actual, even more fascinating account of Jesus' earthly life, based on the four Gospels?

For today's Christian, there is no more important study than the life and ministry of the real, historical Jesus Christ. The writer of the book of Hebrews exhorts us to **"fix our eyes on** Jesus," to **"consider him** who endured such opposition from sinful men." Moreover, Jehovah God himself commanded: "This is my Son, whom I love; with him I am well pleased. **Listen to him!**" (*NIV*, bolding added) While an apologetic of the study of the "*Historical Jesus*," or "*The Case for the Resurrection of Jesus*"[1063] is certainly fine, the primary source of the four Gospels accounts of Matthew, Mark, Luke, and John should be first place, the starting point of any real investigation of Jesus' life and ministry. A life and ministry that viewed the Old Testament as historically true and of the greatest importance to his followers that he would leave behind after his ascension back to heaven.

We return to Wellhausen, who investigated his documentary hypothesis under the worldview of Israelite religion from an evolutionary model: (1) at the beginning it was animistic and spiritistic, (2) gradually developing into polytheism, (3) moving eventually into henotheism (choosing one god out of many), and finally (4) gravitating to monotheism. Wellhausen could not accept that this development took place in a short period, but was an evolution that took more than a millennium. This evolutionary process is no longer held among today's critical scholarship.

Another obstacle was that Wellhausen did not believe in the miraculous and could not accept prophetic statements (for example, Genesis 49) happening before the actual events. This mindset was the catalyst behind his research.[1064] Consequently, Wellhausen investigated the text with this way of thinking and that

---

1063. **Recommended**: Gary R. Habermas, *The Historical Jesus: Ancient Evidence for the Life of Christ* (Joplin, MO: College Press, 1996); Gary R. Habermas, *The Case for the Resurrection of Jesus* (Grand Rapids, MI: Kregel, 2004); Craig A. Evans, *Fabricating Jesus: How Modern Scholars Distort the Gospels* (Downers Grove, IL: IVP Books, 2006); Timothy Paul Jones, *Misquoting Truth: A Guide to the Fallacies of Bart Ehrman's Misquoting Jesus* (Downers Grove, IL: IVP Books, 2007).

1064 Tremper Longman III, and Raymond B. Dillard, *An Introduction to the Old Testament* (Grand Rapids: Zondervan, 2006), 43–44.

state of mind contributed to his discovering the Documentary Hypothesis issues of different uses of the divine name, discrepancies, repetitions (doublets), and differences in style and language, reading his views into the text (eisegesis).

The above facts of this book have easily demonstrated that the evidence of the documentary hypothesis is really no evidence at all. The modern-day critic has to deal with the lack of consensus on the part of his colleagues, who lack in agreement for the explanation of the sources.

> This failure to achieve consensus is represented by the occasional division of source strata into multiple layers (see Smend's J1 and J2) that often occasions the appearance of new sigla (for instance, Eissfeldt's L [aienquelle], Noth's G[rundschrift], Fohrer's N [for Nomadic], and Pfeiffer's S [for Seir]. A further indication of the collapse of the traditional documentary hypothesis is the widely expressed doubt that E was ever an independent source (Voz, Rudolph, Mowinckel; cf. Kaiser, IOT, 42 n. 18). Similar disagreements are also found in the dating of the sources. J has been dated to the period of Solomon by Von Rad, though Schmidt would argue for the seventh century, and Van Seters (1992, 34) has advocated an exile date. While most scholars believe P is postexilic, Haran has argued that it is to be associated with Hezekiah's reforms in the eighth century BC.[1065]

While the lack of consensus is not in and of itself capable of disproving the proposition of sources other than Moses for the writing of the Pentateuch, it does cast even more doubt on the critical scholar's proposal that the new school of the Documentary Hypothesis has any more to offer than the old school of Wellhausen.

As this book has clearly demonstrated, Moses is the inspired author of the Pentateuch. At best, we can accept that it is likely that Joshua may have updated the text in Deuteronomy chapter 34, which speaks of Moses' death, and it is possible that Joshua may have made the reference in Numbers 12:3 that refer to Moses as being 'the humblest man on the face of the earth.'[1066] In addition, we can accept that a later copyist [or even possibly Ezra, another inspired author] updated Genesis 11:28, 31 to read "of the Chaldeans," a name of a land and its inhabitants in the southern portion of Babylonia that *possibly* was not recognized as Chaldea until several hundred years after Moses.

> The origin of the Chaldeans is uncertain but may well be in the west, or else branches of the family may have moved there (cf. Job 1:17). The general name for the area in the earliest period is unknown, since it was part of Sumer (see SHINAR); so it cannot be argued that the qualification of Abraham's home city UR as "of the Chaldeans" (Gen. 11:28, 31; 15:7; as later Neh. 9:7; cf. Acts 7:4) is necessarily a later insertion in the text.[1067]

1065. Ibid., 49–50.

[1066] For the possibility of Moses penning these words, see my comments in the first paragraph of section four.

[1067] Geoffrey W. Bromiley, vol. 1, *The International Standard Bible Encyclopedia, Revised* (Wm. B. Eerdmans, 1988; 2002), 630.

The same would hold true of a copyist updating Genesis 36:31, which reads: "Now these are the kings who reigned in the land of Edom before *any king reigned over the sons of Israel.*" Moses and Joshua were long gone for hundreds of years before Israel ever had a king over them.[1068] The same would hold true again for Genesis 14:14, which reads: When Abram heard that his relative had been taken captive, he led out his trained men, born in his house, three hundred and eighteen, and went in pursuit *as far as Dan.* Dan was an area settled long after Moses death, after the Israelites had conquered the Promise Land. This too is obviously an update as well, making it contemporary to its readers.[1069]

Reference to "Ur of the Chaldeans"[1070] (11:28) identifies the native land of Haran but not necessarily of Terah and his sons Abram and Nahor. In fact, the inclusion of this information for Haran may suggest the ancestral home was elsewhere (for this discussion see comments on 12:1). "Ur of the Chaldeans" occurs three times in Genesis (11:28, 31; 15:7) and once elsewhere (Neh 9:7). Stephen identified the place of God's revelation to Abram as "Mesopotamia" from which he departed: "So he left the land of the Chaldeans and settled in Haran" (Acts 7:3–4). The "land [*chōra*] of the Chaldeans" rather than "Ur of the Chaldeans" is the Septuagint translation, as reflected in Stephen's sermon, which can be explained as either a textual slip due to the prior phrase "land of his birth" or the ancient translator's uncertainty about the identity of the site. J. W. Wevers proposes that due to the apposition of "land of his birth," the translator interpreted "Ur" as a region.[1071, 1072]

As we have already stated, the critic is fond of finding portions of the text that lack secular support, and then summarily dismissing it as not being a real historical account. Once evidence surfaces to support their dismissal as being wrong and premature, they simply never mention this section again, but move on to another. The question that begs to be asked by the logical and reasonable mind is, how many times must this take place before they stop and accept the Bible as sound and reliable history? Let us look at the historicity of the above account of Abraham's men defeating the Mesopotamian kings, for it is historically sound. Information had

---

[1068] It should be noted that even this statement could belong to Moses, even though there were no kings in Israel at this time. How? He would be aware that Jehovah had promised Abraham that he would be so great that kings would come out of him (Gen 17:6) and the preparation for such is mentioned at Deuteronomy 17:14-20.

[1069] It should be noted that this author does not accept higher criticisms unending desire to find source(s) for a book, because they have dissected it to no end. While there are a few details that may have been updated by a copyist, or even the inspired writer Ezra (writer of Chronicles and the book that bears his name), this does not mean that we accept the update, if it is such, as the inspired material that was originally written, unless it was done by another inspired writer like Joshua, Ezra, or Nehemiah, or even possibly Jeremiah. It is also possible that it could be an explanatory addition.

[1070] Hb. "Chaldeans" כַּשְׂדִּים is *kaldu* (Akk.) in Assyrian texts, and the Gk. has καλδαιοι; the original *sd* has undergone a change to *ld* (see R. S. Hess, "Chaldea," *ABD* 1.886–87).

[1071] J. W. Wevers, *Notes on the Greek Text of Genesis*, Septuagint and Cognate Studies 35 (Atlanta: Scholars Press, 1993), 158.

[1072] K. A. Mathews, vol. 1B, *Genesis 11:27-50:26*, electronic ed., Logos Library System; The New American Commentary (Nashville: Broadman & Holman Publishers, 2007), 99–100.

become known in the 20th century that vindicates this account as being historically true, and removes yet another arguing point from those supporters of the documentary hypothesis:

> The name of Chedorlaomer, King of Elam, contains familiar Elamite components: *kudur* meant "servant," and *Lagamar* was a high goddess in the Elamite pantheon. Kitchen (Ancient Orient, p. 44) generally prefers the vocalization Kutir instead of Kudur and gives the references for at least three Elamite royal names of this type. He equates tidal with a Hittite name, Tudkhaliya, attested from the nineteenth century B.C. As for Arioch, one King of Larsa ("El-Larsa") from this era was Eri-aku ("Servant of the Moon-god"), whose name in Akkadian was *Arad-Sin* (with the same meaning). The Mari tablets refer to persons by the name of Ariyuk. The cuneiform of the original of Amraphel, formerly equated with Hammurabi of Babylon, is not demonstrable for the twentieth century (Hammurabi himself dates from the eighteenth century, but there may possibly be a connection with Amorite names like *Amud-pa-ila*, according to H. B. Huffman. . . . It should be added that according to G. Pettinato, the leading epigraphist of the Ebla documents dating from 2400–2250 B.C., mention is made in the Ebla tablets of Sodom (spelled *Si-da-mu*), Gomorrah (spelled in Sumerian cuneiform *I-ma-ar*), and Zoar (*Za-e-ar*). He feels that quite possibly these may be the same cities mentioned in the Abrahamic narrative.[1073]

> W. F. Albright comments: In spite of our failure hitherto to fix the historical horizon of this chapter, we may be certain that its contents are very ancient. There are several words and expressions found nowhere else in the Bible and now known to belong to the second millenium. The names of the towns in Transjordania are also known to be very ancient.[1074]

In the final analysis, based on both the internal and external evidence, we can absolute confidence that Moses was the author of the Pentateuch. The minor additions of Joshua, who was himself an inspired writer, as well as the handful of updates in the text to make it clearer to the then-current reader does no harm to the inspired message that God wished to convey.

1073. Gleason L. Archer, *Encyclopedia of Bible Difficulties* (Grand Rapids: Zondervan, 1982), 90–91.

1074. H. C. Alleman and E. E. Flack, *Old Testament Commentary* (Philadelphia: Fortress, 1954), 14.

CHAPTER 11 The Authorship and Unity of Isaiah

Edward D. Andrews

In **Isaiah 1:1**, we are introduced to Isaiah in his own words as **"the son of Amoz,"** informing his readers that he served as God's prophet **"in the days of Uzziah [52 years], Jotham [16 years], Ahaz [16 years] and Hezekiah [28 years], kings of Judah."** The total reign of these four kings would be 112 years, which means that Isaiah likely began toward the end of Uzziah's reign. He was one of the longest serving prophets of the southern kingdom of Judah, no fewer than 46 years, about 778-732 B.C.E.

Very little is known about the personal life of Isaiah, compared to what we know of the other prophets of the Old Testament. He was married to a "prophetess." (8:3) "It is possible that the 'prophetess' simply refers to the prophet's wife, though there are no other examples of this in Scripture. It is possible that Isaiah's wife had a prophetic gift, but this gift is not affirmed elsewhere."[1075] There are other women within the Old Testament that held the office of a prophetess, making it likely that Isaiah's wife may very well have had this same assignment. – Judges 4:4; 2 Kings 22:14.

Amoz was Isaiah's father, this being the only detail of Amoz that is known. (1:1) We are not told of Isaiah's birth or death, though strong Jewish tradition has it "that the prophet Isaiah was cut in half with a wooden saw. This happened during the reign of King Manasseh. The Old Testament has no record of this incident."[1076] (Compare Heb. 11:37.) His prophetic book places him in Jerusalem with at least two sons with prophetic names and his prophet wife. (Isa. 7:3; 8:1, 3) His years of prophesying for the southern kingdom likely run from 778 B.C.E through the 14th year of Hezekiah's reign, a little after 732 B.C.E. (1:1; 6:1; 36:1) Some contemporary prophets of Isaiah were Micah in the land of Judah and, to the north, Hosea and Oded. – Micah. 1:1; Hos. 1:1; 2 Chronicles 28:6-9.

Life in Judah throughout these 46 years for Isaiah was unstable and chaotic, to say the least. The political element was in constant turmoil, the courts were corrupt to no end, and the religious structure of the nation was filled with pretense and duplicity. Scattered throughout the hill country of Judea were pagan altars to false gods. A case in point would be King Ahaz, who not only allowed this idolatrous worship, "but was an active participant, not only duplicating the sins of Israel's kings, but he also sacrificed his son 'in the fire,' perhaps as an offering to the god Molech."[1077] (2 Ki 16:3, 4; 2 Ch. 28:3, 4) Sadly, this is only a continuation of

---

[1075] E. Ray Clendenen, *New American Commentary: Isaiah 1-39* (B & H Publishing Group, 2007), 222.

[1076] Simon J. Kistemaker and William Hendriksen, vol. 15, *New Testament Commentary: Exposition of Hebrews*, New Testament Commentary (Grand Rapids: Baker Book House, 1953-2001), 355.

[1077] Paul R. House, vol. 8, *1, 2 Kings*, electronic ed., Logos Library System; The New American Commentary (Nashville: Broadman & Holman Publishers, 2001), 336.

a people that were supposed to be in a covenant relationship with Jehovah. – Exodus 19:5-8.

We need not leave the impression that all was lost, for some of Isaiah's contemporaries were working for the restoration of true worship. For instance, King Uzziah "did that which was right in the eyes of Jehovah." However, this was not enough, because "the high places were not taken away: the people still sacrificed and burnt incense in the high places." (2 Ki 15:3, 4) King Jotham followed in his father's footsteps and "did that which was right in the eyes of Jehovah." And like in the case of Uzziah, the people of Jotham's reign "followed corrupt practices." (2 Ch. 27:2) Sadly, Isaiah spent much of his career in a spiritually defunct kingdom. While some kings promoted false worship, others worked for the return of pure worship, with no real effect on the people. As one can imagine, presenting this prophetic message to such stiff-necked people was going to prove none too easy.

Some have looked to the style throughout the book of Isaiah and have suggested two Isaiah's, a "Second Isaiah," "the idea of a multiple authorship of Isaiah has arisen only in the last two centuries. Its simplest, most persuasive form is the ascription of chapters. 1–39 to Isaiah and 40–66 to an anonymous prophet living among the sixth-century exiles in Babylonia."[1078] There is an enormous amount of evidence that there is only one Isaiah, who penned the entire book, centuries before the Babylonian exile.[1079]

Chapters 1 to 6 give the reader the historical setting within Judah and Jerusalem, emphasizing the guilt of Judah before God, as well as the commissioning of Isaiah. Chapters 7 to 12 cover the continuous threats of an invasion, giving the people a hope by means of the Prince of Peace, authorized by Jehovah. Chapters 13 to 35 comprise a succession of announcements against numerous nations and a prophecy of salvation, which is to come from Jehovah. Chapters 36 to 39 cover Hezekiah's reign with significant dealings. Chapters 40 to 66 deal with a release from the Babylonian Empire,[1080] and the return of the Jewish people to Judah and Jerusalem restoring Zion.

Multiple Authorship for the Book of Isaiah

Man is unable to foretell the future with any inevitability. Repeatedly their struggles at prophecy are unsuccessful in the extreme. Therefore, a book full of prophetic books, if true, would attract interest, and even attack. The Bible is just such a book.

The primary cause behind questioning Isaiah's authorship is the same for all other prophetic books. It is their prophetic nature (detailed history written in

---

[1078] D. A. Carson, *New Bible Commentary: 21st Century Edition*, 4th ed. (Leicester, England; Downers Grove, Ill., USA: Inter-Varsity Press, 1994).

[1079] For additional verbal agreements and similarities within Isaiah, cf. G.L. Robinson and R.K. Harrison, "Isaiah," in *The International Standard Bible Encyclopedia*, vol. 2 (Grand Rapids: Eerdmans, 1982), pp. 895–898.

[1080] The Babylonian Empire at the time of prophecy, late eighth century B.C.E., is merely an unknown entity, who is yet to grow into an Empire, unseating the current Assyrian Empire.

advance), which is impossible for the Bible critic or liberal scholar to accept as a reality. (Isaiah 41:21-26; 42:8, 9; 46:8-10) If we are to understand the critic, we must examine their thinking. Therefore, let us look at some aspects of their reasoning.

Prophecy is Contemporary, Meaningful and Applicable to the People

The **important truth for the Bible critic lies in** the understanding that for all occurrences, prophecy pronounced or written in Bible times meant something to the people it was spoken or written to; it was meant to serve as a guide for them if they heeded its counsel. Frequently, it had specific fulfillment for that time, being fulfilled throughout the lifetime of that very generation. Thus, it is true that the penned or spoken words always had some application to the very people who heard them. The words of Isaiah's chapters 40 to 66 pointed out that the Jewish people would see the destruction of their beloved Jerusalem, be taken into exile to Babylon for 70-years, yet freed by the Medo-Persians, Cyrus, the leader of Persia specifically. Thereafter, the Jewish people would be released to their homeland, to rebuild. All of this took place 200 years plus after the days of Isaiah. Therefore, for the critic, **there must have been a second Isaiah writing in 540 B.C.E., just before the return of the Israelites to Jerusalem.**[1081]

That Isaiah penned the book that bears his name was never thought otherwise until the 12th century C.E. This was not the position of Jewish commentator Abraham Ibn Ezra.[1082] "He states in his commentary on Isaiah that the second half of the book, from chapter 40 on, was the work of a prophet who lived during the Babylonian Exile and the early period of the Return to Zion." (Pfeffer 2005, 28)" Progressively, throughout the next two centuries, more and more scholars were adopting this view. The New Bible Dictionary notes:

> Many scholars nowadays deny great portions of the book to Isaiah, not only in the sense that he did not write them down, but in the sense that their subject-matter does not come from him at all. Even chapters

---

[1081] It should be noted that the words of Jehovah by way of Isaiah were very much applicable to his audience of the eighth-century B.C.E. The exile to Babylon (150 years away), was applicable for Isaiah and his audience and started the moment he penned the words. It was a process, which began with their guilt before Jehovah, as outlined in chapters 1:1-6:13.

Judah and Jerusalem's guilt; the commission of Isaiah (1:1–6:13)

Hostile intentions of an enemy invasions and promise of relief (7:1–12:6)

Declaring international desolations (13:1–23:18)

Judgment on the whole world, promise of salvation by Jehovah (24:1–35:10)

Jehovah delivers Judah from Assyria; Babylonian exile foretold (36:1–39:8)

Release from Babylon by the Jehovah God through Cyrus, restoration of Israel, Messiah to come (40:1–66:24)

[1082] Abraham Ibn Ezra (1089-1164) was a Jewish scholar of the Middle Ages, who penned a commentary on ever Old Testament book, as well as poetry and grammatical treatise, being more read than all, with the exception the greatest Jewish scholar of that period, Rashi.

1–35 are believed by some to contain much non-Isaianic material. Some scholars go farther than others, but there is a wide measure of agreement that Isaiah cannot be credited with chapters 13:1–14:23; 21; 24–27; 34–35. In addition, critical scholars are practically unanimous in the view that chapters 40–66 do not come from Isaiah.[1083]

A Dissecting of Isaiah

The Bible critics were not going to stop with this Isaiah II. No, they would go on to challenge Isaiah authorship even further. The above theory, known as the Second Isaiah, or Deutero-Isaiah, only led to a suggested Isaiah III. If Isaiah 40 to 66 could not belong to the First-Isaiah, because of the foreknowledge; then, chapters 13 and 14 must be set aside for the very same reason. The critique goes even further as they continue to cut up the book of Isaiah, with chapters 15 and 16 also receiving a writer of its own, another unknown prophet. Chapters 23 to 27 have been set aside as well, belonging to yet another. Another critic argues that chapters 34 to 35 could not have belonged to the 8th century prophet either, as it resembles chapter 40 to 66 that had already been set aside as not being the First-Isaiah. Bible scholar Charles C. Torrey briefly sums up the result of this irrational reasoning. "The once great 'Prophet of the Exile,'" he says, "has dwindled to a very small figure, and is all but buried in a mass of jumbled fragments." (Blenkinsopp 2003, 27) It should be noted that while Torrey brought down the number of alleged Isaiah writers, he still held many of the liberal positions. Nevertheless, not all scholars agree with such dismembering of the prophetic book that was penned in its entirety by one Isaiah, from the 8th century B.C.E.

The idea that the composer of Isaiah II lived in Babylon was being lost with some scholars. As Dr. Gleason L. Archer points out, "the references to geography, flora, and fauna found in Deutero-Isaiah were far more appropriate to an author living in Syria or Palestine."[1084] Professor Bernard Duhm (1847-1928) introduced the world to three Isaiah, with none of them being the Isaiah of the 8th century B.C.E., nor having lived in Babylon. Duhm argues that Isaiah II penned chapters 40-55 about 540 B.C.E., near the region of Lebanon. Isaiah III, in Jerusalem, penned chapters 56 to 66 at the time of Ezra, 450 B.C.E. Duhm would go on to argue that some of the data within Isaiah was even further removed from Isaiah I, some belonging to the first-century B.C.E. Once they settled on a final set of dates for the dissected Isaiah, it was this criticism that George Adam Smith (1856 – 1942), accepted in his *The Book of Isaiah* (*The Expositor's Bible*, 2 vols., 1888, 1890). This criticism would receive one serious blow, only five years after the death of Smith.

Prior to the discovery of the Dead Sea Scrolls, the oldest manuscripts of the Old Testament were dated to about the ninth and tenth centuries C.E., known as

---

[1083] D. R. W. Wood and I. Howard Marshall, *New Bible Dictionary*, 3rd ed. (Leicester, England; Downers Grove, Ill.: InterVarsity Press, 1996), 514.

[1084] Gleason Leonard Archer, *A Survey of Old Testament Introduction*, 3rd. ed.]. (Chicago: Moody Press, 1998), 368.

the Masoretic texts (MT).[1085] The Isaiah scrolls identified as "1Qisaᵃ" and "1QIsaᵇ" are complete copies of the book of Isaiah, but the latter is the earliest known copy of a complete Bible book, and dates to about 175 B.C.E. Both are from cave 1 of the Dead Sea area. Thus, the idea that some portion of the book of Isaiah was penned in the first-century B.C.E. is not long attainable. Gleason Archer stated that about the two Isaiah scrolls "proved to be word for word identical with the standard Hebrew Bible in more than 95% of the text. The 5% of variation consisted chiefly of obvious slips of the pen and variations in spelling." (Archer 1994, 19) It should be noted that the earlier criticisms of Isaiah did not go unchallenged as a result of the DSS, as numerous scholars throughout the nineteenth-century established that there was but one Isaiah, and he lived and wrote in the eighth-century B.C.E.

Entering the Twentieth-Century

The twentieth-century scholars have attempted to move the date of Isaiah out of the first-century B.C.E., closer toward Isaiah I, in an attempt to lower the number of Isaiah's. Dr. C. C. Torrey mentioned above, argued for just one writer for chapters 34 to 66, who lived in Jerusalem at the close of the fifth century. Torrey did not see these chapters as addressing the exiles, but addressing the people who lived right there in Palestine. To him the mere five mentions of Cyrus and Babylon, were interpolations,[1086] and could be ignored.

Different Themes and Subject Matter

The Bible scholar often uses the Latin term *a priori*, which means to work from something that is already known or self-evident to arrive at a conclusion. Another common term among the scholars can possibly further clarify this biased position. A preconception is an idea; an opinion formed in advance, based on little or no information that reflects bias. The Bible critic approaches the study of the book of Isaiah with his or her own preconception that there is no such thing as advanced knowledge events, history written in advance, prophecy. Therefore, the critic will accept, reject, ignore, or fail to mention evidence based on whether or not it fits the preconceived notion of their antisupernatural mindset. For the critic, it is feasible that a Jewish writer living about 540 B.C.E would be able to surmise the rise of Cyrus the Great, to overthrow Babylon (44:28; 45:1), as he could surmise this from his observation of current affairs. However, it is impossible for the critical mind to accept that a Jewish writer of the eighth century could make such observations because Babylon was not even an empire at that time, and Cyrus was yet to be born for some 150 years.

The idea that God's Word prophesied so specifically as to mention Cyrus by name 150 years in advance may seem foreign to the average Bible reader. However, it is not as uncommon as one might think. God's Word is known to mention people

---

[1085] **Hebrew Bible:** the traditional text of the Hebrew Bible, revised and annotated by Jewish scholars between the 6th and 10th centuries C.E.

[1086] An interpolation is to alter or deliberately falsify a text by adding words to it or removing words from it.

and places hundreds of years in advance. God's prophecy regarding Josiah called for some successor of David to be named as such, and it predicted his acting against false worship in the city of Bethel. (1 Ki 13:1, 2) Over three hundred years later, a king named Josiah fulfilled this prophecy. (2 Ki 22:1; 23:15, 16) Of course, the same critics would just argue that we have another interpolation. However, this argument can be used only so much, before we run into a case where it will not work. In the eighth century B.C.E., Isaiah's contemporary, the prophet Micah predicted that a great leader would be born in the unimportant town of Bethlehem. However, there were two towns in Israel at that time that was named Bethlehem, but this prediction identified which one: Bethlehem Ephrathah, the place of King David's birth. (Micah 5:2; Lu 2:1-7) This is not so easily dismissed, as the Jewish scribes of Herod the Great were aware of these facts. The book *Archaeology and Old Testament Study* states the following concerning the future of Babylon after Cyrus conquered it:

> "These extensive ruins, of which, despite Koldewey's work, only a small proportion has been excavated, have during past centuries been extensively plundered for building materials. Partly in consequence of this, much of the surface now presents an appearance of such chaotic disorder that it is strongly evocative of the prophecies of Isa. xiii. 19–22 and Jer. l. 39 f., the impression of desolation being further heightened by the aridity which marks a large part of the area of the ruins."—Thomas 1967, 41.

Presuppositions

The critic will argue that Isaiah 2:2-4 contains the conversion of the non-Jew, which hardly belongs to the eighth-century B.C.E., but occurs hundreds of years later. Therefore, this passage and all similar ones actually come from a later era in Israelite history. The critic will argue that Isaiah 11:1-9 contains the idea of world peace, and must be removed as belonging to Isaiah I. The critical will argue that a verse like Isaiah 14:26, which speak of judgment that is to befall the whole earth is to be removed, as it is not of the mindset of Isaiah's day. The critic will argue that the apocalyptic nature Isaiah chapters 24 to 27 are of a time in the fifth-century Jewish mindset.

Evidence of One Isaiah

The name of Jehovah God "the Holy One of Israel" is found 12 times in Isaiah chapters 1 to 39 and 13 times in Isaiah chapters 40 to 66, yet this name appears only 6 times in the rest of the Hebrew Old Testament. This interconnects the so-called two Isaiah's together as one. This expression being repeated throughout the whole of the book is of great value in establishing that we have one book, written by one prophet of the eighth-century.—Isa. 1:4; 5:19, 24; 10:20; 12:6; 17:7; 29:19; 30:11, 12, 15; 31:1; 37:23. Also, 41:14, 16, 20; 43:3, 14; 45:11; 47:4; 48:17; 49:7; 54:5; 55:5; 60:9, 14. Compare 2 Kings 19:22; Psa. 71:22; 78:41; 89:18; Jer. 50:29; 51:5.

Another similarity between chapters 1 to 39 and chapters 40 to 66 is a "way" or "highway." (11:16; 35:8; 40:3; 43:19; 49:11; 57:14; 62:10) Yet, another similarity runs through the whole of Isaiah is the idea of a "remnant" or "remaining ones."

(1:9; 6:13; 10:20, 21, 22; 11:11, 12, 16; 14:22, 30; 15:9; 16:14; 17:3, 6; 21:17; 28:5; 37:31; 46:3; 65:8, 9) There is also a recurring reference to "Zion," a term used 29 times in chapters 1 to 39 and 18 times in chapter 40 to 66. (2:3; 4:5; 18:7; 24:23; 27:13; 28:16; 29:8; 30:19; 31:9; 33:5, 20; 34:8; 46:13; 49:14; 51:3; 11; 52:1; 57:13; 59:20; 60:14; 62:1; 11; 65:11; 25; 66:8) Even more, there is another distinctive figure of speech such as the expression, "pangs of a woman in labor." 13:8; 21:3; 26:17, 18; 42:14; 54:1; 66:7.

Literary Style

Another expression found only in Jeremiah 9:12 and Micah 4:4 as well as crossing through both chapters 1 to 39 and 40 to 66: "the mouth of Jehovah hath spoken it." (1:20; 40:5; 58:14) Another title found only in Isaiah and appearing throughout the complete book is: "the Mighty One of Israel." (1:24; 49:26; 60:16) Another phrase common to Exodus 7:19; Psalm 1:3, 119:136, Pro 5:16, Lam 3:48, as well as Isaiah is "streams of water." (30:25; 44:4) The style of this author was to use what was known as emphatic duplication. (2:7, 8; 6:3; 8:9; 24:16, 19; 40:1; 43:11, 25; 48:15; 51:12; 57:19; 62:10) This evidence could be repeated with other terms, some less distinctive, yet nevertheless, it authenticates the book as being of one author.

There is another aspect to the Cyrus evidence that actually works against the two Isaiah criticisms. We are to believe that this Second-Isaiah or some redactor[1087] of about 540 B.C.E. is so skilled at smoothing out a document, attempting to make it as though it were one document, by having numerous terms and phrases show up throughout the alleged two Isaiah's, to then develop the Cyrus of Persia situation. Throughout chapters 41 to 48, there are numerous specific references to Cyrus, or allusions to him and his kingdom. In these references, Cyrus' character and person is developed, as well as there being a prophetic element to his actions that is presented as though being far into the future. If written in the midst of the current affairs, it would be pointless to build a character that is extremely well known, unless you presented him as being a product of prophecy.

Once we get past the idea that such devious thinking would be within the mind of some mysterious writer, who then had the tremendous skills to carry it out; we then must believe that this composer would have possessed knowledge that was beyond his circumstances. Little does the critic realize that he is giving just as much power to the mysterious composer as was given to Isaiah the prophet by Jehovah God. This redactor or Second-Isaiah would have had an extensive knowledge of Israel's governmental affairs from the eighth-century to the sixth century, the ability to deduce from current affairs that Cyrus would level Babylon, and release a remnant to return to Jerusalem (Zion), to rebuild. Further, he would have possessed a knowledge of Canaanite idolatry that is reflective of the first 39 chapters; a subject that had long been a dead issue to the Israelites of the sixth-century. Moreover, he would have had to see centuries later that the Messiah [Jesus], would have had to die for the transgressions of others.—Matt 4:15-16.

[1087] A redactor is a person who edits or revises a document in preparation for publication.

The critic would have his listeners believe that chapters 40 to 66 have no connection to the eighth-century B.C.E. This could not be further from the truth, as one considers Isaiah 44:23f.; 45:8; 50:1; 55:12f.; 56:1; 57:1; 59:3; 61:8; 63:3f.f As was stated earlier Micah is a contemporary of Isaiah, his writing being completed about 16-years after Isaiah, covering 777 – 716 B C.E. There is a great resemblance between what Isaiah wrote in chapters 40 to 66 and what Micah penned: Isaiah 41:15f, and Micah 4:13; Isaiah 47:2f. and Micah 1:11; Isaiah 48:2 and Micah 3:11; Isaiah 49:29 and Micah 7:17; Isaiah 52:12 and Micah 2:13; Isaiah 56:10 and Micah 3:5; Isaiah 58:1 and Micah 3:8. On this Old Testament scholar R. K. Harrison wrote:

> Obviously the same glorious expectation of the future under divine providence, the same broad conception of the nations of the Near East, and the confident expectation that a renewed Israel would return from exile, were characteristic of both prophets. (Harrison 2004, 779)

An Anthology of one Author

An anthology is a book that consists of essays, stories, or poems by different writers.[1088] If one considers that Isaiah did not write the entire book that bears his name in one setting, but different sections over a forty-six-year prophetic career; his book become a collection of his different writings throughout his life. For instance, Isaiah may have penned a section of his work at the age of twenty, and another at the age of thirty, and another at forty-three, and another at fifty-two and the final at sixty-five. This could explain the differences in style and literary expression as we are literally different people through our seventy to eighty-year life. As a result, this anthology of the book of Isaiah would have had each section being written under different circumstances and in different historical settings, making the critics argument not relevant.

The following analogy illustrates in modern terms how the book of Isaiah was written over time. Imagine a newspaper writer, at the age of twenty-three, writing an assignment in 1935 about The Great Depression. Then imagine the same writer, in his forties, embedded with the troops and writing articles about World War II from 1942-1945. Next, imagine the writer in his seventies being asked to come out of retirement to cover the Vietnam Conflict in 1969. Then, in 1991, this same writer in his nineties, who had seen the fall of the Soviet Union and the end of the Cold War, decides to pen one last article in his life. The writer dies in 1995 and several years after his death, a compilation of his articles is published in an anthological book about life in the twentieth-century.

Isaiah 1:1 Updated American Standard Version (UASV)

The vision of Isaiah the son of Amoz, which he saw concerning Judah and Jerusalem in the days of Uzziah, Jotham, Ahaz, and Hezekiah, kings of Judah.

[1088] Inc Merriam-Webster, *Merriam-Webster's Collegiate Dictionary.*, Eleventh ed. (Springfield, Mass.: Merriam-Webster, Inc., 2003).

Isaiah 2:1 Updated American Standard Version (UASV)

The word that Isaiah the son of Amoz saw concerning Judah and Jerusalem.

Isaiah 13:1 Updated American Standard Version (UASV)

The prophetic utterance concerning[1089] Babylon which Isaiah the son of Amoz saw.

The Bible Takes the Witness Stand for Isaiah

As the Bible is a collection of 66 smaller books, all of which are inspired of God, it deserves the opportunity to get on the stand for itself, to testify in its own behalf. It is obvious that first-century Christians believed that the book of Isaiah had just one author. Luke was the writer of the Gospel bearing his name, as well as the Book of Acts. In Acts, Luke tells of an Ethiopian official, who "had come to Jerusalem to worship and was returning, seated in his chariot, and he was reading the prophet Isaiah." (Chapter 53) This is the very portion of Isaiah that is attributed to the Deutero-Isaiah." Acts 8:26-28

Luke 1:1-4 Updated American Standard Version (UASV)

[1] Inasmuch as many have undertaken to compile an account of the things accomplished among us, [2] just as they were handed down to us by those who from the beginning were eyewitnesses and servants of the word, [3] it seemed good to me also, **having followed all things accurately** from the beginning, to **write an orderly account** for you, most excellent Theophilus, [4] so that you may know fully the certainty of the things that you have been taught orally.

Acts 1:1-2 Updated American Standard Version (UASV)

[1] The first account, O Theophilus, I composed about all that Jesus began to do and teach, [2] until the day when he was taken up, after he had given commands through the Holy Spirit to the apostles whom he had chosen.

"The general consensus of both liberal and conservative scholars is that Luke is very accurate as a historian. He's erudite, he's eloquent, his Greek approaches classical quality, he writes as an educated man, and archaeological discoveries are showing over and over again that Luke is accurate in what he has to say."—John McRay (Strobel 1998, 97)

Luke Wrote

Luke 4:17 Updated American Standard Version (UASV)

[17] And the scroll[1090] of the prophet Isaiah was given to him. And he unrolled the scroll and found the place where it was written,

---

[1089] Or *oracle*; a serious, lengthy address kind of prophetic message
[1090] Or *roll*

The words that Jesus would go on to read in verse 18-19 of Luke chapter 4 are found in Isaiah 61:1-2. Does Luke attribute this to the alleged Deutero-Isaiah? No, he specifically says "the prophet Isaiah."

Matthew wrote

Matthew 3:1-3 Updated American Standard Version (UASV)

¹ Now in those days John the Baptist came preaching in the wilderness of Judea, saying, ² "Repent, for the kingdom of heaven has come near."[1091] ³ For this is the one referred to by Isaiah the prophet when he said,

"The voice of one crying out in the wilderness,
'Make ready the way of the Lord,
   make his paths straight.'"[1092]

These prophetic words come from Isaiah 40:3. Does Matthew attribute these prophetic words to some unknown prophet, some Deutero-Isaiah? No, he clearly states that it was "Isaiah the Prophet."

Mark wrote

Mark 1:1-3 Updated American Standard Version (UASV)

¹ The beginning of the gospel of Jesus Christ, [the Son of God].[1093]

² As it is written in Isaiah the prophet;[1094]

"Behold, I send my messenger before your face,
who will prepare your way,

³ the voice of one crying in the wilderness:
'Make ready the way of the Lord,
   make his paths straight.'"

The latter portion of that quotation comes from Isaiah 40:3. Peter played a major role in helping Mark with his Gospel. Therefore, in one verse, we can get the

---

[1091] Matt. 4:17

[1092] Isa. 40:3

[1093] Son of God (υἱοῦ θεοῦ) is absent in ℵ* Θ 28ᶜ *al* by either a human error in copying or an addition by the copyist adding to the title – B D W *al* (e.g., Rev. 1:1). Because of the strong witnesses and the fact that "Son of God" is a theme throughout Mark, it could have been original; thus, it is retained in brackets.

[1094] Some manuscripts that carry no textual weight have *in the prophets*; however, the first part of Mark's quote is actually from Malachi 3:1, the second portion from Isaiah 40:3, which makes it easy to see why some copyist would have altered "Isaiah the prophet." Comfort suggests that Mark's attributing all of it to Isaiah may have been because his Roman audience would like be more familiar with Isaiah. Regardless, Mark does not acknowledge any Deutero-Isaiah.

assessment of two prominent Christians. Neither shows any knowledge of there being another Isaiah, the so-called Deutero-Isaiah.

John Wrote

John 12:36-43 Updated American Standard Version (UASV)

[36] While you have the light, trust[1095] in the light, so that you may become sons of light."

The Jews' Lack of Faith Fulfills Isaiah's Prophecy

Jesus said these things, and he went away and was hidden from them. [37] But though He had performed so many signs before them, yet they were not trusting[1096] in him. [38] So that the word of Isaiah prophet might be fulfilled, which he said:

"Lord, who has trusted in the thing heard from us,
and to whom has the arm of the Lord been revealed?"[1097]

[39] For this reason they could not believe, for Isaiah said again,

[40] "He has blinded their eyes
and he hardened their heart,
so that they would not see with their eyes,
and understand with their heart, and turn,
and I might heal them."[1098]

[41] These things Isaiah said because he saw his glory, and he spoke about him. [42] Nevertheless many even of the rulers believed in him, but because of the Pharisees they were not confessing him, so that they might not be put out of[1099] the synagogue; [43] for they loved the glory of men more than the glory of God.

The apostle John drew from both sides of the alleged two Isaiah's: John 12:38 in Isaiah 53:1 and John 12:40 in Isaiah 6:1. There is no indication that two separate writers were being considered.

[1095] The grammatical construction of *pisteuo* "believe" followed by *eis* "into" plus the accusative causing a different shade of meaning, having faith into Jesus.

[1096] The grammatical construction of *pisteuo* "believe" followed by *eis* "into" plus the accusative causing a different shade of meaning, having faith into Jesus.

[1097] Quotation from Isaiah 53:1

[1098] Quotation from Isaiah 6:10

[1099] Or *expelled from*

Paul wrote

Romans 10:16, 20; 15:12 Updated American Standard Version (UASV)

[16] But they have not all obeyed the gospel. For Isaiah says, "Lord,[1100] who has believed what he has heard from us?"

[20] And Isaiah is very bold and says,

"I was found by those who did not seek me;
I became manifest to those who did not ask for me."[1101]

[12] And again Isaiah says,

"There shall come the root of Jesse,
And he who arises to rule over the Gentiles,
In him shall the Gentiles hope."[1102]

In Paul's letter to the Romans, Paul refers to Isaiah 53:1 in Romans 10:16, Isaiah 65:1 in Romans 10:20, and Isaiah 11:10 in Romans 15:12. Thus, we can see that Paul makes references to both chapters 1-39 and chapters 40-66. The context is quite clear that he is referring to the same writer throughout. Obviously, the writers of the New Testament never had any idea of two, three, or more writers for the Book of Isaiah.

Let us look again to the Dead Sea Scrolls, particularly the Isaiah scroll mentioned earlier, which dates to about 175 B.C.E. This one scroll especially refutes the critical claim of a Deutero-Isaiah. How? Within this document, chapter 40 begins on the last line of a column, with the opening sentence being completed in the next column. Therefore, this suggests that the copyist was not aware of a change from a Proto-Isaiah to a Deutero-Isaiah, or some sort of division at this point.

First-Century Jewish Historian

Flavius Josephus, the first-century Jewish historian makes it quite clear that the prophecies pertaining to Isaiah belonged to Isaiah the prophet, but come from the eighth-century B.C.E. as well. "These things Cyrus knew," Josephus writes, "from reading the book of prophecy which Isaiah had left behind two hundred and ten years earlier." It is also Josephus' position that these very prophecies may have been what contributed to Cyrus releasing the Jews, to return to their homeland, for

---

[1100] Quotation from Isaiah 53:1, which reads, "Who has believed our message? And to whom has the arm of Jehovah been revealed?"

[1101] Quotation from Isa 65:1, which reads, "I have let myself be sought by those who did not ask for me;

I let myself be found by those who did not seek me."

I said, 'Here I am; here I am!' to a nation that was not calling on my name.

[1102] A quotation from Isa 11:10, which reads, "In that day the root of Jesse, who shall stand as a signal for the peoples, to him shall the nations inquire, and his resting place shall be glorious."

Josephus writes that Cyrus was "seized by a strong desire and ambition to do what had been written." *Jewish Antiquities*, Book XI, chapter 1, paragraph 2.

Isaiah the Prophet—Trustworthy

Having looked at a small portion of the evidence, what conclusions should we draw? One inspired writer, who lived in the eighth-century B.C.E., whose father was Amoz, penned the book of Isaiah. This book for 2,000 years was never questioned as belonging to more than one writer. Yes, we openly acknowledge that there is a style shift from chapter 40 forward. However, as was stated earlier, the prophet worked on sections of this writing for 46 years, living in different historical settings. In a lifetime, all of us are different people. Therefore, the way this writer may express something at 21 years of age, would certainly be penned differently at the age of 44. Moreover, Isaiah was commissioned to deliver a variety of messages, some coming as warnings, others as judgment, still others as: "Comfort, comfort my people, says your God." (Isaiah 40:1) There is no doubt that the Israelites were comforted by the promise that they would be released after 70-years of exile in Babylon, to return to their homeland. Below the reader will find four specifically selected books, which offer a far more extensive amount of evidence that the Book of Isaiah is but one Isaiah, from the eight-century B.C.E.

CHAPTER 12 Daniel Misjudged

Edward D. Andrews

You have a critical body that has formulated an opinion of the Bible, especially prophetic books, long before they have ever looked into the evidence. The liberal critical scholar is antisupernatural in their mindset. In other words, any book that would claim to have predicted events hundreds of years in advance are simply misrepresenting itself, as that foreknowledge is impossible. Therefore, the book must have been written after the events, yet written in such a way, as to mislead the reader that it was written hundreds of years before.

This is exactly what these critics say we have in the book of Daniel. However, what do we know about the person and the book itself? Daniel is known historically as a man of uprightness in the extreme. The book that he penned has been regarded highly for thousands of years. The context within says that it is authentic and true history, penned by Daniel, a Jewish prophet, who lived in the seventh and sixth centuries B.C.E. The chronology within the book shows that it covers the time period of 616 to 536 B.C.E., being completed by the latter date.

The New Encyclopædia Britannica acknowledges that the book of Daniel was once "generally considered to be true history, containing genuine prophecy." However, the *Britannica* asserts that in truth, Daniel "was written in a later time of national crisis—when the Jews were suffering severe persecution under [Syrian King] Antiochus IV Epiphanes." This encyclopedia dates the book between 167 and 164 B.C.E. *Britannica* goes on to assert that the writer of the book of Daniel does not prophesy the future but merely presents "events that are past history to him as prophecies of future happenings."

How does a book and a prophet that has enjoyed centuries of a reputable standing, garner such criticism? It actually began just two-hundred years after Christ, with Porphyry, a philosopher, who felt threatened by the rise of Christianity. His way of dealing with this new religion, was to pen fifteen books to undercut it, the twelfth being against Daniel. In the end, Porphyry labeled the book as a forgery, saying that it was written by a second-century B.C.E. Jew. Comparable attacks came in the 18th and 19th centuries. German scholars, who were prejudiced against the supernatural, started modern objections to the Book of Daniel.

As has been stated numerous times in this section, the higher critics and rationalists start with the presupposition that foreknowledge of future events is impossible. As was stated earlier in the chapter on Isaiah, the **important truth for the Bible critic is** the understanding that in all occurrences, prophecy pronounced or written in Bible times meant something to the people of the time it was spoken or written to; it was meant to serve as a guide for them. Frequently, it had specific fulfillment for that time, being fulfilled throughout the lifetime of that very generation. This is actually true; the words always had some application to the very people who heard them. However, the application could be a process of events, starting with the moral condition of the people in their relationship with Jehovah

God, which precipitated the prophetic events that were to unfold, even those prophetic events that were centuries away.

However, it must be noted that while Daniel and Isaiah are both prophetic books, Daniel is also known as an apocalyptic book, as is the book of Revelation. This is not to say that Isaiah does not contain some apocalyptic sections (e.g., Isa 24–27; 56–66) What is assumed by the critical scholar here is that there is a rule that a prophet is understood in his day, to be only speaking of the immediate concerns of the people. They are looking at it more like a proclamation, instead of a future event that could be centuries away. Before addressing this concern, let us define apocalyptic for the reader:

Apocalyptic

This is a term derived from a Greek word meaning "revelation," and used to refer to a pattern of thought and to a form of literature, both dealing with future judgment (eschatology).

Two primary patterns of eschatological thought are found in the Bible, both centered in the conviction that God will act in the near future to save his people and to punish those who oppress them. In prophetic eschatology, the dominant form in the OT, God is expected to act within history to restore man and nature to the perfect condition which existed prior to man's fall. Apocalyptic eschatology, on the other hand, expects God to destroy the old imperfect order before restoring the world to paradise.

Origins of Apocalypticism

In Israel, apocalyptic eschatology evidently flourished under foreign domination.

From the early 6th century B.C., prophetic eschatology began to decline and apocalyptic eschatology became increasingly popular. The Book of Daniel, written during the 6th century B.C., is the earliest example of apocalyptic literature in existence.[1103]

The problem with the modern critic is that he is attempting to look at the Biblical literature through the modern-day mindset. His first error is to believe that a prophetic book was viewed only as a proclamation of current affairs. The Jewish people viewed all prophetic literature just as we would expect, as a book of prophecy. The problem today is that many are not aware of the way they viewed the prophetic literature. While we do not have the space to go into the genre of prophecy and apocalyptic literature extensively, it is recommended that you see Dr. Stein's book in the bibliography at the end of the chapter.

[1103] Walter A. Elwell and Barry J. Beitzel, *Baker Encyclopedia of the Bible* (Grand Rapids, Mich.: Baker Book House, 1988), 122.

Some Rules for Prophecy

- One needs to identify the beginning and end of the prophecy.

- The reader needs to find the historical setting.

- The Bible is a diverse book when it comes to literary styles: narrative, poetic, prophetic, and apocalyptic; also containing parables, metaphors, similes, hyperbole, and other figures of speech. Too often, these alleged errors are the result of a reader taking a figure of speech as literal, or reading a parable as though it is a narrative.

- Many alleged inconsistencies disappear by simply looking at the context. Taking words out of context can distort their meaning.

- Determine if the prophet is foretelling the future. On the other hand, is he simply proclaiming God's will and purpose to the people. (If prophetic, has any portion of it been fulfilled?)

- The concept of a second fulfillment should be set aside in place of implications.

- Does the New Testament expound on this prophecy?

- The reader needs to slow down and carefully read the account, considering exactly what is being said.

- The Bible student needs to understand the level that the Bible intends to be exact in what is written. If Jim told a friend that 650 graduated with him from high school in 1984, it is not challenged, because it is all too clear that he is using rounded numbers and is not meaning to be exactly precise.

- Unexplained does not equal unexplainable.

Digging into the ancient Jewish mindset, we find that it is dualistic. It views all of God's creation, either on the side of God or Satan. Further, the Jewish mind was determined that regardless of how bad things were, God would come to the rescue of his people. The only pessimistic thinking was their understanding that there had to be a major catastrophe that precipitated the rescue. In combining this way of thinking, they believed that there are two systems of things: (1) the current wicked one that man lives in, and (2) the one that is to come, where God will restore things to the way it was before Adam and Eve sinned. Jehovah impressed upon his people, to see His rescue as imminent. The vision that comes to Daniel in the book of Daniel and John in the book of Revelations, comes in one of two ways: (1) in a dreamed vision state or (2) the person in vision is caught up to heaven and shown what is to take place. Frequently, Isaiah, Daniel and John did not understand the vision; they were simply to pen what they saw. (Isa 6:9-10; 8:16; 29:9-14; 44:18; 53:1; Dan 8:15–26; 9:20–27; 10:18–12:4; Rev 7:13–17; 17:7–18) The people readily recognized the symbolism in most of the prophetic literature, and the less common symbolisms in apocalyptic literature were far more complex, which by design, heighten the desire to interpret and understand them. There are two very important points to keep in mind: (1) some were not meant to be understood fully at the time, and (2) only the righteous ones would have insight into these books, while the wicked would refuse to understand the spiritual things.

Daniel 8:26-27 Updated American Standard Version (UASV)

26 The vision of the evenings and the mornings that has been told is true,[1104] but seal up the vision,[1105] for it refers to many days from now."[1106]

27 And I, Daniel, was exhausted and sick for days. Then I got up and carried out the business of the king, and I was disturbed over the vision and no one could understand it.[1107]

Daniel 10:14 Updated American Standard Version (UASV)

14 Now I have come to give you an understanding of what will happen to your people in the end of the days, for it is a vision yet for the days to come."

Daniel 12:3-4 Updated American Standard Version (UASV)

3 And the ones who are wise will shine brightly like the brightness of the expanse of heaven; and those who turn many to righteousness, like the stars forever and ever. 4 But as for you, O Daniel, conceal these words and seal up the book until the time of the end; many will go to and fro,[1108] and knowledge will increase."

Daniel 12:9-10 Updated American Standard Version (UASV)

9He said, "Go your way, Daniel, for the words are shut up and sealed until the time of the end. 10Many shall purify themselves and make themselves white and be refined, but the wicked shall act wickedly. And none of the wicked shall understand, but those who are wise shall understand.

2 Corinthians 4:3-4 Updated American Standard Version (UASV)

3 And even if our gospel is veiled, it is veiled to those who are perishing. 4 In their case the god of this world has blinded the minds of the unbelievers, to keep them from seeing the light of the gospel of the glory of Christ, who is the image of God.

One of the principles of interpreting prophecy is to understand judgment prophecies. If a prophet declares judgment on a people, and they turn around from their bad course, the judgment may be lifted, which does not negate the trueness of the prophetic judgment message. There was simply a change in circumstances. There is a principle that most readers are not aware of:

Jeremiah 18:7-8 Updated American Standard Version (UASV)

7 At one moment I might speak concerning a nation or concerning a kingdom to uproot, to tear down, and to destroy it; 8 and if that nation which I have spoken

---

1104 Lit *truth*; Heb., *'emet*

1105 I.e., keep the vision secret; Heb., *satar*

1106 Lit *for to days many*; I.e., to the distant future

1107 Lit *make* me *understand*

1108 I.e. examine the book thoroughly

against turns from its evil, I will also feel regret over[1109] the calamity that I intended to bring against it.

Another principle that needs to be understood is the language of prophecy. It uses imagery that is common to the people, with the exception of the highly apocalyptic literature. One form of imagery is the cosmic.

Isaiah 13:9-11 Updated American Standard Version (UASV)

⁹ Behold, the day of Jehovah is coming,
  cruel, with wrath and burning anger,
to make the land a desolation;
  and he will destroy its sinners from it.
¹⁰ For the stars of the heavens and their constellations
  will not flash forth their light;
the sun will be dark when it rises,
  and the moon will not shed its light.
¹¹ And I will punish the world for its evil,
  and the wicked for their iniquity;
I will put an end to the arrogance of the proud,
  and lay low the haughtiness of tyrants.

It is often assumed that this sort of imagery is talking about the end of the world, and this is not always the case. Using Isaiah 13 as our example, it is talking about a pronouncement against Babylon, not the end of the world, as can be seen in verse 1. This type of terminology is a way of expressing that God is acting in behalf of man. At times, figurative language can come across as contradicting for the modern-day reader. For example, in chapter 21 of Revelation the walls of Jerusalem are described as being 200 feet thick. The walls are an image of safety and security for the New Jerusalem. However, in verse 25 we read that the gates are never shut. This immediate leads to the question of why have walls that cannot be penetrated, and then leave the gates open? Moreover, if gates are the weakest point to defend, why have twelve of them (vs. 12)? To the modern militaristic mind, this comes off as contradictory, but not to the Jewish-Christian mind of the first-century. Both present the picture of safety. It is so safe that you can leave the gates open. What about the idea of a "fuller meaning" that the prophet was not aware of? As we saw in the above there would be symbolism meant for a day far into the future, but generally speaking, most prophets proclaimed a message that was applicable to their day, and implications for another day. Dr. Robert Stein addresses this issue:

> There are times when a prophetic text appears to have a fulfillment other than what the prophet himself apparently expected. (The following are frequently given as examples: Matt. 1:22–23; 2:15, 17–18; John 12:15; 1 Cor. 10:3–4.) Is it possible that a prophecy may have a deeper meaning or "fuller" sense than the prophet envisioned? . . . Rather than appealing to a "fuller sense" distinct and different from that of the biblical author, however, it may be wiser to see if the supposed

---

[1109] Lit *repent of*, .e., *I will change my mind concerning*, or *I will think better of*, or *I will relent concerning*

sensus plenior is in reality an implication of the author's conscious meaning. Thus, when Paul in 1 Corinthians 9:9 quotes Deuteronomy 25:4 ("do not muzzle an ox while it is treading out the grain") as a justification for ministers of the gospel living off the gospel, this is not a "fuller" meaning of the text unrelated to what the author sought to convey. Rather, it is a legitimate implication of the willed pattern of meaning contained in Deuteronomy 25:4. If as a principle animals should be allowed to share in the benefits of their work, how much more should the "animal" who is made in the image of God and proclaims the Word of God be allowed to share in the benefits of that work! Thus, what Paul is saying is not a fuller and different meaning from what the writer of Deuteronomy meant. On the contrary, although this specific implication was unknown to him, it is part of his conscious and willed pattern of meaning. Perhaps such prophecies as Matthew 1:22–23 and 2:15 are best understood as revealing implications of the original prophecies in Isaiah 7:14 and Hosea 11:1. Whereas in Isaiah's day the prophet meant that a maiden would give birth to a son who was named "Immanuel," that willed meaning also allows for a virgin one day to give birth to a son who would be Immanuel. Whereas God showed his covenantal faithfulness by leading his "son," his children, back from Egypt to the promised land in Moses' day so also did he lead his "Son," Jesus, back from Egypt to the promised land. [1110]

Getting back to Daniel, we can clearly see that his book is prophetic and the only Old Testament apocalyptic book at that, which makes him a special target for the Bible critic. The critic has deemed that Daniel did not pen the book that bears his name, but another writer penned the words some centuries later.[1111] These attacks have become such a reality that most scholars accept the late date of 165 B.C.E., by a pseudonym. As we have learned throughout this book, it is never the majority that establishes something as being true, simply for the fact of being the majority; it is the evidence. If the evidence proves that Daniel did not write the book, then the words are meaningless, and the hope that it contains is not there.

For example, take the allegation made in *The Encyclopedia Americana:* "Many historical details of the earlier periods [such as that of the Babylonian exile] have been badly garbled" in Daniel. Really? We will take up three of those alleged mistakes.

[1110] Robert H. Stein, *A Basic Guide to Interpreting the Bible: Playing by the Rules* (Grand Rapids, MI: Baker Books, 1994), 97.

[1111] Some Bible critics attempt to lessen the charge of forgery by saying that the writer used Daniel as a false name (pseudonym), just as some ancient noncanonical books were written under assumed names. In spite of this, the Bible critic Ferdinand Hitzig held: "The case of the book of Daniel, if it is assigned to any other [writer], is different. Then it becomes a forged writing, and the intention was to deceive his immediate readers, though for their good."

Claims That Belshazzar Is Missing From History

Daniel 5:1, 11, 18, 22, 30 Updated American Standard Version (UASV)

¹ Belshazzar the king made[1112] a great feast for a thousand of his nobles, and he was drinking wine in the presence of the thousand.

¹¹ There is a man in your kingdom in whom is a spirit of the holy gods;[1113] and in the days of your father, enlightenment, insight and wisdom like the wisdom of the gods were found in him. And King Nebuchadnezzar, your father, your father the king, appointed him chief of the magic-practicing priests, conjurers, Chaldeans and diviners.

¹⁸ You, O king, the Most High God granted the kingdom and the greatness and the glory and the majesty to Nebuchadnezzar your father.

²² "But you, his son[1114] Belshazzar, have not humbled your heart, although you knew all of this,

³⁰ That same night Belshazzar the Chaldean king was killed.

In 1850 German scholar Ferdinand Hitzig said in a commentary on the book of Daniel, confidently declaring that Belshazzar was "a figment of the writer's imagination."[1115] His reasoning was that Daniel was missing from history, only found in the book of Daniel itself. Does this not seem a bit premature? Is it so irrational to think that a person might not be readily located by archaeology, a brand new field at the time, especially from a period that was yet to be fully explored? Regardless, in 1854, there was a discovery of some small cylinders in the ancient city of Babylon and Ur, southern Iraq. The cuneiform documents were from King Nabonidus, and they included a prayer for "Belshazzar my firstborn son, the offspring of my heart." This discovery was a mere four years after Hitzig made his rash judgment.

Of course, not all critics would be satisfied. H. F. Talbot made the statement, "This proves nothing." The charge by Talbot was that Belshazzar was likely a mere child, but Daniel has him as being king. Well, this critical remark did not even stay alive as long as Hitzig's had. Within the year, more cuneiform tablets were discovered, this time they stated he had secretaries, as well as a household staff. Obviously, Belshazzar was not a child! However, more was to come, as other tablets explained that Belshazzar was a coregent king while Nabonidus was away from Babylon for years at a time.[1116]

[1112] I.e., held

[1113] Spirit of ... gods Aram., *ruach-'elahin';* Or possibly *the Spirit of the holy God*

[1114] Or *descendant*

[1115] *Das Buch Daniel.* Ferdinand Hitzig. Weidman (Leipzig) 1850.

[1116] When Babylon fell, Nabonidus was away. Therefore, Daniel was correct in that Belshazzar was the king at that time. Critics still try to cling to their Bible difficulty by stating that no secular records state that Belshazzar was a king. When will they quit with this quibbling? Even governors in the Ancient Near East were stated as being kings at times.

One would think that the critic might concede. Still disgruntled, some argued that the Bible calls Belshazzar, the son of Nebuchadnezzar, and not the son of Nabonidus. Others comment that Daniel nowhere mentions the name of Nabonidus. Once again, both arguments are dismantled with a deeper observation. Nabonidus married the daughter of Nebuchadnezzar, making Belshazzar the grandson of Nebuchadnezzar. Both Hebrew and Aramaic language do not have words for "grandfather" or "grandson"; "son of" also means "grandson of" or even "descendant of." (See Matthew 1:1.) Moreover, the account in Daniel does infer that Belshazzar is the son of Nabonidus. When the mysterious handwriting was on the wall, the horrified Belshazzar offered the *third* place in his kingdom, to whoever could interpret it. (Daniel 5:7) The observant reader will notice that Nabonidus held first place in the kingdom, while Daniel held the second place, leaving the third place for the interpreter.

Darius the Mede

One would think that the critic would have learned his lesson from Belshazzar. However, this is just not the case. Daniel 5:31 reads: "and Darius the Mede received the kingdom, being about sixty-two years old." Here again, the critical scholar argues that Darius does not exist, as he has never been found in secular or archaeological records. Therefore, *The New Encyclopædia Britannica* declares that this Darius is "a fictitious character."

There is no doubt that in time; Darius will be unearthed by archaeology, just as Belshazzar has. There is initial information that allows for inferences already. Cuneiform tablets have been discovered that shows Cyrus the Persian did not take over as the "King of Babylon" directly after the conquest. Rather he carried the title "King of the Lands."[1117] W. H Shea suggests, "Whoever bore the title of 'King of Babylon' was a vassal king under Cyrus, not Cyrus himself." Is it possible that Darius is simply a title of a person that was placed in charge of Babylon? Some scholars suggest a man named Gubaru was the real Darius. Secular records do show that Cyrus appointed Gubaru as governor over Babylon, giving him considerable power. Looking to the cuneiform tablets again, we find that Cyrus appointed subgovernors over Babylon. Fascinatingly, Daniel notes that Darius selected 120 satraps to oversee the kingdom of Babylon.—Daniel 6:1.

We should realize that archaeology is continuously bringing unknown people to light all the time, and in time, it may shed more light on Darius. However, for now, and based on the fact that many Bible characters have been established, it is a little ridiculous to consider Darius as "fictitious," worse still to view the whole of the book of Daniel as a fraud. In fact, it is best to see Daniel as a person, who was right there in the midst of that history, giving him access to more court records.

After Belshazzar (King of Babylon), Sargon (Assyrian Monarch), and the like have been assailed with being nonexistent, the Bible critic and liberal scholars do the same with Darius the Mede, and Mordecai in the book of Esther. This illustrates

---

[1117] This evidence is found in royal titles in economic texts, which just so happens to date to the first two years of Cyrus' rule.

the folly of assigning boundless confidence in the ancient secular records, while we wait in secular sources to validate Scripture. Most outside of true conservative Christianity carry the presupposition that the Bible is myth, legend and erroneous until secular sources support it.

Bible critics argued profusely that Belshazzar was not a historical person. Then, evidence came in that substantiated Belshazzar, and the Bible critic just move on to another like Sargon, saying that he was not a real historical person, as though they had never raised such an objection for Belshazzar. Then, evidence came in that substantiated Sargon and the Bible critic would silently move on yet again. This is repeated time after time.

The Bible critics, liberal and moderate Bible scholars believe the Bible is wrong until validated by secular history. They move the goal post of trustworthiness as they please, so that Scripture will never be authentic and true, it will never be trustworthy, and to theses one, it is not the inspired, fully inerrant Word of God, as far as they are concerned.

Why do we continue to cater to these ones, as though we need to appease them somehow?

King Jehoiakim

Daniel 1:1 Updated American Standard Version (UASV)

¹ In the third year of the reign of Jehoiakim king of Judah, Nebuchadnezzar king of Babylon came to Jerusalem and besieged it.

Jeremiah 25:1 Updated American Standard Version (UASV)

¹ The word that came to Jeremiah concerning all the people of Judah, in the fourth year of Jehoiakim the son of Josiah, king of Judah (that was the first year of Nebuchadnezzar king of Babylon),

Jeremiah 46:2 Updated American Standard Version (UASV)

² About Egypt, concerning the army of Pharaoh Neco king of Egypt, which was by the Euphrates River at Carchemish, which Nebuchadnezzar king of Babylon defeated in the fourth year of Jehoiakim the son of Josiah, king of Judah:

The Bible critic finds fault with Daniel 1:1 as it is not in harmony with Jeremiah, who says "in the fourth year of Jehoiakim the son of Josiah, king of Judah (that was the first year of Nebuchadnezzar king of Babylon)." The Bible student who looks a little deeper will find that there is really no contradiction at all. Pharaoh Necho first made Jehoiakim king in 628 B.C.E. Three years would pass before Nebuchadnezzar succeeded his father as King in Babylon, in 624 B.C.E. In 620 B.C.E., Nebuchadnezzar conquered Judah and made Jehoiakim the subordinate king under Babylon. (2 Kings 23:34; 24:1) Therefore, it is all about the perspective of the writer and where he was when penning his book. Daniel wrote from Babylon; therefore, Jehoiakim's third year would have been when he was made a subordinate king to Babylon. Jeremiah on the other hand, wrote from Jerusalem, so he is referring to the time when Jehoiakim was made a subordinate king under Pharaoh Necho.

This so-called discrepancy really just adds more weight to the fact that it was Daniel, who penned the book bearing his name. In addition, it must be remembered that Daniel had Jeremiah's book with him. (Daniel 9:2) Therefore, are we to believe that Daniel was this clever forger, and at the same time, he would contradict the well-known book of Jeremiah, especially in verse 1?

Positive Details

There are many details in the book of Daniel itself, which give credence to its authenticity. For example, Daniel 3:1-6 tells us that Nebuchadnezzar set up a huge image of gold, which his people were to worship. Archaeology has found evidence that credits Nebuchadnezzar with attempts to involve the people more in nationalistic and religious practices. Likewise, Daniel addresses Nebuchadnezzar's arrogant attitude about his many construction plans. (Daniel 4:30) It is not until modern-day archaeology uncovered evidence that we now know Nebuchadnezzar was the person who built much of Babylon. Moreover, his boastful attitude is made quite evident by having his name stamped on the bricks. This fact would not have been something a forger from 167-63 B.C.E. would have known about because the bricks hadn't at that time been unearthed.

The writer of Daniel was very familiar with the differences between Babylonian and Medo-Persian law. The three friends of Daniel were thrown into the fiery furnace for disobeying the Babylonian law, while Daniel, decades later under Persian law, was thrown into a lion's pit for violating the law. (Daniel 3:6; 6:7-9) Archaeology has again proven to be a great help, for they have uncovered an actual letter that shows the fiery furnace was a form of punishment. However, the Medes and Persians would have not used this form of punishment; as fire was sacred to them. Thus, they had other forms of capital punishment.

Another piece of inside knowledge is that Nebuchadnezzar passed and changed laws as he pleased. Darius on the other hand was unable to change a law once it was passed, even one that he himself had commissioned. (Daniel 2:5, 6, 24, 46-49; 3:10, 11, 29; 6:12-16) Historian John C. Whitcomb writes: "Ancient history substantiates this difference between Babylon, where the law was subject to the king, and Medo-Persia, where the king was subject to the law."

Daniel 5:1-4 Updated American Standard Version (UASV)

[1] Belshazzar the king made[1118] a great feast for a thousand of his nobles, and he was drinking wine in the presence of the thousand.

[2] Belshazzar, when he tasted the wine, commanded that the vessels of gold and of silver that Nebuchadnezzar his father[1119] had taken out of the temple in Jerusalem be brought, that the king and his nobles, his wives, and his concubines might drink from them. [3] Then they brought the gold vessels that had been taken out of the temple, the house of God which was in Jerusalem; and the king and his

---

[1118] I.e., held

[1119] Or *predecessor*; also verses 11, 13, 18

nobles, his wives and his concubines drank from them. ⁴ They drank the wine and praised the gods of gold and silver, of bronze, iron, wood and stone.

Archaeology has substantiated these kinds of feasts. The fact that stands out is the mention of women being present at the feast, the "wives, and his concubines" were present as well. Such an idea would have been repugnant to the Greeks and Jews of 167-67 B.C.E. era. This may very well be why the Greek Septuagint version of Daniel removed the mention of these women.[1120] This so-called forger of Daniel would have live during this same time of the Septuagint.

Do External Factors Prove Daniel Is A Forgery?

Even the place of Daniel in the canon of the Hebrew Old Testament is evidence against his having written the book, so says the critics. The Jewish scribes (like Ezra) of ancient Israel arranged the books of the Old Testament into three groups: the Torah, the Prophets, and the Writings. Naturally, we would expect that Daniel would be found among the Prophets, yet they placed him among the Writings. Therefore, the critic makes the argument that Daniel had to of been an unknown when the works of the prophets were being collected. Their theory is that it was placed among the writings, because these were collected last.

However, not all Bible scholarship agree that the ancient scribes placed Daniel in the Writings, and not the Prophets. However, even if it is as they claim, Daniel was added among the Writings; this does nothing to prove that it was penned at a later date. Old Testament Bible scholar Gleason L. Archer states that . . .

> It should be noted that some of the documents in the Kethubhim [Writings] (the third division of the Hebrew Bible) were of great antiquity, such as the book of Job, the Davidic psalms, and the writings of Solomon. Position in the Kethubhim, therefore, is no proof of a late date of composition. Furthermore the statement in Josephus (Contra Apionem. 1:8) quoted previously in chapter 5 indicates strongly that in the first century A.D., Daniel was included among the prophets in the second division of the Old Testament canon; hence it could not have been assigned to the Kethubim until a later period. 349 The Masoretes may have been influenced in this reassignment by the consideration that Daniel was not appointed or ordained as a prophet, but remained a civil servant under the prevailing government throughout his entire career. Second, a large percentage of his writings does not bear the character of prophecy, but rather of history (chaps. 1-6), such as does not appear in any of the books of the canonical prophets.350 Little of that which Daniel wrote is couched in the form of a message from God to His people relayed through the mouth of His spokesman. Rather, the

---

[1120] Hebrew scholar C. F. Keil writes of Daniel 5:3: "The LXX. have here, and also at ver. 23, omitted mention of the women, according to the custom of the Macedonians, Greeks, and Romans."

predominating element consists of prophetic visions granted personally to the author and interpreted to him by angels.[1121]

The critic also turns his attention to the Apocryphal book, Ecclesiasticus, by Jesus Ben Sirach, penned about 180 B.C.E., as evidence that Daniel did not pen the book that bears his name. Ecclesiasticus has a long list of righteous men, of which, Daniel is missing. From this, they conclude that Daniel had to of been an unknown at the time. However, if we follow that line of reasoning; what do we do with the fact that the same list omits: Ezra and Mordecai, good King Jehoshaphat, and the upright man Job; of all the judges, except Samuel.[1122] Simply because the above faithful and righteous men are missing from a list in an apocryphal book, are we to dismiss them as having never existed? The very idea is absurd.

Sources in Favor of Daniel

Ezekiel's references to Daniel must be considered to be one of the strongest arguments for a sixth-century date. No satisfactory explanation exists for the use of the name Daniel by the prophet Ezekiel other than that he and Daniel were contemporaries and that Daniel had already become widely known throughout the Babylonian Empire by the time of Ezekiel's ministry.[1123]

We have in chapter 9 a series of remarkable predictions which defy any other interpretation but that they point to the coming of Christ and His crucifixion [about] A.D. 30, followed by the destruction of the city of Jerusalem within the ensuing decades. In Dan. 9:25–26, it is stated that sixty-nine heptads of years (i.e., 483 years) will ensue between a "decree" to rebuild the walls of Jerusalem, and the cutting off of Messiah the Prince. In 9:25–26, we read: "Know therefore and understand, that from the going forth of the commandment to restore and to build Jerusalem unto the Messiah the Prince shall be seven weeks, and threescore and two weeks.... And after threescore and two weeks shall Messiah be cut off, but not for himself: and the people of the prince that shall come shall destroy the city and the sanctuary."[1124]

[1121] Archer, Gleason (1996-08-01). A Survey of Old Testament Introduction (Kindle Locations 7963-7972). Moody Publishers.

[1122] If we turn our attention to the Apostle Paul's list of faithful men and women found in Hebrews chapter 11; it does appear to mention occasions recorded in Daniel. (Daniel 6:16-24; Hebrews 11:32, 33) Nevertheless, the list by Paul is not an exhaustive list either. Even within his list, Isaiah, Jeremiah, and Ezekiel are not named in the list, but this scarcely demonstrates that they never existed.

[1123] Stephen R. Miller, vol. 18, Daniel, electronic ed., Logos Library System; The New American Commentary (Nashville: Broadman & Holman Publishers, 2001), 42-43.

[1124] Gleason Leonard Archer, A Survey of Old Testament Introduction, 3rd. ed.]. (Chicago: Moody Press, 1998), 445.

The Greatest Evidence for Daniel

First of all, we have the clear testimony of the Lord Jesus Himself in the Olivet discourse. In Matt. 24:15, He refers to "the abomination of desolation, spoken of through [*dia*] Daniel the prophet." The phrase "abomination of desolation" occurs three times in Daniel (9:27; 11:31; 12:11). If these words of Christ are reliably reported, we can only conclude that He believed the historic Daniel to be the personal author of the prophecies containing this phrase. No other interpretation is possible in the light of the preposition *dia*, which refers to personal agency. It is significant that Jesus regarded this "abomination" as something to be brought to pass in a future age rather than being simply the idol of Zeus set up by Antiochus in the temple, as the Maccabean theorists insist.[1125]

While this has certainly been an overview of the evidence in favor of the authenticity of Daniel, there will never be enough to satisfy the critic. One professor at Oxford University wrote: "Nothing is gained by a mere answer to objections, so long as the original prejudice, 'there cannot be supernatural prophecy,' remains." What does this mean? It means that the critic is blinded by his prejudice. However, God has given them the choice of free will.

The Bible critics are ever so vigilant today. They are more prepared than most Christians, and witness about their doubts far more than your average Christian witnesses about his or her faith.

1 Peter 3:15 Updated American Standard Version (UASV)

[15] but sanctify Christ as Lord in your hearts, always being prepared to make a defense[1126] to anyone who asks you for a reason for the hope that is in you; yet do it with gentleness and respect;

Peter says that we must be prepared to make a *defense*. The Greek word behind the English "defense" is *apologia* (apologia), which is actually a legal term that refers to the defense of a defendant in court. Our English apologetics is just what Peter spoke of, having the ability to give a reason to any who may challenge us, or to answer those who are not challenging us but who have honest questions that deserve to be answered.

To whom was the apostle Peter talking? Who was Peter saying needed always to be prepared to make a defense? Was he talking only to the pastors, elders, servants, or was he speaking to all Christians? Peter opens this letter saying, "to the chosen who are residing temporarily in the dispersion in Pontus, Galatia, Cappadocia, Asia, and Bithynia." Who are these "chosen" ones? The College Press NIV Commentary gives us the answer,

---

[1125] Gleason Leonard Archer, *A Survey of Old Testament Introduction*, 3rd. ed.]. (Chicago: Moody Press, 1998), 444.

[1126] Or *argument*; or *explanation*

The Greek text does not include the word "God's," but the translation is a fair one since the clear implication is that God did the choosing. The word Peter uses has a rich biblical heritage. The Jews found their identity and the basis of their lives in the fact that they were God's chosen people (see, e.g., Deut 7:6–8). The New Testament frequently identifies Christians as elect or chosen. In 1 Peter 2:9 Peter will identify Christians as "a chosen people," using the same word ἐκλεκτός (eklektos) here translated "elect." The same word is also used of Christ in 2:4 and 6 (where it is translated "chosen"). Christians are chosen or elect through the chosen or elect One, Jesus Christ. The idea that Christians are God's chosen people is fundamental to Peter's thinking, as is apparent in 1:13–2:10. Peter is already laying the foundation for his appeals to these Christians to live up to their holy calling. (Black and Black 1998)

The "chosen who are residing temporarily in the dispersion" were Christians, who were living among non-Christian Jews and Gentiles. This letter, then, is addressed to all Christians, but the context of chapters 1:3 to 4:11 is mostly addressed to newly baptized Christians. Therefore, all Christians are obligated to 'be prepared to make a defense to anyone who asks us for a reason for the hope that is in us.' Yes, we are all required to defend our hope successfully. If any have not felt they were up to the task, this author by way of Christian publishing House are publishing books to help along those lines. Here is what is available at present, including this publication you are reading,

CONVERSATIONAL EVANGELISM Defending the Faith, Reasoning from the Scriptures, Explaining and Proving, Instructing in Sound Doctrine, and Overturning False Reasoning (Sept. 16, 2015) by Edward D. Andrews

THE CHRISTIAN APOLOGIST: Always Being Prepared to Make a Defense (September 27, 2014) By Edward D. Andrews

THE EVANGELISM HANDBOOK: How All Christians Can Effectively Share God's Word in Their Community (Aug 28, 2013) by Edward D Andrews

OVERCOMING BIBLE DIFFICULTIES Answers to the So-Called Errors and Contradictions (Aug. 04, 2015) by Edward D. Andrews

These first-century Christians in Asia Minor were in a time of difficulty. They were at the time of Peter's letter; about 62-64 C.E. going through some trials, not knowing that many far more severe lie in the not too distant future. Within a few years, the persecution of Christians by Emperor Nero would begin. These new converts had given up former religions, idols, cults and superstitions, their 'the futile ways inherited from your forefathers.' (1 Pet. 1:18) These one's were taking of their old person, and bringing their lives in harmony with God's Word, such as 'malice and deceit and hypocrisy and envy and slander.' (1 Pet. 2:1) Now they were 'no longer living for the lusts of men, but for the will of God.' (1 Pet. 4:2) Their former pagan friends now hated these new Christians, because 'they were surprised when these chosen ones do not join them in the same flood of debauchery, and they maligned them.' (1 Pet. 4:4) In fact, Peter informs us that Satan, the Devil is enraged when one is converted from their former life of debauchery, conformed instead to the Word of God. Peter warned them, "Be sober-minded; be watchful. Your adversary the devil prowls around like a roaring lion, seeking someone to devour." 1 Peter 5:8

Christians have never really had it easy in defending their hope. Peter counsels these new ones, who have next to no experience in coping with trials and persecutions to rejoice, albeit distressed by numerous trials. "**Keep your conduct among the Gentiles honorable**, so that when they speak against you as evildoers, they may see your good deeds and glorify God on the day of visitation." (1 Pet. 2:12) "The end of all things is at hand; therefore **be self-controlled and sober-minded for the sake of your prayers**." 1 Pet. 4:4) "Be sober-minded; be watchful" in the midst of men who continue "living in sensuality, passions, drunkenness, orgies, drinking parties, and lawless idolatry." (1 Pet. 4:3) They should be united under Christ as they 'Have purified their souls by their obedience to the truth for a sincere brotherly love, love one another earnestly from a pure heart." (1 Peter 1:22) "Above all, [they were to] keep loving one another earnestly, since love covers a multitude of sins. Show hospitality to one another without grumbling. As each has received a gift, use it to serve one another, as good stewards of God's varied grace." (1 Pet 4:8-10) 'Finally, all of them, had unity of mind, sympathy, brotherly love, a tender heart, and a humble mind. They did not repay evil for evil or reviling for reviling, but on the contrary, they blessed, for to this they were called, that you may obtain a blessing.' (1 Pet. 3:8-9) If they heeded this counsel, it would have kept them from falling or drifting back into their former ways.

There was one more obligation, if they were to preserve on the right path of conduct, namely, being prepared to make a defense for their hope. "It was revealed to [the prophets] that they were serving not themselves but you, in the things that have now been announced to you through those who preached the good news to you by the Holy Spirit sent from heaven, things into which angels long to look. Therefore, preparing your minds for action, and being sober-minded, set your hope fully on the grace that will be brought to you at the revelation of Jesus Christ." (1 Pet. 1:12-13) Peter went on to tell them that they were "a chosen race, a royal priesthood, a holy nation, a people for his own possession, that you may proclaim the excellencies of him who called you out of darkness into his marvelous light." (1 Pet. 2:9) When should they "proclaim these excellencies"? He writes, "but in your hearts honor Christ the Lord as holy, <u>always</u> **being prepared** to make a defense to anyone who asks you for a reason for the hope that is in you; yet do it with gentleness and respect." 1 Peter 3:15

The world in which we live today is much more vast than that of the first-century up unto the 21st-century. The trials and persecution today are much more intense, which unfortunately we ca watch around the world, by way of the media and social media. The greatest threat to Christianity is Islam, which has been an ardent enemy of Christianity since the seventh-century C.E. They are slaughtering Christians the world over. They view Christians as the big Satan and the Jews as little Satan. In their theology, they are looking to turn the world into one big Islamic state, governed by the Quran. For the more radical aspects of Islam, it is convert to Islam or be killed as an infidel.

The second greatest threat to tradition and conservatism is liberal Christianity. Their continued dissecting of the Scriptures until Moses did not pen the first five books, Isaiah is not the author of the book that bears his name, nor is Daniel the author of the book that bears his name, and the Bible is full of myths and legends, errors and contractions.

Then, as we have seen throughout this publication, there are moderate and liberal Bible scholars, who are advocates of Historical Criticism Methodology, and its sub-criticisms: Source Criticism, Tradition Criticism, Form Criticism, Redaction Criticism, among others.

2 Timothy 2:24-25 Updated American Standard Version (ASV)

[24] For a slave of the Lord does not need to fight, but needs to be kind to all, qualified to teach, showing restraint when wronged, [25] instructing his opponents with gentleness, if perhaps God may grant them repentance leading to accurate knowledge [*epignosis*][1127] of the truth,

Look at the Greek word (*epignosis*) behind the English "knowledge" from above. "It is more intensive than *gnosis*, knowledge, because it expresses a more thorough participation in the acquiring of knowledge on the part of the learner."[1128] The requirement of all of the Lord's servants is that they be able to teach, but not in a quarrelsome way, but in a way to correct opponents with mildness. Why? The purpose of it all is that by God, yet through the Christian teacher, one may come to repentance and begin taking in an accurate knowledge of the truth.

> Some Christians see apologetics as pre-evangelism; it is not the gospel, but it prepares the soil for the gospel.[1129] Others make no such distinction, seeing apologetics, theology, philosophy, and evangelism as deeply entwined facets of the gospel.[1130] Whatever its relation to the gospel, apologetics **is an extremely important enterprise that can profoundly impact unbelievers** and be used as the tool that clears the way to faith in Jesus Christ. (Bold mine.)

> Many Christians did not come to believe as a result of investigating the Bible's authority, the evidence for the resurrection, or as a response to the philosophical arguments for God's existence. They responded to the proclamation of the gospel. Although these people have reasons for their belief, they are deeply personal reasons that often do not make sense to unbelievers. **They know the truth but are not necessarily equipped to share or articulate the truth in a way that is understandable** to those who have questions about their faith. It is quite possible to believe something is true without having a proper understanding of it or the ability to articulate it. (Bold mine.)

> Christians who believe but do not know why are often insecure and comfortable only around other Christians. Defensiveness can quickly

---

[1127] *Epignosis* is a strengthened or intensified form of *gnosis* (*epi*, meaning "additional"), meaning, "true," "real," "full," "complete" or "accurate," depending upon the context. Paul and Peter alone use *epignosis*.

1128. Spiros Zodhiates, *The Complete Word Study Dictionary: New Testament*, Electronic ed. (Chattanooga, TN: AMG Publishers, 2000, c1992, c1993), S. G1922.

[1129] Norman Geisler and Ron Brooks, When Skeptics Ask (Grand Rapids: Baker Books, 1996), 11.

[1130] Greg Bahnsen, Van Til Apologetic (Phillipsburg, NJ: Presbyterian and Reformed, 1998), 43.

surface when challenges arise on issues of faith, morality, and truth because of a lack of information regarding the rational grounds for Christianity. At its worst, this can lead to either a fortress mentality or a belligerent faith, precisely the opposite of the Great Commission Jesus gave in Matthew 28:19–20. The Christian's charge is not to withdraw from the world and lead an insular life. Rather, we must be engaged in the culture, to be salt and light.

The solution to this problem requires believers to become informed in doctrine, the history of their faith, philosophy, logic, and other disciplines as they relate to Christianity. Believers must know the facts, arguments and theology and understand how to employ them in a way that will effectively engage the culture. Believers need Christian apologetics. One of the first tasks of Christian apologetics provides information. A number of widely held assumptions about Christianity can be easily challenged with a little information. This is even true for persons who are generally well-educated.[1131]

The ability to reason with others will take time, practice and patience. For example, if someone reasons with others successfully, that person must be reasonable. In a discussion about the historicity about Jesus, a believer knows the other person denying the existence of Jesus is wrong. Moreover, believers possess a truckload of evidence to support this position. However, it is best sometimes to not unload the truck by dumping the entire load at a listener's feet in one conversation, or in one breath. Being reasonable does not mean that a believer compromises the truth because he or she does not unload on the listener.

The other person will likely make many wrong statements in the conversation, and we should let most of them go unchallenged; rather, focus on a handful of the most crucial pieces of evidence and do not get lost by refuting every wrong statement. He may make bold condemnatory statements about many Christian beliefs, but we need to remain calm and not make a big deal of those statements. Listen carefully to the other person, and stay within the boundaries of the evidence in the conversation. For example, in a conversation on the historicity of Jesus when the listener states, "The New Testament manuscripts were completely corrupted in the copying process for a millennium, to the point that we do not even have the supposed Word of God." The evidence for the historicity of Jesus rests in the first and second century, so it would be a fool's errand to get into an extensive side subject about the restoration of the New Testament text, which took place over the centuries that followed the first two centuries C.E. There will be another day to talk about the history of the Greek New Testament, but today focus on the historicity of Jesus Christ.

God has given humanity free will, meaning each human has the right to choose, even if that choice is unwise. Believers have the assignment of proclaiming "the good news of the kingdom," as well as "making disciples" of redeemable humankind. Therefore, we must not pressure, coerce, or force people to accept the truth of that "Good News." However, all Christians have an obligation to reason

---

[1131] Powell, Doug (2006-07-01). *Holman QuickSource Guide to Christian Apologetics* (Holman Quicksource Guides) (p. 6-7). B&H Publishing. Kindle Edition.

with anyone by respectfully, gently, and mildly overturning their false reasoning, in the attempt that being used by God we may save some.

CHAPTER 13 Bible Difficulties Explained

Edward D. Andrews

IT SEEMS THAT the charge that the Bible contradicts itself has been made more and more in the last 20 years. Generally, those making such claims are merely repeating what they have heard, because most have not even read the Bible, let alone done an in-depth study of it. I do not wish, however, to set aside all concerns as though they have no merit. There are many who raise legitimate questions that seem, on the surface anyway, to be about well-founded contradiction. Sadly, these issues have caused many to lose their faith in God's Word, the Bible. The purpose of this books is, to help its readers to be able to defend the Bible against Bible critics (1 Pet. 3:15), to contend for the faith (Jude 1:3), and help those, who have begun to doubt. – Jude 1:22-23.

Before we begin explaining things, let us jump right in, getting our feet wet, and deal with two major Bible difficulties, so we can see that there are reasonable, logical answers. After that, we will delve deeper into explaining Bible difficulties.

Is God permitting Human Sacrifice?

Judges 11:29-34, 37-40? Updated American Standard Version (UASV)

29 Then the Spirit of the Lord was upon Jephthah, and he passed through Gilead and Manasseh; and passed on to Mizpah of Gilead, and from Mizpah of Gilead he passed on to the sons of Ammon. 30 And Jephthah **made a vow** to Jehovah and said, "If You will indeed give the sons of Ammon into my hand, 31 then it shall be that **whatever** comes out of the doors of my house to meet me when I return in peace from the sons of Ammon, it shall be Jehovah's, and I will offer it up as a burnt offering." 32 So Jephthah crossed over to the sons of Ammon to fight against them; and Jehovah gave them into his hand. 33 He struck them with a very great slaughter from Aroer as far as Minnith, twenty cities, and as far as Abel-keramim. So the sons of Ammon were subdued before the sons of Israel.

34 When Jephthah came to his house at Mizpah, behold, **his daughter was coming out to meet him** with tambourines and with dancing. Now she was his one and only child; besides her he had no son or daughter.

37 And she said to her father, "Let this thing be done for me: leave me alone two months, that I may go up and down on the mountains and weep because of my virginity, I and my companions." 38 And he said, "Go." So he sent her away for two months; and **she left with her companions, and wept on the mountains because of her virginity.** 39 At the end of two months she returned to her father, who **did to her according to the vow that he had made;** and she never known a man.[1132] Thus it became a custom in Israel, 40 that the daughters of Israel went year by year **to commemorate**[1133] **the daughter** of Jephthah the Gileadite four days in the year.

[1132] I.e., *never had relations with a man*

[1133] Or *lament*

It is true; to infer that having the idea of an animal sacrifice would really have not been an impressive vow, which the context requires. Human sacrifice will be repugnant if we are talking about taking a life. Jephthah had no sons, so he likely knew it was the daughter, who would come to greet him.

First, the text does not say he killed his daughter. The idea of some that he did kill her is concluded only by inference. While it is not good policy to interpret backward, using Paul on Judges, he does say humans are to be "**as a living sacrifice.**" Therefore, Jephthah could have offered his daughter at the temple, "as a living sacrifice" in service, like Samuel.

This is not to be taken dismissively, because, under Jewish backgrounds, it is no small thing to offer a **perpetual virginity** as a sacrifice. This would mean Jephthah's lineage would not be carried on, the family name, was no more.

Second, the context says she went out to weep for two months, not mourn her death. It says, "she left with her companions, and **wept on the mountains because of her virginity.**"

If she was facing imminent death, she could have married, and spent that last two months as a married woman. There would be absolutely no reason for her to mourn her virginity if she were not facing perpetual virginity. – Exodus 38:8; 1 Samuel 2:22

Third, it was completely forbidden to offer a human sacrifice. – Leviticus 18:21; 20:2-5; Deuteronomy 12:31; 18:10

Imagine an Israelite believing that he could please God with a human sacrifice that was intended to offer up a human life. To do so would have been a rejection of Jehovah's Sovereignty (the very person you are asking for help), and a rejection of the Law that made them a special people. Worse still, this interpretation would have us believe that Jehovah knew this was coming, allowed the vow, and then aided this type of man to succeed over his enemies.

The last point is simple enough. If such a man as one who would make such a vow, in gross violation of the law, and then carry it out; there is no way he would be mentioned by Paul in Hebrews chapter 11 among the most faithful men and women in Israelite history.

In review, there is no way God would have granted and helped in Jephthah's initial success knowing the vow that was coming because both Jehovah and Jephthah would be as bad as the Canaanites. There is no way that God would accept such a vow and then go on to help Jephthah with his enemies yet again. Then, to allow such a vow to be carried out, to then put Jephthah on the wall of star witnesses for God in Hebrews chapter 11.

Does Isaiah 45:7 mean that God Is the Author of Evil?

Isaiah 45:7 King James Version (KJV)	Isaiah 45:7 English Standard Version (ESV)
7 I form the light, and create darkness: I make peace, and **create evil:** I the Lord do all these things.	7 I form light and create darkness, I make well-being and **create calamity,**

	I am the Lord, who does all these things.[1134]

Encarta Dictionary: (Evil) (1) morally bad: profoundly immoral or wrong (2) deliberately causing great harm, pain, or upset

QUESTION: Is this view of evil always the case? No, as you will see below.

Some apologetic authors try to say, 'we do not understand Isaiah 45:7 correctly, because there are other verses that say God is not evil (1 John 1:5), cannot look approvingly on evil (Hab. 1:13), and cannot be tempted by evil. (James 1:13)' Well, while all of these things are Scripturally true, the question at hand is not: Is God evil, can God approvingly look on evil, or can God be tempted with evil? Those questions are not relevant to the one at hand, as God cannot be those things, and at the same time, he can be the yes to our question. The question is, is God the author, the creator of evil?

We would hardly argue that God was **not just** in his bringing "calamity" or "evil" down on Adam and Eve. Thus, we have Isaiah 45:7 saying that God is the creator of "calamity" or "evil."

Let us begin simple, without trying to be philosophical. When God removed Adam and Eve from the Garden of Eden, he sentenced them and humanity to sickness, old age, and death. (Rom. 5:8; i.e., enforce penalty for sin), which was to bring "calamity" or "evil" upon humankind. Therefore, as we can see "evil" does not always mean wrongdoing. Other examples of God bringing "calamity" or "evil" are Noah and the flood, the Ten Plagues of Egypt, and the destruction of the Canaanites. These acts of evil were not acts of wrongdoing. Rather, they were righteous and just, because God, the Creator of all things, was administering justice to wrongdoers, to sinners. He warned the perfect first couple what the penalty was for sin. He warned the people for a hundred years by Noah's preaching. He warned the Canaanites centuries before.

Nevertheless, there are times, when God extends mercy, refraining from the execution of his righteous judgment to one worthy of calamity. For example, he warned Nineveh, the city of blood, and they repented, so he pardoned them. (Jonah 3:10) God has made it a practice to warn persons of the results of sin, giving them undeservedly many opportunities to change their ways. – Ezekiel 33:11.

God cannot sin; it is impossible for him to do so. So, when did he create evil? Without getting into the eternity of his knowing what he was going to do, and when, let us just say, evil did not exist when he was the only person in existence. We might say the idea of evil existed because he knew what he was going to do. However, the moment he created creatures (spirit and human), the potential for evil came into existence because both have free will to sin (fall short of perfection). Evil became a reality the moment Satan entertained the idea of causing Adam to sin, to get humanity for himself, and then acted on it.

God has the right and is just to bring the *calamity of* or *evil* down on anyone that is an unrepentant sinner. God did not even have to give us the underserved

---

[1134] See Jeremiah 18:11, Lamentations 3:18, and Amos 3:6

kindness of offering us his Son. God is the author or agent of evil regardless of the source books that claim otherwise. If he had never created free will beings, evil would have never gone from the idea of evil to the potential of evil, to the existence of evil. However, God felt that it was better to get the sinful state out of angel and human existence, recover, and then any who would sin thereafter; he would be justified in handing out evil or calamity to only that person or angel alone.

Who among us would argue that he should have created humans and angels like robots, automatons with no free will? The moment he chose the free will, he moved evil from an idea to a potential, and Satan moved it to reality. God has a moral nature that does not bring about evil and sin when he is the only person in existence. However, the moment he created beings in his image, which had the potential to sin, he brought about evil. The moment we have a moral code of good and evil that is placed upon one's with free will; then, we have evil as a potential.

In English, the very comprehensive Hebrew word ra' is variously translated as "bad," "downcast (sad, NASB)," "ugly," "evil," "grievous (distressing, NASB)," "sore," "selfish (stingy, HCSB)," and "envious," depending upon the context. (Gen 2:9; 40:7; 41:3; Ex 33:4; Deut. 6:22; 28:35; Pro 23:6; 28:22)

Evil as an adjective **describes** the **quality of** a class of people, places, or things, or of a specific person, place, or thing

Evil as a noun, **defines** the **nature** of a class of people, places, or things, or of a specific person, place, or thing (e.g., the evil one, evil eye).

We can agree that "evil" is a thing. Create means to bring something into existence, be it people, places, or things, as well something abstract, for lack of a better word at the moment. We would agree that when God was alone evil was not a reality; it did not exist? We would agree that the moment that God created free will creatures (angels and humans), creating humans in his image, with his moral nature, he also brought the potential for evil into existence, and it was realized by Satan?

Inerrancy: Can the Bible Be trusted?

If the Bible is the Word of God, it should be in complete agreement throughout; there should be no contradictions. Yet, the rational mind must ask, why is it that some passages appear to be contradictions when compared with others? For example, Numbers 25:9 tells us that 24,000 died from the scourge, whereas at 1 Corinthians 10:8, the apostle Paul says it was 23,000. This would seem to be a clear error. Before addressing such matters, let us first look at some background information.

Full inerrancy in this book means that the original writings are fully without error in all that they state, as are the words. The words were not dictated (automaton), but the intended meaning is inspired, as are the words that convey that meaning. The Author allowed the writer to use his style of writing, yet controlled the meaning to the extent of not allowing the writer to choose a wrong word, which would not convey the intended meaning. Other more liberal-minded persons hold with *partial inerrancy*, which claims that as far as faith is concerned, this portion of God's Word is without error, but that there are historical, geographical, and scientific errors.

There are several different levels of inerrancy. *Absolute Inerrancy* is the belief that the Bible is fully true and exact in every way; including not only relationships and doctrine, but also science and history. In other words, all information is completely exact. *Full Inerrancy* is the belief that the Bible was not written as a science or historical textbook, but is phenomenological, in that it is written from the human perspective. In other words, speaking of such things as the sun rising, the four corners of the earth or the rounding off of number approximations are all from a human perspective. *Limited Inerrancy* is the belief that the Bible is meant only as a reflection of God's purposes and will, so the science and history is the understanding of the author's day, and is limited. Thus, the Bible is susceptible to errors in these areas. *Inerrancy of Purpose* is the belief that it is only inerrant in the purpose of bringing its readers to a saving faith. The Bible is not about facts, but about persons and relationships, thus, it is subject to error. *Inspired: Not Inerrant* is the belief that its authors are human and thus subject to human error. It should be noted that this author holds the position of full inerrancy.

For many today, the Bible is nothing more than a book written by men. The Bible critic believes the Bible to be full of myths and legends, contradictions, and geographical, historical, and scientific errors. University professor Gerald A. Larue had this to say, "The views of the writers as expressed in the Bible reflect the ideas, beliefs, and concepts current in their own times and are limited by the extent of knowledge in those times."[1135] On the other hand, the Bible's authors claim that their writings were inspired of God, as Holy Spirit moved them along. We will discover shortly that the Bible critics have much to say, but it is inflated or empty.

2 Timothy 3:16-17 Updated American Standard Version (UASV)

[16] All Scripture is inspired by God and profitable for teaching, for reproof, for correction, for training in righteousness; [17] so that the man of God may be fully competent, equipped for every good work.

2 Peter 1:21 Updated American Standard Version (UASV)

[21] for no prophecy was ever produced by the will of man, but men carried along by the Holy Spirit spoke from God.

The question remains as to whether the Bible is a book written by imperfect men and full of errors, or is written by imperfect men, but inspired by God. If the Bible is just another book by imperfect man, there is no hope for humankind. If it is inspired by God and without error, although penned by imperfect men, we have the hope of everything that it offers: a rich, happy life now by applying counsel that lies within and the real life that is to come, everlasting life. This author contends that the Bible is inspired of God and free of human error, although written by imperfect humans.

Before we take on the critics who seem to sift the Scriptures looking for problematic verses, let us take a moment to reflect on how we should approach

---

[1135] Gerald Larue, "The Bible as a Political Weapon," *Free Inquiry* (Summer 1983): 39.

these alleged problem texts. The critic's argument goes something like this: 'If God does not err and the Bible is the Word of God, then the Bible should not have one single error or contradiction, yet it is full of errors and contradictions.' If the Bible is riddled with nothing but contradictions and errors as the critics would have us believe, why, out of 31,173 verses in the Bible, should there be only 2-3 thousand Bible difficulties that are called into question, this being less than ten percent of the whole?

First, let it be said that it is every Christian's obligation to get a deeper understanding of God's Word, just as the apostle Paul told Timothy:

1 Timothy 4:15-16 Updated American Standard Version (UASV)

[15] Practice these things, be absorbed in them, so that your progress will be evident to all. [16] Pay close attention to yourself and to your teaching; persevere in these things, for as you do this you will ensure salvation both for yourself and for those who hear you.

Paul also told the Corinthians:

2 Corinthians 10:4-5 Updated American Standard Version (UASV)

[4] For the weapons of our warfare are not of the flesh[1136] but powerful to God for destroying strongholds.[1137] [5] We are destroying speculations and every lofty thing raised up against the knowledge of God, and we are taking every thought captive to the obedience of Christ,

Paul also told the Philippians:

Philippians 1:7 Updated American Standard Version (UASV)

[7] It is right for me to feel thus about you all, because I hold you in my heart, for you are all partakers with me of grace, both in my imprisonment and in the defense and confirmation of the gospel.

In being able to defend against the modern-day critic, one has to be able to reason from the Scriptures and overturn the critic's argument(s) with mildness. If someone were to approach us about an alleged error or contradiction, what should we do? We should be frank and honest. If we do not have an answer, we should admit such. If the text in question gives the appearance of difficulty, we should admit this as well. If we are unsure as to how we should answer, we can simply say that we will look into it and get back to them, returning with a reasonable answer.

However, we do not want to express disbelief and doubt to our critics, because they will be emboldened in their disbelief. It will put them on the offense and us on the defense. With great confidence, we can express that there is an answer. The Bible has withstood the test of 2,000 years of persecution and interrogation and yet it is the most printed book of all time, currently being translated into 2,287 languages. If these critical questions were so threatening, the Bible would not be the book that it is.

[1136] That is *merely human*

[1137] That is *tearing down false arguments*

When we are pursuing the text in question, be unwavering in purpose, or resolved to find an answer. In some cases, it may take hours of digging to find the solution. Consider this: as we resolve these difficulties, we are also building our faith that God's Word is inerrant. Moreover, we will want to do preventative maintenance in our personal study. As we are doing our Bible reading, take note of these surface discrepancies and resolve them as we work our way through the Bible. We need to make this part of our prayers as well. I recommend the following program. Below are several books that deal with difficult passages. As we daily read and study our Bible from Genesis to Revelation, do not attempt it in one year; make it a four-year program. Use a good exegetical commentary like *The Holman Old/New Testament Commentary* (HOTC/HNTC) or *The New American Commentary* set, and *The Big Book of Bible Difficulties* by Norman L. Geisler, as well as *The Encyclopedia of Bible Difficulties* by Gleason Archer.

We should be aware that men under inspiration penned the originally written books. In fact, we do not have those originals, what textual scholars call autographs, but we do have thousands of copies. The copyists, however, were not inspired; therefore, as one might expect, throughout the first 1,400 years of copying, thousands of errors were transmitted into the texts that were being copied by imperfect hands that were not under inspiration when copying. Yet, the next 450 years saw a restoration of the text by textual scholars from around the world. Therefore, while many of our best literal translations today may not be inspired, they are a mirror-like reflection of the autographs by way of textual criticism.[1138] Therefore, the fallacy could be with the copyist error that has simply not been weeded out. In addition, we must keep in mind that God's Word is without error, but our interpretation and understanding of that Word is not.

It should be noted that the Bible is made up of 66 smaller books that were hand-written over a period of 1,600 years, having some 40 writers of various trades such as shepherd, king, priest, tax collector, governor, physician, copyist, fisherman, and a tentmaker. Therefore, it should not surprise us that some difficulties are encountered as we casually read the Bible. Yet, if one were to take a deeper look, one would find that these difficulties are easily explained. Let us take a few pages to examine some passages that have been under attack.

This chapter's objective is not to be exhaustive, not even close. What we are looking to do is cover a few alleged contradictions and a couple of alleged mistakes. This is to give us a small sampling of the reasonable answers that we will find in the above recommended books. Remember, our Bible is a sword that we must use both offensively and defensively. One must wonder how long a warrior of ancient times would last who was not expertly trained in the use of his weapon. Let us look at a few scriptures that support our need to learn our Bible well so will be able to defend what we believe to be true.

When "false apostles, deceitful workmen, disguising themselves as apostles of Christ" were causing trouble in the congregation in Corinth, the apostle Paul wrote that under such circumstances, we are to *tear down their arguments* and *take every*

[1138] Textual criticism is the study of copies of any written work of which the autograph (original) is unknown, with the purpose of ascertaining the original text. Harold J. Green, Introduction to New Testament Textual Criticism (Peabody, MA: Hendrickson, 1995), 1.

thought captive. (2 Corinthians 10:4, 5; 11:13–15) All who present critical arguments against God's Word, or contrary to it, can have their arguments overturned by the Christian, who is able and ready to defend that Word in mildness. – 2 Timothy 2:24–26.

1 Peter 3:15 Updated American Standard Version (UASV)

¹⁵ but sanctify Christ as Lord in your hearts, always being prepared to make a defense[1139] to anyone who asks you for a reason for the hope that is in you; yet do it with gentleness and respect;

Peter says that we need to be prepared to make a *defense.* The Greek word behind the English 'defense' is *apologia,* which is actually a legal term that refers to the defense of a defendant in court. Our English apologetics is just what Peter spoke of, having the ability to give a reason to any who may challenge us, or to answer those who are not challenging us but who have honest questions that deserve to be answered.

2 Timothy 2:24-25 Updated American Standard Version (UASV)

²⁴ For a slave of the Lord does not need to fight, but needs to be kind to all, qualified to teach, showing restraint when wronged ²⁵ with gentleness correcting those who are in opposition, if perhaps God may grant them repentance leading to accurate knowledge[1140] of the truth,

Look at the Greek word (*epignosis*) behind the English "knowledge" in the above. "It is more intensive than *gnosis* (1108), knowledge because it expresses a more thorough participation in the acquiring of knowledge on the part of the learner."[1141] The requirement of all of the Lord's servants is that they be able to teach, but not in a quarrelsome way, and in a way to correct his opponents with mildness. Why? Because the purpose of it all is that by God, and through the Christian teacher, one may come to repentance and begin taking in an accurate knowledge of the truth.

Inerrancy: Practical Principles to Overcoming Bible Difficulties

Below are several ways of looking at the Bible that enable the reader to see he is not dealing with an error or contradiction, but rather a Bible difficulty.

Different Points of View

At times, you may have two different writers who are writing from two different points of view.

[1139] Or *argument,* or *explanation*

[1140] *Epignosis* is a strengthened or intensified form of *gnosis* (*epi,* meaning "additional"), meaning, "true," "real," "full," "complete" or "accurate," depending upon the context. Paul and Peter alone use *epignosis.*

[1141] Spiros Zodhiates, *The Complete Word Study Dictionary: New Testament,* Electronic ed. (Chattanooga, TN: AMG Publishers, 2000, c1992, c1993), S. G1922.

Numbers 35:14 Updated American Standard Version (UASV)

14 You shall give three cities across the Jordan and three cities you shall give in the land of Canaan; they will be cities of refuge.

Joshua 22:4 Updated American Standard Version (UASV)

4 And now Jehovah your God has given rest to your brothers, as he spoke to them; therefore turn now and go to your tents, to the land of your possession, which Moses the servant of Jehovah gave you beyond the Jordan. [on the other side of the Jordan, ESV]

Here we see that Moses is speaking about the east side of the Jordan when he says "on this side of the Jordan." Joshua, on the other hand, is also speaking about the east side of the Jordan when he says "on the other side of the Jordan." So, who is correct? Both are. When Moses was penning Numbers the Israelites had not yet crossed the Jordan River, so the east side was "this side," the side he was on. On the other hand, when Joshua penned his book, the Israelites had crossed the Jordan, so the east side was just as he had said, "on the other side of the Jordan." Thus, we should not assume that two different writers are writing from the same perspective.

A Careful Reading

At times, it may simply be a case of needing to slow down and carefully read the account, considering exactly what is being said.

Joshua 18:28 Updated American Standard Version (UASV)

28 and Zelah, Haeleph and the Jebusite (that is, Jerusalem), Gibeah, Kiriath; fourteen cities with their villages. This is the inheritance of the sons of Benjamin according to their families.

Judges 1:21 Updated American Standard Version (UASV)

21 But the sons of Benjamin did not drive out the Jebusites who lived in Jerusalem; so the Jebusites have lived with the sons of Benjamin in Jerusalem to this day.

Joshua 15:63 Updated American Standard Version (UASV)

63 But as for the Jebusites, the inhabitants of Jerusalem, the sons of Judah could not drive them out; so the Jebusites live with the sons of Judah at Jerusalem until this day.

Judges 1:8-9 Updated American Standard Version (UASV)

8 And then the sons of Judah fought against Jerusalem and captured it and struck it with the edge of the sword and set the city on fire. 9 And afterward the sons of Judah went down to fight against the Canaanites living in the hill country and in the Negev[1142] and in the Shephelah.[1143]

[1142] I.e. *South*

[1143] I.e., lowland

2 Samuel 5:5-9 Updated American Standard Version (UASV)

⁵ At Hebron he reigned over Judah seven years and six months, and in Jerusalem he reigned thirty-three years over all Israel and Judah.

⁶ And the king and his men went to Jerusalem against the Jebusites, the inhabitants of the land, and they said to David, "You shall not come in here, but the blind and lame will turn you away"; thinking, "David cannot come in here." ⁷ Nevertheless, David captured the stronghold of Zion, that is the city of David. ⁸ And David said on that day, "Whoever would strike the Jebusites, let him get up the water shaft to attack 'the lame and the blind,' who are hated by David's soul." Therefore it is said, "The blind and the lame shall not come into the house." ⁹ And David lived in the stronghold and called it the city of David. And David built all around from the Millo and inward.

There is no doubt that even the advanced Bible reader of many years can come away confused because the above accounts seem to be contradictory. In Joshua 18:28 and Judges 1:21, we see that Jerusalem was an inheritance of the tribe of Benjamin, yet the Benjamites were unable to conquer Jerusalem. However, in Joshua 15:63 we see that the tribe of Judah could not conquer them either, with the reading giving the impression that it was a part of their inheritance. In Judges 1:8, however, Judah was eventually able to conquer Jerusalem and burn it with fire. Yet, to add even more to the confusion, we find at 2 Samuel 5:5–8 that David is said to have conquered Jerusalem hundreds of years later.

Now that we have the particulars let us look at it more clearly. The boundary between Benjamin's inheritances ran right through the middle of Jerusalem. Joshua 8:28 is correct, in that what would later be called the "city of David" was in the territory of Benjamin, but it also in part crossed over the line into the territory of Judah, causing both tribes to go to war against this Jebusite city. It is also true that the tribe of Benjamin was unable to conquer the city and that the tribe of Judah eventually did. However, if you look at Judges 1:9 again, you will see that Judah did not finish the job entirely and moved on to conquer other areas. This allowed the remaining ones to regroup and form a resistance that neither Benjamin nor Judah could overcome, so these Jebusites remained until the time of David, hundreds of years later.

Intended Meaning of Writer

First, the Bible student needs to understand the level that the Bible intends to be exact in what is written. If Jim told a friend that 650 graduated with him from high school in 1984, it is not challenged, because it is all too clear that he is using rounded numbers and is not meaning to be exactly precise. This is how God's Word operates as well. Sometimes it means to be exact, at other times, it is simply rounding numbers, in other cases, the intention of the writer is a general reference, to give readers of that time and succeeding generations some perspective. Did Samuel, the author of judges, intend to pen a book on the chronology of Judges, or was his focus on the falling away, oppression, and the rescue by a judge, repeatedly. Now, it would seem that Jeremiah, the author of 1 Kings was more interested in giving his readers an exact number of years.

Acts 2:41 Updated American Standard Version (UASV)

⁴¹ So those who received his word were baptized, and there were added that day about three thousand souls.

As you can see here, numbers within the Bible are often used with approximations. This is a frequent practice even today, in both written works and verbal conversation.

Acts 7:2-3 Updated American Standard Version (UASV)

² And Stephen said:

"Brothers and fathers, hear me. The God of glory appeared to our father Abraham when he was in Mesopotamia, before he lived in Haran, ³ and said to him, 'Go out from your land and from your kindred and go into the land that I will show you.'

If you were to check the Hebrew Scriptures at Genesis 12:1, you would find that what is claimed to have been said by God to Abraham is not quoted word-for-word; it is simply a paraphrase. This is a normal practice within Scripture and in writing in general.

Numbers 34:15 Updated American Standard Version (UASV)

¹⁵ The two and a half tribes have received their inheritance beyond the Jordan opposite Jericho, eastward toward the sunrising."

Just as you would read in today's local newspaper, the Bible writer has written from the human standpoint, how it appeared to him. The Bible also speaks of "to the end of the earth" (Psalm 46:9), "from the four corners of the earth" (Isa 11:12), and "the four winds of the earth" (Revelation 7:1). These phrases are still used today.

Unexplained Does Not mean Unexplainable

Considering that there are 31,173 verses in the Bible, encompassing 66 books written by about 40 writers, ranging from shepherds to kings, an army general, fishermen, tax collector, a physician and on and on, and being penned over a 1,600 year period, one does find a few hundred Bible difficulties (about one percent). However, 99 percent of those are explainable. Yet no one wants to be so arrogant to say that he can explain them all. It has nothing to do with the inadequacy of God's Word but is based on human understanding. In many cases, science or archaeology and the field of custom and culture of ancient peoples has helped explain difficulties in hundreds of passages. Therefore, there may be less than one percent left to be answered, yet our knowledge of God's Word continues to grow.

Guilty Until Proven Innocent

This is exactly the perception that the critic has of God's Word. The legal principle of being "innocent until proven guilty" afforded mankind in courts of justice is withheld from the very Word of God. What is ironic here is that this policy has contributed to these Bible critics looking foolish over and over again when something comes to light that vindicates the portion of Scripture they are challenging.

Daniel 5:1 Updated American Standard Version (UASV)

[1] Belshazzar the king made[1144] a great feast for a thousand of his nobles, and he was drinking wine in the presence of the thousand.

Bible critics had long claimed that Belshazzar was not known outside of the book Daniel; therefore, they argue that Daniel was mistaken. Yet it hardly seems prudent to argue error from absence of outside evidence. Just because archaeology had not discovered such a person did not mean that Daniel was wrong, or that such a person did not exist. In 1854, some small clay cylinders were discovered in modern-day southern Iraq, which would have been the city of Ur in ancient Babylonia. The cuneiform documents were a prayer of King Nabonidus for "Bel-sar-ussur, my eldest son." These tablets also showed that this "Bel-sar-ussur" had secretaries as well as a household staff. Other tablets were discovered a short time later that showed that the kingship was entrusted to this eldest son as a coregent while his father was away.

He entrusted the 'Camp' to his oldest (son), the firstborn [Belshazzar], the troops everywhere in the country he ordered under his (command). He let (everything) go, entrusted the kingship to him and, himself, he [Nabonidus] started out for a long journey, the (military) forces of Akkad marching with him; he turned towards Tema (deep) in the west."[1145]

Ignoring Literary Styles

The Bible is a diverse book when it comes to literary styles: narrative, poetic, prophetic, and apocalyptic; also containing parables, metaphors, similes, hyperbole, and other figures of speech. Too often, these alleged errors are the result of a reader taking a figure of speech as literal, or reading a parable as though it is a narrative.

Matthew 24:35 Updated American Standard Version (UASV)

[35] Heaven and earth will pass away, but my words will not pass away.

If some do not recognize that they are dealing with a figure of speech, they are bound to come away with the wrong meaning. Some have concluded from Matthew 24:35 that Jesus was speaking of an eventual destruction of the earth. This is hardly the case, as his listeners would not have understood it that way based on their understanding of the Old Testament. They would have understood that he was simply being emphatic about the words he spoke, using hyperbole. What he was conveying is that his words are more enduring than heaven and earth, and with heaven and earth being understood as eternal, this merely conveyed even more so that Jesus' words could be trusted.

[1144] I.e., held

[1145] J. Pritchard, ed., *Ancient Near Eastern Texts* (1974), 313.

Two Accounts of the Same Incident

If you were to speak to officers that take accident reports for their police department, you would find that there is cohesion in the accounts, but each person has merely witnessed aspects that have stood out to them. We will see that this is the case as well with the examples below, which is the same account in two different gospels:

Matthew 8:5 Updated American Standard Version (UASV)

5 When he[1146] had entered Capernaum, a centurion came forward to him, imploring him,

Luke 7:2-3 Updated American Standard Version (UASV)

2 And a centurion's[1147] slave, who was highly regarded[1148] by him, was sick and about to die. 3 When he heard about Jesus, he sent some older men of the Jews[1149] asking him to come and bring his slave safely through.[1150]

Immediately we see the problem of whether the centurion or the elders of the Jews spoke with Jesus. The solution is not really hidden from us. Which of the two accounts is the most detailed account? You are correct if you said, Luke. The centurion sent the elders of the Jews to represent him to Jesus, so; that whatever response Jesus might give, it would be as though he were addressing the centurion; therefore, Matthew gave his readers the basic thought, not seeing the need of mentioning the elders of the Jews aspect. This is how a representative was viewed in the first century, just as some countries see ambassadors today as being the very person they represent. Therefore, both Matthew and Luke are correct.

Man's Fallible Interpretations

Inspiration by God is infallible, without error. Imperfect man and his interpretations over the centuries, as bad as many of them have been, should not cast a shadow over God's inspired Word. The entire Word of God has one meaning and one meaning only for every penned word, which is what God willed to be conveyed by the human writer he chose to use.

The Autograph Alone Is Inspired and Inerrant

It has been argued by conservative scholars that only the autograph manuscripts were inspired and inerrant, not the copying of those manuscripts over the next 3,000 years for the Old Testament and 1,500 years for the New Testament. While I would agree with this position as well, it should be noted that we do not possess the autographs, so to argue that they are inerrant is to speak of nonexistent

---

[1146] That is *Jesus*

[1147] I.e., army officer over a hundred solderiers

[1148] Lit *to whom he was honorable*

[1149] Or *Jewish elders*

[1150] I.e., *save the life of his slave*

documents. However, it should be further understood that through the science of textual criticism, we can establish a mirror reflection of the autograph manuscripts. B. F. Westcott, F. J. A. Hort, F. F. Bruce, and many other textual scholars would agree with Norman L Geisler's assessment: "The New Testament, then, has not only survived in more manuscripts than any other book from antiquity, but it has survived in a purer form than any other great book—*a form that is 99.5 percent pure.*"[1151]

An example of a copyist error can be found in Luke's genealogy of Jesus at Luke 3:35–37. In verse 37 you will find a Cainan, and in verse 36 you will find a second Cainan between Arphaxad (Arpachshad) and Shelah. As one can see from most footnotes in different study Bibles, the Cainan in verse 36 is seen as a scribal error, and is not found in the Hebrew Old Testament, the Samaritan Pentateuch, or the Aramaic Targums, but is found in the Greek Septuagint. (Genesis 10:24; 11:12, 13; 1 Chronicles 1:18, but not 1 Chronicles 1:24) It seems quite unlikely that it was in the earlier copies of the Septuagint, because the first-century Jewish historian Josephus lists Shelah next as the son of Arphaxad, and Josephus normally followed the Septuagint.[1152] So one might ask why this second Cainan is found in the translations at all if this is the case? The manuscripts that do contain this second Cainan are some of the best manuscripts that are used in establishing the original text: 01 B L A¹ 33 (Kainam); A 038 044 0102 A¹³ (Kainan).

Look at the Context

Many alleged inconsistencies disappear by simply looking at the context. Taking words out of context can distort their meaning. *Merriam-Webster's Collegiate Dictionary* defines context as "the parts of a discourse that surround a word or passage and can throw light on its meaning."[1153] Context can also be "the circumstances or events that form the environment within which something exists or takes place." If we were to look in a thesaurus for a synonym, we would find "background" for this second meaning. At 2 Timothy 2:15, the apostle Paul brings home the point of why context is so important: "Do your best to present yourself to God as one approved, a worker who has no need to be ashamed, rightly handling the word of truth."

Ephesians 2:8-9 Updated American Standard Version (UASV)

8 For by grace you have been saved through faith; and that not of yourselves, it is the gift of God; 9 not from works, so that no man may boast.

James 2:26 Updated American Standard Version (UASV)

26 For as the body apart from the spirit[1154] is dead, so also faith apart from works is dead.

[1151] Norman L. Geisler and William E. Nix: *A General Introduction to the Bible* (Chicago, Moody Press, 1980), 367. (Emphasis is mine.)

[1152] *Jewish Antiquities*, I, 146 [vi, 4].

[1153] Merriam-Webster, Inc: *Merriam-Webster's Collegiate Dictionary.* Eleventh ed. (Springfield, Mass.: Merriam-Webster, Inc. 2003).

[1154] Or *breath*

So, which is it? Is salvation possible by faith alone as Paul wrote to the Ephesians, or is faith dead without works as James wrote to his readers? As our subtitle brings out, let us look at the context. In the letter to the Ephesians, the apostle Paul is speaking to the Jewish Christians who were looking to the works of the Mosaic Law as a means to salvation, a righteous standing before God. Paul was telling these legalistic Jewish Christians that this is not so. In fact, this would invalidate Christ's ransom because there would have been no need for it if one could achieve salvation by meticulously keeping the Mosaic Law. (Rom. 5:18) But James was writing to those in a congregation who were concerned with their status before other men, who were looking for prominent positions within the congregation, and not taking care of those that were in need. (Jam. 2:14–17) So, James is merely addressing those who call themselves Christian, but in name only. No person could truly be a Christian and not possess some good works, such as feeding the poor, helping the elderly. This type of work was an evident demonstration of one's Christian personality. Paul was in perfect harmony with James on this. – Romans 10:10; 1 Corinthians 15:58; Ephesians 5:15, 21–33; 6:15; 1 Timothy 4:16; 2 Timothy 4:5; Hebrews 10:23-25.

Inerrancy: Are There Contradictions?

Below I will follow this pattern. I will list the critic's argument first, followed by the text of difficulty, and conclude with an answer to the critic. What should be kept at the forefront of our mind is this: one is simply looking for the best answer, not absoluteness. If there is a reasonable answer to a Bible difficulty, why are the critics able to set them aside with ease? Because they start with the premise that this is not the Word of God, but only a book by imperfect men and full of contradictions; thus, the bias toward errors has blinded their judgment.

Critic: The critic would argue that there was an Adam and Eve, and an Abel who was now dead, so, where did Cain get his wife? This is one of the most common questions by Bible critics.

Genesis 4:17 Updated American Standard Version (UASV)

[17] Cain had sexual relations[1155] with his wife and she conceived, and gave birth to Enoch; and he built a city, and called the name of the city Enoch, after the name of his son, Enoch.

Answer: If one were to read a little further along, they would come to the realization that Adam had a son named Seth; it further adds that Adam "became father to sons *and daughters*." (Genesis 5:4) Adam lived for a total of 800 years after fathering Seth, giving him ample opportunity to father many more sons and daughters. So it could be that Cain married one of his sisters. If he waited until one of his brothers and sisters had a daughter, he could have married one of his nieces once she was old enough. In the beginning, humans were closer to perfection; this explains why they lived longer and why at that time there was little health risk of genetic defects in the case of children born to closely related parents, in contrast to how it is today. As time passed, genetic defects increased and life spans decreased.

[1155] Lit *knew*

Adam lived to see 930 years. Yet Shem, who lived after the Flood, died at 600 years, while Shem's son Arpachshad only lived 438 years, dying before his father died. Abraham saw an even greater decrease in that he only lived 175 years while his grandson Jacob was 147 years when he died. Thus, due to increasing imperfection, God prohibited the marriage of closely related people under the Mosaic Law because of the likelihood of genetic defects.—Leviticus 18:9.

Critic: If God is here hardening Pharaoh's heart, what exactly makes Pharaoh responsible for the decisions he makes?

Exodus 4:21 Updated American Standard Version (UASV)

21 Jehovah said to Moses, "When you go and return to Egypt see that you perform before Pharaoh all the wonders which I have put in your hand; but I will harden his heart so that he will not let the people go.

Answer: This is actually a prophecy. God knew that what he was about to do would contribute to a stubborn and obstinate Pharaoh, who was going to be unwilling to change or give up the Israelites so they could go off to worship their God. Therefore, this is not stating what God is going to do; it is prophesying that Pharaoh's heart will harden because of the actions of God. The fact is, Pharaoh allowed his own heart to harden because he was determined not to agree with Moses' wishes or accept Jehovah's request to let the people go. Moses tells us at Exodus 7:13 (ESV) that "Pharaoh's heart was hardened, and he would not listen to them, as the Lord had said." Again, at 8:15 we read, "When Pharaoh saw that there was a respite, he hardened his heart and would not listen to them, as the Lord had said."

Critic: The Israelites had just received the Ten Commandments, with one commandment being: "You shall not make for yourself a carved image or any likeness of anything that is in heaven above, or that is in the earth beneath, or that is in the water under the earth." Therefore, how is the bronze serpent not a violation of this commandment?

Numbers 21:9 Updated American Standard Version (UASV)

9 And Moses made a bronze serpent and set it on the standard;[1156] and it came about, that if a serpent bit any man, when he looked to the bronze serpent, he lived.

Answer: First, an idol is "a representation or symbol of an object of worship; *broadly*: a false god."[1157] Second, it should be noted that not all images are idols. The bronze serpent was not made for the purpose of worship, or for some passionate devotion or veneration. There were times, however, when images were created with absolutely no intention of it receiving devotion, veneration, or worship, yet were later made into objects of veneration. That is exactly what happened with the copper serpent that Moses had formed in the wilderness. Many centuries later, "in the third year of Hoshea son of Elah, king of Israel, Hezekiah the

---

[1156] I.e., *pole*

[1157] Merriam-Webster, Inc: *Merriam-Webster's Collegiate Dictionary*. Eleventh ed. (Springfield, Mass.: Merriam-Webster, Inc., 2003).

son of Ahaz, king of Judah, began to reign. He removed the high places and broke the pillars and cut down the Asherah. And he broke in pieces the bronze serpent that Moses had made; for until those days the people of Israel had made offerings to it (it was called Nehushtan)."—2 Kings 18:1, 4.

Critic: Deuteronomy 15:11 (NET) says: "*There will never cease to be some poor people in the land;* therefore, I am commanding you to make sure you open your hand to your fellow Israelites who are needy and poor in your land." Is this not a contradiction of Deuteronomy 15:4? Will there be no poor among the Israelites, or will there be poor among them? Which is it?

Deuteronomy 15:4 Updated American Standard Version (UASV)

⁴ However, there will be no poor among you, since Jehovah will surely bless you in the land which Jehovah your God is giving you as an inheritance to possess,

Answer: If you look at the context, Deuteronomy 15:4 is stating that if the Israelites obey Jehovah's command to take care of the poor, "there should not be any poor among" them. Thus, for every poor person, there will be one to take care of that need. If an Israelite fell on hard times, there was to be a fellow Israelite ready to step in to help him through those hard times. Verse 11 stresses the truth of the imperfect world since the rebellion of Adam and inherited sin: there will always be poor among mankind, the Israelites being no different. However, the difference with God's people is that those who were well off financially were to offset conditions for those who fell on difficult times. This is not to be confused with the socialistic welfare systems in the world today. Those Jews were hard-working men, who labored from sunup to sundown to take care of their families. But if disease overtook their herd or unseasonal weather brought about failed crops, an Israelite could sell himself into the service of a fellow Israelite for a period of time; thereafter, he would be back on his feet. And many years down the road, he may very well do the same for another Israelite, who fell on difficult times.

Critic: Joshua 11:23 says that Joshua took the land according to what God had spoken to Moses and handed it on to the nation of Israel as planned. However, in Joshua 13:1, God is telling Joshua that he has grown old and much of the Promised Land has yet to be taken possession of. How can both be true? Is this not a contradiction?

Joshua 11:23 Updated American Standard Version (UASV)

²³ So Joshua took the whole land, according to all that Jehovah had spoken to Moses, and Joshua gave it for an inheritance to Israel according to their divisions by their tribes, and the land had rest from war.

Joshua 13:1 Updated American Standard Version (UASV)

13 Now Joshua was old and advanced in years, and Jehovah said to him, "You are old and advanced in years, and there remains yet very much land to possess.

Answer: No, it is not a contradiction. When the Israelites were to take the land, it was to take place in two different stages: the nation as a whole was to go to war and defeat the 31 kings of this land; thereafter, each Israelite tribe was to take their part of the land based on their individual actions. (Joshua 17:14–18; 18:3)

Joshua fulfilled his role, which is expressed in 11:23 while the individual tribes did not complete their campaigns, which is expressed in 13:1. Even though the individual tribes failed to live up to taking their portion, the remaining Canaanites posed no real threat. Joshua 21:44, *ASV,* reads: "Jehovah gave them rest round about."

Critic: The critic would point out that John 1:18 clearly says that "*no one has ever seen God,*" while Exodus 24:10 explicitly states that Moses and Aaron, Nadab and Abihu, and seventy of the elders of Israel "*saw the God of Israel.*" Worse still, God informs them in Exodus 33:20: "You cannot see my face, for man shall not see me and live." The critic with his knowing smile says, 'This is a blatant contradiction.'

John 1:18 Updated American Standard Version (UASV)

¹⁸ No one has seen God at any time; the only begotten god[1158] who is in the bosom of the Father,[1159] that one has made him fully known.

Exodus 24:10 Updated American Standard Version (UASV)

¹⁰ and they saw the God of Israel; and under his feet was what seemed like a sapphire pavement, as clear as the sky itself.

Exodus 33:20 Updated American Standard Version (UASV)

²⁰ But he [God] said, "You cannot see my face, for no man can see me and live!"

Answer: Exodus 33:20 is one-hundred percent correct: No human could see Jehovah God and live. The apostle Paul at Colossians 1:15 tell us that Christ is the image of the invisible God, and the writer informs us at Hebrews 1:3 that Jesus is the "exact representation of His nature." Yet if you were to read the account of Saul of Tarsus (the apostle Paul), you would see that a mere partial manifestation of Christ's glory blinded Saul – Acts 9:1–18.

When the Bible says that Moses and others have seen God, it is not speaking of *literally* seeing him, because first of all He is an invisible spirit person. It is a *manifestation* of his glory, which is an act of showing or demonstrating his presence, making himself perceptible to the human mind. In fact, it is generally an angelic representative that stands in his place and not him personally. Exodus 24:16 informs us that "the glory of the Lord dwelt on Mount Sinai," not the Lord himself personally. When texts such as Exodus 24:10 explicitly state that Moses and Aaron, Nadab and Abihu, and seventy of the elders of Israel "*saw the God of Israel,*" it is this "glory of the Lord," an angelic representative. This is shown to be the case at Luke 2:9, which reads: "And *an angel of the Lord* appeared to them, and *the glory of the Lord shone around them* [the shepherds], and they were filled with fear."

Many Bible difficulties are cleared up elsewhere in Scripture; for example, in the New Testament, you will find a text clarifying a difficulty from the Old Testament, such as Acts 7:53, which refers to those "who received the law *as delivered by angels* and did not keep it." Support comes from Paul at Galatians

---

¹¹⁵⁸ Jn 1:18: "only-begotten god", P⁶⁶ℵ*BC*Lsyrʰᵐᵍ·ᵖ; **[V1]** "the only-begotten god," P⁷⁵133ℵcopᵇᵒ; **[V2]** "the only-begotten Son." AC³(Wˢ)QYf1.13 MajVgSyrᶜ

¹¹⁵⁹ Or *at the Father's side*

3:19: "Why then the law? It was added because of transgressions until the offspring should come to whom the promise had been made, and it was put in place through angels by an intermediary." The writer of Hebrews chimes in at 2:2 with "For since the message *declared by angels* proved to be reliable, and every transgression or disobedience received a just retribution. . . ." As we travel back to Exodus again, to 19:19 specifically, we find support that it was not God's own voice, which Moses heard; no, it was an angelic representative, for it reads: "Moses was speaking, and God was answering him with a voice." Exodus 33:22–23 also helps us to appreciate that it was the back of these angelic representatives of Jehovah that Moses saw: "While my glory passes by . . . Then I will take away my hand, and you shall see my back, but my face shall not be seen."

Exodus 3:4 states: "God called to him out of the bush, 'Moses, Moses!' And he said, 'Here I am.'" Verse 6 informs us: "I am the God of your father, the God of Abraham, the God of Isaac, and the God of Jacob." Yet, in verse 2 we read: "And the angel of the Lord appeared to him in a flame of fire out of the midst of a bush." Here is another example of using God's Word to clear up what seems to be unclear or difficult to understand at first glance. Thus, while it speaks of the Lord making a direct appearance, it is really an angelic representative. Even today, we hear such comments, as 'the president of the United States is to visit the Middle East later this week.' However, later in the article it is made clear that he is not going personally, but it is one of his high-ranking representatives. Let us close with two examples, starting with,

Genesis 32:24-30 Updated American Standard Version (UASV)

24 And Jacob was left alone, and a man wrestled with him until daybreak. 25 When he saw that he had not prevailed against him, he touched the socket of his thigh; so the socket of Jacob's thigh was dislocated as he wrestled with him. 26 Then he said, "Let me go, for the dawn is breaking." But he said, "I will not let you go unless you bless me." 27 And he said to him, "What is your name?" And he said, "Jacob." 28 And he said, "Your name shall no longer be called Jacob, but Israel,[1160] for you have struggled with God and with men and have prevailed." 29 Then Jacob asked him and said, "Please tell me your name." But he said, "Why is it that you ask my name?" And he blessed him there. 30 So Jacob named the place Peniel,[1161] for he said, "I have seen God face to face, yet my soul has been preserved."

It is all too obvious here that this man is simply a materialized angel in the form of a man, another angelic representative of Jehovah God. Moreover, the reader of this book should have taken in that the Israelites as a whole saw these angelic representatives, and spoke of them as though they were dealing directly with Jehovah God himself.

This proved to be the case in the second example found in the book of Judges where an angelic representative visited Manoah and his wife. Like the above mentioned account, Manoah and his wife treated this angelic representative as if he were Jehovah God himself: "And Manoah said to the angel of the Lord, 'What is your name, so that, when your words come true, we may honor you?' And the

---

[1160] Meaning *he contends with God*

[1161] Meaning *face of God*

angel of the Lord said to him, 'Why do you ask my name, seeing it is wonderful?' Then Manoah knew that he was the angel of the Lord. And Manoah said to his wife, "We shall surely die, *for we have seen God.*" – Judges 13:3–22.

Inerrancy: Are There Mistakes?

I have addressed the alleged contradictions, so it would seem that our job is done here, right? Not hardly. Yes, there are just as many who claim that the Bible is full of mistakes.

Critic: Matthew 27:5 states that Judas hanged himself, whereas Acts 1:18 says, "Falling headlong, he burst open in the middle and all his intestines gushed out."

Matthew 27:5 Updated American Standard Version (UASV)

5 And he threw the pieces of silver into the temple and departed; and he went away and hanged himself.

Acts 1:18

18 (Now this man acquired a field with the price of his wickedness, and falling headlong, he burst open in the middle and all his intestines gushed out.

Answer: Neither Matthew nor Luke made a mistake. What you have is Matthew giving the reader the manner in which Judas committed suicide. On the other hand, Luke is giving the reader of Acts, the result of that suicide. Therefore, instead of a mistake, we have two texts that complement each other, really giving the reader the full picture. Judas came to a tree alongside a cliff that had rocks below. He tied the rope to a branch and the other end around his neck and jumped over the edge of the cliff in an attempt at hanging himself. One of two things could have happened: (1) the limb broke plunging him to the rocks below, or (2) the rope broke with the same result, and he burst open onto the rocks below.

Critic: The apostle Paul made a mistake when he quotes how many people died.

Numbers 25:9 Updated American Standard Version (UASV)

9 The ones who died in the plague were twenty-four thousand.

1 Corinthians 10:8 Updated American Standard Version (UASV)

8 Neither let us commit sexual immorality, as some of them committed sexual immorality, only to fall, twenty-three thousand of them in one day.

Answer: We must keep in mind the above principle that we spoke of, the *Intended Meaning of the Writer.* We live in a far more precise age today, where specificity is highly important. However, we round large numbers off (even estimate) all the time: "there were 237,000 people in Time Square last night." The simplest answer is that the number of people slain was in between 23,000 and 24,000, and both writers rounded the number off. However, there is even another possibility, because the book of Numbers specifically speaks of "all the chiefs of the people" (25:4-5), which could account for the extra 1,000, which is mentioned in

Numbers 24,000. Thus, you have the people killing the chiefs of the people and the plague killing the people. Therefore, both books are correct.

Critic: After 215 years in Egypt, the descendants of Jacob arrived at the Promised Land. As you recall they sinned against God and were sentenced to forty years in the wilderness. But once they entered the Promised Land, they buried Joseph's bones "at Shechem, in the piece of land that *Jacob bought* from the sons of Hamor the father of Shechem," as stated at Joshua 24:32. Yet, when Stephen had to defend himself before the Jewish religious leaders, he said that Joseph was buried "in the tomb that *Abraham had bought* for a sum of silver from the sons of Hamor." Therefore, at once it appears that we have a mistake on the part of Stephen.

Acts 7:15-16 Updated American Standard Version (UASV)

[15] And Jacob went down to Egypt and died, he and our fathers. [16] And they were brought back to Shechem and buried in the tomb that Abraham had bought for a sum of silver from the sons of Hamor in Shechem.

Genesis 23:17-18 Updated American Standard Version (UASV)

[17] So Ephron's field, which was in Machpelah, which faced Mamre, the field and cave which was in it, and all the trees which were in the field, that were in all its border around, were made over [18] to Abraham for a possession in the presence of the sons of Heth, before all who went in at the gate of his city.

Genesis 33:19 Updated American Standard Version (UASV)

[19] And he bought the piece of land where he had pitched his tent from the hand of the sons of Hamor, Shechem's father, for one hundred qesitahs.[1162]

Joshua 24:32 Updated American Standard Version (UASV)

[32] As for the bones of Joseph, which the sons of Israel brought up from Egypt, they buried them at Shechem, in the piece of land that Jacob bought from the sons of Hamor the father of Shechem for one hundred qesitahs.[1163] It became an inheritance of the sons of Joseph.

Answer: If we look back to Genesis 12:6-7, we will find that Abraham's first stop after entering Canaan from Haran was Shechem. It is here that Jehovah told Abraham: "To your offspring I will give this land." At this point Abraham built an altar to Jehovah. It seems reasonable that Abraham would need to purchase this land that had not yet been given to his offspring. While it is true that the Old Testament does not mention this purchase, it is likely that Stephen would be aware of such by way of oral tradition. As Acts chapter seven demonstrates, Stephen had a wide-ranging knowledge of Old Testament history.

Later, Jacob would have had difficulty laying claim to the tract of land that his grandfather Abraham had purchased, because there would have been a new generation of inhabitants of Shechem. This would have been many years after Abraham moved further south and Isaac moved to Beersheba, and including Jacob's

---

[1162] Or *pieces of money*; money of unknown value

[1163] Or *pieces of money*; money of unknown value

twenty years in Paddan-aram (Gen 28:6, 7). The simplest answer is that this land was not in use for about 120 years because of Abraham's extensive travels and Isaac's having moved away, leaving it unused; likely it was put to use by others. So, Jacob simply repurchased what Abraham had bought over a hundred years earlier. This is very similar to the time Isaac had to repurchase the well at Beersheba that Abraham had already purchased earlier. – Genesis 21:27–30; 26:26–32.

Genesis 33:18–20 tells us that 'Jacob bought this land for a hundred pieces of money, from the sons of Hamor.' This same transaction is also mentioned at Joshua 24:32, in reference to transporting Joseph's bones from Egypt, to be buried in Shechem.

We should also address the cave of Machpelah that Abraham had purchased in Hebron from Ephron the Hittite. The word "tomb" is not mentioned until Joshua 24:32, and is in reference to the tract of land in Shechem. Nowhere in the Old Testament does it say that Abraham bought a "tomb." The cave of Machpelah obtained by Abraham would eventually become a family tomb, receiving Sarah's body and, eventually, his own, and those of Isaac, Rebekah, Jacob, and Leah. (Genesis 23:14–19; 25:9; 49:30, 31; 50:13) Gleason L. Archer, Jr., concludes this Bible difficulty, saying:

> The reference to a *mnema* ("tomb") in connection with Shechem must either have been proleptic [to anticipate] for the later use of that shechemite tract for Joseph's tomb (i.e., 'the tomb that Abraham bought' was intended to imply 'the tomb location that Abraham bought"); or else conceivably the dative relative pronoun *ho* was intended elliptically [omission] for *en to topo ho onesato Abraam* ("in the place that Abraham bought") as describing the location of the *mnema* near the Oak of Moreh right outside Shechem. Normally Greek would have used the relative-locative adverb *hou* to express 'in which' or 'where'; but this would have left *onesato* ("bought") without an object in its own clause, and so *ho* was much more suitable in this context. (Archer 1982, 379–81)

Another solution could be that Jacob is being viewed as a representative of Abraham, for he is the grandson of Abraham. This was quite appropriate in Biblical times, to attribute the purchase to Abraham as the Patriarchal family head.

Critic: 2 Samuel 24:1 says that God moved David to count the Israelites, while 1 Chronicles 21:1 Satan, or a resister did. This would seem to be a clear mistake on the part of one of these authors.

2 Samuel 24:1 Updated American Standard Version (UASV)

[1] Now again the anger of Jehovah burned against Israel, and it incited David against them to say, "Go, number Israel and Judah."

1 Chronicles 21:1 Updated American Standard Version (UASV)

[1] Then Satan stood up against Israel and moved David to number Israel.

Answer: In this period of David's reign, Jehovah was very displeased with Israel, and therefore he did not prevent Satan from bringing this sin on them. Often in Scripture, it is spoken of as though God did something when he allowed an event

399

to take place. For example, it is said that God 'hardened Pharaoh's heart' (Exodus 4:21), when he actually allowed the Pharaoh's heart to harden.

Inerrancy: Are There Scientific Errors?

Many truths about God are beyond the scope of science. Science and the Bible are not at odds. In fact, we can thank modern day science as it has helped us to better under the creation of God, from our solar system to the universes, to the human body and mind. What we find is a level of order, precision, design, and sophistication, which points to a Designer, the eyes of many Christians, to an Almighty God, with infinite intelligence and power. The apostle Paul makes this all too clear, when he writes, "For his invisible attributes, namely, his eternal power and divine nature, have been clearly perceived, ever since the creation of the world, in the things that have been made. So they are without excuse." – Romans 1:20.

Back in the seventeenth century, the world-renowned scientist Galileo proved beyond any doubt that the earth was not the center of the universe, nor did the sun orbit the earth. In fact, he proved it to be the other way around (no pun intended), with the earth revolving around the sun. However, he was brought up on charges of heresy by the Catholic Church and ordered to recant his position. Why? From the viewpoint of the Catholic Church, Galileo was contradicting God's Word, the Bible. As it turned out, Galileo and science were correct, and the Church was wrong, for which it issued a formal apology in 1992. However, the point we wish to make here is that in all the controversy, the Bible was never in the wrong. It was a misinterpretation on the part of the Catholic Church and not a fault with the Bible. One will find no place in the Bible that claims the sun orbits the earth. So where would the Church get such an idea? The Church got such an idea from Ptolemy (b. about 85 C.E.), an ancient astronomer, who argued for such an idea.

As it usually turns out, the so-called contradiction between science and God's Word lies at the feet of those who are interpreting Scripture incorrectly. To repeat the sentiments of Galileo when writing to a pupil–Galileo expressed the same sentiments: "Even though Scripture cannot err, its interpreters and expositors can, in various ways. One of these, very serious and very frequent, would be when they always want to stop at the purely literal sense."[1164] I believe that today's scholars, in hindsight, would have no problem agreeing.

While the Bible is not a science textbook, it is scientifically accurate when it touches on matters of science.

The Circle of the Earth Hangs on Nothing

Isaiah 40:22 Updated American Standard Version (UASV)

22 It is he who sits above **the circle of the earth,**
    and its inhabitants are like grasshoppers;
who stretches out the heavens like a curtain,
    and spreads them like a tent to dwell in.

[1164] Letter from Galileo to Benedetto Castelli, December 21, 1613.

More than 2,500 years ago, the prophet Isaiah wrote that the earth is a circle or sphere. First, how would it be possible for Isaiah to know the earth is a circle or sphere, if not from inspiration? Scientific America writes, "As countless photos from space can attest, Earth is round–the "Blue Marble," as astronauts have affectionately dubbed it. Appearances, however, can be deceiving. Planet Earth is not, in fact, perfectly round."[1165] Scientifically speaking, the sun is not perfectly, absolutely 100 percent round but in everyday speech, this verse is both acceptable and accurate, when we keep in mind it is written from a human perspective, not from a scientific perspective. Moreover, Isaiah was not discussing astronomy; he was simply making an inspired observation that man came to realize once he was in space, looking back at the earth, it is round. See the section about title, "Intended Meaning of Writer."

Job 26:7 Updated American Standard Version (UASV)

⁷ "He stretches out the north over empty space
and hangs the earth on nothing.

Here the author describes the earth as hanging upon nothing. Many have never heard of the Greek mathematician and astronomer Eratosthenes. He was born in about 276 B.C.E. and received some of his education in Athens, Greece. In 240 B.C., the "Greek astronomer, geographer, mathematician and librarian Eratosthenes calculates the Earth's circumference. His data was rough, but he wasn't far off."[1166] While man very early on used their God given intelligence to arrive at some outstanding conclusion that were actually very accurate, we learn two points here. Eratosthenes was a very astute scientist, while Isaiah, who wrote some 500 years earlier, was no scientist at all. Moreover, Moses, who wrote the book of Job over 1,230 years before Eratosthenes, knew that the earth hung upon nothing.

How Is the Sun Standing Still Possible?

Joshua 10:13 Updated American Standard Version (UASV)

¹³ And the sun stood still, and the moon stopped,
until the nation avenged themselves of their enemies.
Is this not written in the Book of Jashar? The sun stopped in the midst of heaven and did not hurry to set for about a whole day.

The Canaanites had besieged the Gibeonites, a group of people that gained Jehovah God's backing because they had faith in Him. In this battle, Jehovah helped the Israelites continue their attack by causing "the sun [to stand] still, and the moon stopped, until the nation took vengeance on their enemies." (Jos 10:1-14) Those who accept God as the creator of the universe and life can accept that he would know a way of stopping the earth from rotating. However, there are other ways of understanding this account. We must keep in mind that the Bible speaks from an earthly observer point of view, so it need not be that he stopped the rotation. It

---

[1165] Charles Q. Choi (April 12, 2007). Scientific America. Strange but True: Earth Is Not Round. Retrieved Monday, August 03, 2015.

http://www.scientificamerican.com/article/earth-is-not-round/

[1166] Alfred, Randy (June 19, 2008). "June 19, 240 B.C.E: The Earth Is Round, and It's This Big". Wired. Retrieved Monday, August 03, 2015.

could have been a refraction of solar and lunar light rays, which would have produced the same effect.

Psalm 136:6 Updated American Standard Version (UASV)

⁶ to him who spread out the earth above the waters,
  for his lovingkindness is everlasting;

Hebrews 3:4 Updated American Standard Version (UASV)

⁴ For every house is built by someone, but the builder of all things is God.

2 Kings 20:8-11 Updated American Standard Version (UASV)

⁸ And Hezekiah said to Isaiah, "What shall be the sign that Jehovah will heal me, and that I shall go up to the house of Jehovah on the third day?" ⁹ And Isaiah said, "This shall be the sign to you from Jehovah, that Jehovah will do the thing that he has spoken: shall the shadow go forward ten steps or go back ten steps?" ¹⁰ And Hezekiah answered, "It is an easy thing for the shadow to decline ten steps; no, but let the shadow turn backward ten steps." ¹¹ And Isaiah the prophet cried to Jehovah, and he brought the shadow on the steps back ten steps, by which it had gone down on the steps of Ahaz.

How is it that the stars fought on behalf of Barak?

Judges 5:20 Updated American Standard Version (UASV)

²⁰ From heaven the stars fought, from their courses they fought against Sisera.

Judges 4:15 Updated American Standard Version (UASV)

¹⁵ And Jehovah routed Sisera and all his chariots and all his army with the edge of the sword before Barak; and Sisera alighted from his chariot and fled away on foot.

In the Bible, you have Biblical prose, and Biblical poetry.

Prose: language that is not poetry: (1) writing or speech in its normal continuous form, without the rhythmic or visual line structure of poetry **(2)** ordinary style of expression: writing or speech that is ordinary or matter-of-fact, without embellishment.

Poetry: literature in verse: (1) literary works written in verse, in particular verse writing of high quality, great beauty, emotional sincerity or intensity, or profound insight **(2) beauty or grace:** something that resembles poetry in its beauty, rhythmic grace, or imaginative, elevated, or decorative style.

We have a beautiful example of both of these forms of writing communication in chapters four and five of the book of Judges. Judges, Chapter 4 is a prose account of Deborah and Barak, while Judges Chapter 5 is a poetic account. As we have learned from the above, poetry is less concerned with accuracy than evoking emotions. Poetry has a license to say things like what we find in of 5:20, which is in the poetry chapter: "from heaven the stars fought." This can be said, and the reader is expected not to take the language literally. What we can surmise from it though, is that God was acting against Sisera in some way, there was divine intervention.

Procedures for Handling Biblical Difficulties

1. You need to be completely convinced a reason or understanding exists.

2. You need to have total trust and conviction in the inerrancy of the Scripture as originally written down.

3. You need to study the context and framework of the verse carefully, to establish what the author meant by the words he used. In other words, find the beginning and the end of the context that your passage falls within.

4. You need to understand exegesis: find the historical setting, determine author intent, study key words, and note parallel passages. You need to slow down and carefully read the account, considering exactly what is being said

5. You need to find a reasonable harmonization of parallel passages.

6. You need to consider a variety of trusted Bible commentaries, dictionaries, lexical sources, encyclopedias, as well as books on Bible difficulties.

7. You should investigate as to whether the difficulty is a transmission error in the original text.

8. You must always keep in mind that the historical accuracy of the biblical text is unmatched; that thousands of extant manuscripts some of which date back to the second century B.C. support the transmitted text of Scripture.

9. We must keep in mind that the Bible is a diverse book when it comes to literary styles: narrative, poetic, prophetic, and apocalyptic; also containing parables, metaphors, similes, hyperbole, and other figures of speech. Too often, these alleged errors are the result of a reader taking a figure of speech as literal, or reading a parable as though it is a narrative.

10. The Bible student needs to understand what level that the Bible intends to be exact in what is written. If Jim told a friend that 650 graduated with him from high school in 1984, it is not challenged, because it is all too clear that he is using rounded numbers and is not meaning to be precise.

Bibliography

Aland, Kurt and Barbara. *The Text of the New Testament.* Grand Rapids: Eerdmans, 1987.

Aldrich, C Joseph. *Lifestyle Evangelism.* Portland, OR: Multnoma Press, 1981.

Anders, Max. *Holman New Testament Commentary: vol. 8, Galatians, Ephesians, Philippians, Colossians.* Nashville, TN: Broadman & Holman Publishers, 1999.

Anders, Max, and Trent Butler. *Holman Old Testament Commentary: Isaiah.* Nashiville, TN: B&H Publishing, 2002.

Andrews, Edward D. *THE COMPLETE GUIDE TO BIBLE TRANSLATION: Bible Translation Choices and Principles.* Cambridge: Christian Publishing House, 2012.

—. *THE EVANGELISM HANDBOOK: How All Christians Can Effectively Share God's Word in Their Community.* Cambridge: Christian Publishing House, 2013.

Andrews, Edward D. *An Introduction to Bible Difficulties: So-called Errors and Contradictions.* Cambridge, OH: Christian Publlishing House, 2012.

—. *The Text of the New Testament: A Beginner's Guide to New Testament Textual Criticism.* Cambridge, OH: Bible-Translation.Net Books, 2012.

Archer, Gleason L. *A Survey of Old Testament Introduction (Revised and Expanded).* Chicago: Moody, 1994.

—. *Encyclopedia of Bible Difficulties.* Grand Rapids: Zondervan, 1982.

Arndt, William, Frederick W. Danker, and Walter Bauer. *A Greek-English Lexicon of the New Testament and Other Early Christian Literature. 3rd ed. .* Chicago: University of Chicago Press, 2000.

Arnold, Clinton E. *Zondervan Illustrated Bible Backgrounds Commentary: Matthew, Mark, Luke, vol. 1.* Grand Rapids, MI: Zondervan, 2002.

Baer, Daniel. *The Unquenchable Fire.* Maitland, FL: Xulon Press, 2007.

Bahnsen, Greg, and Van Til. *Apologetic .* (Phillipsburg, NJ: Presbyterian and Reformed, 1998.

Barbour, R. S. *Traditio-Historical Criticism of the Gospels.* London: SPCK, 1972.

Barclay, William. *The Letter to the Hebrews (New Daily Study Bible).* Louisville, KY: Westminster John Knox Press, 2002.

Barnett, Paul. *The Birth of Christianity: The First Twenty Years (After Jesus, Vol. 1) .* Grand Rapids, MI: Wm. B. Eerdmans , 2005.

Barton, John. *The Nature of Biblical Criticism.* Louisville: Westminster John Knox Press, 2007.

Barton, S.C. "'The Communal Dimension of Earliest Christianity'." *JTS 43*, 1992: 399–427.

—. *Discipleship and Family Ties in Mark and Matthew.* Cambridge: Cambridge University Press, 1994.

Bercot, David W. *A Dictionary of Early Christian Beliefs.* Peabody: Hendrickson, 1998.

Berkhof, Louis. *New Testament Introduction.* Grand Rapids: Eerdman-Sevensma, 1915.

—. *Principles of Biblical Interpretation.* . Grand Rapids, MI: Baker House, 1992.

Black, Allen, and Mark C Black. *THE COLLEGE PRESS NIV COMMENTARY 1 & 2 PETER.* Joplin: College Press Publishing Company, 1998.

Blenkinsopp, Joseph. *Isaiah 56-66: A New Translation with Introduction and Commentary.* New York: Anchor Bible, 2003.

Blomberg, Craig L. *Historical Reliability of the Gospels.* Downer Groves, IL: IVP Academic, 2007.

Blomberg, Craig L. "New Testament miracles and Higher Criticism: Climbing Up the Slippery Slope." *JETS 27/4*, December 1984: 436.

Blomberg, Craig L, and Stanley E., Stovell, Beth M Porter Jr. *Biblical Hermeneutics Five Views.* Downers Grove: InterVarsity Press, 2012.

Bock, Darrell L. *"Form Criticism," in New Testament Criticism and Interpretation. Edited by David A. Black and David S. Dockery.* Grand Rapids: Zondervan, 1991.

—. *Studying the Historical Jesus: A Guide to Sources and Methods.* Grand Rapids, MI: Baker, 2002.

—. *The Missing Gospels: Unerthing the Truth Behind Alternative Christianities.* Nashville, TN: Thomas Nelson, 2006.

Bradley, Anthony B. *Liberating Black Theology: The Bible and the Black Experience in America.* Wheaton: Crossway, 2010.

Bray, Gerald. *Biblical Interpretation: Past and Present.* Downers Grove, IL: InterVarsity Press, 1996.

Bridges, Jerry. *The Practice of Godliness* . Colorado Springs, CO: : NavPress, 1983.

Briley, Terry R. *The College Press NIV Commentary: Isaiah.* Joplin, MO: ollege Press Pub, 2000.

Bromiley, Geoffrey W. *The International Standard Bible Encyclopedia (Vol. 1-4).* Grand Rapids, MI: William B. Eerdmans Publishing Co., 1986.

Bruce, F. F. *The New International Commentary on the New Testament: The Epistle to the Hebrews (Revised).* Grand Rapids, MI: William B. Eermans Publishing Company, 1990.

Bucher, Christina. "New Directions in Biblical Interpretation Revisited." *Bretheren Life and Thought 60, no. 1*, Spring 2015: 36.

Bultmann, Rudolf. *The History of the Synoptic Tradition.* Peabody: Hendrickson, 1990.

—. *The History of the Synoptic Tradition. Translated by John Marsh. Revised Edition.* Peabody, MA: Hendrickson, 1963.

Bultmann, Rudolf. "The New Approach to the Synoptic Problem." *Journal of Religion*, July, 1926: 345.

Bultmann, Rudolf, and Frederick C. Translated by Grant. *"The Study of the Synoptic Gospels," in Form Criticism, Two Essays on New Testament Research.* . New York: Harper & Brothers, 1932.

Burge, Gary M. *Interpreting the Fourth Gospel, Guides to New Testament Exegesis, vol. 3.* Grand Rapids, MI: Baker Book House, 1992.

Byrne, James M. *Religion and the Enlightenment from Descartes to Kant.* Louisville: Westminster John Knox Press, 1996.

Caba, Tedl et al.,. *The Apologetics Study Bible: Real Questions, Straight Answers, Stronger Faith.* Nashville: Holman Bible Publishers, 2007.

Caird, George B. "The Study of the Gospels: II. Form Criticism." *Expository Times LXXXVII*, February 1976: 139.

Carson, D. A, and Douglas J Moo. *An Introduction to the New Testament.* Grand Rapids, MI: Zondervan, 2005.

Carson, D. A. *New Bible Commentary: 21st Century Edition. 4th ed.* Downers Grove: Inter-Varisity Press, 1994.

Cassuto, Umberto. *The Documentary Hypothesis: And The Composition of the Pentateuch.* Jerusalem: Shalem Press, 2006.

Coleman, E. Robert. *The Master Plan of Evangelism.* Westwood, NJ: Fleming H. Revell Company, 1964.

Comfort, Philip. *Encountering the Manuscripts: An Introduction to New Testament Paleography and Textual Criticism.* Nashville: Broadman & Holman, 2005.

—. *Encounterring the Manuscripts: An Introduction to New Testament Paleography and Textual Criticism.* Nashville: Broadman & Holman, 2005.

Comfort, Philip W. *New Testament Text and Translation Commentary.* Carol Stream: Tyndale House Publishers, 2008.

Comfort, Philip, and David Barret. *The Text of the Earliest New Testament Greek Manuscripts.* Wheaton: Tyndale House Publishers, 2001.

Cook, Stephen L. "Introduction: Case Studies from the Second Wave of Research in the Social World of the Hebrew Bible," ed. Ronald Simkins and Athalya Brenner." *Semeia 87*, 1999: 1-2.

Cottrell, Peter, and Maxwell Turner. *Linguistics and Biblical Interpretation.* Downers Grove: InterVarsity Press, 1989.

Cruse, C. F. *Eusebius' Eccliatical History.* Peabody, MA: Hendrickson, 1998.

Daly, Mary. *Beyond God the Father: Toward a Philosophy of Liberation.* Boston: Beacon Press, 1973.

Davies, William D. *Invitation to the New Testament, A Guide to Its Main Witnesses.* Garden City, N.Y.: Doubleday, 1966.

Davis, John J. *Paradise to Prison: Studies in Genesis.* Salem: Sheffield, 1975.

Delahaunty, R. J. *Spinoza: Arguments of the Philosophers.* London: Routledge & Kegan Paul Books, 1985.

Dockery, David S., Kenneth A. Matthews, and Robert B. Sloan. *Foundations for Biblical Interpretation.* Nashville: Broadman & Holman Publishers, 1994.

Dodd, C. H. *History and the Gospel.* London: Nisbet, 1938.

Donald A. Hanger, The Jewish Reclamation of Jesus. Eugene: Wipf and Stock, 1997.

Driver, G R. *Canaanite Myths and Legends.* New York: T. & T. Clark, 1971.

Dunn, James D. G. *"The Messianic Secret in Mark," in The Messianic Secret Edited by Christopher Tuckett.* Philadelphia: Fortress, 1983.

Eims, LeRoy. *One to One Evangelism.* Wheaton, IL: Victor Books, 1974, 1990.

Ellingworth, Paul. *The Epistle to the Hebrews: A Commentary on the Greek Text.* Grand Rapids, MI: W.B. Eerdmans, 1993.

Elliott, J.H. *A Home for the Homeless: A Sociological Exegesis of I Peter: Its Situation and Strategy .* London: SCM Press, 1982.

Elliott, John H. "Social-Scientific Criticism of the New Testament: More on Methods and Models." *Semeia 35*, 1986: 6-7.

—. *What is Social Scientific Criticism? .* Minneapolis: Fortress Press, 1993.

Elwell, Walter A. *Evangelical Dictionary of Theology (Second Edition).* Grand Rapids: Baker Academic, 2001.

Elwes, R H M. *A Theologico-political Treatise, and a Political Treatise .* New York, NY: Cosimo Classics , 2005.

Erickson, Milliard J. *Christian Theology.* Grand Rapids, MI: Baker Academic, 1998.

Erickson, Richard J. *A Beginner's Guide to New Testament Exegesis.* Downers Grove: InterVarsity Press, 2005.

Esler, Philip F. *The First Christians in their Social Worlds .* New York: Taylor & Francis, 2007.

—. *The First Christians in their Social Worlds.* New York: Routledge, 1994.

Farmer, William R. *The Synoptic Problem.* Macon, Ga: Mercer University, 1976.

Farnell, F. David. "Historical Criticism vs. Grammatico-Historical Criticism?" *The Jesus Quest*, Quo Vadis Evangelicals: 503-520.

Fasold, Ralph, Jeff Connor-Linton, and ed. *An Introduction to Language and Linguistics*. Cambridge: Cambridge University Press, 2006.

Fee, Gordon D. *New Testament Exegesis: A Handbook for Studemts and Pastors*. Louisville: Westminister John Knox Press, 2002.

Ferguson, Everett. *Backgrounds of Early Christianity*. Grand Rapids, MI: Wm. B. Eerdmans, 2003.

Frame, John M. *Apologetics to the Glory of God*. Phillipsburg: P&R Publishing, 1994.

Frampton, Travis L. *Spinoza and the Rise of Historical Criticism of the Bible*. New York: T&T Clark, 2006.

Free, J. P. *Archaeology and Bible History (Revised amnd Expanded Edition)*. Grand Rapids: Zondervan, 1992.

Friedan, Betty. *The Feminist Mistique* . New York: Dell Publishing, 1963.

Friedman, Richard Elliot. *Who Wrote The Bible*. San Francisco: Harper Collins, 1997.

Friedman, Richard Elliott. *The Bible With Sources Revealed*. Northampton: Harper Collins, 2005.

Garrett, Don. *The Cambridge companion to Spinoza*. Cambridge: Cambridge University Press, 1996.

Geisler, Norman L. *Defending Inerrancy: Affirming the Accuracy of Scripture for a New Generation*. Grand Rapids, MI: Baker Books, 2012.

—. *Inerrancy*. Grand Rapids, MI: Zondervan, 1980.

Geisler, Norman L, and William E Nix. *A General Introduction to the Bible*. Chicago: Moody Press, 1996.

Geisler, Norman L. *"Inductivism, Materialism, and Rationalism: Bacon, Hobbes, and Spinoza," in The Biblical Errancy: An Analysis of Its Philosophical Roots. Edited by Norman Geisler*. Grand Rapids: Zondervan, 1981.

—. *Baker Encyclopedia of Christian Apologetics*. Grand Rapids: Baker Books, 1999.

—. *Biblical Errancy: An Analysis of Its Philosophical Roots*. Eugene, OR: Wipf and Stock Publisher, 1981.

Geisler, Norman L., and Thomas Howe. *The Big Book of Bible Difficulties*. Grand Rapids: Baker Books, 1992.

Geisler, Norman, and David Geisler. *CONVERSATION EVANGELISM: How to Listen and Speak So You Can Be Heard*. Eugene: Harvest House Publishers, 2009.

Geisler, Norman, and Ron Brooks. *When Skeptics Ask* . Grand Rapids, MI: Baker Books, 1996.

Gilson, Etienne, and Thomas Langan. *Modern Philosophy: Descartes to Kant.* New York: Random House, 1963.

Goodspeed, Edgar J. *Matthew, Apostle and Evangelist.* Philadelphia: John C. Winston, 1959.

Goodspeed, J. *Matthew, Apostle and Evangelist.* Philadelphia: John C. Winston, 1959.

Gorman, Michael J. *Elements of Biblical Exegesis: A Basic Guide for Students and Ministers.* Peabody: Hendrickson, 2001.

Green, Joel B, Scot McKnight, and Howard Marshall. *Dictionary of Jesus and the Gospels.* Downers Grove, IL: InterVarsity Press, 1992.

Greenlee, J Harold. *Introduction to New Testament Textual Criticism.* Peabody: Hendrickson, 1995.

Grenz, Stanley J., and Roger E Olsen. *20th Century Theology: God & the World in a Transitional Age.* Downers Gove: Intervarsity Press, 1992.

Grudem, Wayne, Leland Ryken, John C Collins, Vern S Poythress, and Bruce Winter. *Translating Truth: The Case for Essentially Literal Bible Translation.* Wheaton: Crossway Books, 2005.

Guelich, Robert A. *The Sermon on the Mount, A Foundation for Understanding.* Waco, TX: Word, 1982.

Gundry, Robert H. *The Use of the Old Testament in St. Matthew's Gospel.* Leiden: E. J. Brill, 1967.

Gundry, Robert H. "The Language Milieu of First-Century Palestine." *Journal of Biblical Literature 83*, 1964: 408.

Gunkel, Hermann (Translated by Scullion, John J. Edited by Scott, William R.). *The Stories of Genesis.* Berkeley: BIBAL, 1994.

Gunkel, Hermann. *The Stories of Genesis. Translated by John J. Scullion. Edited by William R. Scott.* Berkeley: BIBAL, 1994.

Guthrie, Donald. *Introduction to the New Testament (Revised and Expanded).* Downers Grove, IL: InterVarsity Press, 1990.

Guthrie, George H. *The NIV Application Commentary: Hebrews.* Grand Rapids, MI: Zondervan, 1998.

Gutierrez, Gustavo. *A Theology of Liberation: History, Politics, and Salvation.* Maryknoll, NY: Orbis Books, 1988.

Habib, M. A. R. *A History of Literary Criticism and Theory from Plato to the Present.* Malden: Blackwell Publishing, 2008.

Hagner, Donald. *The New Testament, History, and the Historical Critical Method, in New Testament Criticism and Interpretation.* Grand Rapids: Baker, 2013.

Hanson, K. C., and Douglas E. Oakman. *Palestine in the time of Jesus* . Minneapolis: : Augsburg Press, 1998.

Harris, Robert Laird, Gleason Leonard Archer, and Bruce K Waltke. *Theological Wordbook of the Old Testament.* Chicago: Moody Press, 1999, c1980.

Harrison, Everett F. *Introduction to the New Testament.* Grand Rapids: Eerdmans, 1971.

Hasel, Gerhard F. *Understanding the Living Word of God.* . Mountain View, CA: Pacific Press, 1980.

Hayes, John H, and Carl R Holladay. *Biblical Exegesis: A Beginner's Handbook.* Lousiville, KY: Westminister John Knox Press, 2007.

Hill, Jonathan. *Zondervan Handbook to the History of Christianity.* Oxford: Lion, 2006.

Hindson, Ed, and Ergun Caner. *The Popular Encyclopedia of Apologetics: Surveying the Evidence for the Truth of Christianity.* Eugene: Harvest House, 2008.

Hoerth, Alfred. *Archaeology and the Old Testament.* Grand Rapids: Baker, 1998.

Holbert, John C, and Alyce M McKenzie. *What Not to Say: Avoiding the Common Mistakes that Can Sink Your Sermon.* Lousiville: Westminster Knox Press, 1972.

House, Paul R. *The New American Commentary: 2 Kings* . Nashville: Broadman & Holman Publishers, 2001.

—. *The New American Commentary: Vol. 8., 2 Kings.* Nashville: Broadman & Holman Publishers, 2001.

Howe, Thomas A. *Objectivity in Biblical Interpretation.* North Charleston: CreateSpace, 2015.

Hume, David. *An Enquiry Concerning Human Understanding (vol. 35).* Chicago: Great Books of the Western World, 1952.

Hume, David, and Adam Smith. *An Enquiry Concerning Human Understanding: And Selections from a Treatise of Human Nature.* New York: Barnes & Noble Library of Essential Reading, 2004.

Hutchison, John C. "Darwin's Evolutionary Theory and 19th-Century Natural Theology." *Bibliotheca Sacra 152,* July-September 1995: 334.

Huxley, Thomas H. *Science and Christian Tradition.* New York: D. Appleton, 1899.

Jeremias, Joachim. *New Testament Theology.* New York: Charles Scribner's Sons, 1971.

Johnson, Phillip E. *Darwin on Trial. Second Edition.* Downers Grove: InterVarsity, 1993.

Kaiser, Christopher B. *Creational Theology and the History of Physical Science: The Creationist Tradition from Basil to Bohr.* Leiden: Brill, 1997.

Kaiser, Walter C, and Moises Silva. *Introduction to Biblical Hermeneutics: The Search for Meaning.* Grand Rapids: Zondervan, 1994, 2007.

Käsemann, Ernst. *"The Problem of the Historical Jesus," in Essays on New Testament Themes. Translated by W. J. Montague.* Philadelphia: Fortress Press, 1982.

Kassian, Mary A. *The Feminist Mistake.* Wheaton, IL: Crossway Books, 2005.

Keil, Carl Friedrich, and Franz Delitzsch. *Commentary on the Old Testament.* Peabody, MA: Hendrickson, 1996.

—. *Commentary on the Old Testament.* Peabody, MA: Hendrickson, 2002.

Kelber, Wegner H. *The Oral and the Written Gospel.* Philadelphia: Fortress, 1983.

Keller, Werner. *Archaeology & Science Delve 4,000 Years into the Past to Document THE BIBLE AS HISTORY (2nd Revised ed.).* New York: Hodder and Stoughton, 1980.

Kennedy, D. James. *Evangelism Explosion.* Wheaton, IL: Tyndale House Publishers, 1977.

Kenneth, Boa., and Kruidenier. *Holman New Testament Commentary: Romans, Vol. 6.* Nashville, TN: Broadman & Holman, 2000.

Kimel Jr., Alvin F. Kimel Jr., and ed. *This Is My Name Forever: The Trinity & Gender Language for God.* Downers Grove: InterVarsity Press, 2001.

Kistemaker, Simon J, and William Hendriksen. *New Testament Commentary: vol. 15, Exposition of Hebrews.* Grand Rapids: Baker Book House, 1953-2001.

Kitchen, K A. *On the Reliability of the Old Testament.* Grand Rapids: Eerdmans, 2003.

Kitchen, K. A. *The Ancient Orient and Old Testament.* Downers Grove, IL: InterVarsity Press, 1975.

Krentz, Edgar. *The Historical-Critical Method.* Philadelphia: Fortress Press, 1975.

—. *The Historical-Critical Method.* Philadelphia: Fortress Press, 1975.

Kümmel, Werner Georg. *The New Testament: The History of the Investigation of Its Problems, trans. S. McLean Gilmour and Howard C. Kee.* Nashville: Abingdon Press, 1970.

Kugel, James L. *How to Read the Bible: A Guide to Scripture, Then and Now.* New York: Free Press, 2008.

Ladd, George Eldon. *The New Testament and Criticism.* Grand Rapids: Eerdmans, 1967.

Lantz, Charles Craig. *Hermeneutics: The Art and Science of Biblical Interpretation.* Seattle, WA: Create Space, 2012.

Larsen, L. David. *The Evangelism Mandate.* Wheaton: Crossway Books, 1992.

Larson, Knute. *Holman New Testament Commentary, vol. 9, I & II Thessalonians, I & II Timothy, Titus, Philemon.* Nashville, TN: Broadman & Holman Publishers, 2000.

Lawrence, Paul, and Alan Millard. *The IVP Atlas of Bible History.* Downers Grove, IL: Intervarsity Press, 2006.

Lea, Thomas D. *Holman New Testament Commentary: Hebrews, James.* Nashville, TN: Broadman & Holman Publishers, 1999.

—. *Holman New Testament Commentary: Vol. 10, Hebrews, James.* Nashville, TN: Broadman & Holman Publishers, 1999.

Legaspi, Michael C. *The Death of Scripture and the Rise of Biblical Studies.* Oxford: Oxford University Press, 2010.

Lemche, Niels Peter. *The Old Testament Between Theology and History: A Critical Survey.* Louisville: Westminster John Knox Press, 2008.

Lenski, R. C. H. *Interpretation of the I & II Epistles of Peter the Three Epistles of John, and the Epistle of Jude.* Minneapolis: Augsburg Fortress, 1945, 2008.

—. *The Interpretation of The Acts of the Apostles.* Minneapolis, MN: Ediciones Sigueme, 1961.

Licona, Michael R. *The Resurrection of Jesus, A New Historiographical Approach.* Downers Grove: InterVarsity Press, 2010.

Lightfoot, J. B. *Essays on the Work Entitled Supernatural Religion.* London: Macmillan and Co., 1889.

Lightfoot, Neil R. *How We Got the Bible.* Grand Rapids, MI: Baker Books, 1963, 1988, 2003.

Lightfoot, Richard H. *History and Interpretation in the Gospels.* New York and London: Harper and Brothers, 1934.

Lightfoot, Robert H. *History and Interpretation of the Gospels.* (New York and London: Harper and Brothers, 1934.

Lindsell, Harold. *The Battle for the Bible.* Grand Rapids: Zondervan, 1976.

Linnemann. *Is There A Synoptic Problem? Rethinking the Literary Dependance of the First Three Gospels.* Grand Rapids, MI: Baker Book House, 1992.

Linnemann, Eta. *Biblical Criticism on Trial: How Scientific is "Scientific Theology"?* Grand Rapids: Kregel, 2001.

—. *Historical Criticism of the Bible: Methododology or Ideaology?* Grand Rapid, MI: Kregel Publications, 1990.

Longman, III, Tremper. *Literary Approaches to Biblical Interpretation.* Grand Rapids: Zondervan Publishing House, 1987.

Longman, Tremper III. *Reading the Bible: With Heart & Mind.* Colorado Springs: NavPress, 1997.

MacArthur, John. *The MacArthur Bible Commentary.* Nashville: Thomas Nelson, 2005.

Machen, J. Gresham. "Christianity and Culture." *Princeton Theological Review*, 1913: 7.

—. *The Christian Faith in the Modern World.* Grand Rapids: Eerdmans, 1965 [1936].

Maier, Gerhard. *The End of the Historical-Critical Method. Translated by Edwin W. Leverenz and Rudolf F. Norden.* St. Louis: Concordia, 1977.

Maier, Herhard. *The End of the Historical-Critical Method.* St. Loius, MO: Concordia Publishing House, 1974.

Malina, Bruce.J. *The Social Gospel of Jesus: The Kingdom of God in Mediterranean Perspective.* Minneapolis: Fortress Press, 2001.

Marshall, I. Howard. *A Critical and Exegetical Commentary on the Pastoral Epistles.* New York, London: T&T Clark LTD, 2004.

—. *Historical Criticism, lin New Testament Interpretation.* Grand Rapids: Eerdmans, 1977.

Mayers, Mark K. *Christianity Confronts Culture: A Strategy for Crosscultural Evangelism.* Grand Rapids : Zondervan, 1987.

McCue, Rolland. *Promises Unfulfilled: The Failed Strategy of Modern Evangelism.* Greenville, SC: Ambassador Group, 2004.

McGrath, Alister. "Why Evangelicalism is the Future of Protestantism." *Christianity Today*, June 19, 1995: 18-23.

McKay, K. L. *A New Syntax of the Verb in New Testament Greek.* New York: Peter Lang, 1994.

McKenzie, Stephen L, and Stephen R Hayes. *An Introduction to Biblical Criticism and Their Application: To Each its Own Meaning.* Louisville: John Knox Press, 1999.

McKnight, Edgar V. *Postmodern Use of the Bible: The Emergence of Reader-Oriented Criticism.* Nashville: Abingdon Press, 1988.

—. *What is Form Criticism?* Philadelphia: Fortress, 1969.

McKnight, Edgar V. *"Form and Redaction Criticism." The New Testament and Its Modern Interpreters.* Philadelphia: Fortress Press, 1989.

McRaney, William. *The Art of Personal Evangelism.* Nashville: Broadman & Holman, 2003.

McRay, John. *Archaeology and the New Testament.* Grand Rapids: Baker House Books, 1991.

Metzger, Bruce M. *The Text of the New Testament: Its Transmission, Corruption, and Transmission.* New York: Oxford University Press, 1964, 1968, 1992.

Metzger, Bruce M. *A Textual Commentary on the Greek New Testament.* New York: United Bible Society, 1994.

Mirriam-Webster, Inc. *Mirriam-Webster's Collegiate Dictionary. Eleventh Edition.* Springfield: Mirriam-Webster, Inc., 2003.

Morgan, Robert. *"Rudolf Bultmann," in The Modern Theologians, vol. 1 in An Introduction to Christian Theology in the Twentieth Century. Edited by David F. Ford.* New York: Basil Blackwell, 1989.

Morgenthaler, Sally. *Worship Evangelism.* Grand Rapids: Zondervan Publishing House, 1995.

Morris, Leon. *The Gospel According to Matthew.* Grand Rapids, MI: Inter-Varsity Press, 1992.

Mounce, Robert H. *Matthew, vol. 1 in the New International Biblical Commentary. Edited by W. Ward Gasque.* Peabody, MA: Hendrickson, 1991.

Mounce, William D. *Mounce's Complete Expository Dictionary of Old & New Testament Words.* Grand Rapids, MI: Zondervan, 2006.

Mounce, William D. *Basics of Biblical Greek Grammar.* Grand Rapids: Zonervan, 2009.

Nagel, Thomas. *The View from Nowhere.* New York: Oxford University Press, 1986.

Neil, Stephen, and Tom Wright. *The Interpretation of the New Testament, 1861-1986. Second Edition.* Oxford: Oxford University, 1988.

Nicholson, Ernest. *The Pentateuch in the Twentieth Century: The Legacy of Julius Wellhausen.* New York: Oxford University Press, 1998.

Niessen, Richard. "The virginity of the `almah in Isaiah 7:14." *Bibliotheca Sacra 137*, 1980: 133-50.

Nineham, D. E. "Eyewitness Testimony and the Gospel Tradition—I." *Journal of Theological Studies 9*, April 1958: 13.

Oden, Thomas C. *Ministry Through Word and Sacrament, Classic Pastoral Care.* New York: Crossroad, 1989.

Orchard, Bernard. *J. J. Griesbach: Synoptic and Text - Critical Studies*. Cambridge: Cambridge University Press, 1776-1976, 2005.

Orchard, Bernard, and Thomas R. W. Longstaff. *J. J. Griesbach: Synoptic and text-critical studies 1776-1976.* Cambridge: Cambridge University, 1978.

Osborne, Grant R. *THE HERMENEUTICAL SPIRAL A Comprehensive Introduction to Biblical Interpretation (2nd Edition).* Downers Grove, IL: InterVarsity Press, 2006.

Oswalt, John N. *The NIV Application Commentary: Isaiah.* Grand Rapids, MI: Zondervan, 2003.

Outlaw, W. Stanley. *The Book of Hebrews*. Nashville, TN: Randall House, 2005.

Packer, J. I. *Evangelism and Sovereignty of God.* Downers Grove, Il: InterVarsity Press, 1961.

Packer, J. I. *Evangelism and the Sovereignty of God.* Downers Grove, IL: InterVarsity Press, 1979.

Perrin, Norman. *Rediscovering the Teaching of Jesus.* New York: Harper and Row, 1976.

—. *What is Redaction Criticism?* Philadelphia: Fortress, 1969.

Pink, Arthur Walkington. *An Exposition of Hebrews.* Swengel, PA: Bible Truth Depot, 1954.

—. *Objections to God's Sovereignty Answered.* Bellingham: Logos Bible Software, 2005.

Polhill, John B. *The New American Commentary 26: Acts.* Nashville: Broadman & Holman Publishers, 2001.

Porter, Stanley E. *Handbook to Exegesis of the New Testament.* Leiden, NY: Koninklijke, 1997.

Posterski, C. Donald. *Reinventing Evangelism.* Downers Grove, IL: InterVarsity Press, 1989.

Powell, Doug. *Holman QuickSource Guide to Christian Apologetics.* Nashville, TN: Holman Reference, 2006.

Pratt Jr, Richard L. *Holman New Testament Commentary: I & II Corinthians, vol. 7.* Nashville: Broadman & Holman Publishers, 2000.

Rainer, S. Thomas. *Evangelism in the Twenty-First Century.* Wheaton, IL: Harold Shaw Publishers, 1989.

Rainer, Thom S. *Surprising Insights From the Unchurched and Proven Ways to Reach Them.* Grand Rapids, MI: Zondervan, 2001.

Ramm, Bernard. *Protestant Biblical Interpretation: A Textbook of Hermeneutics, 3rd rev. ed.* Grand Rapids, MI: Baker, 1999.

Rast, Walter E. *Tradition History and the Old Testament.* Philadelphia: Fortress Press, 1972.

Reginald H. Fuller, The New Testament in Current Study. New York: Charles Scribner's Sons, 1962.

Reid, Alvin. *Introduction to Evangelism.* Nashville: Boardman & Holmes , 1998.

Reid, Alvin L. *Radically Unchurched: Who They are and How to Reach Them.* Grand Rapids: Kregel, 2002.

Rendtorff, R. "The Problem of the Process of Transmission in the Pentateuch." *JSOT*, 1990: 101.

Richards, E. Randolph. *Paul And First-Century Letter Writing: Secretaries, Composition and Collection.* Downers Grove: InterVarsity Press, 2004.

Richardson, A, W Schweitzer, and ed. *Biblical Authority for Today.* Philadelphia: Westminster Press, 1951.

Roberts, Alexander, James Donaldson, and Cleveland Coxe. *The Ante-Nicene Fathers Vol.I: Translations of the Writings of the Fathers Down to A.D. 325*. Oak Harbor: Logos , 1997.

Robertson, A. T. *An Introduction to the Textual Criticism of the New Testament.* London: Hodder & Stoughton, 1925.

Robertson, A.T. *Word Pictures in the New Testament.* Oak Harbor, MI: Logos Research Systems, 1933, 1997.

Robinson, G. L., and R. K. Harrison. *The International Standard Bible Encyclopedia, vol. 2.* Grand Rapids: Eerdmans, 1982.

Robinson, John A. T. *Can We Trust the New Testament? "The New Testament Dating Game," Time.* Grand Rapids: Eerdmans, 1977.

—. *Redating the New Testament.* Philadelphia: Fortress, 1976.

Rogers, Jack B, and Donald K. McKim. *The Authority and Interpretation of the Bible, An Historical Approach.* New York: Harper & Row, 1979.

Rooker, Mark F. *The New American Commentary, vol. 3A, Leviticus.* Nashville: Broadman & Holman Publishers, 2000.

Ropes, J. H. *The Synoptic Gospels, 2nd Impression with New Preface.* Cambridge: Harvard University, 1960.

Ruether, Rosemary Radford. *Women-Church: Theology and Practice of Feminist Liturgical Communities.* San Francisco: Harper and Row, 1986.

Russell, Letty M, and ed. *Feminist Interpretation of the Bible.* Philadelphia: Westminster Press, 1985.

Ryken, Leland. *Choosing a Bible: Understanding Bible Translation Differences.* Wheaton: Crossway Books, 2005.

—. *The Word of God in English.* Wheaton: Crossway Books, 2002.

—. *Understanding English Bible Translation: The Case for an Essentially Literal Approach.* Wheaton, IL: Crossway Books, 2009.

Sayce, A. H. *The Early History of the Hebrews.* London: Rivingtons, 1897.

Schweitzer, Albert. *The Quest of the Historical Jesus. Introduction by James M. Robinson. Trans. By W. Montgomery from the first German Edition.* New York: Macmillan, 1906, 1968.

Sisson, Dick. *Evangelism Encounter.* Chicago, IL: Victor Books, 1988.

Smith, Gary. *The New American Commentary: Isaiah 1-39, Vol. 15a.* Nashville, TN: B & H Publishing Group, 2007.

—. *The New American Commentary: Isaiah 40-66, Vol. 15b.* Nashville, TN: B&H Publishing, 2009.

Soulen, Richard N, and R. Kendall Soulen. *Handbook of Biblical Criticism. Edited by Richard N. Soulen.* Atlanta: John Knox, 1981.

Souter, Alexander. *The Text and Canon of the New Testament.* New York: Charles Scribner's Sons, 1913.

Speiser, E. A. *Genesis Anchor Bible 1.* Garden City: Doubleday, 1964.

Spinoza, Baruch. *Theological-Political Treatise, in Complete Works, trans. Samuel Shirley, ed. Michael L. Morgan.* Indianapolis: Hackett Publishing Company, 2002.

Spong, John Shelby. *Living in Sin: A Bishop Rethinks Human Sexuality. .* New York, NY: HaperCollins Publishers, 1990.

Sproul, R.C. *Knowing Scripture. .* Downers Grove, IL: Intervarsity Press, 1978.

Stanton, Elizabeth Cady. *The Woman's Bible .* Seattle, WA: Kindle Edition 2012, 1895.

—. *The Women's Bible.* Boston: Northeastern University Press, 1993.

Stein, Robert H. *A Basic Guide to Interpreting the Bible: Playing by the Rules.* Grand Rapids: Baker Books, 1994.

Stonehouse, , Ned B. *The Origins of the Synoptic Gospels.* Grand Rapids: Eerdmans, 1963.

Strauss, David Friedrich. *A New Life of Jesus. Authorized Translation. Second Edition.* Williams and Norgate: Covent Garden, 1879.

—. *The Life of Jesus Critically Examined. Edited by Peter C. Hodgson. Translated by George Eliot.* Philadelphia: Fortress, 1972.

Streeter, Burnett H. *The Four Gospels, A Study of Origins.* London: Macmillan, 1953.

Streeter, Burnett Hillman. *The Four Gospels, A Study of Origins.* London: Macmillan and Co., 1924.

Stuart, Douglas. *Old Testament Exegesis: A Handbook for Students and Pastors (Fourth Edition).* Louisville: Westminister John Knox Press, 2009.

Tacitus. *The Histories, Books IV-V, Annals Books I-III (Loeb Classical Library No. 249).* Cambridge, MA: Harvard University Press, 1931.

Taylor, Vincent. *The Formation of the Gospel Tradition.* London: Macmillan, 1953.

Tenney, Merrill C. et. al. *Zondervan Pictorial Encyclopedia of the Bible.* Grand Rapids: Zondervan, 1975.

Terry, Milton S. *Biblical Hermeneutics: A Treatise on the Interpretation of the Old and New Testaments.* Grand Rapids: Zondervan, 1883.

Theissen, Gerd. *Psychological aspects of Pauline Theology.* Philadelphia, PA: Fortress Press, 1987.

—. *Sociology of Early Palestinian Christianity. .* Philadelphia, PA : Fortress Press, 1977.

—. *The Social Setting of Pauline Christianity. .* Philadelphia, PA : Fortress Press, 1982.

Theissen, Gerd, and Annette Mertz. *The Historical Jesus: A comprehensive Guide*. Minneapolis, MN: Augsburg Fortress, 1998.

Thiselton, Anthony C. *The Two Horizons: New Testament Hermeneutics and Philosophical Description* . Grand Rapids: Eerdmans, 1980.

Thomas, Robert L. "Current Hermeneutical Trends: Toward Explanation or Obfuscation?" *JETS* , 1996: 241-256.

—. *Evangelical Hermeneutics*. Grand Rapids: Kregel Publications, 2002.

—. *Three Views of the Origins of the Synoptic Gospels*. Grand Rapids, MI: Kregel, 2002.

Thomas, Robert L. ""Current Hermeneutical Trends: Toward Explanation or Obfuscation?" *JETS 39*, June 1996: 241-256.

Thomas, Robert L. "Current Hermeneutical Trends: Toward Explanation or Obfuscation?" *JETS 39* , June 1996: 241-256.

—. *Revelation 1-7: An Exegetical Commentary* . Chicago, IL: Moody Publishers, 1992.

Thomas, Robert L., and F. David Farnell. *THE JESUS CRISIS: The Inroads of Historical Criticism in Evagelical Scholarship*. Grand Rapids, MI: Kregel Publications, 1998.

Torrey, Reuben A., and Edward D. Andrews. *DIFFICULTIES IN THE BIBLE Alleged Errors and Contradictions: Updated and Expanded Edition.* Cambridge: Christian Publishing House, 2012.

Turner, Henry E. W. *Historicity and the Gospel.* London: A. R. Mowbray, 1963.

Vine, W E. *Vine's Expository Dictionary of Old and New Testament Words.* Nashville: Thomas Nelson, 1996.

Virkler, Henry A, and Karelynne Gerber Ayayo. *Hermeneutics: Principles and Processes of Biblical Interpretation.* Grand Rapids, MI: Baker Academic, 1981, 2007.

Wainwright, William J, and ed. *The Oxford Handbook of Philosophy of Religion.* New York: Oxford University, 2005.

Walker, Williston, Richard A Norris, David W Lotz, and Robert T. Handy. *A History of the Christian Church, 4th ed.* New York: Charles Scribner's Sons, 1985.

Wallace, Daniel. *Greek Grammar Beyond the Basics.* Grad Rapids: Zondervan, 1996.

Walsh, Jerome T. *Old Testament Narrative: A Guide to Interpretation.* Louisville: Westminster John Knox Press, 2009.

Walton, John H. *Zondervan Illustrated Bible Backgrounds Commentary (Old Testament) Volume 1: Genesis, Exodus, Leviticus, Numbers, Deuteronomy.* Grand Rapids, MI: Zondervan, 2009.

Walton, John H. "Isaiah 7:14: what's in a name?" *Journal of the Evangelical Theological Society 30*, 1987: 289-306.

Walton, John H., and Sandy. D. Brent. *The Lost World of Scripture, Ancient Literary Culture and Biblical Authority.* Downers Grove: InterVarsity Press, 2013.

Weber, Stuart K. *Holman New Testament Commentary, vol. 1, Matthew.* Nashville, TN: Broadman & Holman Publishers, 2000.

Wegner, Paul D. *A Student's Guide to Textual Criticism of the Bible: Its History Methods & Results.* Downers Grove: InterVarsity Press, 2006.

Wellhausen, Julius. *Prolegomena to the History of Israel .* New York: BiblioBazzar, 1878, 2009.

Westcott, B. F., and Hort F. J. A. *The New Testament in the Original Greek, Vol. 2: Introduction, Appendix.* London: Macmillan and Co., 1882.

Wheelock, Frederic M, and Richard A Lafleur. *Wheelock's Latin, 7th ed.* New York: Harper Collins, 2011.

Whiston, William. *The Works of Josephus.* Peabody, MA: Hendrickson, 1987.

Whitney, Donald S. *Spiritual Disciplines for the Christian Life with Bonus Content (Pilgrimage Growth Guide).* Colorado Springs, CO: Navpress, 1991.

Wolf, Herbert M. "Solution to the Immanuel Prophecy in Isaiah 7:14-8:22." *Journal of Biblical Literature 91* , 1972: 449-56.

Wood, D R W. *New Bible Dictionary (Third Edition).* Downers Grove: InterVarsity Press, 1996.

Woodhead, Linda. "Spiritualising the Sacred: A Critique of Feminist Theology." *Modern Theology*, 1997: 197.

Wright, N. T. *Hebrews for Everyone.* London: Westminster John Knox Press, 2003.

Yarbrough, Robert W. "Evangelical Theology in Germany." *Evangelical Quarterly LXV* , October 1993: 329, 353.

Young, Pamela Dickey. *Feminist Theology/Christian Theology: In Search of Method.* Eugene: Wipf and Stock, 1990.

Zodhiates, Spiros. *The Complete Word Study Dictionary: New Testament.* Chattanooga: AMG Publishers, 2000, c1992, c1993.

Zuck, Roy B. *Basic Bible Interpretation: A Prafctical Guide to Discovering Biblical Truth.* Colorado Springs: David C. Cook, 1991.

Made in the USA
Monee, IL
14 February 2023

27796198R00234